Philippe Barbour

RHÔNE-ALPES

'Sitting on a stray Romanesque capital by
the lavender-surrounded swimming pool,
sipping a local Côtes du Rhône that tastes of
cherries, I'm mulling over how I fell in love
with the Rhône-Alpes that so captivated the
Romantics, who saw in its soaring heights
and frightening depths a reflection of man's
emotional journey through life.'

CADOGANguides

1 Landscape, Drôme

2 Flowers and rooftops, Balazuc
3 Chestnut trees, Ardèche
4 Pont d'Arc, Ardèche
5 Hiking in the gorges, Ardèche

6 Monastery, Loire Gorges
7 Cliousclat, Drôme
8 Morning hilltops, Ardèche

7

8

9 Lavender and sunflower fields, Drôme
10 Mountain chalet
11 Sainte-Croix-en-Jarez
12 Talloires

13

16

13 Mont Blanc massif
14 Skier, Tarentaise
15 Snow-covered chalet
16 Montenvers train, Chamonix

17

18

17 Sunset on the Isère mountains
18 Isère Regional Park
19 Choranche grotto, Isère

20 Grapes, Beaujolais
21 Wine bottles, Beaujolais
22 Montmelas Castle, Beaujolais
23 Wine cellar, Odenas Château

24 Pond in the Dombes
25 Sunflowers, Grignan
26 Grignan

27, 28, 31 Market offerings
29 Les Halles Market, Lyon
30 Chanterelles

Raclette
10,50€/kg

32 Annecy
33 Palais de l'Isle, Annecy
34 Church, Annecy
35 Cloister, Bourg-en-Bresse

40 Casino, Aix-les-Bains
41 Spa, Aix-les-Bains
42 Interior, Pérouges

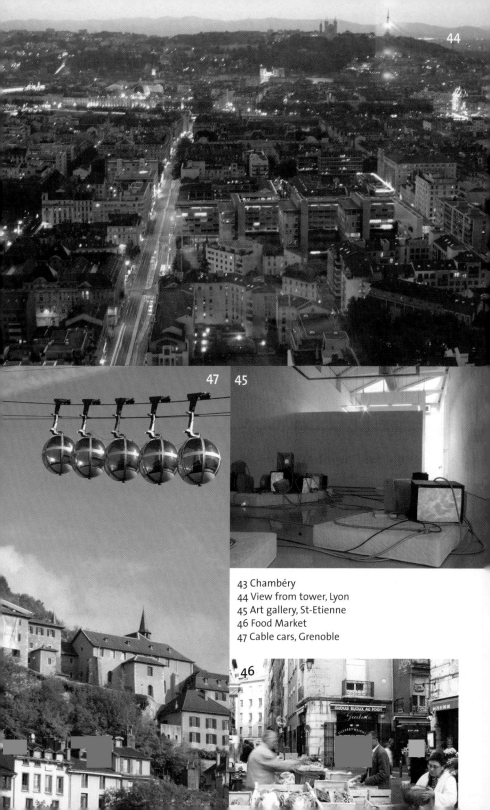

44

47 45

43 Chambéry
44 View from tower, Lyon
45 Art gallery, St-Etienne
46 Food Market
47 Cable cars, Grenoble

46

48 Nightlife, St-Etienne

49 Skyline, Rhône Valley

50 Annecy lake

About the Authors

Philippe Barbour studied French literature at Oxford University. Over the last 10 years he has been completing his French studies with in-depth field work, researching and writing guides for Cadogan. He is the author of their regional guides to Brittany and to the Loire, as well as co-author of *Flying Visits France* (on budget airline destinations) and the country guide to France.

Dave Watts is editor of *Where to Ski and Snowboard*, Britain's leading annual guidebook to winter sports resorts worldwide, and editor-in-chief of *Daily Mail Ski & Snowboard*, Britain's biggest-selling winter sports magazine. After taking up skiing in his 20s he has managed to ski the slopes of virtually every major winter sports resort in Europe and North America. Before that he edited *Which?* magazine and was Assistant Director of Consumers' Association.

Acknowledgements

For this brand new Cadogan guide, Isabelle Faure of the Comité Régional du Tourisme Rhône-Alpes – kindly introduced to me by Gillian Green – set the ball rolling, suggesting it to me and to Dave Watts. She has been a fantastic support and a joy to work with. The press officers of the region's eight *départements*, Nathalie Gaudriot, Colette Dubois, Lucile Clara, Maryse Crumière, Marie-Christine Fustier, Brigitte Roland, Nathalie Rajon, Laetitia Mitton, Joëlle Dubois, Annick Coster, Laurent Collinet and Corinne Raïh, have also been wonderful. They put Dave and me in contact with expert local guides who helped us explore the region in greater depth. These people are too numerous to mention by name here, but know who they are, and we enormously appreciated their help and passion. I would also like to thank Joss Waterfall for her work on chapters 5 and 6 and, on the editorial side, Antonia Cunningham who dealt with matters with appreciable good humour.

I have spent many of the happiest days of my life in the Rhône-Alpes since 1990, when I first visited the hilltop village where my parents bought their paradisiac retirement home. An enormous thank you to them and my family, especially my exceptionally kind grandmother Ninan, for all the special times there. In fact my earliest discoveries of the region were in the 1980s, with Catherine Wastie, who first took me to magical Lyon and walking at night in snowy Beaujolais vineyards, and with John Herbert, who saw me down my first-ever, terrifying ski slope, at Les Arcs – at least I came home intact, unlike John, who almost sliced his ear off. Through the 1990s, Kate Berney was my most faithful Rhône-Alpes companion. We joyously crisscrossed the region on numerous memorable occasions, gorging on culture and restaurants, and even 'discovering' the source of the Loire together. Julia Roberts, Janie Adams and Lynn Kinnear were among the first wave of friends to come to my parents'. Karin Galil, Claire Lofting and Aruna Vasudevan have also spent enchanting butterfly days there. David Stewart ran madly up and down the local hills, while I met my bear of a friend Alan Whysall at the foot of Mont Blanc...which he has conquered *à pied* – he has also lent me useful books on the mountains for my work. John Lotherington has been my rock while preparing this guide, as well as coming out for several splendid trips. Back in London, Andrew Cotton was an angel.

Recently, my nieces and nephew Natasha, Alexandra, Annabelle and Joshua have made times in the Rhône-Alpes particularly joyous. I won't forget Natasha's re-enactment of Hannibal's elephants crossing the Alps. And none of us will forget our mad attempt to conquer Eoupe, the nearest summit to my parents', as a storm broke out. We made it back through the thunder and lightning, luckily leaving me to complete this book in peace.

Isabelle Faure from the Comité Régional du Tourisme Rhône-Alpes would like to thank her colleagues in the region's eight départements for their advice and collaboration, as well as the following team members for their constant support: Valérie Bacquenois, Michèle Bardet, Olivia Cluzet, Laurent Cormier, Lawrence Duval-Montfort and Marie-France Jonte Hornecker.

Contents

Introducing

01
Introduction 1
Guide to the Guide 2

02
History 5

03
Topics 21

04
Food and Drink 27

The Guide

05
Travel 35
Getting There 36
Entry Formalities 39
Getting Around 40

06
Practical A–Z 43

07
Lyon 53
A History of Lyon 55
The Fourvière Hillside and
  Gallo-Roman Lyon 63

Vieux Lyon: Medieval and
  Renaissance Lyon 64
Along the Banks of the
  Saône 66
The Presqu'île de Lyon 67
Up the Croix-Rousse
  Silk-Making Slopes 72
Along the Banks of the
  Rhône 74
Cinema and Invention in
  the Eastern Quarters 76

08
Bresse and Dombes 79
St-Trivier to Bourg-en-
  Bresse 82
Bourg-en-Bresse 85
The Dombes 87

09
Beaujolais 91
Touring the Northern
  Beaujolais Hills 93
From Beaujolais' Brouilly
  Crus through Southern
  Beaujolais-Villages 100
Mont d'Or and
  Monts/Coteaux du
  Lyonnais 103

10
**The Loire to its Source
107**
The Roannais Loire and
  Monts de la Madeleine
  109

The Loire Valley across the
  Forez 115
The Upper Loire from St-
  Etienne to its Source via
  Le Puy-en-Velay 121

11
**West of the Rhône:
Down the Ardèche 125**
Mont Pilat and the
  Northern Ardèche 131
Southern Ardèche 136

12
**Down the Rhône:
From Lyon to the
Provence Border 149**
The Rhône from Lyon to
  Vienne 151
The Rhône from Vienne to
  Valence 160
The Rhône from Valence
  to Montélimar 164
From Montélimar to the
  Languedoc and
  Provence Borders 167

13
**East of the Rhône:
From the Isère into
the Drôme 171**
Western Isère and
  Northern Drôme 174
The Southern Drôme 182

14

The Rhône from Lyon to Lac Léman 197
L'Isle Crémieu from Lyon to the Bugey 199
The Bugey 203
The Valserine and Pays de Gex 210

15

Haute Savoie: From Lac Léman to Mont Blanc 213
Routes from the Lower Arve to Lac Léman 219
Haut Chablais and the Giffre 223
To Mont Blanc via Arve or Aravis 224

16

Savoie's Vanoise Valleys and Oisans 231
Into the Beaufortain 236
The Upper Isère (or Tarentaise) 237
The Arc Valley (or Maurienne) 242
Crossing to the Oisans 245

17

Savoie's Great Lakes 247
Annecy and Lac d'Annecy 249

Lac d'Annecy to Lac du Bourget via the Rhône 256
Les Bauges 258
Lac du Bourget and Aix-les-Bains 260
Chambéry 263
Lac d'Aiguebelette and Avant-Pays Savoyard 265

18

Pre-Alpine Ranges: From Chartreuse to Vercors 267
The Isère Valley below the Western Belledonne 269
The Chartreuse Range 274
Grenoble 276
The Drac, Matheysine and Trièves 280
The Vercors Range 282

19

Winter Sports 285
Haute Savoie 287
Savoie: The Tarentaise Valley 302
Savoie: The Maurienne Valley 319
Isère 325
Ain 333

Maps
Chapter Divisions 3
Lyon 54
Bresse and Dombes 80
Beaujolais 92
The Loire to its Source 108
St-Etienne 119
The Ardèche 126
Mont Pilat and the Northern Ardèche 130
The Southern Ardèche 137
Lyon to Provence 150
Vienne 156
Isère and Drôme 172
East of Lyon: Isère and the Northern Drôme 175
The Southern Drôme 183
From Lyon to Lac Léman 198
Haute Savoie 214
Savoie's Vanoise Valleys 232
Savoie's Great Lakes 248
Annecy 250
Chambéry 265
Pre-Alpine Ranges 268
Grenoble 276

Reference
Language 335
Glossary 337
Index 339

Cadogan Guides
Network House, 1 Ariel Way, London W12 7SL
info@cadoganguides.co.uk
www.cadoganguides.com

The Globe Pequot Press
246 Goose Lane, PO Box 480, Guilford,
Connecticut 06437–0480

Copyright © Philippe Barbour 2004

Cover and photo essay design: Sarah Rianhard-
Gardner
Book design: Andrew Barker
Photography © OLIVIA; © Jean-Luc Rigaux; ©Aline
Perrier
Cover photographs © Jean-Luc Rigaux (front
cover); © OLIVIA (back cover)
Maps © Cadogan Guides,
drawn by Map Creation Ltd
Managing Editor: Natalie Pomier
Editor: Antonia Cunningham
Contributor: Joss Waterfall
Proofreading: Elspeth Anderson
Indexing: Isobel McLean
Production: Navigator Guides

Printed in Italy by Legoprint
A catalogue record for this book is available
from the British Library
ISBN 1-86011-168-8

The author and publishers have made every effort
to ensure the accuracy of the information in this
book at the time of going to press. However, they
cannot accept any responsibility for any loss, injury
or inconvenience resulting from the use of information contained in this guide.

Please help us to keep this guide up to date. We
have done our best to ensure that the information
in this guide is correct at the time of going to press,
but places and facilities are constantly changing,
and standards and prices in hotels and restaurants
fluctuate. We would be delighted to receive any
comments concerning existing entries or omis-
sions. Authors of the best letters will receive a copy
of the Cadogan Guide of their choice.

Introduction

A Guide to the Guide 2

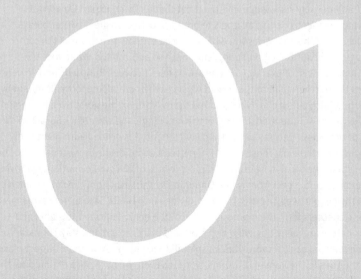

01

Sitting on a stray Romanesque capital by the lavender-surrounded swimming pool, sipping a local Côtes du Rhône that tastes of cherries, I'm mulling over how I fell in love with the Rhône-Alpes that so captivated the Romantics, who saw in its soaring heights and frightening depths a reflection of man's emotional journey through life. My eyes wander distractedly from this introduction I'm preparing, up the stunning mountainsides that encircle me. Above the olive groves, the terraced apricot orchards give way to densely wooded tops from which the odd limestone scar stands out, a reminder of the geological fights that shaped these dramatic parts. Over the nearest summit, I spot a pair of birds of prey circling far above. I'm taking a more relaxed attitude to dinner down at my parents', in their heavenly semi-ruined, semi-restored hill village at a typically awe-inspiring entrance to one of the Rhône-Alpes' pre-alpine ranges. With their vast, dark reptilian backs and huge teeth for mountains, they rise, forbidding yet magnetizing, beyond the fruitful, vinous, bountiful Rhône valley (not just about industry, as you'll see), outer guardians of France's tallest Alpine ranges.

A Guide to the Guide

Olive groves and lavender may only be a feature of the southern Rhône-Alpes, where Drôme and Ardèche meet Provence and Languedoc. But all across this region you'll find nature at its most sensational. It's hard to beat for exhilarating, if challenging, walking, cycling, or pottering about in the car... or for high-energy sports. And these can be practised summer as well as winter. Most think of this region for the most famous concentration of ski resorts in the world, with names like Chamonix, Méribel or Val d'Isère. We certainly don't ignore the immensely important Rhône-Alpes snow season; an intensely knowledgeable, practical chapter by ski expert Dave Watts guides independent skiers of all levels to organize their own great winter breaks.

But the bulk of the book gives you what you need to know to explore all the corners of this magically beautiful region, spring, summer and autumn too. What does the Rhône-Alpes consist of exactly, you may ask? It rises between Burgundy and Provence. It covers the northern half of the French Alps and their pre-alpine foothills bound by the Rhône, which cuts a crinkly path round them. North of the great river, the region also takes in the southernmost ridges of the Jura range, and west of it, the last volcanic slopes of the Massif Central. Larger than Switzerland, it is divided administratively into eight *départements*. Those of the Rhône, Loire and Ardèche lie west of the Rhône. The Ain stands north of it. Isère and Drôme, the bulk of the pre-Revolutionary province of Dauphiné, stretch east from it. The Dauphiné's rival, Savoie, only became French by vote of the people (well, the men) in 1860, divided into Haute Savoie and Savoie.

Touring chapters form the main substance of the book, dedicated to sights and culture, nature and activities, wine and food, and places to eat and stay. They start with the regional capital, **Lyon**, France's splendid second city. A far more august place than little Paris in the Roman centuries, Lyon was even the birthplace of Claudius, the man who conquered England. Many know the city as a gastronomic capital of the

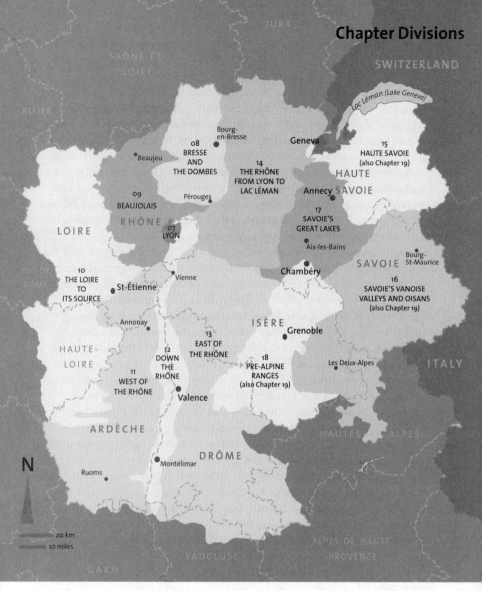

JURA

SWITZERLAND

SAÔNE-ET-
LOIRE

Lac Léman (Lake Geneva)

ALLIER

Bourg-
en-Bresse

08
BRESSE
AND
THE DOMBES

Beaujeu

14
THE RHÔNE
FROM LYON TO
LAC LÉMAN

Geneva

15
HAUTE SAVOIE
(also Chapter 19)

HAUTE

09
BEAUJOLAIS

Pérouges

Annecy

SAVOIE

RHÔNE

17
SAVOIE'S
GREAT LAKES

LOIRE

07
LYON

Aix-les-Bains

Bourg-
St-Maurice

PUY-DE-
DÔME

10
THE LOIRE
TO
ITS SOURCE

St-Étienne

Vienne

Chambéry

SAVOIE

16
SAVOIE'S VANOISE
VALLEYS AND OISANS
(also Chapter 19)

Annonay

13
EAST OF
THE RHÔNE

ISÈRE

Grenoble

HAUTE-
LOIRE

12
DOWN
THE
RHÔNE

18
PRE-ALPINE
RANGES
(also Chapter 19)

Les Deux-Alpes

ITALY

11
WEST OF
THE RHÔNE

Valence

ARDÈCHE

HAUTES-ALPES

N

DRÔME

Montélimar

Ruoms

ALPES DE HAUTE
PROVENCE

20 km
10 miles

VAUCLUSE

GARD

French provinces. Few realize it was also the birthplace of world cinema, thanks to its Lumière boys, or that it is a World Heritage Site.

Just north, either side of the Saône, the rich culinary lowlands of **Bresse and Dombes** face bibulous **Beaujolais**, this flirtatious, busty wine territory flaunting one of the world's most famous wine names. Then we hop over the hills to the **upper reaches of the Loire**, with their magnificent mix of volcanic plains and gorges, stepping quietly round the sinuous, wooded gorges and chestnut terraces of the Ardèche. While much of the *département de la Loire* remains enchantingly undiscovered, that of the Ardèche has gained quite a name for its fabulous gorges and caves.

We don't shy away from tackling the thin strip of **the Rhône valley between Lyon and Provence,** as many cultural and viticultural surprises crop up in the midst of the heavy industry that has given such a false image of the whole region, including a staggering line of medieval castles like vast eagles' eyries. The riverside towns such as Valence, Tournon and Montélimar have been sprucing themselves up, while Vienne conceals one of France's greatest Roman legacies. Then we delve into the delicious rolling orchards and valleys of **western Isère and Drôme.** Beautiful hill villages come two a penny, many with ruined castle, old church, craftspeople and delightful village inn – but then such places exist across the Rhône-Alpes. We then head for the major mountain ranges via the least known stretch of **the Rhône, between Lyon and Lake Geneva** (or Léman as it's called in these parts), but exquisite as a backdrop to a Gothic painting, steep vineyards sweeping down to the water. Here the southern talons of the Jura range stick into the river with savage beauty.

Savoie, an independent, if French-speaking state from medieval times, guarded the vast northwestern Alpine ranges, its foothills bathing their feet in gorgeous great lakes. After lounging a while beside Western Europe's largest lake, glamorous **Léman,** we tackle routes to Europe's tallest, most legendary mountain, **Mont Blanc.** The **Vanoise,** the other range of eternally snow-capped mountains and glaciers wholly within Savoie, is encircled by the huge valleys of the Isère and Arc. Now skiing has conquered its mid-slopes, the Trois Vallées famously offering the most extensive ski domain in the world. But down below, the gritty communities offer history, vibrant Baroque churches swarming with putti, plus wild white-water sports in summer.

Brooding **pre-alpine ranges** line up to the west. Medieval monks found peace in these secretive areas, the *maquisards* hiding places in the war. The string of regional nature parks in **Bauges, Chartreuse** and **Vercors** encourage traditions. Great historic cities spread out below, Chambéry former capital of Savoie, Grenoble former capital of the Dauphiné. **Savoie's great lakes** of Annecy, du Bourget and Aiguebelette nestle beyond, towns like Annecy and Aix-les-Bains rising romantically above the watersides.

At the start of the book, the **Travel** and **Practical A–Z** chapters contain all manner of useful information on practicalities, activities and specialist companies. The **History and Culture** chapter gives an overview of the important people and events to have shaped the Rhône-Alpes, while **Topics** focuses on famous regional features and figures. **Food and Drink** certainly isn't forgotten, this being regarded as the greatest culinary region in France. Also note that the touring chapters include practical boxes with detailed information on tourist offices, market days, local activities, and a splendid selection of truly charming places to eat and stay, whatever your budget.

In short, we hope we've given you the ingredients to enjoy the Rhône-Alpes to the full!

History

The Prehistoric Rhône-Alpes 6
Celts Settle; Hannibal Passes Through 6
Early Christianity and the Dark Ages 7
The Medieval Period 8
Major Medieval Counts 9
Extravagant Late-Gothic Expansion 10
Italian Wars and Wars of Religion 11
The *Ancien Régime* 13
Revolution and Napoleon 15
The Chaotic Course to the Belle Epoque 16
The Two World Wars 18
Speeding into the New Tourist Age 19

02

The Prehistoric Rhône-Alpes

Scraping the surface of hundreds of millions of years of geology, a subject treated with great seriousness by many a French museum, the granite **Massif Central** west of the Rhône arose much earlier than the Alpine ranges to the east, emerging near the end of the **Palaeozoic Era** (c.600 to 225 million years ago). The lands to the east were largely covered by sea water in the **Mesozoic Era** (c.225 to 70 million years ago). Coiled **ammonites** flourished in the waters and **dinosaurs** roamed what lands there were in the **Jurassic**, or middle, period of this era. During the **Cenozoic Era** (from c.70 million years ago), a major geological clash between the earth's tectonic plates led to the emergence of the **Alps**. What had been the seabed in the previous era slipped sideways, forming limestone mountains – north of the Rhône, the **Jura ridges**, and west of the **Combe de Savoie** (a huge Alpine trench), the Rhône-Alpes' **pre-alpine ranges**. The sensational rise of the Alps disturbed the Massif Central, setting off volcanic activity, hence the black basalt stone that predominates there.

As the earth's temperature waxed and waned, glacial meltwaters filled the region's natural depressions, **Lac Léman**, the oldest of the region's great lakes. While the crystalline Alpine mountains proved hard to penetrate, the limestone ranges were easier for waters to cut into, creating vast networks of **underground caverns** from the Bugey in the north to the Ardèche in the south. Archaeologists have found a treasure trove of human and animal remains in these, ranging over tens of thousands of years. Places like the **Musée de l'Ours** in **Entremont-le-Vieux** and the **Musée de la Préhistoire** at **Orgnac** cover the traces, while at the **Grotte de Thaïs** in the Drôme, a bone carved with notches counts among the earliest examples of a human numerical system. The Rhône valley is lined with interesting little museums of prehistory. A fabulous cache of prehistoric art was discovered as recently as the mid-1990s in the **Grotte Chauvet** by **Vallon-Pont-d'Arc**, a one-off find in the region, rivalling Lascaux.

The **last Ice Age** receded some 10,000 years ago. Melting waters formed **lakes** like **Annecy, du Bourget, Aiguebelette** and **Paladru**. During the **Neolithic period** (c.5000–2000 BC), animals were domesticated, and communities greatly appreciated the marshy lakelands, well recorded at Lac de Paladru and Chambéry. The odd standing stone has also left its Neolithic mark here and there. The magical fingers of rock at Le Puy-en-Velay seem to have encouraged early worship. Neolithic finds have even been made as far into the mountains as the Vercors, Tarentaise and Maurienne.

Celts Settle; Hannibal Passes Through

While the **Greeks** set up their colony of Marseille at the mouth of the Rhône around 600BC, bringing olives and vines, through the **Iron Age** (c.600–100BC) following the Bronze Age, **Celtic tribes** established themselves across what would become known as Gaul . The Celts and Greeks seem to have traded by river. The Celts formed the odd hillside settlement, or *oppidum*, a few vestiges revealed in museums by the Rhône. The other side of the Alps, **Rome** grew impressively, and threateningly. On the

Mediterranean, the **Carthaginians** based in North Africa became their main rivals for a time. Their greatest general, **Hannibal**, led history's most famous expedition through the Alps, in 218 BC – with war-trained elephants, to take the Romans by surprise. Until archaeologists unearth the confirmatory pachyderm pooh, people can only speculate which way Hannibal went, but the Col du Petit St-Bernard, Mont Cenis and Buis-les-Baronnies put in claims to having seen the amazing army pass by.

The Romans beat off Hannibal, going from strength to strength. In the 120s BC, they took southern Gaul, creating their much-loved province of Provence, touching on the Rhône-Alpes region. The Celtic tribes to the north were not united, and fought among themselves. **Caesar** claimed that he stepped in at the request of one tribe in the Rhône-Alpes, the Aedui, to oust the pillaging Helvetii (from Switzerland). So began a very long, strong connection between Italy and the Rhône-Alpes. Caesar had the whole of Gaul occupied in the 50s BC, recorded in his *Conquest of Gaul*.

Forget Paris's unimportant little predecessor Lutetia, **Lugdunum** (or **Lyon**), founded in 43BC, swiftly grew into the most significant city in Gaul. Roman emperors were even born in the town, including Claudius and Caracalla. **Vienne** to the south competed with Lyon in trade and, today, boasts an almost finer Roman legacy. The Roman remains at **Aix-les-Bains** recall how classical Italians loved to wallow in a restorative bath. Other Roman vestiges lie along their network of roads through the main valleys.

Early Christianity and the Dark Ages

Frightening batches of early **Christian martyrs** were killed in **Lyon**, but the city also claims to have had one of the first churches in Gaul. By his 313 Edict of Milan, made across the Alps, the Roman Emperor Constantine officially accepted Christianity. Bishops were established in the main cities. **Grenoble** has a rare vestige of a 5th-century baptistery under its bishops' palace, where new converts were fully immersed. **Le Puy-en-Velay** early became devoted to the Virgin Mary.

As the Roman Empire disintegrated in the 5th century, **tribes from the east** moved in, the **Burgondes** to Sabaudia (Land of the Fir, later to become Savoie), pressing on to Lyon, but then kicked out by the **Franks** in 534. Gaul was turning into France. Despite the terrible fighting, major monasteries emerged. Few remains of the **Frankish Merovingian period** (*c.* AD500–751) have been found, but for a riveting if unreliable romp of a read through these times, try **Gregory of Tours'** *History of the Franks*.

After the Arab, or Saracen, invasions of southern France were beaten back in the 8th century, the **Carolingian dynasty** (AD 751–987) took some control of Western Europe. **Charlemagne**, their great unifying figure, created the system of rule by **counts** over his vast territories. He was crowned first so-called **Holy Roman Emperor** by the pope in 800. Monasteries blossomed, but again, very few traces remain. By the Treaty of Verdun of 843, which divided Charlemagne's inheritance among his grandsons, Lyon and much of the Rhône-Alpes fell under the middle kingdom of **Lotheringia**, or **greater Burgundy-Provence**, squeezed between Germany and France. Fragments of primitive late Carolingian churches and carving survive here and there.

The Medieval Period

At the start of the new millennium, as Lotheringia got squeezed out, the Rhône formed part of the western boundary of the loose association of territories nominally ruled by the Holy Roman Emperors . As regards the Rhône-Alpes' lands, the French **Capetian dynasty** (987–1328), which supplanted the Carolingians, remained rather irrelevant for a long time. Here, quasi-independent lordly families amassed large territories, **the houses of Savoie and the Dauphiné** the most significant. In the 11th century, **Humbert aux Blanches Mains** (White Hands – he was supposed to be very pure), Count of Maurienne, received possessions that would grow into the county of Savoie, while **Guigues le Vieux**, Comte d'Albon, came by lands closer to the Rhône, the beginnings of the mighty Dauphiné. West of the Rhône, the little **lords of the Beaujolais and Forez** and the **bishops of the Velay and the Vivarais** lined up as the main holders of power.

Fighting and marriage were employed by the leading regional lords to change the power politics and boundaries down the ensuing medieval centuries. But more local lords often tried to assert themselves too. From the start of the millennium, through to the 15th century, **medieval castles** went up to oversee river fords and river tolls, or on strategic high spots surveying vast tracts, all offering protection to the villagers below in times of conflict. The brutal, sheer-sided **donjons,** or **keeps,** of the Romanesque 11th and 12th centuries were often enlarged and embellished in the Gothic period from the mid-12th to the 15th century, turning into **châteaux**. From the golden-stoned or black volcanic ones in the west of the region to the romantic ones beside swan-covered waters or below daunting ridges out east, they leave a powerful impression on the landscape.

The other great holders of power in medieval times were the varied branches of the **Catholic Church**. These too have left a great architectural legacy. Solid **Romanesque cathedrals** were built in the cities, while many **new churches** and **monasteries** were founded, most often thanks to generous donations by lords believing the monks' prayers would cleanse their souls. The main religious authorities came to compete in territorial power with the feudal lords. **Lyon** saw its **archbishops** strengthen their grip on the city and its surroundings. From 1079, they received the honorific but imposing title of Primate of Gaul. Based close by in Burgundy, the abbey of **Cluny**, long established as one of the powerhouses of Western Europe, exercised its influence over places like **Charlieu** on the Rhône-Alpes' northwest border. Certain **holy figures** focused on founding new orders devoted to prayer and work, or to charitable causes. For information on 11th-century **St Bernard de Menthon,** *see* p.23; in 1084 **St Bruno of Cologne** founded his first strict **Carthusian monastery,** or Chartreuse, in the range that bears the same name.

On the international scene, **Pope Urban II** dropped in on Lyon in 1095 on his European tour whipping up support for the **First Crusade**. In fact, Lyon became the popes' number one stop in medieval Europe outside Italy. Crusading zeal and folly went to the head of many nobles in the 12th and 13th centuries. The **order of the Knights Templars,** bankers to these enterprises, amassed vast riches. Traces of them remain here and there. In 1130, they set up a big centre in **Richerenches**, in what became a papal enclave in the Drôme. With the crusades, relics flowed back from the Middle East in great numbers. However bogus most may have been, they inspired veneration in a credulous population.

Severe **Bernard of Clairvaux** spread the influence of the **Cistercian order**, devoted to rigorous prayer and work, outwards from Burgundy across Western Europe in the early 12th century, reacting to what he saw as Cluny's decadence, even in architecture. The **abbey of Hautecombe** by Lac du Bourget was originally a stern Cistercian establishment, for example. But while some **churches** built in the 11th and 12th centuries (their architecture characterized by **Romanesque** rounded arches) went up in sober style, many were covered with imaginative carvings of symbolic and bestial figures showing man battling it out with his demons, while colourful cartoonish murals depicting Biblical scenes and exemplary saints' lives and martyrdoms were plastered inside. Memorable examples around the Rhône-Alpes include **St-Romain-le-Puy** by the Loire, **Cruas** beside the Rhône, **Die** and **St-Chef** in the Dauphiné, or **Allinges** by Lake Geneva.

In the region's greatest city, Emperor Frederick Barbarossa's Golden Bull (or decree) of 1157 made the **archbishops counts of Lyon**, to be assisted by 32 canons carrying the title of *chanoines-comtes*. They erected castles to guard their substantial territories around the Lyonnais, encroaching on the Beaujolais and Forez to the west. The Lyon monasteries continued to expand separately. Significant protesters emerged against the wealth and materialism of the Catholic Church. A Lyonnais merchant, **Pierre Valdo**, caused a stink in the 12th century with his reforming *Pauvres de Lyon* (to become known as the Vaudois or Waldensians), seen by some historians as precursors of the Protestants, trying to get back to the purer messages of the New Testament.

Major Medieval Counts

Back with the competing regional counts, the **line of Guigues** were in expansionist mode. Despite Bishop St Hugues standing up to them in Grenoble, they took control of the pre-alpine passes around this strategic city. **Guigues IV** was given the nickname of **Dauphin** (Dolphin, but probably from some linguistic contraction for a typical period religious hyperbole such as 'made fine by the grace of God') early in the 12th century. This nickname stuck, the dynasty's lands becoming known as the **Dauphiné**.

The **counts of Savoie** became known as the *Portiers des Alpes*, gatekeepers of the Alps, controlling the major passes of the northwest corner of the whole Alpine arc. **Count Thomas I** bought the town of **Chambéry** in the 13th century. His descendants became major European players, **Pierre II**, incidentally, the man for whom the Savoy Palace in London was built (now site of the Savoy Hotel). Many in this Savoyard dynasty carried the name Amédée. In 1272, **Amédée V** managed, by marriage, to acquire the house of Savoie's most westerly territories, stretching to the Bresse. Before the close of the 13th century, Chambéry had become capital of Savoie. Dauphins and Savoyards fought over their pre-alpine frontiers. Two Dauphins died in skirmishes.

Although the French royal family remained peripheral, the **birth of Gothic style** around Paris in the mid-12th century rapidly had a profound effect on architecture further afield, with its lancet arches and soaring walls of glass supported by flying buttresses. Cities like Lyon and Vienne rebuilt their cathedrals in grand new style.

A new period of zealous monastic activity took off early in the 13th century as charismatic figures like St Francis of Assisi and St Dominic (he of the Inquisition) made an impact across Western Europe. **Franciscan and Dominican orders** were set up in Lyon. Important European Church gatherings were held in the city. Pope Innocent IV even fled there for seven years, escaping the clutches of the Holy Roman Emperor. However, over time, most branches of the Church became increasingly corrupt.

The **Capetians** stepped firmly in on the Rhône-Alpes scene with belligerent **King Philippe le Bel** taking a grip on the French frontiers in the early 14th century. He helped orchestrate the move of the papacy from strife-torn Rome to Avignon, where it remained for much of the century, although Pope Clement V was crowned pontiff in Lyon. Philippe exploited his control of the papacy to attack the Knights Templars, brought to their knees on trumped-up charges. A new order, the **Hospitallers of St John**, took over. **Lyon** and the Lyonnais fell under more direct French royal control from 1312. The **merchants** gained important powers at this time.

Philippe le Bel's descendants seemed cursed. By 1328 there were no direct heirs. The French nobility opted for a new, French dynasty, **the Valois** (1328–1589), **Philippe VI** first of the line. The enraged English king, **Edward III**, believed he had a better claim via his French royal mother, and so began the **Hundred Years War** (played out in two horrendously drawn-out halves, from 1336 to 1380, then 1415 to 1453). The provinces of the Rhône-Alpes lay on the sidelines, although the western territories were affected. During this period, the Valois gained a foothold east of the Rhône. **Count Humbert II** had become Dauphin in 1333. Full of ambition for his province, he created a *Conseil Delphinal* in 1337, and founded the **university of Grenoble**. But he harboured dreams of crusading glory – a crippling enterprise. Having also lost his wife and son, he sold his lordship to the French crown just before the end of Philippe VI's reign, in 1349, diplomats having to-ed and fro-ed by boat over the Rhône to finalize the details, the treaty signed in Lyon. From then on, the heir to the French throne would be known as the Dauphin (equivalent to the English heir becoming Prince of Wales) . At the same time, the catastrophic **Black Death** plague swept across France from 1348, respecting no regional boundaries, decimating populations for centuries to come.

Extravagant Late-Gothic Expansion

Out west, the powerful **Bourbon family** from central France took control, by marriage, of the Roannais and Forez along the Loire. In the east, **the house of Savoie** was reaching the height of its power. Following Amédée VI (nicknamed the Green Count), the Red **Count Amédée VII** bought the county of Nice from the Grimaldi family in 1388, securing an outlet to the Mediterranean. In 1416, Savoie's lords became mightier **dukes** by order of the Holy Roman Emperor Sigismund. The first duke, **Amédée VIII**, extended Savoyard territories to their furthest limits in 1419, going from Neuchâtel (in Switzerland) to Nice, from the Bresse to Piedmont (in Italy). He sought to retire, but the **Great Papal Schism** resulted in his being elected anti-pope Felix V at the Council of Basle of 1439. Resigning nine years later, he helped end the dreadful division in the

Church of Rome. In 1453, the house of Savoie came by one of Christianity's most famous and disputed relics, a cloth said to have been **Christ's burial shroud**, kept at **Chambéry**. The city of Geneva lay within the gift of the dukes through the 15th century, its area, the **Genevois**, repeatedly given as an appanage (a lordly territory for a son to rule over). Here, **Annecy** grew into one of Savoie's most spectacular towns.

In the Dauphiné, one royal Dauphin, the future **Louis XI of France**, and his dynamic administration made a huge difference to Lyon and the province through forward-looking policies from the mid-15th century – the period some historians refer to as the 'good 16th century', going from the 1450s to the 1550s. As well as appreciating **Valence**, where the young Louis set up a prestigious **university**, he also created the powerful **Dauphiné Parlement in Grenoble** (a regional law court run by aristrocrats, not a representative parliament), and encouraged **Lyonnais fairs and new industries** (**silk making, printing** and **banking**) to become of major significance for centuries.

A wily strategist, Louis XI took **Charlotte de Savoie** as his second wife, one of several powerful women from the house of Savoie to exercise influence on the development of the French monarchy. Their eldest daughter, **Anne de France**, became **Anne de Beaujeu**, after the capital of the Beaujolais area, when she was married to Pierre II de Bourbon. Wise and capable, she briefly served as regent of France when her brother **Charles VIII** was too young to reign. She paid attention to her Beaujolais territories, moving the area's capital to **Villefranche** on the Saône, one of many riverside towns in the Rhône-Alpes area to thrive in this period.

Not just the major towns received fine **late-Gothic edifices**, but also smaller centres, particularly remarkable ones going from **Ambierle** or **St-Bonnet-le-Château** out west to **Abondance**, **Bonneval** or **Lanslebourg** far to the east, with countless stunning fortified **medieval villages** (**Pérouges** the most famous) built in between.

For his son and heir Charles, Louis XI had initially lined up supremely well-connected **Marguerite of Austria**, who joined the French royal court on the Loire as an infant, but Anne de Bretagne proved a more useful match. In 1497 Marguerite was married to the Infante Juan of Spain, who promptly died. When her second husband, **Philibert le Beau of Savoie**, expired just three years after their marriage in 1501, she headed off to serve as regent of Flanders, but didn't forget her mother-in-law Marguerite de Bourbon's wishes that she restore the run-down **abbey of Brou**, turning it into one of the most sumptuous churches in the region, with some of the most exquisite tombs in Europe.

Italian Wars and Wars of Religion

While Louis XI had concentrated on domestic policy, **Charles VIII** and his two successors, Louis XII and François I, became obsessed by Italy, going on mad dashes across the Alps to assert inheritance claims there. Charles VIII's foray almost ended in disaster, but his troops managed to drag back a fair amount of booty. Still in crazed conquering mood as he returned, Charles VIII is credited with initiating the first recorded **mountaineering** adventure in France, ordering his men to scale the seemingly inaccessible **Mont Aiguille** on the edge of the Vercors range.

Louise de Savoie, daughter of Philippe II de Savoie and Marguerite de Bourbon, spawned a larger-than-life son, **François I** (king of France from 1515 to 1547), who proved more than a match for Henry VIII of England, but was outdone by Charles of Habsburg, the last becoming both Holy Roman Emperor and King of Spain. Bellicose François turned into a troubling figure either side of the Alps, setting off for glory in Italy, in which he was initially successful, his victory at Marignano in 1516 still cited as one of the great French battles. A much admired old-time French campaigner from the Grenoblois, **Pierre Terrail de Bayard,** 'beyond fear or reproach', knighted the king in recognition of his prowess, an image to serve the royal propaganda legend down the centuries. François wasted a fortune on disastrous Italian campaigns, twisting the arms of Lyon's bankers into lending him money on favourable terms. Lyon even acquired the dubious nickname of *Capitale des Guerres.* At the same time, many city merchants prospered as the crown encouraged national industry at the expense of foreign imports. However, disaster struck at the **Battle of Pavia** in 1525, when the king was captured by troops of the Holy Roman Empire and ransomed at massive expense.

In **Savoie,** the situation became increasingly tense after **Duke Charles III's** brother **Philippe** was made **Count of Geneva** in 1514, and as **Protestant ideas spread** rapidly south after Luther's declarations on reformation of the Church from 1519. Count Philippe pressed for independence. Threatened by the duke, he called on Swiss support; Bernois troops fought off the unwelcome advance, but also overran the Chablais south of Lac Léman, an area to remain predominantly Protestant through the 16th century. François I, picking on easier, closer prey than the Italian states, took on troublesome territories on the edges of his realm and occupied much of Savoie from 1536. West of the Rhône, he put down his upstart cousin, the Duc de Bourbon, confiscating his territories after he had defied him. So Forez and Beaujolais came to be overseen directly by the crown.

But religious matters were about to slide out of control for the French monarchy. Already in the 1530s, François I had been enraged to find an abusive paper pouring scorn on the Catholic Mass pinned to his door. It had been prepared by two Protestant Lyonnais, from the safety of Switzerland. The **Huguenots** recruited more and more minds to Church reform, despite being increasingly persecuted. More playfully, François **Rabelais,** practising as a doctor in Lyon, published his fiendishly clever but bawdy giant satires at the city fairs of the 1530s, *Gargantua* and *Pantagruel* among the most significant French works of the 16th century. Under the farce, he advocated moderation.

The **Catholic Church** tried to put its house in order mid-century with its **Counter-Reformation** agreed at the Councils of Trent. **Claude d'Urfé** represented France at one of the meetings, and when he had his château, the **Bastie d'Urfé** by the Loire, remodelled in Italian Renaissance style, it incorporated symbols emphasizing the Catholic doctrine. The more fanatical **Cardinal François de Tournon,** who had helped negotiate François I's release after his capture at Pavia, successfully pressed the king into signing an order for the extermination of further Vaudois. The cardinal also set up a Catholic college of major influence in the family's home town on the Rhône. François I's first heir, also called François, died in Tournon after catching a cold, so **Henri II** and his wife **Catherine de' Medici** succeeded to the throne. France entered a **war** with the Holy Roman Empire, Henri II's troops humiliated by an army led by **Duke Emmanuel-**

Philibert of Savoie. By the **Treaty of Le Cateau-Cambresis** of 1559, Savoie regained its independence, but the duke moved his capital to Turin, along with the holy shroud.

Inside France, religious hell broke out. In the Rhône-Alpes's lands, **Protestantism** had taken firm root in Lyon and across the Dauphiné and Ardèche, as well as in Savoie. The authorities clamped down increasingly repressively. The first full outbreak of the French **Wars of Religion** occurred in 1562, devastating bouts following over four decades. Two superlative, highly readable serious histories, Emmanuel Le Roy Ladurie's *Le Carnaval de Romans* (a much better read than his better-known *Montaillou*) and Nathalie Zemon-Davis' *Society and Culture in Early Modern France*, brilliantly analyze the situation in the Rhône-Alpes. The first year, Lyon was briefly taken by Protestants after a terrifying fanatical leader from the Dauphiné, the **Baron des Adrets**, led a massacring army through Grenoble, Lyon, Valence and Montbrison. Catholic institutions were violently attacked. At Valence, the royal governor of the Dauphiné was assassinated. Royal and Catholic control reasserted, in 1564 Catherine de' Medici led her young son **Charles IX** on a tour of the country to try and calm matters; a devastating outbreak of the **plague** caused them to leave Lyon in a rush. The divided city was one of the places to suffer most from the 1572 **St Bartholomew's Day massacre of Protestants**. But the numbers that died were tiny compared with the legions wiped out by bouts of the dreaded medieval disease.

In 1577, the Dauphiné got a strong Protestant leader in **Lesdiguières**, close to the head of the Huguenot side, **Henri de Navarre**, who would emerge triumphant. From Savoie, **Duke Charles-Emmanuel** harboured major ambitions, however. When **Henri III**, last of the Valois dynasty, was assassinated in 1589, he even put in a claim to the French throne. But Henri de Navarre took the crown as **Henri IV**, the first of France's **Bourbon monarchs** (1589–1789, restored 1815–1848). Lesdiguières, appointed Lieutenant General in the Dauphiné, defeated the obstreperous Duke Charles-Emmanuel in the early 1590s.

The *Ancien Régime*

Henri IV sought reconciliation, famously converting to Catholicism to be accepted by the Parisian majority, but seeing to the protection of limited Protestant rights in France by the 1598 **Edict of Nantes**. In 1601 he dealt once and for all with troublesome Charles-Emmanuel, taking the north of Savoie, from the Bresse to the Gex, the treaty signed in Lyon, where the dapper Henri had married the stormy **Marie de' Medici** the previous year. Lesdiguières continued to oversee the Dauphiné, encouraging its economy. He even thrived under Henri IV's staunchly Catholic son and successor, **Louis XIII**, having the massive **Château de Vizille** built for himself south of Grenoble.

In Savoie, the most significant figure of the early 17th century was **François de Sales**, a charismatic religious man from a local lordly family, born at the **Château de Thorens**. Preaching a caring Catholicism, he converted recalcitrant parts of Savoie back to the fold. He was helped by the feminine touch of Jeanne de Chantal to set up the new **Order of the Visitation** in **Annecy**. Geneva, however, now lay firmly in the hands of the Protestants, so its Catholic bishopric was moved to this other splendid lake-side city, François de Sales an early incumbent of the post. His *Introduction à la vie dévote* a bestseller through the century, he also helped create the **Académie Florimontane** to encourage high-minded Savoyard literary endeavours, a model for Richelieu's *Académie Française*. But politically, Savoie fell under the thumb of the bullying French Kings Louis through the 17th century, occupied in the 1620s and 1690s.

Across the rest of the Rhône-Alpes, the **Catholic Church** embarked on a campaign of re-conversion through the 17th century, **zealous missionaries** including **St Vincent de Paul** in the Dombes and **St Régis** in the Ardèche and Velay. Although Huguenot centres and *temples* (as their churches were known) were supposedly tolerated, any defiance made them open to attack, as happened horrifically at **Privas** in the Vivarais.

Among the competing, conflicting branches of the Church in the *Ancien Régime* , the powerful **Jesuits** had a major base in Lyon, which produced the most famous Jesuit architect, **Père Martellange**, while Louis XIV's most famous confessor, **Père Lachaise**, taught there. Protestant persecution grew. **Louis XIV's Revocation of the Edict of Nantes** of 1685 cancelled Protestant rights, causing many able Huguenots, particularly skilled craftsmen from the cities, to head into exile. A rare *Ancien Régime* Protestant chapel remains at **Le Poët-Laval** in the Drôme. Up in the small principality of **Trévoux** by the Saône, an influential Jesuit community published its dictionary to counter the anti-establishment questionings of early Enlightenment thinkers. **Madame de Sévigné**, in her correspondence, provided atmospheric observations on aristocratic life down at **Grignan** where her daughter had married the extravagant lord.

Architecture and art counted among the weapons Catholicism used to win back the populace. Savoie, in particular, saw a plethora of new church buildings or lavish redecoration in the **Baroque** style, underlining stories of the Bible, saints and sacraments, all surrounded by swarms of pink putti. Several good museums, sometimes set in old churches, explain the purposes and work of this Savoyard Baroque propaganda campaign, for instance at **Peillonex**, **Moûtiers**, **Séez** or **Lanslebourg**.

In 1713, in the reshuffle of European lands at the end of Louis XIV's warring reign, **Victor-Amédée II of Savoie** gained territories as new King of Piedmont and Sicily, but was slightly downgraded in 1718, to **King of Piedmont and Sardinia**, hence the confusing historical reference around Savoie to the *Etats Sardes* from this period on. The lords of Savoie ruled quite independently for most of the 18th century, although Spanish troops caused havoc during the War of Austrian Succession (1740–48). In architecture, the **neoclassical** style dominated, known as the *style sarde* in Savoie.

Royal-appointed *intendants* oversaw the French regions through the 18th century. **Industry** around the Rhône Valley boomed, notably in silk-making, the mills powered by mountain waters, while vast numbers of workers made the looms clatter in **Lyon**. The city was at the forefront in many domains. In the Monts du Lyonnais, the Perret brothers discovered industrial uses for the pyrite seam at **St-Pierre-la-Palud**, crucial to the development of the massive, lucrative chemical industries along the Rhône. At a Rhône-side village in the Ardèche called **Lafarge**, the Pavin brothers opened a quarry to produce cement, the company to develop into one of the largest in the world in this field, even if its activities scarred the riverbanks. In **St-Etienne**, the well-established craft of arms-making and coal mining both expanded considerably.

On an elevating note, at **Annonay** in the early 1780s, the **Montgolfier brothers** gave birth to the possibility of manned flight with their great balloons. Capping that, in 1786 **Balmat** and **Paccard** became the first men to reach the summit of Mont Blanc by foot, a sensational achievement for the time. More stirring still for French society, two explosive 18th-century authors were based in the region for some time. **Voltaire**'s cutting criticisms of French injustice enflamed the monarchy. Repeatedly forced into exile, he held intellectual court at his **Château de Fernay** on the Swiss frontier. **Rousseau**, born in Geneva, ran away from an unhappy apprenticeship there to **Annecy**, then **Chambéry**, his tearful journey and the formation of his ideas on liberty, justice, education and the general will charted both in his autobiographical *Confessions* and in his novels, several of which feature the Rhône-Alpes. His sensibilities towards the impenetrable forces of nature made him an early model for the Romantic movement in the arts. His political ideas were to have a shattering impact not just on French society, but the world, deformed into grossly simplistic programmes of totalitarian change.

Revolution and Napoleon

The ideas behind the **French Revolution** spread fast. The monarchy reacted repressively towards reform even if suggested by aristocrats. When it tried to shut down the protesting regional *Parlements*, this provoked reaction, notably in **Grenoble**. In the **Journée des Tuiles** of 7 June 1788, protesters against the closure of the Dauphiné *Parlement* threw tiles from the rooftops at royal troops. Some historians interpret this as an important first rumble of Revolution. The three Estates (clergy, nobility and people) of the Dauphiné called for a national meeting of the French Estates. A National Assembly was formed in 1789, one characterful representative from the Rhône-Alpes the *bon vivant* **Brillat-Savarin**; he went on to pen a philosophical classic on French gastronomy, *La Physiologie du goût*. Grenoble boy Henri Beyle recorded his impressions of the Revolution there before becoming one of France's greatest 19th-century novelists under his pseudonym **Stendhal**. His stirring *Le Rouge et le noir* followed a real-life Rhône-side story of a priest's tragic love for a married woman.

In fact, the Revolutionary period passed off relatively peacefully in much of the region, although not in Lyon. France's **Revolutionary wars** with its neighbours broke out in April 1792. General Montesquiou took control of Savoie for the Republic. The Revolution created the administrative **French *départements*** that exist to this day, Savoie briefly made the *département du Mont Blanc*. By 1793, the rabid **Jacobins** were in power in Paris. One of their followers, fanatical Joseph Chalier, tried to install his **Terror** in Lyon. Powerful merchants, supported by the people, executed him instead. In reaction, Robespierre had Lyon terribly punished. The **Château de Vizille**, now converted into an excellent **Museum of the Revolution**, tells of the complex stages in the upheaval, through the arts. The Loire-side textile town of **Roanne** also displays Revolutionary ceramics, the plates declaring their politics with hearty slogans.

Napoleon spent some of his early officer days in **Valence**, before being sent to help crush a silk-workers' revolt in **Lyon**. Dispatched to Egypt to disrupt British trade, he employed **Champollion**, a little genius from Grenoble, to crack the language code of the Rosetta Stone. Back in Europe, Napoleon took control of the Italian Papal States. **Pope Pius VI** was dragged to France, dying in Valence. Assuming total power at the end of the century, Bonaparte appreciated the grandeur of Lyon and his imperial regime brought its silk back into fashion. Napoleon's megalomania went to his head with such horrors as his Russian campaign and he was forced into exile on Elba. But the irrepressible mastermind rose one more time, in 1815, coming up from the Med, avoiding the well guarded Rhône valley, taking a more easterly way via Grenoble still known as the **Route Napoléon**, along which he raised crucial support for his revival. The resurgence was shortlived, ending with **Waterloo** in 1815, the monarchies restored in France and Savoie with **Louis XVIII** and **Victor-Emmanuel I**. Napoleon's family had briefly enjoyed taking the waters of **Aix-les-Bains**. But the best-remembered French visitor here around this time was the sickly **Romantic poet Lamartine**. In 1816, he and the young married consumptive Julie Charles fell madly in love. Julie died before their 1817 rendez-vous, the devastated Lamartine immortalizing her in his famed 'Le Lac'.

The Chaotic Course to the Belle Epoque

French society was so profoundly unsettled by the Revolutionary and Napoleonic upheavals that the new monarchs found it hard to hold the reins – **Charles X** was removed in the 1830 July Revolution and **Louis-Philippe** in the European-wide 1848 Revolution, both punished for trying to be too rigidly disciplined. Austrian troops occupied large parts of Italy, but Savoie kept its independence. Under Victor-Emmanuel I, followed by **Charles-Félix**, huge **fortifications** went up to guard against new French invasions, the impressive **Forts de l'Esseillon** marching down the Arc valley, another series dotted around **Val Cenis**. The French fortified strategic points too, for example vertiginous **Fort l'Ecluse** on the Rhône before Geneva, or **Grenoble**'s heights, bristling with defences. But with restoration came extravagant nostalgia in the arts. Charles-Félix ordered the most ostentatious **neo-Gothic** redecoration of the family mausoleum of the abbey of **Hautecombe**. **Chambéry**'s cathedral and Ste-Chapelle received similar treatment.

Industrial advances were cracking on apace in the Rhône-Alpes, a powerhouse of French progress, albeit at the expense of put-upon workers. In Lyon, **Joseph Jacquard** invented a fiendishly fiddly but time-saving punch-card loom for weaving. The workers, based in new towering blocks, suffered dreadfully, and rebelled periodically, including when their Beaujolais rations were cut. **Laurent Mourguet**'s satirical **Guignol** puppets brought a little light relief (*see* p.24). The Lyonnais manufacturers farmed out increasing amounts of weaving work around the Rhône-Alpes, recalled in countless museums in the region. As to its great rivers, **Marc Seguin**, great-nephew of the Montgolfier brothers, built the first French suspension bridges to span such mighty courses as the Rhône from the mid-1820s. He was also at the forefront of French railway engineering, the first track also opening in the region in the 1820s.

The **French Church** looked for new symbols to boost its image after the Revolution's battering. **Jean Vianney**, a model of a humble priest at **Ars** in the Dombes, was pushed into the limelight as a model of piety, later canonized and declared patron of priests around the world. Architect **Pierre Bossan** was inspired to build an extravaganza of a church for the Curé d'Ars, whose fox-like face smiles out in countless churches around the region. Then a couple of shepherds in a remote corner of the Isère claimed to have witnessed an apparition of the Virgin; the pilgrimage to **Notre-Dame-de-la-Salette** was born. These remain among the most important **pilgrimage** sites in France.

No miracle could save weaving in the Rhône-Alpes, sent into dramatic decline by a fatal combination of silkworm illness, foreign competition and the invention of artificial materials. France's vineyards would later be devastated by a series of illnesses, especially phylloxera, although a Beaujolais man, Victor Pulliat, largely remedied this disaster, by advocating the grafting of American stock onto French vines. The **Second Empire** (1852–1870) under **Napoleon III** and **Empress Eugénie** was an age of technological advances, one **Aristide Bergès** among the first to capture mountain waterpower, along the Isère, generating **hydroelectricity** on a grand scale. It was also a period of great **shopping**, the emperor opening Lyon's Rue Impériale, with its palatial emporia, theatres and banks. In Italy, largely occupied by Austrian troops, the Italians fought for an independent state. The able Piedmont politician **Cavour** (a descendant of the Savoyard de Sales family) and **King Victor-Emmanuel II of Sardinia** negotiated with Napoleon III. In exchange for military success, **France received Savoie** (and Nice) in 1860 – Savoie's men also voted to join France, by 130,533 to 235! Another result, **Victor-Emmanuel II** became the **first King of Italy**. But it ended in tears for Napoleon III, provoked by **Bismarck** into attacking more powerful Prussia, whose armies walked into France. While the **Third Republic** was born, to last until the First World War, the bishop of Lyon ordered the extravaganza of **Notre-Dame de Fourvière** from Bossan, this Marian shrine still receiving one million pilgrims a year.

More light-heartedly, **French skiing** first took off at **Chamrousse** near Grenoble in 1878, when Henri Duhamel bought a pair of Scandinavian skis at a Paris exhibition and went home to try them out. The fashion caught on within a couple of decades. The crack French mountain troops, the **Chasseurs Alpins** (with museums in Grenoble and Albertville) encouraged competitions. Sickly and fashionable aristocrats headed for glamorous **spa resorts** with their exotic new architecture, **Queen Victoria** the most famous visitor to **Aix-les-Bains**, although the British didn't like to mix with the locals. The region was captured by local 19th-century artists in such collections as those at **Morestel** and **Villefranche-sur-Saône**, as well as those in the larger cities. Less formally, a humble postman, **Facteur Cheval**, at **Hauterives** in the Drôme, created a celebrated work of *Architecture Naïve*.

The **Belle Epoque** at the turn from 19th to 20th century saw all manner of brilliant inventors at work in the region. However, when Lyon hosted the major **International Fair of 1894**, it witnessed the traumatic **assassination of French president Sadi Carnot** by **anarchist Santo Caserio**, in turn guillotined in the city. But the next year, the **Lumière brothers** gave birth to the **cinematograph** in Lyon, which, with Paris, was at the forefront of the **automobile age**, nostalgically recalled at the **Château de Rochetaillée**. Work began in 1909 on the **Route des Grandes Alpes**, a 700-km engineering feat of a road linking Lac Léman with the Med via some of Europe's highest mountain passes.

Meanwhile, the Drôme had given France its first president of peasant stock, **Emile Loubet**. Under his term, the cornerstones of the tolerant, secular French Republic were put in place, Church and State crucially separated; the Jewish army officer Alfred Dreyfus, who had been outrageously framed, received a pardon; and the colony-settling Entente Cordiale was signed between France and Britain. As to Lyon's socialist mayor **Edouard Herriot**, he became a major French figure through the first half of the century. In town, he called on progressive architect **Tony Garnier** to develop social housing.

The Two World Wars

The **First World War** front lay well north of the Rhône-Alpes, but men from across France served in the atrocious trenches. A massive arrival of **American troops** was vital in ending the conflict, many black US soldiers stationed for a time in Lyon. After the horrors of the 'Great War', **the first Winter Olympics** took place in 1924 at **Chamonix** and the comedy classic *Clochemerle (see* p.26) put the Beaujolais centre-stage. But France was paranoid about German aggression and in the 1930s the massive **forts of the Maginot line** extended as far as the Alps – you can visit one in the Arc valley. Such defences proved totally ineffective as Germany conquered France with ignominious ease in June 1940 in the **Second World War**. Rule was first split, the Nazis in northern France, the French collaborationist, puppet government led by Marshal Pétain overseeing the southern half of the country from Vichy, just west of the Rhône-Alpes. **Lyon** rapidly developed as **capital of the southern movements of resistance**, many of the most important figures from Lyon *(see* p.77). **Jean Moulin** came along to unify the diverse strands, working exceptionally closely with **de Gaulle** from late 1941.

In November 1942, the Nazis occupied the whole of France after the Allies had successfully taken a footing across in North Africa. The **Gestapo** (the Nazi secret police) set up in **Lyon** under **Klaus Barbie**. The **Italians**, allies of the Germans, were put in command of France's alpine territories. Although generally less fearsome than the Germans, or even the French collaborationist Milice police, they were still another occupying force controlling a large portion of eastern Rhône-Alpes. The King of Italy, **Victor-Emmanuel III**, having yielded too easily to **Mussolini**, finally helped plot that fascist dictator's downfall . While the vast majority of the Rhône-Alpes' population did nothing to act against its occupiers, a proportion collaborated to varying degrees. Disastrously, Moulin was caught in Lyon in July 1943, but not before having helped ensure that de Gaulle's camp was established to take over power come Allied victory.

The German mass call-up forcing young Frenchmen to go to work in Germany caused many to join **Resistance groups**. These grew significantly in ranges such as the **Vercors**, **Chartreuse** and **Aravis**. Resistance fighters also showed exceptional defiance around **Oyonnax** and **Nantua**. As 1944 advanced, the Nazis resorted to desperately heavy-handed atrocities to flush them out. In the Vercors, whole villages were martyred, such as **Vassieux-en-Vercors**. Many compelling but dreadfully upsetting museums recall the war in the region, none more harrowing than that in memory of the Jewish children captured at **Izieu**. Lyon was finally liberated in September 1944.

Speeding into the New Tourist Age

After the Allied victory, **de Gaulle** encouraged French self-reliance. Vast dams were built to provide electricity, not just along the Rhône, where the **Barrage de Génissiat**, completed in 1948, counted for a time as the largest in Europe, but also on the Ain and upper Loire, and along the major Alpine valleys. Nuclear power was pushed to meet the country's massive need for energy, the Rhône seeing huge-funnelled *centrales nucléaires* popping up at regular intervals . Western Europe's leaders, helped by massive American aid, concentrated on peaceful cooperation among themselves, leading to the European Economic Community of 1957, forerunner of the European Union. Even earlier, one of the first prestigious ventures in Western European partnership , **CERN**, at the forefront in nuclear particle physics research, opened on the Rhône-Alpes' border with Switzerland. Nearby, at the spa town of **Divonne**, the calming properties of its cold waters were used to try and treat many victims who survived the Nazi concentration camps. Matters weren't rosy in the French colonies. While the French withdrew from Vietnam, the long, vicious Algerian war ended with the French colonialists leaving by the million; at **Evian** by Lac Léman, the **treaty** was signed in 1962 by which the French government acknowledged Algeria's independence.

In the Rhône-Alpes, attention rapidly turned to tourism, the **mass ski resorts** rising fast. Courchevel was begun as early as 1946. Bold projects followed at the likes of Les Arcs, La Plagne and Tignes up the Isère. At the time, these provided architectural excitement aplenty, and exhilaration for millions. But resorts also went up respecting traditional forms more closely, like Méribel, La Clusaz, La Rosière, and most recently, posh Ste-Foy-Tarentaise. On top of the annual thrill of the ski season, the **Winter Olympics** were held at **Grenoble** in 1968. Towns like this and Lyon boomed industrially, but their first-rate cultural legacies remained curiously unknown. Meanwhile, one of the most famous of all modern architects, **Le Corbusier**, designed the **Couvent de la Tourette** in the **Monts du Lyonnais**, and civic buildings for **Firminy** close to St-Etienne.

Conservation became a concern. Charles Bosson, mayor of **Annecy**, took action to clean up France's most beautiful, but also terribly polluted great lake. Following the Italian lead, France's first **National Park**, the **Vanoise** adjoining that of Gran Paradiso, was created in 1963, in good part to protect the endangered European ibex, although the remit broadened to protecting the environment generally. The new division of the **French regions** occurred in the 1970s, the Rhône-Alpes created as one of the new administrative entities. Plans developed for regional nature parks, to protect exceptionally beautiful traditional areas with balanced policies of conservation and development. It is odd, though, that unlike the tallest mountains of the other continents, Mont Blanc hasn't received protected status, while little can stop Savoie's great glaciers receding, faced by planetary warming. Meantime, the **motorway and TGV** train networks extended across the region, facilitating access down the Rhône and along the furthest Alpine valleys. The first-ever TGV train service in fact opened between Paris and Lyon in 1981.

The **last King of Italy, Humbert II**, was buried at **Hautecombe** in 1983. The war reared its head again in ugly fashion after the extradition of **Klaus Barbie** from Bolivia, where the American authorities had allowed him to 'vanish' in 1951, having briefly served them versus the Communists. The pope visited in 1986, the year before the traumatic **trial in Lyon**. Barbie was found guilty of crimes against humanity and died in gaol.

Strangely, the popular image stuck of the Rhône-Alpes as a region dominated by industry on the economic side, and mass ski resorts on the tourist side . But you'll soon find out how terribly misleading this is, with major industry largely confined to a few sections of valleys, and so many small-scale resorts to be discovered along with innumerable, gorgeous semi-crumbling, semi-restored hill villages. Hippies moved into some during the 1960s, but found the winters a little chilly! Many villages have been given new life by artists, or been spruced up by foreign second-home owners. Some of the prettiest have played the tourist game, joining the association of *Les Plus Beaux Villages de France*. Countless others prove as enchanting, and more peaceful. It is a mystery, though, that in this tourist age, such an exceptionally beautiful French region, so well placed between Burgundy and Provence, should remain so little known to English-speaking visitors outside the snow season. Few know either that a British scientist, **Tim Berners-Lee**, invented the **worldwide web** at CERN.

Even wealthy **Lyon**, despite pouring money into culture and the beautification of its splendid centre, was long bypassed by French tourists. Former French Prime Minister **Raymond Barre** became the city's mayor from 1995 to 2001. During this time Lyon hosted a **G7 world economic summit**, became **headquarters of Interpol** (the international crime-fighting agency), and was **declared a World Heritage Site**; French people suddenly became much more aware of its exceptional 2,000-year legacy, and foreigners are catching on. Modern developments by famous architects such as **Jean Nouvel** and **Renzo Piano** have been going up recently. In fact, although not terribly well known for its towns, the region has other exceptional, dynamic cities like **Annecy**, **Chambéry** and **Grenoble**. Even **St-Etienne**, with its gritty mining and industrial past, has been declared a *Ville d'Art et d'Histoire*, in recognition, especially, of a clutch of fine museums, notably one on **modern art**. The other big centres have created spaces for **cutting-edge creation** too, Lyon, as well as St-Etienne, known for its **Biennales**, definitely a trendy place all round. **Chamonix** was in the news for the wrong reasons at the end of the millennium, with an appalling fatal fire in the Tunnel du Mont Blanc and a particularly lethal avalanche in 1999, the first a freak accident, the second a sadly more regular occurrence – always treat the mountains with great caution.

On a happier note, the old spa towns like **Aix-les-Bains** or **Vals-les-Bains**, long overreliant on French health service patients, have smartened up their acts to offer tourists a good pampering. Poshest of all, **Evian** hosted the **2003 G8 meeting** of advanced industrial countries – a huge police cordon forced the anti-globalization protesters to stay the other, Swiss, side of Lac Léman. Not just such engaged activists, but any visitor can appreciate that, along with a plethora of **museums** and passionately-run smaller *écomusées*, the Rhône-Alpes has seen the creation of far more **natural parks** than any other French region, and exceptionally intelligent **ecological centres** like the **Ecopôle de Chambéon** by the Loire, the **Maison du Marais de Larvours** in the Bugey, **Terre Vivante** in the Trièves, and **Les Jardins de l'Eau du Pré Curieux** at Evian. A vibrant region, rather than one pickled in the past, it now even offers cinema, theatre and jazz in some of its oldest venues, like the Roman theatres of Lyon and Vienne.

Topics

The Taming of the Rhône 22
Alpine Heroes Take On Mont Blanc 23
An *Ancien Régime* Bestseller in Another Loire 23
Why Annonay Celebrates A Lot of Hot Air! 24
Guignol, a French Answer to Punch and Judy 24
From the Ridiculous to the Sublime 24
Lyon Suburb Sees Birth of World Cinema 25
Clochemerle – Poking Fun at the Beaujolais 26
When Lavender Scents the Air 26

03

The Taming of the Rhône

'A raging bull racing down from the Alps,' was the memorable manner France's most famous 19th-century historian, Jules Michelet, described the awesome, muscular River Rhône. It starts its crazed course just the other side of the Swiss St Gotthard pass from the Rhine, rushing first for Lac Léman, splashing into it on the far eastern side, leaving it in the far west, via Geneva. It then takes sharp turns to Lyon before the final swerving leg of its frenzied gallop to the Mediterranean. Between Geneva and Provence, other temperamental waters join forces with it, the Isère and the Drôme from the east, and from the north, the Jura's Ain and Burgundy's Saône. In the west, seasonally crazed then calm torrents plunge down to it from the Massif Central.

The Rhône remained, until recent times, a semi-wild, impetuous creature, on whose bucking back the intrepid traded, the Celts and the Greeks starting the serious business, the Romans leaving a stunning legacy. Gymnastically perched castles vividly recall the importance of frontier tolls and defences in medieval times. Through the *Ancien Régime*, the Rhône remained beyond man's control, although, in 1783, Claude de Jouffray d'Abbans' *Pyroscaphe*, one of the world's earliest steam-powered boats, managed to go up river at Lyon, 'moving without any animal power'! From the 19th century, more assertive efforts were made to straddle the Rhône's back. Marc Seguin of Annonay (great-nephew of the famous Montgolfier brothers – *see* p.24) designed the earliest French suspension bridges, the first one spanning the Rhône in 1825.

Waterpower then began to be exploited for hydroelectricity, although much of the pioneering work on 'white coal' was carried out by Aristide Bergès along the Isère, the second most important river in the Rhône-Alpes. However, the potential of the Rhône was soon put to great use, nearby Bellegarde becoming the first French town to have public lighting. But the river was really only properly tamed after the Compagnie Nationale du Rhône was set up in 1934, controlling navigation, irrigation and, above all, hydroelectricity. A string of vast dams went up, most memorably the Barrage de Génissiat, built around the Second World War, then the largest dam in Europe. Seeking to reassert French national independence, after the war, de Gaulle led France along the route of nuclear power stations, building a string along the Rhône. The raging bull stood in chains, somewhat scarred, well and truly harnessed for heavy-duty work.

You may not think tourism and Rhône go hand in hand. But there are calmer sides to the river beyond industry, with stunning vineyards, museums recalling riverside culture back to prehistoric times, prettified villages, and riverside towns that have recently given themselves a good dusting down. Even Givors, hemmed in by industry, is completely redoing its Maison du Rhône to treat the river with due respect. The ports have been smartened up and offer cruises, plus the summer spectacle of river-jousting, as well as more peaceable activities like fishing. Bourg-St-Andéol on the region's southern river frontier conceals a rare Gallo-Roman relief showing an athletic young man overcoming a formidable bull, a religious sculpture of the Mithraic cult, but well symbolizing the centuries-old struggle with the raging Rhône. How times have changed. Stretches have even been completed of the *Véloroute*, to allow you to cycle happily side by side with the great beast from Geneva to the Med.

Alpine Heroes Take On Mont Blanc

Heading over to tackle Europe's highest peak, one of the Alps' greatest heroes, St Bernard, is said to have been born at the dramatic Château de Menthon on Lac d'Annecy. Legend has it he slipped out of his bedroom window the night before his wedding, to avoid his arranged marriage. Spirited off by an angel, he devoted himself not simply to the religious life around Aosta (in Italy), but also famously set up two monasteries, at the Great St-Bernard and Little St-Bernard passes, the latter on the Rhône-Alpes' Italian border just south of Mont Blanc, protecting travellers from both bandits and the elements. In popular images, Bernard was depicted stamping on the devil; he is certainly credited with making the Alps much more secure for pilgrimage and trade. The Bernardine order created the breed of big dogs named after him, for Alpine rescues, and Pope Pius XI declared the man patron saint of mountaineers.

While the Petit St-Bernard pass allowed travellers to sidestep Mont Blanc, the greatest adventurers in French *alpinisme* took on the highest summit on the continent, at 4,808m. Some claim a group of Englishmen put Chamonix on the map in the 1740s. Summit fever certainly gripped the village from 1760, when Monsieur de Saussure offered a reward to the first person to get to the top of Mont Blanc, then also known as the *Montagne Maudite* (the Cursed Mountain). Messrs Paccard and Balmat were the first to succeed, in 1786, as statues of rather maddened-looking figures recall in Chamonix. De Saussure followed the next year, as did Colonel Beaufoy, the first Englishman. There's some dispute over the first woman to climb Mont Blanc. Marie Paradis reached the top in 1809, but was carried much of the way by friends, so the honour goes to Henriette d'Angerville.

An *Ancien Régime* Bestseller in Another Loire

Somewhat surprisingly, out west, the Rhône-Alpes holds the source of the Loire by its tail, and lays claim to some of the upper reaches of France's longest river. This part of the Loire, and its tributary the Lignon, stars, along with a remarkable number of shepherds and shepherdesses, in one of the greatest literary successes of 17th-century Europe, *L'Astrée*, written by local nobleman Honoré d'Urfé, a pastoral epic that did much to encourage the rage among *Ancien Régime* aristocrats for dressing up as peasants. But the intertwining stories are really about the dreadful complexities of love, *Amour* turning its authority into tragic tyranny in this idyllic country. The local riverbanks serve as the backdrop to the drama from the start, the shepherdess Astrée accusing the good shepherd Céladon of disloyalty. Spurned, he throws himself into the Lignon. Instead of rushing to help, Astrée faints! The story swiftly moves into the realms of higher fantasy as nymphs garlanded with pearls find Céladon on the river bank and carry him to Galathée's castle. The love complications then multiply in this mythological romp. Abridged versions of the massive novel, beloved of the likes of Marie-Antoinette (and also Jean-Jacques Rousseau), now exist, retaining the original's freshness, gambolling good-humour and poignant musings on the agonies of love.

Why Annonay Celebrates A Lot of Hot Air!

Just before the end of the *Ancien Régime*, one of the most significant flights of all time took place at Annonay, thanks to the two brothers, Joseph and Etienne de Montgolfier, who are credited with pioneering hot-air ballooning. The story goes that Joseph began to experiment with the possibilities of hot air after he'd noticed the way his shirt flew up as he tried to dry it over a fire. Late in 1782, he and his brother carried out secretive experiments, lighting fires under the balloons they made from paper and cloth. Rumour spread that they were dabbling in sorcery. But in early June 1783 they held a public demonstration of their invention on Annonay's Place des Cordeliers. The balloon miraculously rose high into the air. Competition hotting up, proceedings moved to Lyon and Paris. The Montgolfiers organized the first flight with live creatures for Louis XIV's court – a cockerel, a duck and a sheep beat the first men into the air, Pilâtre de Rozier and the Marquis d'Arlandes making the first successful recorded manned flight of all time on 21 November 1783. But what of the curious commemorative plate in Annonay's museum depicting a tragic Madame Blanchard apparently making an ill-fated balloon trip in 1782, dying in the process? Nowadays Annonay celebrates hot-air ballooning with its annual early June celebrations, while local companies can organize balloon trips in this cradle of flight.

Guignol, a French Answer to Punch and Judy

French society was profoundly shaken up by the Revolution, but in the 19th century, workers continued to be exploited on a massive scale, among them the *canuts*, the silk workers of Lyon. With bitter-sweet humour, one of their number, the young Laurent Mourguet, who had been made unemployed at the start of the century, dedicated himself to puppetry. To begin with, he followed the traditional stories of the long-established Italian *Commedia dell'Arte* slapstick farce. Such was his success, he became professional in 1804, hired a musician, and created his own characters. Wide-eyed, cheeky Guignol, with his tight black cap, brown frock coat and a long pigtail, wore a Chinese air, but chattered away in Lyonnais dialect, his banter providing working-class commentary on the events of the day. His lady friend Madelon put up with him, grumbling and arguing a lot. His great mate Gnafron, a red-nosed tippler was wedded to Beaujolais. Guignol's puppet characters and stories spread across France, and have now become an institution something akin to Punch and Judy.

From the Ridiculous to the Sublime

Moving from the ridiculous to the sublime, Hector Berlioz was brought up at La Côte St-André in the region, where a renovated museum has just opened in the house of his birth. His hair resembles the plumage of a wild, exotic bird on the many busts of him inside, somehow befitting for such a colourful, passionate figure of the musical world. The composer's father was a forward-looking doctor, among the first to introduce acupuncture into France. On the home front, he oversaw the education of his young son extremely closely, 'my master of languages, literature, history, geography and even music'. Hector moved to Paris to study medicine. But his passion for composing overcame him. Taken into the Paris conservatoire in 1826, by 1830, the brilliant young man had won the prestigious Prix de Rome for one of his earliest compositions, the cantata *Sardanapale*, allowing him to study in Italy. This was the year that produced one of his best-loved pieces, *Symphonie fantastique*. Something of a tormented Romantic dreamer, Berlioz was inspired by literature as much as music, and several English authors, including Byron, had a profound impact on him. But it was Shakespeare's words that stirred him most – helped by the fact that he met and married a Shakespearean actress, Harriet Smithson, with whom he settled, unhappily, in Montmartre. He continued to produce splendid works however, including *Harold en Italie*, a *Requiem*, the opera *Benvenuto Cellini* and the symphony *Roméo et Juliette*, but his style proved too innovative for French audiences, and Berlioz had to make a career principally as a music critic. Although continuing to be spurned by the French, further pieces such as *La Damnation de Faust*, *L'Enfance du Christ*, his *Te Deum*, *Béatrix et Bénédict* and *Les Troyens* were fêted across Europe, where the brilliance of his innovative musical achievements was recognized.

Lyon Suburb Sees Birth of World Cinema

Few people realize that cinema was invented in Lyon. Painter-turned-photo-portraitist, Antoine Lumière laid the foundations for the Lumière boys' revolution in photography and the moving image. His sons Auguste and Louis were born in the Franche-Comté's capital Besançon, in 1862 and 1864 respectively. The family moved to Lyon in 1870. Inventive, sociable Antoine set up his successful studio near Place Bellecour. His bright sons received a fine scientific education at the Martinière school.

Louis was the truly innovative one. At just 17, he invented a technique for instant photography, a major breakthrough. The family built a factory to manufacture these *Etiquette Bleue* films on an industrial scale. And at the start of the 20th century Louis invented autochrome plates for colour photography. In between times he came up with the invention for which he is internationally celebrated – the cinematograph. The patent was registered in February 1895 for this machine that captured moving images on the famed transparent strip with its perforated edges. It gave birth to perhaps the greatest artistic industry of the 20th century, cinema film. Lyon puts on some great cinematic events throughout the year, including those held at the Villa Lumière, one of the sumptuous houses the family built on their fortune, now a major museum. Annecy has become another important centre of cinema, with several festivals, plus a new permanent exhibition on attempts to capture moving images before cinema came into existence. The displays are delightful, allowing you to experiment with the variety of machines dreamt up by pioneering inventors like Joseph Plateau, Emile Reynaud or Etienne Jules Marey. The Rhône-Alpes has also adopted a deliberate policy of encouraging and backing French films set in the region.

Clochemerle – Poking Fun at the Beaujolais

The main joy of touring Beaujolais is exploring its sleepy wine villages, but one of France's comedy classics turns the petty dramas of a fictional one into a national crisis. In October 1922, Barthélemy Piéchut, ambitious fox of a mayor of Clochemerle, and its biggest vineyard owner, decides to build a magnificent new edifice, a Grand Projet well before President Mitterrand's. Piéchut announces his plan to his sidekick, over-earnest teacher Ernest Tafardel, whose lecturing and bad breath the mayor exploits as powerful weapons versus his village adversaries. His big idea? A splendid embodiment of the Republican ideals of liberty, equality and fraternity: a communal urinal. Only he provocatively places it next to the church, within view of the ultra-Catholic, bitter old spinster, the *aride demoiselle* Justine Putet (roughly translated, Justine Tart), one of Gabriel Chevallier's most viciously drawn caricatures.

The battle isn't simply over a urinal of course, the community split between liberal Republican and conservative religious factions, but also between those who can't resist the pleasures of the flesh, and those who want to take their jealous revenge on the unbridled. Such is the brilliance of the comedy and caricatures, you can't help taking pleasure in all the unhappy tales, in which wine and vineyard inheritance play a large part. Even the village priest Ponosse is profoundly affected by Beaujolais wine, his nose 'a hue somewhere between the violet worn by canons of the Church and a cardinal's purple'! To discover the terrible, farcical denouement of the fictional events of 1923, and how this mock-Beaujolais village suffers a storm that makes its slopes run red with 'alcoholic blood', read this deliciously stinging satire for yourselves.

When Lavender Scents the Air

Cultivated in big rounded clumps that look, close up, like ranks of well fed hedge-hogs, from a distance lavender fields mark the landscape of the southern Drôme and Ardèche like corduroy, with their raised lines and deep grooves. In the second half of June, the lavender grows long, mauve-flowered stems that scent the air like a cour-tesan's boudoir, reaching their full, outrageous intensity in July. The careful farming of lavender only took off on a major scale quite recently, in the Belle Epoque before the First World War, when demand from the big perfume houses grew enormously. Before that time, locals would simply go according to need to pick the lavender growing wild on the hillsides, like so many herbs in these dry, warm parts. The work was tough, but song as well as scent would fill the air. *Lavande vraie* (*lavandula augustofolia*) grows with tight tufty ends. *Lavande aspic* (*lavandula latifolia*), has a much more limited growth with two secondary ears. A natural crossing of these two has created *lavandin*, flowering later and less intense, but all three perfume the air deliciously. You can buy all manner of lavender products in the Rhône-Alpes' producing areas and further afield throughout the year, but if you get a chance to see the lavender growing, you'll witness one of the most colourful sights that nature can provide. For good lavender addresses along the way, consult *www.routes-lavande.com*.

Food and Drink

Local Dishes 28
Wines, Liqueurs and World-famous Waters 30
French Menu Reader 31

04

Local Dishes

Jesus is a sausage in food-obsessed Lyon – a sign of how important the culinary is in this region, and how it's treated with both seriousness and good humour. From the chicken-crazed Bresse in the north to the olive- and truffle-mad Drôme in the south, from the mountain chestnuts transformed into divine *marrons glacés* in the west, via the delectable ravioli, walnuts and St-Marcellin cheese of the middle Isère, to the densely flavoured cheeses and hams of Savoie in the east, this region serves up some of the finest produce in France. It can also put on lots of frogs' legs, tripe and brains to upset the sensibilities of soft Anglo-Saxons. The region further spawned Brillat-Savarin, which may sound like a French dish that comes with a complicated sauce, but turns out to have been a brilliant 19th-century *bon vivant* whose philosophising book on the culinary, *La Physiologie du goût*, is still regarded as a classic. 'Tell me what you eat and I will tell you what you are.' is one of his more famous quotes.

The Rhône-Alpes boasts the highest number of **stellar chefs** outside Paris. In fact, in 1938, Fernand Point of La Pyramide in Rhône-side Vienne became the first in France to achieve hallowed Michelin 3-star status. Famous names like Georges Blanc, Paul Bocuse, Alain Chapel, the Troisgros, and Marc Veyrat have followed suit. Before these super-talented chefs, a formidable array of women restaurateurs in the region's capital, *les mères de Lyon*, made the reputation of that city's culinary establishments.

Traditional Lyon grub is copious but not overly sophisticated. Back with that Jésus, it's an exceptionally fat *saucisson* with whitened skin, supposedly looking like a baby wrapped in swaddling clothes! You'll find a huge array of this and other *saucissons* (notably Rosette and Cervelas), plus *quenelles* (see below), cheese, fruit, veg and wines in Lyon's renowned markets. Greater Lyon also boasts an amazing 2,000 restaurants!

In terms of **meats**, the Lyonnais are pork crazy, but will also eat virtually any edible portion of an animal, sometimes under a heavily disguised name – tripe, for example, served up as '*tablier du sapeur* (fireman's apron)'! The love of charcuterie is daunting, to be sampled in the typical little family-run *bouchon* restaurants. Even the traditional Lyonnais elevenses, *mâchons*, involves mountains of charcuterie washed down with a glass of red. To satisfy demand, the provenance of the pigs is rather less certain than that of the pampered *poulets de Bresse*, the most highly regarded chickens in France (*see* p.81). Meadow-grazing lamb from the south can be another treat. In many areas, proud traditions of mountain charcuterie are continued – look out for free-range products such as *jambon à l'ancienne* ham, special *saucissons*, and sausages like *diots*, served in a wine sauce. *Caillettes* are minced meat balls from the Ardèche, mixed with spinach or chard. Plenty of game is caught in the region's woods, but quite a lot of fowl is now specially reared. *Pintadeaux de la Drôme*, guineafowl fed on mountain herbs, have their own *appellation d'origine contrôlée*. Pigeon can also be particularly delicious.

The region's large lakes produce decent amounts of **fish**, although many lake fish and even frogs' legs have to be imported these days. *Féra* (whitefish also known as *lavaret* or *corégone*) is the fine-flavoured exclusive, emblematic fish of the big lakes, often served mashed in a *brandade*. *Omble chevalier*, char, has a reputation for its good taste. *Lotte* (burbot) is quite rare, but *perche* common, while little *perchettes* are fried whole. The lakes yield good salmon and trout, the latter also found in mountain rivers. Down among the Dombes and Forez lakes where carp are reared, frogs' legs are a traditional fast-food speciality! The region's waters yield tasty crayfish too. *Quenelles*, a rather strange concoction, a white dumpling sausage made with cream, egg whites, flour and, usually, *brochet* (pike), can be stodgy, but should be almost as light as a soufflé. The town of Nantua is known for its *quenelles* in crayfish sauce.

Sticking to the savoury, the **olives** of Nyons in the Drôme count among the finest in France, with their own *appellation d'origine contrôlée*. Their oil sells at golden prices. Just west, around Grignan and Richerenches, lie the most prolific **truffle**-producing territories in the country. The southern Ardèche also comes up with these delicacies. Turning to commoner tubers and **vegetables**, potatoes are prepared in various ways, fried in *matafans*, grated in *farçons* or *farcements* or, baked in chunky layers with cream and garlic in Gratin Dauphinois, the region's *pommes de terre* dish par excellence. Polenta, a savoury maize cake, is popular both in Savoie and the Bresse. Splendid vegetables flourish in the valleys, providing all the ingredients for a superb ratatouille, with local herbs to add flavour. Autumn brings wild mushrooms out onto the menus.

The region produces sensational **cheeses**. Cows, sheep and goats are sent into the higher pastures with the *transhumance* at the beginning of the summer season. The dense Alpine meadows ring with *clarines*, the bells of the Abondance, Montbéliard and Tarine cows, in the warm season. Brillat-Savarin declared Beaufort (*see* p. 236) prince of the *gruyères*, the hard mountain cheeses. Its rival, Comté, named after the Franche-Comté or Jura region north of Lac Léman, is produced on the region's frontier. Abondance is another superlative hard *fromage*. The smaller round Tommes come in a variety of styles, Tome des Bauges standing out for its quality, as well as having just one 'm'. Moving to softer varieties, quick-ripening Reblochon has a very long history (*see* p.226), and Vacherin makes a gooey treat. Most internationally famous of all in the **Savoie** cheese stakes are *fondues* and *raclettes*, absolutely delicious dishes of melted cheese, the mix of Emmental, Beaufort and Comté in *fondues* flavoured with local wines, garlic and nutmeg, while simpler Raclette comes with charcuterie and potatoes. Reblochon turns up baked with bacon, potatoes and cream in *tartiflette*, or fried with potatoes and onions in *péla*. In the south of the region, goats' cheese reigns, going from soft, gentle *chèvre frais* to more pungent, hard, aged circles. *Picodons* of the Drôme come from herds grazing in the herb-filled hills. *Ravioles de Royans*, the most delicate of all ravioli, filled with goats' cheese and herbs, cook in just a couple of minutes. The region's blue cheeses tend to be gentle and include Bleu de Bresse, Bleu de Gex, Bleu de Sassenage, and Fourme de Montbrison.

Walnuts thrive in the *département de l'Isère* in particular, long granted their own *appellation d'origine contrôlée*. **Chestnuts** (*see* p.135) were the paupers' staple in the Ardèche in times past. Now they are king, transformed into *marrons glacés*, but also other delicious, sticky preserves like *crème de marrons*. In the Ardèche, countless desserts incorporate chestnuts. The heavenly Mont Blanc pudding (a favourite of the decadent Borgias!) consists of a large meringue filled with chestnut purée, topped by a mountain of whipped cream. Ice cream variations carry the same name and a sweet Vacherin is a somewhat similar. The healthiest **fruit** thrives around the Rhône valley, the quality of the peaches, nectarines, cherries and apricots superlative, with exceptional juice and flavour. Berries come to the fore in the summer Alps.

Regional **cake** specialities include *Gâteau de Savoie*, a light sponge, and brioche or *pogne*, often with bright red lumps of praline (nuts caramelized in sugar). The Rhône-Alpes has fine pâtissiers galore, and some of the best French **chocolate**-makers, the most famous Bernachon, Pralus, Weiss and Valrhôna, the last the best known internationally, its name indicating it's made in the Vallée du Rhône (*see* p.151). But the region's most widely-known confection is **nougat** from Montélimar (*see* p.166).

Wines, Liqueurs and World-famous Waters

'Le vigneron monte à sa vigne, du bord de l'eau jusqu'au cielao.'
('The winemaker climbs to his vines from the waters edge to the sky.')
From a local *vignerons'* song along the Rhône valley.

Vines act like mountaineers in parts of the Rhône-Alpes, struggling up madly steep slopes, be it in the vineyards of the northern Côtes du Rhône, or the very unexpected *vignobles* of Savoie or the Bugey. In other parts, they spread out luxuriantly in the sun, most memorably in the Beaujolais in the north, or in the Côtes du Rhône and Coteaux du Tricastin in the south. All the region's vineyards look gorgeous.

In the northwest, the Beaujolais, Côtes Roannaises, Côtes du Forez and Coteaux du Lyonnais produce light-coloured, easy-drinking ruby wines from the single, Gamay grape variety. The main grape variety for the deeper, fuller bodied reds in the northern Côtes du Rhône is Syrah, that in the south Grenache, with Mourvèdre, Cinsault or Carignan added. For the whites, Viognier is king in the northern Côtes du Rhône, Roussanne and Marsanne noble varieties , while in the south, Grenache Blanc, Clairette and Bourboulenc are the main players. More unusual, highly perfumed varieties dominate in higher climes, like Altesse, Clairette, Jacquère, Roussette and Roussanne in the whites, and Mondeuse in the reds. Perfumed sparkling wines are made at St-Péray on the Rhône, around Die in the Drôme and in the Bugey .

In short, the Rhône-Alpes turns out to be a highly surprising and exhilarating region for wine lovers, and because visiting vineyards is so closely tied with touring, we've included more detailed explanations on the region's main wines in the touring chapters. Special text boxes on wine cover Beaujolais, the northern Côtes du Rhône , Clairette de Die, the Coteaux du Tricastin and southern Côtes du Rhône. Further paragraphs mention the smaller *appellations d'origine contrôlée* dotted around the place .

Potent liqueurs made with a complex concoction of mountain herbs are a heady speciality of the region . Chartreuse is the most famous, a blend of over 100 herbs, coming in brightest yellow or green. Simpler but equally brash-looking Génépi, based on a special plant picked high in the Alps, is popular across Savoie. Among the orchards of the Rhône valley, you'll find excellent distillers of fruit, and nut, liqueurs. To cleanse the palate and clear the head, the region produces some of the most famous of bottled waters, Evian and Badoit (the latter from St-Galmier) leaders in still and sparkling respectively, although you'll find lots of other local brands around.

French Menu Reader

Hors-d'œuvre et Soupes (Starters and Soups)

assiette assortie plate of mixed cold *hors d'œuvre*
bisque shellfish soup
bouchées mini *vol-au-vents*
bouillabaisse famous fish soup of Marseille
bouillon broth
charcuterie mixed cold meats, salami, ham, etc.
consommé clear soup
crudités raw vegetable platter
potage thick vegetable soup
tourrain garlic and bread soup
velouté thick smooth soup, often fish or chicken

Poissons et Coquillages (Crustacés) (Fish and Shellfish)

aiglefin little haddock
alose shad
anchois anchovies
anguille eel
bar sea bass
barbue brill
baudroie anglerfish
belons flat oysters
bigorneau winkle
blanchailles whitebait
brème bream
brochet pike
bulot whelk
cabillaud cod
calmar squid
carrelet plaice
colin hake
congre conger eel
coques cockles
coquillages shellfish
coquilles St-Jacques scallops
crevettes grises/roses shrimp/prawns
daurade sea bream
écrevisse freshwater crayfish
escargots snails
espadon swordfish
esturgeon sturgeon
flétan halibut
friture deep-fried fish
fruits de mer seafood
gambas giant prawns
gigot de mer a large fish cooked whole

grondin red gurnard
hareng herring
homard lobster
huîtres oysters
lamproie lamprey
langouste spiny Mediterranean lobster
langoustines Norwegian lobsters (often called Dublin Bay prawns or scampi)
limande lemon sole
lotte monkfish
loup (de mer) sea bass
maquereau mackerel
merlan whiting
morue salt cod
moules mussels
oursin sea urchin
pagel sea bream
palourdes clams
poulpe octopus
praires small clams
raie skate
rascasse scorpion fish
rouget red mullet
saumon salmon
sole (meunière) sole (with butter and lemon)
St-Pierre John Dory
stockfisch stockfish (wind-dried cod)
telline tiny clam
thon tuna
truite trout
truite saumonée salmon trout

Viandes et Volailles (Meat and Poultry)

agneau lamb
aloyau sirloin
andouillette chitterling (tripe) sausage
biftek beefsteak
blanc breast or white meat
blanquette stew of white meat
bœuf beef
boudin blanc sausage of white meat
boudin noir black pudding
brochette meat (or fish) on a skewer
caille quail
canard, caneton duck, duckling
carré the best end of a cutlet or chop
cassoulet haricot bean stew with sausage, duck, goose, etc.
cervelle brains
chapon capon
châteaubriand porterhouse steak
cheval horsemeat
chevreau kid

civet meat (usually game) stew, in wine and blood sauce

confit meat cooked and preserved in its own fat

côte, côtelette chop, cutlet

cou d'oie farci goose neck stuffed with pork, foie gras and truffles

crépinette small sausage

cuisse thigh or leg

dinde, dindon turkey

épaule shoulder

estouffade a meat stew marinated, fried and then braised

faux-filet sirloin

foie liver

frais de veau veal testicles

fricadelle meatball

gésier gizzard

gibier game

gigot leg of lamb

graisse or *gras* fat

grillade grilled meat, often a mixed grill

grive thrush

jarret knuckle

langue tongue

lapereau young rabbit

lapin rabbit

lard (lardons) bacon (diced bacon)

lièvre hare

maigret (or magret) de canard breast of duck

manchons duck or goose wings

marcassin young wild boar

merguez spicy red sausage

moelle bone marrow

mouton mutton

navarin lamb stew with root vegetables

noix de veau topside of veal

oie goose

os bone

perdreau (or perdrix) partridge

petit salé salt pork

pintade guinea fowl

plat-de-côtes short ribs or rib chops

porc pork

pot au feu meat and vegetables in stock

poulet chicken

poussin baby chicken

quenelles poached dumplings made of fish, fowl or meat

queue de bœuf oxtail

ris (de veau) sweetbreads (veal)

rognons kidneys

rosbif roast beef

rôti roast

sanglier wild boar

saucisson dry sausage, like salami

selle (d'agneau) saddle (of lamb)

steak tartare raw minced beef, often topped with a raw egg yolk

suprême de volaille fillet of chicken breast and wing

tête (de veau) (calf's) head, fatty and usually served with a mustardy vinaigrette

tournedos thick round slice of beef fillet

veau veal

venaison venison

Légumes, Herbes, etc. (Vegetables, herbs, etc.)

ail garlic

aïoli garlic mayonnaise

algue seaweed

artichaut artichoke

asperges asparagus

avocat avocado

basilic basil

betterave beetroot

cannelle cinnamon

cèpes ceps, wild boletus mushrooms

champignons mushrooms

chanterelles wild yellow mushrooms

chicorée curly endive

chou cabbage

choucroute sauerkraut

chou-fleur cauliflower

ciboulette chives

citrouille pumpkin

clou de girofle clove

concombre cucumber

cornichons gherkins

courgettes courgettes (zucchini)

cresson watercress

échalote shallot

endive chicory (endive)

épinards spinach

estragon tarragon

fenouil fennel

fèves broad (fava) beans

flageolets white beans

fleurs de courgette courgette blossoms

frites chips (French fries)

genièvre juniper

gingembre ginger

haricots (rouges, blancs) beans (kidney, white)

haricots verts green (French) beans

jardinière with diced garden vegetables

laurier bay leaf

lentilles lentils
maïs (épis de) sweetcorn (on the cob)
menthe mint
mesclun salad of various leaves
morilles morel mushrooms
moutarde mustard
navet turnip
oignon onion
oseille sorrel
panais parsnip
persil parsley
petits pois peas
piment pimento
pissenlits dandelion greens
poireau leek
pois chiches chickpeas
pois mange-tout sugar peas or mangetout
poivron sweet pepper (capsicum)
pomme de terre potato
potiron pumpkin
primeurs young vegetables
radis radishes
raifort horseradish
riz rice
romarin rosemary
roquette rocket
safran saffron
salade verte green salad
salsifis salsify
sarrasin buckwheat
sarriette savory
sauge sage
seigle rye
serpolet wild thyme
thym thyme

Fruits et Noix (Fruit and Nuts)
abricot apricot
amandes almonds
ananas pineapple
bigarreau black cherry
brugnon nectarine
cacahouètes peanuts
cassis blackcurrant
cerise cherry
citron lemon
citron vert lime
coing quince
fraise (des bois) strawberry (wild)
framboise raspberry
fruit de la passion passion fruit
grenade pomegranate
groseille redcurrant
mandarine tangerine

mangue mango
marron chestnut
mirabelle mirabelle plum
mûre (sauvage) mulberry, blackberry
myrtille bilberry
noisette hazelnut
noix walnut
noix de cajou cashew
noix de coco coconut
pamplemousse grapefruit
pastèque watermelon
pêche (blanche) peach (white)
pignons pine nuts
pistache pistachio
poire pear
pomme apple
prune plum
pruneau prune
raisins (secs) grapes (raisins)
reine-claude greengage plum

Desserts
bavarois mousse or custard in a mould
biscuit biscuit, cracker, cake
bombe ice-cream dessert in a round mould
chausson turnover
clafoutis batter fruit cake
compôte stewed fruit
corbeille de fruits basket of fruit
coulis thick fruit sauce
coupe ice-cream: a scoop or in cup
crème anglaise egg custard
gaufre waffle
génoise rich sponge cake
glace ice-cream
miel honey
œufs à la neige floating islands/meringue on
    a bed of custard
pain d'épice gingerbread
sablé shortbread
savarin a filled cake, shaped like a ring
tarte tropézienne sponge cake filled with
    custard and topped with nuts
truffes chocolate truffles

Cooking Terms and Sauces
aigre-doux sweet and sour
aiguillette thin slice
à l'anglaise boiled
à la bordelaise cooked in wine and diced
    vegetables (usually)
à la diable in spicy mustard sauce
à la grecque cooked in olive oil and lemon
à la jardinière with garden vegetables

à la provençale cooked with tomatoes, garlic and olive oil
allumettes strips of puff pastry
à point medium (for steak)
au feu de bois cooked over a wood fire
au four baked
auvergnat with sausage, bacon and cabbage
barquette pastry boat
beignets fritters
béarnaise sauce of egg yolks, shallots and white wine
bien cuit well-done (for steak)
bleu very rare (for steak)
bordelaise red wine, bone marrow and shallot sauce
broche roasted on a spit
chaud hot
cru raw
cuit cooked
émincé thinly sliced
en croûte cooked in a pastry crust
en papillote baked in buttered paper
épices spices
farci stuffed
feuilleté flaky pastry
flambé set aflame with alcohol
forestière with bacon and mushrooms
fourré stuffed
frit fried
froid cold
fumé smoked
galantine cooked food served in cold jelly
galette flaky pastry case or pancake
garni with vegetables
(au) gratin topped with browned cheese and breadcrumbs
haché minced
marmite casserole
médaillon round piece
mornay cheese sauce
pané breaded
pâte pastry; pasta
pâte brisée shortcrust pastry
pâte à chou choux pastry
pâte feuilletée flaky or puff pastry
paupiette rolled and filled thin slices of fish or meat
parmentier with potatoes
pavé slab
poché poached
pommes allumettes thin chips (fries)
raclette melted cheese with potatoes, onions and pickles
saignant rare steak

salé salted
sucré sweet
timbale pie cooked in a dome-shaped mould
tranche slice
véronique green grape, wine and cream sauce

Miscellaneous
addition bill (check)
carte menu
couteau knife
cuillère spoon
formule à €12 €12 set menu
fourchette fork
menu set menu
poivre pepper
sel salt

Snacks
chips crisps (chips)
crêpe thin pancake
croque-madame toasted ham and cheese sandwich with fried egg
croque-monsieur toasted ham and cheese sandwich
croustade small savoury pastry
frites chips (French fries)
pissaladière a kind of pizza with onions, anchovies, etc.
sandwich canapé open sandwich

Boissons (Drinks)
bière (pression) beer (draught)
(demie) bouteille bottle (half)
brut very dry
citron pressé/orange pressée fresh lemon/orange juice, often served with sugar and a jug of water
doux sweet (wine)
eau-de-vie brandy
eau potable drinking water
glaçons ice cubes
infusion/tisane herbal tea
lait milk
menthe à l'eau peppermint cordial
moelleux semi-dry
mousseux sparkling (wine)
pastis aniseed liqueur
pichet pitcher
pression draught
sec dry
sirop d'orange/de citron orange/lemon squash
verre glass
vin blanc/rosé/rouge white/rosé/red wine

Travel

Getting There 36
By Air **36**
By Sea **37**
By Train **38**
By Bus **39**
By Car **39**
Entry Formalities 39
Getting Around 40
By Air **40**
By Train **40**
By Bus **40**
By Car **40**
By Bicycle **42**
On Foot **42**

05

Getting There

By Air

From the UK and Ireland

The major international airports are Lyon St-Exupéry and Geneva, just across the border in Switzerland. St-Etienne and Grenoble also have direct flights from the UK, and Nîmes airport lies just to the south. Chambéry/Aix also have flights from the UK. Air France, British Airways and British Midland all have frequent flights from the different London airports and several other UK cities, and a number of low-cost carriers now ply these routes as well. Fares have become more competitive in the last few years. On low-cost airlines such as Ryanair, easyJet and Flybe for a one-way flight from the UK to Lyon, St-Etienne or Grenoble, you can get amazing bargains. The usual observations need to be made regarding low-cost airlines, though: fares vary a great deal according to when you travel and how far in advance you book; the really low fares are sometimes only available at inconvenient times; and at popular times, or if you book at short notice, prices leap and can easily be similar to those of major airlines. To qualify for the lowest fares you must also book online, not by phone. Always compare prices, and don't assume the no-frills operators will always be the cheapest.

Many bargain flight tickets are also available from student travel and flight-only agencies.

Airline Carriers

UK and Ireland

Aer Lingus, t IR 0818 365 000, *www.aerlingus.com*. Flights from Dublin to Lyon and Geneva, four times a week.

Air France, t 0845 0845 111, *www.airfrance.com*. Daily from London Heathrow to Lyon.

British Airways, t 0870 850 9850, *www.britishairways.com*. Direct flights to Lyon daily from Heathrow, Birmingham and Manchester; to Geneva daily from London City, Gatwick, Heathrow and Manchester.

easyJet, t 0871 750 0100, *www.easyjet.com*. Daily to Geneva from East Midlands, Gatwick, Luton and Newcastle, and to Lyon and Grenoble from London Stansted.

Flybe, t 0871 700 0535, *www.flybe.com*. From Southampton to Chambéry/Aix and Geneva.

Ryanair, t UK 0871 246 0016, **t** IR 0818 30 30 50, *www.ryanair.com*. London Standsted to St-Etienne daily, and Stansted and Luton to Nîmes daily.

Swiss International Airlines, t 0845 601 0956, *www.swiss.com/uk*. Daily flights to Geneva from Heathrow and London City airport.

USA and Canada

Air France, US **t** 1 800 237 2747, Canada **t** 1 800 667 2747, *www.airfrance.com*. Flights to Paris from Philadelphia, Cincinnati, Atlanta, Boston, Chicago, Houston, Miami, San Francisco, Los Angeles, New York and Washington DC in the US, and from Montreal (3 flights daily), Toronto (1 daily) and Ottawa in Canada.

American Airlines, t 1 800 433 7300, *www.aa.com*. Flights to Paris from Boston, Chicago, Dallas, New York JFK and Miami.

Continental, t US 1 800 231 0856; **t** Canada 1 800 525 0280 *www.continental.com*. Flights to Paris from Houston and Newark.

Delta Airways, t US and Canada (*toll free*) 1 800 241 4141, **t** Canada 1 800 221 1212, *www.delta.com*. Direct flights to Paris from Atlanta, Chicago, Cincinnati, Los Angeles, New York, Philadelphia and San Francisco.

Northwest Airlines, t 1 800 225 2525, *www.nwa.com*. Flights to Paris from Detroit.

United Airlines, t 1 800 538 2929, 1 800 674 46 80 (*toll free*) *www.united.com*. Direct flights to Paris from Chicago, San Francisco and Washington DC.

Students, Discounts and Special Deals

UK and Ireland

Students with ID cards can get reductions on flights, trains and admissions.

Budget Travel, 134 Lower Baggot St, Dublin 2, **t** (01) 661 1866, *www.budgettravel.ie*. Has travelshops all over Ireland.

STA, Priory House, 6 Wright's Lane, London W8 6TA, **t** (020) 7361 6100, *www.statravel.com*. Specializes in student travel.

For the best offers, check the Sunday newspapers, or the websites below.

Lyon St-Exupéry International Airport, t 04 72 22 72 21, *www.lyonairport.com*.

Geneva Cointrin International Airport, t (41) 22 717 71 11, *www.gva.ch*.

From the USA and Canada

There are frequent flights from many parts of North America to Paris, from where you can travel on to Rhône-Alpes by train (*see* p.38). Outside peak seasons (such as any time in fall and winter), you can usually expect to get a scheduled economy flight from New York to Paris from as little as $320–$460. In summer scheduled prices go up, but there are many more non-stop charters available. It can,

however, work out cheaper to fly to Britain – for which there is a bigger range of flights – and then continue your journey. Consider using a low-cost carrier such as easyJet or Ryanair for the last leg. A big choice of charters and discount tickets to France and the UK is available year-round. Check Sunday-paper travel sections for the latest deals, or the specialist flight websites listed below.

By Sea

Crossing to France by ferry – or by the competing 'road route', the Channel Tunnel (*see* p.39) – has many advantages for anyone travelling from Britain, especially with children: you can take your own car, and as

---

Trailfinders, 194 and 215 Kensington High St, London W8 7RG, t (020) 7937 1234, *www.trailfinders.com*. Branches across the UK.

USIT Campus Travel, 52 Grosvenor Gardens, London SW1 0AG, t 0870 240 1010, *www.usit-world.com/services/gateways.htm*. Specialists in student travel, with branches across UK and Ireland.

Useful websites
www.cheapflights.com
www.ebookers.com
www.expedia.com
www.flightmapping.com
www.lastminute.com
www.opodo.com
www.TravelJungle.co.uk
www.travelocity.co.uk

USA and Canada

If you are able to be flexible some great budget deals are available on stand-bys or as courier flights (which usually only allow you to take hand luggage). Check out **Airhitch** or *www.xfares.com* for standby tickets, or the *Yellow Pages* for courier companies. For discounted flights try the newspaper travel pages or the websites listed here.

Air Brokers International, USA, t 1 800 883 3273, *www.airbrokers.com*

Airhitch, USA, t (212) 864 2000, *www.airhitch.org*. Last-minute tickets to Europe.

Last Minute Travel Club, Canada, t (416) 449 5400, USA t 1 877 970 35 00 (*toll free*), *www.lastminuteclub.com*

New Frontiers, USA, t 1 800 677 0720 or (212) 986 3343. Discounted flights and last-minute deals to France, as well as all-inclusive packages.

STA Travel, t 1 800 777 0112, 1 800 781 4070 (*toll free*) *www.statravel.com*. Student and charter flights; branches across the USA.

Travel Avenue, USA, t 1 800 333 3335, *www.travelavenue.com*. Discount flights.

Travel Cuts, t Canada 1 866 246 9762, t US 1 800 592-CUTS (2887), *www.travelcuts.com*. Canada's largest student travel specialist, with branches in most provinces of Canada and across the USA.

Useful websites
www.bestfares.com
www.cheaptrips.com
www.courier.org (courier flights)
www.eurovacations.com
www.expedia.com
www.flights.com
www.fool.com/travel/ (advice on booking over the internet)
www.lowestfare.com
www.orbitz.com
www.priceline.com
www.ricksteves.com (travel advice)
www.traveldiscounts.com
www.travelnow.com

much baggage as you need; children aged 4–15 often get reduced rates, and under-4s go free. The downside of ferry travel can be the cost – fares are often expensive, and vary according to season and demand. All the companies prefer you to book online, and give discounts if you do – but it's best to phone, speak to a human being and ask for details of the cheapest fares available. Then book online to get the discount. Plan your trip well in advance.

Ferry Companies

Brittany Ferries, UK **t** 08705 360 360, IR **t** (021) 4277801, *www.brittanyferries.com*. Wide range of crossings to more westerly ports.
Condor Ferries, **t** 0845 345 2000, *www.condorferries.com*. Also for the more westerly French ports.
Hoverspeed, **t** 08705 240 241, *www.hoverspeed.com*. Speedy Superseacats connect Newhaven and Dieppe (2hrs, end-Mar–end-Sept; 3 sailings daily); and Seacats link Dover

and Calais. This is the fastest sea crossing.
Irish Ferries, **t** IR 1 890 31 31 31, *www.irishferries.com*. Weekly ferries overnight between Rosslare and Cherbourg (12hrs).
Norfolkline, **t** 0870 870 1020, *www.norfolkline.com*. Dover to Dunkerque for car passengers only, but some great deals.
P&O Ferries, **t** 08705 20 20 20, *www.poferries.com*. Dover–Calais, 3–4 sailings hourly.
SeaFrance, **t** 08705 711711, *www.seafrance.com*. Dover–Calais only, but often the cheapest of all the ferry companies.
Transmanche Ferries, **t** 0800 917 1201, *www.transmancheferries.com*. Newhaven–Dieppe.

By Train

The **Eurostar** from London or Ashford to France, followed by the **TGV**, is a civilized way to travel to Rhône-Alpes. Travel from London Waterloo to Paris (Gare du Nord; 2hrs 25mins;

Rail Passes

If you expect to travel a lot by train in France or Europe, rail passes can be an investment. They *must* be purchased in your own country. For discount fares obtainable in France, *see* p.40.

Available in the UK and Ireland

The following are both available from Rail Europe UK, *see* p.39.
Euro Domino. Excellent-value, gives EU residents unlimited travel in France for 3–8 days in a month. The cost ranges from £127 for 3 days to £239 for 8 days (£91–£179 for 12–25-year-olds). Children aged 4–11 travel half-price, and under-4s free.
InterRail. For people of any age who have been EU residents for more than six months. You can travel in zones one, two, three or all three 'zones' of Europe, covering 28 countries. A 12-day pass for one zone costs £125 for under-26s, £182 if you're older. A pass covering all the zones costs £265 for under-26s, £379 for over-26s. The pass also gives you 50% discount on travel from Dover to Calais with P&O or Hoverspeed, and returns on Eurostar trains from £60. InterRail passes cannot be used on UK trains. See *www.interrailnet.com* for more information.

Available in the USA and Canada

The following are all available from Rail Europe USA, *see* p.39.
Eurail. For North Americans only, unlimited 1st-class travel in up to 17 EU countries for 15-day, 21-day, 1-month, 2-month or 3-month periods. Two weeks' travel costs $414 for under-26s; those over 26 can get a 15-day pass for $588, a 21-day pass for $762, or one month consecutive for $946. Children aged 4–11 go half-price, and under-4s free. The more limited **Eurail Selectpass** allows you to travel through 3–5 Eurail countries for 5, 6, 8, 10 or 15 days in a 2-month period for $356–$794 (1st class), or $249–$556 (2nd class). (Not valid in the UK or Morocco.)
France Railpass. Four days of unlimited travel throughout the country in a 1-month period for $218 (reduced to $186 per person for 2 people travelling together), or $252 (1st class).
France Youthpass. Under-26s get the same benefit for $189 (1st class) or $164 (2nd class).
France Seniorpass. Similar benefits to the over-60s for $228 (1st class).
France Rail 'n' Drive. A 6-day pass giving 4 days' unlimited rail travel in France and 2 days' car rental, and which costs from $215.

from £59 return, £50 for under-12s) or Lille (1hr 40mins; from £55 return, £44 for under-12s). In Lille you need to change platform; in Paris, you need to cross from Gare du Nord to Gare de Lyon for the TGV – allow 1 hour. TGV times from Paris are: Lyon (2hrs), Annecy (4hrs), Chambéry (3hrs 5mins), Geneva (3hrs 40mins), Grenoble (3hrs), St-Etienne (2hrs 50mins), Valence (2hrs 30mins). For the cheapest Eurostar fares you must book at least 21 days in advance or include a Saturday night in your stay. Promotional fares are often available off-peak times. Eurostar also offers **Eurostar Plus**, a package that includes a Eurostar ticket and one internal French railway train trip. You may stop off for up to 24 hours *en route*. It must be booked at least two months in advance. A fare to Lyon costs from £79.50. Eurostar also runs a once-weekly direct service to Avignon, just south of Rhône-Alpes, in summer, and twice-weekly direct **ski services** from London or Ashford to Moûtiers, Aime-la-Plagne and Bourg-St-Maurice, with buses to La Plagne, Courchevel, Les Arcs, Méribel and Tignes.
Eurostar, t 08705 186 186, from outside UK **t** 44 1233 617 575; *www.eurostar.co.uk*.
Rail Europe (UK), 178 Piccadilly, London W1J 9AL, **t** 08705 848 848, *www.raileurope.co.uk*. Info and bookings for all European railways.
Rail Europe USA, 226 Westchester Av, White Plains, NY 10064, **t** 1 877 257 2887, *www. raileurope.com*. Take your passport.

By Bus

Eurolines operates regular coach services from London to Paris, Lyon, Grenoble and Chamonix. If you book 30 days in advance, return tickets to Paris can cost as little as £29. The journey to Paris takes 8hrs; Lyon takes 14hrs 15mins, Grenoble 15hrs 45mins and Chamonix 19hrs. Peak-season fares (4 July–7 Sept) are slightly higher. There are discounts for pensioners, under-26s, and under-12s.
Eurolines, t 08705 143 219, *www.eurolines.co.uk*.

By Car

Putting a car on a Shuttle train through the **Channel Tunnel** has become a popular way of getting to France from Britain. It takes only 35mins, and there are up to 4 departures an hour at peak times daily. Hot competition between the Tunnel and the ferries means fares are comparable, but the Tunnel has the added convenience of speed, and that it's not affected by the weather. In the low season, a return ticket for a car and passengers staying over 5 days in France should cost around £160–£200 return, rising to over £300 return in peak periods. Fares also vary by time of day, so it's slightly cheaper to travel at night. There are also frequent special-offer day returns, and 2–3 day deals. Fares are significantly cheaper if you book well in advance, and online.

Whether you arrive in Calais by Tunnel or ferry, you are led pretty painlessly onto an ample network of motorways and trunk roads for your onward journey. To get to Rhône-Alpes you have a fairly long drive; as a guide, the distance from Calais to Lyon is 750km (466 miles), a journey that will take you around 6½hrs. An alternative is to hire a car once you are in Calais; you might start looking into this by comparing prices for the major car rental companies (listed on p.42) or on the website *www.carrentals.co.uk*.

For information on driving, *see* p.40.
Eurotunnel, t 08705 35 35 35, *www.eurotunnel. com*. For Shuttle bookings.

Entry Formalities

EU citizens and holders of full valid US, Canadian, Australian and New Zealand passports do not need a visa to enter France for stays of up to 3 months. Everyone else should check current requirements at the nearest French consulate. If required, the most convenient visa is the *visa de circulation*, allowing for multiple stays of 3 months over a 5-year period. Anyone who plans to stay longer than 3 months in France (including those who don't need a visa for shorter stays) should officially obtain a *carte de séjour* or residence card (this requirement may soon be dropped for EU citizens). Most non-EU citizens should apply for an extended visa through a French consulate at home – a complicated procedure, but you can't get a *carte de séjour* without it. Some visas are exempt from the need for a *carte de séjour*, so seek advice.

Getting Around

By Air

Regular **Air France** services fly from Paris to Lyon, Grenoble and Geneva. For reservations from within France, t 0820 820 820.

By Train

Travelling by rail in France is a joy: French Railways (**SNCF**) trains are sensibly priced and generally clean – and they move. The sleek TGV (*trains à grande vitesse*) allow you to nip, for example, from Paris to Lyon in a mere 2hrs. Inter-City trains are also efficient and quick; Geneva–Lyon takes 1hr 50mins. If you're venturing off the main lines, there's also a decent network of local trains, though in some areas SNCF buses have replaced former train routes. Train and bus services are linked, so you can move painlessly from one to the other, although if your incoming train is late they may not hold the bus back for it.

Fares are very reasonable, even more so if you take advantage of the many discounts (*see* below). When you board a train, you must stamp (*composter*) your ticket in the odd-looking orange machines by the platform entrances. This date-stamps your ticket – if you forget to do it you'll be liable to a fine; also, if you break your journey you must

re-*composter* the ticket. You can book train tickets online inside or outside France, and pay by credit card. For non-TGV trains, SNCF fares vary according to whether you travel in blue off-peak periods(*période bleue*) or white (*blanche*, or *période de pointe*) periods (usually Friday and Sunday evenings and national holidays). All stations dish out little calendars with the cheaper *période bleue* clearly marked. **SNCF information** in English t 08 36 35 39 (*open 7am–10pm*), *www.sncf.com*.

By Bus

Bus services are less extensive than the rail network – they're just about adequate between major towns and cities, but can be more difficult in rural areas. Some bus routes are run by SNCF (replacing old rail routes), but rail passes are still valid. Most larger towns have a central *Gare Routière* (bus station). For details of services, ask at the local tourist office. Country bus services are often timed to fit in with school schedules, leaving a particular village at the crack of dawn and returning in the afternoon.

By Car

Unless you are prepared to stick to major towns, cycle or walk, a car is the only way to see the more remote parts of Rhône-Alpes.

Discount Rail Fares

Most discounts are subject to availibility.

Carte 12–25. For young people aged 12–25 (€48 for one year): 50% discount on TGVs and sleeper (*couchette*) trains, and other trains if the journey begins in a blue period.

Carte Enfant+. Issued to a child aged 4–12, this allows them and up to 4 other people 50% discount on TGVs and sleeper trains, and on other trains if the journey begins in a blue period. Valid for one year, it costs €63.

Carte Senior: For over-60s, gives the same discounts as the previous two for a year, for €49. Also gives 25% off train journeys from France to 25 countries in Europe.

Découverte Séjour. If you set out in a blue period with a return ticket, travel more than 200km and stay at least a Saturday night, you get a 25% discount. Two people travelling together (related, romantically involved or not) are eligible for a **Découverte à Deux** tariff, which gives a discount of 25% on all return journeys in a blue period, or if places are still left, on TGVs or *couchette* trains.

Découverte 12– 26. 25% discount for young people on TGVs and *couchette* trains or other trains, if they begin travel in a blue period.

Découverte Enfant+. Up to 4 people travelling with a child aged 4–12 qualify for a 25% discount on TGVs and *couchette* trains, and on other trains departing in a blue period. Also gives discounts on Avis car hire.

Sénior Découverte. 25% off for the over-60s, travelling on TGVs and *couchettes*, or other trains if they begin travel in a blue period.

This has some snags: the accident rate in France is double that of the UK, and French drivers often behave like a small winged animal departing hell, especially when in a hurry to get anywhere. Tailgating as an immediate preliminary to overtaking is common, and drivers who dither about where they're going (e.g. tourists) are treated with noticeable impatience. The great plus of driving in France, on the other hand, is that traffic densities are low outside cities, so congestion is often remarkably absent.

Drivers must have their driving licence, vehicle registration and up-to-date insurance papers in the car with them. Those with a driving licence from any EU country, the USA, Canada or Australia do not need an international licence. If you take a car to France, you should of course make sure you are properly insured. Under European law all UK motor insurance policies now include basic third-party cover for all EU countries, but it's advisable to get an extension to give you fully comprehensive international cover, which most insurance companies will provide for a limited extra premium. It's also strongly advisable to have breakdown assistance, which many insurance companies can also arrange. Cars from the UK or Ireland require headlamp adjusters. All cars in France are required to have rear seat belts, which must be worn, but note that French law also requires you to have in the car some things that are not usual in Britain: spare bulbs for the car's main lights, and a warning triangle, which should be placed 50m behind the car if you break down.

There are a few points to note when driving in France. First, watch out for *priorité à droite* in towns and villages, an archaic system whereby traffic coming from streets to your right, unless halted by a stop sign and/or a thick white line (sometimes even these are ignored) has right of way. However, this doesn't apply at roundabouts, where you give way to cars already on it. In general the best rule of thumb is to watch out for *Cédez le passage* (Give Way) signs, and treat every intersection with care. Secondly, French drivers rarely respect pedestrian crossings.

Petrol stations can be scarce in rural areas; many keep shop hours, and are shut at night,

on Sunday afternoons, on Mondays, or for lunch. Unleaded fuel is *sans plomb*, and diesel may be called *gazole* or *gasoil*. The cheapest places to buy fuel are the stations attached to supermarkets; the most expensive are on motorways. They are often self-service out of hours, but don't always accept foreign credit cards. Motorway toll stations are generally staffed, and you can pay by cash or card.

Speed limits are 130kph/80mph on *autoroutes* (toll motorways); 110kph/69mph on main highways; 90kph/55mph on other roads; and 50kph/30mph in urban areas. There are few speed cameras, but the police often set up radar traps in laybys. Fines are payable on the spot, and begin at about €90 but can be far more, especially if you fail a breathalyser test. Avoid drinking alcohol when driving; a rigorous campaign against drink-driving has been going for some time and police traps are often set up after Sunday lunch. If you have a breakdown (*une panne*) on major roads or motorways, use the orange emergency phones to contact rescue services or the police. If you're a member of a motoring organization affiliated to the Touring Club de France, ring them; if not, ring the police, t 17.
Autoroute information, *www.autoroutes.fr.*
　Has the current toll rates
Road and traffic information, *www.bison-fute.equipement.gouv.fr.* Site of the French National Traffic Centre, with information on all aspects of driving in France.

Hiring a car

Car hire is relatively expensive in France – an added incentive to bring a car from Britain. If you're travelling from North America, there are big pluses to booking a car in advance through one of the major agencies or online booking services, or looking for a fly-drive travel package with car included. All the major car-hire chains operate in France.

The minimum age for hiring a car varies from 21 to 25 years, and the maximum is 70, depending on the company. Some companies impose surcharges for drivers under 25. Rental conditions are now fairly standard, but check that the price you're quoted includes tax, full insurance and unlimited mileage. *See* box (p.42) for details of the main car hire agencies.

Car Hire Firms

UK and Ireland

Avis, t 08700 100 287, *www.avis.co.uk.*
Budget, t 08701 56 56 56, *www.budget.com.*
easyCar, *www.easycar.com.*
Europcar, t 0870 607 5000, *www.europcar.com.*
Hertz, t 08708 44 88 44, *www.hertz.co.uk.*

USA and Canada

Auto Europe, 39 Commercial St, PO Box 7006, Portland, ME 04112, **t** 1 888 223 5555, **t** (207) 842 2000, *www.autoeurope.com.*
Auto France, PO Box 760, 211 Shadyside Rd, Ramsey, NJ 07446, **t** 800 572 9655, *www.auto-france.com.*
Avis, t 800 230 4898 (USA), **t** 800 272 5871 (Canada), **t** 800 331 2323 (hearing impaired), *www.avis.com.*
Europe by Car, t 800 223 1516 (nationwide), **t** (212) 581 3040 (NY), *www.europebycar.com.*
Europcar, t 877 940 69 00,*www.europcar.com.*
Hertz, t 800 654 3131, **t** 800 654 3001 (international), **t** 800 654 2280 (hearing impaired), *www.hertz.com.*

By Bicycle

Cycling signals as much pain as pleasure in largely mountainous Rhône-Alpes. However, loads of people love the challenge – one of the hazards of driving in the region is suddenly coming upon bands of cyclists pumping up the kinds of inclines that most people require escalators for. French drivers, not always courteous to fellow motorists, usually give cyclists a wide berth – and yet, on any given summer day, half the patients in French hospitals are from accidents on two-wheeled transport. Consider a helmet. Also be aware that theft is fairly common, so make sure your insurance covers your bike or the one you hire.

Getting your own bike to France from the UK and Ireland is fairly easy: Air France, British Airways and some ferry operators will carry them for free. On Eurostar, bikes travel in the guards' vans, with advance reservation and an extra charge. From the USA or Australia most airlines will carry them as long as they're boxed and included in your total baggage weight. Certain French trains (*autotrains*, with a bicycle symbol in the timetable) carry bikes for free; otherwise you have to send them as registered luggage and pay a fee, with delivery 'guaranteed' within 48 hours (delays are common). To find out which trains accept bikes, check the SNCF website, *www.sncf.com.*

You can hire bikes of varying quality at most SNCF stations and in major towns, and you can usually drop your bike off at another station. Private firms hire mountain bikes (VTTs or *vélos tout terrain*) and racing bikes. Rates run at around €10 a day, and you'll have to leave a credit card number or possibly a hefty deposit. Most towns have cycle paths and shelters, and hire points in some car parks. Tourist offices supply touring guides, and the official French IGN mapping agency (*www.ign.fr*) publishes maps for cyclists.

Cyclists' Touring Club, Cotterell House, 69 Meadrow, Godalming, Surrey GU7 3HS, **t** 0870 873 0060, *www.ctc.org.uk*
Fédération Française de Cyclotourisme, 12 Rue Louis Bertrand, 94207 Ivry-sur-Seine, **t** 01 56 20 88 88, *www.ffct.org.* Info and maps.

On Foot

With over 3,900 kilometres of clearly-marked long distance footpaths or *sentiers de Grande Randonnée* (GRs), and a fantastic variety of landscapes, Rhône-Alpes is a superb region to walk in. GR paths, indicated by red-and-white striped signs, are easy to find. As well as the GRs there are shorter *Petites Randonnées* (PRs), usually signalled by single yellow or green stripes, plus *sentiers de Grande Randonnée de Pays* (GRPs), marked by a red and yellow stripe, and any number of variants of the original GR routes, which eventually become paths in their own right. They evolve all the time, and are lovingly maintained by the *Fédération Française de la Randonnée Pédestre* (FFRP), which also produces excellent guides (*topoguides*). The best maps for walking in France are the IGN's 1:25,000 *Série Bleue* and Top 25 series.

Fédération Française de la Randonnée Pédestre (FFRP), 14 Rue Riquet, 75019 Paris, **t** 01 44 89 93 93, *www.ffrp.asso.fr*
Institut Géographique National (IGN), 136 bis Rue de Grenelle, Paris 75700, **t** 01 43 98 80 00, *www.ign.fr.* Maps can be ordered online.

Practical A–Z

Climate and When to Go 44
Crime and the Police 44
Disabled Travellers 44
Eating out 45
Electricity 45
Embassies and Consulates 45
Health and Insurance 45
Major Festivals and Events 46
Money and Banks 47
Opening Hours 47
National Holidays 48
Post, Telephones and the Internet 48
Sport and Activities 48
Tourist Information 50
Where to Stay 50
Specialist Holidays 52

06

Climate and When to Go

Rhône-Alpes has the biggest variation in altitude of any region in Europe, going roughly from sea level to 4,808m on Mont Blanc; the climate therefore varies a good deal. The lower parts of the region spreading out from the Rhône generally have easy climates, reflected in their exceptional agricultural fertility (although snow can fall on their heights as late as April). Spring brings out the orchard blossoms. Summers are lovely, sunny and warm across the region, the heights offering appreciated cooler air. The southern Ardèche and Drôme benefit from particularly mild, warm climates, similar to Languedoc and Provence. September is normally the month for the grape harvest. Autumns are enchanting, vines and trees changing colour.

In the Alps the ski season lasts, for the highest resorts, Dec–April; a few exceptional spots offer nigh on year-round skiing. The smaller resorts of the pre-alpine ranges and the little ones west of the Rhône have shorter, more weather-dependent seasons. In the high mountains, May–June and Sept–Nov are quiet, tourist possibilities limited. The high Alpine summer season runs mid-June to mid-Sept, June best for stunning flower-filled meadows here and in the pre-Alps.

For day-to-day weather information, see the Météo France website, at *www.meteo.fr*.

Crime and the Police

France is a pretty safe country, but be aware that thieves target foreigners, especially their cars and holiday homes. Cars with foreign number plates or that are obviously rented are seen as rich pickings. Be extra careful in cities. Report thefts to the nearest *Gendarmerie* or, in towns, the *Police Nationale*. They will give you an official statement, required for an insurance claim. If your passport is stolen, contact the police and your consulate. Keep photocopies of passports, driving licences and other important documents; this makes life easier if reporting a loss. By law, the French police can stop anyone and demand to see some ID.

Disabled Travellers

When it comes to providing access for all, France is not in the vanguard of nations, but things are changing. Signs in airports and other public places indicate meeting points where help is available and specific needs are catered for. Vehicles equipped to transport disabled people pay reduced tolls on *autoroutes*; you must produce a vehicle registration document showing your status.

The French train service, SNCF, publish a pamphlet called *Mémento du voyageur à mobilité réduite*, on accessible train travel (available from Rail Europe, *see* p.39). On *www.rhonealpes-tourisme.com* there are useful sections on accessible skiing and other outdoor sports and activities.

Access Ability, *www.access-ability.co.uk*. Offers lists of travel companies providing holidays.

Association des Paralysés de France, 17 Bd Auguste Blanqui, 75013 Paris, t 01 40 78 69 00, *www.apf.asso.fr*. French organization providing in-depth local information.

Comité National Français de Liaison pour la Réadaptation des Handicapés, 236 bis Rue de Tolbiac, 75013 Paris, t 01 53 80 66 66, *cnrh@worldnet.net*. Information on facilities for the disabled in France in a booklet.

Holiday Care, 7th Floor, Sunley House, 4 Bedford Park, Croydon, Surrey CR20 2AP, t 0845 124 9971, *www.holidaycare.org.uk*. Information on companies offering holidays abroad for disabled and older people.

RADAR (Royal Association for Disability and Rehabilitation), 12 City Forum, 250 City Rd, London EC1V 8AF, t (020) 7250 3222, *www.radar.org.uk*.

Average Daily Maximum Temperatures in °C (°F)

	Jan	Feb	Mar	April	May	June	July	Aug	Sept	Oct	Nov	Dec
Grenoble	3 (37)	3 (37)	8 (45)	14 (56)	16 (61)	22 (71)	27 (81)	26 (79)	22 (71)	16 (61)	11 (51)	6 (42)
Lyon	7 (44)	6 (42)	11 (51)	16 (61)	17 (63)	25 (77)	27 (81)	27 (81)	24 (75)	17 (63)	10 (50)	8 (45)

SATH (Society for Accessible Travel and Hospitality), 347 5th Ave, Suite 610, New York, NY 10016, **t** (212) 447 7284, *www.sath.org.*

Eating Out

French restaurants generally serve between noon and 2pm and in the evening from 7 to 10pm, with later summer hours; *brasseries* in the cities often stay open continuously.

If service is included it will say *service compris* or *s.c.*; if not, *service non compris* or *s.n.c*, and you should tip between 10 and 15%.

For more information about food, wine and eating out in Rhône-Alpes, and some general help in ordering, *see* **Food and Drink**, p.27.

Electricity

The electric current in France is 220 volts. UK and Irish visitors with electrical appliances from home will need two-pin European plug adaptors, and North Americans with 110v equipment will normally need a voltage transformer as well. Older-style French plug sockets have two round prongs, but there is a new kind of socket with fatter prongs and a third earth prong. Arm yourself with adaptors for all eventualities.

Embassies and Consulates

In France

Canada 35 Av Montaigne, 75008 Paris, **t** 01 44 43 29 00, *www.amb-canada.fr.*
Ireland 4 Rue Rude, 75016 Paris, **t** 01 44 17 67 00, *www.embassyofirelandparis.com.*
UK 24 Rue Childebert, Lyon, **t** 04 72 77 81 70, *www.amb-grandebretagne.fr.*
USA 1 Quai Jules Courmont, Lyon, **t** 04 78 38 33 03, *www.amb-usa.fr.*

Abroad

Canada (Consulates) 25 Rue St Louis, Québec, QC G1R 3Y8, **t** (418) 694 2294, *www.consulfrance -quebec.org*; 1 Place Ville Marie, Suite 2601, H3B 4S3, **t** (514) 878 4385, *www.consul france-montreal.org/consulat/.*
Ireland 36 Ailesbury Rd, Ballsbridge, Dublin 4, **t** (01) 277 5000, *www.ambafrance.ie.*

> ### Restaurant Price Categories
> All restaurants in this guide fall into one of these four price bands, based on a three-course meal without wine for one person. This is also based on set menus, and does not usually reflect prices of luxurious *menu gastronomique* feasts.
>
> | | |
> |---|---|
> | *very expensive* | *over €60* |
> | *expensive* | *€30–60* |
> | *moderate* | *€15–30* |
> | *cheap* | *under €15* |

UK London Consulate: 21 Cromwell Rd, London SW7 2EN, **t** (020) 7073 1200; Embassy: 58 Knightsbridge, London SW1X 7JT, **t** (020) 7073 1000, *www.ambafrance.uk.org.* Edinburgh Consulate: 11 Randolph Crescent, Edinburgh EH3 7TT, **t** (0131) 225 7954, *www.consulfrance-edimbourg.org.*
USA Consulates: 737 North Michigan Av, Suite 2020, Chicago, IL 60611, **t** (312) 787 5359/60/61; 10990 Wilshire Bd, Suite 300, Los Angeles, CA 90024, **t** (310) 235 3200; 934 Fifth Av, New York, NY 10021, **t** (212) 606 3688; Embassy: 4101 Reservoir Rd, NW Washington DC 20007, **t** (202) 944 6000, *www.info-france-usa.org.*

Health and Insurance

Ambulance (SAMU) **t** *15*
Police and ambulance **t** *17*
Fire **t** *18*

In a medical emergency (*un cas d'urgence médicale*), go to the local hospital (*hôpital*, or *centre hospitalier*, or *hôtel-dieu*). You can also call the local *SOS Médecins* (the number will be in the phone book). Local doctors cover night duty. The local papers have details of doctors on call (*médecins de service*) and chemists (*pharmacies*) that open outside normal hours.

All **EU citizens** are entitled to use the French health system, but to do so they should have an **E111** form, which in the UK is available from health centres and post offices. However, be aware that under the French system you, like most French people, still have to pay upfront for medical treatment and reclaim most of the cost later (around 70% of doctors' fees and 35–65% of medicine and prescription charges). (Continued on p.47.)

Major Festivals and Events

A plethora of small festivals and events take place across the region. Find out about them via local tourist offices. Jan–March the ski resorts organize countless snow and winter sports festivals.

January
Valloire, Ice-sculpting contest: for info **t** 04 79 59 03 96, *info@valloire.net* (15–18).
Richerenches, *La Messe de la Truffe:* celebrating France's largest truffle-producing centre (18).

February
Evian, Eurocarnaval (28): *www.eviantourism.com.*
Nyons, *Fête de l'Alicolique:* celebrates the olive oil harvest, **t** 04 75 26 10 35.

March
Grenoble, Grenoble Jazz Festival: over 15 days, *www.jazzgrenoble.com.*
Vallon-Pont-d'Arc, *Raid Nature:* running, canoeing, biking and hiking race (Easter). During **Easter,** egg hunts are held in many towns and villages.

April
Ardèche and **Drôme,** farm-to-farm culinary festival (last weekend of month).
Chambéry, *Grande Braderie:* big flea market on the last Sunday, **t** 04 79 33 42 47.

May
Evian, Musical Stopovers: music festival (6–9), **t** 04 50 26 85 00, *www.royalparcevian.com.*
St-Etienne, Festival of Words and Music: over the second fortnight, **t** 04 77 25 01 13.

June
Annecy, animation film festival: **t** 04 50 10 09 00.
Annonay, hot-air balloon festival, **t** 04 75 33 24 51.
Ardèche, *Ardèchoise* cycling race, *www.ardechoise.com.*
Drôme, *Transhumance:* sheep are taken up to pasture (3rd week), *www.drometourisme.com.*
Lyon, *Festival Les Nuits de Fourvière:* Roman open-air theatre (mid-June–mid-Sept), **t** 04 72 32 00 00, *www.nuits-de-fourviere.org.*
Portes du Soleil, mountain-biking festival for all (end June–beg. July).
Vienne, *Festival de Jazz: www.jazzavienne.com.*
Valence, *Fête des Canaux.*

July
The *Tour de France* always passes through the region in July; see *www.letour.fr.*
Ain, *Fête des Fours à Pain.*
Aix-les-Bains, *Les Aquascenies:* large 3-day festival by the lake, *www.aixlesbains.com.*
Chambéry, International Folklore Festival.
Château de Grignan, *Fêtes Nocturnes:* theatre.
Loire, Musical Summer: *www.loire.fr.*
Saou, Mozart Festival: **t** 04 75 76 02 02.
St-Donat-sur-l'Herbasse, Bach Organ Festival.

August
Aix-les-Bains, *Navig'Aix:* gathering of boats and dinghies, *www.aixlesbains.com.*
Annecy, Lake Festival: *www.lac-annecy.com.*
Chamonix, Mountain Guides' Festival: wild celebrations on their days off (14–15 Aug).

September
Ambronay, classical music festival: *www.fest-ambronay.com.*
Journées du Patrimoine: Open house at a large number of historic venues across France.
Lyon, *Biennale d'Art Contemporain:* art festival (odd years);
Biennale de la Danse: dance festival (even years), *www.biennale-of-lyon.org.*

October
Annecy, *Retour des Alpages* (2nd Sat).
Ardèche chestnut towns, *Les Castagnades:* celebrations on a favourite culinary theme.

November
Beaujeu, Beaujolais Nouveau launch: great wine festival (3rd Thurs), **t** 04 74 07 27 50.
Grenoble, Music Festival (*38ème Rugissants*): at the end of Nov.
St-Etienne, Massenet Biennial: celebrates the 19th-century composer (odd years);
Biennale Design Festival: (even years) **t** 04 77 47 88 05, *www.institutdesign.com.*

December
Lyon, Festival of Lights: with exceptional illuminations around the centre (5–8).
Val Thorens and **L'Alpe d'Huez,** Andros Trophy: car competitions on ice (also held in other locations, check with the tourist office).
Christmas markets are held in many of Rhône-Alpes' main towns and villages.

The leaflet that comes with the E111 explains how to reclaim costs. It doesn't cover all medical needs, however, and to avoid this sort of bureaucracy it can just be better to rely on **private travel insurance**, which as well as medical costs, will also cover you for theft, lost property and a range of other potential problems. Standard travel insurance policies often do not cover sports injuries, so you might need extra cover. Canadian citizens can also officially use the French health system in the same way as EU nationals, but in general for **North Americans** and all non-EU citizens the best option is to have fully comprehensive travel insurance that covers all eventualities – health, loss of property, flight cancellations, emergency repatriation if necessary and so on.

Money and Banks

Dealing with the older French generation you might not know it, but since 1 January 2002 the currency of France has been the **euro**, the symbol for which is €. One euro is divided into 100 cents; there are coins for 1, 2, 5, 10, 20 and 50 cents and for 1 and 2 euros, and notes for 5, 10, 20, 50, 100, 200 and 500 euros. (You can still exchange old French francs free of charge at any Banque de France office: coins until 2005, notes until 2012.)

Exchange rates vary, but in mid-2004 the average pound/euro rate tended to be £1 = €1.51 (so €1 = 66p), while the US dollar/euro rate was around $1 = €0.83 (so €1 = $1.20).

French banks are generally open Mon–Fri 8.30am–12.30pm (or 9–12 noon) and 1.30–4pm. Some branches open on Saturdays, in which case they will be closed on Monday. All banks close early on the day before a public holiday, and are closed on the holiday itself. All banks displaying the '*Change*' sign will exchange foreign currency, generally at better rates than *bureaux de change* (and far better than at railway stations and in hotels). The cheapest places of all to exchange cash are the main post offices, which don't charge commission. Travellers' cheques are the safest way of carrying money, but there can be problems getting them exchanged in small bank branches. Very rarely will you be able to use travellers' cheques directly in payments, as you would in the USA.

The widespread presence of **ATM cashpoints** often makes using them with a credit or debit card the most convenient – and sometimes most economical – way of getting money. The fees can still work out better than bank commission rates. Major credit cards such as Visa and MasterCard are very widely accepted in France, but American Express and Diners Club less so. In smaller hotels and restaurants, especially in rural areas, and *chambres d'hôtes* (bed and breakfast, owners may not accept cards, so it's advisable not to rely on them.

All French plastic now works on the chip-and-pin system. Some self-service petrol stations and bridge toll booths may reject foreign cards.

Credit Card Emergency Numbers
MasterCard, **t** 0800 901387.
American Express, **t** 01 47 77 72 00.
Visa (*Carte Bleue*), **t** 01 42 77 11 90.
Barclaycard, **t** + 44 (0)1604 230 230.

Opening Hours

While many **shops and supermarkets** are now open continuously Tuesday–Saturday from 9 or 10am to 7 or 7.30pm, businesses in smaller towns still close down for lunch from 12 or 12.30pm to 2 or 3pm, or in the summer 4pm. There are local exceptions, but nearly everything shuts down on Mondays, except for grocers and *supermarchés* that open in the afternoon. In many towns, Sunday morning is a big shopping period. **Markets** (daily in the cities, weekly in villages) are usually open mornings only, although clothes, flea and antique markets run into the afternoon.

Most **museums** close for lunch, and often all day on Mondays or Tuesdays, and sometimes for all of November or the entire winter. Hours change with the season: longer summer hours begin in May, June or July, and last until September – usually. Most museums close on national holidays. We've done our best to include opening hours in the text, but please note that they do change regularly. Most museums give discounts if you have a student ID card, or are an EU citizen under 18 or over 65 years old; most charge admissions ranging from €2 to €10. National museums are free if you're under 18.

National Holidays

1 January New Year's Day
Easter Sunday March or April
Easter Monday March or April
1 May *Fête du Travail* (Labour Day)
8 May VE Day, 1945
Ascension Day usually end May
Pentecost (Whitsun) and following Monday
  end May/early June
14 July Bastille Day
15 August Assumption of the Virgin Mary
1 November All Saints' Day
11 November Remembrance Day
25 December Christmas Day

Churches are usually open all day, or closed all day and only open for Mass. Sometimes notes on the door direct you to the *mairie* or priest's house (*presbytère*) where you can pick up the key. There are often admission fees for cloisters, crypts and special chapels.

On French **national holidays** (*see* box), banks, shops, businesses and some museums close; but most restaurants stay open. The French have a healthy approach to holidays: if there is a holiday on a Tuesday or Thursday, they 'make a bridge' (*faire un pont*) to the weekend and make Monday or Friday a holiday too.

Post, Telephones and the Internet

Post offices (PTT or *La Poste*) are easily spotted by their blue bird on yellow logo. There is a main post office located in the centre of all French towns, and many villages also have a smaller, local *Poste*. Main post offices open Mon–Fri 8am–7pm, Sat 8–12 noon; in villages, offices may not open till 9am, often close for lunch, and shut at 4.30–5pm. Ordinary stamps, though, can be bought in any tobacco shop (*tabac*). You can receive letters *poste restante* at any post office. To collect them you will need to show a passport or other ID with a photograph, and may have to pay a small fee.

Most public phone boxes now operate with phone cards (*télécartes*) or credit cards, although a few still accept coins. *Télécartes* are sold at post offices, newsstands and *tabacs*. UK and Irish mobile phones work in France if they have a roaming facility; check with your service provider. North American cellphones will not work without a triband facility. French mobile numbers begin with **t** 06.

N.B. The French have now eliminated separate area codes, so you must dial all 10 digits when calling from within the country.

Calling **from outside France to a French number**, the international French code is 33, then you drop the first zero of the 10-digit number. To call **from within France to an international number**, dial **t** 00, then the country code (UK **44**; US and Canada 1; Ireland 353; Australia 61; New Zealand 64), followed by the area code (minus the first zero for UK numbers) and the number. For the French **operator**, dial **t** 13; for **directory enquiries**, **t** 12, for international directory enquiries, **t** 3212.

Internet cafés are still less common (and more expensive) in France than in other European countries. Main post offices in towns now have perhaps one public web terminal, but there are often long queues to use them, and they are seriously overpriced.

Sports and Activities

Local tourist offices will happily provide you with information, whether you seek adrenalin highs or a more stately form of pursuit; *www. rhonealpes-tourisme.com* is also very useful.

Caving

There are some exceptional caves to explore here. Some hold world records: the Gouffre Jean-Bernard in Haute-Savoie is said to be the world's deepest cave, at a depth of 5,253ft. Cavers must be led by a qualified guide.

Climbing

The Ardèche and the limestone cliffs in the Alpine foothills are favourite spots for climbers; some of the technically toughest climbs can be found near Lyon. For non-experts, the *Via Ferrata* (Prepared Routes) around the region offer routes with steel cables and artificial holds. Organizations offer climbing excursions, led by qualified instructors, throughout the area.

Cycling and Mountain Biking

Rhône-Alpes has great, often challenging terrain for cycling and mountain biking, with an abundance (around 8,379km) of mountain and valley trails. Areas such as La Dombes, which has long, flat routes bordered by plane trees, are ideal for family outings. At the other end of the scale, for biking junkies, are areas such as Isère, Loire and Les Portes du Soleil in Haute-Savoie, the last a paradise for fans of downhill routes – ski lifts operate all summer for them. *See also* p.42, 'By Bicycle'.

Golf

There are over 60 golf courses to putt your way across in Rhône-Alpes, from the high-altitude greens in the Alps, via the banks of Lake Annecy, to those close to the cities (notably Lyon, Grenoble and Geneva) and along the Rhône and Loire valleys. Club addresses are listed on the tourist board website.

Horse-riding

Horse-lovers are well-catered for, with over 6,000km of orange-signposted bridle paths to giddy-up along, and it's a great way to visit the Monts du Forez in the Loire, the Maurienne Valley in Savoie, the Ardèche and the Drôme. 'Horse Hostels' and farms will even accommodate you and your steed along the way. Some of the region's 4,000 riding schools offer one-hour rides with a qualified guide (average cost €12 per person) or riding lessons for beginners; longer, all-inclusive excursions and holidays are also available.

Rhône-Alpes à Cheval, Maison du Tourisme, 14 rue de la République, BP 227, 38019 Grenoble cedex, **t** 04 76 42 85 88, *rhone-alpes-a-cheval@wanadoo.fr*.

Paragliding

Paragliding was founded in Rhône-Alpes in 1978, so it's no surprise that 50 paragliding schools are registered in the region. St Hilaire du Touvet, near Grenoble, is a main centre, but there are many options around the Alps. Swoop down 400–1,800 metres downhill in between five and 60 minutes, accompanied by an expert (around €60pp); details on *www.rhonealpes-tourisme.com*, or contact the *Ligue Rhône-Alpes de Vol Libre*, Chemillieu, 01300 Nattages, **t** 04 79 44 40 78, *www.ffvl.fr*.

Skiing

Rhône-Alpes boasts the best skiing in the world – see chapter 19 for specialist advice on organizing your own independent ski trip. Otherwise, the most economical way to join in is to book a package holiday. **Summer skiing** at Les Deux Alpes and Tignes is guaranteed; that at Alpe d'Huez, La Plagne, Val d'Isère and Val Thorens is more variable according to snow conditions. Check the tourist board websites for details of the resorts, or contact the *Fédération Française de Ski*, 50 Rue des Marquisats, 74011 Annecy Cedex, **t** 04 50 51 40 34, *www.ffs.fr*.

Spas and Fitness

The region has 14 spa centres (all referred to in the touring chapters). Relaxation and health care, fitness and head-to-toe pampering can be enjoyed, for example, at Montbrun-les-Bains, Evian, Aix-les-Bains, Challes-les-Eaux and Vals-les-Bains.

Walking

See 'Getting Around: On Foot' p.44, first.

Rhône-Alpes is the only region in France where you can go **glacier-walking**. Mont Blanc, the Vanoise, the Rateau and the Grande Rousse range are the main centres. You can walk with a guided group or a private guide, June–Sept; trips usually last two days.

Water Sports

The glaciers and alpine rivers of Rhône-Alpes make the region ideal for white-water sports: **rafting**, **canoeing**, **kayaking**, **white-water swimming**, **canyoning** and **tubing** (flying downstream on an inflatable donut) and **hot-dogging** (in an inflatable canoe) are all available to the steely-nerved.

You can **sail** on Lakes Annecy, Geneva/Léman and Le Bourget, all of which have several sailing schools offering courses at all levels. High-altitude sailing is also available at Lakes Monteynard and Mont Cenis. A booklet is available from *Ligue de voile Rhône-Alpes*, **t** 04 79 25 26 89, *www.voile-rhonealpes.org*.

Waterskiing can be done on the Rhône, the Saône and Lakes Monteynard, Annecy, Le Bourget and Geneva May–Oct – even for 4-year-olds! Contact the *Ligue Rhône-Alpes de Ski Nautique*, **t** 04 79 75 78 49, for a list of clubs.

Tourist Information

France has some of the world's best tourist information services. Each of Rhône-Alpes' eight *départements* has its own **Comité Départemental du Tourisme** or **CDT**. They coordinate the local *Offices de Tourisme*, and smaller ones which are sometimes still called *Syndicats d'Initiative*. (Many of these are listed in the touring chapters, but you can also search for details on the region's website.) There's also a regional tourist board (CRT), the *Comité Régional du Tourisme Rhône-Alpes*.

All tourist offices offer excellent free information (often in English). Particularly handy is each *département's* annual visitor's guide (*Loisirs*, or *Lieux de visite* or similar) and the excellent *Bienvenue à la ferme* leaflets, listing farms that sell traditional produce – an essential aid in fine-food hunting. All the CDTs now have good websites, in English as well as French. Addresses of local offices are given throughout this guide. For information on the whole region, contact the very well organized:

Comité Régional du Tourisme Rhône-Alpes, 104 Route de Paris, 69260 Charbonnières-les-Bains, t 04 72 59 21 59, *www.rhonealpes-tourism.co.uk*.

Département Tourist Boards

CDT Ain, 34 Rue Général Delestraint, BP78, 01002 Bourg-en-Bresse, t 04 74 32 31 30, *www.ain-tourisme.com*.

CDT Ardèche, 4 Cours du Palais, 07000 Privas Cedex, t 04 75 64 04 66, *www.ardeche-guide.com*.

CDT Drôme, 8 Rue Baudin, 26000 Valence, t 04 75 82 19 26, *www.drometourisme.com*.

CDT Isère, 14 Rue de la République, BP227, 38019 Grenoble, t 04 76 54 34 36, *www.isere-tourisme.com*.

CDT Loire, 5 Place Jean Jaurès, 42021 St-Etienne Cedex 01, t 04 77 43 24 42, *www.loire.fr*.

CDT Rhône, 35 Rue St-Jean, 69005 Lyon, t 04 72 56 70 40, *www.rhonetourisme.com*.

ATD Savoie, 24 Bd de la Colonne, 73025 Chambéry Cedex, t 04 79 85 12 45, *www.savoie-tourisme.com*.

ATD Haute Savoie, 56 Rue Sommeiller, BP348, 74012 Annecy Cedex, t 04 50 51 32 31, *www.hautesavoie-tourisme.com*.

You might also consult *www.guide-sortir.com*, which offers practical tourist information on a number of the *départements* and areas covered in this guidebook.

French Tourist Offices Abroad

The main website is *www.franceguide.com*.

Australia: Level 20, 25 Bligh St, NSW 2000 Sydney, t (02) 9231 5244.

Canada: 1981 McGill College, Bureau 490, Montreal, Quebec H3A 2W9, t (514) 876 9881.

Ireland:1 Suffolk Street, IEL-2 Dublini t (01) 679 0813

UK: Maison de la France, 178 Piccadilly, London W1J 9AL, t 09068 244 123.

USA: *www.francetourism.com;* New York: 444 Madison Ave, NY 10022, t (410) 286 8310; Chicago: John Hancock Center, Suite 3214, 875 North Michigan Ave, Chicago, IL 60611, t (312) 751 7800; Los Angeles: 9454 Wilshire Blvd, Suite 210, Beverly Hills, CA 90212, t (310) 281 80 44.

Where to Stay

Hotels

We have selected very special hotels in our touring chapters, going from top-of-the-range luxury establishments, via delightful, more moderately priced addresses, to characterful places for those on a tighter budget. Charm and quality have been our main criteria for selection in each category.

Most hotels have a range of rooms and prices. The categories in this guide indicate average prices. They don't include luxury suites, but most top French hotels have them – and they can be amazing – so ask if you're looking for opulence. Most two-star hotel rooms have en suite showers and toilets, while one-stars have a choice of rooms with or without.

French hotels charge for the room, not per person, so families can travel pretty cheaply. People travelling alone don't get such a good deal: single rooms are quite rare, and usually cost two-thirds of the price of a double.

Hotel restaurants are often high quality, and many hotels offer good-value half-board or full-board deals (in summer, some insist on it). Also, try to **book ahead**. It's always advisable for any hotel, and essential in high season.

Hotel umbrella associations, such as **Logis de France** (*www.logis-de-france.fr*), **Relais du**

Hotel Price Ranges

Based on average rates for a double room, with bathroom. In hotels these do not include breakfast, but this is included with the basic price in all *chambres d'hôtes* (B&Bs).

luxury	€230+
very expensive	€150–230
expensive	€100–150
moderate	€60–100
inexpensive	under €60

Silence (*www.relais-du-silence.com*), the charming **Châteaux & Hôtels de France** (*www.chateauxhotels.com*), or the prestigious **Relais et Châteaux** (*www.relaischateaux.fr*), promote independently-owned hotels and their restaurants. The *Logis* – all of which have to be independently-owned, family-run hotels, with their owners resident on the premises – tend to be modest, traditional local hotels. *Logis* membership is a reliable guarantee of comfort. The other three associations are generally more upmarket, *Relais et Châteaux* at the luxury end.

Chambres d'Hôtes or B&Bs

Chambres d'hôtes are very popular in France, and offer different qualities from hotels, being homely and personal. They tend to be better value, but can't offer the same range of facilities as hotels. We have selected exceptionally charming ones. Always book well in advance, especially for French holiday times (Easter, July–Aug). Many can offer guests a *table d'hôte* evening meal, if reserved in advance.

Tourist offices keep lists of local *chambres d'hôtes* , but are not allowed to recommend specific ones. Most country *chambres d'hôtes* are affiliated to the same *Gîtes de France* organization as self-catering *gîtes* (*see* below), which publishes informative annual booklets for each *département*. It classifies its members with one to four *épis* (ears of corn). Another umbrella organization is Clévacances (*see* right), which has more B&Bs in towns. Both organizations have central booking services, but if you can handle French, best call directly.

Gîtes and Self-catering Accommodation

All short-term rented accommodation with its own facilities comes under the French term *gîte*. Most but not all are affiliated to the

Fédération Nationale des Gîtes de France, whose yellow and green *Gîtes de France* symbol is familiar in every part of the country. The other umbrella organization here too is *Clévacances*. Gîte furnishings vary enormously, from opulent to very basic, so make enquiries before you book. Both *Gîtes de France* and *Clévacances* publish guides and have central booking services, or can be contacted through tourist offices.

Useful Contacts

Maison des Gîtes de France Rhône-Alpes, 1 Rue Général Plessier, 69002 Lyon, **t** 04 72 77 17 55, *www.gites-de-france-rhone-alpes.com*.

Fédération Nationale des Locations Clévacances, 54 Bd de l'Embouchure, BP 2166, 31022 Toulouse, **t** 05 61 13 55 66, *www.clevacances.com*.

Brittany Ferries, **t** 08705 360 360, *www.brittanyferries.com*. Agent for *Gîtes de France*; can provide info and bookings.

Vacances en Campagne, Manor Court Yard, Bignor, Pulborough, West Sussex, RH20 1QD, **t** 0870 077 1771, *www.indiv-travellers.com*. Small, independent operator representing an attractive range of country properties.

At Home in France, PO Box 643, Ashland, Oregon 97520, **t** (541) 488 9467, *www.athomeinfrance.com*.

Villas International, 4340 Redwood Highway, Suite D309, San Rafael, CA94903, **t** 1 800 221 2260, *www.villasintl.com*.

Camping

There is a good choice of campsites in Rhône-Alpes, from 4-star luxury sites with swimming pools, restaurants and loads of space, to one-star sites with basic facilities. Virtually every town and village has a no-frills municipal campsite. Camping on farms is popular too, and tends to be cheaper; most are designated as *Campings à la Ferme* by *Gîtes de France* (*see* above).

Rhône-Alpes Tourisme has an official website with a vast range of sites and offers (*www.camping-rhonealpes.co.uk*), and a nationwide guide, the *Guide Officiel Camping-caravaning*, is available in most French bookshops. In summer, book your plot in advance, as even out-of-the-way sites fill up.

Specialist Holidays

La Cuisine de Savoie, Hôtel Million, 73200 Albertville, t 04 79 32 25 15, f 04 79 32 25 36, *www.hotelmillion.com*. A prestigious establishment running week-long cookery courses in English for small groups.

Institut Paul Bocuse, t 04 72 18 02 20, f 04 78 43 33 51, *www.institutpaulbocuse.com*. Offers four cuisine and culture courses in a 19th-century château, with a wine tasting cellar.

Ecole du Grand Chocolat Valrhôna, 26600 Tain l'Hermitage, t 04 75 07 90 90, f 04 75 08 05 17, *www.valrhona.com*. Sensational chocolate-making courses in the Drôme.

Ecole Beaujolaise des Vins, 210 Boulevard Vermorel, BP 317, 69661 Villefranche Cedex, t 04 74 02 22 18, f 04 74 02 22 19, *ecolevins@beaujolais.com*. Wine courses, in English.

Arblaster and Clarke Wine Tours, UK t 01730 893 344, *www.winetours.co.uk*. Fantastic tours by leading wine writers and experts.

Université du Vin, Suze-la-Rousse, Drôme, t 04 75 97 21 30, *www.universite-du-vin.com*. Courses on wine in a great castle, with special lectures. Classes in English possible.

Wine Drive, UK t 01202 603 204, *www.winedrive.com*. Offers good, basic advice on planning a wine holiday in France, from ferry services to regional guides, choice of routes, vineyards and accommodation.

Pavillon Saône, book through H2olidays, Port de Plaisance, 21170 Saint Jean de Losne, France, t 03 80 29 13 81, *www.barginginfrance.com*. Sail a hired cruiser down the Saône.

Peter Deilmann River Cruises, UK t 020 7436 2931, *www.peter-deilmann-river-cruises.co.uk*. Choice of luxury Rhône and Saône cruises.

Travel Renaissance Holidays, 28 South Street, Epsom, Surrey KT18 7PF, t 01372 744 455, *www.travelrenaissance.com*. Luxury Rhône cruises, on boats carrying 50 people or more.

French Golf Holidays, UK t 01277 824 100, *www.frenchgolfholidays.com*. 3–5-night golfing packages in the region.

Golf Par Excellence, UK t 01737 211 818, f 01737 211 820, *www.golfparexcellence.com*.

Belle France, t 0870 405 4056, f 01580 214 011, *www.bellefrance.co.uk*. Independent walking, cycling and boating holidays.

Great Walks of the World, UK t 01935 810 820, *www.greatwalks.net*. Self-explanatory!

Ramblers Holidays, UK t 01707 331 133, *www.ramblersholidays.co.uk*. Walking holidays.

Sentiers de France, t 01 45 69 86 46 *www.sentiersdefrance.com*. Itineraries for walking tours (varying in difficulty and accommodation type). There are four tours in the Rhône-Alpes region.

Sherpa Expeditions, 131a Heston Road, Hounslow, Middlesex TW5 0RF, t 020 8577 2717, *www.sherpaexpeditions.com*. Walking expeditions.

Cycling for Softies, UK t 0161 248 8282, *www.cycling-for-softies.co.uk*. Bicycle tour entitled 'Vineyards of the Rhône', for all energy levels and abilities.

Peak Retreats, UK t 0870 770 0408, *www.peakretreats.co.uk*. Inclusive activity and ski packages. Accommodation options include privately-owned Savoyard-style chalets, some of which have indoor pools.

Esprit Holidays, UK t 01252 618 300, *www.ski-esprit.co.uk*. Ski or summer activity holidays.

Erna Low, UK t 020 7584 2841, or t 0870 750 6820, *www.ernalow.co.uk*. Spa holidays at Les Fermes de Marie, a luxury mountain retreat in 8 converted farms. Also a range of ski and summer destinations in the Alps.

Harris Holidays, UK t 01375 396 688, *www.harris-travel.com*. Value-for-money ski breaks, travelling to the 3 Vallées by coach .

Le Chalet Français, Chamonix, t/f 04 50 54 26 88, *info@lechaletfrancais.com*. Classes in French language and culture; lodgings and meals are in a rustic chalet.

Ecole des Trois Ponts, Château de Matel, 42300 Roanne, t 04 77 71 53 00, f 04 77 71 53 00, *www.3ponts.edu*. Language courses in a lovely setting; also cookery courses in small classes, or combinations of the two.

Experience Language Ltd, 9c Westbourne Terrace, London, t 0845 458 0578, *www.experiencelanguage.co.uk*. Intensive, small-group language courses in Chamonix or St Gervais.

Centre Artistique de Piégon, t 04 75 27 10 43, *www.compu.ch/piegon*. In the southern Drôme. Set up by artist Jean-Pierre Eichenberger in the 1950s. Facilities for solo or group artists: dance studios, music, painting, printing, sculpting and weaving. Ten simple rooms and country food.

Lyon

A Peach of a World Heritage City

A History of Lyon 55
The Fourvière Hillside and Gallo-Roman Lyon 63
Vieux Lyon: Medieval and Renaissance Lyon 64
Along the Banks of the Saône 66
The Presqu'île de Lyon 67
Further down the Presqu'île 68
Up the Croix-Rousse Silk-Making Slopes 72
Along the Banks of the Rhône 74
Cinema and Invention in the Eastern Quarters 76

07

Lyon

4ème

CROIX-ROUSSE

RUE HENON

RUE HENRI GORIUS

BD DES CANUTS

MONTEE DE LA BOUCLE

MONTEE DE LA CROIX-ROUSSE

RUE HENON

GRANDE RUE DE LA CROIX-ROUSSE

Musée d'Art Contemporain

500 metr

500 yards

PONT WINSTON CHURCHILL

Parc de la Tête d'O

RUE CHAZIERE

1er

COURS GENERAL GIRAUD

PLACE DE LA CROIX-ROUSSE

RUE JOSEPHIN SOULARY

COURS D'HERBOUVILLE

Rhône

RUE DUQUESNE

PONT DE LATTRE DE TASSIGNY

AV DE GRANDE BRETAGNE

RUE SULLY

6ème

BD DE LA CROIX-ROUSSE

Gallo-Roman Theatre of the Three Gauls

MONTEE DE LA GRANDE COTE

QUAI ANDRE LASSAGNE

AV MARECHAL FOCH

QUAI ST VINCENT

Saône

QUAI PIERRE SCIZE

Musée des Beaux-Arts

Hôtel de Ville

PLACE DE LA COMEDIE

PONT MORAND

PLACE MARECHAL LYAUTEY

COURS FRANKLIN ROOSEVELT

PLACE KLEBER

RUE CUVIER

St-Paul

QUAI DE LA PECHERIE

PLACE DES TERREAUX

RUE CONSTANTINE

Opéra de Lyon

QUAI J. MOULIN

RUE CREQUI

RUE VAUBAN

FOURVIÈRE

PONT DE LA FEUILLEE

RUE MAJOR MARTIN

RUE PIZAY

RUE DE L'ARBRE SEC

QUAI GENERAL SARRAIL

5ème

Hôtel de Gadagne

Notre-Dame de Fourvière

Musée de la Civilisation Gallo-Romaine

VIEUX LYON

PLACE DU CHANGE

St-Nizier

RUE DE LA PLATIERE

RUE LONGUE

RUE PRESIDENT E. HERRIOT

RUE DE LA REPUBLIQUE

Musée de l'Imprimerie

COURS LAFAYETTE

RUE RABELAIS

Les Hall

PLACE DE FOURVIERE

RUE ST-JEAN

RUE DU BOEUF

RUE DES TROIS MARIES

RUE GRENETTE

PLACE DES CORDELIERS

PONT LAFAYETTE

RUE DE BONNE

Gallo-Roman Theatres

Palais de Justice

PLACE ST-JEAN

PASSARELLE DU PALAIS DE JUSTICE

PRESQU'ÎLE

RUE THOMASSIN

RUE DE LA PART-D

To Gare de la Part-D and Centre Commerc (500 metres)

PLACE ABBE LARUE

RUE DE L'ANTIQUAILLE

MONTEE DU CHEMIN NEUF

RUE TRAMASSAC

Primatiale St-Jean

PLACE DES JACOBINS

RUE DESAVOIE

PLACE DE LA REPUBLIQUE

RUE CHILDEBERT

Préfecture

RUE CHAPONNAY

RUE R. RADISSON

PONT BONAPARTE

RUE GASPARD ANDRE

RUE GASPARIN

PONT WILSON

AV MARECHAL DE SAXE

QUAI TILSITT

RUE ST-GEORGES

2ème

RUE SALA

Hôtel Dieu Hospital

RUE DE LA BARRE

QUAI JULES COURMONT

3ème

RUE VILLEROY

PLACE BELLECOUR

PLACE ANTONIN PONCET

RUE DES MARRONNIERS

Rhône

COURS GAMBE

RUE VICTOR HUGO

RUE AUGUSTE COMTE

RUE DE LA CHARITE

PLACE GAILLETON

RUE GAILLETON

PONT DE LA GUILLOTIERE

Musée Historique des Tissus
Musée des Arts Décoratifs

Basilique St-Martin d'Ainay

PLACE AMPERE

QUAI DOCTEUR GENSOUL

PONT DE L'UNIVERSITE

To Université a Institut Lumiè

RUE CONDE

7ème

Place Carnot

QUAI CLAUDE BERNARD

RUE DE MARSEILLE

Saône

PONT KITCHENER MARECHAL

COURS DE VERDUN GENSOUL VERDUN RECAMIER GALLIENI

COURS DE VERDUN

Gare de Perrache

PONT DE GALLIENI

Centre d'Histoire de la Résistance et de la Déportation

RUE DUGAS MONTBEL

COURS SUCHET

COURS VERDUN-PERRACHE

AV LECLERC

AV JEAN JAURES

AV BERTHELOT

COURS BAYARD

Picture a crate of ripening peaches, with all its variety of hues, and you'll have a notion of Lyon's waterside colours. Traditionally, the Saône has been portrayed as the feminine, graceful half of Lyon's river partnership, the Rhône as the masculine, muscular one, as symbolic statues all around town recall. The two splendid rivers (in fact historically both major working waterways) unite at the end of the long, smart central peninsula, the Presqu'île, heart of the city, with all its grand *Ancien Régime* squares, its great arts museums, and its superb shops, hotels and restaurants.

Lyon's older historic quarters rise west of the Saône, the churches and mansions of Vieux Lyon below the steep Fourvière hill in which the city's major Roman remains lie semi-hidden. From the 15th century, the city became one of Europe's main silk producers, the makers rattling off pieces in ear-splitting numbers in the St-Georges quarter south of the Saône-side cathedral. But in the 19th century, the workers crossed onto the Croix Rousse hill above the Presqu'île, only stopping their manic work to revolt in desperation.

A large swathe of central Lyon going from the Roman hill, across the Presqu'île to the high-rise silk-weavers' houses on Croix Rousse, was declared a UNESCO World Heritage Site in 1998, in recognition of its remarkable urban history going back 2000 years. On top of that, in its posh eastern suburbs, Lyon boasts the site of the first cinema film, shot in 1895 by the Lumière brothers outside their home.

Brash new quarters are racing up now beside the Rhône. Lyon is a vibrant modern city as well as a great historic one. Despite its well-known wartime traumas, these days it looks very self-confident at its core, terribly grand and extremely chic. The French stereotype the Lyonnais as being a bit arrogant, which is somewhat unfair, but they are particularly proud of their city centre – even the underground car parks have been turned into art spaces. It's appropriate that lions are a recurring symbol around town, playing on the city's name, but also reflecting its character. There are even comparisons to be made between Lyon and Paris, without taking things too far – the Lyon conurbation only has around 1.3 million inhabitants, as against Paris' 9.5 million; but it does have plane-lined river quays too, *Bateaux-Mouches* plying its waters, a copy of the top of the Eiffel tower, and a white church glowing on its main hillside, a more central answer to the capital's Sacré Cœur. Plus the city is divided into *arrondissements* like Paris and has a more comfortable metro system. To foreign visitors who may have a completely false notion of the city from its industrial outskirts, the place will come as a wonderful surprise, bursting with interest. Lyon turns out to be a giant, juicy peach to be savoured.

A History of Lyon

Lyon was a far greater city to the Romans than insignificant little Paris, a crossroads of major rivers linking the Mediterranean and northern Europe. A Gaulish settlement called Condate (Confluence), down by the rivers, preceded the Roman one. But the three ancient theatres still visible in town give a clear indication of what a significant Roman city Lugdunum became. The first Italians (there were lots more to come, down the centuries) established themselves on the hill of Fourvière (from *Forum Vetus*, Old Forum) in 43 BC, under one Plancus, after some of their number had been given a

Getting There

By air: Air France flies to Lyon from London Heathrow, easyJet from London Stansted. Lyon-St-Exupéry airport (t 04 72 22 72 21/08 26 80 08 26, www.lyon.aeroport.fr) lies c.25km east of the centre. Satobus shuttle buses (t 04 72 22 71 27, www.satobus.com) leave every 20mins during the day, serving the two central railway stations, Lyon-Part-Dieu east of the Rhône, Lyon-Perrache on the Presqu'île. A regular shuttle bus also links the airport to the separate car-hire area, Avis, Budget, Europcar, Hertz, National/Citer and Sixt represented.

By rail: Paris-Gare de Lyon is 1hr 30mins away; London Waterloo (via Lille) just 5 hrs off.

Getting Around

Lyon has excellent **metro**, **tram** and **bus** systems (for general info, Allo TCL, t 08 20 42 70 00, www.tcl.fr), useful for the northern and eastern quarters.

For **taxis**, try Lyon International Taxis, t 04 78 88 16 16, or Allô Taxis, t 04 78 28 23 23, or see the tourist office website.

Hire **bikes** from the major central car parks (t 04 72 41 65 25, www.lpa.fr). There are also **rickshaws** in the centre: Cyclopolitain, t 08 26 10 00 03.

For **river cruises**, Naviginter, t 04 78 42 96 81, www.naviginter.fr, runs short trips from Quai des Célestins on the Saône, dinner cruises from Quai Claude Bernard on the Rhône.

Tourist Information

Lyon: Place Bellecour, 69002 Lyon, t 04 72 77 69 69, www.lyon-france.com. With a good-value **Lyon City Card**, valid for one, two or three days, you get free access to most museums and guided tours, unlimited free public transport, and free river cruises. The tourist office can reserve hotels and organizes many themed guided tours.

Shopping

The **Presqu'île** between Place des Terreaux and Place Carnot is major shopping territory. Big brand name and department stores stand along Rue de la République and Rue Victor Hugo. Nicknamed the *Carré d'Or*, the specific area between Place des Jacobins, Place de la République, Place des Céléstins and Place Bellecour has the greatest concentration of luxury and fashion boutiques, plus one or two superlative food shops. For upmarket antiques and interior decoration, start with Rue Auguste Comte and Rue de la Charité. Quai de la Pêcherie by the Saône is also interesting for stylish household goods.

At the foot of **Croix-Rousse** hillside, seek out trendy new designers. **Vieux Lyon** is more touristy, with lots of Guignol puppet stores and the odd interesting boutique.

East of the Rhône, foodies visit the modern Halles (covered market). Part-Dieu has a huge typical international mall. For more stylish options east of the river, including the superb Bernachon chocolate shop, try hunting along Cours Roosevelt.

Markets

Stupendous selection. For food, best are the daily Saône-side Quai St-Antoine displays, and the huge market stretching along Bd de la Croix Rousse. The Sunday morning craft market on Quai Rolland west of the Saône is quite a delight.

On the office-block east side of Parc de la Tête d'Or, the *Cité des Antiquaires* antiques market is open Thurs and weekends 10–7 (*closing 1pm in summer*).

Where to Stay

Lyon ✉ 69000

Arrondissement numbers are given after the street addresses. (Change the final zero of the post code for the *arrondissement* address.)

distinctly unpleasant welcome at the bigger Gaulish base of Vienne (*see* p.157) down the Rhône. But the name of their new town paid homage to the Celtic solar god, Lug, facing dramatically towards the rising sun.

Lugdunum rapidly grew into the pre-eminent city in Gaul. Under the first Roman Emperor, Augustus, in 27 BC it was made capital of *Gaule Lyonnaise*, one of three vast

Luxury

★★★★La Villa Florentine, 25 Montée St-Barthélémy, 5e, t 04 72 56 56 56, *www.villaflorentine.com*. Very exclusive location, high on Fourvière hill, in a former convent converted into an Italianate delight. Pool. Enjoy the views from the excellent restaurant too, **Les Terrasses de Lyon** (*very expensive; open eve only Mon–Sat*).

★★★★La Tour Rose, 22 Rue du Bœuf, 5e, t 04 78 92 69 10, *www.slh.com*. Down in the heart of Renaissance Lyon, splendid secretive address set around courtyards with colourful stair towers. Exquisite Lyon silks used in the sumptuous decoration. Superb restaurant (*very expensive; closed Sun, and lunchtimes in Aug*).

★★★★La Cour des Loges, 2 Rue du Bœuf, 5e, t 04 72 77 44 44, *www.courdesloges.com*. Rival of the above, a stunning mix of contemporary design and historic architecture. Exclusive restaurant (*very expensive*).

Expensive

★★★Globe et Cécil, 21 Rue Gasparin, 2e, t 04 78 42 58 95, *www.globeetcecil.com*. Stylish, and the rooms have individual touches.

★★★Beaux-Arts, 75 Rue du Président Herriot, 2e, t 04 78 38 09 50, *www.accorhotels.com*. Art Deco features, plus a few rooms decorated by contemporary artists.

★★★Carlton, 4 Rue Jussieu, 2e, t 04 78 42 56 51, *www.accorhotels.com*. Its glamorous dome stands out in the Presqu'île's shopping district. Rooms in opulent old-fashioned style; some moderately priced.

Moderate

★★★Grand Hôtel des Terreaux, 16 Rue Lanterne, 1er, t 04 78 27 04 10, *www.hotel-lyon.fr*. Smartly renovated rooms in a classic central address, tiny cooling swimming pool cleverly tucked in by the breakfast area. Note that the best rooms fall into the expensive category.

★★★Hôtel des Artistes, 8 Rue G. André, 2e, t 04 78 42 04 88, *www.hoteldesartistes.fr*. Bright, quite simple charm by the Théâtre des Célestins.

★★Au Patio de Morand, 99 Rue de Créqui, 6e, t 04 78 52 62 62, *www.hotel-morand.fr*. Enchanting, intimate, fresh rooms set around a peachy little courtyard close to the best shopping east of the Rhône.

Inexpensive

★★Hôtel Bayard, 23 Place Bellecour, 2e, t 04 78 37 39 64, *www.hotelbayard.com*. With character and quirky décor.

★★L'Elysée, 92 Rue du Président Herriot, 2e, t 04 78 42 03 15, *www.elysee-hotel.com*. Appealing, cosy little rooms at this traditional option.

★★Hôtel du Théâtre, 10 Rue de Savoie, 2e, t 04 78 42 33 32, *www.hoteldutheatre.online.fr*. Good value, stylish, some rooms with nice views.

Eating Out

Very Expensive–Expensive

Léon de Lyon, 1 Rue Pléney, 1er, t 04 72 10 11 12. Superb traditional regional cuisine in warm, panelled, classic restaurant. *Closed Sun and Mon, and most Aug*.

Pierre Orsi, 3 Place Kléber, 6e, t 04 78 89 57 68. Another classic luxury Lyon restaurant, just south of the Parc de la Tête d'Or, in splendid historic house with rose-surrounded terrace. *Closed Sun and Mon*.

Auberge de l'Ile, Ile Barbe, 9e, t 04 78 83 99 49. Up the Saône, on the exclusive Ile Barbe, an exceptional restaurant serving exquisite seasonal dishes. *Closed Sun and Mon, and most of Aug*.

L'Arc en Ciel, 129 Rue Servient, 3e, t 04 78 63 55 00. Part of the Radisson Part-Dieu hotel, sensational location at the top of Lyon's tallest building, the Crédit Lyonnais

territories into which Gaul was divided. Then it effectively became capital of the Three Gauls when the annual tribal gathering was fixed here. The tribes came to meet among themselves, but also to pay homage to the divinities of the empire. A couple of Roman emperors were even born in the city. Claudius (he who conquered England) came into the world here in 10 BC.

skyscraper. Good food to accompany the great views and décor. *Closed Sat lunch and Sun, and mid-July–mid-Aug.*

Moderate

Les Muses de l'Opéra, 7th Floor of the Opera House, 1er, t 04 72 00 45 58. Extraordinary opera-house rooftop location at which to enjoy good cuisine.

Le Vivarais, 1 Place Gailleton, 2e, t 04 78 37 85 15. Smart, on lovely square. A still life animal may watch over you as you sample tasty regional specialities. *Closed Sat lunch and Sun, and most Aug.*

Le Sud, 11 Place Antonin Poncet, 2e, t 04 72 77 80 00. Paul Bocuse's fabled restaurant lies by the Saône north of town (*see* p.66), but he and his team have created four tempting, good-value satellites in Lyon, each devoted to a different cuisine. Here it's Mediterranean.

Bistrot de Lyon, 64 Rue Mercière, t 04 78 38 47 47. Authentic, atmospherically jaded *Belle Epoque* decoration in which to try Lyonnais produce, plus a wide range of seafood.

Brasserie Georges 1836, 30 Cours de Verdun-Perrache, 2e, t 04 72 56 54 54. Huge bustling theatre of a Lyonnais culinary institution behind Perrache station, the smart waiters putting on poised performances, 24 hours a day.

Bouchons

Bouchons are lively, unfussy little family-run restaurants serving simple, stocky regional food and wine at *moderate* prices. A *bouchon* is a cork in French but, specific to Lyon, these restaurants got their name from the first one being set up in stables behind the old town hall where horses were rubbed down, *bouchonné* in French.

Bouchon du Musée, 2 Rue des Forces, 2e, t 04 78 37 71 54. The original one, the traditional fare including tripe and the like.

Au Petit Bouchon Chez Georges, 8 Rue Garet, 1er, t 04 78 28 30 46. Some of the best *bouchon* fare in a delightful atmosphere. *Closed weekends and Aug.*

Chabert et Fils, 11 Rue des Marronniers, 2e, t 04 78 37 01 94. Puppets hang from the ceiling in the lower, vaulted restaurant-cellar of this action-packed typical *bouchon* in a street full of them.

Culture and Nightlife

For listings of what's on, try the tourist office's www.lyon-france.com; *Lyon City News* is its useful regular magazine. *Le Petit Bulletin* is a good free listings magazine widely available. Then there's *Lyon Poche*.

In this highly cultured city, Lyon's Roman **theatres** count among its most dramatic stages in summer. Given that this is where world **cinema** was born, look out for movie events through the year. The daring **opera** house stages challenging, often brilliant productions. The modern Auditorium, home to the Orchestre National de Lyon, presents excellent **music** programmes. The Halle Tony Garnier makes a huge atmospheric venue for **pop concerts**. Further concert and theatre venues are peppered across the city. For **dance**, look at Maison de la Danse. Lyon hosts major cultural *Biennales*, the next ones on contemporary art in 2005 and 2007, those on dance in 2006 and 2008, likewise those of marionettes.

You can swim in the spectacular Rhône-side outdoor baths. A new annual summer attraction is the **Fête des Guinguettes** in mid-July, when the riversides make merry, a beach even laid by the Rhône. Lyon is always beautifully lit at night, but has a spectacular week of illuminations early Dec, the **Festival des Lumières**.

Some of the liveliest spots for **nightlife** include the area around the lower slopes of Croix-Rousse and the Rhône's east bank; Vieux Lyon is more touristy.

Overseen today by a church that seems to think it's a fairytale castle, Lyon boasts one of the very longest Christian histories in France. In fact, it claims to have had the first Christian church in the country. Following a popular uprising in 177 it also got one of the very earliest and biggest batches of Christian martyrs, the most famous being St Pothin, Ste Blandine and St Irénée (or Irenaeus). Gallo-Roman Lugdunum was provided with substantial walls, but these wouldn't stop the arrival of tribes from the east. The Burgondes took hold of Lyon in 470, supplanted in 534 by the Franks.

In the Dark Ages, Lyon became home to influential monasteries, the great one on the Saône's Ile Barbe claimed by legend to have been founded by Longinus, the Roman centurion said to have pierced Jesus' side with a lance as he was crucified, when a drop of holy blood falling into his eye made him see the Christian light. The abbey of St Martin d'Ainay went up on the Presqu'île. Meanwhile, the archbishops acquired power over the city. But life was tough for most, and at Lyon's great Carolingian fairs, Angle and Saxon slaves counted among the prime commodities. By the treaty of Verdun of 843, dividing up Charlemagne's inheritance, Lyon fell under the kingdom of Burgundy-Provence, sandwiched between Germany and France.

In 1032 Lyon was incorporated into the Holy Roman Empire, on its western frontier. The archbishops strengthened their grip on the city, receiving the honorific but imposing title of Primate of Gaul from 1079. In 1095 Pope Urban II dropped in, whipping up European support for the First Crusade to wrest Jerusalem back from Muslim control. Lyon became the popes' number one stop in medieval Europe outside Italy. But the German Holy Roman Emperors, often the pontiffs' biggest bane, kept some sway over Lyon. By Emperor Frederick Barbarossa's Golden Bull (decree) of 1157, the archbishops became counts of the city, aided by 32 canons, who bore the title of *chanoines- comtes de Lyon*. They built castles to guard their substantial territories around the Lyonnais. The monasteries developed separately into huge regional landowners.

Protesters against the Catholic church's abuse of power showed their heads early. Pierre Valdo, a Lyonnais merchant, caused a terrible stir in the 12th century with his reforming *Pauvres de Lyon* (subsequently known as Waldensians or Vaudois), precursors of the Protestants who sought to return to the uncorrupted teachings of the New Testament. In the 13th century, the influential new Franciscan and Dominican orders established monasteries in town. But the archbishops continued to hold the secular as well as the religious strings. Several important European church gatherings were held in the city. Pope Innocent IV even took refuge in Lyon for seven years. In 1254, the pope consecrated the high altar of the revamped, Gothic cathedral. Early in the 14th century, Pope Clement V escaped the bloody chaos of Rome and was crowned in Lyon before taking the new, Provençal pontiff's seat, at Avignon, down the Rhône.

Lyon officially became a part of the French royal realms in 1312. Merchants acquired greater power with the crown, which allowed them a council of 12 to run much of the city. But the workers found their new masters no more charitable than the previous ones and protested frequently at their taxes. The plague also swept Europe, striking all classes from the mid-14th century. From the 15th century, international fairs among the most vibrant in Europe became key to Lyon's exceptional commercial success. Traders flocked from across the continent, Florentine bankers moving in in force to make Lyon one of Europe's major financial centres. Under Louis XI's impetus, the city developed two major industries for the coming centuries: silk-making, the skills imported across the Alps, and printing, first introduced in 1473, by Germans.

At the turn of the 15th–16th centuries, a series of French kings rode off to try to assert inheritance claims to parts of immensely wealthy, but fragmented, Italy and brought back Renaissance learning and luxuries. François I led the most sustained attack on the Italian states, Lyon even nicknamed his *Capitale des Guerres*. The major Florentine bankers in the city, Thomas Gadagne and Robert Albizzi, were forced, hands tied behind their backs, to put a huge 100,000 gold *écus* at the king's disposal.

After Venice and Paris, Lyon became the third most important publishing centre in Europe. But this was a dangerous business, the printed word exploited for protest as well as propaganda. One Lyonnais pamphlet attacked 'the eight or nine hundred years of tyranny of the canon-counts of St-Jean'. Famous and scandalous French Renaissance works were published in Lyon, including work by Rabelais, who was practising as a doctor at the prestigious Hôtel-Dieu, but spending more time hiding his criticisms under the disguise of the traditional giant figures of Gargantua and Pantagruel, his saucy tales published for the fairs of 1532 and 1534.

The French Wars of Religion then wrought massive division and destruction. At the outset in 1562, Protestants took control of the city, attacking churches and imposing Protestant services, but Catholic authority was soon reasserted. The court stayed a time in Lyon in 1564, on a tour to re-establish harmony, but a dreadful bout of the plague caused it to leave in a rush; some 25,000 people died from this prolonged outbreak. By comparison, the number of Protestants killed by fanatical Catholics in the 1572 St Bartholomew's Day Massacres was small, but the psychological impact was terrible. Some Protestant merchants continued to thrive, however.

In 1600, reconciling Henri IV came to Lyon to be married to Marie de' Medici. The town councillors started making exceptional provision for the poor, with the creation from 1617 of the Hospice de la Charité. Nothing could stop the ravages of another attack of the plague from 1628 to 1629 . The town council continued to assert its strength, though, ordering the majestic town hall on Place des Terreaux. Branches of the Church demonstrated their semi-independent power with grand new buildings. The vast Abbaye de St-Pierre, where the daughters of the aristocracy would be educated, rivalled the Hôtel de Ville. The Jesuits had a hugely influential monastery close by, Louis XIV's confessor Père Lachaise among its teachers. Along the Rhône, the major central hospital, or Hôtel-Dieu, expanded in grandiose style.

By 1700, Lyon had grown into a massive city by period standards, with perhaps 100,000 inhabitants, roughly a quarter of Paris. Obsessed by extravagant luxury, the capital's royal court demanded more and more of its silk. No one could match Philippe de Lassalle for the breathtaking finesse of his works. The brilliant Lyonnais sculptors Coysevox, and then his Coustou nephews, went off to serve the court.

Inventiveness bubbled away around Lyon in the 18th century, coming to the boil as the century reached its climax. The first veterinary college in the world opened in the city in 1761, founded by the Lyonnais Claude Bourgelat. The engineer Perrache literally gained ground for the town, reclaiming two kilometres of marshy lands below the Presqu'île. In steam navigation, Claude de Jouffray d'Abbans' *Pyroscaphe* of 1783 was one of the first steam boats in the world. Air travel took a big leap forward here, too, huge crowds witnessing one of the very earliest and most hazardous Montgolfier manned balloon trips, in early 1784. The 100-metre balloon came down in flames, but the navigators survived, treated like heroes by the populace.

If scientific progress advanced rapidly, Lyon's conservative leaders didn't care for the social ideals of the Revolution. A moderate, federalist Girondin attitude prevailed. However, by 1793, the Jacobin fanatics had got the upper hand in France, and the dreaded Joseph Chalier led a mini-Terror in the city, calling for hundreds to be executed and thrown into the Rhône. The federalists, led by the merchants, but supported by the people, rose up and executed the would-be tyrant. Rabid Robespierre and his Parisian National Assembly loathed Lyon with a vengeance by now, declaring that the city's name be eradicated from all maps. Besieged, the Lyonnais suffered bombardments and the ordeal of appalling famine, and finally yielded to their punishment on 9 October 1793. The first purge was aimed at the property of the rich, workers ordered to destroy over one and a half thousand of the finest houses. The city's fortifications were also torn down. The place was temporarily renamed *Ville Affranchie*, 'Freed Town'. The second purge took the form of mass executions, of almost 2,000 people, mostly from the leading strata, including many silk manufacturers. Luxuries like aristocratic silk were clearly out of fashion during the Revolution, the industry collapsing, only to be revived by the vanity of Napoleon's court. Bonaparte came to Lyon to participate in quelling a silk-workers' riot in the 1790s, but returned in 1802 to oversee *La Consulta*, an Italian Assembly at which he was declared President of the new Transalpine Republic – conquered Italy .

Weaving took off with renewed vigour at the start of the 19th century when local man Joseph Jacquard invented a mind-bogglingly complex but time-saving punch-card loom. The Croix-Rousse district became the new heart of the silk industry. Although Jacquard is regarded as a Lyonnais hero, the new machines didn't improve the lot of the ordinary silk-weavers, known as *canuts*, who rose up unsuccessfully on several occasions, most violently in the 1830s. A fatal mix of silkworm illnesses, foreign competition and the invention of artificial silk brought subsequent decline. Many *canuts* transferred to the factories that began to dominate down the Rhône. On a lighter note, a one-time Lyonnais silk-worker, Laurent Mourguet, invented a cast of puppet characters for his satirical Guignol shows, a big hit (*see* p.24).

Sometimes described as the city's answer to Baron Haussmann in Paris, under Claude-Marius Vaïsse, Lyon's centre underwent major changes mid-century, La Tête d'Or park laid out, Rue Impériale (now Rue de la République) cutting an imperious path through the Presqu'île. Opened by Napoleon III and Empress Eugénie, it became home to the region's major banks, including the Crédit Lyonnais, and major news-papers. Fourvière's fantasy church went up in reaction to the humiliating imperial defeat in the Franco-Prussian War of 1870. The Third Republic then stamped its mark, Antoine Gailleton, mayor from 1881 to 1900, even changing the street names to rid Lyon of associations with the Catholic, monarchist past. Hosting the International Fair of 1894, the city suffered the trauma of the assassination of the French President Sadi Carnot by anarchist Santo Caserio . Caserio was guillotined in town.

Much happier news came for Lyon the next year, the Lumière brothers inventing cinema. In 1895, the town, a pioneering centre of the early car industry (*see* Château de Rochetaillée, p.104), also became home to the first automobile club in France. The leftist Edouard Herriot was elected mayor in 1905, and under his long tenure, he encouraged urban projects, including by the visionary architect Tony Garnier. He also played a major part on the national scene through the first half of the 20th century as industry boomed at home.

Inevitably, Lyon suffered from bombardments in the Second World War, while normal city life was affected in various disturbing ways, from bad food shortages to the blowing up of bridges and melting down of statues around town. Lyon rapidly became the most important centre in Pétain-ruled southern France for the movements fighting the Nazis, earning the nickname of Capital of the Resistance (see p.77). But after the Germans took control of the whole country from November 1942, the dreaded Gestapo under Klaus Barbie tracked the Resistance leaders down, possibly aided by collaborators. France's greatest Resistance figure, Jean Moulin, was caught in Lyon in June 1943. In May 1944 US bombings went astray, killing 500 Lyonnais and destroying many buildings. The city was finally liberated on 3 September 1944 by the American 36th Division and the French 1st Armoured Division.

After the war, urban developments raced ahead. These included the business centre of La Part-Dieu, overseen by the fat new pencil of a skyscraper of the Crédit Lyonnais bank, which, despite this proud symbol, became bogged down in problems. In 1981, Lyon became the first French city linked to the capital by high-speed TGV rail link. If Lyon can't compete with Paris in terms of size, it can with Marseille. They fight it out for the title of France's second city, Lyon having a slightly larger agglomeration, but a smaller centre. While Marseille has only slowly been shaking off its image of working-class bad boy getting into terrible scraps and scams, Lyon has a reputation for being a tad snobbish, the clever rich kid investing wisely in prestigious urban projects. Museums, metro, new tramway, even those underground car parks, are world class. Not that the city hasn't had its own social problems, or scandalous leader.

Strong characters have held the powerful post of mayor of Lyon in recent decades, such as Michel Noir who initiated the long-term projects to redevelop the river banks but was brought down by financial improprieties. More traumatically for the whole nation, in 1983, Klaus Barbie was caught in Bolivia, and extradited to Lyon. The year before Barbie's court case, in 1986 Pope John Paul II paid a visit to the city. But Lyon wanted justice, not forgiveness. Barbie's trial, stirring up terrible ghosts of France's past, led to his conviction for crimes against humanity.

Former right-wing French Prime Minister Raymond Barre became mayor of Lyon between 1995 and 2001, the city during this time hosting a G7 economic summit, seeing the opening of Interpol's world headquarters, and, in 1998, celebrating classification as a UNESCO World Heritage Site. This well-merited accolade helped make the French more aware of the city's cultural riches. Under Barre, and his socialist successor Gérard Collomb, the massive redevelopment of Lyon's riverbanks has advanced further. The year 2007 will see important new mayoral elections in France. It will also be important for tourism in Lyon, with the planned opening of the futuristic Confluence Museum, the funky architecture marking the new importance of the point where Saône and Rhône finally fuse.

The Fourvière Hillside and Gallo-Roman Lyon

The bright white Notre-Dame de Fourvière church shining on top of the Fourvière hill labours under the strong illusion that it's a fairytale castle. It is the major landmark in Lyon, visible from so many points in the centre. To get your bearings in town, head up to it first. It is best to take the cable car (*funiculaire* or *ficelle*) from beside the cathedral to avoid the cramp-inducing climb via the various pedestrian paths; consisting of hundreds of steps, these narrow *montées* pass between hushed walled properties, several still concealing monastic institutions on this long-religious slope nicknamed *la colline qui prie* (the praying hill), although graffiti artists have plastered vacuous messages along the way. Reaching the broad **terrace** at the end of the church, you're rewarded with the finest visual map of central Lyon. And on clear days the uninterrupted views eastwards as far as Mont Blanc are magnificent. People stare out with reverence, as though still paying homage to the god Lug. In one sweeping glance you can take in much of the Rhône-Alpes region from here.

'A citadel of superstition', one outraged Republican protester branded showy **Notre-Dame de Fourvière** when it was built. It was ordered by archbishop Monseigneur de Genouilhac just after the Franco-Prussian War of 1870, in gratitude to the Virgin Mary for her supposed role in sparing the city from attack. Conservative Catholics were also appalled by the lavish decorations on this work designed by Pierre Bossan. The ostentatious west front hints at the extravaganza that awaits inside. Everywhere there are floral as well as religious details and lions. The interior feels almost Oriental, built on huge Moorish-looking arches. Mosaics cover floor and walls, much of the decoration devoted to the Virgin, illustrating declarations by the church on her Immaculate Conception, and her status as Mother of God and protectress of France. The crypt is almost on the same scale as the church above, albeit in more sober style. Here, the plethora of plaques of *grâces* and *reconnaissances* indicate what a major pilgrimage destination this is, still receiving one million pilgrims a year.

In fact, there are older places of pilgrimage on the site, the 18th-century **Ancienne Chapelle de la Vierge** housing wildly ornate Baroque altarpieces and topped outside by a big gilded Virgin. She was added in the 19th century, a work by the sculptor Joseph Fabisch. His work proved so popular he went on to make the much-venerated Virgin of Lourdes. The adjoining **Musée d'Art Sacré** (*t 04 78 25 13 01; open April–early Dec daily 10–12 and 2–5.30; adm*) presents sumptuous religious articles. Climb the **basilica observatory** (*open April–Sept Wed–Sun 10.30–12 and 2–6.30, Oct–Mar weekends and public hols 1.30–5.30; adm*) for spectacular views.

Close by on the hilltop, a **metallic tower** sticks out like a copy of the top of Paris' Eiffel Tower – exactly what it is, just grey. Erected in 1893 for an ambitious restaurant owner, at 85m (close on 300ft) it now serves as a television transmitter.

Notre-Dame de Fourvière probably occupies the site of the Gallo-Roman forum of Lugdunum. South along the hillside, admire the remnants of two major **Roman theatres** (*open 9am–nightfall; adm*) built side by side in a spectacular location facing east. These huge structures were only unearthed in the 1930s, after a band of nuns digging their land struck upon an ancient wall; the city took over the excavations. The main theatre originally went up around 15 BC, one of the earliest in Gaul. It doubled in size under Hadrian, seating 10,000. The smaller theatre, or Odeon, dates from around AD 100 and was used for performances of music and poetry. It could seat 3,000. Don't stumble on the outsized paving blocks as you soak up the ancient atmosphere.

Roman Lugdunum was substantially excavated through the 20th century, many finds ending up in the **Musée de la Civilisation Gallo-Romaine** (*t 04 72 38 49 30; open Mar–Oct Tues–Sun 10–6, Nov–Feb Tues–Sun 2–5; adm*) overlooking the two theatres. Its 1970s concrete strata, designed by acclaimed architect Zehrfuss, look a bit drab these days, but are quite sensitively incorporated into the hillside. Although the collections concentrate on how Lugdunum grew so rapidly into a major political and religious centre, they also cover earlier periods in the Rhône-Alpes region, for instance with the processional chariot from La Côte-St-André dating back to 700 BC. Busts of Lyon's founder, Plancus, and the emperors closely associated with the city, help put faces to the Roman names. Models recreate Lugdunum's grandest buildings. The religious sections include cruder devotional items from the Gaulish tradition, and much finer-figured representations of Roman divinities. Separate areas are devoted to Lugdunum's economic life and craftsmen. Among the mosaics, one of the most spectacular depicts a scene at the Roman circus – you can even see what's described as gladiators' graffiti. Roman finds are still being made. In the 1990s, a new hoard of buried Gallo-Roman treasure was found in the suburb of Vaise, now on show here.

Vieux Lyon: Medieval and Renaissance Lyon

Squeezed between Fourvière's hillside and the Saône, the cramped streets of Vieux Lyon are lined with tall mansions, their ground floors often given over to touristy restaurants and boutiques. Gorgeous small squares allow for a little breathing space. This area was home to the archbishops of Lyon and their noble aides, the canon-counts. The most venerable building in Vieux Lyon, the medieval **Primatiale St-Jean**, or **Cathedral of St John**, turns its muscular, rounded back on the Saône. Its finely chiselled west façade overlooks pretty **Place St-Jean**, on which a copper John the Baptist performs a civilized baptism of Christ beneath a small dome. On the front, a splendid rose window attracts attention. Below, although the main statues were torn down, the figures on the carved panels around the portals merely suffered beheadings at the hands of fanatical Protestants. The plethora of scenes proves engrossing, told with medieval chivalric verve, and often violence. Inside, the tall Gothic nave has a sober grandeur, but the place was heavily restored in the 19th century. The swankiest side chapel with its elaborate vaulting was built as the resting place for Charles de Bourbon, long-serving archbishop of Lyon in the 15th century. In the squat Romanesque apse, admire the intense 13th-century stained glass. The transepts, each with their own sets of organ pipes, have bright stained-glass rose windows, while the remarkable childlike 16th-century astronomical clock provides unintentional light entertainment with its chimes and God popping out of a cloud like a figure from a Guignol show. The treasury conceals smaller marvels. The whole area around the cathedral was once occupied by episcopal buildings, portions of which survive in varying states of repair. The notable **Romanesque edifice** beside the Primatiale, with its diminutive arches and patterned bricks, served as the refectory of the canon-counts before being turned into the cathedral choristers' school.

North of the cathedral lie the most touristy streets of Vieux Lyon. The well renovated, fruity-coloured façades of mansions built for wealthy residents in the 15th and 16th centuries loom over the narrow streets. Take the main artery, **Rue St-Jean**, past dramatic Flamboyant Gothic and Renaissance houses, the arcades of the Maison des Avocats most impressive, then on behind the imposing 19th-century Palais de Justice. Don't miss the parallel streets. **Rue des Trois Maries** is graced by the odd religious statue. Reach **Rue du Bœuf** via broad **Rue Neuve St-Jean**, which serves as an intensely touristy square for restaurants. Or try the secretive way to it via the longest *traboule* in town, taking you through five courtyards from 54 Rue St-Jean to 27 Rue du Bœuf. These *traboules* (perhaps a contraction of the Latin, '*transambulare*', 'to walk through') are narrow covered alleys linking the big mansions, offering private paths through the area; while many are now open to the public, they are often dingy and, although the inner courtyards are overseen by picturesque galleries and towers, bins often preside below – greenery might look more fetching. No.16 on Rue du Bœuf conceals the most famous soaring stair towers, the arch-windowed **Tour Rose**.

Following Rue St-Jean north, the street shimmies through a series of sweet squares, teeming with tourist life. **Place de la Baleine** perhaps got its name from whale-meat being shipped in to the nearby quay for Lent; **Place du Gouvernement** was where the *Ancien Régime* governors were based; and **Place du Change** was where Lyon's currency exchange was set up from the time of the fairs. The first exchange building in France was erected here in the 16th century, to be remodelled in the 18th century, the plans by the neoclassical architect Soufflot, making the place look like an elegant theatre. Since the Revolution, it has doubled as Protestant church and concert venue.

Rue Lainerie and **Rue Vernay** lead up to **Place St-Paul**, the medieval **church of St-Paul** signalled by its funnel of a spire . The church interior was drearily renovated some time back, but given murals round the Romanesque apse showing the stages in the saint's life. The local hero of these parts, however, is puppeteer Laurent Mourguet (*see* p.24), a plaque on the square recalling that he lived here from 1795 to 1832.

The name of **Rue Juiverie**, tucked away south of Place St-Paul, recalls the Jewish community who lived and traded here in the Middle Ages, driven out by the French royal purge of Jews in the 14th century. Grand Renaissance houses were built here in the 16th century. The Bullioud mansion, the plushest, was designed, in part, by one of France's most inventive Renaissance architects, the Lyonnais Philibert Delorme, who was inspired by his studies in Italy and allowed to play with his newly acquired classical knowledge in the courtyard. Contorted lions' faces stick out from the later Baroque façade of the **Hôtel des Lions**.

Rue de Gadagne behind **Place du Change** contains the largest mansion in Vieux Lyon, named after one of the most influential Italian banking families to settle in town, chased out of Florence by the mightier Medicis. 'As rich as Gadagne' would become a catchphrase in Lyon though. The huge rambling Renaissance **Hôtel de**

Gadagne (*t 04 78 42 03 61, www.museegadagne.com; open daily exc Tues 10.45–6; adm*) contains two museums. The renovated **Musée Historique de Lyon** offers a major trawl through the city's history, fine fragments on display, such as the capitals rescued from Ile Barbe abbey, as well as covering major episodes in the city's later life, including Revolutionary terror, with telling visual pieces as well as text. The **Musée International de la Marionnette** is devoted to puppets from around the world, but focuses most on local heroes Guignol, Madelon and Gnafron.

Along the Banks of the Saône

An exhilarating string of bridges connects the two banks of the Saône, for charm rivalling the Seine in central Paris. Stroll south along the plane-lined **west bank of the Saône** for one of Lyon's most uplifting walks. Along **Quai de Bondy**, the massive **Palais de Bondy** dates from the early 20th century, a Belle Epoque building with striking *bas-reliefs*, made for exhibitions and performances. Touristy pubs, discos and girlie bars follow in a brash line, but at expansive **Place Fusseret**, enjoy the uplifting view across to the dramatic façade of the church of St-Nizier from one of the big ice-cream parlours with their generous terraces, Nardone set under a huge theatrical mural. The thick trunks of the plane trees along **Quai Romain Rolland** mirror the huge, sober 24 columns of the 19th-century **Palais de Justice**. Designed by Baltard, the extravagant original interior decorations remain in place. This building has witnessed traumatic trials for the nation, including those of Klaus Barbie and Italian anarchist assassin Santo Caserio. Past the rounded back of the cathedral, the **Palais St-Jean** was the archbishops' palace down the centuries, its complex of buildings given their present outer forms by Soufflot in the mid-18th century. Along **Quai Fulchiron**, the spire of the **church of St-Georges** protrudes, a cute neo-Gothic number by the architect Bossan again, although in his opinion, it was a 'youthful error'! The clatter of the looms of Lyon's early weavers once rang out in the now comfortably quiet **St-Georges quarter**. Delightful triangular **Place de la Trinité** has historic connections with Guignol, also recalled in a couple of little museums close by.

Take **Passerelle St-Georges**, one of the many appealing footbridges over the river (even if most of the crossings had to be rebuilt after the war) to walk up the **east bank of the Saône**. Along **Quai Tilsitt** the central synagogue merges self-effacingly into the row of smart apartment blocks. **Quai St-Antoine** hosts the city's major outdoor food market every morning except Monday. Pavement cafés encourage you to pause to admire the Saône and Fourvière. The most noticeable façade along this quay once housed the Antonin monastic order (*see* St-Antoine-l'Abbaye, p.179). It is now home to the **Théâtre des Ateliers**. **Quai de la Pêcherie** hosts Lyon's *bouquinistes*, with their funky metallic outdoor book stalls (*open weekends and holidays*). On **Quai St-Vincent**, the Baroque façade of the **church of St-Vincent** looks like it's been squashed into a strange angle by the bullying buildings shouldering in on either side. Beyond its concave entrance, questionable modern paintings of Christ's story have been added to the cool white neoclassical interior. North, a huge, elaborate ***trompe-l'œil* mural** wraps itself around some of the facades of No.49. The city council has encouraged many such pieces of public art, but none more startling than this one, depicting 24 figures born around Rhône and Saône. The figures go from Emperor Claudius and Ste Blandine, to the best-known Lyonnais faces today, chef Paul Bocuse, literary TV-star Bernard Pivot, film-maker Bertrand Tavernier and charity worker Abbé Pierre, the last often voted as the most admired Frenchman of our times. Delightful triangular **Place Martinière** offers deep shade just above, plus a small traditional covered market.

From **Quai St-Antoine**, embark on a splendid cruise up the Saône, which takes you north as far as the Ile Barbe, the island with its memories of Lyon's oldest monastery. The commentary fills you in on the grand buildings along the elegant banks.

The Presqu'île de Lyon

Cafés spill out around **Place des Terreaux**, big, lively hub of central Lyon, with many splashing fountains, the main one by Bartholdi, better known for his Statue of Liberty. Here, his chubby female charioteer steers four wildly tugging horses, representing river waters dashing to the sea. Rejected by Bordeaux, Lyon happily took her on. The smaller jets shooting out of the paving stones add a contemporary twist . The massive *Ancien Régime* **town hall** overlooks proceedings. Grizzly lions rest their paws over some of the windows, while muscular figures of Hercules and Minerva stand silhouetted above the big, jolly equestrian statue of Henri IV.

Beyond rises the brazen **opera house**, with a classical colonade plus stilted statues below, and a modern glass vault above, designed by ground-breaking contemporary architect Jean Nouvel. Sometimes compared to a Swiss roll cake plonked on top of the older building, it more resembles a tunnel placed high in the sky. Challenging contemporary sculptures and fountains run along the spacious square sloping up from the opera house. Back on Place des Terreaux, the enormously long-faced classical façade of the fine arts museum soberly calls cultural visitors inside.

Musée des Beaux-Arts in the Abbaye St-Pierre

t 04 72 10 17 40; open Wed–Mon 10–6; closed Tues; adm.

The *Ancien Régime* Abbey of Our Ladies of St Peter's, also known as the Palais St-Pierre as it's so grand, served as something of a posh finishing school for daughters of the regional aristocracy. After the Revolution it became Lyon's fine arts museum, one of the most important in France, wholly refurbished in the 1990s. Before entering this vast place, pause for breath in the restful courtyard, now a sculpture garden. It is amusing to see that this part of the former convent now plays host to a plethora of male nudes, including some by Rodin. The former abbey church has been converted into an amazing setting for the contemplation of further sculpture.

Between the two, one of the calmest masterpieces of the museum, Perugino's *Ascension*, greets you in the entrance hall, donated by Pope Pius VII in 1816. A grand Baroque staircase adorned with trumpeting angels, their legs and instruments dangling down, leads you up to the main collections. The first floor has a whole wing devoted to antiquities, another to medieval sculpture and craft pieces, and a third to sculpture and *objets d'art* from the Renaissance to the 20th century. Highlights among the rooms on antiquities include monumental temple doors from Mehamoud in Egypt and the Khore (a representation of a young girl) from the Acropolis in Athens.

Ivories going back to Byzantine and Carolingian times feature among the beautiful sculptures, the medieval European period is represented by many splendid church pieces, while a whole parallel section is devoted to Islamic works. Moving to the French *Ancien Régime*, painted enamels depicting biblical scenes stand out. Non-religious objects such as ceramics, glass, clocks and furniture also feature. The museum has further huge collections of coins and medals on display.

Allegorical dreamscapes typical of Pierre Puvis de Chavannes, a celebrated 19th-century neo-classical artist from Lyon, decorate the staircase leading to the second floor, where the different schools of European painting are well represented. The outstanding Italian works include an allegorical Tintoretto, and three Veroneses, all displaying 'Impressionist' touches well before their time. Bassano's battle scene of 1495, subtitled *Charles VIII receiving the crown of Naples*, illustrates the troubled relationship between France and Italy that affected Lyon so strongly, although apparently there was no such battle! The French *Ancien Régime* collections hold surprises such as works by Simon Vouet, an accomplished classical artist who painted an exceptionally modern self-portrait. An amazing pale-faced knight by a Le Nain brother, along with Jacques Stella's unflinching self-portrait, are further masterpieces in the genre. Then comes the usual avalanche of large-scale religious scenes, not just from courtly France, but also from the mercantile Low Countries. Two major pieces by Rubens are displayed. The Dutch collection has charming small scale landscapes and still lifes too. Then 18th-century French art hits back with the typical excess of the rococco, including Boucher's *The Light of the World* and Greuze's *Lady of Charity*.

The sugary mock-historic style of troubadour painting had Lyon's artistic circle on its knees in early 19th century, Pierre Révoril and Fleury Richard its leading exponents. Then came a wave of Lyon artists influenced by Ingres' neoclassical purity, Hippolyte Flandrin a much-loved exponent. Flower-painting became another Lyon speciality. The Romantics are represented by regional painters too, but also by bigger, national names, Delacroix with two contrasting pieces, Géricault powerfully stirring the emotions as ever, with his study of maddened envy. The Impressionist works, with a handful of Manets, Monets and Degas, make up the second largest collection in France after Paris' Musée d'Orsay, and form a splendid link to the post-Impressionist 20th-century art movements represented.

Further Down the Presqu'île

Rue Chenavard, Rue Herriot and Rue de la République are Lyon's smartest shopping streets, all heading south from Place des Terreaux. Although remarkable buildings stand out on the Presqu'île, you may notice that many of the mansion blocks look plainer on the outside than in a showier city like Paris, or Grenoble, for that matter.

Often in Lyon, the wealthy didn't like to display their fortunes on the outside. One particular decorative feature of the town's wealthy blocks, though, are *lambrequins*, patterned trimmings in wood or iron embellishing the tops of windows.

Look out for some of the Presqu'île's oldest shops along **Rue Paul Chenavard**, which takes you to **Place Meissonnier**, the pale narrow Romanesque façade of the former church of St-Pierre (now part of the fine arts museum, which has a museum shop virtually next door) looking over to a monument recalling a silk-worker's son who made a fortune and left it to Lyon charities. Rue Chenavard continues to the entrance of the **church of St-Nizier**, named after a miracle-working 6th-century bishop of Lyon. Its ornate Gothic forms and gargoyles have been scrubbed clean. Go through the striking central Renaissance porch to see the mainly 19th-century neo-Gothic decoration, although *Notre Dame des Grâces* by the sculptor Coysevox stands out, along with some major paintings. Continuing south, **Rue de Brest** takes over from **Rue Chenavard**. To the west, don't miss gently curving **Rue Mercière** – with the deep crushed-velvet reds of its tall Renaissance facades, it counts among the most stylish of all the streets of the Presqu'île, tempting restaurants lying along its length.

The odd grand façade and decorative detail stand out above very stylish and idiosyncratic shops at the northern end of **Rue du Président Herriot**, which runs parallel to Rue Chenavard and Rue de Brest. Branch off for **Rue Poulaillerie**. The **Musée de l'Imprimerie** (*t* 04 78 37 65 98; open Jan–Dec Wed–Sun 9.30–12 and 2–6; adm), Lyon's well regarded museum of printing, is tucked away in the **Hôtel de la Couronne**. In the courtyard of this lovely Renaissance mansion, a large plaque shows a man and a woman pouring water, representing the city's two rivers. This place served as town hall before the huge Hôtel de Ville was built on Place des Terreaux. The museum goes about its business seriously, tracing the history of writing back to its Middle Eastern roots before concentrating on the 15th-century revolution in printing. The place contains a rare **Gutenberg Bible** (*c*. 1454). On French history, it's fascinating to see a copy of the original **Protestant *Placard Contre la Messe*** of 1534. This explosive piece denounced in crude language 'the pope and all his vermin of cardinals, bishops, priest, monks and other cockroaches...' but also argued a very strong case against the Catholic Mass. It was written by a Lyonnais, Antoine Marcourt, from the safety of Protestant Neuchâtel in Switzerland and was printed by a fellow Lyonnais exile, Pierre de Vingle. One copy was even affixed to the door of François I's bedroom. In his rage, the monarch supported the persecution of Protestants and, after a second placard in January 1535, banned all printing in France for a time. If you tire of the worthy explanatory texts, a whole floor is devoted to fine prints, including Gustave Doré's illustrations of Rabelais' tales. Back along **Rue Herriot**, at Place Francisque Regaud, you might stop at the jaded 19th-century extravaganza, the Café des Négociants. Like Rue Mercière and Rue de Brest, Rue Herriot continues down to Place des Jacobins.

Impressively broad **Rue de la République** came into being as Rue Impériale in the mid-19th century and is lined with grandiose period buildings. Now pedestrianized, locals refer to it as Rue de la Ré and come in droves to the major contemporary departments stores that have taken over many of the most ornate addresses. But the odd family store has survived, and the street is packed with historical memories. A plaque at No. 1 recalls the first public cinema screening ever, on 25 January 1896, the Lumière brothers showing off their amazing new apparatus. The major French banks established swanky offices near the top of the street. The Crédit Lyonnais, founded in 1863 by Henri Germain, opened its office here in 1872. In front of it, President Sadi Carnot was assassinated in 1894, a red stone marking the spot where he was stabbed. **Place de la Bourse** provides a welcome, and greenish, pause along **Rue de la Ré**.

Rue de la Bourse, parallel to the main shopping artery, contains further grand buildings. The Ampère secondary school was previously the seat of the Jesuit order. Louis XIV's celebrated confessor, Père Lachaise, taught here, while Père Martellange became the Jesuits' most renowned architect. He had the **Chapelle de la Trinité** remodelled from 1617; its Baroque interior with painted stucco work and Italian marble statues of the main Jesuit saints has been sumptuously restored.

Back on Rue de la République, the palatial **Palais du Commerce**, smothered with columns, medallions and statues, including a racy image of intertwined naked swimmers representing Rhône and Saône, was built to house a stock exchange, chamber of commerce and commercial court, reflecting the economic dynamism of France's Second Empire. **Place des Cordeliers** is the next square where the shopping artery widens out. To one side stands the 14th-century **church of St-Bonaventure**, once part of an extensive Franciscan monastery. The church has kept its very dark Gothic interior; at one end tapestries illustrate Bonaventure's life, including the saintly man being surprised doing his washing up as the church authorities come to declare him a cardinal. Chillingly, it's said that the last of the *canut* rioters of the 1830s were massacred in the elaborate Sacré Cœur chapel. Further down Rue de la Ré, a few exceptional shops have survived from the 19th century, like the confectioner Voisin and the jeweller Augis. The main Lyonnais newspapers fought it out in this section, *Le Progrès* the main one to have lasted, although no longer based here. **Place de la République**, with its dynamic, sporty-looking swimming-laned fountain and children's carousel, is still overseen by Second Empire buildings. Also cast an eye over the extravagant façades of **Rue Président Carnot**, a development from the Belle Epoque. On the last leg of Rue de la République, the Casino-Kursaal, Lyon's main Belle Epoque music hall, has long been converted into a big cinema complex, while the Bellecour Theatre now houses the major FNAC entertainments department store.

Passage de l'Argue, a slightly jaded covered gallery of shops, connects the north of Place de la République with **Place des Jacobins**, which bears the nickname of the Dominican monastic order established here in the medieval period, although all trace of its highly important monastery has vanished, replaced in the Second Empire by yet more commercial grandeur. The figures of four of Lyon's most famous artists preside on the large central fountain. A trio of smart short shopping streets fan out from the bottom of Place des Jacobins, ultra-chic **Rue Emile Zola**, with its designer clothes shops, jewellers and even *pâtisseries*, most inappropriately named. To the side, **Place des Célestins** carries the title of another medieval religious order whose buildings have long gone, replaced by the **Célestins theatre**, a swanky Belle Epoque number.

Looking enormously vacuous after the shopping streets to the north, **Place Bellecour**, one of the largest squares in Europe, measures some 200 by 300 metres.

It originally served as a military training ground, and feels like it could do with some more action these days. The lonely figure of an imperial, athletic Louis XIV trots across the red-gravel square, like a royal out on a solitary early morning ride. Below, the river gods Saône and Rhône recline on lions, works by the accomplished Coustou brothers. On the south side, the pavilion matching Lyon's tourist office sometimes serves for art exhibitions. The flower stalls bring regular life to this end of the square.

Just east on **Rue des Marronniers**, packed with people and restaurants, you'll find the most compact concentration of *bouchons*, Lyon's traditional, hearty family-run restaurants. Further major shopping arteries lead south. Broad, mainly pedestrian **Rue Victor Hugo** is full of familiar French and international brand names. Parallel **Rue Auguste Comte** draws wealthy shoppers in search of fine antiques and designer interior decorations, but anyone can get a taste for the luxuries of the high life by visiting the duo of museums on **Rue de la Charité** devoted to the refinements of living.

An old sock is much more than simply an old sock when it has managed to survive since Coptic Egyptian times. The ambitious, sumptuous **Musée des Tissus** (*t 04 78 38 42 00; open Tues–Sun 10–5.30; adm*) spreads its net very wide indeed, covering not just the famous silks of Lyon, but textile-making across the world, from ancient times to the present. The collections make the massive, modernized 18th-century Hôtel de Villeroy burst at the seams. The early Christian Copts were amazingly accomplished in the art of weaving, best demonstrated by wonderful funerary cushions celebrating a man's life, and by a masterpiece of cloth depicting 15 varieties of fish swimming through shimmering waters. Moving on swiftly, Greek, Roman, early Persian (or Sassanid) and Byzantine periods are also represented. As regards Western Europe, the pieces go back about one thousand years. Perhaps the most remarkable medieval work comes from England; the 14th-century Tree of Jesse, utterly seductive with its string of coquettish, finger-pointing kings, and its still more flirtatious-looking Virgin. Back with the Middle East, the Persian and Turkish carpets from the 15th to 17th centuries are exceptional large-scale works, the delicacy of the Persian weaving astounding (look out for the elaborate depiction of Layla's story), while in the Turkish pieces, the clarity of design stands out. Lyon's own great silk-weaving tradition is splendidly displayed; its golden age came in the 18th century, when no one could match the skill of Philippe de Lasalle, whose cameo textile portraits for the court look like the most accomplished of paintings.

In contrast to the wide-ranging Musée des Tissus, its neighbour, the **Musée des Arts Décoratifs** (*t 04 78 38 42 00; open daily 10–12 and 2–5.30; adm*) concentrates on *Ancien Régime* furnishings. This, too, is a museum on a grand scale, occupying a mansion that retains its period proportions. The place was built for Jean de Lacroix, adviser to Lyon's Cour des Monnaies. He clearly amassed vast amounts of moneys for himself. In one room, a portrait shows him looking extremely chipper in fine costume. Pastel portraits of more cheerful-looking noblemen admire the décor, all reflected in old mirrors. Splendid ceramics and decorative objects, including a head-spinning number of *cartel* clocks, stand on the gorgeous furniture. Some of the extravagant interiors have been moved here from other Lyon mansions. One of the most ornate shows scenes of Ovid's wild tales. Another is lined with engrossing 19th-century wallpaper illustrating Lyon's riverbanks in that period, the depictions full of architectural details to relish. The museum is also particularly proud of its silver collections, including contemporary creations. The place is so stunningly furnished, it's a just a shame someone doesn't sit down at one of the countless harpsichords and play!

West down Rue Victor Hugo, **Place Ampère** pays its respects to the great Lyonnais scientist (*see* p.104). The restored Romanesque **Basilique St-Martin d'Ainay** nearby formed part of a long influential Benedictine abbey. The medieval builders incorporated the odd Roman cast-off into the architecture. The place retains enchanting Romanesque decoration, but it was heavily restored in the 19th century, Flandrin and Fabisch adding many elements. The abbey provides a calm corner before bustling **Place Carnot**. Huge statues sit in its garden in front of the escalators up to **Lyon-Perrache station**. One represents Liberty stroking a big lion – made to celebrate the centenary of the Revolution in which Lyon proved so difficult to tame.

The station acts as a barrier to the long **southern tip of the Presqu'île**. Redevelopment is under way of this neglected central area. Near the bottom of the peninsula, the **Musée des Confluences** should cause a splash when it opens in 2007. The peninsula ends in a razor-sharp tip like a shark's nose. Across on the Saône-side, a major new **aquarium** (*t 08 20 06 67 66, www.aquariumlyon.fr; open Jan–Dec Tues–Fri 10–6, Sat and Sun 10–7; adm*) overlooks the spit and the cat's cradle of roads. Inside, enjoy big-screen showings of glamorous undersea adventures, exotic fish, and regional species, including the odd amazing huge catfish caught in the Rhône.

Up the Croix-Rousse Silk-Making Slopes

The Croix-Rousse hillside, named after a red stone cross that once stood here, rises to the north of Place des Terreaux. In the 19th century, the place became synonymous with the silk trade that made this area such an intense hive of activity, nicknamed, in contrast to Fourvière, *la colline qui travaille*, the working hill. The steepness of the Croix-Rousse slope was only emphasized by the sheer soaring sides of the extremely tall, severe blocks built specifically for the looms. But before the close of the 19th century, silk manufacturing plummeted. The neglected Croix-Rousse hillside is gradually picking up again, although a strange atmosphere reigns, a kind of eerie, mourning emptiness for the vanished workers.

Before you start up the steep slope, spare a thought for the 80 Jews who were tragically rounded up in a purge in February 1943 immediately behind Place des Terreaux on the now kebab-shop-bustling **Rue Ste-Catherine**. Virtually all the silk-making tradition has vanished in the city, just a few specialist companies still producing items for fashion houses and wealthy clients. The only studio-shop you can visit, the **Atelier de la Soierie** (*closed Sun*), tucked into a courtyard just off the start of **Rue Romarin,** simply prints on silk, rather than weaving, but the process is enthusiastically demonstrated, and the boutique colourful.

Choosing between routes up the Croix-Rousse hillside, before heading up from the western end of Rue Ste-Catherine, pause for a fortifying drink at one of the corner cafés on enchanting **Place Sathonay**, although the statue of an unsteady Lyonnais soldier in the middle acts as a warning against overdoing it. Pass via the stylized little lion fountains up to the rather ignored third Roman theatre of Lyon, the **Amphithéâtre des Trois Gaules**. It has come down in the world since it served as the place where representatives of France's 60 Celtic tribes met under early Roman rule and where Ste Blandine and other early Christian martyrs were fed to the lions in the 2nd century. The most direct route up takes you via the **Montée de la Grande-Côte**, presenting a pretty but unrelenting climb. Further west along the slope, you get great views down on the Saône, from **Place Rouville**, backed by the enormous Maison Brunet silk-house, with supposedly as many windows as days of the year, or from the shaded terraced **Jardin des Chartreux**. Behind, the school-surrounded, Baroque-domed **church of St-Bruno** has been receiving a major clean-up to lure visitors inside again with its glamorous Italian baldaquin and elaborately framed paintings.

Taking the eastern side of the Croix-Rousse slopes, a scattering of gay spots stand along streets skirting east round the base of the hillside, extending along **Rue Romarin** and, across Place Croix Pacquet, into **Rue Royale**. Look along here and **Rue des Petits Feuillants** for atmospheric, trendy little restaurants. **Rue des Fantasques**, a little higher up, offers a panoramic option, with spectacular glimpses onto the local rooftops, the Rhône river and beyond. Up in the streets just west, you'll encounter a mix of bars in what was the heart of the 19th-century silk-making quarters. The Croix-Rousse slope has been being smartened up recently, although trendy-to-louche studenty and sleazy pubs and bars still hang around at the base of the blocks. Just before circular **Place du Forez**, the big *Condition Publique des Soies* on **Rue St-Polycarpe** was where silk was officially weighed in the 19th century. Spot the fine lion's head on the building. The big sober *Ancien Régime* **church of St-Polycarpe** dominates the end of the street. Close to it, off Rue Leynaud, **Passage Thiaffait** is the best example of a recently renovated passageway on Croix-Rousse, with cutting-edge designers opening challenging boutiques. **Rue Burdeau** above contains many massive *soyeux* houses; **Place Chardonnet,** along its length, honours Hilaire de Chardonnet with a statue, over-generously, given that he was one of the principal inventors of synthetic materials, helping to destroy Lyon's traditional silk trade for good. Trendy venues and alternative designer boutiques have opened up nearby. Explore the 19th-century *traboules* or passageways signposted through the neighbourhood, shortcuts (albeit with many steps) to help the *canuts* carry their packages of silk around more easily. The most vertigo-inducing array of stairways is at **Cour des Voraces**, named after the silk-workers' guild that used to meet here. Higher up, quiet, shaded **Place Colbert** offers wonderful views east, more unimpeded yet on **Place Bellevue**.

An alternative exists to climbing the Croix-Rousse hillside on foot; take the metro or a *ficelle*, the latter leaving from below the Amphithéâtre des Trois Gaules. Once you've reached the **Croix-Rousse plateau**, you feel almost like you've reached a separate big town along **Boulevard de la Croix-Rousse**, the broad, flat main street, host to theatrical markets. Jacquard's statue stands in prominent position on **Place de la Croix-Rousse**, where fairs are frequently held. Other principal figures in Lyon's silk-making history stand out on the huge mural nearby.

Along the Banks of the Rhône

Very grand medical history dominates down the **Rhône's west bank**, although walking along this side of the river is severely limited by the very busy road and lack of waterside quays. Past the series of squares opening onto the river above the opera house, the façade of the **Hôtel-Dieu** makes the biggest impression, extending almost a quarter of a mile. First founded as a religious hospital in the 12th century, this place was long recognized as one of the leading medical centres in Europe, and Rabelais practised here in the 16th century. The architect Soufflot designed the majestic river front for it in the 18th century. The massive central dome came crashing down in the fight for Lyon's liberation in 1944, its restoration only completed in 1972. Make your way guiltily past doctors, nurses and patients, then up inside the dome, to visit the **Musée des Hospices Civils de Lyon** (*t 04 72 41 30 42; open Jan–Dec Mon–Fri 1.30–5.30; adm*). This covers the history of Lyon's pioneering medicine, for example its early work with the insane, trying baths in the Rhône to calm them. It also presents pharmaceutical pots, exquisite *bourdaloues* (chamberpots) and historic equipment resembling instruments of torture. It even serves as something of a fine arts museum, with lavish wood-panelled interiors and devotional paintings, the latter once considered an essential part of the cure (or of salvation), rescued from other historic Lyon medical establishments, notably the former Hospice de la Charité.

Sterile **Place Antonin Poncet** (named for a 19th-century Lyonnais surgeon) connects the Rhône to **Place Bellecour**. A lone old **bell tower** stands out mournfully here, sole remnant of that pioneering hospice. A ground-breaking venture when set up by wealthy citizens in the 17th century to provide a soup kitchen for the city's poor, it grew into a fully-fledged hospital. A huge, austere **post office** replaced other dilapidated remnants in the 1930s; go inside for startlingly bright murals on the history of Lyon, gratuitous nudity thrown in for free. Continuing along the river, you pass the smart modern riverside block of the **Sofitel hotel** that replaced a military hospital. Bill Clinton stayed here during the 1996 G7 summit. The pomposity of the monument to the doctor-turned-mayor after whom **Place Gailleton** is named may look comical now, but his bust framed within a triumphal arch gives focus to this delightful square.

The **Rhône's flat eastern bank** is far better geared to walkers and cyclists. On the north side of the Tête d'Or park, the new Rhône-side **Cité Internationale** quarter, its smart cloned blocks designed by Renzo Piano, has been shooting up at a rate of knots, provided with sharp flats and hotel, cinema and casino. The older **Musée d'Art Contemporain** (*t 04 72 69 17 18; open for exhibitions only, Wed–Sun 12–7; adm*) has been swamped by this large life-style statement, but the controversial contemporary art it regularly displays stirs things up. The international **Interpol** headquarters look well protected on the end of the new row. Parts of the Rhône banks just north have been smartened up, but in other areas the sandy riverside has been left quite wild.

The graceful **Tête d'Or park**, supposedly named after a story claiming that a golden head of Christ was buried here, was beautifully laid out in the 19th century, although the rose gardens above the deep green **lake** look a bit aesthetically out of control for British tastes. You might go boating around the string of **islands**, but be prepared for a shock – one of them, which can also be reached via a pedestrian subway, has a moving **war memorial** designed by Tony Garnier, dedicated to 10,000 dead. The extraordinary monument shows a dozen men carrying a coffin, the coffin dressed, the men naked. The park's free **zoo** is undergoing modernization to give the animals more space. To the south, the **botanical garden** has preserved its array of period **greenhouses**, protecting a prestigious array of plants from across the globe.

Continuing south, choose between the riverside or the elegant, spacious **quarters just east**, grandiose public buildings and Parisian-style apartment blocks interspersed with comfortable squares overseen by substantial 19th-century churches. **Cours Roosevelt** offers the most tempting shopping. Behind the very grand **Préfecture** stands one of the most central Arab quarters. The **Halles**, the food-crammed 1970s covered market (east of Pont Lafayette), are where Lyon's celebrity chefs stock up. Among interesting new buildings, cast an eye over the sleek contemporary **Palais de Justice**, or law courts. The heart of the modern **Part-Dieu business and commercial quarter** looks more hackneyed now, but major buildings stand out. Unmissable, the **Crédit Lyonnais skyscraper** rises confidently above the rest, like a big fat pencil to write a big fat cheque in the air – the Crédit Lyonnais bankers were found to be acting with a pie-in-the-sky attitude before the company was taken over. The **Auditorium** is a major concert hall in the shape of a shell. A vacuous piazza stands in front of **Part-Dieu station**, encased in polished red buildings. Opposite, domed skylights bring a bit of natural light into the huge, smart but sterile *Centre Commercial*, or shopping mall. South behind the university quarter, explore Lyon's little Chinese quarter.

The joy of following the **eastern riverside route down the Rhône** is that you get fabulous views not just across to the Presqu'île, but also up to the buildings on the Fourvière hillside, dramatically lit at night. Riverboats are tied to the bank below **Pont de Lattre de Tassigny**, while the odd fisherman tries his luck. The jaded gardens of **Place Maréchal Lyautey** signal the start of **Cours Roosevelt**. Major administrative and university buildings follow behind plane-shaded quays. The best stop in summer is the splendid riverside **open-air pool**, supplied by filtered Rhône water. At night, trendy student bars come to life along the broad pavements, long cruise boats resting below.

Moving to a seriously harrowing subject, the **Centre d'Histoire de la Résistance et de la Déportation** (*t* 04 78 72 23 11; open Jan–Dec Wed–Sun 9–5.30; adm) at 14 Avenue Berthelot (east of Pont Gallieni) occupies the characterless yet chilling buildings of the town's former military hospital, which the dreaded German Gestapo police force took over as its Lyon headquarters in the Second World War. The vital part played by Lyon in the Resistance is thoroughly covered at this excellent Centre (*see* p.77-78), which doesn't shy away from tackling collaboration and other difficult issues.

Although you have to share the Rhône-side way with car parks, you can continue south through fast-developing quarters . The name of the **La Mouche quarter** acts as a reminder that the famous *bateaux-mouches* so closely associated with Seine river cruises were originally made here in the mid-19th century, by Lyonnais entrepreneurs who took some up to a Paris Universal Exhibition, the fashion catching on there. The **Parc des 4 Rives** has been recently planted with trees as well as funky contemporary architecture. As to the staggering former butchers' **Halle Tony Garnier** from the first half of the 20th century, it has been turned into a major concert venue. We end at **Gerland Park**, home to Lyon's highly successful football team. Lyon's huge commercial docklands, scarcely ever noticed by tourists, stretch away from here.

Cinema and Invention in the Eastern Quarters

Discover how cinema came into being at the **Musée Lumière** (*Métro line D to Monplaisir-Lumière stop; t 04 78 78 1895, www.institut-lumiere.org; open Tues–Sun 11–7; adm*) on clearly named **Rue du Premier Film**. This museum occupies the flashy **Villa Lumière**, nicknamed the *Château Lumière* by locals – you'll see why, and realize what a wealthy family the Lumières became. They were a greatly inventive lot. Antoine, father of Louis and Auguste, built up the family fortune selling photographic equipment before his boys came up with cinema (*see* p.25). Antoine loved planning grand houses to flaunt the family's success and enjoy the latest comforts, this villa completed in 1902. The Lumière company kept the property until the 1960s. The next decade, most of other Lumière buildings here were demolished, including the separate lavish villa which Antoine and Louis' families shared, and most of the factory, although it was here that the first cinema film of all time was shot, arguably the most important minute in the history of the moving image, showing the rather banal if engaging sight of Lumière company workers leaving at the end of their day.

You can view this film, and many of the other earliest Lumière shorts, in the villa's basement. Although silent movies, they are accompanied by a delightful modern commentary. But at the start, this museum puts the Lumière brothers' invention in period context, focusing first on pre-cinema attempts to produce moving images. The competition was stiff, the Lumières' greatest rival the American Edison. After inventing cinematography, the Lumières sent out company photographers to shoot images around the world, on display in the sumptuous bedrooms. The centre puts on major cinematic events in the one factory building left. Joyously, this is the very building in front of which the first film of all time was shot.

Not far south, the **Musée Urbain Tony Garnier** (*t 04 78 75 16 75, www. museeurbaintonygarnier.com; open Jan–Dec Tues–Sun 2–6; adm. Murals free.*) celebrates an influential 20th-century Lyonnais architect. Early embracing modernity, Garnier conceived a highly regarded model industrial city. The Lyon authorities employed him on major projects from 1905. A firm believer in providing good-quality housing for the poor, he planned one of the first large-scale low-cost social housing estates in France, the *Cité des Anciens Etats*, built between 1929 and 1933, rebaptized the *Cité Tony Garnier*. A visitor centre introduces Garnier's work. On a guided tour, visit the interior of one of the ground-breaking apartments. Out of doors, 24 huge murals recall Garnier's main projects. The area is now named the *Quartier des Etats Unis* – a US military camp was set up here in the First World War. It's sometimes forgotten that American troops played a crucial role in ending that appalling conflict.

Lyon, Suffering Capital of the Southern French Resistance

A plaque at the entrance to the *Centre d'Histoire de la Résistance* pays homage to the thousands of Jews of the *département* (or county) of the Rhône who were tortured, executed and deported between 1942 and 1945. Jews weren't alone in suffering appallingly. Here at the *Ecole de Santé Militaire* itself, numerous Resistance figures were tortured, most notoriously Jean Moulin, the most famous figure of the whole movement. Speculation as to how the secretive man was captured in June 1943, along with seven other Resistance leaders, in a house in Caluire (north of Croix-Rousse) dominate French memories of Lyon in the war. But extremely important Resistance leaders were at work here before Moulin.

Captain Henri Frenay emerges as the most exceptional character among the Lyon-based groups, one of the few Frenchmen to set about resisting the Germans straight after the French defeat of 1940. Born in Lyon in 1905, this conservative military man was much influenced by his remarkable mistress, the feminist Berty Albrecht. By summer 1941, he had established an intelligence service and secret army, his group named the *Mouvement de Libération Nationale*. It began printing its own newspaper, *Vérités* – the Centre emphasizes the importance of clandestine publications. Frenay brought together people of varied political persuasions and organized an alliance with another resistance group, *Liberté*, run by François de Menthon, a right-wing Catholic Lyon law professor who had moved to a new base at Marseille. Together, they formed *Combat*, the strongest southern Resistance grouping.

'The Red Aristocrat' was the nickname given to the spikier Emmanuel d'Astier de la Vigerie, who established *Libération*, the second-largest early Resistance group in the southern zone, having swung from being an anti-Semitic right-winger to a close ally of the communists. Several pro-Communists in Lyon joined *Libération*. The group also ran a famous newspaper. A third major Resistance group, *Franc-Tireur*, was also founded in Lyon, a little later, in 1941, by Jean-Pierre Lévy.

By summer 1941, *Combat* had a sizable network of secret agents and was in contact with British intelligence in France, but solid backing from abroad was sorely missing. Here Jean Moulin, formerly a top civil servant in Chartres, stepped in. Moulin had been imprisoned there in 1940, when he had refused to let the Germans blame a troop of French North African fighters for atrocities committed by German soldiers. Saved, but relieved of his post, he became a shadowy figure. In July 1941 he met Frenay, via an American agent, Pastor Howard Lee Brooks, to whom he had been introduced through his close links with the French Radical Socialist pre-war minister Pierre Cot (later proved to have been allied to the Soviet Communists). Moulin also met with de Menthon before heading across the Channel in October 1941.

In surely the most important meeting of all for the French Resistance, Moulin met de Gaulle in London and established the most extraordinary trust, the general in exile appointing Moulin his sole representative in southern France, with the role of uniting the quarrelling Resistance factions. Moulin appears in turn to have strongly influenced the stiff military man, making him a much more committed Republican. Evidence of his work on his return to France in January 1942 contradicts any specula-tion that Moulin was ultimately acting for the Communists. In extremely difficult circumstances, he united the factions of Resistance in the south. General Delestraint, another major figure who organized early opposition to the Nazis from Lyon, became head of the Resistance's united military wing, the *Armée Secrète*. All this work led to the foundation of the *Mouvements Unis de la Résistance* (MUR), in January 1943.

But the Gestapo was rapidly uncovering secret networks. In March 1943, a crucial Lyon mailbox was discovered. Frenay's careless second in command, Aubry, disastrously gave away General Delestraint by continuing to use the box. Delestraint was captured and died in Dachau concentration camp. Frenay's mistress Berty Albrecht was caught in Mâcon, but killed herself. Moulin's most trusted agent in northern France, Henri Manhès, was arrested in Paris. Moulin, who had gone to London for a second meeting with de Gaulle, saw this as a disaster and feared for his own safety.

Moulin had been given the vital new task of creating a *Conseil National de la Résistance* (CNR), involving the various old French political parties and unions, to help establish a unified Republican front ready to take control of France once the war ended. On 27 May, an assertive Moulin achieved this, rebutting Communist objections. Crucially, de Gaulle was established as the future French leader, as opposed to General Henri Giraud, US President Franklin D. Roosevelt's preferred choice, sitting in North Africa – Roosevelt loathed the independent-minded de Gaulle.

On 21 June 1943 disaster struck the Resistance in Lyon. Many of its leaders were invited to a secret meeting in Dr Dugoujon's house in Caluire to appoint a new military leader for the *Armée Secrète*. Somehow, the rendez-vous was discovered. Barbie himself came to arrest the group. Controversy has raged since over whether Moulin was betrayed. After the war, René Hardy, who shouldn't strictly have been there, and managed to escape, twice faced trial, but was acquitted. The latest, most commonly accepted theory is that someone accidentally gave away the meeting; even after the arrests, the Gestapo didn't seem to know who Moulin was. Although they discovered his significance, he revealed nothing under torture. The trial of Barbie in Lyon in 1987 didn't solve the outstanding questions, although Barbie claimed that Moulin threw himself down a stairwell of the *Ecole de Santé Militaire* to try to kill himself rather than give away information. Too injured to be interrogated when sent to Paris, he probably expired on the way to Germany. As to Barbie, he died in a French gaol.

Some members of the Lyon Resistance groups who survived the war wrote fascinating books. A confused, angry Frenay hit out at the legend of Moulin. While Moulin may have gone beyond his remit in trying to control as much as coordinate the Resistance across France, the research points time and again to Moulin's great good sense and courage. Jacques Baumel, secretary of MUR, wrote a work that transmits powerfully the terrible climate of fear that existed in Lyon through the war: 'We jumped at the slightest noise outside the window, we froze every time the doorbell rang, we automatically registered every noise in the house. It was in Lyon that I discovered every home has its own music... The strain drove men mad.' Even if the majority of Lyonnais did nothing in terms of active collaboration or resistance, most suffered from major food shortages. Some old people starved to death. The most shocking story came from the Vinatier mental hospital: of its 2,890 patients through the war, 2,000 died of starvation or exposure.

Bresse and Dombes
The Rhône-Alpes, Lowlands

St-Trivier to Bourg-en-Bresse 82
Bourg-en-Bresse 85
The Dombes 87
Along the Dombes' Saône Frontier **89**

08

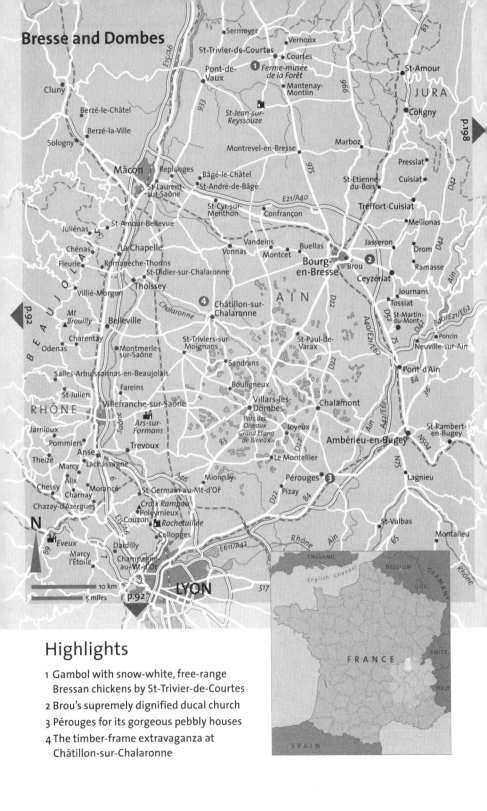

Bresse and Dombes

Sermoyer
Vernoux
St-Trivier-de-Courtes • Courtes
Pont-de- **1** Ferme-musée
Vaux de la Forêt St-Amour

Cluny Mantenay-
Montlin JURA
Berzé-le-Châtel St-Jean-sur- Coligny
Reyssouze
Berzé-la-Ville Marboz
Sologny Montrevel-en-Bresse Pressiat
Replonges Cuisiat
Mâcon St-Etienne-
Bâgé-le-Châtel du-Bois
St-Laurent- St-André-de-Bâgé Treffort-Cuisiat
sur-Saône
St-Cyr-sur- Meillonas
Menthon Confrançon
Juliénas Jasseron Drom
Chénas Vandeins Buellas Ramasse
La Chapelle Montcet Bourg-
Fleurie Vonnas en-Bresse Ceyzériat
Romanèche-Thorins Brou **2**
St-Didier-sur-Chalaronne Journans
Villié-Morgon Thoissey Tossiat
St-Martin-
Mt **4** Châtillon-sur- AIN du-Mont
Brouilly Belleville Chalaronne Poncin
Charentay St-Paul-de- Neuville-sur-Ain
Odenas St-Triviers-sur- Varax
Montmerle- Moignans Pont-d'Ain
sur-Saône Sandrans
Salles-Arbuissonnas-en-Beaujolais Bouligneux Chalamont
St-Julien Fareins Villars-les- St-Rambert-
RHÔNE Villefranche-sur-Saône Dombes en-Bugey
Jarnioux Ars-sur- Parc des Joyeux
Pommiers Formans Oiseaux Ambérieu-en-Bugey
Theizé Anse Trevoux Grand Etang Le Montellier Lagnieu
Marcy Lachassagne de Birieux
Chessy Alix Mionnay Pérouges **3**
Charnay Morancé St-Germain-au-Mt-d'Or Pizay
Chazay-d'Azergues Croix Rampau St-Vulbas
Poleymieux Montalieu
N Couzon Rochetaillée
Eveux Collonges
Marcy Dardilly Rhône Ain
l'Etoile Champagne-
au-Mt-d'Or LYON
10 km
5 miles p.92

p.198

p.92

ENGLAND
BELGIUM GERMANY
English Channel LUX
FRANCE SWITZ
ITALY
SPAIN

Highlights

1 Gambol with snow-white, free-range
  Bressan chickens by St-Trivier-de-Courtes
2 Brou's supremely dignified ducal church
3 Pérouges for its gorgeous pebbly houses
4 The timber-frame extravaganza at
  Châtillon-sur-Chalaronne

Lowlands of the Rhône-Alpes, the Bresse and Dombes lie quietly across the Saône river from ebullient Beaujolais. The Beaujolais hill dwellers referred mockingly to the *ventres jaunes* (yellow bellies) of the Bresse, curiously boasting of themselves as the *boyaux rouges* (red guts). Here we keep Bresse and Beaujolais apart to avoid any disputes. The nickname may relate to the Bressans' farming wealth and keeping their gold tightly in their belts; or perhaps it is a reference to the area becoming a major corn-growing territory when the crop was introduced from the Americas. *Maïs* has many uses. The locals make *gaudes*, like polenta; use cobs to decorate the exteriors of their farms; and in this culinary-mad land feed it to their pampered chickens.

The name Bresse derives from the Roman *brixiae*, French *broussaille* – scrubland; now its fields remain surprisingly green even into the summer. The greater Bresse split in two in Carolingian times, the lords of Savoie came by its southern half in the 13th century, although over-ambitious Duke Charles-Emmanuel lost this (and more

Capering Capons and Culinary Follies

French cookery excels in these flat lands of exceptional culinary traditions, and establishments, such as those of Georges Blanc and Alain Chapel. To see flocks of white capons gambolling about green fields next to timber-frame farms from which corn-cobs hang in decorative bundles is a delight. These chickens are unique in having their own *appellation d'origine contrôlée* (*see* also *www.pouletbresse.com*). But in these Bressan fields, not all is idyllic, as natural laws still apply and predators such as foxes, weasels and crows kill roughly one third of the birds.

When the chicks are about a month old, the males are neutered to remain adolescent capons and both sexes are left to roam the fields. Along with natural pickings, they are fed corn and milk supplements. After 16 weeks, they are usually enclosed and fattened for a fortnight. The female *poulardes* are fattened for slightly longer. Their necks wrung, the birds are wrapped in a tight cloth so that the fat is absorbed more fully into the flesh; a few days later they are elaborately prepared for sale. This process reaches its macabre pinnacle for the big competitions held at Pont-de-Vaux, Montrevel and Bourg-en-Bresse – details include removing the final signs of plumes with tweezers. It is a great honour to win as Bressan farmers see their highly prized (and highly priced) chickens as symbolic of the French quest for quality – their blue legs, white plumes and red crests even reflecting the colours of the French flag! For farms selling direct, look out for '*Produits de la Ferme*' signs.

While the autumn ritual of emptying the Dombes lakes to extract the fish is a fairly obvious, if muddy, event, the locals also delight in hunting down frogs, an art, even if more and more *grenouilles* on French menus are now imported from Eastern Europe. Rolled in flour, fried rapidly in the pan, served in a garlic-butter sauce, frogs' legs are sometimes referred to as the fast food of the area!

For some of the most painstakingly elaborate cuisine in France, try the area's fabled restaurants. The almost legendary, but practically minded, Georges Blanc is claimed to have got a special motorway exit made to service his fabulous restaurant at Vonnas – a town with a mere 2,000 inhabitants. True or not, it indicates the passion, standards and, even, folly involved in producing the finest French food.

mountainous Bugey and Gex to the east – see **Chapter 14**) to Henri IV in 1601. In modern times, the Bresse remains divided between the regions of Burgundy and Rhône-Alpes. We cover the latter half, its capital Bourg-en-Bresse. The culinary having taken on a predominant role, Bourg is now best known for its Bleu de Bresse, but in the 16th century, its magnificent monastery of Brou turned it briefly into an artistic hotbed.

More than 1,000 lakes lie sprinkled across the Dombes, a flat clay plateau south of the Bresse, a secretive, soggy land between the Saône and Ain rivers. Herons colonize the *étangs* all year, and storks fly freely, while migrating birds love the area. The *Parc Ornithologique*, Europe's largest bird centre, presents specimens from all over the globe. The traditional local culinary staples are lake fish and frogs' legs. Romanesque churches show it was well inhabited in early medieval times, when most of the lakes were created. The Dombes retained its semi-independence and regional court through much of the *Ancien Régime*, Trévoux, just north of Lyon, its proud if improbable little capital. But it oversaw dirt-poor territories, evoked in that most splendidly cutting of French films, *Ridicule*, exposing the petty, pitiless court etiquette of Versailles compared with the serious desperation of such an impoverished rural community racked by malaria. Several places in the Dombes clearly knew prosperous times in centuries past, however, such as the exquisite Pérouges, its buildings of pebbles, but much of the architecture across these clay territories looks markedly different from the rest of the Rhône-Alpes region, as it is in brick.

From St-Trivier to Bourg-en-Bresse

For a quietly charming introduction to the Bresse – the first, most northerly section of our region where you arrive heading down the busy A6 motorway or N6 main road from Paris – make for **St-Trivier-de-Courtes**, a tiny fortified town of traditional Bressan brick. In the countryside, look for a rather dispersed flock of fine traditional **Bressan farms**, a few still with their *cheminée sarrasine*, the traditional, local, behatted chimney. Comparisons with minarets are exaggerated, but you can see the connection. The broad hearth below these chimneys was open on all sides to heat the multipurpose main room, or *maison chauffure*. Only about 30 original chimneys still exist, but many timber-frame, brick and *pisé* (straw- and earth-covered) buildings survive, although some in a poor state. North of St-Trivier-de-Courtes, seek out delightful, typical farms just west of **Vernoux**, white chickens running about in their fields. The **Ferme de la Forêt** with its **Ecomusée** at **Courtes** (*open July–Aug daily 10–12 and 2–7, Easter–June and Sept–Oct weekends and public hols same times; adm*) east of town. Although not now in a forest, it dates back to the 17th century and has all the architectural elements that so distinguish the area. Its rustic museum has atmosphere.

The D975 leads south to the capital Bourg-en-Bresse. **Mantenay-Montlin** would be unremarkable were it not for its ten-metre high silver cockerel in front of the **church**. Nearby **St-Jean-sur-Reyssouze** prides itself on its flowers and its **Romanesque church**. Beside **Montrevel**, cluck with delight at two Bressan architectural gems, the traditional **Ferme de Sougey** and the **Manoir de la Charme**.

Getting There and Around

By air: Lyon-St-Exupéry airport is just south of the Dombes.

By rail and bus: Bourg-en-Bresse has good rail links with Lyon and Paris (2hrs by TGV). Mâcon just across the Saône in Burgundy also has a TGV stop outside town, but to catch a bus to Pont-de-Vaux, you must go to the central Mâcon station. Buses from Lyon (Autocars Planche, t 04 74 55 04 21) serve Vonnas, Villars-les-Dombes, Châtillon-sur-Chalaronne and a few other stops, but services are few. For Pérouges, trains from Lyon go to Meximieux; then it's a 15min walk up the hill.

Tourist Information

St-Trivier-de-Courtes: Parc de la Carronière, 01560 St-Trivier-de-Courtes, t 04 74 30 71 89, *www.st-trivier-de-courtes.com*.

Pont-de-Vaux: 2 Rue de Lattre de Tassigny, 01190 Pont-de-Vaux, t 03 85 30 30 02, *www.pontdevaux.com*.

Bourg-en-Bresse: 6 Av Alsace Lorraine, 01000 Bourg-en-Bresse, t 04 74 22 49 40, *www.bourg-en-bresse.org*.

Châtillon-sur-Chalaronne: Place du Champ de Foire, 01400 Châtillon-sur-Chalaronne, t 04 74 55 02 27, *www.ladombes.free.fr*.

Pérouges: Entrée de la Cité, B.P.23, 01800 Pérouges, t 04 74 61 01 14, *www.perouges.org*.

Villars-les-Dombes: 3 Place de l'Hôtel de Ville, 01330 Villars-les-Dombes, t 04 74 98 06 29.

Trévoux: Place du Pont, B.P.108, 01601 Trévoux, t 04 74 00 36 32, *www.mairie-trevoux.fr*.

Market Days

St-Trivier-de-Courtes: Mon morning.
Montrevel-en-Bresse: Tues morning.
Pont-de-Vaux: Wed morning.
Bâgé-le-Châtel: Tues morning.
Vonnas: Thurs morning.
Bourg-en-Bresse: Wed morning and Sat morning.
Châtillon-sur-Chalaronne: Sat morning.
Trévoux: Wed morning and Sat morning.

Activities

The area is flat, so it's good golf territory: two courses south of Bourg, and several below Villars-les-Dombes. Saône river cruises are possible from Pont-de-Vaux and Trévoux.

Where to Stay and Eat

Vernoux ✉ 01560

Ferme-Auberge du Grand Colombier, t 04 74 30 72 00 (*moderate–inexpensive; only open lunchtimes Thurs–Sun and public hols; always book*). Among green, chicken-covered fields, big typical renovated Bressan farm restaurant

As an alternative to cutting across the Bresse, head south via the **Saône valley**. Coming this way, just north of **Sermoyer**, the first village, the **Site des Charmes** presents a wholly unexpected vista of sand dunes. The wide, flat ribbon of land extending south beside the river often floods and is mainly reserved for market gardening and fishermen (although the Resistance made makeshift airfields here during the war). **Pont-de-Vaux** set back east of the Saône, but linked by a shady canal, has built a smart **new marina**. For a leisurely river trip, take a long **cruise** (*contact tourist office*) to Trévoux. Pont-de-Vaux has long been a thriving market town, its valley position making it a rival to more distant Bourg-en-Bresse; and it is still a popular stop on the main French route south. The central **Musée Antoine Chintreuil** (*open Easter–Oct daily exc Tues 2–6; adm*) displays works by a local, 19th-century landscape artist and local ornithological exhibits, for once excluding chickens, although the town goes potty in its December *Concours de Volaille*.

Joined by a venerable old bridge to the imposing southern Burgundian wine merchants' centre of Mâcon, **St-Laurent-sur-Saône** has an interesting church housing serving hearty traditional fare cooked in its old-style oven.

Montrevel ✉ 01340

★★★**Hôtel Le Pillebois**, off D975 between Montrevel and Attignat, **t** 04 74 25 48 44, *www.hotellepillebois* (*inexpensive*). Modern, charming, country hotel, plus pretty restaurant (*expensive–moderate*). Pool.

Chez Léa, 10 Rue d'Etrez, **t** 04 74 30 80 84 (*expensive–moderate*). A cheerful, classic stop for Bressan cuisine. *Closed Sun eve, Mon eve and Wed.*

Le Comptoir, 9 Grand'Rue **t** 04 74 25 45 53 (*moderate*). In the same family as Chez Léa. *Closed Tues eve, Wed, and Sun eve, and mid-Dec–mid-Jan and late-June–mid-July.*

Sermoyer ✉ 01190

Le Clos du Châtelet B&B, **t** 03 85 51 84 37, *www.leclosduchatelet.com* (*moderate*). On the Burgundy frontier, magnificent 18th-century property. Delicious *table d'hôte* (*moderate*). Pool.

Pont-de-Vaux ✉ 01190

★★**Le Raisin**, 2 Place Michel Poisat, **t** 03 85 30 30 97, **e** *hotel.leraisin@wanadoo.fr* (*inexpensive*). Sprawling, popular stop with plain, comfortable, modernish rooms and fine traditional restaurant (*expensive–moderate*).

Closed Jan; restaurant closed Sun pm, Mon, and Tues lunch.

Replonges ✉ 01750

★★★★**La Huchette**, RN79, **t** 04 85 31 03 55, *www.chateauxhotels.com/huchette* (*expensive–moderate*). Close to Mâcon, slightly dated, but spacious, comfortable rooms. Beamed restaurant (*expensive*) with good reputation. Garden with pool. *Closed part of Nov; restaurant closed Mon, and Tues lunch.*

Confrançon ✉ 01310

★★★**Auberge La Sarrasine**, RN79 **t** 03 74 30 25 65, *www.sarrasine.com* (*expensive–moderate*). Bressan farm converted into delightful refined little hotel. Restaurant focuses on the best local specialities. Garden, pool, plus golf close by. *Restaurant closed Wed.*

St-Cyr-sur-Menthon ✉ 01380

La Pilleuse B&B, **t/f** 03 85 36 31 97 (*inexpensive*). Two lovely rooms in very traditional Bressan building, with warm welcome. *Table d'hôte* (*moderate*).

Vonnas ✉ 01540

★★★★**Georges Blanc**, **t** 04 74 50 90 90, *www.georgesblanc.com* (*luxury–very expensive*). For culinary brilliance (*luxury–very expensive*), plus chic contemporary rooms. Pool and tennis court.

some vibrant paintings. Turning our backs on Burgundy and heading east, the few towers standing at almost-circular **Bâgé-le-Châtel** hint at this little village's brief role as as the medieval capital of the Bresse in the 13th century. The main landmark is the church tower, rising over 100 ft. The soaring octagonal tower at neighbouring **St-André-de-Bâgé** recalls that the mighty abbey of Cluny across in Burgundy was master here. The large, sober Romanesque edifice conceals lively medieval carvings.

Close to the motorway exit supposedly built for Georges Blanc, **St-Cyr-sur-Menthon,** with the extensive **Musée de la Bresse** (*t 03 85 36 31 22; open July–Sept daily exc Tues 11–6; April–June and Sept–Oct daily exc Tues and Wed 2–6 plus Sun am; adm*), has been turned into the area's main tourist showcase. The **Domaine des Planons**, a beautiful, traditional farm with double-arcaded galleries, contains an exhibition on traditional farm life and a mini *son-et-lumière*. Stables and barns are part of the exhibition and a few animals, including white fowl, of course, are also kept. A striking sunken contemporary structure has been added to cover aspects of Bresse culture in more detail, with displays on traditional ways and crafts, food and festivities. Farms at the nearby hamlet of **La Mulatière** add to the atmosphere.

L'Ancienne Auberge, t 04 74 50 90 50 (*moderate*). An extra Blanc inn in Belle Epoque style, offers simpler traditional cuisine. *Closed Jan; restaurant closed Mon, Tues, and Wed lunch.*

Montcet ✉ 01310
Les Vignes B&B, t 04 74 24 23 13, *www. wanadoo.perso/chambresdhoteslesvignes* (*inexpensive*). Lovely restored traditional farm by a lake between Vonnas and Bourg. Warm welcome, *table d'hôte* (*moderate*) using garden produce.

Bourg-en-Bresse ✉ 01000
★★★Hôtel de France, 19 Place Bernard, **t** 04 74 23 30 24, *www.grand-hoteldefrance.com* (*moderate*). Central, on a charming square, a stylish stop-off since the early 20th-century. **Chez Blanc**, the restaurant attached, **t** 04 74 45 29 11 (*inexpensive*) is a great place to try food from the Georges Blanc school.
★★★Le Prieuré, 49 Bd de Brou, **t** 04 74 22 44 60, *www.euro-tourisme.com/pub/prieure* (*moderate*). Most rooms in this smart modern hotel look onto Brou church. Calm garden. Several restaurants close by.

Pérouges ✉ 01800
★★★Ostellerie du Vieux Pérouges, Place du Tilleul, **t** 04 74 61 00 88, *www.ostellerie.com* (*very expensive–expensive*). In several splendid buildings off the central square; the beautiful restaurant (*expensive*) is on the square itself.

Châtillon-sur-Chalaronne ✉ 01400
★★★Hôtel de la Tour/Clos de la Tour, Place de la République, **t** 04 74 55 05 12, *www.hotel-latour.com* (*moderate*). Close to the old town, with one part in lovely restored mill in the local style plus garden and pool. Restaurant (*expensive–moderate*). *Restaurant closed Sun eve and Wed.*
La Gourmandine, 142 Rue Pasteur, **t** 04 74 55 15 92 (*moderate–inexpensive*). Adorable riverside terrace to this traditional brick restaurant offering simple menus. *Closed Fri, Sun eve and Mon.*

St-Trivier-sur-Moignans ✉ 01990
La Pampra B&B, t 04 74 55 90 29 (*inexpensive*). Southwest of Châtillon, with great views, pretty rooms in a lovely restored farm. *Table d'hôte* (*moderate*). Pool and court in shaded grounds.

Mionnay ✉ 01390
★★★★Alain Chapel, RN83 **t** 04 78 91 82 02, **e** *chapel@relaischateaux.fr* (*expensive*). Legendary restaurant (*very expensive*), as well as luxury rooms and a well-tended garden. *Closed Jan; restaurant closed Mon, Tues, and Thurs lunch.*

The village of **Vonnas** south by the Veyle river is truly devoted to Georges Blanc's famed restaurants and boutiques, although there is also a **Musée des Attelages** (*open mid-March–mid-Nov Wed–Sun 10–12 and 2–6; adm*) presenting old carriages in an old mill off the central green, which is almost choked by flowers – the villages of the Ain *département* have become a little *parterre*-potty since the start of the French national flower competitions in the 1950s. At nearby **Vandeins**, an oriental-looking Christ greets you at the church; **Buellas** also has a characterful Romanesque church, its porch on wooden pillars called a *galonnière*.

Bourg-en-Bresse

Bourg-en-Bresse, capital of the Bresse, and since the Revolution, of the Ain (pronounced like the French number one, *un*) was, through much of the Middle Ages, a major outpost of Savoie. Briefly seized by the French king François I, the Bresse was returned to the duke of Savoie in 1559. A huge citadel matching that at the new, safer Savoyard capital of Turin went up in Bourg to guard against future attacks by the French – who laid siege to it in 1600, and largely demolished it around 1612. However, a few lively shopping streets slope down the hillside, with the odd remarkable timber-frame house along the way, while the mainly **Gothic church** stands out thanks to its added bright Baroque towers. In the grand grey interior, the wooden stalls are carved with saints, aristocratic faces, jesters and fighting dogs and dragons.

But these pale alongside the artistic riches at **Brou**, an historic suburb a mile east with a splendid **triple-cloistered abbey** (*t 04 74 22 83 83, www.culture.fr/rhone-alpes/brou; open mid-June–mid-Sept daily 9–6, May–mid-June and late Sept daily 9–12.30 and 2–6, rest of year daily 9–12 and 2–5; adm*), much of which houses an art museum. First visit the Flamboyant Gothic church with its Burgundian-style, multi-coloured roof, built between 1513 and 1532. The abbey's main benefactor, Marguerite of Austria, a woman of great importance on the European royal scene, is shown with her second husband Philibert de Savoie on the tympanum of the main façade.

One of the best-connected figures of the early 16th century, Marguerite was born in 1480, daughter of Holy Roman Emperor Maximilian and Mary of Burgundy, later aunt to both Emperor Charles V and François I of France. Dreadfully unlucky with men, she had been engaged to the future Charles VIII of France but, still in her youth, was jilted, for political reasons, in favour of Anne de Bretagne. In 1497 she married the Infante Juan of Spain, but he died a few months later. Philibert le Beau of Savoie scarcely fared better, dying in a hunting accident three years after their marriage in 1501. Undaunted, she remained an exceptionally capable figure and became regent of Flanders for the future Emperor Charles V in 1507. But at Brou she carried out her mother-in-law Marguerite de Bourbon's wishes and rebuilt the abbey in style. Unfortunately, she died two years before the church was officially completed.

Inside the church, you cannot miss the splendid carved stone rood screen and the choir. The tombs of Marguerite and Philibert count among the most elaborate and dignified tombs in France. The couple are each represented twice in idealized form, above in finery, overseen by classical figures and chubby naked *putti*, below in death, Marguerite's body wrapped in a shroud, Philibert's naked, rivalling that of Michelangelo's *David* in beauty. The tombs were designed by Jean de Bruxelles, the highly flattering main figures executed by the German sculptor Conrad Meit. The couple are depicted again in the splendid stained glass, devoted, somewhat understandably, given Marguerite's bad luck with marriage partners, to the theme of resurrection, inspired by engravings by Dürer. The wooden stalls depict intense biblical scenes, while *putti* playing under the seats depict the vices.

Augustinian monks prayed for the lords of the land here up to the Revolution, when the place was just saved from destruction. Two of the cloistered courtyards contain further Gothic figures in stone, but the more rustic, cobbled third proves the prettiest. The vaulted main rooms and the cells have been converted into the Ain's main **fine arts museum**. Medieval religious statues now fill the refectory with life. Amazing 16th-century paintings include a Burgundian triptych of St Jerome and a Flemish Christ flanked by utterly miserable angels, while Marguerite and Philibert crop up again in less idealized fashion, in portraits. Gruesome pieces show two monks flagellating themselves, definitely at the weirder extreme of the religious spectrum, and Gustave Doré's depictions of Dante's *Inferno*, look like a massacre of old men in a sauna. But you can also enjoy some less disturbing Dorés and delightful local landscapes by Chintreuil. Utrillo and Utter also left colourful renditions of Rhône-Alpes scenery. Serene contemporary pieces well suited to the surroundingss stand out in the cloisters. And local crafts have their place too, particularly ceramics produced in Meillonnas, a village reputed for its pottery, situated on the wooded ridge of the Revermont that forms the eastern backdrop to Bourg. Incidentally, **Emaux Bressans Jeanvoine** (*1 Rue Thomas Riboud; closed Sun and Mon*) is the one craftshop in town still making the traditional local enamel jewellery encrusted with bright beads that was particularly fashionable in the Belle Epoque.

An interesting outpost of the Bresse before the Revermont, **St-Etienne-du-Bois**, up the N83, was the cradle of the famous white-plumed Bresse chickens. A couple of stunning old houses (which were often deliberately made to be easily transportable) have been moved here to form **La Maison de Pays en Bresse** (*t 04 74 30 52 54, http://maison.pays.en.bresse.chez.tiscali.fr; open April–Nov Mon–Sat 9.30–6.30; and Sun pm; adm*), one presenting a traditional interior, the other traditional professions in an area that has clung on to Bressan ways, it might be said, pluckily.

The Dombes

Quiet land of so many hundreds of lakes, southwest of Bourg-en-Bresse, the flat plateau of the Dombes extends between the Ain and Saône valleys almost to Lyon. Skirting round the densest region of Dombes lakes, the D22 route south from Bourg follows the Veyle river to **Chalamont**, one of the main centres for the popular tradition of horse breeding in the Dombes, and preserving a little collection of old houses.

But attention further down this route focuses on famously picturesque **Pérouges**, sitting high on the edge of the Dombes plateau above the Ain valley. A dubious story has it that the name derives from Romans from Perugia settling here. It shares a defensive hillside position and, despite the industrial sprawl from Lyon menacing even places this far away, the fortified village remains pretty well protected by its circle of ramparts, although it has lost a whole outer ring of walls. Its very surprising, stern **church** was incorporated into the defensive inner ramparts, and even provided with gun holes. The long, tall Gothic interior contains striking wooden statues, including a tender Madonna offering protection. Pérouges was bitterly fought over between Savoyards and Dauphinois (to the south), notably in 1468, as recalled in a stirring quote on one gateway taunting the '*coquins*' (rascals) who failed to take the place by siege, even if they did run off with doors and locks! Now the village welcomes hordes of visitors via both of its open old gateways.

Many of the houses have outside walls made of the same stones as the cobbled streets, as well as parts of timber-frame and brick; many date from the late 15th century, after the siege. The **Place de la Halle**, its splendid houses hung with decorative corn-cobs, lost its covered market (*halle*) to a fire in 1839, but its linden tree dates back to the Revolution when it was planted as a symbol of liberty. You can see several interiors, as many have been turned into craft shops or restaurants. Take refuge from the trade in the **Musée du Vieux Pérouges** (*open Easter–Oct daily 10–12 and 2–6; adm*) which gathers together pieces of local history in two of the grandest houses, one once belonging to the lords of Savoie. Its tower provides wide views of the area.

The N83 cuts through the heart of the *étangs* of the Dombes and is the most direct route from Bourg-en-Bresse to Lyon. These lakes are all private and many of them well-hidden. At **St-Paul-de-Varax**, the vestiges of the liveliest of Romanesque carvings on its church include an amazing image of a falling angel. The famed Lumière family, inventors of cinema (*see* **Lyon**, p.76), had a château here where they shot one of their very first films, the comedy short *Le Jardinier Arrosé*. The property is still in the family and private, but can be seen along the D17 towards Dompierre-sur-Veyle.

Monks at the serious 19th-century Cistercian **Abbaye de Notre-Dame-des-Dombes** were involved in the transformation of the Dombes into a more healthy area at that time and gave refuge to a number of Jews during the war. The monks have long made *masculine*, a curious mix of fruit jelly and raw meat. Romantically reflected in a lake further south, the ruined **tower of Le Plantay** draws admirers and artists. **Notre-Dame-de-Beaumont** in its sweet location overlooks the Chalaronne. Inside, a lovely series of Gothic wall paintings illustrate the life of the Virgin.

Wild birds are attracted in huge numbers to the Dombes, but at the extremely popular **Parc des Oiseaux** (*t 04 74 98 05 54, www.parc-des-oiseaux.com; open July–Aug daily 9.30am–9.30pm; May–June and Sept daily 9.30–8.30; rest of year check; adm*) by **Villars-les-Dombes**, birds from across the world, including condors even, are kept behind bars. Herons, storks and other 'locals' are free to fly rather tauntingly outside, but it has to be said that the modern aviaries are truly spacious, presenting some 400 species in total. There are also observatories, a large hatching house explaining the park's breeding programme, and snack bars. The **Maison de la Dombes** by the entrance puts on temporary summer exhibitions. The **Route des Etangs de la Dombes** in fact consists of two marked road circuits starting out from Villars-les-Dombes, discreetly signalling points of interest along the way.

Southeast, **Joyeux** offers a pretty picture of a typical Dombes village, while its 19th-century castle was one of a whole pack built as hunting lodges for wealthy Lyonnais. Just south, the keep of the **Château de Montellier** typifies the medieval strongholds of the area, built on mounds known by the curious name of *poyps*. In the 14th century, this was the headquarters of the Thoire-et-Villars family, overlords of huge territories going from the Saône to Lac Léman, later sold to the house of Savoie. Northwest of Villars towards Châtillon, from the road through the village of **Bouligneux**, spot one of the most impressive brick castles of the Dombes, set beside a lake. Tomb effigies of the local lords lie in the church. **Sandrans** has another characteristic *poyp*, and offers **horse-carriage rides** from the **Domaine du Grand Maréchal** (*t 04 74 24 54 96*).

A forest of wooden pillars holds up the splendid dark covered market at the centre of **Châtillon-sur-Chalaronne**, a remarkable village full of the finest timber-frame and brick houses. As to the central church with its steep roof, it looks like it's been transported straight down here from flat medieval Flanders. At the end of its Gothic interior, the stained glass added in the 19th century recalls a major Catholic Reformation figure of the 17th century, St Vincent de Paul, who, although he stayed a mere five months as priest in 1617, found time to found his first religious *Confrérie de la Charité* here, a model for a whole series of similar foundations across France. Organ concerts take place regularly. On the main square, the model trains of the **Musée du Train Miniature** (*open mid-June–mid-Sept Tues–Sun 10–12 and 2–7, otherwise weekends same times; adm*) appeal to aficionados. Pay a visit to the **historic hospital** (see museum times below) across the pretty Chalaronne, signalled by a statue of St Vincent de Paul on the square in front. Its apothecary contains a well-preserved array of pharmaceutical pots made in nearby Meillonnas (*see* p.207), while the emotionally draining, superb triptych of Christ's death and resurrection was commissioned by a rich tanner from Châtillon. A path leads up past a former salt house held on wooden pillars to the modern **Musée Traditions et Vie** (*t 04 74 55 15 70; open July–Aug Tues–Sun 10–12 and 2–7, April–June and Sept Tues–Sun 10–12 and 2–6; Oct–mid-Nov weekends 10–12 and 2–6; adm*) presenting scenes of local rural life at the start of the 20th century. A hop and a skip further up the hill, you come to the remaining walls of the castle, built originally for local squires, but then for several centuries one of Savoie's main Saône frontier fortifications guarding against France.

Along the Dombes' Saône Frontier

Delving in detail into the plant and animal life in the waters around the area, the new **Musée de la Plante Aquatique** (*t 04 74 04 03 09, www.lesjardinsaquatiques.fr; open Tues–Sat 9.30–12 and 2–6.30, Sun and public hols 2–6; adm*) was set up beside the Chalaronne's richly diverse confluence with the Saône at **St-Didier-sur-Chalaronne**.

Given the kiss of life by the dynamic and determined Marc Simonet-Lenglart and his partner Pierre-Albert Almendros, the 17th-century **Château de Fléchères** (*t 04 74 67 86 59; open July–Aug 10–12 and 2.30–6, April–June and Sept–mid-Nov weekends 10–12 and 2.30–6.30; adm*), lies a comfortable distance back from the Saône above Fareins. Having suffered a period of sad neglect, this 17th-century country mansion built for Jean de Sève, a leading Lyon merchant, has made a fine recovery. Most excitingly, the new owners discovered whole expanses of original Italianate murals hidden under whitewash; Pietro Ricci of Lucca, a pupil of Guido Reni, spent the year of 1632 here decorating the interiors. The action-packed works include depictions of a fantasy hunt. The most engrossing cycle portrays the labours of Hercules. Even if the classical hero looks a bit brutish, he shows immense physical energy carrying out his near-impossible tasks.

To be declared patron saint of all the priests in the universe is no mean feat for a humble country boy from the Saône valley, but that's what happened to Jean-Marie Vianney in 1929. A model of 19th-century piety, he went from his birthplace at Dardilly (*see* p.104) across the other side of the Saône to train for the priesthood in Lyon. In 1818, he was sent to serve as parish priest in **Ars-sur-Formans**, leading an exemplary humble life, serving the community. Others couldn't stop themselves promoting his example, though, and a cult grew up around him from 1830. Meanwhile, he developed a special devotion to the martyred virgin Ste Philomène. Although he decried the 'carnival' created around him, which turned him into a Catholic celebrity, he received the *Légion d'Honneur* from Emperor Napoleon III in 1855 before dying in 1859. He was then adopted for an overblown advertising campaign by the French Church, ordering a grandiose new **church** in his honour, creating one of the most popular pilgrimage sites in France, some half a million people still visiting it each year. The architect Pierre Bossan, credited with Lyon's most showy number, Notre-Dame de Fourvière, gave ostentatious Oriental touches to the new edifice, although the plain brick tower of the old village church was kept, sticking out like a sore thumb. Vianney's body has been preserved, his face coated in wax, while a more idealized statue of him stands in a niche surrounded by indecorous gilded putti. Once you've visited Ars, you won't be able to help noticing the kind fox of a face of the Curé d'Ars in statues in countless churches around France.

The Curé d'Ars' house has supposedly been preserved in all the simplicity of Vianney's day, with cloying religious images, but the hagiography gets carried away, with such signs as 'a cassock that the priest ironed himself'. For pilgrims who aren't sated, there's the **Musée de Cires**, a waxworks museum (*t 04 74 00 07 22, www.musee-ars.org; open April–Oct Tues–Sun 10–12 and 2–6; adm*). A monument on the slope above the village recalls Vianney meeting a shepherd boy who helped him on his way to the village when he first arrived. The priest declared: 'You have shown me the way to Ars; I will show you the way to heaven.' It's all too much for non-believers, but the fine views over to Beaujolais are clear for all to enjoy.

Slope-side **Trévoux** surveys a wide bend in the Saône north of Lyon, a dangerous spot on the river, but an obvious point to extract tolls in medieval times. Now the place has the odd riverside restaurant and a **port** from which you can take a long Saône cruise. The **exhibition** (*open April–Sept Mon–Sat 9.30–12 and 2–6.30, Sun and public hols pm only; adm*) attached to the tourist office in an historic building close to the water, recalls the curious local speciality craft, developed by a Jewish community here, of stretching metal, and especially gold, thread. This was just one element that helped make the town rich in contrast to most of the rest of the Dombes, of which it was the tiny independent capital from the start of the 16th century to the eve of the Revolution. During its *Ancien Régime* golden age, it was ruled by a branch of the royal family and was granted its own *Parlement*, or regional law courts from 1676 to 1771. The place also became an important Catholic publishing centre. Grand houses stand along the steep roads up to the plain **Parlement building** (*open May–Sept weekends and public hols, set-time tours via tourist office; adm*), now a more ordinary court, daubed with pompous *trompe l'œils* and figures representing peace and justice. The remnants of a medieval **castle** (*open July–Aug daily exc Thurs 3–6.30 plus weekends 10–12, June and Sept just weekend afternoons; adm*) in ochre stone, with the base of its octagonal keep, stand further up the hillside. Up high, you appreciate what an excellent viewing post Trévoux was, its natural balconies overlooking the Saône, but quite hidden from view from nearby Lyon by the heights of the Mont d'Or (*see p.103*).

Beaujolais
Bacchic Wine Country

Touring the Northern Beaujolais Hills 93
Beaujolais *Crus* Territories between St-Amour
   and Beaujeu **93**
Beaujeu and West of Beaujeu **99**
**From Beaujolais' Brouilly *Crus* through Southern
   Beaujolais-Villages 100**
Southern Beaujolais: Le Pays des Pierres Dorées **101**
Mont d'Or and Monts/Coteaux du Lyonnais 103

Highlights

1 A tour of the *crus* villages and wine cellars
2 Attending the wine festival at Beaujeu
3 Touring the villages of Les Pierres Dorées
4 Automobiles treated like aristocracy at the
  Château de Rochetaillée followed by a meal
  at Paul Bocuse's legendary restaurant

Sloshing across big curvaceous hills west of the Saône, Beaujolais' vines swamp a swathe of countryside between Mâcon, on the southern Burgundian frontier, and the Mont d'Or, almost within spitting distance of Lyon. The vines engulf the Beaujolais' hill villages, although the churches stand out in defiant positions, as though trying with their pencil-sharp spires to put forward some kind of a moral case in this clearly decadent landscape. Many a hilltop Beaujolais village is also overseen by its retired secular lord, the château, too world-weary to put up a fight against the waves of vigorous vines beating at the walls. *Clochemerle*, a joyously wicked novel of the 1930s (*see* p.26), raises to hilarious mock-epic proportions the petty rivalries that rack one fictional Beaujolais wine village, inhabited by a selection of caricatures from *cette race de vignerons montagnards*, this race of mountain winemakers. They, and the real people of Beaujolais, live in a wonderfully inebriating, rolling Bacchic landscape.

Most of the best Beaujolais wines come from the granite northern half of the area, in the triangle of land between Mâcon, Beaujeu and Villefranche. These include the ten top *crus*. Beaujeu, the historic capital from which the area of Beaujolais took its name, has turned into a peaceful backwater, hiding out in the hills beyond the *crus*, but it has one of half a dozen *Pôles Œnologiques*, museums covering Beaujolais wine-making. The town of Romanèche-Thorins by the Saône also has a major wine museum, while workaday Villefranche, modern capital of Beaujolais, has recently been gifted an extensive collection of regional art, giving it a new cultural focus.

South from Villefranche, the wines get lighter, as do the exceptionally beautiful hilltop villages, built in delectable limestone, hence the nickname of the land of *pierres dorées*, golden stones. Press on west beyond the Beaujolais vine line and you enter the quiet, pine-forested Haut-Beaujolais or Beaujolais Vert, untouristy logging hills, the sober half of Beaujolais.

In this chapter we also feature the Mont d'Or and the Monts et Coteaux du Lyonnais. The attractions of the first, the 'golden' mountain separating Beaujolais from the city of Lyon, include a museum in honour of local boy André Ampère, the 'Newton of electricity'; one of the most important collections of cars in France; and one of the country's most celebrated restaurants, run by Paul Bocuse. The Monts et Coteaux du Lyonnais, the continuation south of the sensuous Beaujolais hills, sidle round Lyon's western side. Small surprises hide out here, such as fragments of Roman aqueducts, a wolf reserve and a mining town that boasts the dubious claim of having been at the root of the Rhône valley's explosion in industry. Cherry orchards may be more common than vines in these parts, but the area produces pleasant wines, like Beaujolais, from the Gamay grape.

Touring the Northern Beaujolais Hills

Beaujolais *Crus* Territories between St-Amour and Beaujeu

Be lured into Beaujolais' vinous hills travelling down the Saône from Burgundy, rather than taking the flat valley routes. The most northerly *cru*, the very romantic-sounding **St-Amour**, is named after a Roman soldier who converted to Christianity,

Beaujolais – The Greatest of Gamay Wines

Beaujolais wine, jokingly referred to as Lyon's third river, along with the Saône and the Rhône, has one of the most widely recognized names in the viticultural world. The Beaujolais rectangle of vines stretching south from the Burgundian frontier is just 60 by 20 kilometres, but produces almost as much wine as all of Burgundy. While the name may be very familiar, the variety of its wines proves complex, with 12 *appellations d'origine contrôlée*, not to mention the Beaujolais Nouveau, or *primeur*.

The earliest written record of vines in the Beaujolais dates from 956, although the area's vine-growers claim Roman roots. 'Nasty Gamay' was the none-too-complimentary term said to have been used by the mighty 14th-century Duke of Burgundy, Philippe le Hardi, when he tasted some bad Beaujolais. But good Gamay has been key to Beaujolais' success, although it wasn't until the 17th century that vines became the area's main crop. Popular legend has it that the giant Claude Brosse was responsible for an early marketing coup when he took a cartload of wine to Versailles in the 1680s. Standing out from the crowd, his wine was tasted and approved by the king.

Beaujolais remained popular wine-making territory, with few large estates, most of the smallholders bound to the landowners in a system known as *vigneronnage*. *Négociants*, wine merchants, took on the role of selling the produce. The wine was quaffed in vast quantities by the Lyon workers. On a health note, the town of Beaujeu is proud of the fact that its hospital began auctioning its wines for charity from 1797, a full 64 years before Burgundy's Hospice de Beaune followed suit.

In the 19th century, major crises that affected most wine-making areas of France also hit Beaujolais. First came *pyralis*, a grub more effectively dealt with by boiling water than prayers to the Virgin of Montmerle, whose chapel lay on the wrong, east bank of the Saône. When mildew attacked, the superstitious called for a Virgin to be planted in the Beaujolais; Notre-Dame du Raisin was erected in 1856 on Mont Brouilly. The credulous believed Our Lady of the Grape solved the mildew problem, the rational putting it down to copper sulphate treatment. In the 1880s, nothing could stop the spread of the destructive *phylloxera* insect. Many *vignerons* were forced into factory work. Local scientist Victor Pulliat halted the epidemic by grafting local vinestock onto resistant American vines, but then overproduction became a problem.

After the crippling disasters of two world wars, the 1945 vintage was a classic, and a good omen. Since then, Beaujolais has had one of the greatest marketing successes of all French wine areas, thanks, in large part, to its ruse, begun in 1951, of dashing out Beaujolais Nouveau each November – the temperature in the wine-making kept low, the fermentation shortened, the wine bottled in its infancy. Although the mad rush each autumn to export its *primeur* encourages widespread, heady celebration, it isn't a recipe for giving Beaujolais a good image among wine connoisseurs. Yet Beaujolais' best-made wines can incite the loyalty of a lover.

and unsurprisingly plays on its name to sell the wine from its 310 hectares. Before Juliénas, look out for the **Maison de la Dîme**, the fine galleried storehouse where the monks of St-Vincent-lès-Mâcon received payment in wine from their territories. **Juliénas** is a more substantial *cru*, its well-formed wines made across 600 hectares.

Fashion models of the Rhône-Alpes wine scene, with their transparent ruby robes and often heady perfumes, Beaujolais wines can certainly seduce. All Beaujolais red wines – and they are almost exclusively red – are made from Gamay. In fact, Beaujolais produces most of the world's Gamay wines. Further traditions bind all Beaujolais *vignerons*; even if the pruning and grape yields per hectare vary between the *crus* and the ordinary Beaujolais, all the grapes are harvested by hand. These *vendanges* often start late August, continuing through September.

The best wines of the area, the ten *crus appellations* of Brouilly, Chénas, Chiroubles, Côtes de Brouilly, Fleurie, Juliénas, Moulin à Vent, Morgon, Régnié and St-Amour make up roughly a quarter of all the Beaujolais produced in a year, but stick firmly to their individual identities and have distanced themselves from commoner wines by downplaying or avoiding the name of Beaujolais on their labels. Although many of the *crus* only cover a small number of hectares, their delightful names stick in the mind. They have far more subtlety and staying power than the basic Beaujolais and are at their best between three and seven years old. Since the mid-1990s, the vintages have been good to excellent. Experts detect raspberries, strawberries or cherries, peppery flavours, even cinammon, licorice and cocoa in mature *crus*. The more green-fingered fantasize about peonies, irises, violets and faded roses.

The territories of Beaujolais-Villages, a cut above ordinary Beaujolais AOC, form a sometimes very thin coating round the 10 *crus,* although there are larger pockets around Beaujeu and below Odenas down to the D504, a road that serves as something of a north–south dividing line in Beaujolais wine quality. The 6,000 hectares of Beaujolais-Villages cover 38 parishes, producing roughly a quarter of all Beaujolais wine. A fair amount of Beaujolais-Villages Nouveau is made, although most of this appellation '*fait ses Pâques*', being aged at least until the Easter following harvesting. The plainer, simpler Beaujolais *appellation* wines come mainly from the vines south of the D504, in the gorgeous Pays des Pierres Dorées, although there's also a strip running down from Mâcon to Villefranche close to the Saône. With 10,000 hectares under vine, it makes up about half of all Beaujolais wine, half of which is sold as Beaujolais Nouveau. The area has suffered from a reputation for sloppy vinification by too many winemakers, but through the 1990s, efforts were made to buck them up, and some distinguished producers have emerged in these parts.

For tastings, or *dégustations*, virtually every village has a general wine-selling cellar. Or pick out individual properties bottling their own production; a select number have been granted the label *Secrets de Terroir*, in recognition of their efforts to receive visitors warmly. The official Beaujolais website (*www.beaujolais.com*) includes details on taking Beaujolais wine courses; the Ecole Beaujolaise des Vins at Villefranche-sur-Saône even organizes them in English.

It puts in a claim to being the place where vines were first planted in the Beaujolais. Above the often lively village centre, a big wine cooperative beckons; in this former church turned into the *Cellier de l'Eglise*, Bacchanalian scenes are painted on the walls. Enjoy the views from the nearby Romanesque **Chapelle de la Vâtre**.

Getting There and Around

By Train: The nearest TGV railway stations are at Mâcon and Lyon. Villefranche- and Belleville-sur-Saône also have useful stations.

By Bus: There are limited bus services into some of the hill villages from these two, run by the Transports en Commun du Rhône, t 04 72 61 72 61, *www.rhone.fr*. Le Pays Beaujolais (t 04 74 07 27 50) specializes in tourist taxis.

Tourist Information

For the official website for the whole area, consult *www.beaujolais.com*. For general info on the **Monts du Lyonnais**, consult *www. monts-du-lyonnais.org* and *www.coteaux-lyonnais.com*.

Beaujeu: Square de Grandhan, 69430 Beaujeu, t/f 04 74 69 22 88, *www.beaujeu.com*.

Belleville/Beaujolais-Val de Saône: 68 Rue de la République, 69220 Belleville, t 04 74 66 44 67, *www.ot-beaujolaisvaldesaone.fr*.

Villefranche-sur-Saône: 96 Rue de la Sous-Préfecture, 69400 Villefranche-sur-Saône, t 04 74 07 27 40, *www. villefranche.net*.

Anse/Beaujolais des Pierres Dorées: Place du 8 Mai 1945, 69480 Anse, t 04 74 60 26 16, *www.tourismepierresdorees.com*.

L'Ouest Lyonnais: Domaine de Lacroix-Laval, t 04 78 87 05 21, 69280 Marcy-l'Etoile, e *ot.ouestlyonnais@wanadoo.fr*.

L'Arbresle: 18 Place Sapéon, 69210 L'Arbresle, t 04 74 01 48 87, e *ot.paysdelarbresle@ wanadoo.fr*.

Market Days

Juliénas: Mon morning.
Fleurie: Sat morning.
Villié-Morgon: Thurs morning.

Régnié-Durette: Thurs afternoon.
Beaujeu: Wed morning.
Villefranche-sur-Saône: Mon morning, Fri, and Sun morning.
Anse: Fri morning.
Oingt: Fri morning.
Le Bois d'Oingt: Tues morning.
Bagnols: Fri afternoon.
Chessy-les-Mines: Fri morning.
Châtillon: Sat morning.
Taluyers: Wed and Fri mornings.
L'Arbresle: Fri morning.

Where to Stay and Eat

Juliénas ✉ 69840

★★Chez La Rose, t 04 74 04 41 20, *www.chez-la-rose.fr* (*inexpensive*). Appealing traditional and comfortable hotel on the square, with cheerful restaurant (*expensive–moderate*) or terrace at which to savour local classics. *Closed mid-Dec and Feb; restaurant closed Mon, and lunchtimes Tues, Thurs and Fri.*

Chénas ✉ 69840

Château Lambert B&B, t 04 74 06 77 74, *www.chateau-lambert.com* (*expensive–moderate*). A splendid 17th-century property with some spectacular vineyard views. The rooms are extremely smart. *Table d'hôte* (*moderate*).

Les Platanes de Chénas, at Deschamps, 2km north along D68, t 03 85 36 79 80 (*expensive–moderate*). Enormous restaurant, its bright yellow walls hung with brash paintings. Plenty of room for merry dining on local dishes. Plane-shaded terrace with vineyard views. *Closed Feb, and Tues and Wed outside July–Aug.*

Chénas, smallest of the ten *crus*, with just 280 hectares, produces peppery wines. A tempting stop, the **Château de Chassignol** holds the wine cooperative. The **Moulin à Vent** *cru* extends from the village across 650 hectares to Romanèche-Thorins. It is regarded as the best Beaujolais for ageing, and develops, some say, hints of cocoa. The name comes from a landmark **windmill** (*open in season*) dating from the 15th century.

Down at **Romanèche-Thorins**, the most high-profile wine merchant in these parts, Georges Duboeuf, invites you on a major journey through Beaujolais wine at the **Hameau en Beaujolais** (*t 03 85 35 22 22, www.hameauenbeaujolais.com; open Feb–Dec*

Romanèche-Thorins ✉ 71570

***Les Maritonnes**, Route de Fleurie, **t** 03 85 35 51 70, **e** *mariton@wanadoo.fr* (*moderate*). Charming house, rooms and garden with pool and tennis court. Good country restaurant (*expensive–moderate*). *Closed mid-Dec–Jan.*

Fleurie ✉ 69820

***Des Grands Vins**, La Chapelle des Bois, 1km south by D119E, **t** 04 74 69 81 43, **f** 04 74 69 86 10 (*moderate*). Modern block with annoying neon sign, but in the midst of the vines, with decent rooms, plus wines for sale. Pool. *Closed Dec and Jan.*

Le Cep, Place de l'Eglise, **t** 04 74 04 10 77 (*expensive–moderate*). One of the best restaurants in the Beaujolais, but not pretentious, using fresh farm produce. *Booking essential. Closed Sun and Mon, and Dec and Jan.*

Chiroubles ✉ 69115

La Terrasse du Beaujolais, **t** 04 74 69 90 79 (*expensive–moderate*). Tremendous views from this wonderfully located, popular restaurant. *Closed Mon, and eves outside July and Aug, plus early Dec–Feb.*

Avenas

L'Auberge du Fût d'Avenas, **t** 04 74 69 90 76 (*cheap*). Pleasing country cooking plus displays of local woodwork. *Closed Mon.*

Villié-Morgon ✉ 69910

****Le Villon**, **t** 04 74 69 16 16, **e** *le-villon@liberty surf.fr* (*inexpensive*). Big building with simple rooms with vineyard views. Regional cuisine (*expensive–moderate*), plus pool and tennis court. *Closed late Dec–early Jan; restaurant closed Sun pm and Mon out of season.*

Le Clachet B&B, **t** 04 74 04 24 97, **f** 04 74 69 12 71 (*moderate*). East below Villié, one wing of this substantial farm set around a court-yard offers handsome rooms in sober contemporary style. This being an excellent Beaujolais winemaking property, stock up on Foillard vintages.

Beaujeu ✉ 69430

*****Anne de Beaujeu**, 28 Rue de la République, **t** 04 74 04 87 58, **f** 04 74 69 22 13 (*inexpensive*). Old-fashioned provincial rooms in appealing central townhouse with a courtyard. Grandiose dining room (*expensive–moderate*) plus garden. *Closed early Aug and late Dec–late Jan; restaurant closed Sun pm, Mon, and Tues lunch.*

Vaux-en-Beaujolais ✉ 69460

*****Auberge de Clochemerle**, Rue Gabriel Chevallier, **t** 04 74 03 20 16, *www.georgeslegarde.com* (*inexpensive*). Rooms in a modern annexe, but traditional restaurant (*expensive–moderate*) beside an old house with lovely terrace. *Closed early Aug; restaurant closed Tues and Wed.*

Pizay/St-Jean-d'Ardières ✉ 69220

*****Château de Pizay**, **t** 04 74 66 51 41, **e** *info@chateau-pizay.com* (*very expensive–expensive*). Luxurious hotel on the vine slopes north of Belleville, the grander rooms in the 17th-century castle, modern ones in newer buildings. Restaurant plus courtyard for summer dining (*expensive*). Formal French gardens, pool, tennis court, woods, and vines. With 58 hectares, this is also one of the biggest wine-producing properties in the Beaujolais (visit the *Société Viticole* next door, **t** 04 74 66 26 10).

9–6; *adm*), a plush modern museum set in former railway buildings, the trip ending in the extensive tasting and shopping areas. The new **Jardin en Beaujolais** cleverly combines horticulture and scents with wine tasting.

Back up the vine-covered slopes, cheerful **Fleurie** benefits from a particularly open position and produces a very elegant Beaujolais from its 869 hectares. It also has the oldest wine cooperative in Beaujolais. The chapel perched high on the slope above was built in the 19th century as part of the superstitious efforts to protect the vines from various diseases. **Chiroubles**, the highest of the *cru* villages, stands in a

Villefranche-sur-Saône ✉ 69400
La Grande, 322 Rue de Belleville, **t** 04 74 60 65 81 (*moderate*). Bright dining room and secluded courtyard off a busy road, a lively spot to eat. *Closed Sat–Mon, and most Aug.*

Oingt ✉ 69620
Aux Arts Etc, **t** 04 74 71 12 86 (*moderate–inexpensive*). Both a *café gourmand* serving local dishes and funky art gallery, with little garden with fountain. *Only open Thurs–Sun.*

Bagnols-en-Beaujolais ✉ 69620
★★★★**Château de Bagnols**, **t** 04 74 71 40 00, **e** info@bagnols.com (*luxury*). One of the most luxurious hotels in southeast France. Some of the château rooms are adorned with historic murals. The most ornate stone fireplace oversees the excellent restaurant (*very expensive*). Pool. Concert programme. *Closed Jan–Mar; restaurant closed Sun pm, Mon, and Tues lunch in winter.*

Theizé ✉ 69620
La Ferme du Saint B&B, Le Sens, **t** 04 74 71 15 48, **e** perso.wanadoo.fr/lafermedusaint (*moderate–inexpensive*). Fortified farm with very nice old-style rooms. Pool and mountain bikes.

Alix ✉ 69380
Le Vieux Moulin, **t** 04 78 43 91 66 (*expensive–moderate*). Old stone mill delightfully converted into a tranquil country restaurant. *Closed Mon, Tues, and mid-Aug–mid-Sept.*

Marcy-sur-Anse ✉ 69480
Le Télégraphe, **t** 04 74 60 24 73 (*moderate–cheap; closed Sun*). Popular village restaurant in traditional style offering copious cooking.

Morancé ✉ 69480
Château du Pin, 600 Chemin de la Ronze, **t** 04 37 46 10 10, www.chateauxhotels.com/chateaupin (*luxury–expensive*) Enchantingly restored fortified medieval manor overlooking the Saône valley. Very smart rooms. *Table d'hôte* (*expensive*). Pool.

Collonges-au-Mont d'Or ✉ 69660
Paul Bocuse Auberge du Pont de Collonges, **t** 04 72 42 90 90, www.bocuse.fr (*luxury*). Legendary address run by the famed chef. His fabled, inventive cuisine is served in a deeply colourful restaurant just separated from the Saône by a road.

Marcy l'Etoile ✉ 69280
L'Orangerie de Sébastien, Domaine de Lacroix-Laval, **t** 04 78 87 45 95 (*expensive–moderate*). Smart big restaurant in castle's outbuildings. *Closed Sun eve, Mon and Tues.*

Montrottier ✉ 69770
★★**L'Auberge des Blés d'Or**, **t** 04 74 70 13 56 (*inexpensive*). Lovely country stop 2km from town. Well-presented rooms, delightful rustic dining room (*moderate*) *Restaurant closed evenings and all Tues.*

Festivals and Events

Beaujeu has the biggest and best Beaujolais Nouveau festival, including a candle-lit procession, 3rd Thurs Nov. The Mont-Brouilly pilgrimage takes place 8 Sept. The Château de Lachassagne puts on a *Fête de la Musique* and open days. Domaine de Lacroix-Laval lays on a wide programme of events. Montrottier hosts a huge annual Easter egg hunt.

delightful location too, below a theatre of vines. The wines made from its 370 hectares have marked floral touches.

Vauxrenard, behind Fleurie and Chiroubles towards La Terrasse, is a less well known wine village, but has laid out an educational wine trail through its vines. **La Terrasse** offers one of the best viewing platforms over the northern Beaujolais. Pop over the hill to **Avenas**, a hamlet whose Romanesque church breathes the sobering air of a different age and contains a superlative early medieval altar, Christ appearing more like an emperor than a humble man.

Scattered in the countryside around **Ouroux**, north of Avenas, go in search of many of the farms and sites in the association **Billebaudez en Beaujolais Vert** (*www.billebaudez. com*), putting traditional crafts to the fore. The **Col de Crie** pass has a **Maison d'Accueil** offering general information on such delights as goats -cheese-making, traditional bread- and jam-making, woodworking and logging. It is also a major starting point for walkers, riders and mountain-bikers. Beyond, **Mont St-Rigaud**, the highest peak of the Beaujolais, reaches just over 1,000m, but is easily reached by car.

Back among the vines, the flavour of rich red fruits are found in the larger *crus* south of Chiroubles. **Morgon**, extending across 1,100 hectares, often tastes of cherries. At the centre of the quiet village of **Villié-Morgon**, the modest Château de Fontcrenne has a tempting wine-tasting cellar. Down the vine slopes towards the Saône, the splendid towers of the medieval to Renaissance **Château de Corcelles** (*t 04 74 66 00 21; open Jan–Dec Mon–Sat 10–12 and 2.30–6.30*) draw visitors to its highly commercial cellars.

The tall towers and rounded end of the grand 19th-century church of **Régnié-Durette** are reminiscent of Notre-Dame de Fourvière in Lyon, and were designed by the same architect, Bossan. Several châteaux embellish the surrounding slopes, while the **Grange-Charton** proves an intriguing model wine farm owned by the Hospices de Beaujeu. The makers of Régnié's sharp red-berry-tasting wines fought long and hard to be declared a separate *cru*, and achieved *appellation* status in 1988.

Beaujeu and West of Beaujeu

Hidden in the hills to the west, outside *cru* territory, **Beaujeu** was the medieval capital of Beaujolais after the first castle of the Beaujeu family was built on a high rock above the little town. Today it looks a bit uncomfortably crammed into the narrow valley bottom, the steep slopes above reserved for vineyards. Attention down below focuses around **St Nicolas' church**, the medieval edifice said to have gone up on the site of a lake where Lord Guichard III of Beaujeu's son drowned. On the same square stand two good museums. Behind its timber façade, the lively guided tour round the *Pôle Œnologique* of **Les Sources du Beaujolais** (*t 04 74 69 20 56; open May–Sept daily 10–7, March–April and Oct–Dec Wed–Mon 10–12 and 2–6; adm*) reveals the history of Beaujeu and Beaujolais using amusing modern techniques. The outstanding stone sculptures on display at the more traditional **Musée Marius Audin** (*t 04 74 69 22 88; open same times*) were rescued from Beaujeu's château and church. Apart from sampling local wine in town, the nutty aromas emanating from the **Huilerie Beaujolaise** incite visitors to enter this specialist shop and see how its highly-prized nut and seed oils are made the old-fashioned way. On the culinary trail, visit **L'Escargot de Beaujeu** (*t 04 74 04 84 49*), a snail farm on the Route des Echarmeaux.

In the hills west of Beaujeu, more members of the association **Billebaudez en Beaujolais Vert** may tempt you to explore these wooded territories. Getting on for 1,000m, **Mont Tourvéon**'s panoramic view is said to have appealed to the 16th-century French star-gazer Nostradamus as a place to read the skies. Douglas pines were planted for logging in the Haut-Beaujolais in the 19th century; some of those that have survived around **Claveisolles** have been listed as historic monuments, one reaching 55m in height and claimed to be the tallest tree in France.

From Beaujolais' Brouilly *Crus* through Southern Beaujolais-Villages

Back in Beaujolais wine territory, you come up against a 'mountain covered in vines,' 'Sinai of the Beaujolais' – a couple of the extravagant descriptions used by local author Gabriel Chevallier of totemic Mont Brouilly, its conical shape giving away its volcanic origins. The big Virgin-topped church was built in the mid-19th century on the summit, a sacred spot with inspiring views since pagan times. The exclusive 320 hectares of **Côte de Brouilly** vineyards form a skirt right round the hill.

The more extensive **Brouilly estates**, making up the largest *cru*, with 1,300 hectares, radiate out in a wider circle lower down around the base of the hill, spreading across several parishes. Experts taste raspberries in the wines. **St-Lager** may have been given the grandiose title of *Ville Internationale de la Vigne et du Vin*, and claims to be 'capital of Brouilly', but it's really just a pretty village with charming manors nearby. **Odenas** is signalled by the medieval towers of the otherwise 19th-century **Château de Pierreux**, but the greatest architectural treasure lies hidden in its own separate valley. A magnificently discreet aristocratic property, also the largest wine estate in the Beaujolais, the **Château de la Chaize** dates from 1676, built up to its magnificent if windowless Mansard roofs for François de Lachaise d'Aix, brother of King Louis XIV's famed Jesuit confessor, Père Lachaise. Beyond the beautiful terraced gardens with their statues, topiary and white fences, the estate has 100 hectares under vine.

Charentay, east on the edge of Brouilly territories, offers a charming Romanesque church and old houses. Local legend claims that the superwealthy bankers of the crusades, the Knights Templar, hid their treasure in the nearby **Château d'Arginy** when they were persecuted by the jealous French crown in the 14th century; at that time, Guichard de Beaujeu was nephew of the Templars' Grand Master, Jacques de Molay. All that remains of the castle is its soaring brick **Tour d'Alchimie**.

Leaving the territory of the Beaujolais *crus*, west of the rather misleadingly named town of Belleville, **Capvignes** (*open Easter–Nov Wed–Mon 10–12 and 2–6; adm*) is one of the newest of Beaujolais' half-dozen *Pôles Œnologiques*. This one is set in the restored little Château de Bel-Air, at the back of a modern viticultural college, and focuses on the stages of Beaujolais winemaking in entertaining manner. North of town, the **Maison des Beaujolais** (*t 04 74 66 16 46; open mid-Jan–mid-Dec daily 9am–10pm, but earlier closing Mon and Tues; adm*), a longer-established *Pôle Œnologique* and a major Beaujolais wine-tasting centre, was placed by the busy N6 road at St-Jean-d'Ardières. A surprisingly grand *Ancien Régime* hospital stands on **Belleville**'s main street, breathing a little tourist life into the place, the tour taking you round its ornate pharmacy, down the well-preserved dormitories to the nun's chapel. By the port, the **Maison de la Saône** concentrates on local flora and fauna.

South of Brouilly, you enter the Beaujolais-Villages wine area. First stop for all has to be the urinal of **Vaux-en-Beaujolais**, which has a special place in many a Frenchman's heart – it supposedly served as inspiration for Gabriel Chevallier's *Clochemerle*, one of the cheekiest books in French literature (*see p.26*). The argument as to whether the author only saw the similarity between his fictional Clochemerle and the real Vaux after the novel had been written is of little consequence to the villagers, who milk the connection for all it's worth. There's a merry wine shop with saucy paintings, while a new *Pôle Œnologique* is in the planning.

What a dignified contrast at **Salles-Arbuissonas**. A religious atmosphere still hangs in the air. The beautiful village centres round the buildings of a former medieval priory that came to serve as a finishing school for noblemen's daughters. **St-Julien** below celebrates its famous ancestor, Claude Bernard, the son of a vinegrower who became an eminent scientist in the 19th century, delving into the murky workings of the liver. As *le foie* is a subject of major concern to many a Frenchman, his work, recalled in the village's **Musée Claude Bernard** (*t 04 74 67 51 44; open Wed–Sun 10–12 and 2–5; adm*), is much revered. The tempting local chocolatier makes delicious chocolates flavoured with Beaujolais wine, hardly the ideal recipe for a healthy liver.

Descendants of the treasurer to Anne de Beaujeu for whom the original **Château de Montmelas** was built still own this huge many-walled property, although the castle was redone in enjoyably extravagant neo-Gothic style in the 19th century. Church towers also stand out in the area – the one at the pretty beige-stoned village of **Montmelas** given colourful patterned tiles. Pilgrims and walkers head up to **Notre-Dame-de-la-Délivrance**, a Romanesque chapel at the summit of the Signal de St-Bonnet with spectacular views.

Southern Beaujolais: Le Pays des Pierres Dorées

Apartment blocks rising from the Saône valley signal Beaujolais' modern capital, **Villefranche-sur-Saône**. It took over in importance from more backward Beaujeu as early as 1514, by order of Anne de Beaujeu, who realized its location made it more appropriate as the area's centre. She saw to the restoration of the church of **Notre-Dame des Marais**, its ceiling covered with elaborate tracery and bosses. The town's cultural life has been given a recent boost with the opening of the stylish **Musée Paul Dini** (*t 04 74 68 33 70; open Wed–Fri 11–6.30, weekends 2–6.30; adm*), a grain exchange cleverly transformed to display hundreds of works by artists from Lyon and the Rhône-Alpes region from 1875 to the present, avidly collected by the Dinis.

To begin a tour deep into Pierres Dorées territory, meander west from Villefranche along the Morgon River valley to **Lacenas**, its unmissable long 18th-century *cuvage* in golden stone used regularly for meetings of the *Confrérie des Compagnons du Beaujolais*, a fraternity that has fun promoting the area's wines. South from **Cogny**, a sweet, deeply ochre village, the even more colourful **Jarnioux** cowers below its imposing-looking, many-towered château (*t 04 74 03 80 85; open 1–13 July and 16 Aug–30 Sept Tues and Thurs 9–12, Mon, Wed and Fri 2–6; adm*), one of the most striking in the Beaujolais, long a stronghold for important Lyon families. Once past the two sets of fine gateways, you come upon a rather scrappy scene, however, a refined Renaissance wing knocked into by the later main block. A more characterful, older watchtower soars up on the other side to see over the hill. The few rooms you can visit are sadly dilapidated, but if you're shown around by the owners, their charm makes up for the poor decorative state. **Ville-sur-Jarnioux** has further gorgeous ochre houses. Its church may be medieval, but the murals inside were apparently executed by an Austrian soldier briefly posted here after Napoleon's defeat.

Theizé, to the south, makes a particularly beautiful picture, overlooked by the imposing **Château de Rochebonne** (*t 04 74 71 16 10; open May–Oct Wed–Mon 2–6; adm*), a grand classical castle replacing an earlier one devastated in the Wars of Religion. Now it doubles as a *Pôle Œnologique*, with cellars devoted to the presentation of Beaujolais wine-making, and a cultural centre hosting temporary exhibitions. Admire the *Ancien Régime* features, including the trompe-l'oeil in the lord's chamber.

Its round keep rising high above the village houses, **Oingt** to the west competes with Theizé in the stakes for Beaujolais' most dramatic hilltop silhouette. The *donjon* offers a 360-degree view, but is all that remains of the medieval castle, destroyed by Protestants in the 16th century. However, the church, built to serve the castle, contains carved faces thought to represent members of the medieval lordly family, a powerful line that long ruled over the Azergues valley, one rung down from the lords of Beaujeu. The lanes carry humorous old names, such as the Rue Trayne-Cul (Drag Arse Street). Craftspeople here include a painter, a potter, a wood turner and a weaver. Delicious smells waft out in the morning from the wood-oven *boulangerie*.

Continue west for **St-Laurent-d'Oingt**, its cemetery and church among the vines, the edifice with a welcoming covered wooden porch, a *galonnière*. North, **Ste-Paule** lies on a dramatic slope before you reach the Azergues valley, a medieval boundary of the Beaujolais. Perched on a high rock on the opposite bank, **Ternand**'s name possibly derives from the fact that three streams flow below it. Fortifications were built up here for the archbishops of Lyon, major territorial lords in these parts in the early medieval period. Reds, oranges, blues and greens count among the colours of the local stone houses packed tight around the circular cobbled street, 'like grains in a pomegranate', the locals like to say. Enter the church via its charming *galonnière*. The interior has been spruced up, the church treasure now behind glass. Up the Azergues, at **Chamelet**, go picnicking with donkeys from the **Ferme de la Vieille Route**.

An old wine press stationed outside signals **L'Histoire du Vigneron en Beaujolais** (*t 04 74 71 35 72; open July–15 Sept Tues–Fri 10–7, rest of year Fri only 10–7; adm*) an atmospheric little wine museum on the hillside at **Ronzières** close to Oingt and Le Bois d'Oingt, run by the passionate Jean-Jacques Paire in his country winery. **Le Bois d'Oingt** has retained a few remnants of its fortifications, but **Bagnols** boasts one of the most preserved of all the Beaujolais' castles (*see* Where to Stay and Eat). Its long stone walls, gateways and drawbridge separate it from the village.

For a quicker trip from Villefranche-sur-Saône through the eastern Pays des Pierres Dorées, head down via Limas or **Pommiers**, with its ruddy stones and a church carved with entertaining country animals. Meanwhile, **Anse** down by the Saône once served as a Gallo-Roman garrison on the route north from Lugdunum, in medieval times becoming a strategic post for the archbishops of Lyon, as witnessed by its **Château des Tours**, holding a modest museum (*t 04 74 60 26 16; open for Sat tour at 3.30; adm*).

The D70 up above offers a wonderful route south. Kilometres of stone walls separate the sloping vineyards of the 19th-century **Château de Lachassagne**, one of the grandest properties in the Beaujolais, from its quietly charming village. Abandoned for a quarter century, the place has been undergoing a rapid revival under a Danish-British team. On the way down to the open village of **Marcy**, the square **Tour Chappe** (*open mid-March–Nov Sun 2.30–6; free*) standing on its rise recalls the days before electric telegraphs when, in the first half of the 19th century, a network of 500 such towers was built around France to signal messages round the country.

Pressing south, **Charnay** can claim the grandest village hall in the Beaujolais, occupying part of the big castle in the centre, ordered once again for the archbishops of Lyon. The post office comes with machicolations too, the castle roof glows with coloured tiles in the Burgundian style, and the medieval church is dedicated to the patron saint of travellers, the helpful giant Christopher. Reaching the lower Azergues valley, beside the modest village of **St-Jean-des-Vignes**, set in a lovely open location on a high slope of the southern Beaujolais, the **Espace Pierres Folles** (*t 04 78 43 69 20; open March–Nov Mon–Tues and Thurs–Fri 9–12 and 2–6, Wed and weekends 2–6; adm*), most southerly of the Beaujolais' *Pôles Œnologiques*, takes you back to the geological roots of the region, which is extraordinarily rich in fossils. The modern building wasn't made out of the warm local stone, however, but from reasonably subtle cement, as it was sponsored by the giant company Lafarge, with quarries nearby. The more substantial **Chazay-d'Azergues** has kept vestiges of its fortifications, one gateway overseen by the statue of a naked, muscular Roman soldier, long lance erect. The historic streets bear many other attractive little details.

West along the Azergues, **Châtillon** looks particularly dramatic, its castle towers silhouetted above the river. Although the château is in private hands, you can visit the Romanesque chapel. The wealthy village houses below the hilltop castle and church of **Chessy-les-Mines** are explained by the long lucrative tradition of copper mining. Southwest, **St-Germain-sur-l'Arbresle** stands on the southern frontier of Beaujolais wine-producing territory. A **quarry** for *pierres dorées* has left a big ochre gash in the nearby countryside, and is open to the public. Already, cherry trees pop up among the vines around these parts, presaging the Monts du Lyonnais. However, **Bully** boasts the largest of all Beaujolais cooperatives, producing good-value, widely exported wines.

Mont d'Or and Monts/Coteaux du Lyonnais

Whereas a big flat plain extends east from Lyon, to the west, big sensuous hills wrap themselves around the city. The **Mont d'Or**, a lump of a mountain in golden limestone, separates Beaujolais from Lyon. The summit has been largely occupied by the French military, while the A6 and A46 motorways constrict the mountain to either side. But coming down from Beaujolais via Anse, you can bypass it without taking the *autoroutes* by following the Saône-side roads, a delightful way by which to approach Lyon under densely wooded slopes. This stretch of river is favoured by families of swans and has long been popular with the Lyonnais wishing to escape the bustle of town for some riverside fun, with bathing areas and restaurants. Suburbia has now stretched out comfortably along the Saône, although the odd village like **Couzon-au-Mont-d'Or** has retained a pretty old church in golden stone.

The main valley attraction stands out on the steep east bank, the splendid-looking **Château de Rochetaillée** (*t 04 78 22 18 80; open winter Tues–Sun 9–6, summer Tues–Sun 10–7; adm*) drawing attention to itself with its Burgundian-style coloured roof tiles. A medieval fort was originally built on the spot as a river post for lords of the Dombes (*see* chapter 8), to exact river tolls and guard this frontier between the Holy Roman Empire and France. In the 12th century the mighty Lyon religious authorities took over this lucrative property. Destroyed in the Wars of Religion, the castle was rebuilt in the 17th century, and was subsequently given a major neo-Gothic makeover. It has now become a retirement home for old automobiles, the **Musée de l'Automobile Henri Malartre**, with some of the most aristocratic and eccentric characters of the first generation of cars resting quietly in front of posh fireplaces! Up to the First World War, when France was the world's biggest car producer, Lyon was the second most important centre of production after Paris. Marius Berliet started up possibly the first Lyonnais car-making company. Ironically, it was a car breaker, Henri Malartre, who, from the start of the 1930s, began gathering what was to become one of the most important collections of original and old automobiles in the world. Celebrity numbers include a Lumière brothers Renault, General de Gaulle's Hispano Suiza used after the Liberation, and, most darkly, one of Hitler's armoured Mercedes. On a brighter note, view Edith Piaf's 1950s Paccard, and the Popemobile Renault Espace used by Pope John-Paul II on his visit to France in 1986, taking in Lyon.

Back down on the west bank of the Saône, **Collonges-au-Mont-d'Or** is home to Paul Bocuse's restaurant, which is famous across France. To explore the more traditional Mont d'Or, take the steep country roads up from Curis or Couzon to the unspoilt, golden-stoned village of **Poleymieux** where you will find the **Musée Ampère** (*t 04 78 91 90 77, http://musee-ampere.univ-lyon1.fr; open Jan–Dec daily exc Tues 10–12 and 2–6; adm*), the country retreat of the Lyonnais silk merchant whose son André-Marie Ampère gave his name to the standard unit of electric current, the amp. He spent much of his childhood here, becoming a precocious student, developing an exceptional aptitude for maths. The tragedies of losing his father to the Revolutionary guillotine and his first wife to illness caused him to leave for Paris, where he became a renowned scientist. The museum is old-fashioned, but it has a pleasant old-school feel and clear notices in English and French explaining Ampère's achievements. It also provides very early examples of interactive displays setting off basic experiments.

North above Poleymieux, the **Croix Rampau** is one of the four main peaks of the Mont d'Or, on clear days offering huge views east and west, as far as Mont Blanc one side, and the Puy de Dôme the other, but most of the Mont d'Or's heights are out of bounds, observation posts none too subtly signalling the military's presence.

The slopes of the **Coteaux du Lyonnais** look over their shoulder towards Lyon, the traditional villages in this gently rolling territory planted with Roman aqueducts, Romanesque chapels and vines now expanding to make room for city commuters. Starting this tour west of the A6 motorway, **Dardilly** was the childhood home of the virtuous and charitable Jean-Marie Vianney, who went on to become revered as the model priest (*see* Ars, p.91). The modest family house where he gave charity to the poor has been turned into a museum. The **Domaine de Lacroix-Laval** (*t 04 78 87 87 00, www.lacroixlaval.com; open Jan–Dec Tues–Sun 10–5; adm exc Thurs*) offers a very grand contrast close by, near **Marcy-l'Etoile**, its *Ancien Régime* château surrounded by a sumptuous park. In recent years, it has become an increasingly important cultural country outpost for the Lyonnais. The substantial **doll museum**, once the main attraction, is now an attractive sideshow, with huts where children can watch films away from the adults. The landscaped grounds include deer park and woods. All sorts of events take place here, including gardening shows and outdoor film screenings. A golf course stands nearby, plus the swanky **Charbonnières casino and spa**.

The engineering-mad Romans drew on the resources of the Monts du Lyonnais to provide their city of Lugdunum with plenty of water, building an impressive network of **aqueducts**. Large sections were dug just under the ground, but the most substantial portion left standing above ground is at **Chaponost**, the long row of crumbling arches within view of the big city below. A trail marks out smaller fragments. Small patches of vines also lie scattered around the Coteaux du Lyonnais' slopes, between L'Arbresle, touching on Beaujolais territory, and Givors, Rhône-side Côte Rôtie country. The **Coteaux du Lyonnais wines** gained their own *appellation d'origine contrôlee* in 1984, the vineyards covering over 300 hectares. As in Beaujolais, the reds come from Gamay grapes. A little rosé is also produced, and a little white. Cherry trees compete with the vines and you may see *pêches de vignes*, late-ripening blood peaches, among the rows. In the south, some interesting Coteaux du Lyonnais estates lie around **Taluyers**, its former priory buildings resembling fragments of a castle. The **Domaine du Clos St-Marc** with its barn of a reception room is one of the best to visit and, with 25 hectares under vine, one of the largest. **Mornant**, a sweet medieval village with a fine Gothic church, has preserved a painterly rustic fragment of Roman aqueduct below its hillock, while you can get fine views above **Montagny**.

Starting from Dardilly again to discover the **Monts du Lyonnais**, the N7 road heads for **L'Arbresle**, set in the valley dividing the Beaujolais from the Monts du Lyonnais. Three towers rise above the old centre, putting on a plucky historic show, although an army of modern blocks has taken over the slopes above. The dilapidated 11th-century keep is eclipsed by a rejuvenated Gothic church containing lavish 15th-century stained glass. The third tower dates from the Renaissance. In the compact streets below, the grand houses boast coats of arms in stone. The **Train Touristique des Monts du Lyonnais** (*open June–Sept Sun only; adm*) follows the tight river valley up to **Ste-Foy-l'Argentière**. A monastery built on concrete stilts rises on the wooded heights above **Eveux**, L'Arbresle's neighbour. This **Couvent de la Tourette** (*t 04 74 26 79 70; may be closed for restoration work*) is a concrete classic by the celebrated architect Le Corbusier. A bell tower precariously perched above the most severe and windowless of churches provides the first obvious sign of playfulness in the, at first stark-seeming structure, sadly somewhat neglected.

West of L'Arbresle, explore the cheerful cherry-orchard hills around **Montrottier**, a likeable hilltop town with tall houses curving round the outside, doubling as ramparts, and a huge covered market dating back to Louis XIV's time. South of L'Arbresle, it comes as a shock to discover that this bucolic area is partly responsible for turning the Rhône valley into such an intensely industrial zone. **St-Pierre-la-Palud** had been a copper-mining town in medieval times, but in 1842, the Perret brothers bought the mines and worked out how to extract sulphur from the pyrite that ran in a thick seam under the town. Sulphur became one of the main ingredients for the Rhône valley chemical industries and by the early 1900s, over 1,000 miners worked here. The **Musée de la Mine** (*t 04 74 70 39 66; open March–Nov weekends and public hols 2–6; adm*) covers this harrowing history and, on a brighter note, displays a huge collection of colourful minerals from around the world.

Among the deeply wooded, beautiful hills to the south, a little patch of land has been tamed at the **Parc Animalier de Courzieu** (*t 04 74 70 96 10, www.parc-de-courzieu.fr; open March–Oct daily 10–7; displays pm; adm*), down a deep valley. The place is largely devoted to wolves, the message being that they have been maligned by man. Certainly the pack penned here seems an apathetic bunch, the hassle of hunting removed. With the displays of falconry certain afternoons, the birds of prey have to work harder for their dinner. Twisting hill roads lead up to the high village of **Yzeron,** the **Maison de l'Araire** (*t 04 78 81 07 79; open April–Nov Wed–Thurs and Sat–Sun 2–6; adm*) taking you back to rural life and the Monts du Lyonnais' Roman aqueducts.

The Loire to its Source
Down France's Longest River

The Roannais Loire and Monts de la Madeleine 109
Charlieu **109**
The Loire through the Roannais **113**
The Monts de la Madeleine and Côte Roannaise **114**
The Loire Valley across the Forez 115
Surprising Sights on the Edge of the Forez Plain **115**
The Loire from Feurs to St-Etienne **117**
St-Etienne **118**
The Monts du Forez **120**
**The Upper Loire from St-Etienne to its Source
via Le Puy-en-Velay 121**
Le Puy-en-Velay **122**
The Last Leg of the Loire to its Source **124**

The Loire to its Source

N

10 km
5 miles

ALLIER

Thiers
Courpière
Vollore-Ville
Vollore-Montagne
Cunlhat
PUY-DE-DÔME
Ambert
Monts du Livradois
Arlanc
La Chaise-Dieu
Arlanc
St-André-de-Chalencon
Allègre
Chavaniac-Lafayette
Prades
St-Paulien
Monistrol-d'Allier
St-Vidal
Le-Puy-en-Velay
Cayres
Solignac
Arlempdes
LOZÈRE
Grandrieu

Le Crozet
La Pacaudière
Changy
La Bénisson-Dieu
Brennon
Noailly
Pouilly-sous-Charlieu
Charlieu
Ambierle
St-Haon-le-Châtel
Roanne
Villerest
Commelle
St-Maurice-sur-Loire
Gorges de la Loire
Bully
Dance
Château d'Urfé
Champoly
Cervières
Noirêtable
Pommiers
C. de la Loge
Jeansagnière
Boën
La Bastie d'Urfé
Montverdun
Chalmazel
Trelins
Col du Béal
Sauvain
Marcilly-le-Châtel
Pierre sur Haute
St-Bonnet-le-Courreau
Champdieu
Roche
Montbrison
St-Romain le-Puy
Gumières
St-Just-St-Rambert
Montarcher
Chambles
Estivareilles
St-Bonnet-le-Château
St-Victor-sur-Loire
St-Paul-en-Cornillon
Aurec-sur-Loire
Firminy
Craponne
Valprivas
La Motte-Chalencon
Château de Rochebaron
Bas-en-Basset
Retournac
Château de Lavoûte-Polignac
Yssingeaux
Chaspinhac
Polignac
Le Chambon-sur-Lignon
St-Julien-Chapteuil
Montfaucon-en-Velay
Devesset
St-Agrève
Le Monastier-sur-Gazeille
Mt Mézenc
Les Estables
Borée
St-Martial
Gerbier-de-Jonc
Le Lac d'Issarlès
Source de la Loire
Ste-Eulalie
Usclades-et-Rieutord

Chauffailles
Mont St-Rigaud
Thoissey
Châtillon-sur-Chalaronne
AIN
Chamelet
Villefranche-sur-Saône
Miornay
St-Symphorien-de-Lay
Tarare
Néronde
Violay
Bussières
Rozier-en-Donzy
Panissières
Montrottier
RHÔNE
LYON
Feurs
Montrond-les-Bains
Chazelles-sur-Lyon
St-Galmier
Givors
Rive-de-Gier
Vienne
Lac de Grangent
St-Chamond
St-Étienne
ISÈRE
Le Chambon-Feugerolles
Serrières
Anneyron
Annonay
St-Uze
St-Barthélemy-de-Vals
St-Jean-de-Muzols
Tournon-sur-Rhône
Mauves
Tain-l'Hermitage

HAUTE-LOIRE

LOIRE

Monts du Forez
Monts du Devès

Allier

p.80
p.150
p.126

p.80
p.150
p.126

ENGLAND
BELGIUM
GERMANY
LUX.
English Channel
FRANCE
SWITZ.
ITALY
SPAIN

Highlights

1 Charlieu for its religious legacy in burnished gold
2 Renaissance Bastie-d'Urfé
3 The spectacular pinnacles of le Puy-en-Velay

France's longest, most majestic river, the Loire, takes a stately 1000 km to travel from its source in the volcanic Ardèche mountains to the Atlantic, flowing parallel (but in the opposite direction) to the Rhône and the Saône for the first stretch of its journey. We take you back along this section from the Roannais on the border with Burgundy, via the Forez and Velay, up to Mont Gerbier de Jonc, the green-bouldered giant from which the great river's first streams trickle. You travel along restful farming plains on which Charolais cows graze, through tight gorges, past indolent, slope-side villages and bustling towns. The most dramatic city of the upper Loire is Le Puy-en-Velay, churches and religious statues rising from its rocky pinnacles. Montbrison and St-Galmier offer quieter charms, while former coal-mining St-Etienne has been declared a *Ville d'Art et d'Histoire* for its fine museums.

This part of the Loire offers one of the most secretive retreats in rural France, hidden from view to east and west by the small, blue-ridged Monts de la Madeleine, Monts du Forez, Montagnes du Matin, and the volcanic Velay. Ruined but superbly located medieval castles look down from on high, although the area's most famous château, the Renaissance Bastie d'Urfé, is on the lake-strewn Forez plain. Nearby, the Ecopôle de Chambéon, an amusing nature centre on stilts, focuses on the Loire. Apart from Le Puy, other religious highpoints include Ambierle, Charlieu and wizened old St-Romain-le-Puy. As to cliff-edge St-Bonnet-le-Château, its church not only conceals some of the most delicate murals in southern France, but also sinister mummies, while nowadays the town is devoted to that all-pervasive French ritual – *boules*.

The Roannais Loire and Monts de la Madeleine

After the religious vision in burnished golden stone of Charlieu, here we follow the once heavily working Loire upstream through Roanne and on to the Roannais gorges. We also take you into the dark hills of the Monts de la Madeleine, the barrier in early medieval times between the Roannais, controlled by the counts of Forez, and the territories of the dukes of Bourbon – who eventually took over.

Charlieu

'Monks were masters of the town,' a panel helpfully informs you in the **Centre des Visiteurs** (**t** *04 77 60 09 97, www.amisdesartscharlieu.com; open July–Aug daily 10–12 and 1–7, March–June and Sept–Oct Tues–Sun 10–12.30 and 2–6.30, Feb and Nov–Dec Tues–Sun 10–12.30 and 2–5.30; adm*), a museum housed in a former priory, the oldest religious establishment in a town once clearly packed with them. This *carus locus* (beloved spot, hence the name, Charlieu) developed one of the most glorious collections of monasteries in southeast France as well as a significant merchant community. The **Benedictine priory**, founded in the 9th-century but rebuilt several times from the 10th onwards, suffered terribly during the Revolution. However, its entrance, or narthex, has retained some of France's most memorable Romanesque carvings. Look out for a dumb, fleecy Paschal Lamb peering down from a patterned band so finely carved it resembles cloth, Christ appearing with more dignity in person below it. Elsewhere the wedding at Cana and the Transfiguration feature.

Getting There and Around

By air: Ryanair flies from London to St-Etienne-Bouthéon airport (t 04 77 55 71 71, *www.saint- etienne.aeroport.fr*).

By train: Roanne has a useful train station for the Roannais; otherwise rely on bus services from Roanne (t 04 77 72 28 66). St-Etienne centre has daily fast TGV trains connections with Paris. Regular trains from here serve the towns along the Loire valley, such as Feurs, Montrond, St-Galmier and Le Puy-en-Velay.

By bus: Bus services radiate out from central St-Etienne to the hill towns, and from Le Puy.

Tourist Information

Charlieu: Place St-Philibert, 42190 Charlieu, t 04 77 60 12 42, e *office.tourisme.charlieu@wanadoo.fr*.

Roanne: Cours de la République, 42300 Roanne, t 04 77 71 51 77, *www.leroannais.com*.

Ambierle: Musée Alice Taverne, 42820 Ambierle, t 04 77 65 60 99.

Montbrison: Cloître des St-Cordeliers, t 04 77 96 08 69, *www.loireforez.com*.

Feurs: Place du Forum, t 04 77 26 05 27, *www.officedutourismedefeurs.org*.

Montrond-les-Bains: Av des Sources, 42210 Montrond-les-Bains, t 04 77 94 64 74, *www.montrond-les-bains.com*.

St-Galmier: Bd du Sud, 42330 St-Galmier, t 04 77 54 06 08, *www.ot-stgalmier.fr*.

Chazelles-sur-Lyon: 9 Place Galland, 42140 Chazelles-sur-Lyon, t 04 77 54 98 86, e *ot.chazelles@wanadoo.fr*.

St-Just-St-Rambert: Place de la Paix, 42170 St-Just-St-Rambert, t 04 77 52 05 14, *www.loireforez.com*.

St-Etienne: 16 Av de la Libération, 42000 St Etienne, t 08 92 70 05 42, *www.tourisme-st-etienne.com*.

Chalmazel: Place de l'Eglise, 42920 Chalmazel, t 04 77 24 84 92, *www.perso.wanadoo.fr/otsi.chalmazel/*.

St-Bonnet-le-Château: Place de la République, 42940 St-Bonnet-le-Château, t 04 77 50 52 48, *www.cc-pays-st-bonnet-le-chateau.fr*.

Le Puy-en-Velay: Place du Breuil, 43000 Le Puy-en-Velay, t 04 71 09 38 41, *www.ot-lepuy envelay.fr*.

Le Monastier-sur-Gazeille: 32 Rue St-Pierre, t 04 71 08 37 76, e *oti.paysdumezenc@wanadoo.fr*.

Ste-Eulalie: Le Village, 07510 Ste-Eulalie, t 04 75 38 89 78.

Market Days

Charlieu: Wed and Sat mornings.
Roanne: Tues, Wed, Fri, Sat and Sun mornings.
Ambierle: Thurs morning.
Montbrison: Sat morning.
Feurs: Tues and Fri mornings.
Montrond-les-Bains: Thurs morning.
St-Galmier: Mon morning, Fri afternoon.
Chazelles-sur-Lyon: Tues and Fri mornings.
St-Just-St-Rambert: Thurs, Sat and Sun mornings.
St-Etienne: Every morning.
St-Bonnet-le-Château: Fri morning.
Le Puy-en-Velay: Sat morning.
Le Monastier-sur-Gazeille: Tues morning.

Where to Stay and Eat

Charlieu ✉ 42190

**Relais de l'Abbaye, t 04 77 60 00 88, *www.hotel-relaisdelabbaye-charlieu.fr* (*inexpensive*). Close to the centre. Dull modern architecture, but classy welcome, big comfortable rooms and good restaurant (*moderate*) with terrace. *Closed Jan and end Aug; restaurant closed Sun eve and Mon lunch.*

Pouilly-sous-Charlieu ✉ 42720

La Loire, Rue de la Berge, t 04 77 60 81 36 (*expensive–moderate*). By a bridge over the river, with a charming conservatory. Refined

The modern Centre des Visiteurs presents a good overview of monastic daily life and the various orders established in town. Via the centre, visit the cloister, the chapter house and the priors' chapel, plus a small surviving section of the 11th-century church, with its own tympanum of the Apocalpyse, and an enchanting carving of the sun and the moon, the latter represented childlike, covering its eyes with its hands.

cuisine. *Closed Sun eve, Mon, and Tues lunch, plus certain school hols.*

Noailly ✉ 42640

Château de la Motte B&B, t 04 77 66 64 60, *www.chateaudelamotte.fr.st (moderate).* Near La Bénisson Dieu, cheerful little white castle with six stylish rooms overlooking the park. *Table d'hôte (moderate).* Pool.

Roanne ✉ 42300

★★★★**Troisgros**, Place de la Gare, t 04 77 71 66 97, *www.troisgros.fr (luxury–very expensive).* France's most famous railway station restaurant, serving up the most refined food in the country, plus sleek luxury contemporary bedrooms. *Closed early Aug and Feb school hols; restaurant closed Tues and Wed.* **Le Central**, t 04 77 67 72 72 *(moderate).* The neighbouring, far cheaper Troisgros bistrot option. *Closed Sun and Mon, and Aug.*

Commelle-Vernay ✉ 42120

Château de Chassignol B&B, t 04 77 23 06 57, *www.chateau-chassignol.com (inexpensive).* Simple rooms in rustic country house southeast of Roanne, with square tower. Pool.

St-Maurice-sur-Loire ✉ 42155

L'Echauguette B&B, Rue Guy de la Mure, t 04 77 63 15 89, e *dm.alex@wanadoo.fr (inexpensive).* Run by an enchanting couple, very tasteful village rooms by the gorges.

Ambierle ✉ 42820

Le Prieuré, t 04 77 65 63 24 *(expensive–moderate).* Tempting, stylish central restaurant. *Closed Wed, and late Sept.*

St-Haon-le-Châtel ✉ 42370

Au Natur'elles, t 04 77 62 12 01 *(moderate–cheap).* Lovely central typical simple village inn. *Closed summer Mon, and Tues lunch, winter Mon and Wed, and all of Feb.*

Montrond-les-Bains ✉ 42210

★★★**Hostellerie La Poularde**, t 04 77 54 40 06, *www.la-poularde.com (moderate).* Splendid, artistic restaurant *(very expensive–expensive)* run by Gilles Etéocle at the main crossroads. The stylish suites are well soundproofed. Snazzy contemporary rooms overlook the small pool. *Closed most Jan and mid-Aug; restaurant closed Mon, and Tues lunch.*

St-Galmier ✉ 42330

★★★**La Charpinière**, t 04 77 52 75 00, *www.lacharpiniere.com (moderate).* In lovely shaded grounds below town, a pleasing manor with some air-conditioned rooms, plus **Closerie de la Tour** restaurant *(moderate).* Pool, tennis court and sauna.
★★**Le Forez**, 6 Rue Didier Guetton, t 04 77 54 00 23, *www.leforez.fr (inexpensive).* Spruced up, set around its courtyard. Bright restaurant *(moderate)* serving reliable local cuisine, plus bison and ostrich. *Closed parts Aug; restaurant closed Sun eve and Mon lunch.*

Jeansagnière ✉ 42920

Parc de la Droséra Chalets & Restaurant, t 04 77 24 81 44, *www.parc-de-la-drosera.fr (moderate).* The ten chalets are in fact *gîtes*, normally rented by the week, although weekends are possible. The modern restaurant *(moderate)* serves refined local cuisine. *Restaurant closed eves, and mid-Nov–Feb.*

Chalmazel ✉ 42920

Château de Chalmazel B&B, t 04 77 24 88 09, *www.chateaudechalmazel.com (expensive).* Splendid rooms in historic styles, with modern comforts. *Table d'hôte (moderate).* **Hôtellerie du Béal**, t 04 77 24 86 08 *(moderate).* Pleasing traditional family restaurant .

St-Georges-en-Couzan ✉ 42990

Ferme-Auberge Le Mazet, t 04 77 24 80 95. Substantial stone farm with six rooms.

In Charlieu centre, fine stone and timber-frame buildings have been turned into tempting shops, such as *chocolatier* **Pralus** in the ornate *Maison des Anglais*, English headquarters during the Hundred Years War. On Charlieu's main square, the 13th-century **church of St-Philibert**, its attractive tympanums heavily restored, survived the

Also serves fine farm fare. *Closed Dec and Jan; restaurant closed Sun.*

Auberge La Sarrazine, t 04 77 24 53 59 (*cheap*). Hidden below the castle ruins, farm turned atmospheric restaurant, with terrace and darkly brooding dining room to accompany local *charcuterie. Open daily July–Aug, otherwise weekends April, June and Sept.*

St-Bonnet-le-Courreau ✉ 42940

Jasseries Garnier, t 04 77 76 83 86 (*moderate*). Favourite for Monts du Forez walkers. Lovely local dishes served in traditional farm setting on the heights. *Book. Open July–Aug daily, Feb–June and Sept–Nov weekends.*

St-Bonnet-le-Château ✉ 42380

Le Béfranc, 7 Route d'Augel, **t 04 77 50 54 54, *www.hotel-lebefranc.com* (*inexpensive*). Sober rooms in former *gendarmerie*. Nice dining room (*moderate*). *Closed most Jan.*

La Calèche, 2 Place Marey, **t** 04 77 50 15 58 (*moderate*). Inventive cuisine in typical old central town house. *Closed Sun eve, Tues eve and Wed, and school half-terms.*

St-André-de-Chalencon ✉ 43130

Relais des Seigneurs, Place de l'Eglise, **t 04 71 58 41 41 (*inexpensive*). Caringly renovated little hotel by the church. *Only open mid-July–mid-Sept.*

St-Just-St-Rambert ✉ 42170

Le Neuvième Art, Place du 19 Mars 1962, **t** 04 77 55 87 15 (*expensive*). Fabulous new restaurant opened in the former railway station, where Christophe Roure cooks up a storm. Divinely presented, delicious cuisine.

Le Puy-en-Velay ✉ 43000

***Régina, 34 Bd Maréchal Fayolle, **t** 04 71 09 14 71, *www.hotelrestregina. com* (*inexpensive*). Superb value for modernized rooms on the boulevards, with delicious menus (*moderate*).

Tournayre, 12 Rue Chenebouterie, **t** 04 71 09 58 94 (*expensive–moderate*). Swish restaurant with vaulted dining room for Auvergnat specialities. *Closed Sun eve, Mon, Wed eve, plus Jan and early Sept.*

Le Bateau Ivre, 5 Rue Portail d'Avignon, **t** 04 71 09 67 20 (*moderate*). Cosy restaurant also devoted to Auvergnat traditions. *Closed Sun and Mon, 1 week June, 10 days Nov.*

Chaspinhac ✉ 43700

La Paravent B&B, t 04 71 03 54 75, **e** *micheljourde@wanadoo.fr* (*inexpensive*). Pleasant, spacious, simple rooms. Run by a woman who loves her area. *Table d'hôte* (*cheap*).

Arlempdes ✉ 43490

*Hôtel du Manoir, t 04 71 57 17 14 (*inexpensive*). Appealing old stone hotel below the castle, restaurant (*moderate*) with fine view. *Closed Nov–early Mar.*

Ste-Eulalie ✉ 07510

**Hôtel du Nord, t 04 75 38 80 09, *www. ardeche.tourisme.com/hotel/du-nord* (*inexpensive*). Modern, but in the local style, run by a fisherman; organizes outings. Country cooking (*moderate*). *Closed mid-Nov–late-Feb; restaurant closed Tues pm and Wed.*

Usclades-et-Rieutord ✉ 07510

Ferme de la Besse, t 04 75 38 80 64 (*moderate*). Utterly splendid typical dining room in a farm owned by the same family for five centuries. Feast of traditional cuisine. *Booking essential. Closed Dec–early April.*

Condas/St-Martial ✉ 07310

Le Hameau Gourmand B&B, t 04 75 29 28 44, **e** *condas@free.fr* (*inexpensive*). Lovingly restored by the Quinons, Madame uses local plants for her *table d'hôte* (*moderate*), and even organizes stays on the plant theme.

Revolution better than the priory. It contains remarkable decorations, notably late-Gothic stalls depicting banner-carrying, beautifully robed saints.

The town has a long history of weaving. In the 1820s, silk-making was established here as the workers in Lyon were kicking up a fuss – the story is recalled at the **Musée de la Soierie** (**t** *04 77 60 28 84; open July–Aug daily 10–1 and 2–7; Feb–June and Sept–Dec*

Tues–Sun 2–6; adm), housed in an 18th-century hospital. *Haute couture* dresses made in town include an Yves St-Laurent leopard-print silk number for Catherine Deneuve. Small pieces of silk are also sold. The **Musée Hospitalier** (*same details*) presents a somewhat sanitized version of hospital history, rooms scented with medicinal herbs.

On Charlieu's western outskirts, visit the 14th-century **Couvent des Cordeliers** (*t 04 77 60 07 42; open July–Aug daily 10–1 and 2–7, April–June and Sept–Oct Tues–Sun 10–12.30 and 2–6, Feb–March and Nov–Dec Tues–Sun 2–5; adm*). The church is typically Franciscan, big and plain, but decorated with worn fragments of Gothic paintings, while one side of the cloisters is enlivened by comical cautionary-tale stone carvings.

The Loire through the Roannais

An old barge rests out of the water at **Briennon**, a port on the canal built parallel to the Loire in the 1830s, linking Roanne and Digoin (in Burgundy). The canal's working days, when Briennon was surrounded by tile-making factories, are over, but you can take a tour round **Dhus barge's interiors** (*t 04 77 60 75 79; open June–Aug daily 10–12 and 1.30–7, April–May and Sept–Oct 1.30–7; adm*), which are sweet. The canal is now dedicated to **pleasure boats** – book a mini-cruise or hire a boat at **Marins d'Eau Douce** (*t 04 77 69 92 92*), which also sells local produce and has a minor exhibition of local tiles and pottery. Or play with **model boats** in the inventive **Parc des Canaux** (*same details as for barge*), a water garden by the barge. The church stands well back, but its steeple stands out, brightened by Burgundian-style varnished tiles.

The **Cistercian church** at **La Bénisson Dieu** (*t 04 77 66 64 65; open Easter–11 Nov daily 3–7; adm*) looks, at first, like a vast vulgar Burgundian *pâtisserie* topped by bright tiles, overlooked by a tower with arrow slits. Inside, the worn medieval frescoes include an image of a black Christ with yellow hair. Baroque murals adorn a later chapel.

Formerly a textile town, working-class Loire-side Roanne's trump card is Troisgros, one of France's most famous restaurants (*see p.111*). For the town's history, visit the **Musée des Beaux-Arts Déchelette** (*t 04 77 23 68 77; open Jan–Dec daily exc Tues, and Sun am, 10–12 and 2–6; adm*), in an *Ancien Régime* mansion. Its finest collections are of Gallo-Roman finds and revolutionary pottery, the plates declaring their politics.

South, in the **Roannais gorges**, hire boats at the little ports around a 30km-long lake created by the **Barrage de Villerest**, completed in 1982. Engineering enthusiasts visit the dam; the more frivolous play in pedalos. Along the west bank, **St-Jean-St-Maurice-sur-Loire** seems ready to go for a swim in the water. It has a new port, but has retained a few picturesque medieval fortifications. The medieval pilgrim on the church exterior indicates that this lay on a pilgrimage route. Inside, the Roman martyr Maurice is shown run through with a sword. The statue of St Nicholas recalls that he was patron saint of the Loire mariners. **Bully** has another pleasure port, while **Le Pêt d'Ane**, a calm meander near **Dancé** is a particularly picturesque spot . A Romanesque church stands proudly above the vegetable plots in rustic **Pommiers**, part of a walled priory, some of whose defences survive. The church was built in colourful stone, while the dark interior conceals charming Gothic wall paintings of Christ's life.

Following the Loire's east bank from Roanne, the road hugs the river to the spectacular neo-Gothic **Château de la Roche** (*t 04 77 64 97 68; open July–Aug daily*

10.30–12 and 2–7, March–June and Sept–Oct daily exc Wed 2–7, most Nov daily exc Mon and Wed 2–6; adm), which stands in the midst of the waters, accessible by a low walkway. The interior includes exhibitions on Loire river trading and the Villerest dam. The gentle hills to the east, known as the **Montagnes du Matin**, separate this stretch of the Loire from the Beaujolais' hills. Entering the **Château de St-Marcel-de-Félines** (*t 04 77 63 23 08; open July–Aug Sun and Mon 2–6, Easter–June and Sept–Oct Sun and public hols 2–6; adm*), not just lions, but sphinxes greet you in the eccentric little courtyard. Dating back to early medieval times, the castle had its heyday in the *Ancien Régime*, when the Talaru family from Chalmazel lived here. In the delightful salons, charming wood panelling features Italianate landscapes, natures mortes (including a still life with hamster!) and bouquets; a menacing Joan of Arc looks ready to stab any passing Englishman. For views, head to the wood-porched **chapel of Notre-Dame** above the village of **Néronde**, or east beyond Violay for the **Tour de Matagrin**.

Local craft traditions are recalled at **Bussières** with its modern **Musée du Tissage** (*t 04 77 27 33 95; open July–Aug daily 3–6, Mar–June and Sept–Oct Wed–Sun 3–6; adm*), featuring textiles and at **Panissières** with a new **Musée de la Cravate** (*t 04 77 28 77 86; open 1st Sun in month 2.30–6; adm*). You can also visit a tie-maker here. The blushing remains of Benedictine priory buildings at **Pouilly-lès-Feurs** are made of the local pink-tinged granite.

The Monts de la Madeleine and Côte Roannaise

As an alternative to following the Loire, west of Briennon, head for the **Monts de la Madeleine**, along delightful hillside roads that take you through fortified villages, now hardly menacing, but like mellowed old warriors reminiscing about glories past.

Above **La Pacaudière**, church and medieval watchtower keep company on **Le Crozet**'s hilltop. The compact, historic village below retains its old gateways and fine old houses made of Charlieu stone. One contains a **local history museum** (*t 04 77 64 31 57*). The east-facing **Côte Roannaise vineyards** start from **Changy** below Le Crozet, their 160-hectare line stretching along the lower slopes of the Monts de la Madeleine to **St-Jean-St-Maurice**. Round here, Gamay goes by the pseudonym St-Romain and produces fresh *appellation d'origine contrôlée* reds and rosés in Beaujolais style.

Vines climb the slopes to proud **Ambierle**, with its brightly roofed **Gothic church**, its entrance carved with twisting vines. Built in the 15th century, it was the centre of a Benedictine priory dating back to the end of the Dark Ages. Inside, the local nobility displayed their vanity – heraldry decorates the column capitals and ceiling bosses and, below the lovely stained glass in the choir, a fine 15th-century Flemish altarpiece shows magnificent donors. The tomb of Monseigneur Jean-Marie Odin, from Ambierle, first bishop of Galveston, Texas, in 1840, then bishop of New Orleans, is also here. For traditional crafts, walk to the **Musée Alice Taverne** (*t 04 77 65 60 99; open Feb– Nov daily 10–12 and 2–6; adm*) – peasant remedies include cow pats for burns, and for sore eyes, alum mixed with the white of an egg laid on a Thursday and washed with urine!

Seventeen towers once protected **St-Haon-le-Châtel**. Seek out their remains along the picturesquely run-down ramparts. The **church**, a solid 12th-century edifice, has recently restored murals. Below, seek out the secretive **Jardin du Moyen-Age** garden.

The Loire Valley across the Forez

A couple of extraordinary volcanic hillocks emerge from the flat **Forez plain** along this stretch of the Loire, both summits occupied by monks from the early Middle Ages. However, the most fascinating edifice is the Renaissance Château de La Bastie d'Urfé below. Although these sights leave Montbrison (capital of the counts of Forez, and, until St-Etienne muscled in in the mid-19th century, also capital of the *département de la Loire*) in the shade, it is quietly charming.

The **Monts du Forez** separate the Rhône-Alpes from the Auvergne and, although you scarcely get a glimpse of the neighbouring Auvergnat lands from this side, the scenery is captivating. The cows produce milk for *Fourme de Montbrison* blue cheese. Walkers head for the *jasseries*, mainly abandoned summer farms on the bare heights. In snow, skiers take on the single piste off the highpoint of the Monts du Forez, Pierre-sur-Haute, landing up near Chalmazel, typical of the unspoilt local villages with their red-tiled roofs. This trail ends with a real cliff-hanger, St-Bonnet-le-Château.

Surprising Sights on the Edge of the Forez Plain

The early medieval d'Urfé lords lived high in the Forez mountains, but in the 13th century acquired lands on the Loire plain and came down to settle at their manor of **La Bastie d'Urfé** (*t 04 77 97 54 68, www.ladiana.com; open July–Aug daily 10–12 and 1–6; April–June and Sept–Oct daily 10–12 and 2.30–6; Nov–Mar daily exc Tues 2–5; adm*). Claude d'Urfé (1501–1558) fought beside François I in the wars in Italy and represented him at the first round of the crucial Council of Trent in 1546, reinforcing the doctrine of the Catholic Church against Protestantism. He became French ambassador to the Vatican under François' successor, Henri II, before serving as tutor to the royal heir.

Enamoured with Italy, Claude rebuilt the family manor in the Renaissance style. Neglected after the Revolution, it has now been restored. A fashionable sphinx, symbol of wisdom, greets visitors to the clever perspectival Renaissance gallery. The sand-and-shell-plastered grotto is crammed with saucy delights, including a mischievous Pan lurking against one pillar – in the past, it wasn't just the fake stalagtites that shot out water! The chapel sent out a much more elevated Catholic message emphasizing the Holy Trinity and the Eucharist via a stunning decorative ensemble executed by accomplished artists. Further rooms are well furnished, hung with fine tapestries illustrating a literary masterpiece written by Claude's great-nephew Honoré d'Urfé (1567–1625), brought up at the castle (*see* p.23).

The jet-black fortified **priory of Montverdun** (*t 04 77 97 53 33, www.montverdun.com; open April–Oct Mon–Sat 2–6, Sun 3–7, rest of year Tues–Sat 2–6; adm*) atop one of the unmissable volcanic hillocks on the Forez plain is made of the local basalt rock. Inside the church stands a statue of St Porchaire – said to have had his eyes gouged out by marauding Saracens; hence the sinister-looking orbs he holds in his hands .

The **Côtes du Forez vineyards** are a mere 10 hectares larger than those of the Côte Roannaise, covering 170 in all; since the year 2000, the wines have won the same right to *appellation d'origine contrôlée* status. The mainly Gamay vineyards lie scattered on the slopes between Boën-sur-Lignon and Montbrison. **Boën-sur-Lignon**'s sober 18th-century château houses a **wine museum** (*t 04 77 24 08 12, www.boen-sur-lignon.fr.st; open mid-Jan–mid-Dec Tues–Sun 2.30–6.30; adm*). Seek out the **Cave des Vignerons Foréziens** (*t 04 77 24 00 12, e vignerons.foreziens@wanadoo.fr; open daily exc Sun am 9–12 and 2–7*) in nearby Trelins, where a large amount of the wine is made and sold. Following the lower Forez slopes, look out for the crenellated ruins of the **Château Ste-Anne** by Marcilly. Nearby, the **Volerie du Forez** (*t 04 77 97 59 14; open mid-March– Oct; displays July–Aug daily at 3 and 4.30, otherwise Wed, weekends and public hols at 3; adm*) offers regular displays of falconry. **Champdieu**'s priory (*t 04 77 97 17 29; open mid- May–mid-Sept Mon–Fri 10–12 and 2–6; adm*) was fortified in the Hundred Years' War. The refectory holds some entertaining medieval murals. Nearby, the 17th-century **Château de Vaugirard** (*t 04 77 58 33 88; open June– Sept daily exc Fri and Sat 2–6; adm*) contains a couple of merry chambers illustrating later courtly life.

Capital of the medieval counts of Forez, **Montbrison** boasted their main castle and their main church. Guy IV, one of the most important in the lordly line, a man of culture as well as of war, commissioned the biggest Gothic church in the Forez, **Notre-Dame de l'Espérance**. Begun in 1224, due to wars and financial problems, it took 250 years to complete – without even enough money to pay for statues on the façade. The lofty interior holds the tomb of Guy IV, wearing the bonnet of a Sorbonne professor, a sign of his erudition. Given that the **Salle La Diana** (*t 04 77 96 01 10, www. ladiana.com; open Jan–Dec Wed and Sat 9–12 and 2–5; adm*) behind the church was constructed so hurriedly in 1296 to celebrate the marriage of his grandson, Count Jean I of Forez, to Alise de Viennois, it has survived quite well. But there wasn't time to employ noble materials. Making up for this, the count covered the hall's ceiling with heraldry, 1,700 squares repeating the aristocratic connections of the two families. A couple of rooms off it form the **Montbrison archaeological museum**. The **Musée d'Allard** (*t 04 77 96 39 15; open Jan–Dec daily exc Tues 2–6; adm*) presents minerals, carved stones, stuffed birds, and church fonts, plus the **Musée de la Poupée**, with some 600 dolls, including Gégé *poupées*, made in Montbrison until 1980. Almost nothing remains of the counts' castle, but smart historic houses line the main streets, while flowers deck out the sides of the central Vizézy stream. The Saturday market stretches a full mile.

Standing out on a volcanic rock south of town, **St-Romain-le-Puy**'s amazing **priory church** (*t 04 77 76 92 10; open June–Aug daily exc Tues 11–12 and 2–7, April–May and Sept–Oct daily exc Tues 2.30–4.30; adm*) has a magnetic effect. Close up, it looks crooked, not surprisingly as it dates back in part to the 10th century. On the blotched stone around the apse, a frieze of worn animals and symbols spells out a message to the initiated, that man's spiritual journey is a struggle given the burden of original sin. The interior is covered with frescoes. Certain murals represent saint Romain having his tongue cut off for preaching Christianity, then being imprisoned and murdered, his evil killer replacing his fat sword in its scabbard. Further murals include semi-vanished figures thought to represent the early Christian martyrs of Lyon, Saint Pothin and Saint Irénée (also known as Irenaeus). Intertwining capitals decorate the church, while the crypt contains memorable carvings, the peacock carrying a rainbow on its back a symbol of hope. The rare *viognier* white wine made here sells as Vin d'Aldebertus, after one of the most important figures in the priory's history.

The Loire from Feurs to St-Etienne

The name of the Forez plain derives from that of **Feurs**, main Gallo-Roman centre along this stretch of the Loire, recalled in fragments at the sleepy **Musée d'Archéologie** (*t 04 77 26 24 48; open daily exc Sat 2–6; adm*) just outside the pleasant grid-plan centre of this low-key town. The museum also focuses on local equine history, in particular the popular trotter races staged at Feurs. The largest ornithological reserve in the Rhône-Alpes hides out on the flats by the Loire. Rarely will you come across a more joyously presented wildlife centre than the **Ecopôle du Forez** (*t 04 77 41 46 60, www.frapna.org; open daily 2–6, or 7 Sun; adm*), a wooden ark on stilts set up in the late 1980s, when big new lakes were created in 400 hectares previously ravaged by gravel quarrying. Birds flock here and beavers have been introduced.

Once guarding a ford across the Loire for the counts of Forez, the ruined **Château de Montrond-les-Bains** (*t 04 77 94 50 31; open July–Aug daily exc Tues 10.30–12.30 and 1.30–7, April–June and Sept Wed–Sun 10–12.30 and 1.30–5.30; adm*) still casts its shadow over the riverside. Built in the 12th century, embellished in the 16th, largely destroyed at the Revolution, its restored remains contain a rather wooden **local history museum**. As the name indicates, Montrond-les-Bains has a thermal establishment. Set up to treat medical conditions, this **Station Thermale** (*t 04 77 94 64 74*) now welcomes tourists for pamperings, even if it looks a bit clinical.

St-Galmier hides its tourist light under a bushel, although it stands out so attractively on a hilltop handily close to St-Etienne's airport and produces internationally imbibed Badoit natural sparkling water. In medieval times, the counts of Forez had a castle built on the hilltop, two sets of ramparts added below. This well-defended 'Balcony on the Forez' became one of the family's favoured residences. A few vestiges of the ramparts remain, but the castle precinct has disappeared, except for the major Gothic church. The towering belfry was added in the 19th century, along with neo-Gothic decoration inside, notably startlingly bright stained glass, by the local Mauvernay workshops. But a couple of exceptionally refined Gothic Virgins also stand out. In the lanes descending steeply from here, admire the fine 15th- and 16th-century houses and the tiny chapel of **Notre-Dame des Pauvres**. The lower town honours Augustin Badoit, who began marketing the local waters so successfully in the mid-19th century, with a statue, although the Romans had, of course, already found them first. Visitors can pay to see the Badoit bottling factory, where one million bottles are filled a day (ask at the tourist office). St-Galmier also offers the waters of a big outdoor pool, regular horse races and gambling at its casino.

Up in the hills, the misleadingly named **Chazelles-sur-Lyon** has no connection with the metropolis the other side of the Beaujolais. It's the sleepiest kind of provincial French town, but with a lively **Musée du Chapeau** (*t 04 77 94 23 29, www.museedu chapeau.com; open July–Aug daily 2–6, rest of year daily exc Tues 2–6; adm*), on hats.

Back in the busier valley, the Loire splits **St-Just-St-Rambert** in two. As to its **Musée des Civilisations** (*t 04 77 52 03 11; open Jan–Dec daily exc Tues 2–6; adm*), it's divided into sections on local history, world cultures, and caricatures, the last producing the most laughs. The defensive old church is guarded by a fortified bell tower. The **Loire**

gorges twisting and turning west of St-Etienne provide high natural drama just out of sight of the sprawling city. This area has become a welcome retreat for the *Stéphanois*, as the building of the **Barrage de Grangent**, a hydroelectric dam from the 1960s, created another major Loire lake, the **Lac de Grangent**, with opportunities for swimming and water sports. Because of towering cliffs, you can't get close to the river along the west bank, but from the high villages of **Essalois** and **Chambles** you get sensational views, with a splendidly picturesque ruined castle on the **island of Grangent**. For the most breathtaking views, clamber round the distinctly crumbling remains of Essalois' castle, or climb the more solid tower at Chambles. Both look down towards the sweet waterside village of **St-Victor-sur-Loire**, its adorable marina tucked into an inlet, the Château de Grangent a tempting destination in the midst of the waters. South, the **Château de St-Paul-en-Cornillon** occupies another dramatic height, a couple of the chambers in this lordly nest open to visitors.

St-Etienne

St-Etienne is familiar to the British because of its periodically very successful football team and also because it has become a cheap-flight destination. But it's not an obvious tourist stop, even if, like Rome, it boasts of being built on seven hills. In fact, this city of 300,000 sprawls over far more hills, slag heaps adding to its confusing geography. History isn't St-Etienne's strong point either, but manufacturing has been. From the Middle Ages, the locals specialized in making arms. Coal mining took off too. Trade in weapons boomed so much that during the Revolution the town briefly changed name to Armeville. Activities diversified in the 19th century, the French associating St-Etienne with the joy of bicycle-making as well as put-upon miners. Its friendly people have experienced upheavals as these industries collapsed, but it has the retail giant Casino, prestigious educational establishments and lots of budding small businesses. It has also established itself as quite a centre of pioneering design, putting on an international *biennale* (next one 2006) covering innovation from fashion to architecture. And it plays host every two years to a Pierre Boulez festival (next one 2006 also), celebrating the world-famed challenging contemporary composer from the region.

More surprisingly, the town has been declared a *Ville d'Art et d'Histoire*, its main strength an array of major museums. The modest **Musée du Vieux St-Etienne** (*t 04 77 74 57 79, www.vieux-saint-etienne.com; open Jan–Dec Tues–Sat 2.30–6; adm*) isn't among the most ambitious, but stands in the small historic quarter, near **Place du Peuple**. Trendy bars and restaurants radiate out from the appealing little triangular intersection of **Place Neuve**. Keen church visitors could pay their respects at the **Grand'Eglise** on Place Boivin, dedicated to the town's patron, Stephen. The 15th-century façade appears to have melted like candle wax into intriguing, Gaudiesque forms. Head north into the central shopping streets, too tightly packed to be entirely comfortable. A few large squares allow you to breath more easily. **Place Jean Jaurès** forms the pleasing green hub of central St-Etienne. Although overseen by a dull town hall and greyer cathedral, cheerful restaurants and cafés congregate along its sides.

Head out of town for the main museums. The substantial **Musée de la Mine** (*t 04 77 43 83 23; open Jan–Dec daily exc Tues, guided tours weekdays 10.30 and 3.30, weekends*

2.15; adm) set in a disused mine just to the west looks dismal on the outside, but is in part run by enthusiastic former miners. To the south, the **Musée d'Art et d'Industrie** (*t 04 77 49 73 00; open Jan–Dec daily exc Tues 10–6; adm*) has moved into one of the most splendid buildings in town, and explains the city's craft traditions with panache. Broad, tree-lined Cours Fauriel makes a grand winding exit from town, the **Astronef Planétarium** (*t 04 77 33 43 01, check times on www.sideral.com; April–Oct Wed and weekends shows at 3.30 and 4.45, Oct–March Wed and weekends 2.15, 3.30 and 4.45; adm*) along the way. Out on the eastern ringroad, don't mistake the **Musée d'Art Moderne** (*t 04 77 79 52 52; open Jan–Dec daily exc Tues 10–6; adm*) for an enormous bathroom showroom. This is a serious, challenging gallery. Most aptly for this industrial city, Fernand Léger's industrialized figures stand out, the central woman in his *Trois Femmes* with hair curving like a sheet of black metal. There are further shocking images of women by the likes of Picasso, Dubuffet and Warhol. But one of the museum's most provocative collections is of Surrealists' favourite Victor Brauner, whose liberated subconscious couldn't keep phalluses out of the picture. West of St-Etienne, modern architecture triumphs in the satellite town of **Firminy**, claiming the largest array of buildings designed by the ground-breaking Le Corbusier.

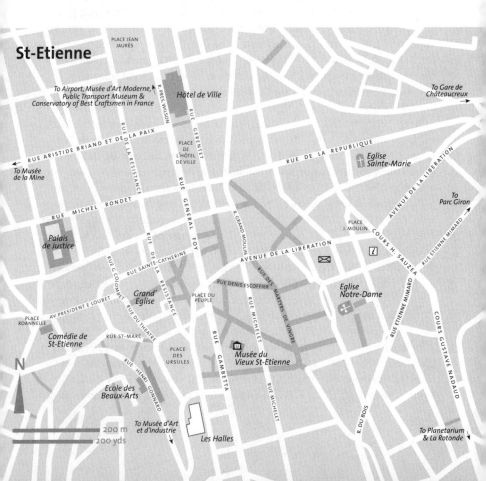

The Monts du Forez

The forested mountain roads leading south from the A72 motorway (Exit 4) are a delight looking down across the Loire's Forez plain. Above **Champoly**, walk to the remains of the medieval **Château d'Urfé** (*free*) for good views. Simple Gothic arches lead into the fortified hilltop village of **Cervières**, prettily run-down by time. A truncated **church** survives, a plump-cheeked peasant Mary standing inside. Opposite, the fine granite **Maison des Grenadières** (*t 04 77 24 98 71, www.grenadieres. com; open April–Oct daily exc Tues 2.30–6; Feb–March and Nov, weekends 2.30–6; adm*) attractively presents the local tradition of embroidering gold emblems for the French forces, megalomaniac leaders and top fashion houses. Beyond the scruffy but sporty valley town of **Noirétable**, seek Christian elevation at the high-perched convent of **Notre-Dame de l'Hermitage** (although the religious shop proves tacky). Around the **Col de la Loge**, you get spectacular glimpses of the Auvergne region. Sights across the *département* of the Loire, plus a few in neighbouring Auvergne, have been reproduced in scale models curiously placed among the clumps of heather at the **Parc de la Droséra** (*t 04 77 24 81 44, www.parc-de-la-drosera.fr; open daily March–mid-Nov 10–7; adm*). The imposing **Château de Talaru** (*t 04 77 24 88 09, ww.chateaude chalmazel. com; July–Aug daily 2–6, June and Sept weekends 2–6; adm*) stands guard at one end of the valley village of **Chalmazel**, which is at the bottom of a straight ski slope coming down from **Pierre sur Haute**, at 1,634m high, the highest point in the Forez range. It turns into one of the region's most endearingly rustic ski resorts on the rare occasions the snow sticks. The castle was built for the local Talaru lords, guardians in medieval times of the **Col de Béal**, the exposed, barren pass leading into the Auvergne.

Cheese pervades the air in the *fromage* capital of the Forez, the cheese-obsessed village of **Sauvain**, high on the Forez slope, with superb views across the Loire. The simple Gothic church is protected by a circle of old houses. Just beyond, visit the **craft cheese shops** and the **Maison Sauvagnarde** (*t 04 77 76 85 21; open July–Aug Tues–Sun 2.30–6.30, June and Sept Sun 2.30–6.30; adm*) dedicated to local traditions, cheese-making included. The **Maison de la Fourme** indicates cheese-making properties to visit nearby. Staring arrogantly out from an amazingly spectacular height to the east, the awesome, if ruined, ramparts of the hilltop **Forteresse de Couzan** (*t 04 77 96 01 10, www.ladiana.com; open mid-June–mid-Sept daily 2.30–6.30; adm*), built for the Damas family, bitter rivals of the counts of Forez, dominate the meeting of several wooded valleys. Follow the twisting high Forez road south through further attractive, peaceful hillside villages with views like **St-Bonnet-le-Courreau**, **Roche** and **Gumières**. Tiny hilltop **Montarcher** wins out for cuteness and panoramas, with the most exquisite views from its church, which seems to grow straight out of the rock.

Coming back down to earth, Estivareilles' **Musée d'Histoire du 20ème Siècle** (*t 04 77 50 29 20; open Jan–Dec daily 2–6; adm*) makes a valiant if overambitious attempt to cover recent European history but the **Ecomusée** at the more attractive if equally sleepy neighbouring village of **Usson-en-Forez** (*t 04 7750 67 97, www.usson-en-forez.fr;*

open Jan–Dec daily 2–6; adm) has more appeal, as it sticks to what it knows best, local life, traditions and legends.

Finish the high Forez trail with the high drama of **St-Bonnet-le-Château**. *Boules*-lovers from far and wide visit this historic hillside town, self-styled *Capitale Mondiale de la Boule*, no mean claim in a country where people adore this leisurely sport, some 10 million reckoned to practise it on a casual basis, half a million registered as regular practitioners. St-Bonnet-le-Château has gained pre-eminence in this sphere as home to one of France's major metallic boules makers, Obut, and its **Musée International Pétanque et Boules** (*t 04 77 50 15 33, e musee@petanque.com; open June–Sept Mon 1.30–6; Tues–Fri 8.30–12 and 1.30–6.30; Sat 10–12.30 and 2–6; Oct–May Mon 1.30–5.30; Tues–Fri 8.30–12 and 1.30–5.30; Sat 1.30–5; adm*). At this appealing centre, glean all sorts of information on the sport, from antiquity to the present day (passing via the major schism between *boules* and *pétanque*), from its stars to the abject, comical humiliation reserved for total losers, the kissing of Fanny's bottom, explained with gravitas. To avoid such public ignominy, there's no substitute for practice, and you can invest in fine *boules* and the true *boulomane's* accoutrements in the shop.

On a more elevated note, make for the **church** (*must book tour via tourist office to see mummies and murals; adm*) beyond the slightly jaded old squares and streets lined by tall mansions, signalling how this little merchants' town once prospered from its metal-working trade (hence the *boules*). The Gothic edifice stands aloof on its cliffside terrace, its main entrance reached by a bridge. The views at the back of the church are breath-taking. The interior offers a lesson in sober Gothic style at first sight. But the place has skeletons in the cupboard. On the guided tour you're taken down to a chamber whose walls are hung with scary brown mummies, not from antiquity, but thought to date from the end of the 17th century, when they died here of natural causes, their bodies buried in ground containing alum and arsenic, natural chemicals that preserved them in this leathery state, with horrifying grimaces. In heavenly contrast, the tour also takes you round to a lower chapel concealing one of the most uplifting arrays of frescoes in southeast France, probably commissioned for Anne, Duchess of Bourbon and Countess of Forez. In the Annunciation scene, the Virgin appears blonde, but turns brunette for the sumptuous arrival of the three kings. The musical angels on the ceiling play a whole array of medieval instruments although many of them wear pained expressions. After such a fantastic Forez finale, we rejoin the Loire valley below St-Etienne.

The Upper Loire from St-Etienne to its Source via Le Puy-en-Velay

Increasingly dark-stoned castles line the way up to the source of the Loire, reflecting these old volcanic territories. Le Puy-en-Velay has put the vestiges of its explosive geological past to stunning Christian use. The very early stages of the river cut through gorges lined by curious rock formations, as at elephantine Arlempdes, while the even more curious round lake of Issarlès is explained by its position in a volcanic crater. You reach the source of the Loire at the mighty pyramid of the Mont Gerbier-de-Jonc, outdone in majesty by neighbouring Mont Mézenc.

Pressing south via Aurec-sur-Loire, high above **Bas-en-Basset**, you can only reach the **Château de Rochebaron** by a steep hillside walk. **Retournac** down by the Loire has recently revived its lace-making traditions, and opened a **lace museum**. A detour west takes you past the sweet village of **St-André-de-Chalencon** to the exceptional hamlet of **Chalencon** with its adorable chequered church lost in its deeply wooded valley.

Continuing down the Loire, the darkly picturesque **Château de Lavoûte-Polignac** (*open July–Sept daily 10–12.30 and 2–6.30; June daily 2–5; May weekends and hols 2–5; Easter hols daily 2.30–5; adm*) stands guard over a meander in the river, one of the many impressive homes of the powerful Auvergnat Polignac family, one of the most hated aristocratic clans in France at the Revolution. Abandoned during that period, the castle was restored in the late 19th century. It now looks sorry for itself inside, though the guided tour can offer an absorbing insight into the family. In an even more ruined state, but an even more dramatic location atop a volcanic platform, the same family's medieval **Château de Polignac** (*open June–Sept daily 10–7; Easter– May and Oct pm only; adm*) still commands respect. This tremendous medieval stage-set was the family base until they moved to Lavoûte in the 18th century. From here, look down on the cathedral city of Le Puy-en-Velay, set in its natural basin surrounded by conical volcanic mountains. West, the well-preserved **Château de St-Vidal** (*open July–Aug daily 2–6.30; adm*) looks a bit like a children's picture-book image of a medieval fort with its square shape and round corner towers, all built in forbidding black rock.

Le Puy-en-Velay

Thin pinnacles of volcanic rock make the skyline of Le Puy-en-Velay unforgettable and, from distant times, inspired religious veneration. A rock known as the Feverish Stone, possibly part of an earlier Neolithic dolmen, became a significant place of worship in Gallo-Roman times. With the coming of Christianity, Le Puy early embraced the cult of the Virgin Mary, the first church to her probably built in the 5th century.

A huge statue of the Virgin, and another of St Joseph, both 19th-century, stand high on two pinnacles. On another rises one of the most eccentric churches in France, perhaps built for Bishop Gothescalk. Tradition has it that he set out in 950 on the first major pilgrimage from Le Puy to Santiago de Compostela in northern Spain. During the Middle Ages, the place developed into one of the four most important meeting points in France for this popular spiritual journey. The craft of lace-making, probably established in the 15th century, became a second source of renown. Large numbers of women were still employed producing hand-made *dentelle* until World War I.

One of the most memorable streets in France, steep, many-stepped **Rue des Tables**, leads up to the **cathedral**. Its huge black porch gapes wide open, like the mouth of a biblical leviathan. The alternating stones and columns of the sheer wall above provide a virtuoso display of Romanesque decoration. Rising to the left of the cathedral façade stand the imposing **Hôtel Dieu**, or hospital, and a castle-like building surrounding the cathedral cloister. The whole complex looks like a well-defended holy citadel. Enter the cathedral via its massive porch, the size of a decent church, and a piece of extraordinarily bold architecture, an extension built out from the hilltop. Pilgrims in centuries past would have climbed up to pop straight out of the floor in the centre of the nave; you now go up via side stairs. The cathedral interior was restored with a heavy hand in the 19th and 20th centuries. Devout pilgrims still venerate the curious Black Virgin. The original was said to have been brought back from the Orient by a medieval French king – it's now thought she may have been a representation of the ancient Egyptian goddess Isis. But the original was destroyed at the Revolution. The copy shows Jesus popping his head out of his mother's clothing like a baby kangaroo. The sacristy houses a mixed bag of further religious curiosities.

A labyrinth of religious buildings surrounds the cathedral. The **Chapelle du St-Sacrement** once served as the library of the cathedral school, one wall decorated in the 16th century with marvellous depictions of the liberal arts as enthroned women in period attire. The overrestored **cloisters** (*open July–Aug 9–6.30; mid-May–June and most Sept 9–12 and 2–6.30; rest of year 9–12 and 2–5; adm*) and the rooms around it house an important museum of religious art. The most striking elements include the medieval wall paintings in the chapterhouse and a 16th-century embroidered coat made for the Black Virgin, featuring a splendid Tree of Jesse depicting Christ's lineage.

Gather your energies to walk up to the enormous sickly pink **Notre-Dame de France** (*open mid-March–Sept 9–7; rest of year 10–5; adm*) stuck on top of the nearby **Rocher Corneille** in the 19th century. So striking from a distance, this Virgin turns out to be a bit of a monstrosity close up. Designed by Jean-Marie Bonnassieux, she measures over 50ft in height and weighs in at over one hundred tons. You can actually climb up inside her long graffiti-covered innards to get a head-spinning view of the city.

Back down at **Place des Tables**, take Rue Raphaël for the **Centre d'Enseignement de la Dentelle au Fuseau** (*open mid-June–mid-Sept weekdays 9–12 and 1.30–5.30, Sat 9.30–4.30; rest of year weekdays 10–12 and 2–5; adm*). This presents a video on lace-making in Le Puy-en-Velay, and small exhibitions. Adjoining **Place du Clauzel** and **Place du Martouret** form the heart of the old secular town. The neoclassical **Hôtel de Ville** was completed in 1766, in time to witness the guillotining of over 40 people, including 18 priests, and the burning in 1794 of the original Black Virgin. The other side of the town hall, imposing **Rue Pannessac** curves from Place du Plot to the stocky gateway of the **Tour Pannessac**, a remnant of medieval defences.

A grandiose area developed on the flat to the south in the 19th century, stretching from **Place du Breuil** via the shaded *boules*-players' **Vinay Gardens** to the substantial **Musée Crozatier** (*open mid-June–mid-Sept daily 10–12 and 2–6; May–mid-June and late Sept daily exc Tues 10–12 and 2–6; rest of year daily exc Sun am and Tues 10–12 and 2–4; adm*), the place crammed with a confusion of artefacts, regional arts and lace well represented. To the west, the **church of St-Laurent** stands close to the Borne river. St Dominic, founder in Toulouse of the Inquisition, came to visit in the 13th century and a Dominican monastery was set up. In the Hundred Years' War, the fearsome French leader Bertrand du Guesclin died besieging Châteauneuf-de-Randon not far south, explaining why his entrails ended up here, along with his tomb effigy.

Isolated high above another atmospheric corner of town, two hundred and sixty steps lead up another staggering pinnacle to the crooked little **Chapelle St-Michel**

d'Aiguilhe (*open May–Sept 9–6.30; mid March April and Oct–mid-Nov 9.30–12 and 2–5.30; Feb–mid-March, plus Christmas hols 2–7; adm*). Before the climb, consider saying a quick prayer at the simple **Oratoire St-Grégoire** below and visiting the Espace St-Michel, which briefly explains the geology of the area as well as the cult of St Michael. The story goes that Bishop Gothescalk had the extraordinary chapel built in the bellicose archangel's honour on his return from his pilgrimage to Santiago; the architecture certainly appears to contain Spanish to Moorish touches. In the fabulous cave-like interior, nooks and crannies display intriguing religious items. If captivated by the pinnacles of Le Puy, head out to **Espaly** to acquaint yourself with the enormous **Joseph** (*open July–Aug 2–7; adm*), surrounded by more sickly 19th-century religious confections. As with Notre-Dame de France, you can climb up inside.

The Last Leg of the Loire to its Source

A string of more or less ruined medieval forts marks the banks of the Loire south from Le Puy. Head a little east to marvel at the dark purples, blacks and oranges of **Le Monastier-sur-Gazeille**'s exceptional church, a remnant of the most important abbey in the Velay in medieval times. The stocky castle behind is less colourful, but with its black volcanic sides and its crinkled red-tiled roofs has plenty of character too, although the **Musée Municipal** (*open July–Aug Tues–Sun 10.30–12 and 2–6, June and Sept–Oct Tues–Sun 2–5; adm*) is just a modest affair. It cursorily recalls that Robert Louis Stevenson stayed for a month here in 1878, observing the villagers' antics before heading off on his travels with a donkey through the Cévennes.

Back by the Loire, you hit upon dark gorges before **Arlempdes**, a village standing in a wonderfully dramatic location, the remnants of its fort clinging to the back of a monster of a rock. Here, the Loire makes an important turn. The almost perfectly round **Lac d'Issarlès** is a natural wonder created by water collecting in an old volcanic crater, although tourism has now made its mark, and visitors fight for space on the thin pebble beach in high summer. Up towards the beginnings of Loire, *sucs*, huge majestic round-topped volcanic mountains, seem to protect the source of the great river. The landscapes look ancient – it would barely be a big surprise to see a dinosaur or two wandering around. The villages can look grey and exposed, and spring comes late, although green and orange lichens add blotches of colour, while *ski de fond* signs indicate that people enjoy Nordic skiing here in winter. To appreciate traditional life, visit the welcoming, atmospheric farms at **Ste-Eulalie** –ask at the tourist office.

Mont Gerbier de Jonc, birthplace of the Loire, a near deity of a river to this day, looks almost man-made, seemingly built up of a great mound of boulders, snow-covered or stained with green lichens. The first waters of the Loire dribble rather inconspicuously down the side of the pyramid. Perhaps pass via the very battered but quite beautiful ruins of the **Chartreuse de Bonnefoy**, or cast an eye on the shimmering stone roofs of **Borée**, or then freshen up on warm days at the pretty **Lac de St-Martial** before scaling Mont Gerbier de Jonc's still more impressive brother, the **Mont Mézenc**, at 1,754m offering timeless views all round. These two brooding mountains form part of France's surprisingly easterly *division des eaux*, the line separating the river waters flowing to the Atlantic from those heading for the Mediterranean.

West of the Rhône
Down the Ardèche

Mont Pilat and the Northern Ardèche 131
Mont Pilat **131**
Northern Ardèche **132**
River Valleys to Privas and Vals-les-Bains **134**
Southern Ardèche 136
The Upper Ardèche River and the Southwest **136**
Vals-les-Bains and Aubenas **136**
Up to the Source of the Ardèche **140**
Savage Southwest Ardèche **141**
From Aubenas to Les Vans **142**
The Middle and Southern *Gorges de l'Ardèche* **143**
The Middle Ardèche River from Vogüé to
    Vallon-Pont-d'Arc 143
The Southern Ardèche River Gorges and Caves **146**

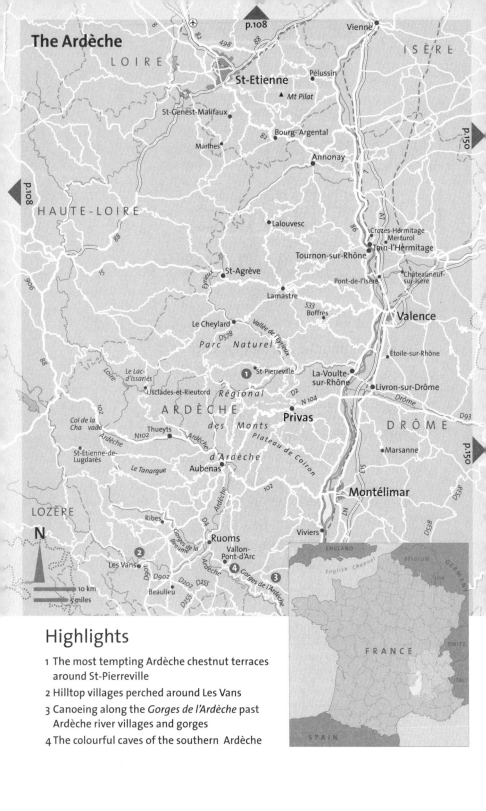

The Ardèche

p.108
p.150
p.108
p.150

LOIRE

ISÈRE

Vienne

St-Etienne

Pélussin

▲ Mt Pilat

St-Genest-Malifaux

Marlhes

Bourg-Argental

Annonay

HAUTE-LOIRE

Lalouvesc

Crozes-Hermitage
Mercurol
Tain-l'Hermitage

Tournon-sur-Rhône

St-Agrève

Pont-de-l'Isère

Châteauneuf-
sur-Isère

Lamastre

Boffres

Valence

Le Cheylard

Vallée de l'Eyrieux

Parc Naturel

St-Pierreville

La-Voulte-
sur-Rhône

Le Lac-
d'Issarlès

Étoile-sur-Rhône

Usclades-et-Rieutord

Régional

Privas

Livron-sur-Drôme

ARDÈCHE

des Monts

Plateau de Coiron

DRÔME

Col de la
Chavade

Thueyts

St-Étienne-
de-Lugdarès

d'Ardèche

Marsanne

Le Tanargue

Aubenas

LOZÈRE

Ribes

Viviers

Montélimar

N

Ruoms

Les Vans

Gorges de la Beaume

Vallon-
Pont-d'Arc

Gorges de l'Ardèche

Beaulieu

10 km

5 miles

Highlights

1 The most tempting Ardèche chestnut terraces
   around St-Pierreville
2 Hilltop villages perched around Les Vans
3 Canoeing along the *Gorges de l'Ardèche* past
   Ardèche river villages and gorges
4 The colourful caves of the southern Ardèche

ENGLAND
BELGIUM
GERMANY
English Channel
LUX
FRANCE
SWITZ
ITALY
SPAIN

There's scarcely a single straight road in the tortuous *département de l'Ardèche* once you've left the west bank of the Rhône (*see* chaper 12), and scarcely a road that isn't beautiful. Although a testing drive, almost all the winding ways through the densely wooded valleys and gorges crossed by old stone bridges prove a delight for passengers. This mountainous area (also known as the Vivarais, after its ancient southern town of Viviers, *see* p.167) dips dramatically down from the Massif Central. In the south, Vivarais and Cévennes mountains touch. Protestantism was quickly adopted from the 16th century in these poor regions sharing a history of religious persecution.

As to the rocks and old stone houses across the *département*, they tend towards the dark and moody because of the area's volcanic past. Rivers hurtle down from the old craters through twisting Ardéchois valleys – sensational, but hardly conducive to agriculture. Farmers down the centuries painstakingly built up layers of terracing on these difficult lands. Mainstay of the year were chestnuts, not to be turned into delicious *marrons glacés* as they are today, but into flour, for human and animal use alike – this wasn't the territory of wealthy men. The influence of Lyon's silk-makers radiated far and wide and silk farms and textile factories were established in the area, although these traditions have now died out, leaving derelict *filatures*, now being converted into silk museums and trendy hotels. Fruit flourishes in the more generous valleys towards the Rhône, and small-scale wine-making survived the 19th-century crises. In recent decades the quality of Ardéchois wines has been rising. (For information on the well-established northern Côtes du Rhône wines, *see* pp.158–9.)

The Rhône passing down one side of the *département* and the Loire beginning along the other, the Ardèche river itself cuts a jagged path across the southern half of the Vivarais. Its source lies close to that of the Loire, but while the latter sets off on its leisurely 1,000 km journey to the Atlantic, the Ardèche does a mere 100km sprint to reach the Rhône. Starting at breakneck speed, it slows down, its curious rock forma-tions lined with enchanting villages in a *département* packed with them. Beyond Vallon-Pont-d'Arc come the major Gorges de l'Ardèche, a head-spinning canyon beloved of canoeists, climbers and potholers. Amazing cool caves hide out around here. A sensational one only discovered in the mid-1990s conceals one of the world's greatest caches of prehistoric art. This Grotte Chauvet will never be opened to the public, but the building of its replica is under way.

So much for the heavily touristy parts of the *département*. But in the north, and out west, where large swathes come under the protection of the *Parc Naturel Régional des Monts d'Ardèche*, it remains largely unspoilt. Or rather, many of the centuries-old terraces were abandoned, its villages falling partly into ruin, although a large number of Brits as well as Belgians, and even northern European Protestants whose ancestors fled into exile from here, have been helping to restore the ruins. One restoration brought the unlikely pairing of dippy English journalist Nigel Farrell and his utterly sensible Sikh house-buying partner Nippi Singh to British attention on the Channel 4 programme *A Place in France*, following life in Ardèche through the seasons. This chapter also includes the surprise of the little Mont Pilat, squeezed between industrial sections of the Rhône and the Gier valleys, but an almost unbelievably rustic, unknown range connected to northern Ardèche.

Getting There and Around

By bus and train: For the Pilat, in the west, buses from St-Etienne (which has a major railway station) serve Le Bessat, St-Genest-Malifaux, Jonzieux, Marlhes and Bourg-Argental. East, Vienne has good rail services. Buses from Lyon to Annonay pass through a few parishes on the east side of the Pilat. For information on times, consult Maison du Parc below. For northern Ardèche, join a bus from the Rhône valley rail stations, such as Vienne, Tournon, or Valence. Autocars Charrière, **t** 04 75 64 10 19, has plenty of buses running to and from Privas weekdays, few at weekends and during holidays. A handful of Courriers Rhodaniens **t** 04 75 81 09 09 buses go weekdays from the Rhône to Annonay. St-Félicien, Boucieu-le-Roi and Lamastre can be reached by the odd bus from the Rhône.

Tourist Information

For general information on the **Parc Naturel Régional des Monts d'Ardèche**, *www.parc-monts-ardeche.fr*.

Pélussin: Maison du Parc du Mont Pilat, 42410 Pélussin, **t** 04 74 87 52 00, *www.parc-naturel-pilat.fr*.

St-Genest-Malifaux: 1 Rue du Feuillage, 42660 St-Genest-Malifaux, **t** 04 77 51 23 84, **e** *ot.haut-pilat@wanadoo.fr*.

Bourg-Argental: 18 Place de la Liberté, 42220 Bourg-Argental, **t** 04 77 39 63 49, **e** *otbourgargental@aol.com*.

Annonay: Place des Cordeliers, 07100 Annonay, **t** 04 75 33 24 51, *www.inforoutes-ardeche.fr/annotour*; also see *www.ardeche-verte.com*.

Lalouvesc: Rue St-Régis, 07520 Lalouvesc, **t** 04 76 67 84 20.

St-Félicien: Place de l'Hôtel de Ville, 07410 St-Félicien, **t/f** 04 75 06 06 12 .

Lamastre: Place Montgolfier, 07270 Lamastre, **t** 04 75 06 48 99, *www.valleedudoux.com*.

Désaignes: Porte du Bourg-de-l'Homme, 07570 Désaignes, **t** 04 75 06 61 19.

St-Agrève: Hôtel de Ville, 07320 St-Agrève, **t/f** 04 75 30 15 06.

Le Cheylard: Place de la Poste, 07160 Le Cheylard, **t** 04 75 29 18 71.

St-Pierreville: Place du Clos, 07190 St-Pierreville, **t** 04 75 66 64 64.

Privas: 3 Pl du Général de Gaulle, 07000 Privas, **t** 04 75 64 33 35, *www.paysdeprivas.com*.

Market Days

Pélussin: Sat morning.
St-Genest-Malifaux: Thurs and Sun mornings.
Bourg-Argental: Thurs and Sun mornings
Annonay: Wed and Sat mornings.
Lamastre: Tues and Sat mornings.
St-Agrève: Mon morning.
Le Cheylard: Wed morning.
Privas: Wed and Sat mornings.

Sports and Activities

The Pilat is much appreciated for high-energy sports. In winter, there is cross-country skiing around the highest crests, **Le Bessat** the main centre, while Graix boasts four little downhill pistes (*for info*, **t** 04 74 87 52 00 *or Allo Neige*, **t** 04 77 20 43 43); in summer the dare-devil can try mountainbiking or devalkarting (in go-karts without engines, **t** 04 77 20 43 43). The **Sentier Flore** from Le Bessat down to Malleval offers a more tranquil 22km hiking trail. The **Bureau des Guides et Moniteurs du Pilat** (**t** 06 76 04 61 05, **e** *guides.pilat@liberty-surf.fr*), an association of sports guides, is based at Rochetaillée. Paragliders set off from the Crêt de l'Œillon and other locations (**t** 04 74 87 52 00). There are also *accrobranche* treetop assault courses: consult *www.accrobranche.org*.

In northern Ardèche, for Annonay hot-air ballooning, try: **Ardèche Montgolfières**, **t** 04 75 69 39 39, *www.ardeche-montgolfieres.fr*; **Montgolfières d'Annonay**, **t** 04 75 67 57 56, *www.ima7.com/MA/index.html*; or **Annonay Concept**, **t** 04 75 33 22 11, **e** *ballons.chaise@wanadoo.fr*. The annual Annonay ballooning festival takes place early June. The Golf St-Clair lies outside Annonay. Mountain biking is big in this terrain; contact *http://perso.wanadoo.fr/cyclotourisme.ardeche*.

Where to Stay and Eat

Ste-Croix-en-Jarez ✉ 42800

★**Le Prieuré**, **t** 04 77 20 20 09, **f** 04 77 20 20 80 (*inexpensive*). Four simple rooms in the gateway. Rustic restaurant (*moderate*). *Closed Jan–mid-Feb; restaurant closed Mon.*

Colombier-sous-Pilat ✉ 42220
Auberge de Vernolon, t 04 77 51 56 58, e *aubergevernolon@wanadoo.fr* (*cheap*). Isolated high up, not far from the tallest Pilat crests, basic, good-value B&B rooms, with spacious barn where rustic country cooking is served. *Closed Mon–Fri outside July and Aug; booking essential.*

St-Genest-Malifaux ✉ 42660
Auberge de la Diligence Ferme-Auberge, Le Château du Bois, t 04 77 39 04 99 (*inexpensive*). Fortified pink-stone farm close to Mont Chaussitre attached to an agricultural school, with basic *gîte d'étape* group accommodation and restaurant using local produce (*moderate–cheap*). *Closed Mon–Thurs outside July and Aug, when open daily.*

St-Julien-Molin-Molette ✉ 42220
La Rivoire B&B, t 04 77 39 65 44, *www. larivoire.net* (*inexpensive*). Serious, solid farm with round tower above the N82 south of Bourg-Argental. Neat rooms. Fresh farm produce with the *table d'hôte* (*moderate*).

St-Bonnet-le-Froid ✉ 43290
****Auberge et Clos des Cimes**, t 04 71 59 93 72, e *contact@regismarcon.fr* (*very expensive*). Pinnacle of regional cuisine taken to the refined heights. Stylish contemporary rooms. *Closed mid-Dec–mid-March and Tues and Wed; restaurant closed Mon eve (out of season), Tues and Wed.*

Lamastre ✉ 07270
***Le Midi Barattéro-Perrier**, Place Seignobos, t 04 75 06 41 50, f 04 75 06 49 75 (*moderate*). Old-fashioned central hotel with comfortable rooms and splendid menus (*expensive*) in classic French provincial style. *Closed late-Dec–mid-Feb; restaurant closed Fri eve, Sun eve and Mon.*

St-Agrève ✉ 07320
***Domaine de Rilhac**, t 04 75 30 20 20, e *hotel_rilhac@yahoo.fr* (*moderate*). Old stone converted farm 2km south. Very tasty

cuisine (*expensive–moderate*). *Closed Jan–Feb; restaurant closed Tues eve, Wed, and Thurs lunch.*

Boffres ✉ 07440
Domaine de Reiller B&B, t 04 75 58 15 14, *www.reiller.com* (*inexpensive*). Traditional stone architecture set among chestnut woods, with a pool and pleasant views. *Table d'hôte* (*moderate*).

St-Pierreville ✉ 07190
****Hôtel des Voyageurs**, t 04 75 66 60 08 (*inexpensive*). Traditional option, with fishing expertise to hand. Restaurant. Pool. *Closed Dec–Feb.*

Antraigues-sur-Volane ✉ 07530
La Manufacture, t 04 75 38 77 35, *www.art-de-vie-lamanufacture.com* (*expensive; but moderate if 2 nights plus*). Exciting contemporary mill conversion with big, calm rooms. Spa and relaxation spaces, plus pool and court. Restaurant (*cheap barbecue, eve only*). **La Remise, Pont de l'Huile**, t 04 75 38 70 74 (*moderate*). Passionate chef serving fresh regional cuisine in a converted barn. *Closed Fri and Sun eve out of season, plus late June, early Sept and mid-Dec–early Jan.*

St-Julien-du-Serre ✉ 07200
Mas de Bourlenc B&B, t/f 04 75 37 69 95 (*inexpensive*). Lost in the hills a few km above Aubenas, with splendid views. *Table d'hôte* (*moderate*).

Privas ✉ 07000
***La Chaumette Portes des Suds**, Av du Vanel, t 04 75 64 30 66, *www.hotel chaumette.fr* (*moderate*). Modern, pretty rooms in the centre. Pool. Refined restaurant (*moderate*). *Restaurant closed Sat lunch.*

Rochessauve ✉ 07210
Château de Rochessauve B&B, t 04 75 65 07 06, *www.chateau-de-rochessauve.com* (*expensive*). Sensationally restored rustic property with charming courtyard. Antique-dealer owners also run courses on furniture care. Tasteful rooms, delightful garden, pool with view, plus hearty *table d'hôte* (*expensive*).

Mont Pilat and the Northern Ardèche

Mont Pilat

Short, precipitous routes lead into the Pilat heights from the Rhône or Gier and you're soon away from the industry below into a world of rustic high plateaux and forests stretching below rocky peaks. Although the Pilat's villages are now quiet, those in the valleys have an industrial past, recalled in a scattering of museums. The Mont Pilat was made into a regional nature park in 1974. Its name derives from a legend in which a Roman emperor called for the body of Pontius Pilate to be brought up the Rhône; it is said that, at Vienne, locals stole it and left it in the mountains to the west – their tops becoming barren, Pilate haunting the range. Several peaks have tortured piles of rocks known as *chirats*, but they date from the end of the last ice age.

The most extraordinary village in the Pilat, one of *Les Plus Beaux Villages de France*, **Ste-Croix-en-Jarez** is a former fortified monastery. Legend says that it was founded in the 1280s after a pious lady, Béatrix de Roussillon, had a vision of a silver cross pointing to the spot. For five centuries Carthusian monks prayed and worked here, developing the economy of the Pilat. The last were thrown out during the Revolution and the locals from nearby Pavezin converted the cells into unusual homes rather than removing the stone. The village is centred around the two monastic courtyards divided by a substantial church. The main church, dating from the 17th century, preserves its carved wood stalls and paintings of three imploring saints. You only see the earlier, medieval chapter house and sacristy on a guided tour, the latter with fine medieval murals. Attention turns to industry near the village of **La Terrasse-sur-Dorlay**, the **Maison des Tresses et Lacets** (*t 04 77 20 91 06; open Feb–Dec daily exc Tues and Sat 2.30–6, but open Sat in July and Aug; adm*) recalling how the local waters were used to power machines to make braid. The machinery swings into action on guided tours.

Pélussin stands in an airy, open location looking east. The **Maison du Parc** (*open Easter hols–11 Nov daily 9.30–12.30 and 2–6, rest of year weekdays exc Thurs am, plus Sat am, 10–12.30 and 2–6*) offers a helpful introduction to the regional nature park. The bases for Pilat skiing are **Le Bessat** and **Graix**. The Pélussin area is famous for the quality of it fruit, especially apples, and a delightful orchard-lined road heads for **Malleval** (*see* p.160). The village of **Lupé** has a restored medieval **château** and a pretty church.

Forests surround the highest peaks of the Pilat where, from the 18th century, pines were planted to provide wooden posts for the coalmines around St-Etienne. But there was pastureland up high too, and herds are now being reintroduced to stop the forest encroaching. **The Crêt de l'Œillon** reaches 1,362m, and boasts better views than the highest of the Pilat range, the **Crêt de la Perdrix**, at 1,432m. Both are topped by curious piles of *chirats*. West, the eagle's eyrie of **Rochetaillée** is made even more dramatic by its ruined castle and its church, and offers plunging views on the industrial Gier valley.

To enjoy the southwestern Pilat heights at their best, take the easy moorland walk to the cross on **Mont Chaussitre** affording spectacular views west onto the volcano tops of the Velay. South a bit, a duckboard path leads to the **Gimel peat bog**. Lovely, solid traditional farms mark the ways down west from Mont Chaussitre, a few selling local produce. At **Jonzieux**, the tradition of producing ornate trimmings for textiles is occasionally relived at the **Maison de la Passementerie** *(t 04 77 39 93 38; open May–mid-Oct Sundays 2.30–6.30; adm)*. **Marlhes** is marked out by Catholicism, its village church practically the size of a cathedral. Although the Ardèche to the south and the Velay to the west became Protestant, the Pilat remained strongly Catholic. The Marlhes edifice sends a forceful message from the Church. Traditionally, in these isolated parts, laywomen could take on pastoral roles for their communities. They were known as *béates* – the last retired in 1930. You can find out about them at the old-style **Maison de la Béate** *(t 04 77 51 24 70; open mid-July–Sept Sundays and public hols, 2.30–6.30)* in the hamlet of **Allier**. Head for **St-Régis du Coin** to visit one of the most interesting traditional Pilat country properties, **La Ferme des Champs**.

Down in the Deûme valley, **Bourg-Argental** has retained fragments of historic charm. Racy Romanesque carvings saved from an earlier structure enliven the doorway to the otherwise much later church, events in Jesus' childhood featuring below a surprisingly friendly Christ of the Apocalypse. The **Maison du Châtelet** *(t 04 77 39 63 49; open mid-June–late-Sept daily 9.30–12.30 and 2.30–6.30, May–mid-June Mon and Fri 2–6, Tues–Thurs 9–12, weekends 9–12 and 2–6, rest of year Mon and Fri 2–6, Tues–Thurs and Sat 9–12; adm)*, a sturdy 16th-century townhouse, has been turned both into a centre presenting the Parc du Pilat, and a local museum, with a heart-warming film on the textile-making tradition. The disused factories at **St-Julien-Molin-Molette** are a reminder that this village used to supply textiles and arms to St-Etienne. Now, craftspeople, notably woodworkers, have set up, while clever pieces of art are displayed out in the open, bringing a touch of invention to the slightly drab surroundings.

Northern Ardèche

Drunken-looking roads swerve down through the northern half of the *département de l'Ardèche*. We steer you along the routes to the most rewarding villages and towns, castle ruins and religious halts – although conflict between Protestantism and Catholicism was strong in these parts. Below St-Agrève, we cover the northern half of the *Parc Régional Naturel des Monts d'Ardèche.*.

Towns aren't exactly the *département de l'Ardèche's* strong point, and **Annonay**, the largest, a worn-out industrial centre encircled by mountains, is hardly an obvious tourist stop. But it is here that the local Montgolfier brothers *(see p.24)* escaped into the skies, by inventing the hot-air balloon. You can find out about them at the gritty black-stone **Musée Vivarois César Filhol** *(t 04 75 67 67 93, www.mairie-annonay.fr; open July–Aug daily, rest of year Wed and weekends 2.30–6; adm)*, which also has sections on local history and artists. The Montgolfiers aren't the only technical whizzkids from Annonay. Their great-nephew, the engineer Marc Seguin, designed the first French suspension bridges, put up over the Rhône, and in 1826, one of the earliest French railway lines, linking Lyon and St-Etienne. A statue of the Montgolfier brothers stands out on one square; Marc Seguin presides over another.

By the river in the suburb of **Davézieux**, at the birthplace of the Montgolfier brothers, the **Musée des Papeteries Canson & Montgolfier** (*t 04 75 69 88 00; open July–Aug daily, rest of year Wed and Sun 2.30–6; adm*) concentrates on paper-making, old machines creaking into action on the tour. **Peaugres safari park** (*t 04 75 33 00 32, www.safari-peaugres.com; open July–Aug daily 9.30–6, April–June daily 9.30–5, rest of year daily 10–4; adm*) nearby has two popular trails, one in your firmly sealed car, one on foot.

South from Annonay, you enter rural religious territory. St-Pierre-aux-Liens at **Quintenas** is a fortified church; southwest, pilgrims head for **Notre-Dame d'Ay**, perched above the valley, to venerate its Black Virgin; west, the Romanesque priory of **Veyrine** hides in a gentle hamlet. The Ay valley continues up to **Lalouvesc**, a more showy religious stop among pine forests. The imposing 19th-century neo-Byzantine church was built by Pierre Bossan (designer of Lyon's showy Fourvière church, *see* p.63) and dedicated to St Régis, a 17th-century Jesuit missionary priest sent to the remoter parts of the Vivarais and the Velay. He features in a lot of the visual propaganda.

Surrounded by mountain pastures with goats producing little *caillé doux* cheeses, **St-Félicien** makes an open, airy slope-side stop east of Lalouvesc. The place goes mad once a year over one of the biggest (non-competitive) cycling events in Europe, the *Ardéchoise*, which starts from here at the end of June. On its height above the Doux valley, **Boucieu-le-Roi** was, through the Gothic period, seat of the royal representative in the *Haut Vivarais*, until Annonay usurped its role. It has retained its legacy of rather fine stone houses. The former **château** was taken over by the religious order of the Holy Sacrament, a small museum, the **Maison Pierre Vigne** (*t 04 75 06 76 74; open Jan–Dec Tues–Sun 2.30–5.30*), recalling its zealous Catholic missionary founder.

Pine-forested ways lead to the lively country-crossroads town of **Lamastre**, overseen by the ruins of the **Château de Pécheylard**. In the old upper quarter of **Macheville**, the much-transformed Romanesque church has kept its period carved capitals. At a junction of mountain rivers, the Doux is the main waterway passing through Lamastre. The century-old **Chemin de Fer du Vivarais** steam train swerves alarmingly down the valley to **Tournon-sur-Rhône** (*see* p.162). Further upstream, a favourite local bathing spot is watched over by the overgrown ruins of the **Château de Retourtour**. Battered by the Wars of Religion, when it was one of the largest towns in the Ardèche, **Désaignes** by the Doux managed to keep several of its medieval gateways. Its quiet streets lead to the rough medieval **château** (*t 04 75 06 61 19; open July–Sept Tues–Sun 3–7, April–June and Oct weekends 2–6; adm*), containing displays on local history.

St-Agrève lies exposed at over 1,000m on a high plateau to the west. Strung along one simple main street below the cone of the Mont Chiniac, a stop has existed here between Le Puy-en-Velay and the Rhône since pre-Roman times. The martyr after-whom it is named was a 7th-century bishop of Le Puy who came to a sticky end on Mont Chiniac. Nothing historic remains in town because this Huguenot stronghold was decimated in the Wars of Religion. The **Galerie du Besset** (*www.galerielebesset.com*) has opened St-Agrève's horizons to contemporary art, including British artists. Climb the **Mont Chiniac** to appreciate the grandiose ancient landscapes, or take the old-style **Train de la Galoche** into the Velay area in the Auvergne. **Lac de Devesset** to the north is surrounded by woods and a popular base for watersports.

River Valleys to Privas and Vals-les-Bains

Here we head into the wild valleys of the **Parc Naturel Régional des Monts d'Ardèche**. The steep, winding roads can be exhilarating, but at times also difficult and desolate, with very few houses around. The **Eyrieux river**, starting up by St-Agrève, twists below the deceptive ruins of the medieval **Château de Rochebonne** (*free*), semi-camouflaged by the granite from which they rise. This stronghold was destroyed during the Wars of Religion. The vertiginous views reach well beyond the Eyrieux valley. Above **Le Cheylard**, a little valley town of narrow streets, is the medieval **Château de la Chèze** (*t 04 75 29 45 93, e aspb.lacheze@club-internet.fr; tour mid-July–mid-Aug at 4, April–mid-July and mid-Aug–Oct Wed 10–4*), which survived the strife of centuries until the Germans torched it in the Second World War. Now in the midst of a camp site, it's slowly being restored. Craft delights in town include the **Riou** *chocolaterie* and the **Bijoux GL** jeweller's factory shop selling items that attract fashion houses such as Christian Lacroix. If you follow the lower Eyrieux valley to Privas, detour to **Chalencon**, a fortified village that was populated by staunch Protestants and consequently largely destroyed by order of Richelieu. The Protestant church contains a portable altar that hints at the hard times.

From Le Cheylard, you can branch off south along the D578 following the **Dorne valley**. At the high pastures of **Mézilhac**, look for the turning to Marcols-les-Eaux and St-Pierreville. The gorge road to them, east along the **Glueyre valley**, counts among the most beautiful terraced chestnut routes in the whole *département*. **St-Pierreville**, set in a tremendous location, pays its respects to the venerable provider of centuries past (*see* box) with its **Maison du Châtaignier** (*t 04 75 66 64 33; open July–Aug Mon–Fri 11–12.30 and 2.30–6, April–June and Sept–mid-Nov Wed, Sun and public hols 2–6; adm*), while the **Musée Vivant de la Laine et du Mouton** (*t 04 75 66 66 11, www.ardelaine.fr; open July–Aug daily tours 11, 3, 3.30, 4, 4.30 and 5; Feb–June and Dec Wed, Sun and hols 3; adm*) devotes itself to the sheep that traditionally grazed beneath the chestnut trees; much of the time, this is as much a woollen clothes shop as a museum, but the tours on wool-making are instructive. The **Route du Châtaignier** entices you with further stops among the chestnut trees, and at local farms offering produce and teas.

From St-Pierreville, there are only ridiculously contorted routes to **Privas**. Try a western loop going via **St-Julien-du-Gua**, the **Col de la Fayolle** and **Pourchères**. Or take an eastern loop, briefly rejoining the Eyrieux valley before taking the D2 south. Branch off for the hamlet of **Le Bouschet** near Pranles, where the long and painful story of Vivarais Protestantism, its persistence and persecution, is recalled in the old house holding the **Musée du Vivarais Protestant** (*t 04 75 64 22 74, e lblache@wanadoo.fr; open mid-June–mid-Sept daily exc Sun am and Mon 10–12 and 2–6, April–mid-June and mid-Sept–Oct daily exc Sun am and Mon 2.30–6; adm*) focusing on two extraordinary Protestants, Pierre Durand and his sister Marie, born here in the early 18th century. The diminutive Romanesque church of **Pranles** on its separate hillock contains remarkable carved capitals. A track nearby leads you down by foot to the **Mandy mill**.

For such an unassuming country town with a sweet old heart, it comes as a surprise to learn that **Privas** is administrative capital of the whole *département de l'Ardèche*. It's better known as capital of *crème de marron* and *marrons glacés*. Beyond the eye-

From Paupers' Nosh to Posh *Marrons Glacés*

In the past, local pigs and people alike depended on chestnuts for much of the year. Known as *l'arbre à pain*, the bread tree, the chestnut harvest was roasted, smoked, and also made into flour, hence the nickname. The trees are among the latest-flowering in France, blossoming in June. There are many varieties, 60 traditional ones. The long-established Comballe gives a fine fruit, but the Bouche Rouge are used for *marrons glacés*. Crosses of US-Japanese varieties have also been brought in, giving bigger, fuller fruit, if less tasty ones, but they have proved more susceptible to disease and the groves were decimated in the 1960s. Communities such as St-Pierreville were hard hit. A vaccine discovered in the 1970s saved the remaining trees.

For harvesting, the *Ardéchois* invented savage-looking implements to knock down and shell the chestnuts, notably vicious shoes with sharp points on the sole. Now they are shaken on to nets, the shells or burs (*bogues*) removed by machine. The shells open, the distinction emerges between an ordinary *châtaigne*, a chestnut divided into several separate sections, and a *marron*, a whole, undivided chestnut. When candied, these become *marrons glacés*. The two main Ardèche producers are Faugier of Privas (out on the road to Montélimar) and Sabaton outside Aubenas. *Crème de marrons* and other sweet chestnut spreads are less refined but equally delicious.

sore concrete tower of the town hall, appealing old squares climb up to the pleasingly solid stone penitentiary. Privas suffered badly after espousing Protestantism in the Wars of Religion, butbecame one of the main Huguenot strongholds accepted at the end of the conflict. However, when in 1629 the populace defied the regional governor and attacked the castle because a Catholic became lord, Richelieu and Louis XIII camped outside town along with 20,000 troops and, although the Cardinal tried to stop the carnage, many Privas Protestants died. One local girl who escaped was adopted by Richelieu, and became known as *La Fortunée de Privas*. To improve relations, the royalists built the bridge over the Ouvèze. **Coux**, a forward defensive post for Privas in times past, has managed to keep its well-armoured head above the urban sprawl east of town. South from Privas, dramatic twisting country roads lead across the **Plateau du Coiron**. The N104 main road heads west via the **Col de l'Escrinet**, a major pass into the southern half of the *département*, with stunning views towards Aubenas.

Up backwith the Mézilhac country crossroads, to the west of its pass, several rivers hurtle south from close to the Mont Gerbier de Jonc (*see* p.124) along parallel valleys to join the Ardèche river. Along the Bourges white-water road trip, don't miss the **Cascade du Ray-Pic**, a spectacular volcanic waterfall in most seasons, a good half-hour walk from the car park. The intrepid might try the roads along the parallel **Bézorgues valley**.

The **Volane valley** route is slightly better known. Prettier inside than out, **Antraigues-sur-Volane** sits remote atop its volcanic hill, surrounded by green-lichen-covered slopes, and was a significant centre of the *maquis* in the Second World War; the main square, renamed Place de la Résistance, is popular for boules; a metal *boulomane* counts among many sculptures in the village, made by locals, helped by the numerous crafts-people here. The ruins of the **Château du Crau** stand out on the border of a volcanic crater, a tempting walking destination through typical chestnut woods.

The contorted routes east of Antraigues offer beautiful country roads. Head for hill-side **Genestelle**, where you feel you're on top of the world. By St-Michel, seek out the dramatic ruins of the **Château de Boulogne**, perched above two ravines. Additions in the 16th century explain the glamorous Renaissance twists, such as the stunning gateway, but the place was in good part demolished in the 19th century.

Southern Ardèche
The Upper Ardèche River and Savage Southwest

Vals-les-Bains tucked into its deep valley and Aubenas on its high ridge stand close together at the northeast corner of the triangle of land we cover here. This section extends across the southwest corner of the *département* between the N102 road, following the ravine of the upper Ardèche river, and the D104, which leads to some of the most cheerful small Ardéchois towns. The wild, mountainous areas of the Tanargue and the Vivarais Cévenol fan out between these two roads.

Vals-les-Bains and Aubenas

Every six hours, a geyser spurts into life at **Vals-les-Bains**, an amusing symbol for this cheery old spa town straddling the Volane. In the 17th century, the springs acquired a medical reputation and Mme de Sévigné and Jean-Jacques Rousseau (*see* p.189 and p.254) counted among illustrious visitors. Grand hotels went up in the Belle Epoque. During the First World War, American soldiers recuperated here. Vals' water was also bottled and became popular in France long before many of its younger rivals.

On the east bank of the Volane, the early 20th-century bottling factory is still going strong. Opposite temptingly unhealthy food shops, the smoked-glass modern **spa** offers relaxation breaks as well as medical treatments. The geyser, in the pretty public garden, performs better in hotter weather. There's also an Olympic-size outdoor swim-ming pool. For more leisurely exercise, stroll to the 1920s **Pavillon St-Jean** close to Pont St-Jean, a good place to taste from three of the local springs (*open to all May–September*). Several bridges span the Volane. Pretty gardens also extend along the west bank. On the main shopping street, **La Maison Champanhet** (*t 04 75 37 81 60, e lamaisonchampanhet@yahoo.fr; open mid-July–mid-Aug daily 10–12.30 and 3.30–8, mid-June–mid-July and mid-Aug–mid-Sept daily exc Mon 10–12 and 2–6, mid-March–mid-June and mid-Sept–mid-Oct daily exc Mon, Wed and pm weekends 10–12 and 2–6; adm*) is a grand town house recently converted into the local museum, telling the history of Vals and the family that once owned the house.

Aubenas sits high on its ridge above the Ardèche, its turreted castle and domed chapel dramatically silhouetted against the sky. Once you've scaled its defensive flanks, it is a pleasure to stroll round its scruffily merry old streets and squares (though the number of car parks is frustrating). While both soaring keep and the Gothic towers in front of the massive **château** (*t 04 75 87 81 11; open July–Aug Tues–Sat 11–12.15 and 2–6.15, June and Sept Tues–Sat 10.30–12.15 and 2–3.30, rest of year Tues, Thurs, Fri and Sat 2–3.30; adm*) were built for the medieval Montlaurs, the brightly coloured

The Southern Ardèche

Getting Around

By train: The closest rail links are Valence, Montélimar, Pierrelatte and Pont-St-Esprit. Avignon TGV station (with once a week summer service direct from London) is near.

By bus: Compagnie Sotra, t 04 75 35 09 02, runs buses from Montélimar, Autocar Charrière, t 04 75 35 68 60, from Valence. Services are limited Sundays. Regular coach services from Montélimar and Valence serve Aubenas, Vals-les-Bains and Largentière. Joyeuse and Les Vans are on the line between Montélimar and Alès. Compagnie Sotra also runs to Vogüé. Autocar Faure, t 04 75 88 03 55, serves Ruoms. For Vallon-Pont-d'Arc, Faure goes from Montélimar, Sotra from Avignon.

Tourist Information

Vals-les-Bains: 116 Rue Jean Jaurès, 07600 Vals-les-Bains, t 04 75 37 49 27, www.vals-les-bains.com.

Aubenas: 4 Bd Gambetta, B.P.208, 07204 Aubenas, t 04 75 89 02 03, www.aubenas-tourisme.com.

Largentière: 8 Rue Camille Vielfaure, 07110 Largentière, t 04 75 39 14 28, www.largentiere.net.

Joyeuse: Route D104, 07260 Joyeuse, t 04 75 39 56 76, e joyeuse@fnotsi.net.

Les Vans: Place Léopold Ollier, 07140 Les Vans, t 04 75 37 24 48, www.les-vans.com.

Vogüé: t/f 04 75 37 01 17, e vogue@fnotsi.net.

Ruoms: t 04 75 93 91 90, e ruoms@fnotsi.net.

Vallon-Pont-d'Arc: Place de la Gare, 07150 Vallon-Pont-d'Arc, t 04 75 88 04 01, www.vallon-pont-darc.com.

St-Martin-d'Ardèche: Place de l'Eglise, 07700 St-Martin-d'Ardèche, t/f 04 75 98 70 91, e st-martin-dardeche@fnotsi.net.

Market Days

Vals-les-Bains: Sun morning; in summer, evening markets Wed and Thurs.

Aubenas: Sat morning extravaganza.

Largentière: Tues morning. July and Aug, Fri evening market.

Joyeuse: Wed morning. In July and Aug, look out for evening markets.

Les Vans: Sat morning; mid-June–mid-Aug evening markets on Tues.

Vogüé: July–Aug, Mon morning.

Ruoms: Fri morning.

Vallon-Pont-d'Arc: Thurs morning; July–Aug, also Tues morning.

St-Martin-d'Ardèche: mid-June–mid-Sept, Wed morning and Sun morning.

Sports and Activities

Canoeing is wildly popular on the Ardèche; contact the *Comité Départemental de Canoë-Kayak*, t 04 75 88 00 41, e cdck@wanadoo.fr.

For **rockclimbing**, contact CDFFME, t 04 75 64 85 54, www.ffme.fr/cd07, for **potholing**, t 04 75 39 72 71. Keen **walkers** consult the *Comité Départemental de la Randonnée Pédestre*, t 04 75 64 27 91, e cdrp07@wanadoo.fr.

Vallon-Pont-d'Arc is a sports-crazy centre. It organizes an annual April *Nature Raid* endurance race (contact tourist office).

Where to Stay and Eat

Vals-les-Bains ✉ 07600

Château Clément B&B, La Chataigneraie, t 04 75 87 40 13, www.chateauclement.com (*very expensive–expensive*). This sumptuous home built for a Vals water magnate has been beautifully restored and has its own pool. Owner, *pâtissier* Eric organizes half-day

roofs date from the 17th century, when the Burgundian d'Ornanos took control. Enter the château via one of the twin main doors, each with its own staircase. Through the sober inner courtyard, the grand *Ancien Régime* staircase was added for the de Vogüés, an up-and-coming family from central Ardèche who moved here (*see* p.144) in the late 1730s. Pillaged at the Revolution, some of the *Ancien Régime* panelled rooms remain. Further up, a few chambers are devoted to regional artists. Climb the keep for a medieval guard's view of the surrounding territories.

cookery courses, his specialities are chocolate and *marrons glacés*.

***Grand Hôtel des Bains**, Montée des Bains, t 04 75 37 42 13, *www.hotel-des-bains.com* (*expensive–inexpensive*). 19th-century extravaganza behind the spa. Stylish, lively restaurant (*expensive–moderate*). Pool and garden. *Closed Nov–Mar.*

***Le Vivarais**, Rue Claude Expilly, t 04 75 94 65 85, f 04 75 94 65 85 (*expensive–inexpensive*). Belle Epoque, with wide range of pleasant old-fashioned rooms looking onto the river. Well-regarded regional cuisine (*expensive*). Pool. *Closed Feb.*

Neyrac-les-Bains ✉ 07380

***Hôtel du Levant**, t 04 75 36 41 07, e *hotellevant@wanadoo.fr* (*inexpensive*). Relaxing spa hotel with traditional rooms. Restaurant (*expensive– moderate*) has elaborate cuisine and great shaded terrace. *Closed 11 Nov–mid-Jan; restaurant closed Sun eve.*

Aubenas ✉ 07200

Le Fournil, 34 Rue du 4 Septembre, t 04 75 93 58 68 (*moderate*). Vaulted dining room plus courtyard, where fine regional cuisine is served. *Closed Sun, Mon, and late-June–early July, plus short school hols.*

L'Entracte, 2 Bd Gambetta, t 04 75 35 90 68 (*moderate–cheap*). Fantastic views and value for simple local menus at this large-windowed restaurant looking out to a semicircle of mountains. *Closed Mon and late-June–early July.*

Vinezac ✉ 07110

**La Bastide du Soleil, Le Bourg, t 04 75 36 91 66, e *bastidesoleil@chateauxhotels.com* (*expensive*). Wonderful stone building in the centre of the village, with a few simple

elegant rooms. The restaurant (*moderate–expensive*) turns towards Provence in its cuisine and spreads outside on warm days. *Restaurant closed Tues and Wed.*

Uzer ✉ 07110

Château d'Uzer B&B, t 04 75 36 89 21, *www.chateau-uzer.com* (*moderate*). Magical restored castle and keep, with most stylish, airy rooms. *Table d'hôte* (*moderate*). Pool and great exotic garden.

Largentière ✉ 07110

***Domaine de l'Eau Vive**, Le Roubreau, t 04 75 89 20 53, *www.domaineeauvive.com* (*moderate*). Recent conversion of big 19th-century riverside mill, poshest rooms with luxury bathrooms. Big restaurant (*moderate*). *Closed Jan.*

Sanilhac ✉ 07110

**La Tour de Brison, t 04 75 39 29 00, *www.belinbrison.com* (*inexpensive*). Nicely modernized rooms in typical old hillside house with spectacular views. Fine food (*moderate; must book*). Great pool. Tennis court. *Closed Nov–Mar.*

Les Vans ✉ 07140

**Mas de l'Espaïre, Bois de Païolive, t 04 75 94 95 01, *www.hotel-espaire.fr* (*moderate*). Spacious rooms in tranquil silk farm 6km to south, meals for guests only, served on the splendid shaded terrace by the pool. *Closed mid-Nov–mid-Mar.*

**Le Carmel, 7 Montée du Carmel, t 04 75 94 99 60, e *lecarmel@wanadoo.fr* (*moderate*). Delightful rambling converted convent above the centre. Fine cuisine (*moderate*). *Closed most of period mid-Nov–Mar.*

Originally part of a Benedictine convent, the many-sided **Dôme St-Benoît** also bears the stamp of the d'Ornanos' decorative scheme. Converted into a grain market at the Revolution, inside it retains the d'Ornano mausoleum and presents other religious artefacts. Aubenas became a Protestant stronghold in the Wars of Religion, the medieval **church of St-Laurent** devastated, two Jesuit priests murdered. The Jesuits imposed strict Catholicism afterwards. St-Laurent was rebuilt in uninspiring style, but inside, it contains a dynamic Baroque woodcarving, a legacy from the town's Jesuit college. In the main scene, the Virgin looks like she's throwing the baby Jesus in the air.

Le Grangousier, Rue Courte, t 04 75 94 90 86 (*moderate; closed Tues and Wed exc July–Aug*). Regional fare in fabulous historic house. *Closed mid-Nov–Feb.*

Ribes ✉ 07260

Auberge du Côqou, Le Haut-Grand-Val, t 04 75 39 44 39 (*moderate*). Lost up in the wooded hills, locals love making the stomach-churning journey up here to savour the dedicated chef's rustic local delights (*book,as only open Fri pm and weekends*).

Beaulieu ✉ 07460

★★★Hôtel de la Santoline, t 04 75 39 01 91, *lasantoline.com* (*moderate*). Lovely sprawling rustic stone hunting lodge lost in the deeply picturesque *garrigue* southeast of Les Vans. Colourful bedrooms, fresh cuisine (*moderate*) and pool. *Closed Oct–April.*

St-Pons ✉ 07580

★★★La Mère Biquette, Les Allignols, t 04 75 36 72 61, e merebiquette@wanadoo.fr (*moderate*). At the end of a quiet valley, with goats around, country retreat, plus pleasant restaurant (*moderate; check when closed*). Pool and court. *Closed mid-Nov–mid-Feb.*

St-Maurice d'Ardèche ✉ 07200

★★Domaine du Cros d'Auzon, t 04 75 37 75 86, *www.hotel-cros-auzon.com* (*inexpensive*). Very good location right close to the river between Vogüé and Balazuc. Nice stone architecture and reasonable rooms. Restaurant. Pool. Court. *Closed Oct–Mar.*

St-Alban-Auriolles ✉ 07120

La Villa St-Patrice B&B, t 04 75 39 37 78, *www.villastpatrice.com*

(*expensive–moderate*). Spacious village house with splendid rooms.

Grospierres ✉ 07120

★★★La Ferme de Bournet, Bournet, t 04 75 39 08 35, *www.fermedebournet.com* (*moderate*). Exclusive address with handful of rooms in a farm built out of an old fortified manor. Big restaurant, La Bergerie, (*moderate; closed Mon*) with vaulted dining room and terrace. Pool.

Vallon-Pont-d'Arc ✉ 07150

★★Hôtel du Tourisme et du Pont d'Arc, t 04 75 88 02 12, *www.hotel-tourisme-pont-darc.com* (*inexpensive*). Practical central town option with modern rooms. Big restaurant with terrace (*moderate*). *Closed Dec–Feb.*

Labastide-de-Virac ✉ 07150

Le Mas Rêvé B&B, t 04 75 38 69 13, *www.lemasreve.com* (*moderate*). Within a stone's throw of the Ardèche gorges, splendid, spacious 17th-century converted farm. *Table d'hôte* (*moderate*). Pool. *Closed mid-Nov–mid-Mar.*

La Petite Auberge, t 04 75 38 61 94 (*moderate*). Lovely stylish terrace on the edge of the village, a sweet address for nice traditional cuisine. *Closed Oct–Mar.*

Vagnas ✉ 07150

Le Mas d'Alzon B&B, t/f 04 75 38 67 33 (*moderate*). Lovingly restored farm close to Labastide. Pool and garden.

Up to the Source of the Ardèche

Heading up the exceptionally steep Ardèche river valley from Vals or Aubenas, traces of volcanic lava flows still mark the way. By the adorable village of **Jaujac**, set to become home to the **Maison du Parc**, introducing the *Parc Régional Naturel des Monts d'Ardèche*, go walking inside a volcano crater. Above the Ardèche, the sensational silhouette of the medieval **Château de Ventadour** (*t 04 75 38 00 92; open July–mid-Oct weekdays 9–12 and 2–7, weekends 2–7; adm*) tempts you to explore. At **Chirols,** the **Ecomusée du Moulinage** (*t 04 75 94 54 07, e ecomuseechirols@worldonline. fr; open*

June–Sept Wed–Mon 2–7; adm) recalls the local silk industry. Press on north for **Montpezat-sous-Bauzon**, backed by a series of volcanic tops. Below, the Romanesque church of **Notre-Dame-de-Prévenchère** displays solid character.

Back close to the Ardèche, **Meyras** has feisty historic character, with its old houses and its church fronted by an intimidating volcanic-stone entrance. It became a thermal stop in Roman times, but now boasts one of the most private, peaceful spas in France, **Neyrac-les-Bains' Thermes de Neyrac** (*t 04 75 36 46 00, e thermes-deneyrac@wanadoo.fr*), tucked away in woods across the N102.

By **Thueyts**, built on a terrace above a solidified lava flow, you really feel you're leaving civilization, although the simple **Musée Ardèche Autrefois** (*t 04 75 36 46 27; open July–Aug daily 9–12 and 2–6, April–June and Sept–Oct Thursday–Tues 9–12 and 2–6; adm*) recalls old peasant traditions. Rewarding walks lead, one to the **Château de Blou**, only open for exhibitions, but set in pleasant grounds, another to the **Pont du Diable**, a Roman, rather than devil's, bridge, where people often bathe. Walk down for the **Chaussée des Géants**, a stairway cut into the lava flow. The N102 climbs relentlessy, following the Ardèche river almost to its source beside **La Chavade**.

Savage Southwest Ardèche

Daunting lines of mountains descend from the Massif Central between the N102 and D104, presenting a tough adventure even by car, the reward savage scenery. Once the snows clear, the mountaintops are covered in green lichen, giving them an alien look before the purple heather flowers. The most northerly mountain line in this area, the **Massif du Tanargue** isn't for the lily-livered. Out in the *département*'s Far West, Christian civilization makes a grandiose statement at **St-Etienne-de-Lugdarès** with a huge church built in bands of volcanic stone. In the shadow of a huge mountain, the little spa town of **St-Laurent-les-Bains** offers hot natural springs and treatments at the **Centre Thermal de St-Laurent** (*t 04 66 69 72 72, www.st-laurent-les-bains.com*).

In the 19th century, Trappist Benedictines set up at the isolated, now-modernized **Notre-Dame des Neiges**. Watch a video about the order – its most famous monk, Charles de Foucauld, became a renowned explorer in North Africa. Robert Louis Stevenson (of the same generation) stopped here on his journey recorded in *Travels with a Donkey in the Cévennes*. The abbey shop sells the fruits of the monks' labour. The D4 leads south along the top of heathery slopes, the massive **Mont Lozère**, highest peak of the Cévennes, out west. To journey into dark, lost terrain, join the upper **Drobie valley** for **Le Mas**, its substantial houses built to combat winter cold, and for **Sablières**, where even the roofs are of stone to keep all in place versus the harsh elements.

For an alternative route through the Tanargue mountains, head for the **Col de la Croix de Bauzon**, snowy territory in winter. Twig-thin branches to mark the edges of the roads indicate that this is not sophisticated ski territory. The Baume river sets out on its dramatic journey to join the Ardèche's waters from **Loubaresse**, with massive views down the valley. You then plunge into very pretty, if narrow, gorges to Joyeuse (*see p.142*). By **Ribes** you reach civilization in the form of terraced vines that practically encircle this airy hilltop village. Before Ribes, a turning leads into the boulder-strewn western valley of the Drobie – a sunbather's secret paradise in summer. A hair-raising detour along poor roads takes you up high via lost hamlets to the **Ron des Fades** (*outdoors; donations welcome*) at **Pourcharesse**, where an eccentric local builder has recreated local sights in miniature, and also presents outsized carved chestnuts!

From Aubenas to Les Vans

The easier route skirting the edge of the *département*'s savage southwest, running parallel to the middle section of the Ardèche river, takes you along the D104, from which you can visit a string of appealing if unkempt towns and villages close to the road. Or start by taking a back road from Aubenas to the dead-end delight of **Ailhon**, with its scattering of hamlets, its main Romanesque church, and its arboretum. With castle and rampart ruins, the lovingly restored village of **Vinezac** among its vines makes a good next port of call. Gargoyles hang out from the medieval church. Prehistoric men probably worshipped at the nearby menhirs and dolmens.

As the name suggests, silver (*argent*) was discovered long ago at the dramatic hill town of **Largentière**. In medieval times, bishops of Viviers controlled its mining, and minted coins. Silver mining continued on a small scale up to 1980. The **castle** (*rarely open; check at tourist office*), built for the bishops, stamps its military authority over the historic centre, rising above the tall spire of the restored **Gothic church**, although a messy modern hospital besieges the castle walls. The streets and vaulted passage-ways running down the hill towards the **Porte des Recollets**, the gateway that still stands guard by the Ligne river, are appealing. On the opposite bank stands a melodramatic law court. The hilltop village of **Montréal** has a splendid **château** (*t 04 75 89 91 81; open July–Aug daily exc Sat 10–12.30 and 2.30–7, April–June and Sept–Nov daily tour at 3; adm*) mirroring Largentière's. In season, the **Roseraie de Berty** (*t 04 75 88 30 56, www.roseraie-de-berty.fr.st; open late-May–late-June Mon–Sat 10–12.30 and 2–6; adm*) 6km away attracts garden lovers with the scent of its 600 rose varieties.

Joyeuse, a happy enough little hillside town, lives up to its name, although many traces of stern fortifications remain. The castle has been transformed into the town hall. Nearby, the pleasingly provocative **Maison de la Caricature** (*t 04 75 39 30 14; open July–Aug daily 10–12.30 and 3–7.30, April–June Tues–Sat 10–12.30 and 3–7.30, Sun pm only; adm*) features small exhibitions by cutting-edge artists in one of the nicest old houses up by the sharp-spired church on its charming square. By the entrance to the church, the **Musée de la Châtaigneraie** (*t 04 75 39 90 66; open July–Aug Tues–Sat 10–12.30 and 3–7, Sun and Mon 3–7, mid-March–June and Sept–mid-Nov Tues–Sat 9–12 and 2–6, Sun and Mon 2–6; adm*) has taken over the premises of a former monastery, treating Ardèche chestnuts and chestnut trees once again with all the seriousness they deserve (*see p.135*). Some comically eccentric pieces of rural chestnut furniture add a lighter note. The main old street along the crest of the hill has interesting shops and restaurants. To reach the more ordinary main shopping drag, pass through steep dark passageways under the ramparts. Southwest of Joyeuse, on the first slopes before the wild mountains further west, you encounter villages surrounded by fertile terracing, those at **Planzolles** given over to vines. **Faugères** has for centuries huddled around its priory. **Payzac** grows olives as well as vines, producing an excellent oil.

In a wide basin of land surrounded by layered hills that look like they've been decapitated sprawls the laid-back town of **Les Vans**. A large statue in the café-filled main square honours Léopold Ollier, a 19th-century doctor and an early pioneer in skin- grafts. The area around is major olive country, **L'Olivier de Vincent** an irresistible shop in the centre devoted to olive products in all their forms. The passionate man who runs it has his own mill, but there are several others that can be visited (*contact the tourist office*).

Churches and chapels occupy some precarious positions on the heights around Les Vans, good objectives for a wander. So too are the villages. A picturesque château with corner towers oversees **Chambonas**, reached via the largest Gothic bridge in the region. The castle is private, but look in at the images of the Romanesque church. In a beautiful barn at the hamlet of **Sièlves**, visit the pig-mad **Musée Vivant du Cochon** (*open April–Sept Wed–Sun 11–7; Oct, and Christmas hols–March, Wed and weekends 2–6; adm*).

Just west of Les Vans, little **Naves** is perched precariously on the side of a circus of stratified rock. Beyond the cobbled, arched lanes with the odd craft shop, the church stands in suicidal position. Further west up the Chassezac valley, find the track for **Thines**. As dead ends go, this remote hamlet offers one of the most enchanting on its densely wooded slope. There are no car parks or pavements up there, just sliced rocks to walk on. The roofs are of stone as well. Slashed, one-eyed statues of saints stare madly from the church doorway. A monument recalls *maquisards*, Resistance fighters who hid out in these remote parts. A crooked old shop sells local produce.

South from Les Vans, the amazingly shaped boulders look as though they've been strewn by giants around the cork oak **Païolive forest**. **Banne**'s twin villages stand higher up just to the south, the defensive medieval castle camouflaged like a bunker, the upper village pressed against it. Dreamy, open country roads, the D901, D202, then D255, cut through gently undulating fertile lands east from here to the more barren scrubland and deep drama of the southern Ardèche gorges.

The Middle and Southern Gorges de l'Ardèche

A string of stunning villages lines the middle stretch of the Ardèche between Aubenas and Ruoms. Lumpy, elephantine rock formations oversee the bright pebble beaches where canoeists take to the waters in droves. Between Vallon-Pont-d'Arc and St-Martin, the Ardèche cuts a massive trench through the high limestone plateau. Several hundred feet deep, the Gorges de l'Ardèche count among the most famous canyons in France, one of the country's most sensational stretches of river. Signs point to fabulous caves hidden here and there. So many sensational attractions make the middle and southern stretches of the Ardèche river heavily touristy, but head just a little away from the main action, and quieter attractions await around yet more enchanting but less competitive villages, often surrounded by vines or even lavender.

The Middle Ardèche River from Vogüé to Vallon-Pont-d'Arc

Before heading down the Ardèche river from Aubenas, try an elating detour east for two villages, **St-Laurent-sous-Coiron** and **Mirabel,** hanging startlingly on the black bottom lip of the **Plateau de Colron**. From their cliff-edge positions, you get vertiginous views south. Above the volcanic village of Mirabel, its church sometimes serving for art exhibitions, climb the black medieval tower that stands lone guard.

Although *alba* usually means 'white' in Latin languages, a black castle dramatically rises above the village of **Alba-la-Romaine**. Or more precisely, a black-and-white castle stands above Alba-the-medieval. Confusing. Truth is, through the Roman centuries, a sizable town existed down the slope. The major element left, built in light limestone, is the discreet remnants of an **ancient theatre**, with an **archaeological site** (*t 04 75 52 45 15; open year round; theatre free, adm for site*) alongside. The theatre seated 3,000, signalling just how important this outpost once was. But it would lose its position as an early Christian bishopric to Viviers (*see p.167*) and Alba was abandoned. In medieval times, a castle was built higher up, protecting a tight-packed village, the architecture mixing the black basalt of the hilltop with the white limestone already quarried below. The **Salle d'Exposition** tucked away in a corner displays Gallo-Roman objects, from an exquisite if headless naked divinity to a superb mosaic of colourful fish. The robust **château** (*t 04 75 52 42 90, e chateau.alba@wanadoo.fr; late June–mid-Sept daily 10–12 and 3–7, April–June and mid-Sept–Nov 2–6; adm*), heavily restored in 19th-century style, has long welcomed contemporary art for regular exhibitions.

Vineyards proliferate around Alba and the Escoutay valley. Seek out **Valvignières** south among the vines, its wines lauded since Roman times, the **cooperative** (*t 04 75 52 60 60; open Jan–Dec Mon–Sat 8–12 and 1.30–5.30*) now selling a variety of good-value single variety wines, while the sleepy shell of a village has preserved portions of medieval ramparts and a church with impressive spire. East, the village of **St-Thomé** stands aloof and neglected by time up on its thin crest of rock, while south, **Gras**, a medieval village with a fortified church, has been left in peace by the tourist world.

Back west with the Ardèche river, built against a curving rockface in the valley side, the superb square **Château of Vogüé** (*t 04 75 37 01 95, www.chateaudevogue.net; open July–mid-Sept daily 10.30–6, April–June Thurs–Sun 2–6, mid-Sept–Oct weekends 2-6; tours; adm*), flanked by rounded towers, stands slightly aloof above the other village houses, although its Roman-tiled roofs match those below. Its history is closely linked with the aristocratic de Vogüés for whom the castle was first built. Dispossessed during the Hundred Years' War, the family came back after the Wars of Religion, the castle largely redone in the 17th century. However, in 1736, the ambitious line shifted headquarters to Aubenas, then further afield. This castle fell into ruin after the family lost everything during the Revolution, but a de Vogüé bought it back and restored it. From the terraced garden, you get a lovely view of the Ardèche's waters. So do you from the riverbank row of houses with canoeing centres and cafés. Take in the old ensemble from the other side, and you're presented with a real, living picture postcard, not surprisingly a member of the association of *Les Plus Beaux Villages de France*. Pretty **Lanas** is more low key, with a couple of very simple-looking hotels by the bridge. **Rochecolombe**, also delightful, stands back, away from the rush of the river, dramatic castle ruins running along a crest above the sloping village.

Balazuc tumbles down to the Ardèche. You must negotiate a dark warren of narrow streets on foot to reach the water. A few craft shops hide out here. A 19th-century church with soaring spire rises above the old village along with the triple arch of the Romanesque church's bell tower. Balazuc remained a Catholic island as Protestantism spread like a wave across the Ardèche during the Wars of Religion. At the end of rampart ruins, you stumble on the remains of an early medieval castle. *The Stones of Balazuc* by John Merriman take you on a fascinating journey through a thousand years of the place's history. At the foot of the village, you emerge into a wonderful rocky riverside landscape, curious-shaped cliffs lining up along the Ardèche. In summer, bathers and canoeists jostle for space on the pebble beach. Cross the waters for a stunning view of the whole village. A long but rewarding walk south along the river takes you to the **Ferme Ecovillage du Viel-Audon** (*t 04 75 37 73 80*), a farm renowned not just for producing excellent goats' cheese and weaving its own silk, but also for recycling everything. Move on to appreciate the **Cirque de Gens**, a spectacular natural meander in the Ardèche below Chauzon. Rockclimbers love this challenging spot.

Ruoms, a stop on the flat and on a slightly larger scale, is a major tourist point, with lots of boutiques selling the tools necessary for enjoying a typical family holiday along the river. The pale local stone is so beautiful it has been quarried and exported around southeast France, going into the building of such famous structures as the Pont d'Avignon on the Rhône just beyond our region. Some locals assert that the base of New York's Statue of Liberty (a gift from the French nation to the USA) comes from here, although there's no evidence for this claim. The place's new wine museum **Vinimage** (*t 04 75 93 85 00, www.vinimage.tm.fr; open April–Oct Tues–Sun 10–12.30 and 2–6.30; adm*) has taken over an old tannery on the church square. You're given a *tastevin* on the tour; at the end put it to use in the *dégustation*. Four **wine-touring circuits** lie within easy reach of town, inciting you to go in search of individual properties. A short way east of Ruoms, in sleepy hillside **Lagorce**, **Ma Magnanerie** (*t 04 75 88 01 27; open July–Aug daily 10–12 and 2.30–6.30, May–June and Sept daily 2.30–6.30; adm*) is a simple museum on silk-making, silk scarves on sale in the shop.

Cross the Ardèche river by Ruoms for further extraordinary riverside sights. Take the D4 north for the dramatic limestone side of the **Défilé de Ruoms**. Best of all, branch off for **Labeaume**, a truly fairytale-like village, its castle (private and impossibly inaccessible) perched on a needle of rock. The old houses standing along smooth-stoned lanes below have been beautifully restored, with improbable corner gardens. The church porch stands on two huge columns like outsized stilts. Enormous plane trees create columns in front of the Baume river, tributary of the Ardèche, forming a dark roof of leaves in the hot season under which the cafés sprawl out. Most enchanting of all is the riverside itself. Huge rocks line up like a row of stone elephants, their trunks dipping down to drink from the pebbly water. In summer, you can swim here.

The **Mas de la Vignasse** (*t 04 75 39 65 07, www.musee.daudet.free.fr; open July–Aug daily visits at 11 and 12, and on the hour 2–6, April–June and first half Sept daily visits on the hour 2–5; adm*) is a traditional farm in which 15 generations of the Reynaud family lived in virtual independence, with their own bread oven and milling wheels. Adeline Reynaud was mother of Alphonse Daudet, one of southern France's favourite 19th-century writers, hence the memorabilia on this much-loved figure. **St-Alban-Auriolles** and **Chandolas** sit in the midst of fragrant *garrigue* concealing Neolithic dolmens.

The Southern Ardèche River Gorges and Caves

Now for the really major natural drama of the Gorges de l'Ardèche. Two big tourist events have occurred since the war to totally transform **Vallon-Pont-d'Arc**, located just before the high thrills of the Ardèche gorges. First, the new tourist era took off with an explosion in canoeing. Rockclimbing and potholing attracted further enthusiasts. All this sporty activity turned the appealing town with its stocky squares and jovial café terraces into a honey pot, and it is now crammed with touristy shops.

In the mid-1990s came the discovery, a short way east of town, of one of the best prehistoric finds in the world. The **Exposition sur la Grotte Chauvet-Pont-d'Arc** (*t 04 75 37 17 68, e cerpv.pontdarc@wanadoo.fr; open June–Aug Tues–Sun 10–1 and 3–8, mid-March–May and Sept–mid-Nov Tues–Sun 10–12 and 2–5.30; adm*) offers amazing glimpses of thes treasures. In 1994 three dedicated local potholers squeezed into a fabulous cavern filled with arguably the greatest prehistoric cave paintings ever. The walls were covered with an even wider variety of animals than at the celebrated Lascaux cave in the Dordogne. Lascaux's paintings were almost wholly ruined by uncontrolled tourism. Learning from this mistake, the Grotte Chauvet will never be opened to the public. A replica is being made, to open in a few years' time. In the meantime, there is an excellent half-hour film that shows the cave paintings in all their beauty. Such is their finesse, it's hard to believe that they were painted *c.* 30,000 years ago, making them virtually the earliest cave art ever discovered. As well as the deer, horses and mammoths, the prides of prehistoric lions, gatherings of prehistoric bears, and the unforgettable array of prehistoric rhinos take your breath away. One figure is thought to represent a hyena, another a leopard – if so, unique in cave art discovered to date.

Close by, at the heart of the tourist action, the **Hôtel de Ville** (*t 04 75 88 02 06, e mairie.vallon-pontdarc@wanadoo.fr; open Jan–Dec, Mon–Fri 8–12 and 1.30–5; adm*) or town hall (also known as the château), a grand 17th-century building constructed for the local Counts of Vallon, holds remarkable Aubusson tapestries illustrating in heroic fantasies the ruthless crusader Godefroy de Bouillon.

In the countryside away from the gorges, quaint villages lie like lizards immobile on rocks in the sun. Head south from Vallon via Salavas for **Labastide-de-Virac**. The little lanes all lead up to the friendliest-looking of village castles. Crowning the hill, the **Château des Roure** (*t 04 75 38 61 13, www.chateaudesroure.com; open July–Aug daily 10–7, April–June and Sept daily exc Wed 2–6; adm*) proves atmospherically rustic, the pleasant self-guided tour revolving around the silk-worm farming trade that once employed so much of the community. But there are more sinister tales retold along the way. The deeply peaceful hamlet of **Les Crottes** hiding out on the flat near Labastide remembers its inhabitants martyred by Germans in 1944, in revenge for a successful Resistance attack on a convoy near here.

Set among scrubland and vineyards, the most famous swallow hole in the Ardèche, and one of the largest in Europe, the **Aven d'Orgnac** (*t 04 75 38 65 10, www.orgnac. com; open July–Aug daily 9.30–6.30, April–June and Sept daily 9.30–5.30, Oct–Nov daily 9.30–12 and 2–5.15, Christmas hols and Jan–March daily 10.30–12 and 2–4.45; adm*) lies 135m underground. Taken down by lift, you're shown just a few caves out of a whole network. The major swallow hole is enormous, a curious cool house for weird stalagmites forming a bizarre cartoon copse of tree trunks in stone. The collection includes the largest stalagmite in France, rocketing up 24m.

Prehistoric finds of major significance have been made in the area, displayed in the **Musée Régional de la Préhistoire** by the aven. This is a serious educational museum to reflect an area declared a *Grand Site de France*. The place concentrates on the 350,000 or so years that *homo erectus* has lived around the southern gorges of the Ardèche, from the early Palaeolithic, when he busied himself preparing flint tools, to the great leap forward in sophistication of Cro-Magnon man, some 40,000 years ago. The story goes as far as the more developed Bronze and Iron Ages, with a superb bronze dagger from the 2nd millennium BC among the most remarkable objects.

The caves are much smaller at the nearby **Aven de la Forestière** (*t 04 75 38 63 08; open July–Aug daily 10–7, April–June and Sept 10–6; adm*), but refined. With only 60 steps, access is much easier than to most of the Ardèche's other subterranean sites. The deep red stains come from iron oxyde rather than ancient blood of the hairy rhinoceros, among prehistoric remains found down here.

Half of France seems to have canoed down the major **Gorges de l'Ardèche** (starting just south of Vallon-Pont-d'Arc) at some time or other. In fact, half of France may seem to be doing so if you visit in summer, with the queues of canoes in the waters almost matching the queues of cars on the road up above. The full canoe trip down the gorges from Vallon covers some 30 km. Hardy hikers take the roadless national GR paths along the south side of the river. Before reaching the corniche road, you pass a couple of small caves. Still wet (and slippery), a sign that its formations are still growing, the entrance to the **Grotte des Tunnels** (*t 04 75 88 03 73; open April–Sept daily 9am–9.30pm; adm*) was, until quite recently, a blacksmith's workshop and goat pen – disappearing goats gave a clue as to the cave beyond. The **Grotte des Huguenots** (*t 04 75 88 06 71, e ercotp@wanadoo.fr; open mid-June–Aug daily 10–7; adm*) hid Protestants during the Wars of Religion; the exhibition inside explains cave formations. Then comes one of the most stunning natural phenomenon in France . Nature occasionally carves out bridges of stone; rarely do they come more picturesque than the **Pont d'Arc**, spanning the Ardèche river across 66m, the arch a full 30m high. Canoes pass beneath like shoals of exotic fish. In summer, bathers venture into the bright emerald waters.

The **corniche road** rises rapidly onto the high plateau, a scrubby wilderness broken only by the vast canyon of the Ardèche valley. Space is limited at the various car parks along the way; gawp down sheer apricot-coloured limestone walls towards the black snake of a river heading towards the Rhône. The entrance to the **Grotte de la Madeleine** (*t 04 75 04 22 20, www.grottemadeleine.com; open July–Aug daily 9–7, April–June and Sept daily 10–6, Oct daily 10–5; adm*) stands beside one of the most breathtaking views down on the gorges. The tour takes you on a roller-coaster one-kilometre walk to two vast caverns in particular, the most grandiose in the Ardèche.

Several attractions are gathered together at the **Aven de Marzal** (*t 04 75 04 38 07, e brey@wanadoo.fr; open April–Sept daily 10.30–6; March and Oct–Nov just Sun 10.30–6; adm*). Large dinosaur models lurk in the twisting paths of the Zoo. The small **Musée du Monde Souterrain** pays homage to pioneering potholers who came up with such

Sorting Your *Grottes* from your *Avens*

Grottes and *Avens* are a major feature of the area. Most of these sensational caves were dug into the limestone by underground rivers eating away at the rock, or were caused by the collapse of fragile strata. The waters changed course hundreds of thousands of years ago, finding other paths through the limestone at lower levels. In the vacated, dripping caverns, stalagtites and stalagmites ('*les stalagtites tombent, les stalagmites montent*') built up over the millennia from an accumulation of limestone deposits from individual droplets. Other concretions formed, like drapery, or vast cauliflowers. A concentration of oxydized minerals has caused vivid colour in some caves. As animals and mankind evolved, they took refuge in some caves, or were accidentally trapped and died in them, enabling archaeologists to recover prehistoric material. In recent centuries, locals, notably shepherds, sheltered in the caves, while in times of conflict such as the Wars of Religion or the Second World War, oppressed Protestants and *maquisards* hid in them. The Ardèche caves divide into two types: *grottes* tend to be more horizontal, following the course of ancient rivers; *avens*, or swallow holes, are vertical, natural wells. Cave systems are still being discovered in the Ardèche, and in the mid-1990s, sensational prehistoric art was found in the Grotte Chauvet (*see* p.146).

finds as the impressively fanged skull of a sabre tooth tiger. The *aven* is somewhat sinister, not good for vertigo sufferers, with hundreds of steps. It turns out to be named after a man killed by an angry shepherd who pushed him and his dog down this hole. At the bottom, there are impressive concretions, although the name of the Salle des Diamants, covered with calcite crystals, rather exaggerates the effect.

For a more restful visit, head to picturesque **St-Remèze**, where you will find nearby the fresh new, laboratory-white **Musée de la Lavande** (*t 04 75 04 37 26, www.ardeche lavandes.com; open May–Sept daily 10–7, April and Oct daily 10–5; adm*). **Bidon** has an interesting small geological museum, the **Musée de la Vie** (*t 04 75 04 08 79; open April–mid-Nov daily 10–6; adm*), run by a passionate archaeologist. Monsieur may allow you to feel a piece of mammoth hair if you're lucky.

The **Grotte de St-Marcel** (*t 04 75 04 38 07; open July–Aug daily 10–7, mid-March–June and Sept daily 10–6, Oct–mid-Nov daily 10–5; adm*) isn't at the gently touristy St-Marcel-d'Ardèche at all, but 12 kilometres southwest, beside the Gorges de l'Ardèche. A relatively easy ramp of steps leads down to the first massive cave, known as the Galerie des Peintres because of its naturally colourful walls. Other impressive caves include the Cascade des Gours, boasting an extraordinary natural cascade of rock pools like giant oyster shells, filled with the clearest water. Ravel's *Boléro* plays when you enter the largest of the caves, the vast Salle de la Cathédrale, reaching up to 60m in height; here, the stalagmites really do resemble organ tubes.

By **St-Martin-d'Ardèche**, you've descended back down to the riverside, the place where many of the canoe trips end. The village feels lively and cheerful in season, loads of snack bars catering to the tired adventurers at the end of their gorgeous voyage. A neo-Gothic bridge connects St-Martin to aloof **Aiguèze**, perched dramatically on the opposite bank, its crenellated ramparts merging with the cliff, guardedly surveying the southern frontier of the Ardèche.

Down the Rhône
From Lyon to the Provence Border

The Rhône from Lyon to Vienne 151
The Rhône from Vienne to Valence 160
The Rhône from Valence to Montélimar 164
From Montélimar to the Languedoc
   and Provence Borders 167

12

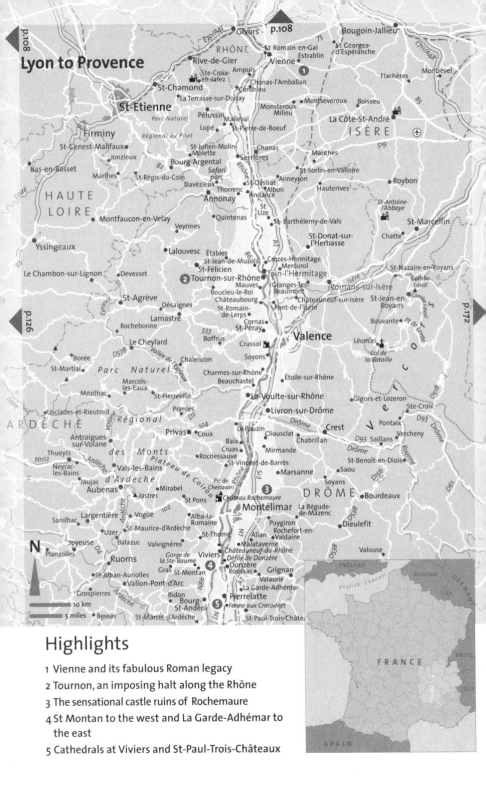

Lyon to Provence

p.108
p.108
p.126
p.172

RHÔNE

Givors
Rive-de-Gier
Ste-Croix-en-Jarez
St-Chamond
La Terrasse-sur-Dorlay
St-Etienne
Parc Naturel
Firminy
St-Genest-Malifaux
Jonzieux
Bas-en-Basset
Marlhes
St-Régis-du-Coin
Davézieux
HAUTE LOIRE
Montfaucon-en-Velay
Yssingeaux
Le Chambon-sur-Lignon
Devesset
Lalouvesc
St-Agrève
Lamastre
Rochebonne
Le Cheylard
Borée
St-Martial
Mézilhac
Parc Naturel
Marcols-les-Eaux
St-Pierreville
Pranles
Usclades-et-Rieutord
Régional
Privas
Coux
Antraigues-sur-Volane
Thueyts
Neyrac-les-Bains
Jaujac
Vals-les-Bains
Aubenas
Mirabel
des Monts
Plateau de Coiron
Largentière
Vogüé
Sanilhac
Uzer
Balazuc
Joyeuse
Ruoms
Planzolles
ARDÈCHE
St-Alban-Auriolles
Vallon-Pont-d'Arc
Grospierres
Bessas
St-Marcel-d'Ardèche

Pélussin
Malleval
Lupé
St-Pierre-de-Boeuf
St-Julien-Molin-Molette
Bourg-Argental
Safari parc
Thorrenc
Annonay
Veyrines
Quintenas
Étables
St-Jean-de-Muzols
St-Félicien
Tournon-sur-Rhône
Mauves
Boucieu-le-Roi
Châteaubourg
Désaignes
St-Romain-de-Lerps
Boffrus
Chalencon
Charmes-sur-Rhône
Beauchastel
La-Voulte-sur-Rhône
Le Pouzin
Baix
Cruas
Rochessauve
Pic de Chenavari
St Pons
Château Rochemaure
Alba-la-Romaine
St-Maurice-d'Ardèche
St-Thomé
Valvignères
Gorge de la Ste-Baume
Gras
St-Montan
Bidon
Bourg-St-Andéol

Ampuis
Condrieu
Chonas-l'Amballan
Monsteroux-Milieu
Chanas
Serrières
St-Désirat
Andance
St Uze
St-Barthélemy-de-Vals
Crozes-Hermitage
Merdurol
Tain-l'Hermitage
Granges-les-Beaumont
Châteauneuf-sur-Isère
Pont-de-l'Isère
Cornas
St-Péray
Crussol
Soyons
Valence
Étoile-sur-Rhône
Livron-sur-Drôme
Gigors-et-Lozeron
Clousclat
Mirmande
St-Vincent-de-Barrès
Marsanne
Montélimar
Château-Rochemaure
Châteauneuf-du-Rhône
Malataverne
Allan
Viviers
Donzère
Roussas
La Garde-Adhémar
Pierrelatte
Ferme aux Crocodiles
St-Paul-Trois-Château

E70/A47
St Romain-en-Gal
Estrablin
Vienne ①
Montseveroux
Montrevel
Boisseu
ISÈRE
La Côte-St-André
Manthes
St-Sorlin-en-Valloire
Anneyron
Hauterives
Roybon
St-Antoine-l'Abbaye
St-Marcellin
Chatte
St-Donat-sur-l'Herbasse
St-Nazaire-en-Royans
Combe Laval
Romans-sur-Isère
St-Jean-en-Royans
Bouvante
VERCORS
Léoncel
Col de la Bataille
Ste-Croix
Pontaix
Crest
Vercheny
Chabrillan
Saillans
Drôme
St-Benoît-en-Diois
Saou
DRÔME
Soyans
Bourdeaux
La Bégude-de-Mazenc
Puygiron
Rochefort-en-Valdaine
Dieulefit
Valdaine
Valouse
Grignan
Valaurie

Bougoin-Jallieu
St Georges-d'Espéranche
Flachères

FRANCE

N
10 km
5 miles

Highlights

1 Vienne and its fabulous Roman legacy
2 Tournon, an imposing halt along the Rhône
3 The sensational castle ruins of Rochemaure
4 St Montan to the west and La Garde-Adhémar to the east
5 Cathedrals at Viviers and St-Paul-Trois-Châteaux

For those of you who have the misfortune of having to rush straight down the Rhône between Lyon and Provence without getting off the main valley roads, here we concentrate on the very narrow strip of land these roads take up, one that has given the vast and varied region of the Rhône-Alpes such a misleading tourist image. Millions rush as fast as possible along the extremely busy three major arteries: the A7 motorway, and the N7 and N86 main roads just east and west of the Rhône. There are fine attractions right by these routes, or just a ridge away, and we will tempt you with those, but first let's get the negatives out of the way.

True, this industrial band has been dubbed France's 'chemical corridor' and contains some of the most intense concentration of plant in France. Cement quarries scar the valley banks and many of the factories, as well as the nuclear installations, have been built to make use of the Rhône's energy. These large-scale enterprises have generated wealth for the region, but have marred the undoubted natural beauty of this ribbon of land. Electricity pylons are as much a feature of the landscape as woods or vines. On top of that, it's scarcely a secret that the Rhône valley here has a terrible wind problem. From south of Valence, the notorious Mistral makes its regular violent escape. It is, however, a blessing as well as a curse, clearing the air, chasing away clouds and making way for those intense blue skies that presage Provence. From the confluence of the Drôme and the Rhône, the weather turns markedly more Mediterranean.

Starting to feel more positive? And see how, below Lyon, sensationally steep vineyards cling pluckily to the valley cliffs. These northern Côtes du Rhône vines produce some of the greatest wines in southern France. Dense fruit orchards planted in more generous patches yield not just superb crops, but also liqueurs. Montélimar has long been reputed for its nougat, while superlative Valrhôna (see where the name comes from?) chocolate is also produced along here. So there are sweet culinary reasons to stop. And cultural ones too. Many a dramatic castle ruin looks down on the valley roads, along with hill-top villages, the artistically minded Cliousclat and Mirmande among the finest. But the most surprisingly arresting places are the towns. If you take the trouble to penetrate their dusty commercial outskirts, Vienne offers one of the most staggering Roman legacies in France; Tournon and Tain-l'Hermitage face each other in the most beautiful, vine-covered locations along this stretch; and Valence, where Napoleon enjoyed his cherry-picking days, is spied on across the Rhône by the sensational ruins of the medieval Château de Crussol. Historic Montélimar hides coyly under thick layers of plane trees. We end with two unknown little gems, both with stunning cathedrals, Viviers west of the Rhône, St-Paul-Trois-Châteaux to the east. These two alone should leave you with a definite desire to press further into the Ardèche, Isère and Drôme (*see* chapters 11 and 13).

The Rhône from Lyon to Vienne

From Lyon, the three major Rhône valley roads rush south through industrial quarters to converge on Vienne. Before that, a cluster of routes knot around **Givors**, but a new **Halte Fluviale**, or little port, attracts yachting tourists who use the Rhône as a short

Getting There and Around

By train: Vienne is just 20mins from Lyon-Part-Dieu by train. Valence's TGV station stands 10km east of town (to which it's connected by shuttle bus) with rapid links across France – Paris is 2hrs 30mins away. Avignon TGV station, with a direct weekly summer link with London, lies just south of the Ardèche and the Drôme. Tain-l'Hermitage, Montélimar and Pierrelatte have useful train stations too.

By bus: Buses link the valley towns. For river cruises, *see* pp.157, 161, 162, 164.

Tourist Information

Givors: Maison du Rhône, 1 Place Liberté, 69700 Givors, **t** 04 78 07 41 38, **e** *office.tourisme.fleuve@wanadoo.fr*.

Vienne: Cours Brillier, 38200 Vienne, **t** 04 74 53 80 30, *www.vienne-tourisme.com*.

Condrieu: Place du Séquoia, 69420 Condrieu, **t** 04 74 56 62 83.

Albon: Maison de la Valloire, 26140 Albon, **t** 04 75 03 17 05, *www.lavalloire.com*.

Tournon-sur-Rhône: Hôtel de la Tourette, 07300 Tournon-sur-Rhône, **t** 04 75 08 10 23, *www.valleedudoux.com*.

Tain-l'Hermitage: 70 Ave Jean Jaurès, 26600 Tain-l'Hermitage, **t** 04 75 08 06 81, *www.tain-tourisme.com*.

Valence: Parvis de la Gare, 26000 Valence, **t** 08 92 70 70 99, *www.tourisme-valence.com*.

La Voulte-sur-Rhône: Place Etienne Jarjeat, 07800 La Voulte-sur-Rhône, **t** 04 75 62 44 36, *www.ardechepleincoeur.com*.

Montélimar: Allées Provençales, 26200 Montélimar, **t** 04 75 01 00 20, *www.montelimar-tourisme.com*.

Viviers: 5 Place Riquet, 07220 Viviers, **t** 04 75 52 77 00, **e** *viviers@fnotsi.net*.

Bourg-St-Andéol: Place du Champ de Mars, 07700 Bourg-St-Andéol, **t** 04 75 54 54 20, **e** *otbsa@wanadoo.fr*.

La Garde-Adhémar: Rue Marquis de la Baume, 26700 La Garde-Adhémar, **t/f** 04 75 04 40 10, *www.la.garde-adhemar.com*.

St-Paul-Trois-Châteaux: Rue de la République, 26130 St-Paul-Trois-Châteaux, **t** 04 75 96 59 60, *www.office-tourisme-tricastin.com*.

Market Days

Givors: Wed, Fri and Sun mornings.
Vienne: Every morning; Sat extravaganza.
Tournon-sur-Rhône: Sat morning.
Tain-l'Hermitage: Sat morning.
St-Péray: Wed morning.
Valence: Sat morning.
La Voulte-sur-Rhône: Fri morning.
Montélimar: Wed morning and Sat morning.
Viviers: Tues morning.
Bourg-St-Andéol: Wed morning.
St-Paul-Trois-Châteaux: Tues morning. Truffle market Nov–Mar Sun morning.

Festivals and Events

Many of the Rhône-side towns and villages put on summer festivals by and on the river, with races, jousting and even waterskiing.

Vienne Jazz Festival, the first fortnight in July, is the most important jazz event in France. Look out for local wine festivals too.

Where to Stay and Eat

Vienne ⊠ 38200

****La Pyramide, 14 Bd Fernand Point, **t** 04 74 53 01 96, *www.lapyramide.com* (*very expensive*). Bright modern Provençal chic in splendid rooms, but known above all as a temple of *haute cuisine* – the street is even named after Fernand Point, the legendary chef who made its name, the first ever to be awarded three Michelin stars. *Closed Feb–mid-Mar; restaurant closed Sun and Mon.*

Le Cloître, 2 Rue des Cloîtres, **t** 04 74 31 93 57 (*expensive–moderate; closed Sun*). Romantic restaurant by the cathedral; refined cuisine.

Le Pré Neuf B&B, 9 Rue des Guillemottes, **t** 04 74 31 70 11, *www.membres.lycos.fr/preneuf1* (*inexpensive*). 1.5km up towards hospital. Pleasant B&B in property with wall-surrounded garden.

Estrablin ⊠ 38780

***La Gabetière, 7km east of Vienne on D502, **t** 04 74 58 01 31 (*inexpensive*). Utterly charming 16th-century manor, and a bargain, with spacious salons, tasteful rooms hung with art, plus pool in shaded grounds.

Chonas-l'Amballan ✉ 38121

**Domaine de Clairefontaine/Les Jardins de Clairefontaine, Chemin des Fontanettes, t 04 74 58 81 52, *www.domaine-de-claire-fontaine.fr (moderate–inexpensive)*. Set back in large gardens on the Rhône's east bank, characterful old-fashioned hotel with reputed restaurant (*very expensive–expensive*). Tennis court. *Restaurant closed out of season; also closed Sun eve, Mon, and Tues lunch, plus mid-Aug, and mid-Dec–mid-Jan.*

Condrieu ✉ 69420

****Beau-Rivage, 2 Rue du Beau Rivage, t 04 74 56 82 82, *www.hotel-beaurivage.com (expensive)*. By the Rhône, pleasing rooms even if the architecture's a mixed bag. Fine traditional restaurant (*very expensive–expensive*), with a terrace beside the river.

Serrières ✉ 07340

**Hôtel Schaeffer, 34 Quai Jules Roche, t 04 75 34 00 07, *www.hotel-schaeffer.com (inexpensive)*. Standing out among the simpler cafés by the bridge, well located traditional riverside hotel. Good restaurant (*expensive*) with river views and mural. *Closed Jan; restaurant closed Tues high summer, otherwise Sat lunch, Sun eve and Mon.*

Albon ✉ 26140

Domaine des Buis, by golf course, t/f 04 75 03 14 14, *www.domaine-des-buis.com (expensive– moderate)*. Exclusive 18th-century house built in the pebbles of the area. Spacious rooms with luxurious bathrooms. Pool in lovely leafy garden. *Closed Dec–Feb.*

Etables ✉ 07300

Domaine du Moulin B&B, t 04 75 06 88 68, *www.chateaudomainedumoulin.com (moderate)*. Splendid 15th-century manor once owned by diet guru Michel Montignac, now run by a Dutch family. High quality restaurant. Pool. *Closed Nov–Easter.*

Tournon-sur-Rhône ✉ 07300

Le Chaudron, 7 Rue St-Antoine, t 04 75 08 17 90 (*moderate; closed Thurs eve and Sun*). On pedestrian street, restaurant reputed for Ardèche specialities and excellent wines. *Closed most of Aug.*

Tain-l'Hermitage ✉ 26600

***Reynaud, 82 Av Roosevelt, t 04 75 07 22 10 (*moderate*). New rooms with great views onto the Rhône, plus good restaurant (*expensive*) in stylish old building. Pool. *Closed early Jan and late Nov; restaurant closed Sun eve, Mon, and Tues lunch.*

Rive Gauche, 17 Rue Joseph Péala, t 04 75 07 05 90 (*expensive*). Exciting modern restaurant with liner decoration, looking across the Rhône. Cuisine top notch. *Closed Sun eve and Mon, and most Jan.*

Pont de l'Isère ✉ 26600

***Michel Chabran, 29 Avenue du 45ème Parallèle, t 04 75 84 60 09, e *chabran@ michelchabran.fr (expensive–moderate)*. Delicious smart restaurant (*expensive; closed high summer Wed lunch and Thurs lunch, rest of year Wed lunch and Sun eve*) with superb local wine list and lovely sunny patio, plus a dozen reasonable rooms.

Valence ✉ 26000

****Maison Pic, 285 Av Victor Hugo, t 04 75 44 15 32, *www.pic-valence.com (luxury–very expensive)*. One of the great stops on the N7 well before the motorway was built, proudly run family establishment, a bastion of superlative cuisine (*very expensive–expensive; out of season closed Sun eve, Mon and Tues lunch*) and comfort, although the big road outside isn't appealing. Try less elaborate dishes at **L'Auberge du Pin** (t 04 75 44 53 86, *moderate, out of season closed Wed*).

**Hôtel de France, 16 Bd de Gaulle, t 04 75 43 00 87, *www.hotel-valence.com (inexpensive)*. Renovated option close to the historic heart.

Bistrot des Clercs, 48 Grande Rue, t 04 75 55 55 15 (*moderate; closed Sun*). In the central house where Napoleon stayed, good food from the Chabran stable (*see Pont d'Isère above*).

Soyons ✉ 07130

****/***Domaine de Soyons, N86, t 04 75 60 83 55, *www.ledomainedesoyons.com (very expensive–expensive)*. Plusher rooms in the stylish main 19th-century block, more rustic Provençal ones in the outbuildings. Smart restaurant (*expensive*) with verandah. Pool and tennis court. *Closed Nov–Feb; restaurant closed Jan, and Mon out of season.*

Charmes-sur-Rhône ✉ 07800

★★★**Autour d'une Fontaine**, Rue Paul Bertois, t 04 75 60 80 10, www.autourdunefontaine. com (moderate). Delightful bright rooms in stylish little hotel. Striking restaurant (expensive–moderate) and relaxing terrace. Restaurant closed Sun pm and Mon.

Le Pouzin ✉ 07250

★★★★**La Cardinale et sa Résidence**, Quai du Rhône, t 04 75 85 80 40, www.lacardinale. com (luxury). Farm converted into a very smart, bright hotel, with pool in large grounds; 3km away at Baix, the main restaurant (expensive) in a grand old house has lovely views of the Rhône.

Cliousclat ✉ 26270

★★★**La Treille Muscate**, t 04 75 63 13 10, www.latreillemuscate.com (moderate). Adorable, in the heart of the village, with fine pottery plates among the decorations. Pleasing Provençal-style cuisine (moderate). Closed Dec–Feb; restaurant closed Wed.

Mirmande ✉ 26270

★★**La Capitelle**, Rue du Rempart, t 04 75 63 02 72, www.lacapitelle.com (moderate). Tasteful rooms in this fine village house, plus vaulted restaurant (moderate) serving good regional cuisine. Closed Dec–Feb.

Goriou B&B, t 04 75 63 01 15, f 04 75 63 14 06 (inexpensive). Joyously artistic touches all around this lovely property at the foot of the village. Run with charm.

Montélimar ✉ 26200

Le Chalet du Parc, Allées Provençales, t 04 75 51 16 42 (moderate). Contemporary glass-sided dining room with terraces tacked on to an old villa in the public gardens. Refreshing for a Provençal meal, opposite the café-lined Allées Provençales. Closed Mon eve and Tues.

Bourg-St-Andéol ✉ 07700

Le Cloître Gabriac B&B, 8 Rue Paul Mazet, t 04 75 54 66 62, e dalbard.pierre@wanadoo.fr (expensive). Extremely stylish, spacious rooms in property with splendid garden terrace above the Rhône. Outdoor Jacuzzi.

Digoine B&B, Quai de Madier de Montjau t 04 75 54 61 07, www.digoine.com

(moderate). In a mansion looking on to the Rhône, very colourful themed rooms. Table d'hôte (moderate).

Malataverne ✉ 26780

★★★**Le Domaine du Colombier**, Route de Donzère, t 04 75 90 86 86, e domainecolombier @voila.fr (expensive–moderate). An oasis close to motorway exit 18, a converted medieval religious establishment with bright rooms and good restaurant (expensive– moderate). Pool. Restaurant closed Sun.

Valaurie ✉ 26230

★★★**Le Moulin de Valaurie**, Le Foulon, t 04 75 97 21 90, www.lemoulindevalaurie.com (expensive). Set quietly down from the village, a lovely restored mill, plus fine restaurant (moderate). Restaurant closed Sun eve, Mon.

★★★**Domaine Les Méjeonnes**, Les Méjeonnes, t 04 75 98 60 60, www.mejeonnes.com (moderate). Converted farm with sweet rooms and restaurant (moderate). Pool. Restaurant closed Wed lunch.

La Garde-Adhémar ✉ 26700

★★★**Le Logis de l'Escalin**, Les Martines, t 04 75 04 41 32, www.lescalin.com (moderate). Charming, outside the village. Enchanting restaurant (expensive–moderate). Pool. Restaurant closed Sun eve and Mon.

St-Paul-Trois-Châteaux ✉ 26130

★★★★**Villa Augusta**, 14 Rue du Serre Blanc, t 04 75 97 29 29, www.villaaugusta-hotel. com (very expensive–expensive). Italianate magic in new hotel opened by the Pourcels, renowned for their cuisine (expensive).

★★★**Hôtel L'Esplan**, 15 Place de l'Esplan, t 04 75 96 64 64, www.esplan-provence.com (moderate). Behind its 16th-century front on a central square, quite stylish, even if the modern modifications look a bit chaotic. Air-conditioned rooms, enclosed patio, smart dining room (expensive–moderate). Closed mid-Dec–mid-Jan; restaurant closed Sat lunch, plus Sun eve out of season.

La Chapelle, Impasse L de Bimard, t 04 75 96 60 88 (expensive–moderate). Tucked away in a courtyard among the ruins of the bishops' chapel, wonderful secret restaurant. Closed Sun eve, Mon, and Tues eve.

cut from the Mediterranean to the Channel (thus also avoiding the stormy Atlantic), although it can be tough sailing against the current. In the past, sailors used oars and sails, or even pulled their vessels from the bank. By Givors' riverside, spot the statue paying homage to the mighty Rhône river god and visit the **Maison du Rhône**, undergoing renovations, but reopening soon to present the river between Lyon and Provence with the respect it deserves. The town is also proud of its funky **Etoile** contemporary housing project by Jean Renaudie, in the shape of stars. For the Mont Pilat park, a short, steep world away, *see* p.131.

Amazing secrets of the very glamorous past life of Vienne and its sibling St-Romain across the river have been unearthed in recent times. These places may look scruffy at first, but take the time to acquaint yourselves with them – especially lovable, slightly tatty old Vienne, an exceptional grandee steadily dribbling antiquities, although it is being revived and spruced up to look more and more presentable. This was a very important place in Gallo-Roman and early Christian times. Main settlement of the powerful Celtic Allobroges tribe from the 3rd century BC, it was taken over by the Romans after they conquered these territories at the northern limit of their beloved Provence.

Vienne enjoyed a period of immense trading prosperity from the 1st century AD to the 3rd, as did **St-Romain-en-Gal**. Head there first to appreciate the magnificence of the area's ancient legacy at the superlative modern **Musée et Site Archéologique** (*t 04 74 53 74 01; open Tues–Sun winter 10–5, summer 10–6; adm*), presenting fabulous finds in a contemporary glass block by the Rhône. The traders ordered sumptuous dwellings; over 250 mosaic floors have been uncovered either side of the river, making this one of the most prolific areas for such art in the Roman world. Some tell mythological stories, others are just decorative. There are also outstanding Gallo-Roman mural paintings, models of Vienne and St-Romain-en-Gal in ancient times, and all the other archaeological finds typically associated with Roman towns – statues of gods, tools, amphorae – creating a highly evocative picture of Vienne's Gallo-Roman life. Don't miss the luxurious latrines rescued for posterity! Outside lies an extensive archaeological site, with its network of streets and partially reconstructed villas.

Vienne itself seems overwhelmed by the weight of its cultural legacy. On its hillside, the ruined medieval bishops' castle peers wearily on the town; the 19th-century church with massive statue of the Virgin stands more confidently; most obvious is the modern hospital, a slightly unfortunate symbol of Vienne's decrepitude. But fear not, this ancient town really has a feisty old heart. Vienne's museums share the same opening times (*April–Oct Tues–Sun (the Roman theatre also open Mon April–Aug) 9.30–1 and 2–6, Nov–March Tues–Sat 9.30–12.30 and 2–5 plus Sun 2–5.30; adm*) – if visiting them all, invest in the cheap all-in-one ticket, valid 48 hours, from the tourist office. Vienne's **Roman theatre** (*t 04 74 85 39 23*) lies snugly embedded in the hillside, yet with over 40 tiers counts among the largest built in Gaul. Today the place hosts the prestigious Vienne summer jazz festival, as made clear in colourful style in a big recent outdoor **mural** illustrating Vienne's history on the back of the **town theatre**, its 1930s front concealing an Italianate interior, offering an elegant covered venue. The impressive corner arches in the nearby archaeological **Jardin de Cybèle** may have

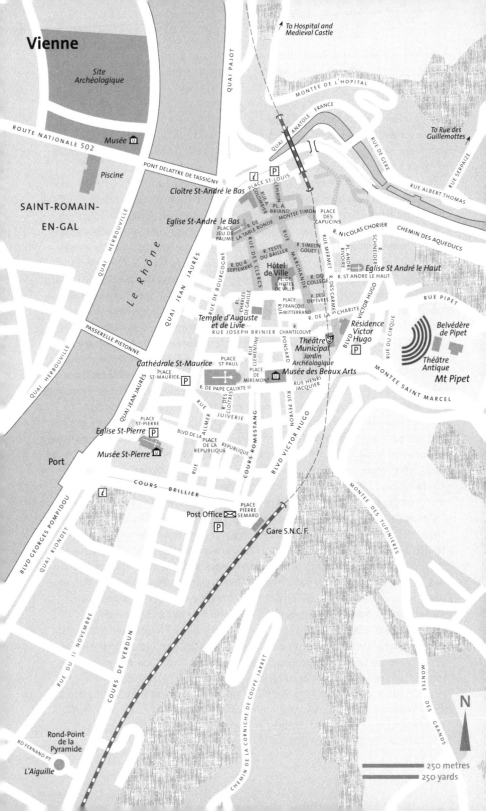

Vienne

Site Archéologique

ROUTE NATIONALE 502

SAINT-ROMAIN-EN-GAL

Musée 🏛

Piscine

PONT DELATTRE DE TASSIGNY

QUAI PAJOT

↑ To Hospital and Medieval Castle

MONTEE DE L'HOPITAL

QUAI ANATOLE FRANCE

RUE DE GÈRE

To Rue des Guillemottes →

RUE SERPAIZE

RUE ALBERT THOMAS

QUAI HERBOUVILLE

Le Rhône

QUAI JEAN JAURÈS

PASSERELLE PIETONNE

QUAI HERBOUVILLE

Port

Cloître St-André le Bas

PLACE ST-LOUIS

Eglise St-André le Bas

PLACE JEU DE PAUME LA TABLE RONDE

R. DE COLOMBIER

R. DE L'EPERON

PL. A. BRIAND

MONTEE TIMON

PLACE DES CAPUCINS

R. NICOLAS CHORIER

CHEMIN DES AQUEDUCS

R. DU 4 SEPTEMBRE

R. TESTE DU BAILLER

R. SIMEON GOUET

R. MERMET

RUE DES CLERCS

RUE MARCHANDE

PL. ANDRE RIVOIRE

R. SCHNEIDER

Eglise St André le Haut

RUE DE BOURGOGNE

Hôtel de Ville

R. DU COLLEGE

R. ST ANDRE LE HAUT

PL. CHARLES DE GAULLE

PLACE FRANCOIS MITTERRAND

R. DES ORFÈVRES

R. DES CARMES

R. DE LA CHARITE

RUE VICTOR HUGO

RUE PIPET

Belvédère de Pipet

Temple d'Auguste et de Livie

RUE JOSEPH BRINIER

RUE CLEMENTINE

RUE CHANTELOUVE

PONSARD

Théâtre Municipal

Résidence Victor Hugo

BLVD VICTOR HUGO

RUE DU CIRQUE

Théâtre Antique

Mt Pipet

Cathédrale St-Maurice

PLACE ST-MAURICE

PLACE ST PAUL

PLACE DE MIREMONT

Jardin Archéologique

Musée des Beaux Arts

RUE HENRI JACQUIER

MONTEE SAINT MARCEL

Eglise St-Pierre

Musée St-Pierre 🏛

QUAI JEAN JAURÈS

PLACE ST-PIERRE

RUE JUIVERIE

R. DE PAPE CALIXTE II

R. DES CLOITRES

RUE DE L'ALLMER

BLVD DE LA REPUBLIQUE

PLACE DE LA REPUBLIQUE

RUE DE L'ALLMER

COURS ROMESTANG

RUE PEYRON

RUE VICTOR HUGO

COURS BRILLIER

BLVD GEORGES POMPIDOU

QUAI RIONDET

Post Office ✉

PLACE PIERRE SEMARD

Gare S.N.C.F.

MONTEE DES TUPINIERES

RUE DU 11 NOVEMBRE

COURS DE VERDUN

CHEMIN DE LA CORNICHE DE COUPE JARRET

MONTEE DES GRANDS

Rond-Point de la Pyramide

BD FERNAND PT

L'Aiguille

N ▲

━━━━ 250 metres
━━━━ 250 yards

formed one angle of the extensive Roman forum. At the south end, the ancient structure was thought once to have been a temple to the Roman nature goddess.

Sitting squarely in the middle of **Place de Miremont**, the grand 1820s granary has long housed the distinctly old-fashioned **Musée des Beaux-Arts et d'Archéologie (t** 04 74 85 50 42). A mammoth's tusk and Neolithic tomb signal inhabitants here before the Allobroges, from whose times just the odd metallic object remains. Buried Gallo-Roman treasure discovered in the 1980s is a highlight. Possibly hidden from the invading barbarian hordes, the exceptional banqueting pieces include two exquisite silver platters, one decorated with exotic animals and men at work, the other with recumbent women. The collections of ornate *Ancien Régime* and 19th-century paintings and ceramics seem fussy by comparison.

Skirting round the massive medieval cathedral, perhaps going via the tree- and café-lined **Cours Romestang**, then **Place de la République**, you arrive at the battered **church of St Peter (t** 04 74 85 20 35), with some of the oldest Christian roots in Vienne. But since the 19th century, this has been used as a chaotic storehouse for all sorts of truly extraordinary Gallo-Roman fragments taken from around town, archaeological pornography of the highest order. A beautiful, monumental classical face greets you at the entrance; more unusual figures follow, including dancers disporting themselves in distinctly Indian style. Also root out the remnants of remarkable early Christian tombs. The one engraved with peacocks pecking at grapes may have been made for Léonien, an abbot of prime importance when a monastery was founded on this spot in the 6th century. The grey, neglected church is essentially Romanesque. The rest of the monastery has vanished, but in 1349 witnessed the first meeting on the sale of the Dauphiné region to the French crown (*see* pp.161 and 162). However, it would take until 1450 for Dauphin Louis II (later Louis XI) to take away control of Vienne from its archbishops. The brutish **Tour des Valois** the other side of the pedestrian river crossing recalls the centuries when the Rhône served as the frontier between France and the Holy Roman Empire. Vienne has just revived its riverside with a new **port** in front of the tourist office and public gardens. Try a short **cruise on the Rhône** from here.

Before focusing on the cathedral, just north of it, Vienne's most exceptional Roman monument still stands out proudly in the very heart of town, the **Temple of Augustus and Livia** on **Place Charles de Gaulle**. Its columns may look chipped, and the place may have undergone major surgery in the 19th century, but the building stamps Roman imperial authority on the centre to this day. The tower of the law courts presides over the building. Wonderful cafés allow you to pay homage from a comfortable seat.

Vienne's several medieval churches, highly visible to travellers along the Rhône, help recall what an extremely important Christian centre this was. The former **Cathédrale St-Maurice** resembles Lyon's muscular Primatiale St-Jean from the front. Various structures succeeded each other on the site from perhaps as early as the 3rd century. In the 8th, the establishment came by the supposed head of the Roman military convert Maurice, martyred with his men in Switzerland. After King Boson of Burgundy had established a base here in the 9th century, donations followed from that line of rulers, for whom the cathedral became a final resting place. The present cathedral is a mix of the Romanesque and the Gothic. Among the delightful decorations in the

Northern Côtes du Rhône Wine Exclusives

What a contrast with the wines of Beaujolais just a little way north of Lyon (*see* p.94). Here not far south of that city, instead of those light 'feminine' numbers, your palate is confronted by big, beefy wines, the finest, brooding ones remaining quite impenetrable for the first few years. Even the whites have muscle in these parts, the finest giving the great reds a run for their money in ageing potential, a rarity. And rare many of these wines are.

Wine experts agree that some of the very finest vintages in the world, both red and white, are made along this narrow stretch of the Rhône valley. You pay not just for the high quality and rarity, but also for the difficult working conditions – some of the steepest patches of vines can only be reached by ladder! All told, these are extremely exclusive, slightly awkward numbers. Many estates produce only small quantities and sell via merchant families and companies (the *négociants*), who also tend their own vines. They market internationally rather than locally, despite their manic tendency to plaster their names on every little section of vineyard wall belonging to them. There is the odd high-quality cooperative, merchant's shop, and property happy to receive visitors. The Côtes du Rhône's official body, the *Interprofession des Vins A.O.C. Côtes du Rhône* (www.rhone-wines.com or www.vins-rhone.com) offers introductory information on the many *appellations*. Get hold of the latest slim *Route des Vins* brochures, with details on properties you can visit. Most of the viticultural action takes place on the west bank of the Rhône, although the dramatic hills of Hermitage and Crozes-Hermitage rise above the east bank. In the reds, the Syrah grape reigns supreme. These wines wear deep purple robes, in such contrast to the light red chiffon of Beaujolais. Barrels are often used for their ageing. For the whites, Viognier gives the intensely mature fruit flavours of Condrieu. Marsanne and Roussane mix power with fragrance in the other whites.

Immediately below St-Romain-en-Gal, the first almost legendary *cru* (fine wine) is **Côte Rôtie**, the Burnt Slope, a world-class ambassador for the northern Côtes du Rhône. Its mature reds typify the serious side of the area, smoky and meaty, with plenty of blackcurrant accompaniment. Condrieu and Château-Grillet produce some of the finest whites in France. The **Condrieu** vineyards only extend over some 250

three late-Gothic portals, look out for the adorable musical angels. Sixty high Romanesque capitals survive inside the nave, with their amusing carved decorations. Leave by the north door to admire more wonderful stone carving, some taken from much earlier Gallo-Roman architecture, hardly a surprise in this city!

The most interesting historic streets, the network dating in part to medieval times, lead up to the other main Christian stop, St-André-le-Bas, from the Roman temple, or from spacious **Place François Mitterrand**, the latter hosting the daily market, with the impressively arcaded **town hall** to one side. Towers stick out high above the lively shopping drags, built to provide wealthy inhabitants with fresher air and more light. **Rue des Clercs**, lined by the arcades of 15th-century shops, became the home to popular Lyon puppeteer Laurent Mourguet (*see* p.24). **Rue des Orfèvres** boasts some of the finest towers, continuing into **Rue Marchande**. The big church of **St-André-le-Bas** hectares; **Château-Grillet** is a single-property *cru* covering under ten! Sweet scents emerge intensely of peaches and apricots. Yet in taste these are serious, dry numbers, with complex layers of flavours.

Next come the vineyards of the less exclusive **St-Joseph** *appellation*. The quality of this west bank wine varies, the 1,700 hectares stretching from Chavanay to Guilherand (opposite Valence). For tourists, these can be particularly attractive, easier to find, costing less, and producing delicious surprises. The Syrah seems to soften rapidly in these parts. The whites, from Marsanne and Roussane, tend to be more middle-of-the-road. Two small *crus* stand out just before the St-Joseph *appellation* comes to an end. **Cornas**' wines, produced from 220 hectares of Syrah, are so impenetrable they can look like they've been dragged up from the bottom of the Rhône. They are considered among the greatest 'peasant-style' wines in France. In total contrast, **St-Péray** produces light whites and frothy sparkling wines from 160 hectares of Marsanne and Roussane, quaffable and improving fast.

Sober-sounding **Hermitage** is the exceptionally high-quality red *appellation* on the east bank, covering some 320 hectares. Its stupendously powerful wines start out bursting with tangy ripeness, pepperiness mixed with the blackcurrants, but also have a tarry tinge, as in a great Bordeaux. Spicy tastes emerge with age. While the odd great **Crozes-Hermitage** is made, most are pale relations of the Hermitages. The Crozes-Hermitage vines sprawl over more than 2,550 hectares of hillsides. Wine experts talk of herbal flavours in the reds, which dominate, taking up around 90 per cent of the *appellation*.

Across the northern Côtes du Rhône area, 1997, 1998 and 1999 were classic years. The year 2000 reds are already rich and ripe, although not a match for the exceptional depth of the 1990s, one of the finest of all post-war vintages. The whites of 2000 were truly exceptional, however. 2001 continued a long good run, although 2002 was mediocre by comparison. The tiny sun-baked yields of 2003 are promising to turn out exceptionally powerful. Experts recommend keeping the finest Côte Rôtie, Cornas and Hermitage reds at least five years before opening, and they can develop for a good quarter century. Best drink the easier reds like Crozes-Hermitage and St-Joseph between three and six years of age.

contains just a few mighty capitals, a couple Roman, a couple with Romanesque interpretations of biblical stories. But the main interest is in the **Cloître St-André-le-Bas** (*t 04 74 85 18 49*), its greying Romanesque cloister held on elegant columns with animal decorations. The mass of epitaphs on the walls behind stretch from the 5th to the 18th century, making an exceptional collage indicating the age of Vienne's Christian past. Contemporary art shows provide quite a contrast in further spaces. Down closer to the river, the **Salle du Patrimoine** (*free*) offers clear, brief introductions to the main stages in Vienne's history, Roman vaults hidden behind the place, of course!

South of the centre, seek out one last Gallo-Roman remain, the **Aiguille**, claimed, in one of the more far-fetched Christian legends, to be the tomb of Pontius Pilate (*see* Mont Pilat, p.131). In fact the imposing arch topped by a soaring obelisk probably formed the centrepiece of a Roman circus. Also, consider climbing **Mont Pipet**, the

Roman theatre at your feet, to enjoy almost as good views as the Black Virgin atop the church. The view along the Rhône proves surprisingly unspoilt, the vines of Condrieu to the south, those of the recently renewed Vienne vineyards to the north.

The Rhône from Vienne to Valence

Heading down the **west bank of the Rhône**, immediately below St-Romain-en-Gal, you enter **Côte Rôtie country**, although the vines fight it out with factories. For keen cyclists, a 5km track has been laid through the vineyards to **Ampuis**, part of the much greater project to create an uninterrupted cycle route along the Rhône from Geneva to the Mediterranean. Ampuis looks a bit scruffy, despite some of the richest Côtes du Rhône family companies having bases here. An oasis along this heavily industrial stretch, the small **Centre d'Observation de la Nature de l'Ile de Beurre** (*t 04 74 56 62 62; open Jan–Dec Mon–Sat 8–12 and 1–5, Sun and public hols 2–5; adm*) introduces the natural life of this protected Rhône island attracting many birds.

Condrieu, long a mariners' village as well as a winemakers' one, has a pleasant port. One of the finest houses, the Maison de la Gabelle, where salt was taxed, serves as a reminder that this was one of the most precious commodities transported along the Rhône down the millennia, brought up from the salt pans beside the Mediterranean. **Georges Vernay**, one of the most acclaimed believers in the place's Viognier wines has a welcoming cellar (*open Mon–Sat; tasting charge if you don't buy*). Climb the very steep lanes to tour the dramatic vineyards spreading up towards the Pilat. At **St-Pierre-de-Boeuf**, the Rhône's waters have been cleverly diverted to feed the **Rivière Artificielle**, a man-made white-water rafting course. There are the calmer waters of the lake for other water sports. Tucked out of sight from the Rhône, **Malleval** (Evil Vale) sounds menacing, and the old hilltop village with its dark stone buildings is somewhat shunned, but it proves quite adorable. The place is so well protected by higher hills that cacti as well as vines thrive on its slopes.

At **Arcoules**, you enter the Rhône-side territories of the *département de l'Ardèche*, getting off to a very fruity start, thick ranks of orchards challenging the power station installations. With its broad flat riverbank, **Serrières** was an obvious spot for a useful port. Although local fishermen appreciate the place, the vacuous riverside could be made more enticing for tourists beyond the water-jousting tournaments. However, the **church of St-Sornin** (*t 04 75 34 00 46; open 2nd week June–3rd week Sept Tues–Sun; adm*) holds the newly spruced up **Musée des Mariniers**. Mariners' colourful processional crosses brighten the interior, along with restored medieval murals. (For **Peaugres safari park** *see* p.133).

While factories hug the river around St-Désirat, the **Cave St-Désirat** (*t 04 75 34 22 05, www.cave-saint-desirat.com*) stands out in a sea of fruit. The excellent big shop stocks Condrieu and St-Josephs and much simpler, cheaper *vins de pays*, made by grape variety. Divine aromas of fruit liqueurs fill the air at the nearby **Musée de l'Alambic** (*t 04 75 34 23 11, www.jeangauthier.com; open July–Aug weekdays 8am–7pm, weekends 10–7, rest of year weekdays 8–12 and 2–6.30, weekends 10–12 and 2–6.30; adm*) and

Gauthier fruit liqueur shop. Again, there's a big selection. A collection of copper stills is displayed at the heart of the distillery in stilted set pieces with life-size automata.

The fortunes of the inhabitants of riverside **Andance** were tied for centuries to the Rhône. It has the oldest-serving suspension bridge on the Rhône, built in 1827. The place has recently tidied up its spacious quay to encourage the huge *bateaux-hôtels* that cruise up the Rhône to stop. For a journey transporting you rapidly into the savage atmosphere typical of northern Ardèche, head for **Thorrenc**, cowering hamlet and defensive castle (*not open*) caught in a time-trap in their densely wooded gorge. At **St-Jean-de-Muzols**, turn onto the D238 to discover the **Maison Delas**, a reputable family wine business taken over by a Champagne house, who keep it open daily.

Taking the **east bank of the Rhône** from Vienne, steering clear of St-Alban-St-Maurice's nuclear power station, at **St-Rambert-d'Albon** you enter the *département de la Drôme*, the Albon area once the powerbase of the medieval family that won and ruled over the substantial province of the Dauphiné spreading east from this stretch of the river. One of their number overstretched himself and was forced to sell the Dauphiné to the French crown in the mid-14th century. From then on, the heir to the French throne was given these territories to practise ruling, and would be known as the Dauphin (Dolphin). Up on its height, the isolated **Tour d'Albon** signals what was once the lordly headquarters, a sorry remnant, if with fine views.

Down below, the **Golf Club d'Albon** has one of the Drôme's three 18-hole golf courses (*t 04 75 03 03 90*). Northeast at **Anneyron** the **Lafuma factory store** (*open Mon–Sat*) sells good-quality outdoor wear and accessories, while **Jars** specializes in high-quality pottery. Winding wooded gorges lead from the Rhône to **St-Uze**, devoted to porcelain since the early 19th-century thanks to the discovery of the magical ingredient, kaolin, nearby. Learn more at the old-fashioned **Maison de la Céramique** (*t 04 75 03 98 01; open mid-March–Oct Wed, Thurs and Sun 10–12 and 2–7, Fri and Sat 2–7; adm*) and pick up traditional pieces at the factory store. As much a natural as a Neolithic curiosity, seek out the cromlechs (stone circles) at **St-Barthélemy-de-Vals**.

Tain-l'Hermitage looks a bit drab compared with **Tournon** across the water, although the addition of a sleek modern cruise liner of a building by the Rhône has added a note of glamour. But the outstanding element here is the vine-baldened hills behind town, forming quite a backdrop, their pates sticking out high above the river. By the Rhône, enjoy the mercifully quiet quays on foot. Set in a stylish former river merchant's house, the **Musée de Tain-l'Hermitage** (*t 04 75 07 15 54; open April–Sept weekends 3–7; adm*) is an art museum run with passion. The terribly busy **N7** cuts mercilessly through the centre of town. The cramped **Valrhôna chocolate shop** south along it attracts chocoholics like bees to the hive. The most famous winemaker and merchant in these parts, the irrepressible **Michel Chapoutier** (*www.chapoutier.com*), champion of organic methods as well as the highest quality, has a modern tasting room (*open daily, 18 Avenue du Dr. Paul Durand*) towards the railway station. The big **Tain-l'Hermitage wine cooperative** lies beyond, on a calm vine-covered slope, and has a very spacious, well-presented boutique.

Best of all, go for a wander in the bacchic hills above town, where vines have colonized almost every inch of ground. Follow the **Route des Belvédères** and walk along the ridges to the **Chapelle de l'Hermitage** to appreciate some of the most dreamy views along the whole of the Rhône, the river cutting a romantic ribbon across the plain to Valence, mountains rising to east and west. Away from the river, try some friendly wine-making addresses among the hilly vineyards of **Mercurol**, in Crozes-Hermitage territory. Southeast at **Châteauneuf-sur-Isère**, the renowned **Paul Jaboulet Aîné wine company**, rival to Chapoutier in northern Côtes du Rhône supremacy, has opened **Vinéum** (*t 04 75 84 68 93, www.jaboulet.com*), spectacular cellars in a former quarry, but you'll need to phone to see if you can join a group visit.

Tournon and Tain-l'Hermitage were linked in 1825 by the first suspension bridge in continental Europe, designed by Marc Seguin (*see p.22*). Sadly, this was destroyed in 1965 to make way for the larger ships plying the Rhône. However, a slightly later one survives, the long footbridge linking both banks. Its château rising straight out of the riverside rock, historic **Tournon** imposes a stop for anyone coming down the Rhône's west bank. Up the hill, the odd isolated tower marks the line of the town's former **outer ramparts**, although small cohorts of vines have scaled these walls, viticulture winning over military culture. Down by the river, rows of huge planes shade the car parks in front of the small port. Major buildings near the water include the **Lycée Faure**, originally a religious school founded in the mid-16th century by the raging Catholic Cardinal François de Tournon. Head into the old town via appealing shopping streets, venturing into the shadowy Gothic **church of St-Julien** for sobering murals tracing Christ's life. Jesus' donkey is sniffed at by a dog as he arrives in Jerusalem, where he is brought before Pontius Pilate, seemingly wearing cardinal's robes.

The **château** (*t 04 75 08 10 31, open June–Aug daily 2–6, late-March–May and Sept–Oct Thurs–Tues 2–6; adm*) aloof on its rock was built in stages from the 10th to the 16th centuries. Apparently this strategic seat served as the headquarters for French royal negotiations to buy the province of the Dauphiné across the Rhône in the 14th century. Tournon lords held major court posts in the 15th and 16th centuries. Just de Tournon was killed fighting alongside François I at the disastrous Battle of Pavia of 1525, at which the sovereign was captured. François de Tournon, Just's brother, negotiated with the Holy Roman Emperor Charles V for the king's release.

A demoralizing royal tragedy took place in town in 153; the young heir to the French throne (also called François) died here in agonizing sickness. As to Hélène de Tournon, daughter of Just II, some claim her tragic love story made her the model for Shakespeare's Ophelia in *Hamlet*. The family line came to an end in the mid-17th century, the castle then long serving as a prison. The displays beyond the tremendous nail-covered door consider the Rhône mariners as well as the aristocratic Tournons. The place also serves as the town's art museum. The high-perched chapel boasts a stunning triptych, Christ rising to heaven in a flaming ball, an extraordinary falling skeleton contrasting with his ascent. The work includes a superb portrait of the donor, Cardinal François, with dog.

Keen walkers could tackle Tournon's former ramparts by following the **Sentier des Tours**. For an unstrenuous way to explore the area, book a **cruise up the Rhône**, allowing you to take in the vineyards and castle at leisurely pace; or head up into the rugged, scarcely populated Ardèche hills by the **Chemin de Fer du Vivarais** (*t 04 75 08*

20 30; July–Aug daily; May–June and Sept Tues–Sun; April and Oct Wed, Sun and public hols; adm) up the dramatically twisting Doux valley. Or then again, follow the locals to **Douce-Plage** (*c.* 5km along the Lamastre road) for a refreshing summer dip.

While Tournon is often described as the cradle of St-Joseph wine, around **Mauves**, you enter the area of the largest St-Joseph producers. Above Mauves, follow the dramatic **Corniche du Rhône**, or **Route Panoramique**, for spectacular views from the heights of **St-Romain-de-Lerps**. On the Rhône's bank, you pass impressively defensive **Châteaubourg**, the village below its castle (*not open*) clearly subservient. After **Cornas'** secretive theatre of vines, the vineyards of **St-Péray** surround that sweet little town. The place is quite eclipsed, though, by the spectacular bone-white ruins of the medieval **castle of Crussol** (*free*) lying like a huge battered snail's shell on the very steep hillside. Bastet de Crussol decided to have a castle built on this ridiculously difficult spot 230m above the Valence plain in the 12th century. Later members of the family presumably had enough of the hair-raising route home and headed off to play greater roles on the national stage. In the 17th century, the castle was partly destroyed. But what remains is, with Rochemaure (*see* p.165), by far the most sensational castle ruin along the Rhône. The reward if you make it up the treacherously slippery paths (take great care) is amazing views east to the Vercors mountains. As the sun descends, the castle casts a huge shadow across the Valence plain.

The young Napoleon is said to have appreciated his stay in **Valence** as a young army officer, arriving by boat in November 1785 and enjoying flirting with the daughters of the local bourgeoisie, cherry-picking, reading voraciously, and even penning a passionate military novel. The story goes, however, that he almost died on the perilous climb to the top of Crussol castle – how different European history might have been if that tourist outing had ended otherwise! As it was, Napoleon left in August 1786 to help put down a silk-workers' riot in Lyon, briefly returning to the same elite regiment in 1791. Valence had a very long military past, originally founded as a Roman garrison. Its merchants long prospered from controlling the salt trade. Pope Pius VI didn't have as good a time in Valence as Bonaparte, ignominiously dragged from Rome as far as here once the imperious *petit caporal* was setting about brief European domination. The sickly pontiff died here in 1799. His body was eventually returned to Italy, the Rhône-side city receiving a bust by way of thanks.

Although in a central location, the **Cathédrale St-Apollinaire** turns its back on the main central square. Much reconstructed in the 17th century, the edifice retains the form and certain fragments of the Romanesque original. Inside, the bust of Pope Pius VI stands out in the colonnaded ambulatory. Occupying the plain 18th-century bishop's palace, the town's **Musée des Beaux-Arts** (*t 04 75 79 20 80, www.musee-valence.org; open mid-June–Sept Tues–Sun 10–12 and 2–6.45, Oct–mid-June Tues–Sun 2–5.45; adm*) starts with a collection of remarkable Roman mosaics, the most startling starring a beefy, naked Hercules performing his twelve labours with club-swinging gusto. Classical ruins feature in the best-known collection of pictures in the museum, dramatic red crayon drawings by the *Ancien Régime* artist Hubert Robert. The odd portrait of important figures in Valentinois history draws attention, including one of Jean-Etienne Championnet, one of Napoleon's brilliant boy-generals, from Valence.

The end of the cathedral sticks unapologetically out into **Place des Clercs**, now the lively centre of the old town, along with **Place de l'Université** hub of the spectacular Saturday morning market. The main old shopping streets lead off these squares, including the stylish **Grande Rue**, which boasts the liveliest façade in town, the well-named **Maison des Têtes**, containing a small, free permanent exhibition on Valence's history. But the main interest is on the outside, reflecting a golden period when fairs and a reputed university brought prosperity to Valence – this façade was commissioned by a professor of law and leading town councillor. Classical allusions feature from the heads on high representing the winds, via Fortune and Time gadding about naked on the first floor, to nine philosophers presiding over the ground floor. On the town guided tour you see the elaborate courtyard, and that of the **Maison Dupré-Latour** on parallel **Rue Perrolerie**. At the bottom of that street, the restful 16th-century classical funerary monument of **Le Pendentif** stands in a quiet corner, while at the other end, appealing restaurant terraces spread out on little **Place de la Pierre**.

Just up **Rue St-James**, the **Temple**, or Protestant church, occupies the former Catholic St Rufus priory where pilgrims used to stop on their way down the Rhône. An aside in English Church history, in the 12th century, one Nicholas Breakspear made quite an impression when he joined the order here; he went on to become the only English pope, Adrian IV. In the 18th century the church interior was decorated with fine stucco, while Napoleon later ordered the obelisk honouring Championnet. On grandiose **Place de la Liberté**, the 19th-century **Hôtel de Ville** and **theatre** with their massive egos vie for attention. Continue to **Place St-Jean**, embellished with a light covered market, looked down upon by the **Eglise St-Jean-Baptiste**.

Wide **boulevards** encircle the historic centre, following the course of former ramparts. To the south lies the enormous **Champ de Mars**, the biggest terrace in Valence. The statue once again stars Championnet. Behind, a further array of bright shopping streets line up, but the view west tempts you down into the shaded **Parc Jouvet**, with a magical ring of towering planes under which the *boules* players gather. The gates at the end stop anyone running out onto the thundering roads cutting the Valentinois off from their river. For a day-trip out on the Rhône, contact **Bateaux Taxi Valentinois** (*t 06 85 08 44 26*).

The Rhône from Valence to Montélimar

Following the **west bank of the Rhône**, **Soyons** appears to have been the place to head in prehistoric times for butchering mammoths along the river. A hoard of the woolly creatures' bones was unearthed here in the 1980s. This mysterious story counts among the most compelling told in the unassuming but interesting **Musée Archéologique** (*t 04 75 60 88 86, e musee.soyons@wanadoo.fr; has undergone restoration; check times*). Evidence of continuous human habitation is displayed here going back 150,000 years. The separate archaeological site of **La Brégoule** uncovers a comparatively short 10,000 years of civilization.

Model trains clamber round the tortuous local terrain recreated in reduced version at **Ardèche Miniature** (*t 04 75 60 96 58, www.ardeche-miniatures.com; open June–Sept daily 10–7, Feb–May and Oct–Nov Tues-Sun 2–6; adm*). Real pretty old villages with castle ruins follow at **Charmes-sur-Rhône** and at **Beauchastel**. Leave civilization totally behind for the craggy ruins of the **Château de Pierre-Gourde** just rising out of the dense greenery, a dozen melting layers of hills disappearing to the west. A black castle (*t 04 75 62 44 36; open mid-June–Aug Wed only at 10.30; adm*) dominates **La Voulte-sur-Rhône**, its Gothic to Renaissance forms at one time hosting the estates general of the whole Languedoc region. Among the dark arcaded streets, the church of St-Vincent treasures a beautifully carved 16th-century marble altarpiece. An array of fossilized animals including a 150-million-year-old octopus have been gathered by a passionate collector at the **Musée de Paléontologie** (*t 04 75 62 44 94, www.musee-fossiles.com; open July–Aug Sun–Fri 10–6, Feb–June and Sept–Dec Sun–Fri 2–5.30; adm*).

One of the worst victims of the Rhône valley's massive industrialization, **Cruas** boasts one of the most splendid religious edifices along the river. Pope Urban II consecrated the **church** (*t 04 75 49 59 20, www.cruas.com; open April–Sept Mon–Sat visits at 11, 3 and 5, Sun at 3.30 and 5.30, off season Mon, Tues, Thurs and Fri visits at 2.30 and 4.30, Sat at 10; adm*) in the late 11th century. The abbey of which it was a part became a powerful establishment, ruling over extensive territories, with up to 100 monks at home here. They held on doggedly through the Wars of Religion, defending themselves up in the compact fort on the hillside. A bishop of Viviers rang the death knell for the abbey, closing it in the 18th century. Just the abbey church remains. In its lower part, admire the finely carved capitals. Down in the Carolingian crypt, the motifs look far more primitive, one figure in wildly uplifting prayer. The upper church was reserved for the monks. The intriguing mosaic formed part of the original 11th-century symbolic decorations. Later medieval murals illustrate exemplary martyrdoms. For a divine little country detour avoiding Cruas, branch off the N86 north of Baix onto the D22, then join the D2 south, a cheerful, peaceful route, a world away from the Rhône-side industry. Below **St-Vincent-de-Barrès**, a hill village marked out by crumbling towers, seek out **Il Etait Une Soie** (*t 04 75 65 93 40, www.iletaitunesoie.com; open May–Sept Tues–Sun 3–7; adm*), a farm where the region's silk-making traditions are lovingly recalled, with regular little theatrical performances.

Shooting up at the top of what some unfortunate French brochures translate as a volcanic 'dick', the most startling of all Rhône valley castles balances on top of the amazing pinnacle at **Rochemaure**. The medieval fort was for a time the stronghold of one of the branches of the Adhémar family from Montélimar. Restored in the 19th century, the ramparts extend further along the high ridge, protecting an upper village. For another amazing view head west to the **Pic de Chenavari**, reached by foot.

On the **east bank of the Rhône below Valence**, the **A7** and **N7** get involved in a slightly twisted race to Montélimar. Protected from them by remnants of its ramparts, **Etoile-sur-Rhône** has kept its historic atmosphere. Closer to the Rhône, certain vineyards around Livron produce a rare Brézème, sought-after Côtes du Rhône. South from Loriol, take to the slopes for two enchanting neighbouring artistic old villages. **Cliousclat** keeps very tightly in its shell, protecting itself from modern encroachments. This is a potters' village where the houses really are as tightly packed as pieces in a kiln. Visit the many galleries, and the old-style **Musée Histoire de Poteries** (*t 04 75 63 15 60; open July–Aug daily 10–1 and 2–7, April–June and Sept–Nov Tues–Sun 2–6; adm*), still operating the old-fashioned way. **Mirmande** faces the Rhône valley with more open defiance, built in layers up a pudding-shaped hill. Early in the 20th century many locals abandoned their houses for the valley. But Mirmande then welcomed an artists' colony when Cubist painter André Lhote fell in love with the place in the 1920s. Stylishly restored, it remains a favourite with an intellectual and artistic crowd, a couple of galleries on the way up to the church, which serves as something of a cultural centre. A beautiful forest road leads to **Marsanne**, once Mirmande's rival, in a panoramic spot above the Roubion plain leading to Montélimar, contorted peaks rising to the east. The ruins of a castle tumble down the hillside. Clamber up to what remains of medieval **St-Félix**. Below, the 19th-century stamps its mark confidently. Marsanne was the birthplace in 1838 of the first 'peasant president', Emile Loubet (*see below*). Down to Montélimar, it's hard to wipe the vast chimneys of the Cruas nuclear power station from the corner of your eye, one quite cynically daubed with a huge image of a child playing innocently on a beach.

Its compact historic kernel caught between major nuclear installations along the Rhône, the name of **Montélimar** does conjure up very sweet images for French children. Before the A7 motorway was opened in the late 1960s, legions of families would stop in town to buy a bag or two of nougat, in part to keep the children quiet on the journey, their teeth almost literally glued together. Approaching the old town, the

Nougat de Montélimar

The almonds, pistachios and honey mixed with whites of egg to make nougat make you think of a Moorish dessert, and legend has it that this was one of the delights brought over to France by way of the Arabs. One version of the story claims the recipe arrived with the 8th-century Moorish incursions into southern France; another that it was an Adhémar lord who came back from crusade with a native cook in tow, who whipped up culinary delicacies for his new master's delight. But it's only in the 16th century that there's clear evidence of almond trees being planted in the region. One highly placed ambassador for Montélimar's confectionery at the start of the 20th century was long-time mayor Emile Loubet, who made it to top post of President of France. A staunch Republican, as well as seeing to the pardoning of the framed Jewish soldier Alfred Dreyfus, the quintessential Republican separation of French Church and State, and the signing of the Entente Cordiale with Britain, he apparently spoilt all his guests with Montélimar's sticky sweets.

To see how nougat is made, visit one of the 15 producers in town. Just north of the main boulevards, the central Nougaterie Chaudron d'Or is one of the smallest and friendliest. The maker with the biggest reputation has moved his premises to a new commercial zone off the main southern road out of the centre. Despite the dull surrounds, Arnaud Soubeyran, tireless modern-day ambassador for nougat, has created a swanky shop, with a corner turned into a Musée du Nougat (*t 04 75 51 01 35, www.nougatsoubeyran.com; open Mon–Sat 9–7, Sun 10–12 and 2.30–6.30*).

relentless commercial zones hardly look appealing, although many a nougat shop still lines the way, while the trendy-to-tacky new art and craft centre **Au Fil du Temps** to the north calls for attention.

Traffic dashes incessantly round the boulevards that encircle the historic kernel. But the wonderful shade of layers of plane trees (up to six rows deep) of the **Allées Provençales** should tempt you to stop. Most of the historic streets are reserved for pedestrians. From a few, you get fleeting glimpses of the medieval castle on the hill, a short but steep climb away. Around the 11th century, the Adhémar family took up home here on Monteil hill, which became the Mont-Adhémar, hence Montélimar. Although you don't feel the presence of the Rhône in Montélimar, their solid keep surveyed the valley down to the Donzère straights, where tough little mountains tighten their grip around the river's throat. The Adhémar family subsequently split into several competing hilltop factions, one branch taking to La Garde-Adhémar, another to Rochemaure, a third to Grignan. As to the merchants of Monteil, they were early granted franchises from taxes. The acquisitive popes of Avignon, not far south, ensured that many monasteries were built in the town when they gained control in the 14th century, but the place suffered terribly in the Wars of Religion. Calmer times followed with the planting of mulberries for silk-making and almonds for nougat.

Montélimar's semi-ruined feudal **Château des Adhémar** (*t 04 75 00 62 30; open April–Oct daily 9.30–11.30 and 2–5.30; Nov–March Wed–Mon, same times; adm*) looks slightly Moorish. It has been given a new lease of life as a *Centre d'Art Contemporain*, holding retrospectives on major international artists, and inviting newer talents to fill the empty medieval chambers with bold works for a season. Montélimar's ramparts brought down in the 19th century, one *Ancien Régime* gateway survives at the northern end of the main street, **Rue Pierre Julien**. Explore the maze of unfussy to scruffy lanes and squares off this main artery. Many facades have been painted in cheerful powder-puff colours, one of the brightest, a former religious building, converted into the curious but stylish **Musée de la Miniature** (*t 04 75 53 79 24; open July–Aug daily 10–6; Feb–June and Sept–Dec Wed–Sun 2–6; adm*) dedicated to miniature works of art. On the outskirts of Montélimar, fans of military aviation shoot off to the **Musée Européen de l'Avion de Chasse** (*t 04 75 53 79 49, www.meacmtl.com; open weekdays 1.30–5.30, weekends 2.30–6.30; adm*). Golfers head for the 18-hole **Golf de la Valdaine** (*t 04 75 00 71 33*) east at Montboucher-sur-Jabron.

From Montélimar to the Languedoc and Provence Borders

A tiara in stone crowns the fine cathedral of **Viviers**, a startling if neglected town on its hilltop **above the west bank of the Rhône**. Its Gallo-Roman name, Vivarium, probably derived from *viviers*, fishponds by the river, supplying the city of Alba-la-Romaine (*see* p.144). Then Bishop Ausonne made the big move from Alba to here, a new city by the Rhône. It grew to such importance that it gave its name to a whole mountainous area west of the river, the Vivarais, roughly equivalent to the present-day *département* of Ardèche. Despite feeling semi-abandoned now, the place still has a bishop, as it has had since the 5th century. Large episcopal buildings stand out in the lower town.

It's a steep climb to the hilltop **cathedral**, protected within a precinct of tall white stone walls. The windowless, aisleless nave is of staggering proportions, an awesome religious cave, in some way rivalling the celebrated natural grottoes of the Ardèche gorges close by (*see* p.146). Consecrated by Pope Calixtus II in 1119, the place still feels strongly Romanesque, although apparently largely redone in the 18th century. Seven splendid Gothic windows in the choir signal clearly how that end was rebuilt in the late 15th century. A major cycle of 18th-century Gobelin tapestries below illustrates episodes in Christ's life. They've kept their fresh colours, but also the sickly sweet tone favoured in *Ancien Régime* storytelling. The separate campanile towers 40m into the air, doubling as a huge defensive post, but from the terrace beyond, the views are marred by industry. The liveliest thing in the dying streets below is the façade of the grand **Maison Noël Albert**, a striking carving showing victorious knights on horseback, their vigour seeming somewhat ironic today. From the lower town, a splendid avenue of squat plane trees leads to the picturesque **port**.

Below Viviers, the Rhône valley narrows into the extremely tight **Défilé de Donzère**, cliffs closing dramatically in on the river. **St-Montan**, named after a 5th-century religious man who sought refuge from the world here, today offers a refreshing haven away from the roar of the main Rhône valley roads. Streams congregate at the bottom of the village, whose lovingly restored roofs you can appreciate by climbing beyond the main church and the cobbled maze of steep lanes up to the substantial crenallated remnants of a castle, which stomps to the top of the pyramidal hill, guarding the entrance to the unspoilt rocky terrain of the **Gorge de la Ste Baume**, wild parts appreciated by rockclimbers and potholers.

Its quays backed by major merchants' houses may now be quiet, but **Bourg-St-Andéol** makes a last surprisingly rich historic stop on the Ardèche side of the Rhône. The place carries the name of a 2nd-century Christian martyr savagely put to death by order of Emperor Septimus Severus, enraged at witnessing his success in converting the locals. Andéol's dismembered body was thrown in the Rhône. Christianity was never an innocent cult, however. In their early days in Gaul, Christians smashed rival religions like Mithraism. This cult, introduced to the Roman empire from Persia, featured a young saviour killing a formidable bull, symbol of evil. A **Mithraic carving** has miraculously survived below the terraces of a rustic public garden near the centre. Although badly defaced, you can make out the caped young hero stabbing the bull. Hope springs from his act, corn sprouting from the beast's tail. Sun and moon oversee proceedings, the former wearing rays like an early Statue of Liberty.

Old Christian buildings triumph above the quays. A powerful octagonal tower rises from the heavily restored **Romanesque church**. Nearby, the very substantial **Palais des Evêques** (*t 04 75 54 41 76; open June–Sept Wed, Thurs, Sat and Sun 3.30–7.30; adm*) long served as a residence of the bishops of Viviers. Battered by the centuries, only just being revived, certain Gothic features still stand out on the outside, and spacious fireplaces within. Under the 17th-century Monseigneur de la Baume de Suze, bishop of Viviers at just 17, certain chambers were embellished with painted ceilings. Cultural events are now being staged in this sprawling edifice. Another grand building above the Rhône, the **Hôtel Doize** houses the **Musée de la Dentelle** (*t 04 75 54 00 73 between 10am and 8pm for appointment*), a private lace museum run by a British woman passionate about her craft, on which she organizes courses. For one of the most stunning views over the Rhône, taking in much of the gorgeous *département* of the Drôme, climb the D4 from Bourg towards Vallon.

Côtes du Rhône vines stretch south from Bourg-St-Andéol. Above historic **St-Marcel-d'Ardèche**, tucked away on its hillside, almonds and other trees also thrive, while below **St-Just**, truffle oaks and peach orchards have been planted close to the Rhône. On the border with the *département du Gard* in the Languedoc region, one last, lovely sandy beach stretches along the Ardèche riverbank by a romantically ruined bridge. For the Ardèche gorges a little west, *see* p.146. If you want to continue south, consult Cadogan *South of France*.

Heading south from Montélimar along the **Rhône's east bank**, keeping close to the river, **Châteauneuf-sur-Rhône**, with its old line of ramparts running down the hill, still looks a feisty medieval military village, but the place really is embattled by industry. Set some way back from the Rhône, the old **Allan** on its ridge was totally abandoned long ago, leaving an impressive array of ruins stretching along the hillside like a mighty, vanished fort. A back road leads to somewhat better preserved **Roussas** on its dramatic ridge, several churches vying for attention along with the restored ruins of its castle. The steep narrow lanes of **Valaurie** protect a couple of art galleries in a hilltop village well known for having attracted a close-knit intellectual crowd. For gorgeous Grignan to the east, *see* p.189.

Stood defiantly on its high terrace above the Rhône, **La Garde-Adhémar** has to contend with noisy Rhône valley traffic below. But enchantingly restored, this splendid village has the character to deal with the situation. Its serene Romanesque church confidently overlooking the valley offers a calm refuge and the comfort of a solid peasant Virgin and child. Just below, explore the enchanting herb garden, its plants colour-coded according to their medicinal properties. The rest of the village turns its back on the Rhône, with plenty of resources to look in on itself, including delightful houses, craft shops and cafés. The neglected ruins of the **Chapelle du Val des Nymphes** lie hidden a few kilometres east. To the south, a tower rises from the rock-top hamlet of **Clansayes**, a landmark visible from afar, topped by a big Virgin who looks quite dismayed at the nuclear power station visible down in the Rhône valley. French people go in their hundreds of thousands to visit the Tricastin nuclear installations beside **Pierrelatte** every year, while the bizarre **Ferme aux Crocodiles** (*t 04 75 04 33 73, www.lafermeauxcrocodiles.com; open March–Sept daily 9.30–7, Oct–Feb daily 9.30–5; adm*) also attracts huge numbers. Its waters are heated by the warmth generated by the power station, providing a suitable habitat for a whole range of crocodile species, living in exotic surroundings.

We end the chapter with a forgotten joy hidden just out of sight of the Rhône, an ancient little city still surrounded in good part by medieval walls, adorable **St-Paul-Trois-Châteaux**. Those of you hoping from the name to discover three castles here will be sorely disappointed, as there are none. But the **Romanesque cathedral** helps make up for that, a remarkable edifice that incorporates fragments of previous Roman buildings. In fact, the place is named after a Bishop Paul who served here in the late-Roman period; and this tiny spot would remain a bishopric up until the Revolution. The cathedral's almost total lack of windows clearly indicates its pre-Gothic roots, built mainly in the 11th and 12th centuries. Intriguing features make up for the lack of openings. Look out for the noble carved heads squashed in above the main door, itself an accomplished piece of carving. Wander round the outside of the building looking out for stonemasons' marks and even tiny rough carvings of warriors. In the dauntingly tall interior, a mosaic in the apse depicts a naïve Jerusalem. Elsewhere, carved details and patches of medieval murals add to the intrigue.

The lands east of here are the most prolific truffle-producing territories in France, hence the **Maison de la Truffe et du Tricastin** (*t 04 75 96 61 29; open daily exc Mon morning, and Sun out of season, 9–12 and 2–6; adm*) in the shadow of the cathedral. Explanations get a little overtechnical for the uninitiated – take the tour CD for assistance. You can buy samples of the massively priced 'black diamonds' here. Explore the enchanting maze of squares away from the cathedral. Vines proliferate in the lands to the east too, producing excellent-value Coteaux du Tricastin and Côtes du Rhône wines, while at nearby Suze-la-Rousse, the old castle has been converted into a university of wine! For more details, read the next chapter. If you head south from here, Cadogan's *Provence* guide focuses on that region.

East of the Rhône
From the Isère into the Drôme

Western Isère and Northern Drôme 174
Into Western Isère's Lands of Glacial Pebbles **174**
The Culinary Isère Valley below the Vercors **178**
The Pebbly Northern Drôme **180**
Romans-sur-Isère **181**
The Southern Drôme 182
Up the Drôme into the Diois **182**
Into the Drôme Provençale **188**
To Dieulefit and Grignan **189**
Into the Baronnies Range **193**

13

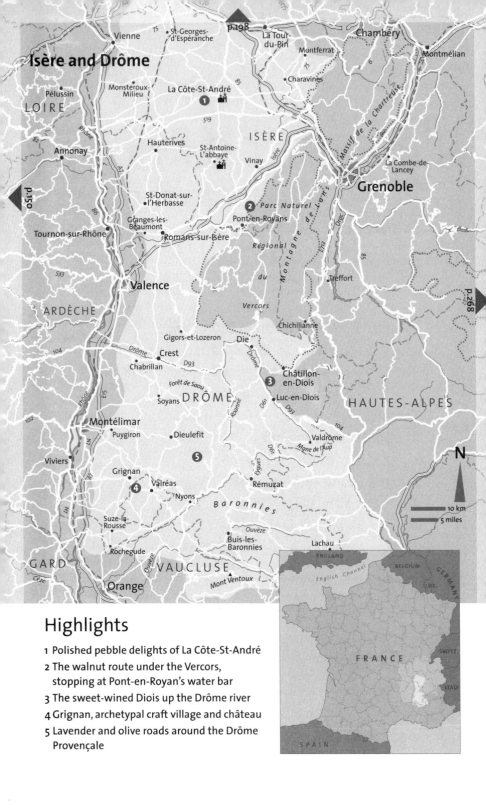

Highlights

1 Polished pebble delights of La Côte-St-André
2 The walnut route under the Vercors, stopping at Pont-en-Royan's water bar
3 The sweet-wined Diois up the Drôme river
4 Grignan, archetypal craft village and château
5 Lavender and olive roads around the Drôme Provençale

The sharp wolves' ears of pre-alpine ranges rising menacingly in the background, the lands we look on so fondly here roll playfully down to the Rhône. The Isère and the Drôme are the main rivers that trip west to join their master through the area we cover in this chapter, consisting of the western, less elevated halves of the two *départements* named after these rivers. Historically, these territories fell within the province of the Dauphiné, joined to the French crown in the 14th century. In contrast with the tortuous Ardèche on the other side of the Rhône, these are generous, open lands. Instead of dark-stoned villages, the slopes are sprinkled with cheerful places in lighter tones. And instead of eking a living from meagre terraces and narrow valleys, the farmers have benefited from exceptionally fertile lands.

In the northern half, the round glacial stones of the valleys have long been put to decorative effect in the traditional architecture. A 19th-century postman got rather carried away by these polished pebbles, and created one of the most famous follies in France, the *Palais Idéal du Facteur Cheval, Architecture Naïve* at Hauterives. You can also admire typical architecture in places such as La Côte-St-André, bourgeois birthplace of that ecstatic figure of 19th-century high culture, Berlioz, or at the beautiful religious halt of St-Antoine-l'Abbaye, headquarters of medically-minded medieval monks. Further east, around the pleasingly low-key Lac de Paladru, the traditional, steeply curving Dauphiné roofs with their fish-scale tiles serve as a reminder that the winters get harsher nearer the mountains. The walnut orchards lining the Isère banks below the forbidding Vercors range also signal fresher climes, but refreshment is the order of the day at Pont-en-Royans, with the most joyous new museum on water.

South of the shoe-addicts' dream of Romans-sur-Isère, sunnier southern orchards of peaches, nectarines, cherries and apricots prevail. And down in the very south, you enter the positively paradisiac Drôme Provençale, the southern slice of the *département* where not just fruit orchards and vines proliferate, but also lavender and olive trees. As if that weren't bountiful enough, black diamonds are unearthed under the oak trees – this is the largest truffle-producing area in France, the centre of this closely guarded crop the former Knights' Templar fortified village of Richerenches.

Major castles occupy high points in these parts, like Crest, with the tallest keep in France, Grignan, intimately associated with that most refined of *Ancien Régime* correspondents, Madame de Sévigné, or Suze-la-Rousse, now home to the wicked-sounding *Université du Vin*. While leaving the vicious, chilling pre-alpine heights of the Chartreuse and Vercors well alone here, we do venture into the friendlier, more southerly Diois and Baronnies *montagnettes*, where you encounter an extraordinary, quieter Cowboys-and-Indians landscape, huge bald limestone mountaintops rising high above the smaller patches of crops, goats grazing on the mid-slopes, majestic birds of prey taking in the gorgeous territories, circling high above.

Western Isère and Northern Drôme
Into Western Isère's Lands of Glacial Pebbles

We start at that ancient geographical dividing line between territories, the A43 motorway between Lyon and Chambéry. For those interested in contemporary architecture, **L'Isle d'Abeau** has plenty to show, a new town that has sprung up since the 1970s, a spacious modern satellite for the Lyonnais. Neighbouring **Bourgoin-Jallieu**, by contrast, has long-established working-class credentials, which in these parts means clothes-making. Its pompous claim to have been French capital of *l'ennoblissement textile* since the 17th century really signifies that the speciality here was printing on cloth. The tradition has lost out to cheaper international labour and computers, but even at the end of the millennium, one or two specialist local companies were still painstakingly working the old-fashioned way for leading fashion brands. In the bustling commercial centre, the **Musée de Bourgoin-Jallieu** (*t 04 74 28 19 74; open Jan–Dec Tues–Sun 10–12 and 2–6; adm*) traces the path of this dying industry in real style. Plus the place serves as a local art museum. And the original selection of sumptuous scarves comes at knockdown prices.

La Tour-du-Pin may have been the centre of the last branch of independent medieval lords of the Dauphiné (*see* p.161), but the place continued to thrive, to go by the Renaissance houses, while in the **church** hangs a remarkably sensitive 16th-century triptych by Georg Pencz, a pupil of Dürer; movingly, he donated it in thanks for the care he received at the local hospital.

If you leave the Rhône valley south of Vienne, go via the crumbling pebble and earth village of **Monsteroux** to **Montseveroux,** standing proud on its hill ridge with views, its old golden-stoned castle bought by the community in the 19th century, now converted into a delightful town hall and school. Continue east to the stunningly flat former glacial **Plaine de la Bièvre**, the view onto the unbroken patchwork of fields like a natural masterpiece of abstract art. Mountains fill the backdrops east and west.

Its Romanesque church signalled by a brick and pebble tower, its old covered market held up on an impressive six rows of wooden pillars, a slope-side town above the plain, **La Côte-St-André** has many appealing aspects. But the main attraction is the renovated **Musée Hector Berlioz** (*t 04 74 20 24 88, www.musee-hector-berlioz.com; open June–Sept daily exc Tues 10–7, Oct–May daily exc Tues 10–6; adm*) in honour of the composer of such ecstatic pieces as *Les Nuits d'été*. The museum, situated in the substantial townhouse where the great composer was born, introduces Berlioz in the context of early 19th-century political upheaval and the Romantic movement it helped to spawn, and then gives an overview of his life and work (*see* p.24). The tour of the house, which has a strong 19th-century bourgeois feel, takes you from the kitchen, via the grand salons, to the bedrooms, with mementoes from Hector's life, such as his first instruments (a guitar and a *flageolet*, the latter a type of recorder, not a bean) and numerous portraits and statues. The top floor concentrates on Berlioz's writing as well as his music and the interactive posts allow you to listen to short

East of Lyon: Isère and the Northern Drôme

extracts. Down in the basement, you can appreciate longer pieces in the small auditorium.

Passionate chocolate lovers may sniff out a particularly tempting chocolate shop on the lively main shopping street by the museum, run by the same man who directs the **Paradis du Chocolat** (*t 04 74 20 35 89, www.paradis-chocolat.com; open weekends and public and school hols 2–6; adm*), at the top of the town, in the much-abused remnants of the château, now resembling a factory as much as a castle. Chock-a-block with information on chocolate history, culture and commerce, this museum

Getting Around

By train: Romans-sur-Isère and St-Marcellin have railway stations on the line from Valence to Grenoble.

By bus: Bus services for the area go from Valence or Romans.

Tourist Information

La Côte-St-André: Pl Berlioz, 38260 La Côte-St-André, **t** 04 74 20 61 43, www.cc-bievre-liers.fr.
Pont-en-Royans: 38680 Pont-en-Royans, **t** 04 76 36 09 10, www.ot-pont-en-royans.com.
St-Jean-en-Royans: 13 Place de l'Eglise, 26190 St-Jean-en-Royans, **t** 04 75 48 61 39, www.royans.com.
St-Antoine-l'Abbaye: Place Gilibert, 38160 St-Antoine-l'Abbaye, **t** 04 76 36 44 46, **e** stantoine.tourisme@wanadoo.fr.
Hauterives: Place de la Galaure, 26390 Hauterives, **t** 04 75 68 86 82 .
Romans-sur-Isère: Place Jean Jaurès, 26100 Romans-sur-Isère, **t** 04 75 02 28 72.

Market Days

La Côte-St-André: Thurs morning.
Charavines: Sun morning.
St-Jean-en-Royans: Sat afternoon.
Hauterives: Tues morning.
Romans-sur-Isère: Tues, Wed, Fri, Sat and Sun.

Where to Stay and Eat

Césarges ✉ 38300

Château de Césarges B&B, **t** 04 74 93 20 42, **f** 04 74 28 61 49 (*inexpensive*). Bargain characterful rooms in this big block of a building below Bourgoin.

Bossieu ✉ 38260

Le Cellier B&B, **t** 04 74 54 32 85, **f** 04 74 54 29 04 (*inexpensive*). Superb spacious white B&B rooms in towered property once owned by the abbey of Bonnevaux, with splendid views, looking down beyond the horses in the paddock and across the Bièvre plain. *Table d'hôte* (*moderate*).

St-Georges-d'Espéranche ✉ 38790

Castel d'Espéranche, **t** 04 74 59 18 45 (*expensive–moderate*). One of Europe's most famous medieval castle architects, Jacques d'Espéranche (builder of Edward I's great edifices in north Wales), came from here; appropriately , this atmospheric restaurant is partly in a 13th-century guards' tower, the service sometimes in costume. *Closed Mon–Wed, plus Mar and Nov*.

La Côte-St-André ✉ 38260

★★Hôtel de France, Place St-André, **t** 04 74 20 25 99, **f** 04 74 20 35 30 (*inexpensive*).

proves a tad hard to swallow, although you can buy lots of chocolate. You're also treated to an impassioned lecture on true chocolate-making by the owner.

The three parallel diagonal valleys of the Bourbre, Bièvre and Ainan form a splendidly undulating area known as the **Pays des Trois Vallées** east of the A48 motorway, south of the A43. This patch on the borders of the Dauphiné and Savoie was long ruled over by the lords of Clermont. The intimidating **Château de Virieu** (**t** 04 74 88 20 10, www.chateaudevirieu.com; open July–Aug Tues–Sun 2–6; Easter–June and Sept–Oct weekends and public hols 2–6; adm) stands arrogantly high above the little town with a lovely old covered market grovelling at its feet. The castle's roofs are covered with distinctive Dauphiné tiles like brown fish scales. Although a medieval stronghold of the Clermonts, it was for a leading Grenoblois that the towers went up. The formidable place has never been disturbed by wars. The entrance looks so forbidding you can understand why. Enter the courtyard via a door covered with over 1,000 sharp nails, and you're greeted by five cannons, a gift from Louis XIII when he visited in 1622. The military theme continues through the handful of chambers you see inside.

Welcoming rooms in old building by the church, with a fine traditional country restaurant (*expensive*) . *Restaurant closed Sun eve and Mon.*

Charavines ✉ 38850

**Beau Rivage, 115 Rue Principale, t 04 76 06 61 08, f 04 76 06 66 58 (*inexpensive*). Big hotel and restaurant (*moderate*) making the most of their lake-side setting. *Closed Christmas–Jan; restaurant closed Sun eve, plus Mon, and Tues eve out of season.*
Hôtel des Bains, 365 Rue Principale, t 04 76 06 60 20 (*moderate–inexpensive*). Actually now just a nice lakeside restaurant for fish fry-ups . *Closed Jan–mid-Feb.*

Montferrat ✉ 38620

Auberge Féfête, Le Vernay, t 04 76 32 40 46 (*moderate*). Refined cuisine at this intimate family restaurant on the northern end of Paladru lake. *Closed late April and late Oct.*

St-Ondras ✉ 38490

Le Pas de l'Ane B&B, t 04 76 32 01 78, f 04 76 32 67 67 (*moderate*). Spacious Dauphiné property up from Virieu. *Table d'hôte (moderate).*

St-Antoine-l'Abbaye ✉ 38160

Auberge de l'Abbaye, t 04 76 36 42 83 (*expensive–moderate;*). Lovely food in wonderful location on the square facing the abbey. *Closed Jan and Tues out of season.*
L'Antonin B&B, t 04 76 36 41 53 (*inexpensive*). Lovely old village house. *Table d'hôte (cheap).*

Hauterives ✉ 26390

**Le Relais, t 04 75 68 81 12, f 04 75 68 92 42 (*cheap*). Traditional house of pebbles, with reasonable rooms and decent cuisine (*moderate*). *Closed mid-Jan–end Feb; restaurant closed Sun eve outside summer, and Mon.*
Les Beaumes de Tersanne B&B, t 04 75 68 90 56, e *romanat@free.fr* (*inexpensive*). Neatly restored traditional farm outside the village, serving *table d'hôte* (*moderate*)

Romans-sur-Isère ✉ 26100

***L'Orée du Parc, 6 Ave Gambetta, t 04 75 70 26 12, *www.hotel-oreeparc.com* (*expensive*). Practical address for shopaholics, so close to Marques Avenue. Pool.
La Charrette, 15 Place de l'Horloge, t 04 75 02 04 25 (*cheap*). Lovely terrace at the foot of the Tour Jacquemart, offering local ravioli or dish of the day. *Closed Sun.*

Granges-lès-Beaumont ✉ 26600

Les Cèdres, t 04 75 71 50 67 (*expensive*). Splendid village restaurant west of Romans. *Closed Mon and Tues, and mid-Aug–mid-Sept.*

Close by, the **Lac de Paladru** may be a poor relation of the more glamorous great lakes of Savoie to the east, but you can find pleasant, good-value little family resorts around its emerald-blue waters, with thin pebbly beaches and clusters of boats. And this lake, the fifth largest natural one in France, formed with the melting of the last Ice Age, has an exceptional pre-tourist prehistory, explained at the **Musée du Lac de Paladru** (*t 04 76 55 77 47, www.museelacdepaladru.com; open July–Aug Tues–Sun 3–7, June and Sept Tues–Sun 2–6, May weekends and public hols 2–6; adm*) at **Charavines**. In the lake's shallow waters, submerged remains have been discovered, not just of medieval settlements from around the year 1000, but also of Neolithic ones dating back some 5,000 years. The lake has kept the finds in a good state of preservation. For a long time, the theory was that these communities were built on stilts above the water, but now it's thought they went up in periods when the globe warmed and the waters receded, only to be inundated later. Charavines has a gentle family holiday feel. In the hills above, the older villages boast houses topped with superb wide-brimmed sloping Dauphiné roofs. Seek out the **Grange Louisias**, sporting a wonderful thatched hat and earthen walls. The enchanting Vergers de Louisas farm produces superlative fruit jams and drinks. The **Grange Dimière**, or tithe barn, of the abbey of the Chartreuse de la Silve-Bénite (*same times as Musée du Lac*) recalls the importance of this religious establishment as well as serving for exhibitions. Behind its moat, the **Château de Longpra** (*t 04 76 07 63 48; open June–Oct daily 2–6; adm*) to the east presents a refined model of Dauphinois good living, kitted out with superb woodwork by the reputed Hache family in the 18th century. For more interesting religious architecture, visit the church at **St-Geoire-en-Valdaine** and **Chirens priory**.

The Culinary Isère Valley below the Vercors

The Isère river emerges from its staggering mountain journey (*see* chapter 16) via a narrow gap between the Chartreuse and Vercors ranges north of Grenoble, close to **Voiron**. Daunting pre-alpine slopes as a backdrop, the town's 19th-century **church of St Bruno**, designed by the great Gothic revivalist Viollet-le-Duc, responds with soaring twin spires and colourful roof, while the smaller, less showy, older **church of St Peter,** built on a Gallo-Roman site, is more modest, but of interest. The ruins of the medieval **Barral tower** recall that this strategic spot served as a forward post of Savoie until the mid-14th century. The Chartreuse range so closely linked with the monks of its famous charterhouse (*see* p.275), this monastery's influence spread into the valley. The immense underground **Caves de la Grande Chartreuse** (*t 04 76 05 81 77, www. chartreuse.fr; open April–Oct daily 9–6.30, rest of year daily 9–11.30 and 2–5.30; free*) are where the violently green and yellow Chartreuse liqueurs have been made since the 1930s, but the secret herbal recipe that the monks received at the start of the 17th century is not revealed on the popular tour. Simpler fruit liqueurs are also on offer.

Three busy roads accompany the Isère on its last leg to join the Rhône, running below the sheer wall of the Vercors range. The valley itself is lined by the black forks of walnut trunks, in orchards that produce *appellation d'origine contrôlée* nuts, and whose glossy foliage shines in the summer sunshine. In the hillsides just to the north, white cattle graze in lush pastures beside wide-brimmed farms where the milk is collected for melting St-Marcellin cheese, one of the best *fromages* in the region. This valley produces an astonishing array of exceptional culinary delights, *ravioles de Royans* the most delicate little ravioli you can imagine, stuffed with cheese and herbs, almost translucent when cooked, a divine fast food on menus across the Dauphiné. In the hills above Tullins, the **priory of Notre-Dame-de-Parménie** lies in a superb spot. The village of **Vinay** is capital of walnuts, while it's after the busy town of **St-Marcellin** that the delicious cheese is named. **Chatte**'s Clermont castle may not be open to the public, but you can see walnut oil being made at the **Moulin à Huile de Léon**. Also at Chatte is the popular **Jardin Ferroviaire** or Railway Garden (*t 04 76 38 54 55, www.jardin-ferroviaire.com; open April–June daily 10-7; July–Aug daily 10-8; Sept weekdays 2-4, weekends 10-;, Feb, Nov, Dec 2–4pm weekends, public holidays and zone A school holidays; Mar and Oct 10–7, weekends, public holidays and school holidays; adm*), a remarkable miniature world created in the late 1980s by Christian Abric and now one of the finest networks of outdoor garden trains in Europe.

South of the Isère, the pocket of country known as **the Royans**, tucked right under the sensational vertical sides of the Vercors range, has the most dramatic of backdrops. At **Pont-en-Royans**, below a huge wooded wall of rock, the old riverside houses look as if they they're about to jump into the clear waters of the Bourne rushing down from the heights. Jets of water freshen the air at the wonderfully playful **Musée de l'Eau** (*t 04 76 36 15 53; open July–Aug daily 10–6; rest of year Tues–Sun outside school hols 10–12 and 2–5.30; adm*), a brilliantly designed modern museum that offers the most appealing introduction to Vercors ecology and waterpower. At the end of the visit, taste H$_2$O vintages from around the world at the water bar. The traditional wood-working town of **St-Jean-en-Royans** specialized in tableware, hence the term *tabletterie* around the place. The *Ancien Régime* **church** with its stocky stone tower contains beautiful carved stalls rescued from the former monastic Chartreuse du Val Ste-Marie. For walnut oil and walnut products, try **Cave Noisel** in a restored mill, explained with passion. At **Les Cuillères du Royans** on the Route de Lente you can see traditional wooden spoons being made.

St-Nazaire-en-Royans lies close to the confluence of Bourne and Isère, the Vercors still a spectacular backdrop. The **aqueduct** adds to the drama, although the lorries along the busy road reduce the charm. Much of the place's history has been wiped out by wars, but its red-tinged rocks above the green Bourne waters still create quite an effect. Near town, the **Grotte de Thaïs** (*t 04 75 48 45 76; open July–Aug daily 10–12 and 2–5, June and Sept weekdays 2–5, April–May and Oct only Sun and public hols 10–12 and 2–5; adm*) boasts exceptionally colourful walls, plus surprising concretions and nooks. This cave is well known for its prehistoric finds. Among the tools and weapons, a bone with notches counts among the earliest pieces of evidence of a human numerical system. Get out on the water by taking the paddle boat *Royans-Vercors* (*t 04 76 64 43 42, www.bateau-a-roue.com; operates April–mid-Oct, times variable; adm*) plying between here and **La Sône**, the latter with startling water gardens, the **Jardin des Fontaines Pétrifiantes** (*t 04 76 64 43 42, www.jardin-des-fontaines.com; open May–mid-Oct*) set among limestone waterfalls. Get up onto St-Nazaire's spectacular **aqueduct** by taking the lift (*t 04 75 48 49 80; open April–Oct; adm*). The structure dates from 1876, built to bring water down from the Vercors to irrigate the crops on the often parched Valence plain. (For Romans-sur-Isère, *see* p.181.)

No amount of water could soothe the agonizing burning pains and dreadful convulsions suffered by the patients in the religious foundation of **St-Antoine-l'Abbaye** west of St-Marcellin. In medieval times, ergotism, a terrible wheat-borne fungal illness, could ravage communities, and a religious order called the Antonins developed here in the 13th century to look after those afflicted by the illness, which became known as St Anthony's Fire. The place contained relics of St Anthony, one of the greatest figures of the early Christian centuries, reputed to have experienced torment during his days as a hermit in the desert. He was adopted as the patron saint of the medieval order that spread across Europe. Work began on a great Gothic church here in the 13th century, but it was not completed until the 15th. This was the most successful period in the abbey's history; from the 16th century it fell into decline. A large portion of the complex has survived, and is slowly being restored. The

church contains many riches, including wall paintings. In the choir, a tapestry cycle of finest Aubusson work depicts scenes in the life of Joseph. The **Musée Le Noviciat** (*t 04 76 36 40 68; open July–Aug daily 11–12.30 and 1.30–6; rest of year daily exc Tues 2–6; adm*) in adjoining buildings houses a permanent collection on the Antonins and presents a changing programme of contemporary art exhibitions.

Roybon in the midst of the high, wooded Chambaran plateau, boasts the distinction of one of three miniature copies made of Bartholdi's Statue of Liberty, plus a church decorated with pebbles in typical local herringbone patterns. Nearby, there's a big lake for swimming, while the **Parc Naturel du Chambaran** reserves 300 hectares for wild animals, notably deer, to wander round with a certain degree of freedom.

The Pebbly Northern Drôme

The endearing old dog of a **priory** at **Manthes** and some of the old houses at **Moras-en-Valloire** demonstrate again how glacial valley stones have long been employed as a matter of course in local architecture. But at **Hauterives**, a local postman, Ferdinand Cheval, fell, almost literally, in love with the pebbles of the area. Having tripped over one in 1879, he picked it up, took it home, and began on a crazy building programme that lasted 34 years, creating the **Palais Idéal du Facteur Cheval** (*t 04 75 68 81 19, www.facteurcheval.com; open July–Aug daily 9–12.30 and 1.30–7.30; April–June and Sept daily 9.30–12.30 and 1.30–6.30; Feb–Mar and Oct–Nov daily 9.30–12.30 and 1.30–5.30; Dec–early Jan daily 9.30–12.30 and 1.30–4.30; adm*). All this in the back garden of a quiet Drômois village house where you'd really just expect to find a well-tended vegetable plot. After the grottoes came a tomb for the family, in Egypto-Christian form. A Hindu-style temple followed, guarded by giants. And so on, the various constructions all cemented together, topped by concrete vegetation. *'Monument original'*, reads one of the most understated quotes among many more vacuous, arrogant ones written across the architecture. But actually Cheval's vision isn't wholly original. A thwarted traveller, unable to afford trips to the exotic locations he might read about in the magazines of the time, he plundered visual ideas and vague notions of foreign cultures to create his own fantasy world in his backyard. Models of great buildings from around the globe were stuck on here and there. The whole clutter of the so-called *Palais Idéal* is at one and the same time admirable, entertaining, laughable and lamentable. The building's title is to be taken with a strong pinch of salt.

From *Architecture Naïve* to *Art Brut* – more disturbing, disturbed, grotesque, hilarious, anti-establishment works hang out in **L'Art en Marche** (*t 04 75 68 95 40; open daily 10–12 and 2–6; adm*). As well as seeing a very wide array of works, you can trace the history of *Art Brut*. While you feel the naivety in Postman Cheval's enterprise, many of the artists here are clearly more knowing. A further eccentric attraction in Hauterives, **Les Labyrinthes Végétaux** (*t 04 75 68 86 82; open May–mid-Sept 11–7; adm*) gets you entangled in four hectares of shrubs and lavender, although the main lavender territories of the Drôme lie to the south.

Part of the priory buildings sitting pretty at the top of the village of **St-Donat-sur-l'Herbasse** have been given the grandiose title of **Palais Délphinal** (of the Dauphiné) (*t 04 75 45 15 32; guided tours July–Aug 2.30–6; adm*). Reaching the medieval religious buildings via steep streets, you'll see how the place was savaged in the Wars of Religion. Just a Gothic end stands behind the 20th-century church (which has an exceptional organ), and just one side of the cloister, but decorated with entertaining carvings. The 'palace' hosts exhibitions, the church fine organ concerts.

Romans-sur-Isère

Shoe addicts should hotfoot it south for riverside **Romans-sur-Isère**, a bustling town where several of France's top shoe designers are based, including Robert Clergerie, Stéphane Kélian and Charles Jourdan. The place has a long tradition of tanning, which explains why it became a major centre of shoe manufacturing from the mid-19th century. A truly remarkable piece of historical research on 16th-century Romans was carried out by the contemporary French historian Emmanuel Le Roy Ladurie and *Le Carnaval de Romans* is a much more fascinating book for the general reader than his more widely known *Montaillou*, although hard to find in English.

The utterly startling **Musée International de la Chaussure** (*t 04 75 05 51 81, www. ville-romans.com; open July–Aug Mon–Sat 10–6, Sun 2–6; Jan–June and Sept–Dec daily Tues–Sat 10–5, Sun 2–5.45; adm*) offers a voyage into the sole of civilizations. It has very successfully set up shop in an immense Italianate convent to present, via its visual and explanatory history of footwear, truly surprising insights into the customs of past centuries and cultures. Famous shoes are treated like relics, safe behind glass. The big chapel serves for extraordinary exhibitions of footware. On the trail of the modern shoe, Romans has attracted all manner of brands. Look in particular along the **Côte des Cordeliers**. Another interesting street of more varied shops, **Côte Jacquemart** slopes down from the medieval **Tour Jacquemart**, which, despite its butch looks, proves high-pitched when its bells ring. At the riverside **church of St-Barnard**, battered Romanesque sculptures greet you at the spot where Bishop Barnard of Vienne created an abbey in the 9th century, leading to the creation of Romans. Inside, the early medieval structure was enlarged in Gothic times. Some murals have survived from the redecoration. The rare 16th-century embroideries of the Mystery of the Passion are kept under lock and key in the **Chapelle du Saint-Sacrement** (*open for guided tours only, mid-June–mid-Sept daily exc Sun am 10–12 and 3–6; adm*).

Up beyond **Place Jean Jaurès**, the main, vast rectangular square stretching out from the Tour Jacquemart, **Marques Avenue** lies along Avenue Gambetta. Setting up hard on the heels of the shoe shops, this brand shopping outlet village has very stylishly taken over a former policemen's training college.

The Southern Drôme
Up the Drôme into the Diois

East from its confluence with the Rhône, the Drôme valley gradually leaves the busy industrial activity behind and, once past the imposing tower guarding Crest, becomes increasingly dramatic, embellished by patches of lavender and vines producing Clairette de Die, named after a rustic little city beneath the vast walls of the Vercors.

Chabrillan, with its ruined castle and the remains of its ramparts still partially protecting it, makes a first potential stop, one of many Drômois villages to have started displays around a botanical theme, here peonies.

Adventurous tourists abseil down the **Tour de Crest** (*t 04 75 25 32 53, www.mairie-crest.fr/tour; open June–Aug daily 10–7; May and 1st half Sept daily 10–12.30 and 2–6.30; Feb–April and 2nd half Sept daily 2–6; Nov–Jan weekends 2–6; adm*), the massive medieval donjon rising far above the town of Crest. You need a strong head for heights, as it claims to be the tallest keep in France, with over 50m of sheer walls. The building stands firmly astride the narrow ridge of rock after which the whole town is named. A truly awesome piece of military architecture, it actually consists of three towers incorporated one into the other, all backed by the highest wall of all, the *mur bouclier*. The bishops of Die originally owned this castle – the local nobility, the Comtes de Valentinois, made do with a *château inférieur*, that is, one further down the slope. From the 13th century, the two were in conflict. The counts took full control in the 14th century, joining the two castles with further walls, and were powerful enough to mint coins in the tower. But the line of counts died out in 1419. The French crown, the new owner, passed the place on to various absentee nobles.

Crest became a Catholic stronghold during the Wars of Religion, the castle resisting a major Protestant attack in 1577 and serving as a prison. Although Louis XIII ordered the destruction of all the fortifications, local protests saved the tower. It then received

Sparkling Clairette de Die

The main centre selling sparkling Clairette de Die is the modern wine cooperative **Jaillance** (*t 04 75 22 30 00, www.jaillance.com; open July–Aug daily 9–7, rest of year daily 9–12.30 and 2–6.30*), outside Die, representing some 90 per cent of growers and roughly three quarters of total production. This highly perfumed wine gained the right to its *appellation d'origine contrôlée* in 1942, but it has much, much older credentials, as you gather in the somewhat over-poetic tour through the cooperative cellars. Pliny the Elder sang the praises of this wine produced by the Gallo-Roman Vocontii tribe back in the 1st century; they had apparently already found a way of making it sparkle naturally, by keeping their amphorae in the cool river waters. These are high altitude vineyards for winemaking, the 1,300 hectares planted up to 700m above sea level, extending from Aouste-sur-Sye to Luc-en-Diois. But the south-facing slopes receive large quantities of southern sunshine. Despite the name, the main grape in Clairette de Die is in fact muscat blanc. It gives so much perfume and sweetness. Clairette only represents around 10 per cent of the mix.

The Southern Drôme

St-Jean-en-Royans

Valence

ARDÈCHE

† Léoncel

Col de la Bataille

ISÈRE

Drac

Gigors-et-Lozeron

Col de Rousset

Chichilianne

Le Percy

Montagne de Glandasse

Livron-sur-Drôme

Beaufort-sur-Gervanne

Ste-Croix

Die

Col de Menée

Drôme

Crest

Pontaix

D93

Cliousclat

Aouste

D93 Saillans

Vercheny

Drôme

Châtillon-en-Diois

Chabrillan

Mirmande

Drôme

St-Benoît-en-Diois

Rimon-et-Savel

Roanne

Marsanne

Forêt de Saou

Saou

Pennes-le-Sec

Recoubeau-Jansac

D06

Aucelon

Luc-en-Diois

Soyans

Col de la Chaudière

Col de Gourdon

D61

Bourdeaux

DRÔME

Montélimar

La Bégude-de-Mazenc

D538

Col de Cabre

104

Puygiron

La Motte-Chalancon

Rochefort-en-Valdaine

Le Poët-Laval

Dieulefit

Roanne

D61

Valdrôme

Mgne de l'Aup

Notre-Dame-d'Aiguebelle

Valouse

Bois de Grignan

Taulignan

Villeperdrix

St-May

Eygues

Gorges

HAUTES-ALPES

Valaurie

Grignan

Le Pègue

Rousset-les-Vignes

Rémuzat

La Garde d'Adhémar

D538

Condorcet

Venterol

Eygues

Le-Poët-Sigillat

Valréas

Aubres

Les Pilles

Montségur-sur-Lauzon

Richerenches

Nyons

Baronnies

Étoile-St-Cyrice

Vinsobres

Ste-Jalle

St-Auban-sur-l'Ouvèze

Col de Perty

Suze-la-Rousse

Mirabel-aux-Barronnies

D538

Piégon

Col d'Ey

Eygues

Mérindol-les-Oliviers

La Roche-sur-le-Buis

Ouvèze

Eygalayes

Lachau

Eygues

Vaison-la-Romaine

Buis-les-Baronnies

Rochegude

Ouvèze

Pierrelongue

Plaisians

Séderon

Sérignan-du-Comtat

Séguret

Mollans-sur-Ouvèze

Brantes

Barret-de-Lioure

Sablet

Montbrun-les-Bains

Orange

Gigondas

Malaucène

Toulerenc

Montmirail

VAUCLUSE

Mont Ventoux

Ferrassières

N

10 km

5 miles

persecuted Protestant guests, who started the tower's unusual art collection, of protest graffiti. The tower saw its last prisoners, who added scrawled political slogans, after an uprising in the 1850s against the future Napoleon III. Inside the impressive interior, admire all kinds of medieval provisions against sieges. Also take in the amazing ideal city carved in wood on a door rescued from Crest's church. The

Getting Around

By train: Crest and Die lie on the rail line from Valence to Gap. Montélimar has the nearest train station for the Drôme Provençale and Baronnies; catch buses east from there.

By bus: Services run by Cariane Drôme (t 04 75 44 10 33) and the SNCF (t 04 75 25 05 81) from Valence serve Crest, Die and Luc-en-Diois.

Tourist Information

Crest: Place du Dr Maurice Rozier, 26400 Crest, t 04 75 25 11 38, www.crest-tourisme.com.

Saillans: Montée Soubeyranne, 26340 Saillans, t 04 75 21 51 05, e ot.saillans@wanadoo.fr.

Die: Rue des Jardins, 26150 Die, t 04 75 22 03 03, www.diois-tourisme.com.

Châtillon-en-Diois: t/f 04 75 21 10 07.

Luc-en-Diois: t/f 04 75 21 34 14.

Dieulefit: 1 Place de l'Eglise, 26220 Dieulefit, t 04 75 46 42 49, www.tourisme-pays-dieulefit.com.

Grignan: Place Jeu de Ballon, 26230 Grignan, t 04 75 46 56 75, www.guideweb.com/grignan.

Suze-la-Rousse: Ave des Côtes du Rhône, 26790 Suze-la-Rousse, t 04 75 04 81 41, e ot-suze-la-rousse@wanadoo.fr.

Nyons: Place de la Libération, 26110 Nyons, t 04 75 26 10 35, www.nyonstourisme.com.

Rémuzat: t 04 75 27 85 71, www.remuzat.com.

Buis-les-Baronnies: 2 Place du Quinconce, 26170 Buis-les-Baronnies, t 04 75 28 04 59, www.buislesbaronnies.com.

Market Days

Crest: Tues and Sat morning.
Saillans: Sun morning.
Die: Wed and Sat morning.
Châtillon-en-Diois: Fri morning.
Luc-en-Diois: Fri morning.
Dieulefit: Fri morning.
Grignan: Tues morning.
Suze-la-Rousse: Fri morning.
Nyons: Thurs morning, and Sun morning, June–Sept.
Buis-les-Baronnies: Wed and Sat morning.
Montbrun-les-Bains: Sat morning.

Festivals

Interesting musical events in southern Drôme: the **Château de Grignan season** (*Feb–April*), the **Le Poët-Laval cycle** (*May–Sept*), the acclaimed **Saou Mozart festival** (*July*), the **Crest jazz festival** (*August*) and the **Grignan jazz festival** (*Nov*). Grignan also hosts a **festival of correspondence** (*July*) and summer-evening **theatre in the castle** (*July–Aug*). **Wine festivals** can pop up throughout the year.

Where to Stay and Eat

Saou ✉ 26400

L'Oiseau sur sa Branche, t 04 75 76 02 03 (*moderate*). Enchanting restaurant in the village, mad about local goats' cheese. *Closed Mon and Tues out of season, and Jan.*

L'Auberge de l'Etang, t 04 75 76 05 70 (*cheap*). Country inn with simple menus in a beautiful setting under limestone walls.

Bourdeaux ✉ 26460

Seeger Perrin B&B, t 04 75 53 38 51 (*inexpensive*). Former girls' school converted into comfortable rooms. *Table d'hôte* (*moderate*).

La Chaudière ✉ 26340

L'Arche de 3 Becs B&B, Ferme Couteau, t 04 75 21 59 32, www.3becs.com (*inexpensive*). Simple welcoming country stop in beautiful spot. Good access for the disabled. Covered pool. *Table d'hôte* (*cheap*).

Die ✉ 26150

★★Le St-Domingue, t 04 75 22 03 08, f 04 75 22 10 65 (*cheap*). Basic traditional hotel with friendly old-style restaurant (*moderate–cheap*). Pool. *Restaurant closed Mon.*

---

medieval nobility, who had the luxuries of fireplaces and latrines, lived on the third floor. From the top, you're rewarded with fabulous views along the Drôme valley.

You also enjoy a view down on the theatre of Roman tiles formed by the roofs of the **old town**. The main shopping street with Provençal pottery and gifts passes below the white pillars of the temple-like 19th-century **church** on the narrow market square.

Châtillon-en-Diois ✉ 26410

**Le Mont Barral, Les Nonières, Treschenu-Crayers, t 04 75 21 12 21, *www.hotelmont barral-vercors.com* (*inexpensive*). A very traditional French country hotel with solid country cooking (*moderate*). Covered pool. Tennis court. *Closed mid-Nov–mid-Feb; restaurant closed Tues eve and Wed.*

Recoubeau Jansac ✉ 26310

Chaffois B&B, Les Banous, Jansac, t/f 04 75 21 30 46 (*inexpensive*). Cosy bright rooms up in the high slope-side old village of Jansac. Well run by young members of a local farming family. *Table d'hôte* (*cheap*).

Dieulefit ✉ 26220

Villa Marie B&B, t 04 75 46 89 19, *mjmancel@club-internet.fr* (*moderate*). Smart 19th-century property in large garden, with pool. *Table d'hôte* (*moderate*).

Domaine de la Fayence B&B, t 04 75 46 35 10, *www.domainedelafayence.com* (*moderate–inexpensive*). Classic converted farm. *Table d'hôte* (*moderate*). Pool. Court.

Auberge des Brises, Route de Nyons, t 04 75 46 41 49 (*moderate*). Nice country cooking under linden trees 1.5km outside town. *Closed Tues, plus Mon eve and Wed out of season, and mid-Jan–mid-Mar.*

Le Poët-Laval ✉ 26160

***Les Hospitaliers, t 04 75 46 22 32, *www.hotel-les-hospitaliers.com* (*expensive–moderate*). Divine little hotel up in the semi-ruined hillside village. Delicious cuisine (*expensive*). Pool. *Closed mid-Nov–mid-Dec and Jan–mid-Mar; restaurant closed low season Mon and Tues.*

Grignan ✉ 26230

****Manoir de la Roseraie, Route de Valréas, t 04 75 46 58 15, *www.manoirdelaroseraie.com* (*very expensive*). Exclusive 19th-century walled property below the village with pool and tennis. Stylish restaurant (*expensive*).

Closed half of Dec and early Jan–mid-Feb; restaurant closed Tues, Wed out of season.

***Au Clair de la Plume, Place du Mail, t 04 75 91 81 30, *www.chateauxhotels.com/clairplume* (*expensive*). Romantic hotel in the village, rooms overlooking a delightful garden where teas are served. *Closed late-Jan–Feb.*

Montségur-sur-Lauzon ✉ 26130

**Auberge des Tarraïettes, t 04 75 98 13 24, *www.auberge-des-tarraiettes.com* (*inexpensive*). Set back in its scruffily appealing courtyard-garden off the village round-about, nice welcoming old inn with practical rooms and pleasing restaurant (*moderate*). *Restaurant closed Sun eve and Mon.*

Suze-la-Rousse ✉ 26790

Les Aiguières B&B, t 04 75 98 40 80 (*moderate*). Good rooms, plus pool with view of château. *Table d'hôte* (*moderate*) – Madame does thematic dinners around regional wines.

Rochegude ✉ 26790

****Château de Rochegude, t 04 75 97 21 10, *www.chateauderochegude.com* (*luxury–very expensive*). Amazing converted hilltop castle offering lordly luxury. Fine courtyard as well as dining room for meals (*very expensive–expensive*). Pool and court. *Closed most Nov.*

Café du Cours, Cours de l'Apparent, t 04 75 98 24 83 (*cheap*). At the other end of the scale, charming village café. *Closed Tues out of season.*

Vinsobres ✉ 26110

Auberge du Petit Bistrot, t 04 75 27 61 90 (*moderate–cheap*). Enchanting village restaurant by the fountain.

Nyons ✉ 26110

La Bastide des Monges, Route d'Orange, t 04 75 26 99 69, *www.bastidedesmonges.com* (*expensive–moderate*). Among the vines

Either side of the church, climb the *calades*, the dilapidated cobbled lanes, in search of pretty covered **washhouses**. To go **canoeing**, go east to **Aouste** and **Cap Plein Air** (t *04 75 76 70 66*), where the vineyards producing sparkling Clairette de Die begin.

Continuing east, the Drôme valley becomes increasingly rural and beautiful, overseen by the well-named **Trois Becs**, a clutch of three peaks that resemble young west of town, smartly restored roadside farmhouse with views to Mont Ventoux. Pool. *Closed mid-Oct–Easter.*

Une Autre Maison, Place de la République, **t** 04 75 26 43 09, *www.uneautremaison.com* (*expensive*). Its lush little garden with tiny pool leads to the high-standard restaurant (*expensive*). Bright themed little rooms with rustically trendy North African touches. *Closed Nov–Feb; restaurant closed Sun eve, Mon, and weekday lunchtimes.*

★★★Le Colombet, Place de la Libération, **t** 04 75 26 03 66, *www.hotelcolombet.com* (*moderate*). Pleasant traditional French provincial hotel with restaurant (*moderate*) at the heart of the action. *Closed late Nov–late Jan.*

Aubres ✉ 26110

Auberge du Vieux Village, **t** 04 75 26 12 89, **e** *auberge.aubres@wanadoo.fr* (*moderate*). Built on the castle ruins of a hilltop village east of Nyons, many rooms have their own terraces. Fantastic views from the restaurant (*moderate*) with terrace. Pool. *Restaurant closed Wed.*

Les Pilles/Condorcet ✉ 26110

La Charrette Bleue, Route de Gap, **t** 04 75 27 72 33 (*moderate*). Cheerful roadside restaurant serving reliably excellent Provençal cuisine. *Closed Wed high season, Tues, Wed and Sun eve low season, plus mid-Dec–Jan.*

Valouse ✉ 26110

★★★Le Hameau de Valouse, **t** 04 75 27 72 05, *www.hameau-de-valouse.com* (*moderate*). Delightful huddle of stone houses turned peaceful hotel off the D130, the mountainous route between Dieulefit and Nyons. Pleasant simple restaurant (*moderate*). Pool. *Closed Nov–Feb; restaurant closed Mon and Tues.*

Mirabel-aux-Baronnies ✉ 26110

La Baronnie B&B, **t** 04 75 27 12 97, *www. labaronnie.net* (*expensive–moderate*). Calm,

retreat at foot of the village, with pool. *Table d'hôte* (*Tues and Sat; moderate*).

Mollans-sur-Ouvèze ✉ 26170

★★Le St-Marc, Ave de l'Ancienne Gare, **t** 04 75 28 70 01, *www.saintmarc.com* (*inexpensive*). Charming village hotel with welcoming garden, colourful rooms and nice restaurant (*moderate*). Pool and court. *Closed Nov–Mar; restaurant closed lunchtimes exc Sun.*

Buis-les-Baronnies ✉ 26170

★★Sous l'Olivier, Quartier du Menon, **t** 04 75 28 01 04 , **f** 04 75 28 16 49 (*inexpensive*). Pleasant modern rooms, pool, tennis court and sauna, plus restaurant (*cheap*).

L'Ancienne Cure B&B, **t** 04 75 28 22 08, *www.anciennecure.com* (*moderate*). Enchanting rooms in central house by the church. *Table d'hôte* (*moderate*).

Plaisians ✉ 26170

Auberge de la Clue, Place de l'Eglise, **t** 04 75 28 01 17 (*moderate*). Old-style generosity at this delightful inn. *Closed Mon, and weekends out of season, plus Oct.*

St-Auban-sur-l'Ouvèze ✉ 26170

La Clavelière, **t** 04 75 28 61 07 (*inexpensive*). Lovely simple traditional village inn along the ramparts. Handful of rooms and unpretentious restaurant (*moderate–cheap*). Pool. *Closed Nov–Mar; restaurant closed Sat lunch.*

Ferrassières ✉ 26570

Château de la Gabelle B&B, **t** 04 75 28 80 54, *www.chateau-la-gabelle.com* (*moderate*). A property bathing in lavender, run by a woman devoted to her property and her produce. *Table d'hôte* (*moderate*).

Eygalayes ✉ 26560

Les Forges Ste-Marie, **t/f** 04 75 28 42 77, **e** *Isabelle.muse@wanadoo.fr* (*inexpensive*). For tranquillity lost in southeast Drôme. Lavender spa tub. *Table d'hôte* (*moderate*).

birds greedily poking their beaks up to be fed. Down below, you arrive in lavender-growing territory. The **Route de la Lavande** association (*www.routes-lavande.com*), spanning the Rhône-Alpes region and Provence, has created itineraries for drivers, cyclists and walkers. While the lavender fields this far north aren't as extensive as in the Drôme Provençale , they flower well into August, offering a later season than further south. One lavender trail takes you towards the Vercors via **Beaufort-sur-Gervanne**, a lovely old fortified village, a few towers remaining. For healthy natural herbal products, try the particularly nice shop at the **Domaine des Arômes Sanoflore** (*t 04 75 76 46 60, www.sanoflore.net*), with its herbal garden at **Gigors-et-Lozeron**, a village with splendid views down on the Gervanne valley from its perch.

Or take a delicious detour south from Crest for **Saou**, an enchanting village at the entrance to the magical, secretive **Forêt de Saou**, sloping up to catch the Trois Becs unawares from behind. At **Soyans**, climb to the eccentric **Musée de l'Œuf** (*t 04 75 76 00 15, www.lemuseedeloeuf; open June–Sept daily exc Tues 3.30–7; adm*) at the top of the village, and enjoy the medieval surroundings as well as the owner's extensive, eccentric egg collections. Rough remnants of castle stick out above laid-back **Bourdeaux**. Take the D156 road round the Trois Becs via the **Col de la Chaudière**, offering amazing distant views to the highest Alpine peaks.

Back down by the Drôme river, wrinkly old **Saillans** has preserved its character, with its hunched, narrow streets and arches, its fountains and old houses. The **church** clings on to its Romanesque details. Saillans' vines produce Clairette (*see* p.182), but the place also once lived off silk-making, recalled at **La Magnanerie** (*t 04 75 21 56 60; open May–Sept daily 10–7; adm*). At the end of the serious tour you see how silk is unwoven from its cocoon. Canoeing is popular here, with **Eaux Vives Aventures** (*t 04 75 21 55 71*) and **Lido Location** (*t 04 75 21 54 20*). You can even canoe by moonlight.

Off the D93, head south up the Roanne valley for attractive **St-Benoît-en-Diois**. Explore refreshing bathing spots in the waters of the Roanne, and further villages perched up winding roads to the south, like **Rimon-et-Savel**, **Pennes-le-Sec** or **Aucelon**.

Back close to the D93, the **Musée de la Clairette** (*t 04 75 21 73 77; www.caves-carod. com; open Jan–Dec weekdays 8–12 and 2–6, weekends and public hols 9.30–12 and 2–6; free*) at **Vercheny** is attached to a wine producer, offering re-creations of wine-making scenes from the start of the last century. From the **Camping Les Acacias** (*t 04 75 21 72 51*), there are more canoeing possibilities. **Pontaix** looks in danger of toppling into the Drôme. You can fall in canoeing with **Aloa'venture** (*t 04 75 21 13 63*). The next dramatic village close to the river is **Ste-Croix**.

Dwarfed by the sheer, massive 2,000m wall of yellow limestone of the Montagne de Glandasse, southern rampart of the Vercors mountain range, it seems unbelievable that such a tiny, remote town as **Die** served so long as a cathedral city. The little place has ancient roots. Roman traces remain, such as the **St-Marcel arch**. Further vestiges are displayed in the **Musée d'Histoire** (*check opening times at tourist office*) on the main shopping street, an appealing line cutting through Die's compact centre – the historic town is still bound by its medieval walls. The museum also covers prehistory in the area, and the particularly painful period of religious division through the *Ancien Régime*, when Die suffered as a Protestant centre.

Standing out in white stone in the centre, the **cathedral**, originally Romanesque, was ransacked by Protestants in the 16th century and largely rebuilt in the 17th century. There are still a few Romanesque carved capitals under the entrance tower. Elaborate altars in the nave recall the 17th-century period of Catholic revival.

More extraordinary still, is the **mosaic** in the quite separate private **chapel of the bishops of Die** (*contact the tourist office for visits*), which is a rare, sumptuous medieval piece from the 12th century, covering the floor like a carpet. Four faces spit out water, thought to represent four great biblical rivers. From the pointed star in the centre, 12 lines branch out, possibly symbolizing the months or the 12 tribes of Israel. The chapel walls teem with big-breasted grotesques, snails and butterflies on wallpaper, ordered by an extravagant 18th-century bishop.

The D518, one of the most sensational hairpin-bend roads in France, winds north from Die to the **Col de Rousset**, a spectacular and head-spinning route up into the Vercors mountain range (*see* p.282). Take a look at a detailed road map before you undertake the journey. Continuing along the Drôme valley, look out for the remains of the **abbey of Valcroissant** (*t 04 75 22 12 70; July–Aug tours weekdays exc Tues at 5*), now a farm. Branching east up the Bèz valley to **Châtillon-en-Diois**, lovely stone huts for the vineyard-workers are sprinkled among the vines. This area produces whites, reds, rosés and sparkling wines. Occasional patches of lavender also survive up here. Follow the botanical trail leading through the village's quiet, charming lanes, looking out for the remains of its ramparts and three church bell towers (one a ruin). Some claim Hannibal and his elephants came this way on their way through the highest Alps to Rome (*see* p.6), although there is no evidence for this.

Back with the upper Drôme valley, walnut orchards line the way. Just above Luc, the D61 branches south, taking in fabulous villages, **Chalancon** the most dramatic, pressed against a curving mountainside. Friendly, open, relaxed **Luc-en-Diois** attracts lively, but laid-back, high-energy sportspeople into rockclimbing and hang-gliding. A chaos of grey boulders tumble down the steep valley at the **Saut de la Drôme**. Up above, there are restful pools of turquoise waters. A very peaceful flat stretch of valley road follows. The D306 continues past the hamlet of **Valdrôme**, up past the sources of the Drôme, to arguably France's most discreet ski resort. Here, the *département de la Drôme* comes to a natural end with the barrage formed by the **Montagne de l'Aup**.

Into the Drôme Provençale

In the mesmerizing countryside east of Montélimar, elegant pyramidal mountains slope down to olive groves and cherry and apricot orchards, while the flats are carpeted with vines and lavender and oaks are planted in rows to encourage truffles to grow. Crafts thrive in the sculptural villages – Grignan, almost crushed by its castle being the archetype. The little towns such as Dieulefit, Nyons and Buis-les-Baronnies have a relaxing feel. To the east, the Baronnies rivers run through many narrow gorges. Bald-topped Mont Ventoux and the Montagne de Lure, guardians of northwest Provence, loom over the quiet range – the Baronnies mark the historic boundary between the Dauphiné region and Provence.

To Dieulefit and Grignan

Following the Jabron, below **Puygiron** with its private château, castle ruins don't come much more uplifting and tranquil than those by **Rochefort-en-Valdaine**, some of which have been restored (*t 04 75 46 62 16, open mid-July–Aug daily 3–7, mid-March–mid-July Sun and public hols 2–6; free*). The **Monastère de la Trappe d'Aiguebelle** tucked away in its own valley dates back to the 12th century, but has been heavily restored. As well as the church, there's a well-stocked store selling produce from French monasteries, including liqueurs and fruits cordials under the Aiguebelle label.

Continuing along the Jabron valley, branch off for the **Vieux Village** of **Le Poët-Laval**, a member of the association of *Les Plus Beaux Villages de France*. Beautiful it is, if semi-ruined on its steep hillside, its main church just a shell. Its small **Musée du Protestantisme Dauphinois** (*t 04 75 46 46 33, www.museeduprotestantismedauphinois. org; open April–Sept daily exc Fri, and Sun am, 11–12 and 3–6.30; adm*) recalls the sufferings experienced by the people in these parts for adopting Protestantism, and preserves a rare Protestant chapel, one of the few to have survived in the whole Rhône-Alpes region. War-time Resistance is also recalled. In recent decades, the devoted Morin family have given the place a real cultural boost, opening the enchanting hotel, redoing the **hilltop castle** (*t 04 75 46 44 12, open July–mid-Sept daily 11–12.30 and 3–7; adm*), once home to a branch of the knightly order of St John of Jerusalem, and putting on quite intriguing art exhibitions at the **Centre d'Art Raymond du Puy** (*t 04 75 46 49 38, www.centre-art-drome.com; open April–May and early July–mid-Sept daily 11–12 and 3–7; adm*), featuring rare works by leading 20th-century artists. Also look up the atmospheric café-cum-bookshop, *La Bouquinerie*.

Dieulefit, 'God made it', has made it rich through modelling clay of its own. The streets of this hippy-chic town are filled with potters. The traditional style is of simple glazes in blue, green, yellow or caramel – typically Provençal – but a clutch of more-experimental-to-wacky artists have also opened up shop, while an imaginative glassblower works the other side of the Jabron. The **Maison de la Terre** (*t 04 75 90 61 80, www.ceramique.com/dieulefit; open April–Oct Tues–Sun 10–12.30 and 2–7; adm*) holds splendid pottery exhibitions. The outskirts of town are the rather curious location for a Club Med holiday village, drawing a surprisingly glamorous crowd to the local cafés. A stunning mountain route leads east from Dieulefit, the D130 road narrowing into tight gorges, patches of lavender clinging to the slopes towards the **Défilé des Trente Pas**. The irresistible **D538 lavender route** leads south to Grignan.

The haughty aristocratic **Château de Grignan** (*t 04 75 91 83 55; open April–Oct daily 9.30–11.30 and 2–5.30; Nov–Mar closed Tues; adm*) sits dramatically aloof on its rock above the village houses. This substantial French Renaissance castle lost its head at the Revolution, but its fascinating *Ancien Régime* connections are brought to the fore on the tours. Mme de Sévigné, the court socialite and prolific letter-writer of Louis XIV's day, spent three long periods here thanks to her daughter, recording her impressions in her correspondence. She loved the good days, but the mistral wind almost drove her crazy...and she eventually died here towards the close of the 17th century. Her daughter, Françoise-Marguerite, also quite a character and a fine catch,

The Coteaux du Tricastin

The Coteaux du Tricastin are named after the Celtic tribe that was based in these parts before the Romans arrived. Evidence has been unearthed of one of the largest Roman wine estates ever found across the Empire having existed here. Essentially a part of the Côtes du Rhône, the Coteaux du Tricastin cover around 2,600 hectares in a triangle of land between Montélimar, Grignan and St-Paul-Trois-Châteaux. Bargains are to be had, as the name isn't as well known as that of wines bearing the simpler title of Côtes du Rhône, but the vintages can share similar power and reliability. The Grignan *Caveau* is a good place to start discovering this *appellation*, as it represents 27 producers, the bulk of them, both cooperatives and individual properties. After tasting, the *caveau* employees can organize a visit to the properties. Alternatively, try the walking trail through the vines around Grignan, but also taking you through the splendid carpet of lavender laid out around the village. Beyond, in the wider landscapes of the Coteaux du Tricastin, vines tend to triumph.

was regarded as one of the brightest beauties of her day. In 1669 she had married François, Comte de Grignan, who spent vast sums on lavish entertainment. The couple's daughter, Pauline, was forced to sell the family castle in 1732 to pay off his debts. On the tour round some 20 modestly furnished rooms, the lives of the castle's other significant owners are also explained. Afterwards, go out on to what is surely one of the most decadent terraces in southern France, gloriously located on the flat roof of the substantial church below.

In this intensely artistic village, beautiful old roses perfume the air in season. Run with passion, the appealing **Musée de la Typographie et du Livre** (*t 04 75 46 57 16; open daily exc Mon am 10–12 and 2–6; adm*) celebrates the art of making books, the dedicated small team printing its own charming works. This place also fits in a courtyard café and a bookshop specializing in famous correspondence, including that of Mme de Sévigné, who is buried in the vast Gothic cave of a **church** against the hillside, reached through a thick arch of white roses. Among other crafts shops up in the village, the five artisans who've clubbed together to form **Roue Libre** produce particularly joyous pieces in a variety of media. Down close to the colonnaded town hall, the round, colonnaded **village washhouse** looks like a temple to laundering, while a **statue** shows a young Madame de Sévigné concentrating on her writing, quill in hand. The **Caveau des Coteaux du Tricastin** (*t 04 75 46 55 96; open April–Sept daily 10.30–1.30 and 2.30–7.30; free*) in the tourist office's courtyard offers an introduction to this curiosity of an *appellation* where the vines share the land with lavender and truffle oaks (*see above*). East of Grignan, the **Village Provençal Miniature** (*t 04 75 46 91 68; open July–Aug daily 10–7, rest of summer daily 10–12 and 2–7, winter daily exc Tues 10–12 and 2–6; adm*) proves amusing with its array of Provençal figures made by *santonniers*, local traditional specialist craftspeople.

Just **south of Grignan**, the emaciated **Tour de Chamaret** (*t 06 82 10 80 35; open 10–1 and 3–7weekends and daily July–Aug ; adm*), the very tall remnants of a medieval keep, towers over a pretty village and overlooks a curious historical anomaly to the east, a **Provençal papal enclave**, which belonged to the papacy through the Middle Ages.

Encircled by the Drôme, it has been administered by the *département* of the Vaucluse in Provence since the Revolution, and stretches out around the pleasing historic town of **Valréas**, proud of its premier position in the world of carton-making, a subject covered, along with printing, by its **museum**. The lands around Grignan are the most prolific truffle-producing territories in France, whole patches of truffle oaks planted in neat rows to encourage the crop. **Richerenches** in the papal enclave holds the biggest truffle market in France, every Sunday in mid-winter. Truffles bring money now, but the name of this little place, and its mighty defences, indicate it was a wealthy centre long before. While most of the historic villages in these parts were built on defensive hills and slopes, this one is on the flat, presenting an almost perfect square of fortifications, round towers marking the corners. Panels along the streets help visitors build up a picture of the Knights Templars for whom this *commanderie* was founded in 1130. The mighty chivalric order became hugely wealthy, controlling much of the finances raised for the crusades, buying vast territories overseen by such *commanderies*. But its members were viciously destroyed in the early 14th century by a jealous King Philippe le Bel of France, who pressurized Pope Clement V in Avignon into excommunicating them and then had them tried on trumped-up charges including idolatry and sodomy. A rival knightly order, the Hospitallers of St John of Jerusalem, took over many of their properties, such as this one.

As at Grignan, the medieval **Château de Suze-la-Rousse** (*t 04 75 04 81 44; open April–Oct daily 9.30–11.30 and 2–5.30, rest of year daily exc Tues, same times; adm*) sits snobbishly on a solid pedestal of rock above the village grovelling at its feet. The nickname of La Rousse probably derives from the slight ruddiness of its stones. Standing out so imposingly from afar, close up, the crenellated, round-towered château looks severe. But note the fine coat of arms, plus the caricature sticking its tongue out at

Not So Sober Wines

From the castle windows of Suze-la-Rousse, you look down on a sea of Côtes du Rhône vines (*www.rhone-wines.com*) stretching out across the wide Eygues valley. Follow the exceptionally picturesque wine route east to Nyons, the ends of the rows marked by blood-red roses (planted to spot mildew as well as for aesthetic reasons). The Baronnies hills and the Mont Ventoux make a perfect photographic backdrop. A huge wine cooperative stands on the outskirts of each village, that of the Cellier des Dauphins on the edge of Tulette the most enormous and daunting, the others on a more human scale. But be tempted into trying individual properties too. This area produces excellent powerful wines, generally extremely reliable and reasonable value. Each of the villages has a Provençal feel, with plane-tree-shaded squares and trickling fountains. A couple of the parishes have earned the distinction of labelling their wine Côtes du Rhône-Villages. Contrary to expectation, the hilarious-sounding (and delectable) village of Vinsobres is said to take its name from the Latin for 'above the vines', rather than from *vignerons'* humour. The fact that the place has two churches indicatesdivisive religious times in the past. A notice on the top *temple* explains the painful Protestant history of the place. Now Vinsobres' big-pebbled architecture running up the hillside looks blissful, surrounded by ranks of vines.

you, as you arrive at the moat. The inner courtyard proves amazingly ornate, embellished in an elaborate classical style as a wedding gift for Comte François de la Baume, one of the castle's most powerful owners. A fierce Catholic during the Wars of Religion, he served as governor of Provence. Although the gargoyles aren't original, the coats of arms and symbols below signal the family's proud military history, while the bishop's hat recalls that the generous gift was made by François' episcopal uncle. A later family bishop ordered the magnificent double staircase inside, redone after the Revolution. The family line only died out in 1958. You can tour the wood-panelled chambers on one floor, which are sadly empty when not hosting exhibitions, although a couple of intriguing murals of cavalry scenes stand out. One is said to represent the battle for Montélimar in 1587 at which François de la Baume was mortally wounded while fighting the Protestants who had taken the town. Much of the rest of the castle is occupied by the **Université du Vin** (*t* 04 75 97 21 30, *www. universite-du-vin.com*), installed in these sumptuous surroundings since 1978. The name proves a bit misleading though, as anyone can enrol on a wine course here. They even run the odd class in English. The installations for studying oenology range from the superb to the outrageous, the former chapel converted into a tasting room!

Another well-located rock-top castle stands out from the centre of the charming village of **Rochegude**, marking the Rhône-Alpes frontier with Provence, on which it turns its back. The castle has been transformed into a splendid luxury hotel (*see* p.185)

A further stunning wine route leads east from Grignan to Nyons, avoiding the papal enclave altogether, taking you under the mountain tops of the Lance and the Vaux, ranged like huge, neat pyramids along the route. The historic villages below huddle in tight circles. At **Taulignan**, the outer houses form a defensive ring with towers, but now only the fountains disturb the peace. Beyond the walls, a former school with arcaded front has been converted into the **Musée de la Soie** (*t* 04 75 53 12 96, *www. atelier-museedelasoie-taulignan.com; open July–Aug daily 10–6, Feb–June and Sept–Nov daily 10–12.30 and 1.30–5.30; adm*) charting the history of silk making both in the region and around this village, where young girls lacking family support were sent to work to build up their dowries. All is presented in spick-and-span fashion, some old machines creaking partially into action, while the shop sells Lyon silk scarves and ties. Quiet, withdrawn **Le Pègue** contains a surprisingly interesting **Musée Archéologique** (*t* 04 75 53 68 21; *www.museearcheolepegue.com; open June–Sept daily exc Wed 2–6; adm*) run with great passion. A pre-Roman Celtic settlement of some importance surveyed the edge of the very wide plain from up on its height, the views stretching over to northern Provence and the Cévennes the other side of the Rhône. Delightful **Rousset-les-Vignes** looks down from mid-slope onto a sea of vines; this is in the most northerly area of Côtes du Rhône-Villages production, the local properties offering up some excellent reliable wines. But the chapel of **Notre-Dame de Beauvoir** has nothing to do with it, remaining aloof, the only human construction on the green pyramidal hills above. Most picturesque and defensive of all the villages, **Venterol** hides like a snail in its shell, as though trying to shut its eyes to all the beauty that surrounds it.

Olives are the main crop associated with **Nyons**, the place almost synonymous with its golden oil, sold at near golden prices, although vineyards and orchards also abound around town. The gourmet Tanche olives here have been granted the distinction of their own *appellation d'origine contrôlée*. The friendly town hosts the **Institut du Monde de l'Olivier** (*open Mon–Thurs 8.30–12.30 and 1.30–5.0; adm*) by the central squares, with exhibitions on olive-related subjects. A spectacular single-arched **medieval bridge** spans the turquoise waters of the Eygues. By the 14th century, when it was built, the bourgeois of Nyons were already entitled by charter to sell and transport their olive oil. Beside the bridge, along with shops selling olive products, visit a couple of atmospheric old oil-making mills hidden under the houses at the **Vieux Moulins à Huile** (*t 04 75 26 11 00, http://vieuxmoulins.free.fr; open July–Aug daily exc Sun pm, visits at 10.30, 11.30, 3, 4 and 5; Feb–June and Sept–Dec Tues–Sat, visits same times; adm*). Beyond its culinary pleasures, and its use in lamps, olive oil was employed in the making of soap, and an 18th-century soap-making chamber has also been unearthed here, looking like an ancient archaeological site. The soap wasn't made for personal hygiene back then, but to soften the cloth made in the region, notably at Dieulefit. Continuing upstream, the **Scourtinerie** (*t 04 75 26 33 52; open Jan–Dec daily 9.30–12 and 2–6; adm*) provides another curious visit related to olives. *Scourtins* were the traditional round mats through which the oil was filtered, the natural fibres often coming from far afield. The manufacturing of *scourtins* flourished until the disastrous frost of 1956, when many olive trees died and demand collapsed. But the Fret family decided to branch out, using the Catherine-wheel-like looms to make pieces from table mats to carpets, all circular of course.

From the scruffily charming central **Place des Arcades**, dark covered alleyways lead up to the exotic neo-Gothic calvary of the **Tour Randonne** at the top of the old town. Wandering west along Eygues, the **Distillerie Bleu Provence** (*t 04 75 26 10 42; shop open all year; guided tour July–Aug Mon–Sat at 5, adm*) often scents the riverside air with a heady lavender perfume. You can see the old-fashioned process in action in high summer, while the shop sells a range of lavender products. Close to the new indoor-and-outdoor **pool complex** stands a small **riverside herb garden**. A bit north, the **Musée de l'Olive** may be terribly old fashioned, a messy single-room display covering the history, legends and traditions around *l'olivier*, but the neighbouring modern **cooperative** proves more exciting, selling all manner of olive products, fine local produce generally and wine, including by the pump. A lovely book, *La Charrette bleue* by René Barjavel, recalls his family's life running a *boulangerie* in Nyons, revealing all sorts of details on traditional life in these parts, from the deep-rooted division between Catholics and Protestants to the tricks of the local wind, the *pontias*.

Into the Baronnies Range

From the Tour Randonne, Nyons looks like a stopper wedged into the narrow entrance to the gorgeous Baronnies, named after the little local lords, and not that barren little mountains, as olive and cherry trees, vines and lavender find patches in which to thrive. The symbol of this range though is the apricot; it produces the most divine variety, plump, deep orange and bursting with juice, a completely different fruit from the pale, insipid things you tend to find in most supermarkets. Crumbling, semi-abandoned, semi-restored villages cling to the hillsides. In summer you may encounter a lone goatherd guarding his or her flock; these parts produce excellent goat's cheese, *picodons*.

Two stupendously beautiful routes lead from Nyons to Buis-les-Baronnies, one looping north round the western Baronnies mountains, the other looping south of them. Both included on the **Route de l'Olivier**, this whole area is classified as a *Site Remarquable du Goût*, recognizing the exceptional mix of agricultural traditions and landscapes. The **northern way** first winds along the **Eygues river gorges**, the different strata reading like thick pages in the book of geology. Before turning off along the languorous **Ennuye valley**, explore the villages hiding up in the limestone rocks above the Eygues, **Villeperdrix** hidden from the road, **St-May**'s beautiful necklace of houses set on the wrinkliest of old skin of rocks. Climb up to its tiny triangular cliff-top cemetery to appreciate the high spiny dinosaur mountains peering hungrily down. Beyond the meagre ruins of the **Abbaye de Bodon** above, follow the signs for 'Vautours' where, in the morning, you may be able to see vultures from across the valley. The swirling of these birds (with up to three-metre wing spans) is awesome. The indigenous population of the southern Alps was destroyed in the 19th century by improved husbandry hygiene, poisoned carcasses left out to get rid of wolves, and hunters. The birds have been reintroduced here, from Spain, since 1996. Learn many more details on this colony, now numbering over 100, down in **Rémuzat** far below its Table Mountain, at the charmingly run **Maison des Vautours** (*t 04 75 27 85 71; open April–mid-Sept daily exc Mon, and Thurs am, 10–12 and 2–5; otherwise weekends 10–12 and 2–5; adm*). Book here for walks with a nature specialist.

Back on the way to Buis, **Ste-Jalle**, with its diminished castle and two churches signals the entrance to an exceptionally beautiful, tranquil, fruitful bowl of land totally encircled by *montagnettes*. The thick shade of the village's wide plane alley is beloved of *boules* players. Perched dramatically on the rim of the bowl, the most distinctive element to **Le Poët-Sigillat**'s silhouette is its open-gated belltower. To the south, paragliders often circle like colourful dragonflies above the **Col d'Ey**, the high pass leading down to Buis.

The **southern way** from Nyons to Buis takes you through vine and olive country via **Mirabel-aux-Baronnies** to join the **Ouvèze valley**. Up in the village of **Piégon**, wine seems to have turned the head of a modern sculptor who has made an enormous outdoors piece in homage to the vine. Nipping across to the Ouvèze just above **Vaison-la-Romaine** (*see* Cadogan *Provence*), you come to **Mollans-sur-Ouvèze**, its natural fortification a massive lump of a rock, topped by an impressive medieval keep. Down below, the **Moulin à Huile Chauvet** (*t/f 04 75 28 90 12; open July–Sept daily 10–12.30 and 2.30–7, April–June weekends and public hols, same times; adm*) still turns the old-fashioned way. By the river, the cutest, least assuming chapel stands one side of the water, an enchanting colonnaded washhouse the other. At **Pierrelongue**, a 19th-century church has startlingly perched itself on a thinner ridge of rock, inciting walkers and pilgrims alike to take on the almost irrestible challenge of climbing up to it. Befittingly, the place has a **Musée d'Art Religieux**. *Tilleuls*, linden or lime trees, beautify the routes all around Buis-les-Baronnies, their plump forms yielding the flowers that go into making one of France's most popular infusions. In early summer, you may see wooden ladders propped against many a tree for the traditional harvest.

Hannibal and his elephants may possibly have sneaked through **Buis-les-Baronnies**, set against the backdrop of a bony dinosaur dorsal of a mountain, on their epic journey to take on Rome. But until the archaeological elephant droppings have been unearthed, it remains pure speculation as to whether the Carthaginian's extraordinary warhorses drank at the fountains here. This semi-forgotten town and its environs certainly attracted a hippy crowd from the 1960s, as did many of the semi-ruined villages of the southern Drôme and the Ardèche, even if the slightly harsher winters than expected made many of them run back to their home comforts. A residue remained here, however, topped up in season by young followers. Between ancient and modern times, the medieval barons had a solid little town built in their little mountains. Arcades of planes bring shade to the cafés along the main boulevard encircling the compact old centre. Within, the enchanting, eccentric arcades lining **Place du Marché** were apparently built by Swiss settlers in the 15th century, each plump arch adopting a slightly different pose. Among the narrow lanes beyond, look out for the lovely simple **cloister** of the converted Dominican monastery before the sturdy restored **church**, and for the mix of old butchers and new oil and herbal shops. It's not just linden trees that thrive in the fragrant Baronnies; aromatic herbs generally proliferate, as explained at the **Maison des Plantes Arômatiques et Médicinales** (*t 04 75 28 04 59; open July–Aug Mon–Sat 9–12 and 3–7, Sun and public hols 10–12 and 3–6; April–June and Sept Mon–Sat 9–12 and 2–6, Sun and public hols 10–12 and 3–6; Oct–March Mon–Sat 9–12 and 2–5, Sun and public hols 10–12 and 3–6; adm*) above the tourist office, although the panels and videos concentrate on linden and lavender in particular. The presentation is a tad dry, as is the herb garden outside.

To breath in the scents of the Baronnies at first hand, take the **Menon valley** east of Buis, olive groves thriving on one steep side, apricot orchards on the other. **La Roche-sur-le-Buis** sits among a cascade of big boulders, the remains of a castle clinging desperately to the highest one. The gravestones in the adorable tiny cemetery are almost choked by deliberately dense planting, with a miniature **Musée des Arts et Traditions** (*t 04 75 28 01 42; open on request; free*) next door focusing on old ways.

Pressing east, a gorgeous, unspoilt country route takes you up to the **source of the Ouvèze**. As well as apricot orchards and lavender fields, this tranquil corner is marked by wrinkled ridges of rock dragged up from the ocean in a distant era. According to a plaque in the most peaceful hilltop village of **St-Auban-sur-l'Ouvèze**, America recognizes the important role that François d'Albert, Comte de Rions, who died here in 1802, played in its War of Independence against Britain. Continue up to the **Col de Perty** for startling views of some of the Alps' eternally snow-capped peaks.

A still more dramatic route follows the southern frontier of the Drôme from Buis-les-Baronnies in the sensational black shadow of the **Mont Ventoux**. Clinging defiantly to its slope, facing the deeply forested northern flank of Provence's great Windy One, **Brantes** is a delicious isolated fortified village that lies in the neighbouring region, but should really be claimed by the *département de la Drôme*.

A ruined French Renaissance château gives the finishing touch to the fine silhouette of **Montbrun-les-Bains**, a substantial old village climbing its hillside via a series of stone terraces. It's a member of the association of *Les Plus Beaux Villages de France*, but not overprettified. Through the gateways, the medieval church contains surprisingly ornate *Ancien Régime* decorations. The *châtelain* most remembered in these parts, Charles Dupuy-Montbrun, became one of the most feared Protestant campaigners in the Wars of Religion, fighting alongside the Baron des Adrets. He is said to have gone to war with a sword in one hand, and a Bible in the other. After terrorizing Catholic communities around the Rhône valley, he suffered a blow when his castle was destroyed; but it was he who ordered the fine Renaissance one whose remains you now see. He eventually got his comeuppance, condemned to death for stealing Polish treasure from Henri III. It's a crying shame that modern houses have been so insensitively dotted around the valley below. The eggy smell emanating from here signals the posh thermal establishment with its classical style colonnade, apparently partly modelled on Baden-Baden in Germany. General relaxation treatments are now on offer at these **Thermes de Montbrun** (*t 04 75 28 80 75*).

Lost in a narrow valley to the north, the gathering of towers overseen by the imposing square keep of the **Château d'Aulan** (*t 04 75 28 80 00; open July–Aug daily 10–12 and 2–6.30; adm*) comes as a big surprise along the unoccupied **Gorges de Toulourenc**. You wonder what on earth the medieval lords might have been trying to protect in this barren landscape, but this was once a strategic gateway to Provence, on a salt trading route. Although a stone keep was built here perhaps as early as the 12th century, the one you see is a 19th-century reconstruction and, all told, the place has a slightly scruffy neo-Gothic look. Restored in engagingly amateurish manner since the war, when it served as a refuge for Resistance fighters, now cluttered with family memorabilia and bric-a-brac, the pleasure of the tour comes from anecdotes the objects engender on the adventurous past of the Suarez-d'Aulan family.

East of Montbrun, the countryside remains magnificently unspoilt. From around the village of **Barret-de-Lioure**, marked out by three wooden crosses perched on a rock in the midst of this high, deep valley, enjoy spectacular views back along the north flank of the Mont Ventoux. A war monument recalls three local Resistance fighters caught out in this tight valley. Around **Ferrassières** you reach the most southerly frontier of the Rhône-Alpes region, the expansive lavender-covered slopes descending gently and generously into Provence. Old stone huts known as *bories* scattered in the fields around the open village add to the photogenic surrounds. The **Château de la Gabelle**, one of the finest lavender properties to visit, has a lovely lavender boutique.

Heading back north round the forbidding Montagne d'Albion, follow the **Méouges valley**. The village of **Séderon** lies protected in a narrow section of the valley. Reaching the southeastern limits of the *département de la Drôme*, **Lachau**, with its castle and little squares with fountains, has the charms you'll have come to expect of Drôme villages. The Méouges then runs into Provence, through bright gorges leading to the natural sliding doors of rockmaking fortified **Sisteron** one of the most impressive gateways into that region.

The Rhône from Lyon to Lac Léman

The Isle Crémieu, Bugey and Gex

L'Isle Crémieu from Lyon to the Bugey 199
The Bugey 203
The Bulk of the Bugey **203**
The Revermont, Ain Valley and Northern Bugey 2**07**
The Valserine and Pays de Gex 210

14

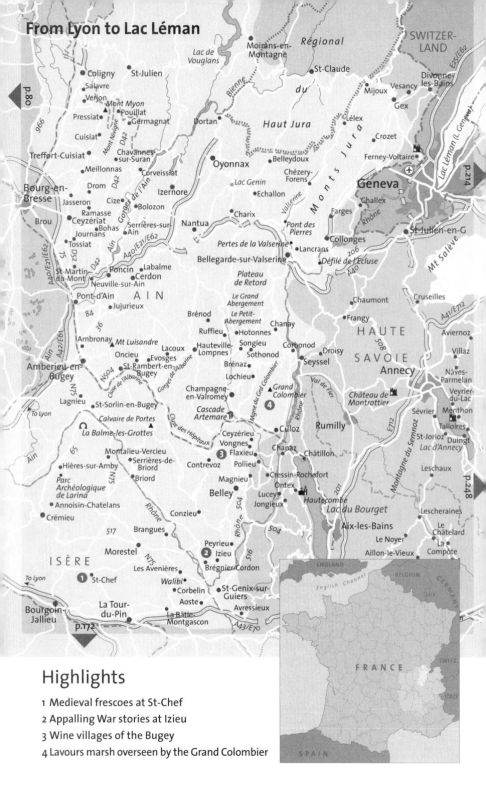

From Lyon to Lac Léman

Highlights

1 Medieval frescoes at St-Chef
2 Appalling War stories at Izieu
3 Wine villages of the Bugey
4 Lavours marsh overseen by the Grand Colombier

Here we take you up a splendidly little-known section of the Rhône, from the gently rolling lands east beyond Lyon airport, via the Bugey and Gex, spectacular southern spines of the Jura range, to the doorstep of Geneva. Along with the Bresse, this batch of territories stretching from the Saône to the border with the feisty Swiss enclave came firmly under the French royal thumb when Henri IV put down the troublesome expansionist Duke Charles-Emmanuel I of Savoie in 1601.

We stay mainly north of the Rhône in this chapter, although we start with l'Isle Crémieu just to the south, which is not an island, but a limestone plateau that forms an arrowhead of territory that juts out into the river. The big tourist thrills here are the Grottes de la Balme and the Walibi amusement park, but the routes around valley and plateau, despite the odd major industrial blip, also offer attractive small cultural stops.

The bigger, more viciously barbed arrowhead of the Bugey proceeds south into the river. This magical, secretive territory extends roughly from the A40 motorway between Ambronay and Bellegarde in the north to its very sharp point at Izieu in the south. It offers an unspoilt, natural roller-coaster ride up on to flower-filled, panoramic plateaux, down along straight dark diagonal gorges known as *cluses*, in the east bumping into the exceptionally broad-shouldered Grand Colombier, the Bugey's most impressive bodybuilder of a mountain. Way below its muscular frame lie the most beautiful flat marshes and utterly enchanting rolls of vine-covered slopes. This convivial countryside produced the most famous French writer on good living, Brillat-Savarin, from the cathedral town of Belley. But the Bugey's history is by no means all joyous, Nantua and Izieu retelling Second World War tragedies.

Back with our sweet tourist times, moving north, we offer delightful asides along the Revermont, the unspoilt wooden ridge above the Bresse, and along the Ain, a river almost as spectacularly dammed as the Rhône, before heading over to the Gex above Bellegarde. In these parts bordering on the Franche-Comté region, where the bulk of the French Jura mountains rise, the similarities with that old province become clearer and clearer in the architecture (especially the characteristic church towers topped by a little dome resembling a military hat) as well as the Comté cheese-making and pine-forested, wood-working surrounds. The Gex spans both sides of the highest of all the French Jura ridges, the Valserine valley to the west lost in time, continuing the old Comtois traditions. But the great curving slope to the east has been transformed by its proximity to Geneva, peering over it to Lac Léman. Political stirrer Voltaire sought refuge from the angered French monarchy in this frontier territory at the end of the *Ancien Régime*; now it's home to one of the earliest successful European cooperative ventures in science and technology, CERN. The Gex's horn of territory forms part of the wider *Parc Naturel Régional du Haut-Jura*.

L'Isle Crémieu from Lyon to the Bugey

Start a tour of the so-called **Isle Crémieu** with the old fortified town of **Crémieu** itself, at the entrance to the plateau east of Lyon-St-Exupéry, a pleasant first or last

Getting Around

By air and train: Lyon-St-Exupéry airport lies at one end of this area, Geneva airport at the other. By train, Culoz and Bellegarde are on the fast line from Paris to Geneva. The closest station for L'Isle Crémieu is Bourgoin-Jallieu, from Lyon.

Tourist Information

Crémieu: 9 Place de la Nation, t 04 74 90 45 13, www.ville-cremieu.fr.

Morestel: 100 Place des Halles, t 04 74 80 19 59, www.morestel.com.

Ambérieu-en-Bugey: Pl Robert Marcelpoil, t 04 74 38 18 17, www.ville-amberieuenbugey.fr.

St-Rambert-en-Bugey: 7 Ave de l'Europe, t 04 74 36 32 86, www.tourisme-albarine.com.

Hauteville-Lompnes: 15 Rue Nationale, t 04 74 35 39 73, www.plateau-hauteville.com.

Champagne-en-Valromey: Maison de Pays, t 04 79 87 51 04, www.valromeyretord.com.

Culoz: 6 Rue de la Mairie, t 04 79 87 00 30, www.interarb.com/culoz/.

Belley: 34 Grande Rue, t 04 79 81 29 06, e ot_belley@club-internet.fr.

Seyssel: Maison de Pays, Chemin de la Fontaine, t 04 50 59 26 56, e otseyssel@wanadoo.fr.

Cerdon: Place Allombert, t 04 74 39 93 02, e perso@wanadoo.fr/si.cerdon.

Pont-d'Ain: Crfr. des 4 Vents, t 04 74 39 05 84.

Poncin: 10 Place Bichat, t 04 74 37 23 14.

Nantua: Place de la Déportation, t 04 74 75 00 05, www.ville-nantua.com.

Bellegarde: 24 Place Victor Bérard, t 04 50 48 48 68, www.pays-de-gex.org.

Lélex-Mijoux: BP 2, t 04 50 20 91 43, www.monts-jura.com.

Gex: Square Jean Clerc, t 04 50 41 53 85, www.pays-de-gex-lafaucille.com.

Divonne-les-Bains: Rue des Bains, t 04 50 20 01 22, www.divonnelesbains.com.

Ferney-Voltaire: 26 Grand'Rue, t 04 50 28 09 16, www.ferney-voltaire.net.

Market Days

Crémieu: Wed.
Lagnieu: Mon.
Ambérieu-en-Bugey: Wed, Fri and Sat.
St-Rambert-en-Bugey: Thurs.
Hauteville-Lompnes: Thurs and Sat.
Champagne-en-Valromey: Thurs.
Culoz: Wed.
Belley: Sat.
Seyssel: Sat.
Jujurieux: Tues.
Cerdon: Fri.
Treffort-Cuisiat: Fri.
Pont-d'Ain: Sat.
Poncin: Mon.
Nantua: Sat.
Bellegarde: Thurs.
Gex: Sat.
Divonne-les-Bains: Fri and Sun.
Ferney-Voltaire: Wed and Sat.

Where to Stay and Eat

Crémieu ✉ 38460

**Auberge de la Chaite, Place des Tilleuls, t 04 74 90 76 63, f 04 74 90 88 08 (*inexpensive*). Quite central, nice rooms on garden side. Traditional restaurant (*moderate– cheap; closed Sun eve and Mon*) with terrace. *Closed late-April–early May.*

Bouvesse-Quirieu ✉ 38390

Moulin d'Arche, t 04 74 88 61 61 (*moderate*). Atmospheric 16th-century mill known for its organic bread, offering a copious country menu summer weekends. *Open Fri eve–Sun eve only; closed late-Sept–mid-May.*

Morestel ✉ 38510

***Hotel de France, 319 Grande Rue, t 04 74 80 04 77, f 04 74 33 07 47 (*moderate– inexpensive*). Pre-Revolution roadside inn rejuvenated just a tad, with traditional restaurant (*moderate*). *Restaurant closed Sun eve and Mon.*

Faverges-de-la-Tour ✉ 38110

****Château de Faverges de la Tour, t 04 74 97 42 52, www.faverges.com (*luxury–very expensive*). Superb 19th-century castle plus converted farm, rooms in grand style. Splendid grounds, pool, court and private 9-hole golf course. Exclusive restaurant (*very expensive–expensive*) in vaulted cellars. *Closed Oct–mid-May; restaurant closed lunchtimes Mon–Wed.*

Ruffieu ✉ 01260

Le Relais St-Didier, t 04 79 87 71 60, **e**
relaisstdidier@wanadoo.fr (*cheap*). Very likeable bargain village inn decked with flowers.
Simple rooms being redone. Modern, fresh
cuisine (*moderate–cheap*). *Closed most Jan,
plus late Nov; restaurant closed Sun pm.*

Châtillon-en-Michaille ✉ 01200

★Auberge Le Catray, Plateau de Retord **t** 04 50
56 56 25 (*inexpensive*). Breathtaking location,
on the edge of the high plateau west of
Bellegarde. Basic rooms. Lovely terrace for
dining (*moderate*) on mountain products or
more elaborate cuisine. *Closed 2 wks Sept/
2 wks Nov; restaurant closed Mon and Tues.*

Artemare ✉ 01510

★★Hôtel Michallet, Rue de la Poste, **t** 04 79 87
39 33, **f** 04 79 87 39 20 (*inexpensive*).
Traditional little country town hotel with
spacious rooms. Restaurant (*moderate*), with
shaded terrace. *Closed early Sept and early
Jan; restaurant closed Sun pm and Mon.*

Contrevoz ✉ 01300

Auberge de Contrevoz, La Plumardière, **t** 04 79
81 82 54 (*moderate*). Delightful, stylish
country restaurant with terrace, 8km northwest of Belley on D32. *Closed Sun eve, Mon
and Thurs, plus Christmas–Jan.*

Ceyzérieux ✉ 01350

Relais du Marais, t 04 79 87 01 61,
e *relaisdu marais@wanadoo.fr* (*inexpensive*).
Simple but appealing village hotel. Basic
rooms, nice Bugey menus (*moderate*), superb
pool. *Restaurant closed Mon.*

Avrissieu ✉ 01350

Le Pressoir et la Forge B&B, t 04 79 87 92 56
(*inexpensive*). Crammed with Bugey
character, with a wine press for company in
one apartment – the rooms have kitch-
enettes. *Closed Nov–Mar.*

Belley ✉ 01300

La Fine Fourchette, N504, **t** 04 79 81 59 33
(*expensive–moderate; closed Sun pm and
Mon*). 3km southeast above the road,
looking over a lake, high standard traditional
French cuisine. *Closed Christmas–early Jan.*

Jasseron ✉ 01250

Auberge de la Terrasse, t 04 74 25 05 77
(*moderate*). Unpretentious lively village inn,
local cuisine nicely done. *Closed Sun eve and
Mon, and 2nd half Aug and most Jan.*

Meillonnas ✉ 01370

Auberge au Vieux Meillonnas, t 04 74 51 34 46
(*moderate*). Stone and cobs and *soigné*
cuisine. *Closed Tues eve and Wed.*

Mijoux ✉ 01410

★★Le Soleil, Rue Royale, **t** 04 50 41 31 04,
www.hotellesoleilmijoux.com (*inexpensive*).
Good traditional central village option.
Copious food (*cheap*). Pool. *Closed Nov.*

Gex/Col de la Faucille ✉ 01170

★★★La Mainaz, Col de la Faucille, **t** 04 50 41 31
10, *www.la-mainaz.com* (*moderate*).
Wonderful views on to Lac Léman and the
Alps beside the pass. Darkly furnished rooms
with balconies. Fantastic vistas too from the
dining room (*expensive*). *Closed Nov–early
Dec; restaurant closed Sun eve and Mon.*

Divonne-les-Bains ✉ 01220

★★★★Château de Divonne, 115 Rue des Bains,
t 04 50 20 00 32, **e** *divonne@grandesetapes.fr*
(*luxury–expensive*). Up on the heights, exclusive 19th-century number with views onto
Lac Léman and Mont Blanc. Splendid restaurant (*luxury*). Pool and court in grounds.
★★★★Grand Hôtel, Ave des Thermes, **t** 04 50 40
34 34, **e** *info@domaine-de-divonne.com*
(*luxury*). Swish hotel with casino and
crooners in the heart of town. Restaurants
(*very expensive–expensive*). Pool, plus golf
course and spa centre nearby. *Closed Feb;
restaurant closed Sun eve and Mon.*
Le Pavillon du Golf, Route de Gex, **t** 04 50 40
34 13 (*moderate*). By golf course, restaurant
in beautiful building. Superb terrace for
summer dining. *Closed Tues out of season.*

Ferney-Voltaire ✉ 01210

★★Hôtel de France, 1 Rue de Genève, **t** 04 50 40
63 87, **e** *hotelfranceferney@wanadoo.fr*
(*moderate*). Attractive house where Voltaire's
secretary lived. Pleasant rooms. Rustic
restaurant (*moderate*). *Closed late-Dec–early
Jan; restaurant closed Sun and Mon.*

stop if using that airport, avoiding the big city's outskirts. The remnants of the medieval **Château Délphinal** look down from one hill, those of a Benedictine priory from another. Below, ramparts and impressive gateways remain, while the church builders cleverly adapted one defensive tower to serve as the base for the soaring spire! In the heart of town, attention centres on the splendid covered market. The local limestone provided blocks for building, but also thin slices for roofing, in what is called *lauze*. At **Annoisin-Chatelans** admire the effects in the houses, and discover more about the techniques at the **Musée de la Lauze** (*t 04 74 83 11 28; open late Jan–Dec daily exc Tues 9–5; adm*).

To the north, the **Plateau de Larina** proved a popular lookout post above the Rhône down the civilizations. Archaeological traces have been unearthed going from Neolithic huts and a Roman temple through to Carolingian times. The archaeological site is free, while the exceptionally long historical trail is explained more fully at the **Maison du Patrimoine de Hières-sur-Amby** (*t 04 74 95 19 10, www.mairie-hieres-sur-amby.com; open March–Oct daily 2-6; rest of year Mon–Fri 2–5; adm*). Today, however, the area around is marked by the nuclear power station across the Rhône at St-Vulbas. Along the valley's southern edge, waters infiltrated the plateau and formed underground rivers and lakes. The **Grottes de la Balme** (*t 04 74 90 63 76, www. grotteslabalme.com; open April–Sept daily 10–12 and 2–6; Feb–Mar and Oct–mid-Dec; check weekend visiting times; adm*) provide sensational evidence. Two chapels greet you at the entrance to these extraordinary caves, seemingly appreciated by prehistoric man as well as by François I, whose image features.

Reaching L'Isle Crémieu's northern point, the riverside road then shoots south below the cliff edge on the easterly side of the plateau. **Montalieu** shares with Serrières-de-Briord across the river the expanse of water created by a dam on the Rhône, now used for water sports. Close to several islands in the river, from the quietly seductive village of **Brangues**, a church tower rises in the Franche-Comté style. This edifice witnessed a terrible *crime passionnel* in 1827, when Antoine Berthet, a trainee priest consumed with jealousy, tried to shoot dead Mme Michoud de la Tour during a service. The scandal served as inspiration for one of the greatest French 19th-century novels, cruelly exposing the shock of a young man's loss of innocence, *Le Rouge et le Noir* (*Scarlet and Black*), by the greatest writer from Grenoble and the Dauphiné, Stendhal. The local castle was owned by another famous French writer, the committed Catholic Paul Claudel, buried here in 1955. The **Espace d'Exposition Claudel et Stendhal** (*t 04 74 80 32 14; open July–Aug daily exc Tues 10–12 and 3–7; May–June weekends and public hols 10–12 and 3–7; April and Sept–Nov Sun 2–6; adm*) follows the stories of these two exceptional literary figures.

Landscape painters led by Auguste Ravier were attracted to **Morestel** in the 19th century. The **Maison Ravier** (*t 04 74 80 06 80, www.maisonravier.com; open Mar–Oct daily exc Tues 2.30–6.30; adm*) concentrates on the pre-Impressionist master, in his Dauphiné house, while the **Maison du Pays des Couleurs** (*t 04 74 80 39 30; open Feb–mid-Dec Tues–Fri 10–12 and 2.30–5.30, Sun 2.30–5.30; free*) fills you in on the movement, with a small permanent display, plus temporary exhibitions. Nowadays the busy N75 crossing through the village has diminished the tranquillity of the place, even if the medieval church tower and keep still make their presence felt, the latter turned in summer into another space for exhibitions. The abbey church dominating quiet **St-Chef** (*t 04 74 27 73 83; open Jan–Dec Sun only*) may look plain on the outside, but conceals one of the most splendid, colourful displays of medieval wall paintings in the Rhône-Alpes. The most arresting images depict scenes from the fiery Apocalypse. Christ reigns in triumph in the apse. Around him, the variety of angels reveal the mastery of the artists. The **Musée Maison du Patrimoine** (*t 04 74 92 59 92; open 3 Jan–Nov daily exc Tues 10–12 and 2.30–6.30; adm*) covers the history of the abbey as well as its murals, plus local celebrities.

The **Musée du Tisserand** (*t 04 74 83 08 99, www.batie-montgascon.com; open Jan–Dec Wed–Sat plus Sun pm 9–12 and 2–5; adm*) at **La Bâtie-Montgascon** focuses on working-class weaving, which took off in a major way when workers driven out of Lyon by their desperate riots in the 1830s settled here. The place offers good demonstrations. A section is also devoted to bicycle history. Aoste takes you much further back in time with its **Musée Gallo-Romain** (*t 04 76 32 58 27, www.musee-archeologique-aoste.com; open Jan–Nov weekdays exc Tues 10–12 and 2–6, weekends 2–6; adm*). The area's cooking pots apparently became known across the Roman Empire, although this museum covers Gallo-Roman life beyond the culinary. To the east lies the Guiers river (*see p.266*), frontier between France and Savoie until the latter joined France in 1860. The **Parc Walibi** amusement park (*t 04 74 33 71 80, www.sixflagseurope.com; open July–Aug daily 10–9, June daily 10–5; May and Sept–Oct weekends and public hols 10–5; adm*) attracts families from far and wide with all manner of rides at **Les Avenières**.

The Bugey

The Bulk of the Bugey

The stretch of the Rhône from industrial Lagnieu to country Izieu forms the western edge of the Bugey's arrowhead. **St-Sorlin-en-Bugey** has kept its centuries-old charm, its church crowned by a lovely dome. One house boasts an old painted front showing the giant St Christopher crossing a river, the child Jesus on his shoulders. Climb to the **Col des Portes** for a winding route up and over into the central Bugey. Back down by the river at **Serrières-de-Briord**, the **Point Vert lake** overseen by the flanks of the **Molard de Don** provides a big expanse of water for fishing, swimming or boating. **Briord** has a little pleasure port on the Rhône. The small patches of vines around Montagnieu and Seillonnaz on the steep side of the **Montagne de Souhait** produce a typical fragrant Bugey sparkling wine from the Roussette grape. A dramatic waterfall descends from the southern Bugey mountains to beside **Glandieu**. At **Brégnier-Cordon**, the **Maison des Isles du Rhône** (*t 04 79 87 26 62*) focuses on the islands and their flora and fauna at this major turning point in the river.

The idyllic village of **Izieu**, at the very southern tip of the Bugey, was the setting for an horrific event in the Second World War, recalled in the harrowing **Maison Mémorial** (*t 04 79 87 21 05, www.izieu.alma.fr; open mid-June–mid-Sept daily 10–6.30;*

mid-Jan–mid-June and mid-Sept–mid-Dec weekdays 9–5, weekends 10–6; adm), in an isolated farm on the hillside. This place became a secret refuge for Jewish children rescued from persecuted families, many from Eastern Europe. But on 6 April 1944 the Gestapo came and took away 44 of them and their teachers; 47 would die in Auschwitz; three others would be shot in Estonia; and just one survived to reveal the horror. Klaus Barbie, the Gestapo head in Lyon, at his trial in 1987 (covered in a film here), denied that he gave the order for the Izieu raid, but it seems highly unlikely that he didn't know about it. After the traumatic case, this spot was turned into this exceptionally important museum, with the support of Sabine Zlatin, director of the clandestine school, who was by chance away the day of the tragedy, and of civil servant Wiltzer, who had found the farm in the first place. The beauty of the site just adds to the agony of the story. Seeing the children's happy photos and lovely drawings and letters is absolutely heartrending. The barn has been converted into a museum that confronts the terrible ghosts of France's as well as Germany's anti-Semitism. The anti-Jewish laws that Pétain's Vichy government promulgated following the Nazi example are unflinchingly exposed. In all, some 76,000 Jews were deported from France, around a quarter of the entire Jewish population in the country in 1939. Around 43,000 were gassed in concentration camps. Just 2,500 survived. The 63,000 Resistance figures and political objectors deported are also remembered. 37,000 of these returned alive.

For sensational paths into the heart of the Bugey, back west you could start from **Ambérieu-en-Bugey**, the remnants of towers around this rail and aviation town indicating it was a major stronghold close to the Dauphiné and Savoie frontier in medieval times. Up in the hills, the pure medieval defensive forms of the **Château des Allymes** (*t 04 74 38 06 07, open May–Aug daily 10–12 and 2–6; Mar–April and Sept–Oct daily 2–5.30; Nov daily 2–4; Dec–Feb weekends 2–6; adm*) went up for the Dauphiné side, while the Savoyards sat on the height of Mont Luisandre. Les Allymes preserves the memory of the treaty negotiated by local lord René de Lucinge by which the duke of Savoie gave up his rights to Bresse, Bugey and Gex in 1601. The N504 road leads along the Albarine valley, this section marked by the textile industry. **St-Rambert-en-Bugey**, with its **Ecomusée des Traditions Bugistes** (*t 04 74 36 32 86; open June–Oct Tues–Sat 9–12 and 2–6, Sun 2.30–5.30; rest of yearTues–Sat 9–12 and 2–5; adm*) concentrating on traditional crafts from 1850 to 1940, is overseen by further defensive towers.

The long, tight **Cluse des Hôpitaux gorge** leads directly to Belley, but tackle the dramatic terrain to the north to discover the most enchanting parts of the Bugey. Climb to the village of **Oncieu** for a magnificent little detour, and continue round via **Evosges**. The village of **Lacoux** lies hidden up its own dramatic, boulder-strewn gorge. It lost its school some time ago, but this has been converted into an energetic **Centre d'Art Contemporain** (*t 04 74 35 25 61, www.cac-lacoux.com; check on spring, summer and autumn exhibitions; free*), regularly shocking visitors with its cutting-edge exhibitions. Attracting a curious mix of the ultra-sporty and the very sickly, **Hauteville-Lompnes** further up the Albarine is appreciated by both because of its pure air. The skies are so clear around here that an **observatory** (*t 04 79 87 67 31, www.astroval. free.fr; open daily 2–6; adm*) has been set up at the **Col de Lèbe**. If your astronomical

French is up to it, book in advance for a night course here; or during the day, you can follow an introductory trail.

Maybe try a delicious country loop around the high plateau north from Hauteville to join Ruffieu, going via **Champdor**, with its remarkable *Ancien Régime* castle, on to **Brénod**, with its cheese-making *Fruitière*, then round to the butch sister country villages of **Le Petit Abergement** and **Le Grand Abergement**, their well-built traditional farms with big rounded gates. All this high terrain turns into cross-country skiing territory when it snows. From Le Grand Abergement, roads head north up across the almost wholly houseless **Plateau de Retord**, renowned for its spring daffodils as well as its summer flowers, devoted attention in a little museum at **Les Plans d'Hotonnes**. To the north, walkers head for the isolated **Chapelle de Retord**, a 19th-century sanctuary on a spot consecrated by the great 17th-century Catholic Reformation figure of Savoie, St François de Sales (*see* p.254). It has gained a certain comical reputation for the annual August ceremony to bless cars! On the eastern edge of the plateau, utterly spectacular views open out to the Alps.

Back with rustic Ruffieu, or neighbouring Hotonnes, the enchanting views southwards will tempt you down into the **Valromey**, the romantic wide valley of the Seran river that cuts through the centre of the Bugey. Famous writers sought refuge and inspiration here in the first half of the 20th century, including the avant-garde American Gertrude Stein. The villages have preserved a wonderful unspoilt feel to this day, their old communal bread ovens still in place, and sometimes even the *travail*, where horses were shoed. The western route goes via **Ruffieu**, lovingly restored and utterly tranquil. Then potter through the quiet villages around the D31. The church at **Champagne-en-Valromey** conceals the remnants of a beautiful 16th-century triptych. By **Cerveyrieu**, admire the waterfall of the Seran before the pleasant stop of **Artemare**.

The eastern route takes you from Hotonnes under the mighty wooded flank of Le Grand Colombier. The **Grotte du Pic** by **Songieu** was favoured by Neolithic men, while Songieu itself served for centuries as medieval capital of the Valromey. It has kept vestiges of its period castle. The next villages have retained signs of their connection with the Abbey of Arvières, founded in the 12th century way up on the wooded heights of Le Grand Colombier, but in ruins; now a **Jardin Ethnobotanique** (*t 04 79 87 02 06, www.multimania.com/arvieres; open mid-May–mid-Oct Wed–Sun; adm for tour*) occupies the site, covering plants from the Neolithic to the discovery of the New World. The **château** at **Sothonod** belonged to the Artaud family, whose St Arthaud created the abbey. **Brénaz**'s church contains an altar rescued from the religious establishment. **Lochieu**'s church holds relics of St Arthaud. The wider traditions and culture of the Valromey are beautifully presented in the **Musée du Bugey-Valromey** (*t 04 79 87 52 23; open April–Oct Sun and public hols 10–6, Mon and Thurs–Sat 2–6; adm*) spread around a fine Renaissance house. As well as the more typical historical displays, one section is devoted to outstanding contemporary woodwork.

Distinctly alarming mountain routes climb up into the dense woods of **Le Grand Colombier** from Lochieu and Virieu-le-Petit, not roads for the faint-hearted. The reward at the top of the Bugey's giant is fantastic views over Lac du Bourget and the

Alps beyond. Then tremendously precipitous ways twist down to the stretch of the Rhône marking not just the eastern side of the Bugey's arrowhead, but also an historic divide between France and Savoie. That explains why the enchanting riverside town of **Seyssel**, an important port for Rhône mariners down the centuries, has two distinct settlements (*see also* p.257), each provided with its own church and other social amenities. On the Bugey side, contemporary artists put on regular shows at the *Ateliers de la Poudrière*. Seyssel is well known for its wines. Although the AOC **vineyards** only cover some 90 hectares, however they embellish both banks. Stay on the Bugey side to find wine estates to visit. Seek them out around enchanting villages like **Corbonod** or **Chanay**, heading towards Bellegarde.

Below the Grand Colombier's southern flank you come upon a magical flat marsh, the **Marais de Lavours**, created around the Séran's confluence with the Rhône, now a protected nature reserve. **Culoz** keeps its feet dry, clinging to the Grand Colombier's lower slopes. Take a splendid lesson on the marsh habitat by going to the unspoilt village of **Aignoz**, the houses provided with intricately divided barn doors. The wonderful new **Maison du Marais de Lavours** (*t 04 79 87 90 39; open June–Aug daily 10–7; April–May and Sept 2–6.30; Feb–Mar and Oct–Nov weekends 2–6; adm*) reveals the frog-eat-frog world of this beautiful marsh in most engaging style. It's the kind of place to get even difficult adolescents to feel passionate about the natural food chain rather than food chains, with gripping, gory film footage. Go walking into the marsh on what is apparently the longest boardwalk on stilts in Europe, 2.4km in length.

Delicious villages bask in the gorgeous **vineyards** covering the slopes west of this marsh. Don't miss **Vongnes**, whose reds not only employ Gamay and Pinot Noir, but also the rarer Manicle and Mondeuse. The place has a **wine museum** (*t 04 79 87 92 32; open daily 9–12 and 2–7; free*) in a wine property run with great good humour. Virtually all the villages down to Belley have kept their traditional features. Seek out delightful places like **Flaxieu** and **Pollieu**. The quite wild **Lac de Barterand** has a much-appreciated strip of beach, and the surprise of a giant sculpted figure of Gargantua. Beside **Cressin-Rochefort**, its old houses sitting below a medieval castle, a large artificial lake offers all manner of water sports on the canal running parallel to the Rhône. Below **Magnieu** lies the river stop serving Belley.

Centrepiece of **Belley**, the Gothic **cathedral** has an impressive choir almost as long as the nave, the latter redone in the 19th century, when a grand organ was also added. The extravagant decoration inside includes double rows of stained glass in the choir, plus side chapels draped with fake cloth. A very ornate reliquary chest contains remnants of the city's important 12th-century bishop, Anthelme. The curving main street with its substantial houses was the address of Brillat-Savarin, Belley's most famous son and its one-time mayor, a peculiarly French concoction, a figure who represented the region's Third Estate at the 1789 Revolution, but who also wrote the Bible on French good living, *La Physiologie du Goût*, a philosophical culinary classic published in 1826. For a glimpse of good country living, explore more of the typical villages south of Belley towards Izieu (*see* pp.203-4) like **Conzieu** with its medieval church and its lakes. It was due to the generosity of an American woman who appreciated the Bugey, Grace Whitney-Hoff, that **Peyrieu** became the first village in France to put up a monument to its dead from the First World War, as early as 1919.

The Revermont, Ain Valley and Northern Bugey

This section covers another gem of a largely undiscovered land, the triangle between Ambronay, Coligny and Oyonnax. The **Revermont** west of the Ain forms the dreamy backdrop to the Bresse (*see* Chapter 8) and offers a gentle introduction to the mountainous Jura terrain to the east. To appreciate the stone villages resting sleepily along the western slope of the Revermont, join the D52 above Pont-d'Ain, this road the dividing line between the flat *poulet de Bresse* plain, and the green, wooded, vertical world that leads to Lake Geneva. The well-exposed ridge was wine-producing territory in times past, although only **Pétillant de Gravelles** is made now, a perfumed sparkling wine. Religion still marks the way. **St-Martin-du-Mont**'s church was built for a venerated 16th-century Pietà. A 16th-century cross stands in front of the Gothic church at **Tossiat**, containing remnants of murals. At **Journans**, a gilded St Vincent, patron saint of winemakers, counts among the church treasures. **Ceyzériat**'s steeple draws attention with its twisted spire, while inside it boasts 15th-century stained glass. **Jasseron**'s church conceals carved delights from different epochs.

Since the *Ancien Régime*, **Meillonnas** has retained its reputation for pottery, ateliers signalled around the neatly kept village, whose very street name signs are made in ceramics. Flowers often feature among the motifs on the traditional ware, and the lanes are well provided with real blooms. Having served as the main centre of production in the 18th century, the castle may soon be devoted to Meillonnas pottery again, with plans for a new museum. A stylish dome stands out on **Treffort**'s hillock, the odd fountain splashing along this village's very steep streets, the houses provided with handy wine cellars. The Gothic church retains wooden stalls representing the life of regional monastic hero St Bruno (*see* p.275), works rescued from the Charterhouse of Sélignat further east. Just one or two vestiges of a medieval castle stand out to one side. At **Cuisiat**, a pretty hillside village, the old school has been turned into the charming **Musée du Revermont** (*t 04 74 51 32 42; open 1st Sun in April–Oct, Sun and bank hols 10–6, Mon and Thurs–Sat 2–6; adm*), which recalls the vanished winemaking traditions in these parts as well as local pottery. The sweet gardens behind put forgotten fruit and veg to the fore.

You then reach the tallest, pyramidal tops of the Revermont slopes, their highest point at 768m along the **Mont Nivigne**. As to **Mont Myon**, it's a favourite spot for hang-gliding, the extraordinary flying machines circling like colourful birds of prey in the skies. French champion Jean-Marc Caron often displays his skills here. A **Sentier Mémorial**, a steep track lined with contemporary sculptures, leads walkers down to **Pressiat**, a village partially destroyed by German soldiers towards the close of the war, although the Gothic church survived with its 15th-century murals. Beyond **Verjon**, a village with a pretty bridge, and **Salavre**, tucked in its valley, **Vergongeat**'s hosts of daffodils draw crowds in March. **Coligny** brings you back to the busy modern world, although a gorgeous Roman statue of Apollo and a Gaulish calendar counted among antique treasures discovered here in the 19th century, copies held in the *Mairie* of this historic lordly town on the border with the Franche-Comté.

Over the first Revermont ridge, the D42 and D59 follow the route of **the Suran**, the river flowing through the midst of the range. You might join the valley at **Pouillat**, with its isolated Gothic church. The other side, **Germagnat** in its delightful location has a medieval church containing a gilded Baroque altarpiece. Press further up for the castle ruins. The church at **Chavannes-sur-Suran** protects *Ancien Régime* works rescued from the nearby **Chartreuse de Sélignat**, reoccupied by monks from the 1920s, and onto which you can get a fabulous view by climbing a track between Arnans and Corveissiat. Vestiges of castles line the routes south, the romantic ruins of the **Château de Bohas** the result of German destruction in 1944. Also seek out the dramatic silhouette of the **Donjon de Buenc** and the vestiges of the **Château de Beaurepaire**. The Suran then joins the Ain.

Compared with the tranquil Revermont, the **Ain valley** has been much more visibly marked by man's intervention, with not just factories to the south, but also a large number of dams further north. The wooded banks and unnaturally bright waters of the middle section we cover here provide a pleasing riverside journey. Starting back with **Pont-d'Ain**, this strategic river crossing stands in a corner where Bresse, Dombes and Bugey meet. The remnants of the castle help recall that Louise de Savoie, mother of one of France's most ambitious kings, François I, came into the world here, although the 19th-century hillside church draws more attention these days.

The beautiful form of **Ambronay**'s hillside **abbey** beckons seductively across the wide expanse of the Ain valley in these parts. This very well-located monastery was founded in 800 for Barnard, a former officer to Emperor Charlemagne. Just a few signs remain of the Carolingian building, but the church and cloisters are largely in uplifting Gothic style. One doorway is graced by an engrossing Resurrection scene. The cool Gothic interior contains tender period murals and stained glass, soberly carved wooden stalls and a remarkable stone Pietà, Christ rigid in death on the knees of his shocked mother. A door leads into the beautiful Gothic cloisters.

Imposing châteaux line up along the wooded slope at **Jujurieux**, also dramatically visible from far across the Ain valley. This place long lived off silk-making, a large factory still standing out in the centre, built from the 1830s for Claude Bonnet, a local who became one of Lyon's biggest silk merchants, the company's working girls leading a cloistered life here until the Second World War. The factory specialized in high-quality work for leading fashion houses until the turn of the millennium; it has now been turned into a **silk museum** (*open May–mid-June daily exc Tues 2.30–6; mid-June–mid-Sept daily exc Tues and weekend mornings 10–12.30 and 2.30–6; adm*).

Steep **vineyards** crop up most surprisingly in unlikely corners of the mountainous eastern half of the Rhône-Alpes region, but perhaps nowhere more dramatically than around the sprawling village of **Cerdon**, hidden in the bottom of a deep bowl of land surrounded by limestone-topped heights. The vineyards seem to be trying desperately to climb up and out over the rim. Far below, in the tight village streets, as well as sampling and buying the extraordinarily perfumed local wines, visit the **Cuivrerie** (*t 04 74 39 96 44; open high summer daily; adm*), an old copper-making factory still using old machinery to produce vats, cups, medals and the like. The **church** perched above the village has a cemetery happily surrounded by vines, while a solid white Virgin oversees proceedings from an even higher rock. Every evening, two villagers walk up to light her with candles. Along the high main N84 road east, the *Monument aux Morts du Val d'Enfer*, with its naked-breasted female figure flying from the stone, is meant to recall the Resistance fighters from the Ain and Bugey who died in the Second World War. Further along, at the **Grotte de Labalme** (*t 04 74 37 36 79; open July–Aug daily 10–6; Easter–June and Sept–Oct weekends; adm*), visitors take a train into a series of caves with weirdly shaped geological formations, where the local cheesemakers used to age their *fromages*. You have to be a little crazy to take the nearby **Fantasticâble**, strapped in like a bobsleigh rider, to whistle down an aerial cable offering you a bird's eye views over Cerdon at up to 100 kph!

West back by the Ain, **Poncin** has kept something of a medieval fortified air and arcades. At **Neuville-sur-Ain** with its sturdy stone bridge, the old riverside houses give one reason to stop, the traditional oil mill still at work another. Heading up the Ain, the **Allement dam** has helped create a river lake with water sports by **Merpuis**. By **Serrières-sur-Ain**, the locals were provided with a new, single-span bridge after the dam caused the waters to rise. Climb east to the **Col de Berthiand** for dramatic views. Continuing up the Ain's meanders, between **Bolozon** and **Cize**, marvel at the bold late-19th-century **double viaduct** crossing the waters on huge arches. Restored after its destruction in 1944, the lower level serves for cars, the upper for trains. The corniche road along the west bank of the river provides the more dramatic route to the border with Franche-Comté. For the best view of the medieval **Château de Conflans** marking the regional frontier, carry on up to **St-Maurice-d'Echazeaux**.

The **Oignin valley** parallel to the Ain conceals the odd surprise, such as small fragments of a Roman temple at **Izernore**, but the heavily industrial **Ange valley** and area around **Oyonnax** has long been nicknamed Plastics Valley after the traditional craft-making skills (especially of elaborate comb-making in wood and horn) were superseded. During the Second World War, the feisty town witnessed an extraordinarily defiant march by Resistance members on 11 November 1943, paying their respects to the Allied dead of the First World War. **Dortan** may have been destroyed in the Second World War, but still defends its long-held position as one of the world's major producers of chessboards. Gothic masons showed off their carving skills in saucy sculptures at the church of **Arbent**.

Its shockingly bright glacial lake, overseen by dramatic limestone cliffs popular for summer swimming and boating, **Nantua** makes one of the Bugey's most arresting semi-forgotten towns. The settlement grew up around an abbey founded in the Dark Ages by Amand, said to have converted the henchmen sent to assassinate him into the new monastery's first monks! The atmospheric medieval **church of St Michael** had most of the Romanesque decorations round the doorway hammered off in later violence, but the Last Supper's table remains set. In the Gothic interior, the pillars curve disconcertingly under the pressure. The striking painting by Delacroix in the choir depicts an alarmingly beautiful, foreshortened St Sebastian. Stories of Second World War martyrdom in the Ain and Haut-Jura are told nearby, the former prison

turned into the harrowing **Musée de l'Histoire de la Résistance et de la Déportation**
(*t 04 74 75 07 50; open May–Sept Tues–Sun 10–1 and 2–6; adm*), the cells put to
effective use. Many successful operations are charted, and the help from the Allies –
the first American DC3 Dakota to land in France did so here. Among the most
extraordinary objects on display is a wedding dress made from material recuperated
from parachutes used in Allied drops. But in terrible revenge for the strong local
Resistance activity, and as the Germans hadn't managed to unearth the *maquisards*,
many of the menfolk of Nantua between 18 and 40 years of age were rounded up and
sent to the concentration camp of Buchenwald. Beside the lake, a chillingly large
memorial pays homage to them.

Northeast of Nantua head via the pretty old hamlets around **Charix** to another
popular if wilder, higher lake, **Lac Genin**, where people swim in summer, but go ice-
skating in winter. Past **Echallon**, a pyramidal war monument in the prairies recalls
Allied parachute drops to Resistance groups. A vast bird appears to have been drawn
in the rocks at the **Cirque de la Fauconnière**, a natural wonder of the Jura range.

The Valserine and Pays de Gex

The deeply industrial town of **Bellegarde** at the confluence of the Valserine and the
Rhône marks a crossroads between different areas. Although down at heel today, a
massive amount of hydroelectric power was harnessed to power industry here in the
19th century, Bellegarde claiming to have been the first town in France to get electric
lighting. Then in 1937 work began on the enormous Rhône **Barrage de Génissiat** south
of town, for some time the largest dam in Europe, but only completed after the war, in
1948, after that helping to supply the country with electricity.

North of Bellegarde, the Valserine's waters are constricted in a tight gulley by
Lancrans known as **Les Pertes de la Valserine**, which can be discovered on a 2-hour
walking round tour. Climbing to the villages around **Pont-des-Pierres**, the views
open out dramatically. Beyond, you enter the secretive Valserine valley, seeming
quite cut off from the rest of the world. While France acquired most of these
territories at the start of the 17th century, the Spanish Holy Roman Emperors held
on to this valley route, helping their armies travel between their southern and the
northern territories, bypassing France. Now, the Valserine is renowned for its
tranquillity, its streams much appreciated by fishermen.

Although overlooked by a dramatic natural theatre of rock, at **Chézery-Forens** the
valley widens out to offer high pastures. The cows' milk goes into making Bleu de Gex
cheese and Comté at the modern *fromagerie*. Passers-by through the year stock up on
sausages at the traditional butcher's in **Lélex**, but when the snows come, the place
offers cross-country and downhill skiing along with its neighbour. **Mijoux** provides
plenty of amusement at any time, in the series of modern murals illustrating
traditional trades on the outside of the village houses, in the jewellery on sale at the
major shop doubling as the **Musée des Pierres Fines et Précieuses** (*t 04 50 41 31 72,
www. vuillermoz.fr; open Jan–Dec Tues–Sun 10–12 and 2–6.30; free*), continuing the

local tradition of cutting and polishing semi-precious stones, and, across the frontier river close to the church, in a vegetable plot protected by a fence made entirely of colourful old skis!

The staggering views across Lac Léman and the Alps from the **Col de la Faucille** come as a breathtaking shock. From the pass, walkers follow the GR9, a splendid path along the highest crest of the French Jura, the **Monts-Jura**. Plunging down towards Geneva, the Pays de Gex was controlled through the early Middle Ages by the counts of that city. In the 13th century one branch set up an independent barony in the steep town of **Gex**, with its sloping squares. But in the mid-14th century, the house of Savoie gained control. For a taste of the traditional rural Pays de Gex, visit the village of **Vesancy** with its castle tower, church and rustic houses still surrounded by orchards.

In the suburban sprawl below, particularly in the border town of **Divonne**, you see the influence of booming Geneva. You can practically feel Swiss money in the air; indeed, the locals asked to join Switzerland in the 19th century, but only the lakeside communities were admitted. However, with the creation of *Zone Franche du Pays de Gex*, the rest of the area has benefited since 1815 from exceptional tax breaks, while Divonne has long attracted Swiss wealth both because of its spa and its show-time casino, although the Helvetian authorities have recently loosened their gambling laws, diminishing Divonne's popularity. One passionate inhabitant runs regular guided tours around the **natural springs** in town. Many people who suffered so traumatically in Nazi concentration camps were sent to Divonne's **cold-water spa** after the war to try to help them recover. Now the place caters both to depressives and to those in need of relaxation, a **golf course** next door.

This border territory appealed to that provocative campaigning Enlightenment iconoclast Voltaire, who sought safety from the enraged French royal authorities at **Ferney-Voltaire** from 1754 on. He hardly slummed it. In fact, he had the **Château de Ferney** (*t 04 50 28 09 16, www.ferney-voltaire.org; open June–Sept – check for times of visits; adm*) rebuilt in classical style for himself and his niece-cum-mistress, Marie Louise Denis. From 1760, this became his favourite residence. On the intelligent tour you're given a vivid picture of Voltaire's life, with plenty of *Ancien Régime* visuals. As well as entertaining lavishly at Ferney and encouraging local enterprise, from here he mounted his famously successful defence of the Protestant Calas, wrongly accused of the murder of his Catholic son, while the Caprony mill at Divonne provided the paper on which the first editions of his fantastic work *Candide* was printed. Today the château tries to follow in Voltaire's footsteps with a vibrant cultural programme.

For an even more intellectually challenging visit, book a tour of **CERN** (*t 00 41 227 67 61 11; adm*), the European Centre for Nuclear Particle Research, between Prévessin and St-Genis-Pouilly. One of the earliest cooperative Western European ventures after the war, this laboratory was set up in 1954 and is a world-leader in atomic particle research. Although such high-brow physics may bring to mind frightening thoughts of the nuclear age, the projects here also aim to forward much more benign technologies, and are playing a significant part in the quest to get to the root of the creation of the universe and the tiniest particles from which it is formed. Put your thinking caps on if you wish to follow the demanding three-hour visit. The less taxing option is to head a bit up the Monts Jura slopes to enjoy a natural curve of such exceptionally pleasing proportions as to satisfy even the most demanding of mathematicians. Explore the peaceful villages along the way.

You come out at the **Défilé de l'Ecluse**, the most alarming strategic post along the gully of the Rhône valley separating Jura and Alps, a spot where France, Switzerland and Savoie met in times past. The dauntingly defensive steps of **Fort l'Ecluse** (*t 04 50 59 68 45, www.fortlecluse.fr.st; open late-June–mid-Sept Tues–Sat 2–7, Sun 3–7; adm*) climb the very steep, rocky slope, an awesome frontier fortress. Prepare yourselves for the more than 1,100 steps of the underground staircase leading up from the *Ancien Régime* parts to the 19th-century fortified terraces far above, offering superb plunging views on the gorge. Displays and screenings help tell the history of this chilling, awesome strategic military site. To follow the Rhône up to Geneva, you have to enter Swiss territory.

Haute Savoie
From Lac Léman to Mont Blanc

Routes from the Lower Arve to Lac Léman 219
Lac Léman rather than Lake Geneva **220**
Haut Chablais and the Giffre 223
To Mont Blanc via Arve or Aravis 224
Coming Face to Face with Mont Blanc **227**

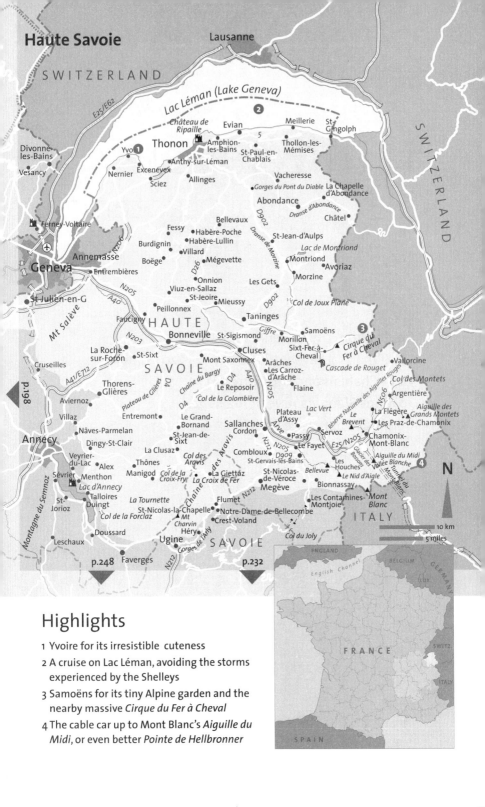

Haute Savoie

SWITZERLAND

Lausanne

Lac Léman (Lake Geneva) ②

Château de Ripaille

Evian

Meillerie

St-Gingolph

Divonne-les-Bains

Vesancy

Ferney-Voltaire

Yvo ①

Thonon

Amphion-les-Bains

St-Paul-en-Chablais

Thollon-les-Mémises

SWITZERLAND

Nernier

Excenevex

Anthy-sur-Léman

Sciez

Allinges

Vacheresse

Gorges du Pont du Diable

La Chapelle d'Abondance

Geneva

Annemasse

Entremblères

Fessy

Burdignin

Boëge

Habère-Poche

Habère-Lullin

Villard

Mégevette

Bellevaux

St-Jean-d'Aulps

Abondance

Dranse d'Abondance

Châtel

Lac de Montriond

Montriond

Avoriaz

St-Julien-en-G

Onnion

Viuz-en-Sallaz

St-Joeire

Mieussy

Les Gets

Morzine

Col de Joux Plane

Peillonnex

Faucigny

HAUTE

Taninges

Bonneville

St-Sigismond

Giffre

Morillon

Samoëns ③

Cirque du Fer à Cheval

La Roche-sur-Foron

St-Sixt

Cluses

Sixt-Fer-à-Cheval

Vallorcine

Cruseilles

Mont Saxonnex

Arâches

Les Carroz-d'Arâche

Cascade de Rouget

Thorens-Glières

Chaîne du Bargy

Le Reposoir

Flaine

Col des Montets

Aviernoz

Plateau de Glières

Col de la Colombière

Plateau d'Assy

Lac Vert

Réserve Naturelle des Aiguilles Rouges

Argentière

Aiguille des Grands Montets

Villaz

Entremont

Le Grand-Bornand

Sallanches

Cordon

Passy

Servoz

Le Brevent

La Flégère

Les Praz-de-Chamonix

Nâves-Parmelan

Dingy-St-Clair

St-Jean-de-Sixt

Combloux

Le Fayet

Chamonix-Mont-Blanc

Annecy

La Clusaz

Col des Aravis

St-Gervais-les-Bains

Les Houches

Aiguille du Midi ④

Vallée Blanche

Veyrier-du-Lac

Alex

Thônes

Manigod

Col de la Croix-Fry

La Giettaz

St-Nicolas-de-Véroce

Bellevue

Le Nid d'Aigle

Sévrier

Menthon

La Croix de Fer

Megève

Bionnassay

St-Jorioz

Talloires

Duingt

Lac d'Annecy

La Tournette

Flumet

Les Contamines-Montjoie

Mont Blanc

ITALY

Leschaux

Doussard

Col de la Forclaz

St-Nicolas-la-Chapelle

Mt Charvin

Héry

Notre-Dame-de-Bellecombe

Crest-Voland

Col du Joly

Favergès

Ugine

Gorges de l'Arly

SAVOIE

10 km

5 miles

N

p.198

p.248

p.232

Highlights

1 Yvoire for its irresistible cuteness

2 A cruise on Lac Léman, avoiding the storms experienced by the Shelleys

3 Samoëns for its tiny Alpine garden and the nearby massive *Cirque du Fer à Cheval*

4 The cable car up to Mont Blanc's *Aiguille du Midi*, or even better *Pointe de Hellbronner*

ENGLAND

BELGIUM

GERMANY

LUX.

English Channel

FRANCE

SWITZ.

ITALY

SPAIN

Haute Savoie really has an enormous amount to boast about, with the biggest lake in Western Europe and the tallest, most impressive mountain on the continent. Breathtaking as these natural wonders are, Haute Savoie shouldn't crow too selfishly, as it shares them, the Mont Blanc range with Italy and Switzerland, while only the southern shore of Lake Geneva, that great blue croissant on the maps, is French – and always referred to in these parts as Lac Léman. The whole region of Savoie has historically been French-speaking. When joined to France by vote in 1860, it was divided into two *départements*, Haute (Upper) Savoie in the north, plain Savoie to the south. Its flag, like the Swiss, consists of a white cross on red background; you can tell them apart by the fact that the arms of Savoie's cross reach right to the edge. The region has its own little independence movement in the *Ligue Savoisienne*, polling very poorly in elections, but plastering signs everywhere for a *Savoie Libre*.

In this chapter we cover the Haute Savoie areas of Faucigny, stretching along the broad Arve valley, and of the Chablais, rising between this valley and Lac Léman. We also tackle the traditional Bornes pre-alpine range, ending with the awesome wall of the Aravis, before taking you across to Chamonix and Mont Blanc.

Despite being so utterly gorgeous, Lac Léman's name may derive rather unpoetically from an ancient word for mud, although the more romantic etymologists opt for roots in the Celtic for elm. In little corners close to the lake, vines thrive, Bas (Lower) Chablais producing refreshing wines to accompany the lake fish. Swanky Evian is of course famous for its pure spring water and luxury spa centre. Neighbouring Thonon may be less well known, but is more important historically. Its vinous Château de Ripaille became the retirement home of one of Savoie's most remarkable dukes, who served for a brief period as an alternative pope. Chablais turned Protestant after the invasion of new ideas and armies from Switzerland in the 16th century. The most famous figure in its history, however, is a steadfast Catholic who crops up time and again across Savoie – St François de Sales, revered for his sensitive work in restoring regional faith in the Catholic Church in the 17th century.

In the much higher Haut Chablais there are plenty of enchanting traditional places to visit out of the snow season, among the highlights Samoëns and Abondance. The latter produces one of the great Savoyard cheeses. Visiting most parts of Savoie in summer, ringing *clarine* cowbells accompany you through fabulous flower-strewn pastures to gorgeous lakes, and to waterfalls cascading from stupendous heights. Just don't expect to be alone; the summer season in particular is short, tourists often as numerous as gnats. But all come here to gasp in wonder at the natural grandeur.

Before Chamonix, we pause to pose in the glamorous, more traditional resorts around the Aravis chain, offering much more picturesque routes to Mont Blanc than via the industrial Arve. Megève established itself between the wars as one of the most chic of all the ski resorts, the St-Tropez of the Alps. Closer to Lac d'Annecy, Thorens-Glières and Thônes have important historic tales to tell. Right below Mont Blanc, Chamonix may look chaotic, but always has excitement in the air as palpable as falling snow, even in the height of summer. The *Aiguilles* (Needles), viciously sharp peaks surrounding the greatest summit, add to the high drama, but Mont Blanc itself rises magnificently above the rest like an otherworldly deity of a meringue, sometimes majestically aloof, at other times mysteriously lost in cloud. To appreciate the Mont Blanc range at its best, climb closer to the summits by foot, cable car or tram. You can even fly over by helicopter. Whichever way you choose, the experience is unforgettable; at such high altitude, it may literally take your breath away.

Routes from the Lower Arve to Lac Léman

The Rhône coming down from its source in the Swiss Alps to the east is the main river to supply the immense Lac Léman, and the main river to leave it, via Swiss Geneva in the west. The most interesting route bypassing this thorny Swiss enclave is the D41 over **Mont Salève** (or even the GR hiking path along it), offering a spectacular arrival in Haute Savoie, dominating Lac Léman, spying on Geneva, its huge fountain spurting high into the air. The N206 then heads straight for the lake. But a series of enchanting parallel mountain roads lead north off the D907, which follows the course of the **Foron valley**. Nicknamed the Vallée Verte, one forested route goes up the **Menoge valley**, through **Boëge**, with its typical colonnaded covered market, past **Villard** and **Burdignin**, villages which compete in grand churches, to the hamlets of the **Habères**. Or at Boëge, branch west for **Fessy**, with its **Musée d'Art et de Folklore** (*t 04 50 39 46 30; open June–Oct daily 2–6.30*) displaying a huge collection of objects representing traditional Chablais life. The impressive forms of the **Château d'Avully** (*t 04 50 36 11 59, e chateaudavully@wanadoo.fr; open July–Aug daily 2–6, rest of year Sun 2–6; adm*) nearby recall lordly medieval Chablais, as do the murals inside, while the historical sections cover the eight centuries of the independent state of Savoie, from 1032 to 1860. The topiary gardens provide light relief.

Over the passes, the heights offer staggering views north. From the vestiges of the two **Châteaux des Allinges** (*free*) perched ridiculously close together on their promontory, you get sensational views onto Lac Léman. The older of the ruins, **Allinges-le-Vieux** became a stronghold of the lords of Faucigny in early medieval times, traditionally supporters of the Dauphiné counts. The disgruntled counts of Savoie built right next door to put the wind up the Faucignys, eventually pushing them out in the 14th century. Despite its name, **Allinges-le-Neuf's chapel** (*t 04 50 72 01 30; open July–Aug, variable times, so call first; adm*) contains an awe-inspiring 11th-century Apocalypse Christ in Majesty, the oldest painting to survive in Savoie. François de Sales settled here for a time from 1594, as he battled to bring the Chablais back into the Catholic fold through persuasive rhetoric.

Back between Foron and Arve valleys, the sober **abbey church at Peillonnex** (*t 04 50 36 89 18, www.paysalp.asso.fr; open July–Aug Wed–Fri and Sun tours at 2,3,4 and 5, rest of year 1st Sun of month, same times; adm*) overlooks proceedings dispassionately from its delightful mid-slope terrace, an ancient yew tree providing centuries of company. When the Romanesque buildings were rebuilt after Swiss troops had devastated the place in the 16th century, the church was provided with an extravaganza of Baroque altarpieces. The theatrical levels of decoration are well explained on a commentary covering the history of the Baroque movement generally as well as the

Getting Around

By air: Geneva airport lies very close by.

By train: Reach Thonon and Evian from Geneva, Paris via Bellegarde, or direct on rapid TGV trains in high season winter and summer. The main Arve valley towns have good rail links, but the connection to Chamonix can be slow. Most villages to Vallorcine have a station too.

By bus: **Chamonix bus**, t 04 50 53 05 55, serves the whole Arve valley. The main bus company for Upper Savoie is **SAT**: for **north-west area**, t 04 50 38 42 08 or 04 50 37 22 13 for **Thonon**, t 04 50 71 00 88 for **Haut-Chablais**, t 04 50 98 07 81 for **Sallanches** or **Megève** to **Chamonix**, t 04 50 53 01 15. *Also see* **Frossard CFTI**, t 04 50 26 41 32, and **Alpbus Fournier**, t 04 50 03 70 09.

Tourist Information

For sights, both French and Swiss, around **Lac Léman**, see *www.leman-sans-frontiere.com*. For information across the **Mont-Blanc** area, consult *www.pays-du-mont-blanc.com*. For the specialist ski resorts, *see* **chapter 19**.

Viuz-en-Sallaz: Route du Fer à Cheval, 74250 Viuz-en-Sallaz, t 04 50 36 86 24, *www.alpesduleman.com*.

Bellevaux: Bâtiment Les Contamines, 74470 Bellevaux t 04 50 73 71 53, *www.bellevaux.com*.

Yvoire: Place de la Mairie, 74140 Yvoire, t 04 50 72 80 21, *www.presquile-leman.com*.

Thonon-les-Bains: Place du Marché, 74200 Thonon-les-Bains, t 04 50 71 55 55, *www.thononlesbains.com*.

Evian-les-Bains: Place d'Allinges, 74501 Evian, t 04 50 75 04 26, *www.eviantourism.com*.

Thollon-les-Mémises: 74500 Thollon-les-Mémises, t 04 50 70 90 01, *www.thollonlesmemises.com*.

Abondance: 74360 Abondance, t 04 50 73 02 90, *www.abondance.org*.

St-Jean-d'Aulps: Domaine des Arches, 74430 St-Jean-d'Aulps, t 04 50 79 65 09, *www.saintjeandaulps.com*.

Samoëns: Place de l'Ancienne Gare, 74340 Samoëns, t 04 50 34 40 28, *www.samoens.com*.

Sixt-Fer-à-Cheval: Place de la Gare, 74740 Sixt, t 04 50 34 49 36, *www.sixteracheval.com*.

La Roche-sur-Foron: Place Andrevetan, 74800 La Roche-sur-Foron, t 04 50 03 36 68, *www.larochesurforon.com*.

Bonneville: Place de l'Hôtel de Ville, 74130 Bonneville, t 04 50 97 38 37, e *officetourisme-bonneville@wanadoo.fr*.

Cluses: 100 Place du 11 Novembre, 74300 Cluses, t 04 50 98 31 79, *www.cluses.com*.

Sallanches: 32 Quai de l'Hôtel de Ville, 74700 Sallanches, t 04 50 58 04 25, *www.sallanches.com*.

Thorens-Glières: 22 Place de la Mairie, 74570 Thorens-Glières, t 04 50 22 40 31, e *ot.thorens@infonie.fr*.

Thônes: Place Avet, 74230 Thônes, t 04 50 02 00 26, *www.thones-tourisme.com*.

La Giettaz: 73590 La Giettaz, t 04 79 32 91 90, *www.la-giettaz.com*.

Flumet: Ave de Savoie, 73590 Flumet, t 04 79 31 61 08, *www.flumet-montblanc.com*.

Notre-Dame-de-Bellecombe: 73590 Notre-Dame-de-Bellecombe, t 04 79 31 61 40, *www.ot-ndb.com*.

Crest-Voland: 73590 Crest-Voland, t 04 79 31 62 57, *www.crestvoland-cohennoz.com*.

Megève: 70 Rue Monseigneur Conseil, 74120 Megève, t 04 50 21 27 28, *www.megeve.com*.

Combloux: B.P.38, 74920 Combloux, t 04 50 58 60 49, *www.combloux.com*.

St-Gervais: 115 Ave du Mont Paccard, 74170 St-Gervais, t 04 50 47 76 08, *www.st-gervais.net*.

Chamonix-Mont-Blanc: 85 Place du Triangle de l'Amitié, 74400 Chamonix, t 04 50 53 00 24, *www. chamonix.com*.

Vallorcine: Le Betté, 74660 Vallorcine, t 04 50 54 60 71, *www.vallorcine.com*.

Market Days

Viuz-en-Sallaz: Mon morning.
Bellevaux: Mon morning.
Thonon-les-Bains: Thurs morning.
Evian-les-Bains: Tues morning.
Châtel: Wed morning.
Morzine: Wed morning.
Les Gets: Thurs morning.
Samoëns: Wed morning.
Sixt-Fer-à-Cheval: (crafts July–Aug) Tues pm.
La Roche-sur-Foron: Thurs morning.
Bonneville: Tues and Fri mornings.
Sallanches: Sat morning.
Thônes: Sat morning.

Megève: Fri morning.
Combloux: Wed morning.
St-Gervais: Thurs morning (plus Sun morning July–Aug).
Chamonix-Mont-Blanc: Sat morning (plus Tues morning July–Aug)

Activities

Cruises across Lac Léman from Thonon and Evian are run by **Companie Générale de Navigation, t** 04 50 71 14 71 or 00 41 848 811 848, e *info@cgn.ch*. Best Léman **beaches** are at **Excenevex** (sandy), **Thonon** (around Ripaille peninsula) and **Evian** (*with pools by the beach; open May-Sept; adm*), boat hire, sailing, rowing, diving and water-skiing possible. Also try **Anthy** or **Amphion**. Other lakes for swimming include the Lac Bleu at **Morillon** and the Lac Bleu at **La Beunaz** (St-Paul-en-Chablais).

For **mountain biking**, Les Gets and Morzine are renowned, but in summer possibilities are vast. **White-water rafting** is very popular in the Giffre valley – contact **Sixt**, **Samoëns** or **Morzine** tourist offices for addresses such as **Sixt Aventure-Passion, t** 04 50 34 16 85 or **Morzine Aventure Passion, t** 04 50 72 15 12.

Paragliding was born in these parts. The first courses were started by **Les Choucas, t** 04 50 43 02 13, at **Praz-de-Lys-Sommand**. One of the inventors of the sport, Jean-Claude Betemps, runs a school at **Thollon-les-Mémises, t** 04 50 70 95 75. Or try **Pégase Air Samoëns, t** 04 50 34 95 80. The Mont Salève is also popular.

For **spa pamperings**, Evian has a renowned centre, **Les Thermes Evian, t** 04 50 75 02 30, *www.lesthermesevian.com*. The **Thermes de Thonon, t** 04 50 26 17 22, have been specially renovated, while the **Thermes de St-Gervais, t** 04 50 47 54 54, *www.thermes-st-gervais.fr*, are reputed for mud treatments.

For **Mont Blanc**, *see also* box on p.229.

Where to Stay and Eat

Yvoire ✉ 74140
★★★Le Pré de la Cure, t 04 50 72 83 58, e *lepredelacure@wanadoo.fr* (*moderate*). Modern, picturesque hotel outside the main gate. Excellent restaurant (*moderate*). Pool. *Closed mid-Nov–early Mar.*

★★★Hôtel du Port, t 04 50 72 80 17, e *hotelduport.yvoire@wanadoo.fr* (*expensive*). Irresistible, by the port. Four rooms, but more spacious restaurant (*expensive*) with lovely terrace. *Closed mid-Oct–early Mar; restaurant closed Wed out of season.*

Sciez-sur-Léman ✉ 74140
★★★★Château de Coudrée, Bonnatrait, **t** 04 50 72 62 33, e *coudree@chateauxhotels.com* (*very expensive–expensive*). Magical lake-side location, a 12th-century keep encased in later wings. Classic cuisine (*very expensive–expensive*). Pool and court. *Closed Nov–early Dec.*

Anthy-sur-Léman ✉ 74200
★★★Auberge d'Anthy, t 04 50 70 35 00, *www.auberge-anthy.com* (*inexpensive*). Excellent value, renovated family inn. Smart rooms, fine restaurant (*moderate*). *Closed most Jan; restaurant closed Sun eve and Mon.*

Thonon-les-Bains ✉ 74200
★★Alpazur, 8 Ave Général Leclerc, **t** 04 50 71 37 25, e *hotel-alpazur@mailme.net* (*inexpensive*). Ask for a lake view in this neat 1970s building down by the cute central port. *Closed mid-Nov–Jan.*

Prieuré, 68 Grande Rue, **t** 04 50 71 31 89 (*expensive*). Venerable restaurant close to the central churches. *Closed Sun eve, Mon, and Tues lunch.*

Le Scampi, 1 Ave du Léman, **t** 04 50 71 10 04 (*moderate*). Central too – fish with views! *Closed Mon, and early April and mid-Nov.*

Evian-les-Bains ✉ 74500
★★★★Royal and **★★★★Ermitage** (*luxury*), **t** for both 04 50 26 85 00, e *hotelroyal@royalparcevian.com* or *hotelermitage@royalparcevian.com*. Very luxurious, linked palatial hotels up on the heights, with all manner of facilities and restaurants (*luxury–expensive*). *Closed early Nov–early Feb.*

★★Hôtel de France, 59 Rue Nationale, **t** 04 50 75 00 36, e *hotel-france-evian@wanadoo.fr* (*inexpensive*). Decent plain central option down on main pedestrian shopping street. *Closed mid-Nov–mid-Dec.*

Thollon-les-Mémises ✉ 74500
★★Bon Séjour, t 04 50 70 92 65, *www.bon-sejour.com* (*inexpensive*). Sweet old-

styled family hotel. Good traditional cuisine (*moderate*). *Closed Nov–mid-Dec.*

Morzine ✉ 74110

★★★**La Bergerie**, Rue du Téléphérique, t 04 50 79 13 69, *www.hotel-bergerie.com* (*expensive–moderate*). Jolly stop in a resort with several good chalet-hotels. Pool. *Closed mid-April–June and mid-Sept–mid-Dec.*

Samoëns ✉ 74340

★★**Le Moulin du Bathieu**, t 04 50 34 48 07, e *moulin-du-bathieu@wanadoo.fr* (*moderate*). Picturesque chalet up among meadows (signs for Samoëns 1600). Savoyard cuisine (*moderate*). *Closed May and Nov–mid-Dec.*

Manigod-Thônes ✉ 74230

★★★**La Croix-Fry**, t 04 50 44 90 16, *www. hotel chaletcroix-fry.com* (*luxury–very expensive*). High-perched former farm, beamed rooms with wooden furniture, some with amazing views. *Table d'hôte* (*expensive–moderate*) for those staying at the hotel. Heated pool. *Closed mid-Sept–mid-Dec and mid-April–mid-June.*

La Clusaz /Le Grand-Bornand

See **Winter Sports**, p.301.

Flumet ✉ 73590

La Ferme du Rocher, Le Pracet, t 04 79 31 80 30 (*moderate; always book*). Adorable dining rooms in lovingly done-up farm north along the Arly, traditional cuisine on the menus.

St-Nicolas-la-Chapelle ✉ 73590

★★**L'Eau Vive**, t 04 79 31 60 46, *www.hotel-eauvive.com* (*inexpensive*). Appealing chalet, simple restaurant (*moderate*), lively owners, Monsieur a mountain guide. *Closed Easter–May and Oct–mid-Dec.*
La Ferme du Mont Charvin B&B, Les Passieux, t 04 79 31 62 89 (*cheap*). True farm with basic rooms run by a woman devoted to Reblochon and old ways. Delicious farm produce at the *table d'hôte*.

Notre-Dame-de-Bellecombe ✉ 73590

★★**Le Tétras**, Les Frasses, t 04 79 31 61 70, *www.hotel-tetras.com* (*inexpensive*). Appealing, in high location. Pool.

Ferme de Victorine, Le Planay, t 04 79 31 63 46 (*moderate*). Delightfully restored farm near Les Saisies, for regional cuisine. *Closed mid-June–early July and mid-Nov–mid-Dec.*

Crest-Voland ✉ 73590

★★**Le Mont Charvin**, Le Cernix, t 04 79 31 61 21, *www.hotel-montcharvin.com* (*inexpensive*). Friendly, balconies with view and little outdoor pool. *Open late-June–early-Sept.*

Megève

See **Winter Sports**, p.297.

Cordon ✉ 74700

★★★**Les Roches Fleuries**, t 04 50 58 06 71, *www. rochesfleuries.com* (*expensive*). Stunning Mont Blanc views from the balconied rooms of this enchanting, quiet hotel. Two good restaurants (*expensive–moderate*), one refined, one Savoyard. Heated pool. *Closed mid-Sept–mid-Dec and early April–early May.*

Combloux ✉ 74920

★★★**Au Cœur des Prés**, t 04 50 93 36 55, f 04 50 58 69 14, (*moderate*). Excellent chalet, many rooms with splendid Mont Blanc views. Good restaurant (*moderate*) with views too. *Closed early April–May and Oct–mid-Dec.*

St-Gervais ✉ 74170

★★★**Chalet Hôtel Igloo**, 3120 Route des Crêtes, t 04 50 93 05 84, *www.ligloo.com* (*expensive*). By Mont Arbois' summit, comfortable rooms and great views of Mont Blanc. Hearty cooking (*moderate*). *Closed mid-April–mid-June and mid-Sept–mid-Dec.*
Chalet Rémy, Le Bettex, t 04 50 93 11 85, f 04 50 93 14 45 (*inexpensive*). 18th-century farm packed with old-fashioned atmosphere. Basic little rooms. Copious local cooking (*moderate*). *Closed early Nov–mid-Dec.*

St-Nicolas-de-Véroce ✉ 74190

L'Etape, t 04 50 93 20 95 (*cheap*). 3km above village, charming chalet eyrie in stunning location looking to Mont Blanc. Simple, pleasant rooms. Good family cooking.

Chamonix-Mont-Blanc, Les Houches and Argentière

See **Winter Sports**, p.294.

riot of detail here, including prophets dangling from the cornices. St François de Sales features of course, gazing devotedly up to God.

At **Viuz-en-Sallaz** with its views as far as Mont Blanc, the ultra-modern **Paysalp** (*t 04 50 36 89 18, www.paysalp.asso.fr; July–Aug daily 2–6, rest of year Mon–Sat 10–12 and 2–5; adm*) presents a vast number of regional craft objects and costumes collected by the Hermanns, staunch defenders of popular culture across the whole arc of Europe's Alps, but in curiously characterless surroundings. The *fruitière*, or cheese-making area, is also ultra-modern (*view the process July and Aug daily at 9.15; rest of year weekends only*). The plainer, separate **Musée Paysan** (*t 04 50 36 89 18, www. paysalp.asso.fr; open July–Aug daily 2–6, rest of year 1st Sun of every month 2–5; adm*) covers Savoyard rural life and traditions from 1850 to 1950. The *pele* (from the word *poêle*, stove) was the only room lived in in winter, because of its heat, while in summer families decamped up the slopes to their *chalets d'alpage*, moving their cattle to higher pastures.

The D26 offers a lovely route up from **St-Jeoire** to **Thonon**. A massive landslide in 1943 created a huge natural dam across the Brevon river, creating the **Lac de Vallon**, pretty walking country, but bathing is forbidden in its dangerous waters. Amidst these relatively unspoilt mountains, **Bellevaux** quietly defends its traditions with its **Musée de l'Histoire** and **Musée de la Faune** (*t 04 50 73 71 53; only open hols at appointed times pm*), while a pretty new garden lies below its muscular church.

Lac Léman rather than Lake Geneva

Reaching the panoramic, 73-km-long crescent of water of **Lac Léman** (almost 14km at its widest), you may feel more like you've arrived at the edge of a sea. Virtually the whole southern side of the lake is French, although the Swiss have grabbed hold of both ends. In the west, we ignore the enclave of Geneva sticking its defiant Protestant tongue out at France. Between Douvaine and the lake, the **Musée Milouti** (*t 04 50 94 10 55; open July–Aug daily 3–7; adm*) occupies the Granges de Serviette, typical 17th-century barns where old Chablais crafts are recalled. Join the French lake-side at Chens-sur-Léman. **Nernier** occupies a particularly lovely promontory at the end of the so-called 'Petit Lac', the thin, mainly Swiss, western tail of Lac Léman. **Yvoire**, where the views broaden out to take in the much wider, deeper **Grand Lac**, is as absurdly cute as a village in a fairytale. Its church spire looks as though it's wrapped in silver foil, like an elaborate confection. It shines out above the gorgeous old stone houses smothered in flowers in summer. But tourists crawl over the place like an infestation of ants in high season. The enchanting port is lined with delectable cafés, overseen by a picture-book **castle**. For a floral experience appealing to all the senses, visit its **Jardin des Cinq Sens** (*t 04 50 72 88 80, www.jardin5sens.net; open mid-May–mid-Sept daily 10–7; mid-April– mid-May daily 11–6; mid-Sept–mid-Oct daily 1–5; adm*). Very posh **Excenevex** just south boasts the nicest sandy beach on the French side of the lake. The waterside at **Anthy** has kept a more traditional aspect, with tiny port, fish stall and pebbly beach. For those really wishing to delve into the prehistoric lake-side communities, try Sciez's **Musée de la Préhistoire** (*t 04 50 72 53 28; open July–Aug Wed 10–12 and 3–6, Sat 10–12; adm*). The more dynamic **Les Aigles du Léman** (*t 04 50 72 72 26,* *www.lesaiglesduleman.fr; open mid-April–early Sept daily 10-7; adm*) offers all manner of shows featuring hundreds of animals, ranging well beyond eagles.

Split in two by its cliff, imposing **Thonon-les-Bains** was historic capital of the Chablais. Down below, it has a good beach, a sizeable marina and a few old fishermen's cottages, some still used by professionals, one batch containing a modest fishing museum, the **Ecomusée de la Pêche** (*t 04 50 70 69 49; open July–Aug daily 10–12 and 2.30–6.30, June and Sept Wed–Sun 2.30–6.30; adm*). Connected by cable car, the historic and shopping quarters stand high on their promontory. On the cliff edge, regional culture is celebrated at the **Musée du Chablais** (*t 04 50 70 69 49; open July–Aug daily 10–12 and 2.30–6.30, rest of year for exhibitions Wed–Sun 2.30–6.30; adm*), set in a grand house. Nearby, the interconnecting **churches of St-François de Sales** and **St-Hippolyte** vie for attention with their over-elaborate decorations. The older, a Gothic structure, had its interior plastered with ornate Baroque additions. It witnessed François de Sales preaching to the town's recalcitrant Protestants and winning them over. Maurice Denis covered the later church with big bold classical-style biblical scenes, all tinged with his distinctive pinks and mauves. A particularly fine cheese shop, Boujon, stands on Rue St-Sébastien.

Surrounded by vineyards on the flats east of town, the impressive **Château de Ripaille** (*t 04 50 26 64 44, www.ripaille.com; open July–Aug daily 12.30–6.30; April–June and Sept daily 10.30–12 and 2–6; Feb–March and Oct–Nov daily 2.45–4.15; adm*) served as a hunting lodge for the lords of Savoie. Duke Amédée VIII enlarged it and retired here with six like-minded gentlemen to devote himself, up to a point, to a pious life, drawing the line at the table; hence, apparently, the French expression *'faire ripaille'* for enjoying a hearty banquet. However, as the Papal Schism split the Church, Amédée was elected anti-pope Felix V at the Council of Basle of 1439. Resigning nine years later, he helped end the dreadful division. From the 17th century to the Revolution, Carthusian monks settled here. On the tour you're shown their kitchens and wine press. But the bulk of the interiors were redecorated in the 19th and 20th centuries in mock Gothic style with an Art Nouveau twist and are geared to receptions. The forest behind contains the **Clairière des Justes**, a national memorial to French people who rescued Jews through the Second World War, and an **Arboretum** (*t 04 50 26 28 22; open May–Sept Tues–Sun 10–7, Oct–Nov Tues–Sun 10–4.30; free*), the latter damaged in the major 1999 storms. The swanky new development of **Port-Ripaille** lies hidden on the wooded end of the peninsula. The other side of the Dranse estuary, **Amphion** offers another popular, open summer waterside halt.

The year 1789 was a revolutionary one for **Evian** – that is the year when its mineral water was 'discovered', thanks to a sickly marquis, de Lessert, who came to take the waters at nearby Amphion for his kidney stones. To little effect. At Evian, he tried St Catherine's spring, below a certain Monsieur Cachat's garden. That appeared to do the trick. News of the water's miraculous power soon spread, doctors prescribing it, Cachat fencing off the spring to make his fortune. Bottling took off in earnest from 1826, while the first public baths went up in 1827. The *Société des Eaux d'Evian*, created in 1869, drilled for and bought further springs, financed refreshment pavilions, hotels, theatre and casino, and the place grew into a highly fashionable spa resort, attracting the extremely wealthy. Although taking the waters has become less common these days, bottled mineral water is all the rage, and Evian is apparently the world's largest producer, filling some 4 million bottles a day at the **Eaux Minérales d'Evian factory** (*t 04 50 26 93 23, www.evian.fr; open Jan–Dec weekdays, by appointment only*) located, somewhat ironically, at Amphion.

The glamorous crowd go yachting on the lake from Evian's swanky **marina** opposite Swiss Lausanne. Clearly, a **boat trip** (*t 00 41 848 811 848, www.cgn.ch*) is *de rigueur*, but the immaculately manicured promenade offers a relaxing alternative view from dry land. The town behind proves a jumble, just the odd historic fragment jutting out, but all is undergoing major renovation. Along the front, the irreverent **casino** mocks the shape of a Greek-cross church, and is only separated from the real **church** by an elaborate mock-Renaissance villa, now the **town hall**, but originally built for the Lumière family of cinema fame (*see* p.25) – enter during working hours for a free peak at a Belle Epoque decorative extravaganza. The place was very slightly damaged during demonstrations at the G8 summit held in town in 2003, although a police cordon kept most of the protesters on the Swiss side of the lake, which bore the brunt of their rage. Evian, with its very grand hotels, has hosted many major international conferences as well as well-heeled honeymooners. Most seriously, the *Accords d'Evian* of 1962 saw the French government officially acknowledge Algeria's independence. The luxury hotels now stand aloof high on the hillside, but remnants of palatial lakeside blocks can still be made out on the front, along with the jaded old thermal establishment – a much more contemporary glass-covered **Thermes** has made it redundant. Up on the main pedestrian shopping street, the Art Nouveau **Evian Buvette Thermale** (*open mid-June–mid-Sept daily 10.30–12.30 and 3–7; early May–mid-June and late Sept daily 2.30–6.30; free*) cuts a dash. Just above, top up on Evian water for free at the public fountains. A short boat trip takes you to **Les Jardins de l'Eau du Pré Curieux** (*reserve via tourist office, May–Sept Wed–Sun 10.15, 1.30 and 3; adm*), a lakeside garden cleverly set out to show the different aspects of wetland ecosystems, from torrents to marshes, the swish villa dedicated to exhibitions. The separate, more traditional **Musée du Pré Lude** (*open mid-June–Sept Tues–Sun 10.30–12 and 3–7; adm*) on the main road behind covers local crafts in a renovated farm.

Pressing east, the Chablais mountains descend practically to the water. Clinging to the lakeside, **Meillerie** has a delightful quay. A rock here is dedicated to Jean-Jacques Rousseau (*see* pp.264–5), who set some of the events in his hugely influential, idealistic novel, *La Nouvelle Héloïse*, in the village. In the book, the protagonists Julie and St-Preux seek refuge here from a storm on the lake...just as Byron and Shelley had to in real life when they were on their famous literary holiday on Lac Léman in 1816, during which their travelling companion, Mary Shelley, spawned that most famous of literary monsters, *Frankenstein*. They were staying in Swiss territory, but **St-Gingolph** on the border doesn't know which side it's on. No need to cross customs to visit the **Musée des Barques du Léman** (*t 00 41 244 827 024, www.st-gingolph.ch/musee; open mid-June–mid-Sept daily 2–5.30, April–mid-June and mid-Sept–Oct Sat 2–5.30; adm*) a pleasant museum on boating on Lake Geneva set in part of the schoolish castle.

Haut Chablais and the Giffre

Dranse is the Savoyard word for a torrent and a trip up the **Gorges de la Dranse** above Thonon, much favoured by white-water rafters, plunges you into rocky mountain terrain. This river gets its force from the three separate *dranses* that join at Bioge. The **Dranse d'Abondance** valley takes you up via the historic town of **Abondance**, overseen by its **abbey** (*t 04 50 81 60 54; open Christmas–Oct daily 10–12 and 2–5; adm*), one of the most important in medieval Savoie, its cloisters decorated with striking remnants of 15th-century frescoes, a mix of Gothic elegance and naivety. Abondance is also a slightly smoky hard cheese, a small version of Beaufort. Thick, creamy Vacherin is produced here too. From **La Chapelle d'Abondance**, climb the GR5 hiking path to admire cows and flowers in the well-named **nature reserve of Vacheresse**. The well-located south-facing chalets of **Châtel** by the Swiss border bask in sunshine late into the afternoon, although mad sporting types take the hair-raising **Fantasticâble**, going up to 100kph down the cable from Plaine Dranse! The twisting D228 road takes you on a startling route to the Lac de Montriond or to Avoriaz and its lake.

The more usual way to these spots is via the **Dranse de Morzine** valley, also known as the **Vallée d'Aulps**, from Thonon. This road is the start of the famous old 700-km French Alpine motoring **Route des Grandes Alpes** (*www.routedesgrandesalpes.com*) from Lac Léman to Menton on the Med, but you can only scale all the highest passes in summer. The **Gorges du Pont du Diable** (*t 04 50 72 10 39, www.les-gorges-du-pont-du-diable.com; open May–Sept daily 9–7; adm*) were carved into tortuous curves by raging waters. The romantic early Gothic ruins of the **Abbaye d'Aulps** (*t 04 50 72 15 15, www.valleedaulps.com; guided tours May–Sept Fri at 11*) speak calmly of the former importance of this Benedictine religious centre, a rival to the abbey of Abondance. However, wealth and power went to the monks' heads and François de Sales had to put the house back in order, although it fell into terminal decline in the 18th century. A surviving barn is being turned into a cultural centre.

Narrow hairpin bends lead to the emerald-green **Lac de Montriond** and the traditional village of **Ardent** above. Mountain bikers swarm over the slopes of the linked Portes du Soleil resorts that follow (*see* p.287), their ski lifts open to bikes in summer. The distinctive beige slate roofs of the attractive, roomy valley-bottom chalets of **Morzine** take on silvery tones in the sunshine. Visit a traditional slate worker at the **Ardoisière des 7 Pieds** (*t 04 50 79 12 21, www.ardoise-morzine.com; open summer tours, Tue and Fri at 10.30 and 5; adm*). Chic boutiques line the main street, but the centre lacks cohesion despite the church with its spiked onion dome. The high-energy resort of **Avoriaz** may be perched way up high, but is lively year round with sports fanatics. **Les Gets**, with its friendly array of chalets and curious **Musée de la Musique Mécanique** (*t 04 50 79 85 75, www.lemuseedesgets.free.fr; open July–Aug daily 10–12 and 2.30–7.20, Jan–June and Sept–Oct daily 2.30–7.30; adm*) hosted the 2004 mountain-bike world championship. Consider trying devalkarting (go-karting down a mountainside) here!

Fruit trees and waterfalls pepper the surprisingly generous, fertile **Giffre valley**, a scattering of delightful old hamlets on its slopes, the traditional chalets often with a smaller *mazot* alongside, in which precious objects were stored separately in case of a chalet fire. **Taninges** makes the first stop, for the Gothic ruins of the **Chartreuse de Mélan**, founded by a lady of Faucigny, only destroyed as recently as the 1960s. What's left acts as an atmospheric setting for summer exhibitions of contemporary art. West, the typical village of **Mieussy**, its flash, Flamboyant Gothic church with onion-bulb steeple added on, took its place in the history of extreme sports in 1978 as the place where paragliding was born, or the art of 'armchair flight' as it's been nicknamed!

East of Taninges, the pretty hamlets are all outdone by higgledy-piggledy **Samoëns**, actually reached most dramatically from Morzine, via the lofty **Col de Joux Plane**, close to which a visit to the 18th-century **Ecomusée Ferme du Clos Parchet** (*t 04 50 34 46 69; tours July–Aug Tues and Thurs at 3, March–June and Sept–mid-Oct Thurs at 2.30; book at Samoëns tourist office; adm*) proves absorbing. The stonemasons of the Giffre (and of Samoëns in particular), nicknamed the *frahans*, became renowned for their craft across France. Beyond the village covered market lies the rose-surrounded church, its door guarded by two ancient Chinese-looking lions, a feature adopted from northern Italy. To one side rises the delightful **Alpine garden** (*free*) created by a local girl made good, co-founder of the celebrated Seine-side Samaritaine department store in Paris. Neighbouring **Sixt-Fer-à-Cheval** is surrounded by hamlets, chapels and crosses, signalling the religious influence of its abbey in times past, parts of which remain around the main square. Learn more about its history, and that of the valley and its special natural environment, at **La Maison de la Réserve Naturelle de Sixt**. The village is also a member of the association of *Les Plus Beaux Villages de France*.

East, you hit against the huge **Cirque du Fer à Cheval** (*fee for cars*), the most over-whelming dead end in the Alps, where the limestone rocks of the pre-alpine ranges bang into the granite of the mighty Mont Blanc range. Sensational waterfalls drop from the great heights encircling you. Legends of golden-hoofed ibex, their feet powdered with precious metal, led prospectors to the maddest acts of mountaineering folly to find seams. Most notoriously, Mont Blanc's conqueror Jacques Balmat died on the highest peak, the Ruan, chancing his luck once too often.

To Mont Blanc via Arve or Aravis

Taking the more obvious, busy Arve valley, the main settlements are industrial, but many have historic hearts. **La Roche-sur-Foron** oversees the lower Arve. Climb from the medieval town – for centuries a centre of the medieval counts of Geneva, closely related to Savoie's lords – to the tower commanding impressive views. At **Bonneville**, Duke Charles-Félix of Savoie looks down on the Arve standing on his 100ft-column, commemorating the taming of the river from 1826. The town was provided with grand neoclassical buildings on **Place du Marquet**. The **castle** dating back to medieval times and the **Musée Départemental de la Résistance** are undergoing restoration.

Avoid the main roads to Cluses by taking a hair-raising route along the **Gorges du Bronze**. From Notre-Dame-de-l'Assomption church at the resort of **Mont-Saxonnex** the views reach north to the Jura mountains. Up the D4, the **Chartreuse du Reposoir** makes a magnificent sight nestling in its valley, but is out of bounds, occupied by a Carmelite order. Originally a clock-making centre, industrial **Cluses** has specialized in *décolletage* since the 20th century, which has nothing to do with women's fashion, but everything to do with precision machine parts; learn about this, along with the older traditional craft from which it was born, in the **Musée de l'Horlogerie** (*t 04 50 89 13 02; open year round Mon–Sat 10–12 and 2–6; plus Sun pm July– Aug; adm*). For a clock centre that has kept its historic heart beating, head for **Arâches**, also known for rock-climbing and canyoning. **Flaine**, a high, purpose-built ski resort resembling a vision of a bureaucrats' retirement city, does have a summer season, and the **Désert de Platé** reached by its **Grandes Platières cable car** (*open early July–early Sept*) offers an extraordinary blinding white limestone hiking landscape, Mont Blanc as backdrop.

By **Sallanches**, you've passed round the barrier of the Aravis chain, and Mont Blanc completely fills the end of the Arve valley. Destroyed by fire in 1840, a new town was built with arcaded streets typical of 19th-century Savoie. The interior of the **Eglise St-Jacques** was restored with a riot of decoration. The plain 14th-century **Château des Rubins** (*t 04 50 58 32 13, www.rubinsnature-asso.fr; open July–Aug daily exc weekend mornings 9–6.30, rest of year daily exc weekend mornings and public hols 9–12 and 2–6; adm*) presents Alpine nature, a good place for interactive learning on a rainy day. **Les Ilettes** offers three lakes at the foot of the *Aiguilles Rouges*, lifeguards in situ in summer. Climb above the valley north of Sallanches for the Parking du Burzier at the **Alpage de Doran**, then take the trail of well over an hour to see *gypaètes*, bearded vultures, recently reintroduced after disappearing at the start of the 20th century.

The most direct way from Annecy to the Arve is via the A41 motorway or parallel N203. But seek out much more intriguing mountain roads **through the Aravis**. The picturesque slopes road via **Nâves-Parmelan** and **Aviernoz** takes you to the **Château de Thorens** (*t 04 50 22 42 02; open June–Sept daily 2–6; adm*), its lovely array of restored towers calling for attention, as does its connections with famous Savoyards. Built by a count of Geneva as a gift for a devoted vassal, a later count confiscated it from a barbarically behaved one. It was then sold to François de Sales – not the famous religious figure, but his father. However, the future St François was born in a nearby oratory in 1567. The family had a good eye for art. Splendid 16th-century Antwerp tapestries illustrate the story of Tobit. The most remarkable paintings include a girlish boy of a Saint Stephen by Marco d'Oggiono and a later Van Dyck representing a duke of Savoie. Of equal interest for Savoyards are the objects that belonged to the local saintly hero, and to a distant and distinguished politician of a descendant, Camillo Cavour, both of exceptional importance in regional history. The most bizarre relic among the many portraits of the seductive Catholic preacher François de Sales is an ornate scissor case said to contain a slice of his heart! Cavour negotiated the ceding of Savoie to France in exchange for military help to expel the Austrian army occupying northern Italy and thus unify the peninsula. The couple of rooms devoted to him include the ornate table on which the all-important treaty was signed in Turin.

A road leads up to the gentle high pastures of the **Plateau des Glières**. A large **monument** inaugurated in 1973 pays homage to the Second World War Resistance fighters up here, even if it looks at first sight more like an advert for local cheese makers. Some 500 *maquisards* hid out here in the winter of 1944, receiving some of the earliest Allied munitions supplies dropped by parachute. The Vichy military tried

Pull the Udder One: the Story of Reblochon Cheese

A comic tale showing how the local Aravis farmers hoodwinked their medieval landlords recounts how Reblochon cheese came into being around Thônes. In the 13th century, renting farmers had to give their masters a return in proportion to the amount of milk their cows produced. But when the landlords came to measure this, the farmers deliberately only did a partial milking to lower the figure. Once the *patron* had gone, they did a second milking (*reblocher* meaning to pull the udders a second time), producing a rich fat result, excellent for making cheese. It takes a full nine litres of milk to make a kilo of Reblochon. These soft, early eating cheeses are ripened for just three or four weeks.

in vain to dislodge them. Then in March 1944, a German force quite out of proportion with the resisters, perhaps over 10,000 strong, was sent to eradicate the enemy. While 100 *maquisards* died, many more Germans fell. The Nazis wrought their revenge on nearby communities. Below the southern end of Les Glières, on the road from Annecy to Thônes, the **Cimetière des Glières** trapped in a tight gorge became the moving resting place of many of these *maquis* martyrs, the stirring **Musée de la Résistance** (*t 04 50 32 18 38; open June–mid-Sept daily 10–12 2–7; free*) attached to the cemetery recalling their heroism, and resistance across Haute Savoie.

Everyday Savoyard traditions are recalled in and around **Thônes**, its arcaded, rounded main square sitting picturesquely under the western wall of the Aravis. The onion-bulb **church** contains the obligatory Baroque altarpiece, but also plaques recalling the war dead, including from a German bombing. The central **Musée du Pays de Thônes** (*t 04 50 02 96 92; open July–Aug 10–12 and 3–7, Jan–June and Sept–Dec daily exc Sun 9–12, plus Mon, Wed and Sat 2–5.30; adm*) looks none-too-exciting, but contains nicely carved wooden objects, the wood theme continued in the **Ecomusée du Bois** (*t 04 50 32 18 10; open July–Aug daily exc Wed 10–12 and 2.30–5.30, April–June and Sept–Oct Tues and Thurs tour only at 4, Sun 2.30–5.30; adm*) out of town at an old sawmill up the tall, tight **Montremont valley** with old farms that seem to date from a different era.

Two routes lead from Thônes to La Clusaz. The chalet-filled valley one up to **Manigod** is exceptionally attractive, with pastures cut like windows into the slopes. Explore further traditional hamlets to the south. The road via the **Col de la Croix-Fry** leads to the modern resort of **La Clusaz**, most appealing with its polished wooden chalets climbing out of a steep bowl. Head north for the more traditionally picturesque chalets scattered around the higher resort of **Le Grand-Bornand**, a restored 19th-century farm serving as home to the **Maison du Patrimoine** (*t 04 50 02 79 18; open July–Aug Tues–Sat 10–12 and 3–5.30, Sun 4–7; mid–late-June and first half Sept Tues, Wed and Fri 3–5; Christmas–Easter Tues–Sat 3–5.30; adm*) presenting traditional Aravis life. Continue up to the **Col de la Colombière** passing via **Le Chinaillon** with some ancient chalets. This way forms part of the **Route des Grandes Alpes**, while the sensational GR96 runs further up the Aravis. South, the Route continues via La Clusaz up to the **Col des Aravis**, the single high, tooth-gap pass through the range, where tourist pandemonium often breaks out because of the spectacular view of Mont Blanc.

Swooping down the steep eastern side of the Aravis chain, the more daring take the **Route de la Soif**, a track leading through very exposed pastures, where chamois, mouflons and bearded vultures hang out, to **Chaucisse**, the old hamlet's church roof in wood resembling a dog's shaggy coat. Taking the more conventional route, a solid Baroque church marks the centre of **La Giettaz**. It has welcoming saints in its sky-blue altarpiece and fine stained glass. The little house of **A la Rencontre du Passé** (*t 04 79 32 92 29 ; open July–Aug Tues and Thurs 3–6, Jan–March Tues and Thurs 9.30–12 and 3–6; adm*) invites you in to discover an old-style Savoyard interior. For modern woodwork, cast an eye on André Porret's wooden furniture and sculpture shop below. Traditional **Flumet** at a crossroads right down in the Arly valley has a defensive medieval heart and medieval church. The place could be made more attractive, but its cheese cooperative and charcuteries are good places to pick up local culinary specialities, the church has just been restored, and plans are afoot to tackle the riverside mill.

The little resorts around the Arly above Flumet make a change from the flash big boys to the north, settled around charming traditional villages. Climb to **St-Nicolas-la-Chapelle**, gilded Baroque altarpieces and gory paintings filling the big church with its silvery spire. Heading south to Ugine, the narrow **Arly gorges** look forbidding, but take the dramatic, winding route via **Héry** and its waterfall up towards **Mont Charvin** (2,407m), highpoint of the Aravis chain, for awesome vistas from in front of the sheer cliff. **Ugine** looks clearly industrial down in the valley, known for its stainless steel, although it does have an historic core. The **Musée du Crest-Cherel** (*t 04 79 89 00 40; open mid-June–mid-Sept daily exc Tues 2–6; adm*) in the restored castle covers local non-industrial traditions. Back above Flumet, wooden sculptures by a local electric saw artist bring fun to the resorts of **Notre-Dame-de-Bellecombe** and **Crest-Voland**, the latter lying in stunning location on an open promontory backed by wonderful shaded woods, looking not just down the Arly, but also far down the Isère valley to the Bauges and Belledonne ranges. For splendid forest walks, head on to **Le Cohennoz**.

At **Megève** north up the Arly, you'll find the Hermès boutique handily close to the church, the latter filled, appropriately enough, with gilded Baroque altarpieces. Although the **Musée du Haut Val d'Arly** (*t 04 50 91 81 00; open Jan–mid-April and July–mid-Sept Mon–Sat 2.30–6; adm*) occupies an olde-style chalet absolutely crammed with objects associated with traditional Alpine crafts, Megève was totally rebranded by Noémie de Rothschild in the 1920s, and has since catered especially to the mega-rich as a kind of St-Tropez of the snows. Pricey art, craft and culinary shops certainly aren't lacking; however, Mont Blanc lies tantalizingly out of sight unless you head far up the surrounding summits. If you overindulge in Megève, do penance by taking the popular walk above town along the steep calvary path marked by little altars, views of plump-looking summits all around.

Coming Face to Face with Mont Blanc

Reaching the wonderful twin villages of **Combloux** and **Cordon** high above the Arve, marvel at some of the most staggering views of **Mont Blanc** from their steep sides, the monstrously large triangular summit totally blocking the end of the valley. Combloux has big fat farms liberally scattered on its slopes, but is outdone in quaintness by quieter Cordon. Both boast typical colourful Baroque churches. **St-Gervais-les-Bains** is the traditional base for the ascent of Mont Blanc's summit, although you can't see much of Europe's ultimate mountain from this cheerful resort. With large Belle Epoque hotels across from the Baroque church and a broad main square, it makes an appealing stop, but can become choked with traffic. Down the valley at **Le Fayet**, a long, lush, shaded public garden leads to the revived **spa centre**.

But most visitors come to join the mountaineers on the highest train journey in France. Heaving up on to the shoulders of the Mont-Blanc range like a determined little caterpillar, the spectacular **Tramway du Mont-Blanc** (*t 04 50 47 51 83; runs mid-June–Sept and mid-Dec–mid-April; adm*) from **Le Fayet** or **St-Gervais** may be the highest, steepest line in France, but clearly it isn't one of the fastest. With its spectacular pauses for breath, walkers can get on and off at **Montivon**, **Col de Voza** or **Bellevue** before the terminus, the **Nid d'Aigle**, or *Eagle's Eyrie*. Built before the First World War, the line takes you up almost 1,800m, leaving you at a very heady 2,732m; the original intention was to take visitors right to the summit of Mont Blanc by rail, but the technical obstacles stopped travellers being offered such an easy option. From the end of the line, the views of the Bionnassay glacier will take your breath away.

As a somewhat simpler option to admire Mont Blanc, head up from St-Gervais to **St-Nicolas-de-Véroce**, with one of the most captivating churches in the area, its cemetery, surely one of the most uplifting in France, looking across to the summit. There are further chapels to discover far down below on the way to **Les Contamines-Montjoie**, a rather exclusive ski resort hidden at the end its own valley. Magical **Bionnassay**, up a side road, puts in a (false) claim to being the closest village to the summit of Mont Blanc. Enter one of the characterful old chalets by visiting the **Ecomusée de la Vieille Maison** (*t 04 50 93 40 78; open mid-July–Aug Tues–Sat, 2-hour guided tour only at 2.30 and 4.30*) run by an earnestly enthusiastic local. Walkers in search of a burst of adrenaline-pumping adventure, try the exciting walk to the *Nid d'Aigle*, taking on glacier territory with fixed ladders.

Back at the Arve, for a relatively peaceful way in these busy parts, head up the north side of the valley from Sallanches, offering some of the finest views of Mont Blanc. Thanks to the persuasive Canon Devémy, **Passy**'s church doubles as a modern art gallery, **Notre-Dame de Toute Grâce** bursting with the most colourful Christian art by an amazing array of the most famous artists of the first half of the 20th century. Architect Novarina's chalet of a church went up through the war. Flowers are replaced on the façade by a fan of Fernand Léger's bright mosaics. Among the bold to garish works inside, the most alarming, Jean Lurçat's tapestry clash between Apocalyptic Good and Evil, depicts a combative female statue-of-liberty figure facing up to the seven-headed monster. By contrast below, the bowed, gouged crucifixion Christ by Germaine Richier has a simple power. Over the side altars, the economical lines of Matisse's St Dominic contrast with the frenzied activity in Bonnard's St François de Sales, who appears to be suffering from a terrible bout of bishop's sunburn. Look out too for the gorgeous array of stained-glass windows and the calm, totemic figures carved on the beams. The metallic green **Lac Vert** with rocks spaced out over its limpid waters is overseen to one side by what resemble the funnels of a great stone ocean

Rubbing Noses with Mont Blanc

The third most visited natural site in the world, any close encounter with the majestic meringue of Mont Blanc (4,808m) proves unforgettable. However, special trips are expensive, and the weather high up is unpredictable – consider staying a few days to see the summit properly. And go to other parts of the Rhône-Alpes to walk alone. However, this is the most famous area for Alpine hiking in Europe, the natural high drama unbeatable. For the ultimate experience of climbing Mont Blanc's summit, you must contact the reputed **Compagnie des Guides de Chamonix**, t 04 50 53 00 24. At local tourist offices, pick up maps of the innumerable, well-signed easier hiking paths. Always take weather predictions very seriously. The lakes, especially high up west of the Arve, make for extremely popular destinations. Seasonal cafés, village inns and Alpine refuges mean the need for food, drink and comfort are surprisingly well catered for; in the higher spots, provisions are heli-coptered in! The lucky spot chamois and ibex, marmots rushing away as the odd golden eagle circles. For the keenest walkers, the 170-km **Tour du Mont-Blanc** is a famous challenge taking you through Switzerland and Italy as well as France.

You might try a magical tour of Mont Blanc by hot-air balloon (**Objectif Ballons du Mont-Blanc**, t 04 50 58 08 46, *www.alpes-montgolfiere.com*) or by helicopter (t 04 50 54 13 82, *www.helico.fr*). For even more exhilaration, there are several paragliding companies (e.g. **Les Ailes du Mont-Blanc**, t 04 50 53 96 72, *www.lesailesdumontblanc. com*; **Kaïlash Adventure**, t 06 83 29 43 67, *www.kailashadventure.com*; or **Summits Parapente**, t 04 50 53 50 14, *www.summits.fr*). Easier options for less adventurous mortals include several exhilarating cable-car trips around Chamonix. Many are run by the **Compagnie du Mont-Blanc** (*www.compagniedumontblanc.fr*).

The **Aiguille du Midi** (reservations, t 04 50 53 30 80 or 04 50 53 22 75) is the closest most visitors come to the top of Mont Blanc; the first viewing platform isn't of much interest, the second is stupendous, the third even better, at 3,842m (*c.* 12,000ft) still almost 1,000m below the summit. The climbers seem ant-sized. From level two the most magical of all cable-car rides whisks you over sparkling glaciers to the Hellbronner peak on the Italian border. Many locals say the finest views of Mont Blanc are to be had from the heights west of Chamonix. Take the cable car to **Le Brévent** (reservations, t 04 50 53 13 18 or t 04 50 53 22 75) at just over 2,500m, or go to Les Praz, north of town, to take the cable car for **La Flégère** (reservations, t 04 50 53 18 58 or t 04 50 53 22 75).

The journey by little red mountain train to the **Mer de Glace glacier** (from Montenvers station behind Chamonix railway station; reservations, t 04 50 53 12 54 or t 04 50 53 22 75) is less spectacular, taking you to *c.* 2,000m. In summer the *Mer de Glace* can look grubby. Its main attraction is an ice grotto. Further up are displays on crystals and fauna, and a café from which to watch parties walking on the glacier; contact the tourist office well in advance to join them.

Around Chamonix, rock-climbing, canyoning, white-water rafting and mountain-biking are all possibile. The *Compagnie des Guides* also puts on a programme of mountaineering activities for youngsters (contact **Cham Aventure**, t 04 50 53 55 70).

liner. From chalet-strewn **Servoz**, spectacularl views open out on to Mont Blanc. A well-maintained track allows you to walk along the beautiful **Gorges de la Diosaz**.

Approaching Chamonix, **Les Houches** may be the closest village to Mont Blanc's summit but lies trapped in the valley. **The Parc Animalier du Merlet** (*t 04 50 53 47 89; open July–Aug daily 9.30–7.30, May–June and Sept daily 10–6; adm*) further up allows you almost to rub noses with shy mountain wildlife such as ibex, chamois and marmots. To appreciate the largest ice river in Europe, which flows down 3,500m of mountainside, reach the **Chalet du Glacier des Bossons** (*t 04 50 53 03 89; open mid-May–Sept daily*) at 1,425m either by foot or by cable car. As well as stunning views, there are chilling displays on air catastrophes in the Mont Blanc range.

Torrents of tourists race through the centre of **Chamonix** like the bubbling waters of the Arve. It's not that the place is particularly beautiful – in fact it's developed in scrappy manner, but it exudes excitement. The maddened statues of Balmat and Paccard point up to Mont Blanc's summit, which they were the first to conquer, from beside the heavily touristy shopping quarter by the river. The **Musée Alpin de Chamonix** (*t 04 50 53 25 93; open June–mid-Oct daily 2–7, Jan–May daily 3–7, plus school hols 10–12; adm*) stands back a little from the crowds, in one of the huge but dilapidated Belle Epoque hotels scattered around the centre, recalling the resort's glamorous heyday. Displays go into detail on the many major events to have taken place in these parts, from the conquest of Mont Blanc (*see* p.23) to the first Winter Olympic Games, held here in 1924. Separate temporary exhibitions on Alpine themes are held in the slick modern architecture of the **Espace Tairraz** (named after a family fascinated by the Alps for generations) beyond the offices of the legendary **Compagnie des Guides** beside the richly gilded interior of the town's **Baroque church**, the main feature of historic little Chamonix before it was swamped by tourists and hotels.

Huge glaciers curve menacingly down the mountainsides towards the small centre of **Argentière**, an old settlement as well as a ski resort, its churches nestling close to the source of the Arve. Get up close to the glaciers, even in summer, by taking the **cable car** up to the **Aiguille des Grands Montets** (*reserve tickets in advance, t 04 50 54 00 71*); the magical view up the white valley ends with **Mont Dolent**, its peak marking the point where France, Switzerland and Italy meet.

The atmosphere changes heading for **Vallorcine**, entering the **Réserve Naturelle des Aiguilles Rouges**. The official **Chalet** (*t 04 50 54 08 06; open June–Aug daily 9.30–12.30 and 1.30–6.30, first fortnight Sept daily 10–12.30 and 1.30–6; free*) at the **Col des Montets** offers slightly old-fashioned displays on the geology, flora and fauna of the valley, strewn with interesting plants growing amidst big boulders that turn green in summer, a world apart from the glacial grandeur of the Arve, but with great walking, and more traditional communities on the way to the Swiss frontier. Until the 19th century, this valley was completely cut off from the world by winter snows, and back in the Middle Ages was apparently almost as populated with bears as people, hence the name of the village of Vallorcine. At the border hamlet, the **Musée Barberine** (*t 04 50 54 63 19; open July–Aug 2–6; adm*) recalls traditional ways in an old farm. To end with a sensational view over Haute Savoie and the Swiss Alps, why not walk up via the **Bérard waterfall** to **Mont Buet**, its peak at a relatively manageable 3,099m?

Savoie's Vanoise Valleys and Oisans

Into the Beaufortain 236
The Upper Isère (or Tarentaise) 237
The Arc Valley (or Maurienne) 242
Crossing to the Oisans 245

16

Highlights

1 Hauteluce, Boudin and Conflans, idyllic villages
2 Cathedral city of St-Jean-de-Maurienne
3 The flurry of Baroque churches around Lanslebourg and Lanslevillard
4 Walks and natural grandeur around Pralognan

The second greatest French Alpine range, the Massif de la Vanoise rises almost immediately south of the Mont Blanc range. Encircled by the Isère river to the north and the Arc to the south, the centre of the Vanoise, with its stunning solid peaks and its mammoth glaciers, has been pretty well preserved from human encroachment, and was declared France's first national park in 1963. Its highest peaks reach around 3,800m, aloof above the highest pistes – many of the most reputed ski resorts in the world stand along the sensational slopes of the jagged upper Isère valley (*see* chapter 19), ending with Val d'Isère. The equally awesome sides of the Arc valley have smaller resorts, but more formidable forts, recalling the days when this was a jealously guarded frontier. The Arc also developed more industrial muscle. Although many of the factories have closed, the locals are going back to the gym to hone their beautiful brawn to show off to tourists.

These two intimidatingly grand Vanoise valleys are almost better known as the Tarentaise and Maurienne respectively, reflecting historical territories. The little city of Moûtiers and ancient Aime count among the most interesting historic stops in the Tarentaise. As to the delightful cathedral city of St-Jean-de-Maurienne, it was the cradle of the lordly house of Savoie, via Humbert aux Blanches Mains (White Hands – he was reputed for his purity), back in the 11th century. The main cultural surprise the valleys share is a string of extraordinarily decorated churches, both Baroque and Gothic. The Baroque swarm with putti so lively you could imagine them flying out after you on your discoveries of the natural wonders in these parts. For many, the summer season is devoted to walking or more daring sports.

It makes most sense to present the two Vanoise valleys in a loop, as once you've explored as far as Val d'Isère or Bonneval-sur-Arc, it's very much worthwhile climbing to the other side via the highest road pass in Europe, the Col de l'Iseran, at 2,764m, assuming it's open. There are smaller, enchanting delights off this obvious touring circle. Definitely climb into the centre of the park by car or by foot to visit charming Champagny-en-Vanoise and remote Pralognan-en-Vanoise. And off towards the Col du Petit St-Bernard, the resort of La Rosière clings to the most sensational summer spot along the Isère. Host of the Winter Olympics in 1992, Albertville west along the river, along with snooty Conflans looking down its nose at it, acts as our starting point round the Vanoise. But before taking this loop, stop in the Beaufortain, beautiful link between Mont Blanc and Vanoise ranges. The cows, almost up to their necks in flowers and grasses in summer, produce the finest of cheeses, the *Coopérative Laitière* at Beaufort the main centre of production. Hauteluce nearby can put in a fair claim to being one of the most heavenly villages in the French Alps.

At the end of the chapter, we sneak across to the Oisans via Valloire and the high passes of the Col du Galibier and Col du Lautaret, on the sensational dividing line between northern and southern French Alps, this route only open a few short summer months. We then take you under La Meije, most impressive, eternally snow-capped height of the third major Alpine range, the Ecrins, to explore the ravine of the Romanche valley close to Grenoble.

Getting Around

By train: Albertville , Moûtiers, Aime-La Plagne, Bourg-St-Maurice, St-Jean-de-Maurienne and Modane have good TGV links.

By bus: Catch valley buses from these stops. For Val d'Arly and Beaufortain, use services from Albertville – **STA**, **t** 04 79 32 08 88, runs to Crest-Voland, Flumet-Megève, La Giettaz, and Hauteluce-Les Saisies; **Blanc**, **t** 04 79 38 10 50, serves Beaufort-Arêches. Grenoble bus services take you to the Oisans.

Tourist Information

For the tourist offices of the major ski resorts, *see* **Winter Sports**.

Aime: Ave de Tarentaise, 73212 Aime, **t** 04 79 55 67 00, *www.aimesavoie.com*.

Albertville: Place de l'Europe, 73204 Albertville, **t** 04 79 32 04 22, *www.albertville.com*.

Aussois: t 04 79 20 30 80, *www.aussois.com*.

Beaufort: Grande Rue, 73270 Beaufort **t** 04 79 38 37 57, *www.areches-beaufort.com* or *www.lebeaufortain. com*.

Bessans: 73480 Bessans, **t** 04 79 05 96 52, *www.bessans.com*.

Bonneval-sur-Arc: 73480 Bonneval-sur-Arc, **t** 04 79 05 95 95, *www.bonneval-sur-arc.com*.

Bourg-St-Maurice: 105 Place de la Gare, 73700 Bourg-St-Maurice, **t** 04 79 07 04 92, *www.bourgstmaurice.com*.

Champagny-en-Vanoise: Le Centre, 73350 Champagny-en-Vanoise, **t** 04 79 55 06 55, *www.champagny.com*.

Haute-Maurienne/Lanslebourg: Rue du Mont-Cenis, 73480 Lanslebourg, **t** 04 79 05 91 57, *www.hautemaurienne.com*.

Moûtiers: Place St-Pierre, 73600 Moûtiers, **t** 04 79 24 04 23, *www.ot-moutiers.com*.

Pralognan-la-Vanoise: Ave de Chasseforêt, 73710 Pralognan-la-Vanoise, **t** 04 79 08 79 08, *www.pralognan.com*.

Séez: Rue Célestin Fréppaz, 73700 Séez, **t** 04 79 41 00 15, *www.seezsaintbernard.com*.

St-Jean-de-Maurienne: L'Ancien Evêché, 73300 St-Jean-de-Maurienne, **t** 04 79 83 51 51, *www.saintjeandemaurienne.com*.

Val Cenis/Lanslevillard: Rue Sous l'Eglise, 73480 Lanslevillard-Valcenis **t** 04 79 05 23 66, *www.valcenis.com*.

Venosc/Vallée du Vénéon: La Condamine, **t** 04 76 80 06 82, *info@venosc.com*.

Market Days

Beaufort: Wed.

Albertville: Wed, Thurs and Sat.

Moûtiers: Tues and Fri.

Champagny-en-Vanoise: Tues.

Pralognan-la-Vanoise: Tues and Fri.

Aime: Thurs.

Bourg-St-Maurice: Sat.

Séez: Thurs.

Bessans: Mon.

Lanslevillard: Wed.

Aussois: Tues.

St-Jean-de-Maurienne: Sat.

Where to Stay and Eat

Beaufort ✉ 73270

★★Grand Mont, Place de l'Eglise, **t** 04 79 38 33 36, **f** 04 79 38 39 07 (*inexpensive*). Smart and comfortable by the church. Regional cuisine (*moderate*).Half-board compulsory in high season. *Closed late-April–mid-May and Oct.*

Arêches ✉ 73270

★★Grand Mont, Route du Grand Mont, **t** 04 79 38 10 67, *www.le-grand-mont.fr* (*inexpensive*). Same name as above, but comfortable option in central Arêches, with restaurant (*moderate-cheap; closed Sun out of season*).

★★Poncellamont, Route de Carroz, **t** 04 79 38 10 23, **f** 04 79 38 13 98 (*inexpensive*). More old-fashioned option in flowery chalet. Good traditional cuisine (*moderate*). *Closed mid-April–May and Oct–Christmas; restaurant closed Sun eve and Mon out of season.*

Les Saisies ✉ 73620

★★★Le Calgary, **t** 04 79 38 98 38, *www.hotelcalgary.com* (*expensive*). High quality big modern chalet. Spacious rooms. Good restaurant (*moderate*). Pool. *Closed late April–late June and early Sept–mid-Dec.*

Lac de Roselend ✉ 73270

La Pierre Menta, Col du Pré, **t** 04 79 38 92 45 (*moderate–cheap*). To eat enjoying the great view down onto the lake . *Closed mid-Oct–early May; by reservation only evenings.*

Albertville ✉ 73200

★★★Million, 8 Place de la Liberté, **t** 04 79 32 25 15, *www.hotelmillion.com* (*very expensive–expensive*). Excellent central hotel. Spacious rooms. Exquisite restaurant (*very expensive–moderate*). *Closed early May; restaurant closed Sat lunch, Sun pm and Mon.*

Conflans ✉ 73200

Le Ligismond, Place de Conflans, **t** 04 79 37 71 29 (*moderate*). Great terrace on main square, with vaulted room too for traditional cuisine. *Closed Sun eve and Mon.*

Pralognan-la-Vanoise ✉ 73710

★★Le Grand Bec, **t** 04 79 08 71 10, **e** *grand_bec@wanadoo.fr* (*moderate*). Balconies on all sides, rooms in regional style as well as the cuisine (moderate). Pool and court. *Closed late April–May and mid-Sept–mid-Dec.*

★★Les Airelles, Les Darbelays, **t** 04 79 08 70 32, **f** 04 79 08 73 51 (*moderate*). Modern, appealing chalet beside forest c.1km from village, its balconied rooms with great mountain views. Decent restaurant (*moderate*). Pool. *Closed late April–May and late Sept–mid-Dec.*

La Rosière ✉ 73700

★★Plein Soleil, **t** 04 79 06 80 43, **f** 04 79 06 83 65 (*inexpensive*). Fabulous views from this cheerful little hotel.

For recommendations for the resorts of **Val d'Isère and Tignes**, *see* **Winter Sports**, p.317.

Bonneval-sur-Arc ✉ 73480

Le Pré Catin, **t** 04 79 05 95 07 (*moderate*). Enchanting, doing more than just traditional raclettes. *Closed Sun eve and Mon, and late April–mid-June and late Sept–mid-Dec.*

Bessans ✉ 73480

Gîte d'Etape Le Petit Bonheur, **t** 04 79 05 06 71, **f** 04 79 05 16 75 (*inexpensive*). Bargain half-board; rooms for four. Friendly stop.

Lanslevillard ✉ 73480

★★Nanook, **t** 04 79 05 91 24, *www.hotelnanook.com* (*inexpensive*). One of several simple but pleasant options here, run by Franco-British

couple. Restaurant (*moderate*). *Open mid-June–mid-Sept.*

Lanslebourg ✉ 73480

★★★Hôtel Club Le Val Cenis, Sablon, **t** 04 79 05 80 31, *www.mmv.fr* (*moderate–inexpensive*). Good standard appealing big hotel with pool. *In summer, open July–late-Aug.*

Le Terroir Savoyard, Montée du Coin, **t** 04 79 05 82 31 (*moderate*). Lots of regional specialities, served below the church.

Aussois ✉ 73500

★★★Hôtel du Soleil, 15 Rue de l'Eglise, **t** 04 79 20 32 42, **f** 04 79 20 37 78 (*inexpensive*). Cosy central rooms. Restaurant (*moderate; evenings by reservation only*). Jacuzzi. *Closed mid-April–mid-June and mid-Oct–mid-Dec.*

St-Jean-de-Maurienne ✉ 73300

★★Hôtel du Nord, Rue St-Antoine, **t** 04 79 64 02 08, *www.hoteldunord.net* (*inexpensive*). Central, with standard rooms, but big atmospheric vaulted stables turned jolly regional restaurant (*moderate*). *Closed 2 weeks April; restaurant closed Sun eve, Mon, and Tues lunch outside July–Aug.*

Le Châtel ✉ 73300

Café-Grange Le Châtel, **t** 04 79 64 25 77 (*cheap*). Splendid location above St-Jean-de-Maurienne, family village inn with terrace for tasty charcuterie and cheeses. *Closed Wed, and Sat lunch, and Jan–Mar.*

For recommendations for ski resorts of **La Toussuire, St-Sorlin-sur-Arves, Valloire, l'Alpe d'Huez and Les Deux-Alpes**, *see* **Winter Sports**.

Venosc ✉ 38520

★Château de la Muzelle, Bourg d'Arud, **t** 04 76 80 06 71, **f** 04 76 80 20 44 (*inexpensive*). Bargain hamlet mini-château, basic accommodation. Restaurant (*moderate–cheap*) with broad terrace, and nice garden. *Open summer only, June–mid-Sept.*

★Les Amis de la Montagne, Le Courtil, **t** 04 76 11 10 00, *www.hotel-venosc-deux-alpes.com* (*moderate–inexpensive*). Dynamic and sweet family stop in main village. Wide choice of menus (*moderate*). *Closed mid-April–mid-June and early Sept–mid-Dec.*

Into the Beaufortain

The N212 Val d'Arly road from Sallanches to Albertville via Megève (*see* pp.227 and 296) is the main road link between the Mont Blanc and Vanoise ranges. Branch off it for the **Col des Saisies** and the delicious pasturelands of the **Beaufortain**. Up high, the well-planned modern resort of **Les Saisies**, a bit of a one-street cowboy-like ski village, was built for cross-country sport and makes easyish walking territoy. During the Second World War, the open terrain up here proved a good dropping point for munitions for the Resistance. Heavenly **Hauteluce**, one of the prettiest villages in Savoie, high on its steep slope above the Dorinet river, casts a coquettish sideways glance towards Mont Blanc. Its many-layered, spiked onion steeple draws you to its Baroque **church**, but a faded skeleton with scythe on the sundial isn't there to remind you that this is a land where the meadow grasses are still cut by hand. Inside, the acrobatic Christ balanced on the main beam sports a gilded loincloth, while putti heads float miraculously at his feet. An **Ecomusée** (*t 04 79 38 80 31; open July–Aug Tues pm–Sat 10–12 and 3–7; adm*) recalls traditional Savoyard ways, while bars offer superb terrace views. The ruins of the **Châteaux de Beaufort** lie down in the valley. Continue further up for the hamlet of **Belleville**, its chapel with enchanting medieval murals. From the **Col du Joly** appreciate splendid views to Mont Blanc.

Beaufort, synonymous with one of the greatest of French cheeses, is also a big, burly traditional village with beefy Baroque church at the meeting of Doron and Argentine valleys. The **church** is dedicated to saint Maxime, credited with converting the Tarentaise to Christianity. But more traditional Fathers of the Church sit enthroned on the remarkable 18th-century pulpit in the clean-lined Baroque edifice. The cows that graze in the exquisite pastures cut out of deep dark forests around produce rich milk,

Beaufort Cheese, Prince of Gruyères

Beaufort cheese, a *fromage* as dense in subtle flavours as foie gras, was deemed '*prince des gruyères*' by the great French bon vivant, Brillat-Savarin (*see* p.29). It was granted its *appellation d'origine contrôlée* in 1968. The area of production covers large swathes of pastures not just in the Beaufortain, but also the Maurienne and Tarentaise. Some 800 farmers keep the beloved Tarine cows, and some 40 centres are allowed to make Beaufort cheese. In summer, the farmers send their cattle *en alpage* for around 100 days. They gradually climb the mountain slopes to the highest pastures, then munch their way back down again, this endurance exercise in Alpine eating now regulated by electric fencing. The traditional farmers follow the cattle, staying in the old wooden *fermes d'alpage* only used in summer. It's a gruelling summer schedule for them, having to work long days in Spartan conditions. The milking done, the milk collected, the Beaufort *fromages* are made in big rounds each weighing between 40 and 50 kilos and most distinctive because of their concave sides, derived from the beechwood circles in which they're pressed. But it's the cows' exceptionally rich diet, the painstaking curdling process and the special *morge* bacteria working on the Beaufort that, combined, give it such a profound, distinctive taste. The cheeses are cellared, often for half a year and more, before being sold.

much of it turned into cheese at Beaufort's **Coopérative Laitière** (*t 04 79 38 33 62; open July–Aug daily 8–12.30 and 2–7, rest of year daily exc Sun and public hols 8–12 and 2–6; adm*). The sight of thousands upon thousands of rounds of *fromage* in the cellars bowls visitors over. A film, available in English, explains the cheese-making process well. Beaufort is also well known for its association with the novelist Roger Frison-Roche, a passionate mountaineer who spent his boyhood holidays nearby and used the Alps as a background for his the gripping novels.

South of Beaufort, a tortuously beautiful road leads to the picturesque, protected traditional Alpine chalet villages of **Arèches** and **Boudin**, although once the snows melt, many of the houses are left exposed with corrugated roofing. The wood-surrounded pastures, and the more open ones around the big, bare sides of the **Lac de Roselend**, ring with the sound of cowbells in summer. This very large artificial lake created by the construction of a massive dam in 1961 looks peaceful enough, but generates enormous amounts of hydroelectric power. The area's name derives from the pink-flowering rhododendrons on the slopes. According to legend, the distinctive **Pierre Menta peak** was kicked over here from the Aravis chain (marked by a tooth-like gap in its middle) by the frustrated giant Gargantua, who was finding that he had bitten off more than he could chew with Mont Blanc. Above, you can take an austere, almost treeless, houseless and completely resortless shortcut to **Bourg-St-Maurice** avoiding the Isère valley's huge meanders by going via the **Col de Méraillet**, with its superlative views of Mont Blanc, across the eerie **Cormet de Roselend**.

For a challenging-to- (at times) chilling route onto the southern end of the Mont Blanc range, branch off via **Les Chapieux**'s rich pastures up to **Ville des Glaciers**. The walk past the ruins of the **Auberge des Mottets** takes you along a section of the famed **Tour du Mont Blanc hiking route**, huge glaciers and spiky *Aiguilles* (or Needles) forming the sensational backdrop as you reach the **Col de la Seigne**, once an important way into Italy's Aosta valley. From here you get frightening views onto the less familiar, far more daunting Italian face of Monte Bianco.

Alternatively, heading west of Beaufort to Albertville, **Villard-sur-Doron** and **Queige** have churches concealing interesting interiors, the calm, resigned Pietà in the latter contrasting with the typical Baroque show. A winding mountain road above Villard brings you to the **Signal de Bisanne** (also reachable from Les Saisies), with remarkable views. Beyond Queige, make a most attractive detour to the hamlet of **Les Pointières**.

The Upper Isère (or Tarentaise)

Set on a big elbow in the Isère, where the Arly joins forces with it, industrial **Albertville**'s main claim to fame is having hosted the Winter Olympics in 1992, as recalled in the **Maison des Jeux Olympiques d'Hiver** (*t 04 79 37 75 71; open mid-June–Sept daily 10–7, Feb–mid-June daily exc Tues 2–6; adm*). A fairly modern creation anyway, the town was named after its founder in 1836, Charles-Albert of Savoie. The grandiose administrative buildings left from that time were upstaged by the rebuilding of central Place de l'Europe for the Olympics, in somewhat extravagant salmon-pink Italianate neo-fascist style. On a nearby rocky outcrop, the much older, deeply atmospheric village of **Conflans** looks down its nose at Albertville. Its ramparts and gateways protected magnificent dwellings built on the proceeds of prosperous trading on the route between the Rhône and northern Italy. The **Grand-Place** with its picturesque oval fountain and many flowers, and the arcaded Maison Rouge, actually look most Italian. The muscular brick mansion holds the **Musée d'Art et d'Histoire** (*t 04 79 37 86 86; open mid-June–Sept daily 10–7, Feb–mid-June daily exc Tues 2–6; adm*), with quite interesting religious pieces as well as rooms dedicated to the place's military past – it was even the original home of the elite mountaineering *Chasseurs Alpins*. The whole village beyond looks almost over-prettified now, the place laying on thick its olde medieval charms, craft shops and restaurants with broad terraces competing with each other. Even the church seduces with its saints painted on the outside, while the Baroque attractions within include dynamic pulpit figures. From a broad esplanade one side of the village, wide views open up of the Isère valley beyond the 16th-century **castle of Manuel de Locatel** (undergoing restoration).

Stubs of medieval castles stick out at the start of the high slopes between Albertville and Moûtiers, their towers overwhelmed by the vast expanses of woods above. The **Château de Chantemerle** was once the summer residence of the Moûtiers bishops. The one at **Blay** went up in flames in the 17th century. The **castle of Feissons**, by contrast, has been restored. There is one little-known road link between the Isère and Arc valleys beyond the formidable Col de l'Iseran, far off by the sources of both these great mountain rivers – it's the short mountainous route via the Col de la Madeleine, only completed in 1968. Head up through chestnut woods to the memorably named village of **Pussy**, its church containing a typically ornate Baroque altar. You then enter wild gorges to which **Bonneval** and **Celliers** cling dramatically. At the **Col de la Madeleine**, among high pastures, enjoy splendid views over both Vanoise and Mont Blanc ranges. The way then winds down via the ski resort of **St-François-Longchamp**. This road has gained a certain notoriety as a punishing route for the Tour de France cyclists.

Continuing to the next big elbow-turn in the Isère, the historic town of **Moûtiers** has a pleasing Italianate heart. A fine stone bridge spans the bounding river close to the **cathedral**, a mix of Romanesque and Gothic. Exquisite small medieval religious objects are displayed in the treasury, while the life-size Crucifixion and Entombment draw you into those terrible episodes in Christ's life. Moûtiers was the clear capital of the Tarentaise for centuries until the ski resorts took pride of place. Now, most visitors to Savoie ignore the town, so easily bypassed these days. Even if the local population has suffered from a decline in industry, the substantial old houses in the centre have been given colourful licks of paint, lending them a bright feel. The **bishops' palace** houses a tempting **Musée des Traditions Populaires** (*t 04 79 24 04 23; open Mon–Sat 9–12 and 2–6; adm*) celebrating Baroque art and local traditions.

On any map, you'll notice how flailing tentacular roads lead up a series of valleys south of Moûtiers, heading to the really major skiing territories of the **Trois Vallées** (*see p.304*). Although these valleys come into full tourist bloom in the winter ski season, there is their natural beauty to explore in summer, plus the usual array of

Baroque churches, hiking trails and mad Alpine summer sports. The short valley to
Valmorel turned to skiing later than the rest and developed with more restraint.
Make the detour west to **Doucy** for its refined altarpiece, including a distressing 19th-
century painting of the crucifixion of St Andrew. The **Vallée de Belleville** leading to
Val-Thorens has the most character in summer, with its string of chapels and mountain lakes. The **Chapelle Notre-Dame des Grâces** before **St-Jean-de-Belleville** gleams
with 19th-century painted vaults as well as 18th-century altarpieces, and the church
of **St-Martin-de-Belleville** contains a major retable. Above the latter village, **Notre-
Dame de la Vie** on its rock has been a particularly significant place of worship since
medieval times, although later kitted out with the obligatory Baroque frills. **Val-
Thorens** may not be everyone's cup of tea architecturally, but the scenery is
spectacular, as are the sporting possibilities. Exclusive **Méribel**, its heliport tucked
away down its own private wooded valley, is the Isère resort with the most style. The
high road connecting Méribel and messy Courchevel passes through that rarity in
these parts, a genuine old settlement, **Méribel-Village**.

Especially delightful small resorts hide out east of **Courchevel**, heading for the heart
of the Vanoise and its national park below vast peaks and glaciers. At **Bozel**, the church
has all the usual bright Baroque attributes, plus a lovely gallery within, while the
stocky, misleadingly named **Tour Sarrazine** didn't go up at the time of the Saracens,
but for the powerful medieval lordly family of these parts. Recently graced with an
upbeat modern sundial, it holds exhibitions. Attractive **Champagny-le-Bas** is a village
made up entirely of chalets, with no modern excrescencies whatsoever. Its orange-
hued church crowning the hillock in front of it makes it all the more appealing. Inside,
the Baroque retable, the silliest in Savoie, looks like it's being attacked by a swarm of
pink doll-like putti. The gilded figures on the main beam display slightly more dignity.
A precipitous road hanging to a cliff edge leads to **Champagny-d'en-Haut** and a
delightful flat, generous valley with old hamlets strung along it, one of the most
unspoilt roads in the range, the sound of the torrent accompanying you along the
way. Hiking paths head into the park, its massive summits and glaciers snow-covered
year round. Surrounded by breathtaking peaks, **Pralognan-la-Vanoise** lies along a
separate, tighter, more forested high route, in a large clearing at 1,400m, making a
peaceful base for superb walks to mountain lakes and heights, the scenery reminiscent of those gorgeous Ansel Adams photographs of American mountains.

The **GR55 hiking path** crosses the Vanoise beside Pralognan, heading south for the
Col d'Aussois below the **Dent Parrachée**, totemic peak in the south of the range, and
east, skirting round stunning glaciers and another of the park's most striking peaks,
the **Pointe de la Grande Casse**, which carries the nickname of the *Pointe Matthews*, in
memory of a British climber who, along with French companions, carved more than
1,000 steps here in 1860 to help walkers reach the summit. Not something the agile
ibex would be fussed about. It was first and foremost for this endangered species
with its trademark thick, ridged horns that the Vanoise National Park was originally
created, although the park's remit has spread to take in considerate, well-planned
tourism, including 600km of marked trails and some 40 mountain refuges for
dedicated walkers.

Back way down by the Isère, the cheery, open town of **Aime** has an inordinately long history for these parts, stones bearing Roman inscriptions on show in the crypt of the severe 11th-century **Romanesque church**, built in part from pebbles gathered from the river bed. In the cubic medieval forms of the main church, a few fragments of frescoes remain in place, including one showing a boyish God creating Adam and Eve. But the major scene to have survived depicts the New Testament Massacre of the Innocents. Aime also has a more typical **Baroque parish church** provided with two sundials outside, and a plethora of painted details within. To the north, the **Chapelle St Sigismond** has been turned into the Haute Tarentaise's archaeological and ethnographic **Musée Pierre Borrione** (*t 04 79 55 67 00; open July–Aug daily 10–12.30 and 2–6.30; adm*), including fragments from Roman Aime as well as rare minerals and fossils. Baroque art also gets a look in, plus the story of La Plagne's mines.

South of Aime, modern **La Plagne** consists of a handful of ski resorts (*see* p.309) in different styles. This, and the massive string of experimental resorts of **Les Arcs** (*see* p.309) have a sporty summer season catering to mass-market holidays. Between the two, more traditional **Landry** stands out for its delightfully located church with spiked onion dome, and three sundials on the outside. Higher up, **Peisey-Nancroix** claims the highest pointed steeple in the Tarentaise. No fewer than seven Baroque retables fight for attention inside. For an interesting saunter round an 18th- to 19th-century silver-bearing mine, wander round **Le Palais de la Mine – Circuit des Monts d'Argent** (*free*) at **Peisey**. The **Sanctuaire Notre-Dame des Vernettes** is a much-appreciated goal for pilgrims who go up by foot to this Baroque gem with magnificent views of **Mont Pourri**, the mighty northeast marker of the Vanoise at 3,779m. Press on to **Les Lanches**, from which you can join the GR5 walking trail.

The pretty old hamlets huddling together on their high perches on the north side of the valley between Aime and Bourg-St-Maurice offer quite a contrast to the massive resorts opposite. The GR5 continues north to **Pierre Menta**. Traditional rural ways are kept going by the inhabitants, who've rebaptized their stretch of valley *Le Versant du Soleil* (The Sunny Side). At **La Côte d'Aime**, pay a visit to the **Fruitière**, explaining the tradition of collective Beaufort cheese-making here and presenting local craft objects, while a real life oldie will take you on a guided visit of a traditional house. **Vulmix** has a chapel hiding a whole colourful 15th-century fresco cycle telling how saint Grat found the head of St John the Baptist in the Holy Land and brought it back to the pope; the scene where he presents what looks like the holy man's dentures to the pontiff can't help but raise a smile. Closer to home, St-Jean-de-Maurienne would receive other supposed bits of the Christ's great cousin (*see* p.244).

Bourg-St-Maurice in the valley bottom spreads out at another of the major elbows in the Isère. It may serve as a major gateway to the ski resorts in winter, but canoeists and rafters take to the river here in large numbers in summer. Its lively waters have even hosted world canoeing championships. It also has a sprightly main shopping street and a cheese cooperative. Unfortunately, the local torrents ruined the parish church in the 19th century, but somehow the Baroque interiors were restored within the new neoclassical structure. North above town, standing way on high at 2,000m, the **Fort de la Plate** (*t 04 79 60 59 00*) on its dramatic crest is nowadays transformed from June to November into a farmers' showcase. Bourg-St-Maurice's valley-bottom neighbour, the former tanning town of **Séez**, conceals several Baroque attractions. The rich **church of St Peter** contains an outrageous image of Christ on the cross sporting what can only be described as a gold lamé disco loincloth. Sometimes those Baroque artists just didn't quite set the right tone. The **Espace Baroque Tarentaise St-Eloi** (*t 04 79 40 10 38; open July–Aug daily exc Sun am 10–12 and 2–7, 2nd half June and 1st half Sept Mon–Sat 2–6; adm*) enlightens visitors about the aims of Baroque art in these parts, including demonstrations of the crafts involved.

A serpenting road takes you to **La Rosière**, in arguably the most spectacular location of all the Isère ski resorts, perched at 1,850m, overlooking a sharp turn in the river's course, layer upon layer of mountains receding into the distance to south and west. It's a phenomenal spot to appreciate at any time of year, although it is a tad surprising to find a golf course nearby. Continuing up to the **Col du Petit St-Bernard**, this was once a much more important pass into Italy. The rather grim-looking remnants of the **Hospice du Petit-St-Bernard** (*on this saintly figure, see* p.23), offering shelter to travellers from medieval times, are being restored. The **Chanousia Alpine botanical garden** (*t 04 79 41 00 15; open July–mid-Sept daily exc Sat 9–1 and 2–7; adm*), created up here at over 2,000m by a dedicated abbot at the end of the 19th century, has also been revived. At the pass itself, Mont Blanc suddenly pops up looking startlingly close, although actually far away. The road leads down to the famous Italian resort below Monte Bianco, **Courmayeur**.

Heading south towards the source of the Isère, in summer, try the vertiginous route from La Rosière past the whitewashed **church of Le Châtelard**, standing out like an Alpine lighthouse on the massive, near vertical slopes, and the pretty hamlet of **Le Moulin**, to reach the splendid stepped chalets of **Le Miroir**. **Ste-Foy-la-Tarentaise**, a spanking new, exclusive resort, is worth a look for the high quality of its architecture, but further along the slopes hamlets like **Le Monal** or **La Gurraz** are quite extraordinarily pickled in the past, very tricky to reach, and best approached discreetly, as you can feel like an intruder in such startling mountain hideaways.

Down by the big, artificial **Lac du Chevril** with an unmissable vast mural covering the side of one of the biggest dams in the world, a road leads up to **Tignes**. The **Espace Patrimoine Le Cœur de Tignes** (*t 04 79 40 04 40; open Jan–March and July–Aug Mon–Sat 3–7; adm*) recalls not just the traumatic times in 1952 when the village of Tignes-Les-Boisses was deliberately drowned, but also centuries of history and the emergence of the modern high ski resort of Tignes, its fortresses of ski apartments built in a wide open bowl surrounded by sensational eternal snowy peaks and glaciers which offer almost year-round skiing, as well as other sporting possibilities in summer. **Val d'Isère**, the final, more exclusive resort set deep at the end of the valley, has more style, and a glamorous reputation, although it looks somewhat bedraggled once out of its white winter furs. Above town, hardy walkers head out early to spot ibex and chamois in the **Gran Paradiso Park**, which extends across from Italy to join this high, wild corner of the Vanoise National Park where these rare, shy creatures are well protected. Marmots also abound in this area, getting up early to avoid the summer traffic going over the challenging **Col de l'Iseran**, Europe's highest road pass at 2,764m. When this was laid in the 1930s, the **Route des Grandes Alpes** (*www.routedesgrandesalpes.com*) linking Lake Léman (or Geneva) with the Mediterranean was complete – the Tarentaise and Maurienne were finally joined together by more than a mule track.

The Arc Valley (or Maurienne)

Heading down the Arc river with its metallic green and blue tinges, its valley may be more industrial and more heavily fortified than the upper Isère, but the old villages near the river's source have preserved much of their character and their ornate churches. Orange lichen tinges the stone roofs of **Bonneval-sur-Arc** in summer, the houses turning into tourist shops. Up towards the source of the river, make an expedition up to ultra-traditional **L'Ecot**. Walkers climb to the peak of **Les Evettes** for stunning 360-degree views. The GR5 hiking path takes the other bank of the Arc. The fact that the old hamlet of **Le Villaron** is only accessible on foot makes it all the more irresistible. Across the river, the **Avérole valley** offers an even calmer walking retreat, most of it closed to traffic, its meadows covered in a profusion of flowers in summer.

It seems incredible that such a remote place as **Bessans** should have been largely destroyed during the war, but the duo of church and chapel on their hillock mercifully survived, conserving one of the most elaborate and engrossing ensembles of Savoyard Christian art. Worn frescoes of noble figures and exotic beasts, plus traces of a complicated tale involving Christ and a pair of golden sandals, feature on the outside of the **Chapelle St-Antoine** (*small adm*). The interior is covered in exceptionally vibrant paintings, 40 naive panels representing episodes in Jesus' life, but the tight-lipped participants sport late-Gothic fashions. The **main church** contains a bright array of saints' statues. However, the major woodworking obsession in the village today is for crude and colourful devils, a tradition started by Etienne Vincendet in the mid-19th century as a snub to the local priest, and now flourishing for tourists.

At **Lanslevillard**, the amazing Gothic-decorated **Chapelle St-Sébastien** is covered, head to toe, inside with further splendid naive frescoes on the lives of Christ and Sebastian – the arrow-pierced saint was invoked against the agonizing plague, and one Sébastien Turbil who survived the dreaded disease commissioned these. The crowds once again show off Gothic fashions, while the drama is striking, particularly from Judas' kiss, his hair turning devilish. Lanslevillard's larger twin, **Lanslebourg**, has less charm, but its **Espace Baroque Maurienne** (*t 04 79 05 90 42, www.hautemaurienne.com; open late-Dec–late April, Mon–Wed 9.30–12, Thurs and Fri 3.30–7.15; mid-June –mid-Sept, Mon–Wed 9.30–12, Thurs, Fri and Sun 3.30–6.30; adm*) in a converted church offers a good introduction to local Baroque. Also, here or at Lanslevillard's town hall, pick up the keys for the **Circuit Chapelles**, inciting you to follow a kind of treasure hunt to an array of chapels hidden on the nearby mountainsides, each interior devoted to a different local theme.

A rather barren route leads up from Lanslebourg via the **Col du Mont-Cenis** to Susa in Italy. This was one of the most important passes through the western Alps from classical times. The English artist J. W. Turner memorably got stuck in a storm, as he was carried over by sedan-chair and sleigh (as was the way), a drama he recorded in sketches. Beyond the pass, the route follows the major, morose **Lac du Mont Cenis**, its natural size trebled by various dams constructed through the 20th century, drowning a former travellers' hospice and Napoleonic border barracks; all the history is explained in the **Musée de la Pyramide** (*open July–Aug daily 10–12.30 and 2–6, June and Sept weekends 2–6 ; adm*) in the basement of the curiously shaped contemporary lake-side structure that doubles as a chapel. Also visit the **Maison Franco-Italienne** (*t 04 79 05 86 36; open July–Aug weekdays 10–6; free*), merrily presenting geology, nature, history and traditions both sides of the frontier. From 1862 to 1947, the Mont-Cenis plateau and high pastures lay under Italian rule, its army building a chain of forts, now destinations for walkers, the **Fort de Ronce** the easiest to take on.

West along the Arc, the cows that graze the pastures of **Termignon** produce a very rare but distinctive blue cheese. One branch of the GR5 hiking trail leads up into the glacial heights of the Vanoise. The other side of the Arc, in the quiet village of **Sollières-Envers**, the recent **Musée d'Archéologie** (*t 04 79 20 59 33; open mid-June–mid-Sept Tues–Sun 3–6.30, Jan–mid-April Sat–Mon 2.30–6; adm*) is dedicated to the surprising finds of prehistoric men made in these parts, notably at the **Grotte des Balmes**, recreated here, and revealing the earliest traces of human agriculture in the French Alps, going back to Neolithic times.

The Arc valley soon turns more industrial though, and the slopes bristle with **forts**, many of which you can visit (*t 04 79 20 30 80, or see www.savoie-patrimoine.com*). A handful, known collectively as the **Forts de l'Esseillon**, were built between 1817 and 1834 to defend Savoie from France, the most sensational, the **Barrage de l'Esseillon**, with half a dozen levels of fortifications stepping stiffly down the mountainside, as though on a military march. As to **Fort St-Gobain** (*t 04 79 05 16 52, www.fortifications-maurienne.com; open July–Aug daily 10–12 and 2–7, April–June and Sept–Nov Fri–Mon 10–12 and 2–7; adm*), it formed part of the 1930s French Maginot line, which extended as far down as the Alps, and provides a chilling visit as well as memories of the vain attempts to keep the Germans (and Italians) out. The village of **Avrieux** among these forts boasts one of the most extravagant Baroque churches in the valley, dedicated to Thomas à Becket, represented in six naïve colourful carved scenes. The **Chapelle Notre-Dame-des-Neiges** virtually next door is covered with further elaborate decorations, including intriguing grisaille paintings on its tower, executed by the same artistic priest who painted the vices and virtues on the main church.

Aussois, a high, sunny resort on the plateau above, faces the summits of the Italian frontier, but is overseen by the dramatic **Dent Parrachée**. In the old village, a hellfire *Last Judgement* greets you at the entrance to the Baroque church, but it's all floating putti within, while Christian figures stand dramatically on the main beam. East of the resort, seek out the **Parc Archéologique des Lozes**, with two trails leading you to prehistoric engravings on the rocks and the towering monoliths, which pop their heads out above the pines. One of the menhirs reaches almost 100m, but these aren't man-made, rather a remarkable natural curiosity. The **Fort Marie-Christine**, part of the Esseillon defences, now acts, among other things, as an introductory centre to the

Vanoise National Park. A section of the GR5 hiking network leads up from Aussois past big lakes into the heart of the Vanoise via the **Col d'Aussois**.

Modane stands at one end of the expensive **Tunnel de Fréjus** into Italy. Heavy industry has left its mark in the bottom of the Arc valley to the west, but a remarkable trio of mountains, the **Aiguilles d'Arves**, draw the attention upwards to their spearheads. Far down below, most of the factories have shut in recent times, leading to economic troubles. But tourism is developing in response. Discover traditional villages hiding on the slopes above, such as **Mont-Denis**, with its crafts and high pastures.

Don't dismiss **St-Jean-de-Maurienne** because of the huge Péchiney aluminium works down in the valley. The bright historic centre boasts extremely dignified monuments below mountainsides marked by high crosses. Beside a soaring **keep-cum-bell tower** stands one of the most intriguing **cathedrals** in the whole Rhône-Alpes region, given a classical front, but mainly dating from medieval times. It held revered relics, three supposed fingers of St John the Baptist, brought back by 6th-century Sainte Thècle – small matter that some 180 fingers of the Baptist have been recorded around the Christian world! A few intriguing, highly carved stones from a Carolingian cathedral were incorporated into the Romanesque structure, much of which remains. Then ambitious bishops transformed the building in the late-Gothic period. Staggering religious decorations from this era adorn the choir, notably a towering *ciborium* (to contain the eucharistic bread and wine), and walnut-wood stalls. The latter were supremely carved, probably by German craftsmen, with 300 images, mostly prophets and saints, both international and local. Via the adjoining Gothic cloister, an entrance leads down to the crypt, containing rough Carolingian carvings. Opposite the cathedral, the massive **bishops' palace** stands out in vibrant colour, one part housing the **Musée des Costumes et Traditions Populaires** (*t 04 79 83 51 51; open July–mid-Sept Mon–Sat 10–12 and 2–6, Jan–April Tues–Wed 4–6; adm*), a rambling collection. Wandering round, you see some ostentatious *Ancien Régime* decorations.

On the edge of the centre, the **Musée Opinel** (*t 04 79 64 04 78; open Jan–Dec daily exc Sun and public hols 9–12 and 2–7; adm*) celebrates one of the most famous pocket-knife makers in France. Although the quite atmospheric workshop here stopped churning out knives in the 1960s, manufacture moving to Chambéry, the family company's story is still celebrated on the spot. It dates back to the 19th century, when the skilful knife-makers practised their craft on their stomachs – dogs warming their legs in winter! The picking of mountain herbs to make Mont Corbier liqueur sounds rather more appealing, and the history of herbal alcohols is traced at the curious **Musée du Mont Corbier** (*t 04 79 64 00 24; open July–Aug Mon–Sat 10–12 and 2–7, rest of year Tues–Fri; adm*), the local heady concoction invented by a 19th-century priest who pedalled its supposed medicinal qualities in outrageous advertising claims. The liqueur does have pleasant hints of liquorice and mint.

While the bishops of St-Jean ruled the roost for so long in town, the local lords observed them from their perch across the Arc valley, at **Le Châtel**, an enchanting mountainside village in an exceptional spot. This eyrie was the birthplace of the mighty house of Savoie, just the ruins of a castle now standing aloof to one side. The ever-so-worthy Humbert aux Blanches-Mains came from these parts, and is considered father of the dynasty, taking command not just of the Maurienne, but also of Savoie in the 11th century.

Above St-Jean, follow a head-spinning loop of roads round the **eastern side of the Belledonne** range, old villages and small new ski resorts along the way. Make it up the dead-end to **Jarrier** for its Baroque church. Then **Fontcouverte** boasts another of interest. Taking a loop within a loop to the ski station of **La Toussuire**, there's a fine potter at **Les Ensembles**. Further up, **St-Sorlin-sur-Arve** has a very pretty church and a Beaufort cheese cooperative (*t 04 79 59 70 16; tours daily 9–11.30*). At the top of the tour, the **Col de la Croix de Fer** and **Col du Glandon** are surrounded by sinister craggy peaks, the massive **Grandes Rousses** dominating to the south, although Mont Blanc glows in the northern distance. The **Villards valley** races back down to the Arc.

The main Arc roads between St-Jean-de-Maurienne and the river's confluence with the Isère may be brutish, big factories lurking in the valley bottom, the huge impenetrable wooded slopes above intimidating, but little country routes offer some relief. For instance try the D75 to the picturesquely ruined château and church at **Epierre**, then visit the delightful **Musée du Félicien** (*t 04 79 44 33 67, museedufelicien.ifrance.com; open Feb–Nov daily exc Tues 2.30–6.30; adm*) at **Argentine**, recalling local valley history and traditions, and life across the very varied seasons. Across the valley at **St-Georges-des-Hurtières**, **Le Grand Filon** (*t 04 79 36 11 05, www.grand-filon.com; open April–mid-Dec; adm*) takes you deep into the mining history of these parts in a quite slick modern presentation. Above ground, admire a traditional glassblower (*t 04 79 44 35 39; open July–Aug Wed–Sun 9–12 and 2–6.30, rest of year Wed–Sun 2–5*) at work.

Crossing to the Oisans

The staggering passes linking northern and southern French Alps take you across from the Vanoise to the Ecrins range, but only in summer. Set exclusively in its own valley between the two, sports-crazy **Valloire** feels curiously like a Far West town of the French Alps, with an air of isolation and mad excitement, set in its own bowl of mountains. The exuberance continues inside the broad-shouldered Baroque church. Two of the highest road passes in Europe then lead you across to the southern Alps, the **Col du Galibier** (2,646m) offering some of the most magnificent mountain views of any in the Alps; to the north your gaze trips nimbly over the Vanoise peaks to Mont Blanc, while to the south, the vast summits of the **Ecrins** loom large, in particular La Meije. Leaving the northern, Savoie Alps behind, dropping down to the **Col du Lautaret** (2,058m), a profusion of meadow flowers add dashes of colour to the scenery, while the surprisingly exposed but flourishing **Jardin Alpin** (*www.ac-grenoble.fr/jardin/jardins.htm*) presents a hugely varied display of mountain plants from across the globe among its open rockeries and streams.

The two amazing passes stand roughly at the halfway point of the **Route des Grandes Alpes** (*www.routedesgrandesalpes.com*) from Lac Léman to the Med, but rather than heading south into the southern Alpine ski area of Serre-Chevalier before Briançon, we branch west into **the Oisans**, an area of huge mountains and modern resorts on the northwest corner of the Ecrins, the third mightiest range of the French Alps. Although just outside the Rhône-Alpes region, the emblematic, most spectacular of the Ecrins mountains, the awesome **La Meije**, its eternally white triangular peak rising almost to 4,000m, surveys the Romanche valley. A fabulous cable-car ride takes you up towards it from the traditional village of **La Grave**, facing the mighty mountain with a mix of cowardice and courage down in the **Romanche valley**.

This Romanche has to circle round La Meije coming down from the heart of the Ecrins. Then its **Combe de Malaval** leads west to the two huge modern Oisans resorts, L'Alpe d'Huez (*see* p.325)and Les Deux-Alpes(*see* p.328). These offer mass-market holidays in summer as well as winter, their cool high altitude and sports facilities appreciated by many. **Les Deux-Alpes** is really like a modern town that's been transferred wholesale up into a long, spacious dead end in the mountains, although the **Musée Chasal Lento** (*t 04 76 80 23 97; open Christmas–April and July–Aug daily 10–12 and 3–7; adm*) at **Mont-de-Lans** along the way proves quite fascinating.

L'Alpe d'Huez is similar in feel, but the sensational **Route Pastorale** you can take up to it from the valley **Lac du Chambon** seems to transport you to a different world, or at least several generations back. You pass the vestiges of a medieval silver mine lost way up in these mountains, testimony to the extraordinary lengths to which men could go in search of precious metals. Visit the open archaeological site at **Brandes-en-Oisans**, Besse's **Maison des Alpages de l'Isère** (*t 04 76 80 19 09; open Jan–Dec Thurs–Tues 10–12 and 3–7; adm*), or the little **Musée d'Huez et de l'Oisans** (*t 04 76 11 21 74, www.musee.alpedhuez.com; open July–Aug and Dec–March daily 10–12 and 3–7; adm*) in the midst of L'Alpe d'Huez's mayhem of buildings, to focus on the history and traditions of the area. The views south across the Ecrins are hard to beat. A whole network of major hiking trails allows you to appreciate them to the full.

A classic mountain road leads south of the Romanche, avoiding any large, modern resorts, up the **Vénéon valley**, the road passing close to waterfalls and alongside the stream's splashing turquoise waters, reaching deep into the Ecrins range. Stock up on woodwork and pottery, honey and silks at **Venosc**, just about the prettiest village in all the Ecrins, all cobbled and cute, connected by **cable car** to Les Deux-Alpes, but the latter's modernity totally out of sight and mind. Beyond **St-Christophe-en-Oisans**, with its **Musée d'Alpinisme** (*t 04 76 79 52 25, www.musee-alpinisme.com; open June–Sept daily 10–12 and 2.30–7; adm*) relating exciting tales of mountain conquests in the Ecrins, by **Les Etages** and **La Bérarde**, you're rewarded with fantastic views of the range's highest peaks, the glaciers crystal clear on good summer days.

The valley bottom town of **Le Bourg d'Oisans** is a lively place, packed with tourist shops. Up by the church, the **Musée des Minéraux et de la Faune** (*t 04 76 80 27 54, www.oisans.com/musee.bo; open Jan–Oct summer daily 10–6, rest of year daily pm; adm*) contains a stunning collection of crystals gathered in the Alps, plus stuffed animals representing the wildlife of the Ecrins. Head south via the D526 and take one of the dead end roads up either the **Valsenestre** or **Bonne valleys**. Only by walking can you penetrate the more secretive corners of the Ecrins. The Romanche gorges turn more industrial leading to Vizille and Grenoble, with the odd industrial museum, difficult to focus on with the magnificent mountain scenery behind.

Savoie's Great Lakes

Annecy and Lac d'Annecy 249
Lac d'Annecy to Lac du Bourget via the Rhône 256
Les Bauges 258
Lac du Bourget and Aix-les-Bains 260
Chambéry 263
Lac d'Aiguebelette and Avant-Pays Savoyard 265

17

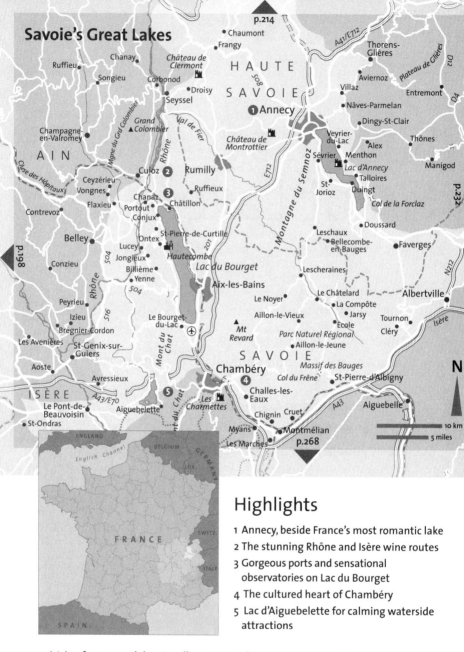

Savoie's Great Lakes

p.214

Chaumont
Frangy
HAUTE

Ruffieu
Chanay
Château de Clermont
SAVOIE

Songieu
Corbonod
Aviernoz
Plateau de Glières

Champagne-en-Valromey
Droisy
Villaz
Entremont

Seyssel
Annecy
Nâves-Parmelan

AIN
Grand Colombier
Château de Montrottier
Dingy-St-Clair

Cuioz
Rumilly
Veyrier-du-Lac
Alex
Thônes

Ceyzérieu
Vongnes
Ruffieux
Sévrier
Menthon
Manigod

Flaxieu
Chanaz
Châtillon
St-Jorioz
Lac d'Annecy
Talloires

Contrevoz
Portout
Conjux
Duingt

Belley
Ontex
St-Pierre-de-Curtille
Leschaux
Doussard

Lucey
Hautecombe
Bellecombe-en-Bauges
Faverges

Conzieu
Jongieux
Billième
Lac du Bourget
Lescheraines

Peyrieu
Yenne
Aix-les-Bains
Le Châtelard
Albertville

Izieu
Le Noyer
La Compôte
Jarsy

Brégnier-Cordon
Le Bourget-du-Lac
Aillon-le-Vieux
Ecole
Tournon
Cléry

Les Avenières
Mt Revard
Parc Naturel Régional
Aillon-le-Jeune

St-Genix-sur-Guiers
SAVOIE

Aoste
Chambéry
Massif des Bauges

Avressieux
Col du Frêne
St-Pierre-d'Albigny

ISÈRE
Aiguebelette
Les Charmettes
Challes-les-Eaux
Aiguebelle

Le Pont-de-Beauvoisin
Chignin
Cruet

St-Ondras
Myans
Montmélian

Les Marches
p.268

10 km
5 miles

N

ENGLAND
English Channel
BELGIUM
GERMANY

FRANCE
SWITZ.

ITALY

SPAIN

Highlights

1 Annecy, beside France's most romantic lake
2 The stunning Rhône and Isère wine routes
3 Gorgeous ports and sensational observatories on Lac du Bourget
4 The cultured heart of Chambéry
5 Lac d'Aiguebelette for calming waterside attractions

A trio of gorgeous lakes, Lac d'Annecy, Lac du Bourget and Lac d'Aiguebelette, settled themselves very comfortably into splendid locations in the pre-alpine ranges southwest of their older, larger cousin Lac Léman as the massive glaciers of the last Ice Age melted. Surely the most romantic lake in France, Lac d'Annecy attracts a glamorous crowd. Posh little ports offer all types of boat to get out on its magical waters, the mountains reflected in its depths. Macho castles survey the scene, those of Menthon and Duingt looking particularly unashamedly down, that at Annecy more discreet, but long an important feudal centre, long home to the counts of the Genevois (the wider area around Geneva). The beautiful arcaded streets below, along with a clutch of grand churches, stretch out beside the canals around the Thiou river.

More fascinating castles lie within easy reach of Lac d'Annecy – Alex, converted into a startling contemporary art centre, Montrottier, above the tortured Gorges du Fier, crammed with art and artefacts, Chaumont, in total ruins but still atmospheric, Clermont, a thriving Renaissance cultural centre. Beyond Clermont, enchanting vineyards lead down the Rhône valley to Lac du Bourget. The alternative route between Lac d'Annecy and Lac du Bourget takes you up into a peaceful, self-contained land detached from the cosmopolitan, noisy lakes; Les Bauges proves a shaggily forested mountain range, where old ways have been preserved in the traditional villages and old crafts continue at gentle pace – although there are major hang-gliding centres too. Vines grip the slopes below the nature reserve of the eastern heights.

To appreciate the natural grandeur of Lac du Bourget at its best, explore the northern end, with an adorable string of tiny harbours and stunning viewing points, including the promontory abbey of Hautecombe, the last resting place of the dukes of Savoie and the kings of Italy. Towns cluster round the southern end, Le Bourget, after which the lake is named, eclipsed by Aix-les-Bains and Chambéry. Now undergoing something of a revival, the waters of Aix were discovered by the Romans and much appreciated by the Victorians, while Chambéry, a splendid historic city, was capital of Savoie for much of the medieval period and, for a while, home, before it was moved to Turin for greater safety from the French, to one of Christianity's most revered and disputed relics, a shroud said to have covered Christ's body at his death.

Little-known, much smaller Lac d'Aiguebelette takes you away from all the frenzy to a calmer pre-alpine lake where motorboats are forbidden and fishermen and ducks rule the roost, putting up with the odd hearty rower. The Avant-Pays Savoyard beyond now looks dreamily down over the neighbouring historic province of the Dauphiné, although the Guiers river was once a much fought-over frontier.

Annecy and Lac d'Annecy

The canal-criss-crossed, chocolate-box-pretty city of Annecy hides somewhat coyly by the northwest corner of its lake, although modern Annecy has sprawled across the north side. In fact, submerged remnants going back to Neolithic times have been found along the north shore. The medieval town grew up around the 12th-century castle, built by the counts of Geneva as one of their main bases and serving as something of a capital to them for a time. After the death of Robert of Geneva, Annecy was purchased in 1401 by Amédée VIII of Savoie, and from mid-15th to mid-17th centuries, its lordship was reserved for junior members of the house of Savoie, trade prospering.

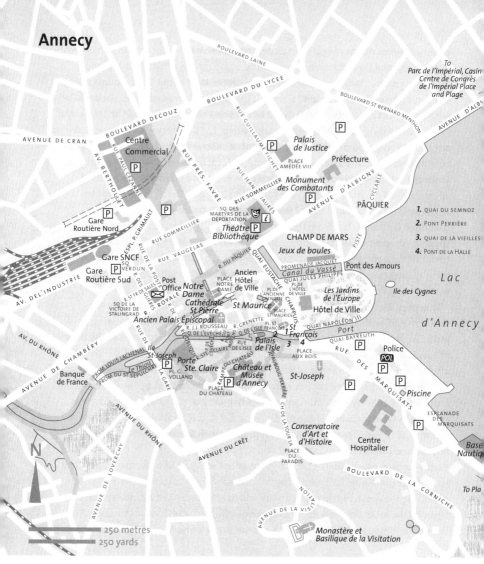

Annecy

To
Parc de l'Impérial, Casino
Centre de Congrès
de l'Impérial Place
and Plage

AVENUE D'ALBI

1. QUAI DU SEMNOZ
2. PONT PERRIÈRE
3. QUAI DE LA VIEILLES
4. PONT DE LA HALLE

Lac

d'Annecy

Île des Cygnes

250 metres
250 yards

With the splits caused by the Reformation in the 16th century, Annecy acquired wider religious importance. Geneva had become the stronghold of Protestantism, the city's monastic communities expelled. Many moved to Annecy, which became the seat of a new bishopric for the Genevois. The most famous of the exiled bishops was the charismatic François de Sales, who devoted his life to gentle but persuasive preaching of a virtuous Catholic life (*see also* Chapter 15). In 1610 he established the charitable Order of the Visitation at Annecy with Jeanne de Chantal (grandmother of that superlative socialite at the Sun King's court, Mme de Sévigné – *see* 'Grignan', p.189). He was also a founder member here of the *Académie Florimontane*, a high-minded cultural institution set up to encourage good writing and good morals in the literary arts, a model for Cardinal Richelieu's slightly later *Académie Française*. François

Getting Around

By air: Look out for cheap Flybe flights from Southampton to Aix-les-Bains/Chambéry

By train: Regular trains from Paris-Gare de Lyon serve Annecy, Aix-les-Bains and Chambéry. Vions-Chanaz and Chindrieux have local stations north of Lac du Bourget. For the Avant-Pays Savoyard and Aiguebelette, there's a reasonable selection of local railway stations, at Le Pont de Beauvoisin, Lépin-le-Lac and Aiguebelette-le-Lac.

By bus: For Les Bauges, use **Voyages Francony, t** 04 79 54 81 23, **f** 04 79 54 83 61.

Tourist Information

For special themed short stays and out-of-season savings organized via the Savoie tourist authorities, *see www. lemeilleurdesalpes.com*.

Annecy: Centre Bonlieu, 1 Rue Jean Jaurès, 74000 Annecy, **t** 04 50 45 00 33, *www. lac-annecy.com*.

Le Châtelard/Les Bauges: Maison du Parc, **t** 04 79 54 84 28, *www.lesbauges.com*. Also see *www.pnr-massif-bauges.fr*.

Aillon-le-Jeune: 73340 Aillon-le-Jeune, **t** 04 79 54 63 65, *www.lesaillons.com*.

Ruffieux: Maison de Chautagne, 73310 Ruffieux, **t** 04 79 54 54 72, *www.chautagne.com*.

Yenne: 52 Place Charles Dullin, 73170 Yenne, **t** 04 79 36 71 54, **e** *yenne.tourisme@wanadoo.fr*.

Le Bourget-du-Lac: Place Général Sevez, 73371 Le Bourget-du-Lac, **t** 04 79 25 01 99.

Aix-les-Bains: Rue Monard, 73100 Aix-les-Bains, **t** 04 79 88 68 00, *www.aixlesbains.com*.

Chambéry: 24 Bd de la Colonne, 73000 Chambéry, **t** 04 79 33 42 47, *www.chambery-tourisme.com*.

Avant-Pays Savoyard: Bouvent, 73470 Novalaise, **t** 04 79 36 09 29, *www.avant-pays-savoyard.com*.

Lépin-le-Lac/Aiguebelette: Place de la Gare, 73610 Lépin-le-Lac, **t** 04 79 36 00 02, *www.lac-aiguebelette.com*.

St-Genix-sur-Guiers: Rue du Faubourg, 73240 St-Genix-sur-Guiers, **t** 04 76 31 63 16, *www.valguiers.com*.

Le Pont-de-Beauvoisin: Rue Gambetta, 38480 Le Pont-de-Beauvoisin, **t** 04 76 32 70 74, **e** *tourisme.cclvg@wanadoo.fr*.

Market Days

Annecy: Tues, Fri and Sun mornings.
Le Châtelard: summer only, Fri morning.
Yenne: Thurs morning.
Le Bourget-du-Lac: Thurs morning.
Aix-les-Bains: Wed all day and Sat morning.
Chambéry: Tues and Sat mornings.
Novalaise: Wed and Sun mornings.
St-Genix-sur-Guiers: Wed morning.
Le Pont-de-Beauvoisin: Mon morning.

Lake Activities

For boat trips on Lac d'Annecy: Try **Compagnie des Bateaux du Lac d'Annecy, t** 04 50 51 08 40, *www.annecy-croisieres.com*, **Groupement des Loueurs de Bateaux de Haute-Savoie, t** 04 50 66 01 75, and **Bateaux Dupraz, t** 04 50 52 42 99, *www.bateauxdupraz. com*. For Lac du Bourget: Try Aix-les-Bains tourist office, or, from Chanaz, **du Lac du Bourget et du Haut-Rhône, t** 04 79 88 92 09 or **t** 04 79 88 33 21, *www.gwel.com* or **Bateaux de Chanaz, t** 04 79 54 29 13, **f** 04 79 63 41 63.

For helicopter flights from the lakeside airports, there are **Héli-Alpes, t** 04 50 27 35 45, or **Hélijet, t** 04 79 54 46 30. **Ski Vol, t** 04 79 08 41 72, and **Takamaka, t** 04 50 45 60 61, offer balloon trips. For parachuting, try *www. veloce-skydive.com/chambery*, **t** 04 79 54 42 93. The tourist offices have information on sailing, canoeing, rowing, windsurfing, diving, cycling and rock-climbing, among other activities – make arrangements early.

Where to Stay and Eat

Annecy ✉ **74000**

★★★★**L'Impérial Palace**, Allée de l'Impérial, **t** 04 50 09 30 00, *www.hotel-imperial-palace.com* (*luxury*). Huge, swanky hotel beside the lake north of the centre. Four restaurants with lake views, **La Voile** (*expensive*) the most exclusive, the others more reasonable. Flash casino.

★★★**Palais de l'Isle**, 13 Rue Perrière, **t** 04 50 45 86 87, *www.hoteldupalaisdelisle.com* (*moderate*). Wonderfully located in house on the main (sometimes noisy) central canal, tight stairways leading to modern rooms.

***Les Trésoms**, 3 Bd de la Corniche, t 04 50 51 43 84, *www.lestresoms.com* (*very expensive–expensive*). Charming big house, with pool, on the slope south of the centre. Artistic touches, including stylish rooms with lake views. Panoramic restaurant **La Rotonde** (*very expensive– expensive*).

****Nouvel Hôtel**, 37 Rue Vaugelas, t 04 50 45 05 78, *www.nouvelhotel.com* (*inexpensive*). Actually in a remarkable Art Deco building, well-kept rooms in the shopping quarter.

***Central**, 6 Rue Royale, t 04 50 45 05 37, *www.lac-annecy.com* (*inexpensive*). Central, calm.

Auberge de Savoie, 1 Place St-François de Sales, t 04 50 45 03 05 (*expensive–moderate*). Annecy's canal-sides are packed with touristy restaurants; sample lake fish at this excellent address at the heart of the action. *Closed Tues and Wed, plus early Jan, late April–early May and late Aug–early Sept.*

L'Atelier Gourmand, 2 Rue St-Maurice, t 04 50 51 19 71 (*very expensive–moderate*). More exclusive, the chef also putting his art on the walls. *Closed Sun pm, Mon, and Tues lunch, plus late Aug and early Jan.*

Ciboulette, Cour du Pré Carré, 10 Rue Vaugelas, t 04 50 45 74 57 (*expensive–moderate*). Gastronomic address in exclusive courtyard off one of the main arcaded streets lined with more basic options. *Closed Sun and Mon, and most July.*

Talloires ✉ 74290

*****Auberge du Père Bise**, t 04 50 60 72 01, e *reception@perebise.com* (*luxury*). Exceptional, with private lake-side beach. Sumptuous rooms with views. Lake fish dressed up in the first-rate restaurant (*luxury–very expensive*). *Closed Christmas–mid-Mar; restaurant closed Tues lunch and Fri lunch in season, Tues and Wed out of season.*

*****L'Abbaye**, Chemin des Moines, t 04 50 60 77 33, e *abbaye@alp-link.com* (*luxury–very expensive*). Former Benedictine abbey now with piano bar, solarium, and private beach. Rooms around a graceful 17th-century cloister. Good restaurant (*very expensive–expensive*). *Closed late Dec and most Jan.*

****Villa des Fleurs**, Route du Port, t 04 50 60 71 14, e *lavilladesfleurs@wanadoo.fr* (*moderate*). More secretive chalet hotel with cute rooms, serving good lake fish

(*expensive*). *Closed mid-Nov–mid-Dec and late Jan; closed Sun pm, Mon, and Tues lunch.*

Veyrier-du-Lac ✉ 74290

******Auberge de l'Eridan**, 13 Vieille Route des Pensières, t 04 50 60 24 00, e *contact@marcveyrat.fr* (*luxury*). Fabulous lakeside hotel, and fabulously expensive. Luxurious rooms. Owner Marc Veyrat is one of the country's star chefs. *Closed Nov–mid-May; restaurant closed weekday lunch, Mon pm, and Tues pm outside July–Aug.*

Aviernoz ✉ 74570

****Auberge Camelia**, t 04 50 22 44 24, e *info@hotelcamelia.com* (*inexpensive*). Comfortable village inn northeast of Lac d'Annecy, run by a very friendly British couple.

Motz ✉ 73310

Auberge de Motz, t 06 76 60 93 12 (*inexpensive*). Model of a new bargain village inn in a cleanly restored old building, with neat plain rooms. Pleasant restaurant (*moderate*).

Ruffieux ✉ 73310

Lachat B&B, Chez M et Mme Baltz, t 04 79 54 20 18, e *baltz.gite@infonie.fr* (*inexpensive*). Sweet room in fantastic location among high vineyards looking down on the Rhône.

Chanaz ✉ 73310

Auberge de Savières, t 04 79 54 56 16 (*moderate*). For its wonderful terraces by the canal; local fish dishes. *Closed Jan–mid-Mar.*

Jongieux ✉ 73170

Auberge Les Morainières, Coteau Marestel, t 04 79 44 09 39. Refined cuisine in a dining room in cellars in the heart of the Marestel vineyards, or on the terrace with melting views. *Closed Sun eve, Mon and Thurs.*

St Jean de Chevelu ✉ 73170

****Hôtel de la Source**, Route du Col du Chat, t/f 04 79 36 8016, *www.hotel-lasource.com* (*inexpensive*). Very decent, with great views, reasonable rooms, tasty cuisine (*moderate*).

Grésy-sur-Isère ✉ 73460

***Tour du Pacoret**, t 04 79 37 91 59, e *info@hotel-pacoret-savoie.com* (*moderate*). Atmospheric hotel, rooms in medieval tower overlooking the Isère valley. Restaurant (*expensive–moderate*) in new wing with terrace; try the local wines. Pool *Closed mid-Oct–April; restaurant closed Tues, plus Wed lunch outside July–Aug.*

Aillon-le-Jeune ✉ 73340
La Grangerie B&B, t 04 79 54 64 71, *www.lagrangerie.com* (*inexpensive*). Simple rooms in old farm above the ski resort Copious *table d'hôte* (*cheap*).

Aix-les-Bains ✉ 73100
★★★Le Manoir, 37 Rue Georges 1er, **t** 04 79 61 44 00, **e** *Hotel-le-Manoir@wanadoo.fr* (*expensive–moderate*). Smart address close to the new Thermes. Restaurant (*expensive–moderate*) and garden. Indoor pool. *Closed mid-Dec.*
★★★Astoria, 7 Place des Thermes, **t** 04 79 35 12 28, **e** *hotel.astoria-savoie@wanadoo.fr* (*moderate*). In the heart of town, stylish rooms beyond the Art Deco entrance and restaurant (*moderate*). *Closed early Dec.*
★★Au Petit Vatel, 11 Rue du Temple, **t** 04 79 35 04 80, *www.petit-vatel.com* (*inexpensive*). Old-style charm and simple rooms, by the Anglican church. Traditional regional cuisine (*moderate*). *Closed Jan.*
★★Davat, 21 Chemin des Bateliers, Le Grand Port, **t** 04 79 63 40 40, *www.davat.fr* (*inexpensive*). Pleasant traditional hotel just behind the port. Garden where meals (*moderate*) can be served. *Closed Jan and Feb; restaurant closed Sun eve and Mon.*

Chambéry ✉ 73000
★★★★Château de Candie, Rue du Bois de Candie, **t** 04 79 96 63 00, **e** *candie@icor.fr* (*luxury–expensive*). Beautifully furnished fortress above town. The modern dining room (*expensive*) serves up trompe-l'œil decorations with refined cuisine. Pool. *Restaurant closed Mon, Tues lunch, and Sat lunch June–July, plus Sun pm rest of year.*
★★★Les Princes, 4 Rue de Boigne, **t** 04 79 33 45 36, **e** *hoteldesprinces@ wanadoo.fr* (*inexpensive*). Comfortable, themed rooms.
★★Le Savoyard, 35 Place Monge, **t** 04 79 33 36 55, **e** *Savoyard@noos.fr* (*inexpensive*). Cheerful, on a main boulevard. Restaurant (*moderate*) serving Savoie classics. *Restaurant closed Sun.*

★★Les Pervenches, Chemin des Charmettes, **t** 04 79 33 34 26, *www.pervenches.net* (*inexpensive*). Delightful spot close to Rousseau's house 2km above town. Old-fashioned rooms; traditional restaurant (*moderate*). *Restaurant closed Sun pm and Mon.*
Le Saint Réal, 86 Rue St-Réal, **t** 04 79 70 09 33 (*very expensive–expensive*). Brilliant restaurant in historic central house *Closed Sun.*
Le Tonneau, Rue St-Antoine, **t** 04 79 33 78 26 (*moderate*). Traditional cuisine in a relaxed brasserie. *Closed Sun pm and Mon.*
La Maniguette, Rue Juiverie, **t** 04 79 62 25 26 (*moderate*). Trendy, serving an interesting single menu. *Closed Aug and Christmas; restaurant closed Sun, Mon and Tues lunch.*
L'Hypoténuse, Carré Curial, **t** 04 79 85 80 15 (*moderate*). Imaginative cuisine and décor. *Closed Spring hols and late July–mid-Aug; restaurant closed Sun and Mon.*
Le Bistrot, 6 Rue du Théâtre, **t** 04 79 75 10 78 (*moderate–cheap*). Excellent deal for Savoie specialities. *Closed Sun and Mon lunch.*

Challes-les-Eaux ✉ 73190
★★★Château des Comtes de Challes, 247 Montée du Château, **t** 04 79 72 86 71, **f** 04 79 72 83 83 (*very expensive–moderate*). Variety of rooms, some magnificent, in fortified medieval manor and outbuildings, with fine views. Pleasing restaurant (*expensive*). Pool.

Aiguebelette Port ✉ 73610
Les Belles Rives, t 04 79 36 05 03, *www.bellesrives-berthet.com* (*moderate*). Enchanting waterside address, serving lake specialities. *Closed Dec–Feb.*

St-Alban-de-Montbel ✉ 73610
La Chesneraie B&B, t 04 79 36 04 33, *www.lachesneraie.com* (*moderate*). Wonderful place, built for an opera singer at the start of the early 20th century in an operatic setting. Extremely well furnished rooms with dramatic views. Caring *table d'hôte.*

Novalaise-Lac ✉ 73470
★★Novalaise-Plage, t 04 79 36 02 19, *www.novalaiseplage.com* (*inexpensive*). Nice, with own beach. Tasty fish restaurant (*expensive–cheap*) with terrace. *Closed Oct–Mar; restaurant closed winter Mon eve and Tues.*

de Sales was buried in Annecy, canonized in 1665, and proclaimed patron saint of writers and journalists in 1923, when the Basilica of the Visitation was being built above town – it now stands out more than the castle from afar, along with a few unfortunate modern apartment blocks. In 1728, the young Jean-Jacques Rousseau arrived in town, fleeing misery as an engraver's apprentice in Geneva. At the Convent of the Visitation, he met a slightly older Swiss in exile, the eccentric, kind-hearted, potion-concocting divorcee and Catholic convert, Madame de Warens. It was *sympathie* if not love at first sight and the woman he would call his *Maman*, his real mother having died giving birth to him, gave him enormous support.

While Annecy became capital of the *département de la Haute Savoie* when Savoie became French, its lake grew increasingly polluted as industry developed in 19th and 20th centuries. After the war, its dynamic mayor, Charles Bosson, set about reviving it and the waters are now among the clearest and healthiest in Europe, winning prizes and plaudits, although the hordes of visitors can be hard to regulate. As to national flower awards, Annecy won so often that it was banned from taking part! To appreciate the lake in its full glory, take a boat trip out from **Annecy's port** (*see* p.251).

Heading into the tourist-packed, arcaded canal-side streets, start on the **Pont sur le Thiou**, from where the town's most celebrated building, the **Palais de l'Isle** (*open June– Sept daily 10.30–6; rest of year daily exc Tues 10–12 and 2–5; adm*), resembles a stone vessel anchored in the midst of the river. It dates back to the 12th century, and has served as residence, prison, mint, and law courts. It now contains the **Musée de l'Histoire d'Annecy**, offering a light introduction to local history. The basic-looking **Café des Arts** also on the island puts on Savoyard events. Looking in the other direction from the bridge, the grand scrolled front of the **church of St-François de Sales** signals the location of the first monastery of the Order of the Visitation. Now restored, the church was badly damaged during the Revolution and the tombs of François de Sales and Jeanne de Chantal demolished. North, the Dominican Gothic barn of **St-Maurice** is the oldest church in Annecy, but only dating from 1422. Look out for the creepy funeral picture for Philibert de Monthouz and the *Deposition* by Pourbus the Elder.

Walk along the gorgeous colourful quays or almost equally lovely parallel **Rue Grenette** and **Rue Jean-Jacques Rousseau** for the **Cathedral of St-Pierre**, with its striking Gothic to Renaissance façade. Built for the Franciscans in 1535, it was converted into the bishops' seat with the move from Geneva. Dramatic *chiaroscuro* paintings stand out inside, another *Deposition* attributed to Caravaggio. The **Bishops' Palace** now houses a school of music and the *Académie Florimontane*. The tempting shops of **Rue Filaterie** lead you up to more enchanting quays before the fourth central church of note, imposing **Notre-Dame-de-Liesse**, signalled by its tall, leaning bell tower rising above a bright square. It was rebuilt after the Revolution, its classical front topped by a gilded statue of the Virgin and Child. Murals brighten the dull classicism inside, although the figures' faces aren't well executed. An English church hides in the elegant house next door. Among other arcaded streets, don't miss **Rue du Pâquier** and the **Hôtel de Sales**, a mansion embellished with figures of the seasons. Its continuation, **Rue Royale**, is a major, but more mundane shopping artery. Further modern shopping quarters lie to the north.

Crossing south of the Thiou via one of many photogenic bridges, arcaded **Rue Ste-Claire** curves irresistibly around the base of the castle's rock, the main thoroughfare of medieval Annecy, now lively night and day. The **Château d'Annecy** (*t 04 50 33 87 30, e musees@ville-annecy.fr; open June–Sept daily 10.30–6; rest of year daily exc Tues 10–12 and 2–5; adm*) is a short walk up the hill, but a world away from the tourist crowds. The enormous 13th-century **Tour de la Reine** forms the oldest part of this massive ensemble. The 14th–15th-century Gothic **Logis Vieux** and the 16th-century, Renaissance **Logis Nemours** contain a regional museum filled with religious statues and all-too-pretty paintings of Annecy. The **Observatoire Régional des Lacs Alpins**, set apart in the **Logis Perrière**, delves into the formation of the region's lakes and their ecology.

The **Conservatoire d'Art et d'Histoire** (*t 04 50 51 02 33; open Mon–Fri 10–12 and 2–6; free*) further out occupies the plain seminary where, until 1970, trainee priests were educated. It now contains a mixed bag of art, including exotic faces sculpted by Evariste Jonchère on his early 20th-century world travels, and contemporary works from the Lyon school. Most excitingly, a new interactive section devoted to pre-cinema experiments in moving images occupies the former chapel. Up on its height, the showy white **church of the Visitation**, consecrated in 1949, holds relics of François de Sales and Jeanne de Chantal. Pilgrims go to venerate them in large numbers.

Down at the lake, the waterside teems with activity, offering many pleasures, including a narrow **beach** and **open-air pools** (*fee for both*) just south of town and the central, well-shaded **Jardins de l'Europe**, laid out in the Belle Epoque, the patronizing statue of Berthollet recalling a celebrated 19th-century scientist from Lac d'Annecy. Opposite, the name of diminutive **Ile aux Cygnes** evokes the countless swans around Annecy, but panels explain the diversity of fowl and fish in the crystal-clear waters. Cross the refreshingly plane-shaded **Canal du Vassé** via the well-named **Pont des Amours** for the north shore, the lawns vacuous, but some of the most memorable views of all on Lac d'Annecy opening up to the south as you approach the unmissable wedding-cake **Imperial Hotel**, in front of which you'll find another **beach** (*fee*) with sporting facilities, and romantic rose gardens to be enjoyed by all.

Layers of peaks receding into the distance beyond huge showy molar tooth-like mountains, **Lac d'Annecy** is so magnetically dramatic that although it may be one of the largest lakes in the country, its lakesides often feel crowded. On the **eastern shore**, posh **Veyrier-du-Lac** has two public beaches. Delightful **Menthon-St-Bernard** with its beach is overseen by the spectacular **Château de Menthon** (*t 04 50 60 12 05; open July–Aug daily 12–6; May–June and Sept Fri, weekends and public hols 2–6; adm*), its magical many-towered silhouette perhaps an inspiration for Walt Disney, its history an extraordinary story. The castle dates back to the 12th century, but its exceptionally important lordly family settled on this rock still earlier. It has never left.

The château is claimed as the birthplace of **St Bernard**, an Alpine hero (*see* p.23), in 1008 . While Bernard flew off to do his charitable work, the medieval lords who stayed served as some of the most powerful figures under the counts of Geneva, guarding a strategic route. Three major towers went up, the Tour du Lac, the keep, and the Tour des Armes. The local populace could seek refuge in the courtyard in times of trouble. Made more comfortable at the Renaissance, the castle was added to in the 18th century with the building of the façade overlooking the lake. Then in the late-19th century, René de Menthon ordered decorative additions, including turrets, to give the place a more Romantic air. On the tour, you see half-a-dozen grand rooms, with many images of St Bernard, but also other fine family portraits and pieces of furniture. The library holds a magnificent collection of works. You may hear the extraordinary story of François de Menthon, father of the present owner, one of the founding figures of the Resistance (*see* p.79), then a Minister of Justice for de Gaulle and French prosecutor at the Nuremberg military tribunal.

Lakeside resorts don't come more chic than **Talloires**, with its swanky port, fabulous array of waterside hotels and restaurants, and its golf course. The **Roc de Chère** promontory is so rich in flora it's been turned into a nature reserve. Towards Thônes, the **Château d'Arenthon** *(t 04 50 02 87 52, e info@fondation-salomon.com; open July–Oct Wed–Fri 2–7, weekends 11–7; Feb–May Thurs–Sun 2–7; adm)* above the pretty village of **Alex** wears a defiant air opposite a massive wall of limestone. It's been given a bold make-over, the Salomon family, renowned in the Alps for making its fortune through ski manufacturing, turning it into a centre for contemporary art exhibitions. The gardens are planted with more discreet contemporary sculptures.

Consider following **the lake's west bank** from Annecy by bike, given the excellent cycle path. At **Sévrier**, with its spectacular views of the toothy mountains opposite, the **beach** *(fee in summer)* and **marina** attract the most attention. Up by the smart neo-Gothic church, Savoyard traditions are recalled in the enthusiastically run **Musée du Costume Savoyard** *(t 04 50 52 41 05, www.echo-de-nos-montagnes.com; open mid-June–mid-Sept daily, exc Sun am and Mon, 10–12 and 2.30–6.30; May–mid-June and late Sept daily, exc Sun and Mon, 2–6; adm)*. Along the main road, the Paccard foundry, celebrated at the **Musée de la Cloche** *(t 04 50 52 47 11; open June–Sept daily exc Sun am, 10–12 and 2.30–6.30; rest of year daily exc Sun am and Mon 10–12 and 2.30–5.30; adm)*, has been making bells the old-fashioned way for eight generations. Numerous copies of the Philadelphia Liberty Bell have been cast by Paccard. Charming lakeside **St-Jorioz** has a good expanse of beach, while a sensational private château once owned by the de Sales family sticks out from the peninsula of **Duingt**. Nature lovers explore the marshy reedbeds at the southern end of the lake by **Doussard**, which also benefits from a good beach. This place goes by the nickname of 'the source of the lake', as most of the waters that feed Lac d'Annecy enter here.

Lac d'Annecy to Lac du Bourget via the Rhône

This section of the great river long formed a piece of the frontier between Savoie and France, the Savoie side sometimes referred to as Le Petit Bugey in contrast to le Grand Bugey opposite (*see* chapter 14). The Clermont family were masters of these parts in former times. The easiest fort to reach from Annecy, medieval **Château de Montrottier** *(t 04 50 46 23 02, www.chateaudemontrottier.com; open June–Aug daily 10–12 and 2–7, mid-March–May daily exc Tues 10–12 and 2–6; adm)* boasts especially grand views from its soaring 15th-century keep. Inside are the collections of Léon

Marès, bequeathed to the *Académie Florimontane*. Among jaded weapons, tapestries and Napoleonic artefacts, the finest works are the Vischers' supremely masterful Renaissance bronzes of the *Battle of the Centaurs*, commissioned by the super-rich Fuggers of Augsburg, but rejected because they featured too many naked buttocks! Nearby, the path along the precipitous **Gorges du Fier** (*t 04 50 46 23 07; open mid-June–mid-Sept daily 9–7, mid-March–mid-June and mid-Sept–mid-Oct daily 9–12 and 2–6; adm*) reveals how the rocks here have been drilled down by the power of the waters. At the hamlet of **Lagnat** by Vaulx, the Moumen family has created a host of intriguing gardens and wooden structures in their **Jardins Secrets** (*t 04 50 60 53 18, www.jardins-secrets.com; open late July–early Sept daily 1.30–7; April–late July weekends and public hols 1.30–7; Sept–Oct Sun 1.30–6; adm*). West along the Fier, **Rumilly**, little capital of this little area known as the Albanais, was once a more important town and has some fine arcaded houses.

Northwest of Annecy the N508 leads to the **Montagne de Vuache**, a dramatic hiking path crossing its ridge, the view giving onto Geneva. Its lower eastern slopes are still covered with orchards. On its protruding southern rump, scramble up to the battered white ruins of the **Château de Chaumont** (*free*) to appreciate commanding views. Vines ski down the steep slopes to **Frangy**, a town on the trout-teeming Usses river, and on the route of pilgrims from Geneva to Santiago in Spain. Confusingly, it's the Altesse grape that produces the local AOC Roussette de Savoie, a respectable sweet white wine. The story goes that the variety was brought back from Cyprus.

The **Château de Clermont** (*t 04 50 69 63 15; open May–Sept daily 10.30–6.30; adm*) standing in a wonderfully confident location on its hill was transformed in the 16th century from a sturdy Savoyard home into a more graceful Renaissance residence for Monseigneur Gallois de Regard, a local who spent much of his life at the Vatican. The place remains devoted to the Renaissance, with a fine collection of furniture. In summer, cultural exhibitions and events add life to the place, the balustraded arcades serving as backdrop to performances. The dignified hillside church is listed as well. Climbing across **Montagne des Princes** via the peaceable village of **Droisy**, look longingly back at Mont Blanc before stepping on the breaks down to Rhône-side **Seyssel**.

Twins separated by the cruel Rhône, there are in fact two Seyssels (*see also* p.206) defying the river that once regularly tore into them. On each bank, a completely separate town developed, the Savoie side venerating its stone Virgin, the west side its black Virgin. In both, important communities of mariners carried out their river trade, their special barges known as *seysselannes*, as recalled at the modest new **Maison du Rhône** (*t 04 50 56 77 04; open mid-June–mid-Sept daily exc Tues 10.30–12.30 and 2–6; April–mid-June and mid-Sept–Nov Wed, Fri and weekends same times; adm*). A big Virgin stands concernedly atop the suspension bridge that has linked the two sides since the 1840s; the Rhône swept earlier crossings away. Now, a dam has tamed the river through this narrow, wildly beautiful section. The name of Seyssel is strongly associated with wine-making, although the extent of the vineyards is tiny, making it one of the smallest producers in France. Although vines grow down the east bank, the wineries you can visit are on the equally lovely western slopes.

The huge dark flanks of the **Montagne du Gros Foug** and the **Grand Colombier** lie like primordial sleeping monsters on either side of the narrow stretch of the lovely, vine-covered Rhône-side stretch known as the **Chautagne**. On the flat, below **Châteaufort**, at the confluence of the Fier and the Rhône, the **Espace Nature** (*most sections free*) lies in a romantic spot, allowing you to appreciate the Rhône at close quarters, as well as providing lots of sporting facilities. The gorgeous **Chautagne vineyards** stretch south from **Motz**, with its Baroque church on high. **Ruffieux** boasts a huge wine cooperative. Surprisingly, red production outdoes the white here. The village looks over a vast, intriguing poplar plantation, one of the largest in Europe, which you can cycle round.

Stick to the Rhône for attractive **Vions** and **Chanaz**, the latter an especially delightful historic frontier village linked to Lac du Bourget by a canal lined with restaurants. In the pretty lanes behind, seek out specialist craft shops and, further up the slope, a mill making walnut oil. A stunning wine route continues south along the steep slopes above the Rhône, **Mont de la Charvaz** separating the valley from Lac du Bourget. A dramatic **château** that sells *Vins de Savoie* stands above **Lucey** with its onion-bulb church. **Jongieux**'s scattering of wine hamlets lie below very steep vineyards. The stunning semicircle of mountains at the back of the **Mont du Chat** acts as a backdrop to **Billième**. **La Chapelle St-Romain** stands on a hillock amid the vines. This wine route is so magically beautiful, the landscapes look like they've been lifted from the background of a great Gothic painting. **Yenne**, its ancestor by the Rhône founded in Roman times, retains its medieval character and arcaded houses. The church conceals intriguing Romanesque and Gothic elements. The town has culinary traditions too, known for its feather-light *Gâteau de Savoie* sponge cake, while its cheese cooperative specializes in organic produce. The **Défilé de Pierre Châtel** leads down to the Rhône, the spectacularly perched **Chartreuse of Pierre Châtel**, built on the site of a fortress of the counts of Savoie, now in private hands, but to be spied on from the GR9 hiking path.

Les Bauges

Although rising between ever so popular Lac d'Annecy and Lac du Bourget, the heavily wooded pre-alpine range of Les Bauges feels lost in time. Huge limestone walls rise around it, protecting its secretive heart. The range was declared a regional nature park in 1995. Woodworking used to be the major craft, *argenterie des Bauges* an ironic name for its once-common tableware, made from wood rather than silver. In cheese terms, *Tome des Bauges* differentiates itself from the rest of this type of Savoyard *fromage*, spelling itself with just one 'm', granted its own *appellation d'origine contrôlée* in 2003. On Les Bauges' eastern side sloping down to the stretch of the Isère valley known as the Combe de Savoie, try some intriguing Savoie wines. The summits above are a protected reserve where ibex and rare flora hide out.

From the southern tip of Lac d'Annecy, you can skirt round the largest peaks via **Faverges** and **Albertville** to follow the **Combe de Savoie**. Or head up from Faverges towards the **Col de Tamié**, **Seythenex** with impressive waterfall plus underground caves (*t 04 50 44 55 97, www.cascade.fr; open May–mid-Sept 10–5.30; adm*). The **abbey of Tamié** (*t 04 79 31 15 50, www.tamie-abbaye.com; open daily 10–12 and 2.30–6*) is a reminder that medieval monks largely oversaw the development of Les Bauges. A shop sells the abbey's cheese, a video presenting the life of the Trappist order here. The **Fort de Tamié** (*t 04 79 32 30 17; open daily 10.30–7; adm*), opposite, was a major piece of French 19th-century frontier building, now taken over by local enthusiasts bringing cultural life to this dramatic defensive spot above the Isère.

Along the **Combe de Savoie**, a steep slope-side road takes you through surprising vineyards. Past **Cléry**, with its well-located Romanesque church, follow the D201. **Grésy's Ecomusée** (*t 04 79 37 94 36, www.perso.wanadoo.fr/lescoteauxdusalin; open Jan–Dec; adm*), in the main area of vineyards, preserves the memory of many local old crafts. The medieval **Château de Miolans** (*t 04 79 28 57 04; open April–Sept daily; adm*) looks forbiddingly down on the confluence of Isère and Arc. The lords who occupied this powerful location were close to the house of Savoie, which inherited it in the 16th century, turning the gift into a prison. The Marquis de Sade was incarcerated here in 1772, but escaped. The slope-side town of **St-Pierre d'Albigny** has retained quaint old wooden shop fronts, a wine route signalling wineries nearby, while the dead end of **Montlambert** attracts paragliders. The impressive **Château de la Rive** by **Cruet** yielded its rare medieval frescoes of knightly tales to the Chambéry history museum. **Arbin** has long been associated with a nice, light red wine, produced from the Mondeuse grape, which developed here. **Montmélian** lies in a dramatic riverside location below the shapely **Roche du Guet**. This strategically located town was once thoroughly fortified. Although its defences were torn down under Louis XIV, it has retained grand houses and is now proud home of the **Musée Régional de la Vigne et du Vin** (*t 04 79 84 42 23; open July–Sept daily exc Mon am and Sun am 9.30–12 and 2–6.30; adm*) covering a couple of millennia of wine-making in Savoie with style.

The wine trail continues along the **Cluse de Chambéry**, a valley left over by a glacier. **Les Marches** has another wine museum, the **Musée du Vigneron** (*t 04 79 28 13 32; open mid-July–Sept daily 2–7, April–mid-July and Oct–Christmas weekends 2–7; adm*), plus the **Moulin de la Tourne** (*t 04 79 28 13 31, Moulin-a-papier.com; open May–Sept daily tours at 3 and 4; mid-Jan–April and Oct–mid-Dec, tour Mon, Wed, Sat and Sun at 4; adm*), a mill still making paper the traditional way. The molar tooth of the **Mont Granier** above marks the northern end of the Chartreuse range (*see* p.274). A huge chunk fell off it in a deluvian rainstorm in 1248. Communities were destroyed, most horrifically St-André, but **Myans** below survived, so the superstitious claimed, thanks to the protection of its Black Virgin. Its church still attracts pilgrims. While the black figure is inside, a gilded 19th-century Virgin stands triumphantly outside. The boulders of the **Abymes de Myans** still act as reminder of the trauma. Rocks sit immovably among the vineyards to **Apremont**, another village synonymous with a distinctive Savoie wine, a white made from the Jacquère grape. The other side of the valley, around **Chignin**, the beautifully located vineyards surveyed by ruined medieval towers make the most reputed local white wines under the *appellations* Chignin and Chignin Bergeron. **St-Jeoire-Prieuré** has a sober church, sole remnant of its priory. **Challes-les-Eaux** became a major medicinal **spa centre** in the 19th century, along with the usual diversionary accoutrements like its plush casino, and is still going strong.

For the straight route from Lac d'Annecy into the centre of the Bauges, head over the dramatic **Montagne du Semnoz**, with splendid views back to Lac du Bourget. Beyond the **Col de Leschaux**, branch off for **Bellecombe-en-Bauges**, with its traditional big farms and 19th-century saw operated by water power. South, walk to the crevasse leap of the **Pont du Diable** (Devil's Bridge). **Lescheraines** lies at an open crossroads practically at the centre of the range, by the fish-rich Chéran river. It has one lake for anglers, another for swimmers. **Le Châtelard**, 'capital' of Les Bauges, has preserved old shop fronts along its narrow main street, craftspeople and an art gallery established here. The 19th-century church proudly presents its own set of murals. Delightful little barns stand out in the fields as you arrive at airier **La Compôte**, hang-gliding a major pull. At **Ecole**, the **Maison Faune et Flore** (*t 04 79 52 22 56, www. pnr-massif-bauges.fr; open late-June–mid-Sept Tues–Sat 10–7, May–late-June and mid-Sept–Oct weekends 1.30–6 ; adm*) presents the natural world of Les Bauges in modern but mellow style. The chocolate maker (*open pm daily*) at **Jarsy** may tempt you there. Up the exceptionally narrow **Vallon de Bellevaux**, a short forest walk leads you to **Notre-Dame de Bellevaux**, a 19th-century chapel on the site of another former medieval monastery.

Back with Lescheraines, a wooded route takes you to pretty **Le Noyer**, home to several good-humoured craftspeople, including a wood turner and the *Sanglier Philosophe* (*Philosophical Wild Boar*) herbalist! The road continues into the cross-country ski domains of **La Féclaz**. A splendid walk takes you from here to the **Croix du Nivolet**, a landmark of a cross way above Chambéry. Climb by car to **Mont Revard** for the most sensational view over the **Lac du Bourget**.

Sticking to the centre of the Bauges, the delectable **Aillon valley** cuts north-south through the heart of the range, lined by sugarloaf mountains. A *Sentier Botanique* at **Aillon-le-Jeune** leads you on a wild orchid trail (*best mid-May–mid-July*). See how the reputed Tome des Bauges is made in the old village's neat **Fruitière-Ecomusée du Val d'Aillon** (*t 04 79 54 60 28; open Jan–Dec daily 9–12 and 3–7.30*). East through the chalet-strewn slopes of Aillon's little ski resort, **La Correrie** with its chapel and ruined façade recall the location of one more of the major medieval monasteries in Les Bauges. A new cultural centre is being planned here.

Lac du Bourget and Aix-les-Bains

For much the most charming little ports on Lac du Bourget (the largest natural lake wholly located in France) explore the havens at its northern end. **Châtillon**'s marina and beach hide in an enchanting spot below a picturesque **castle** (*t 04 79 54 28 15; open mid–April–mid-Nov Wed 2–5; adm*) on a pimple of a hill above. In early medieval times, this château held the key to the lake, which was known as the Lac de Châtillon up to the 13th century – the lordly family then moved to Le Bourget, hence the name change. **Portout** boasts a sweet brand-new marina tucked out of sight from the lake, plus Gallo-Romans pots from its archaeological site displayed in the **Musée des Potiers** (*t 04 79 52 11 84; open July–Aug daily 2.30–6.30, mid-April–June and Sept–mid-Oct Fri–Mon 2.30–5.30; adm*). **Conjux**, in more open position beside the lake, has a beach, and a clutch of professional fishermen still working there. For one of the most breathtaking views over the lake, brave the scary road from **Chaudieu** behind

Châtillon to **La Chambotte's** belvedere, the sight to be enjoyed with calming tea and scones, a tradition maintained here since Queen Victoria's day.

On the west side of the lake, the majestic **Abbaye d'Hautecombe** (*t 04 79 54 26 12, www.chemin-neuf.org/hautecombe; open Jan–Dec daily exc Tues 10–11.15 and 2–5*) looks like a mighty stone vessel about to launch into the waters from its promontory. A Cistercian foundation turned ducal and royal mausoleum, it's now home to the religious *Communauté du Chemin Neuf*. The monastery dates back to 1135. A power-house of Savoie, sending missions to the crusades, two of its abbots became pope in the 13th century, Celestine IV – for just 17 days – and Nicholas III – for slightly longer. In its very prosperous 14th century, a chapel was constructed here to house the tombs of the counts (and later, dukes) of Savoie. Over 40 members of the family would be buried inside, up until the start of the 16th century, when the abbey fell into dire decline. The ruins became a favoured destination for tormented Romantics, most harrowingly the poet Lamartine and his fated love Julie Charles (*see* p.262). Charles-Félix of Savoie had the place sumptuously restored in 19th-century neo-Gothic style by Ernesto Melano, northern Italian artists adding a wealth of sculptures and decorative flourishes, while a religious community was reinstalled. Crammed with Romantic statues and paintings, the church looks more like a celebration of revivalism than a quiet resting place, troubadour style triumphing, but the last king of Italy, Umberto II of the house of Savoie, was buried here as recently as 1983. Go via peaceful, pastoral **St-Pierre-de-Curtille**, with its curiosity of a circular church, for an unforgettable view down Lac du Bourget from the belvedere at **Ontex**.

Southwest, climb to the most distinctive peak overlooking Lac du Bourget, the sharp **Dent du Chat**, or Cat's Tooth. A very silly legend says the name derives from the story of a dishonest fisherman. Desperate at not hooking any fish for some time, he vowed to throw back the first creature he did catch, for luck. But when he landed a big fat pike, he forgot his promise and kept the fish. The next rapid catch surprised him, of a sweet kitten, which he also pocketed, but it grew into a monster that devoured every 20th person to cross its path, and was only killed by a brave soldier who got wise to the pattern. For the best views, walk to the nearby **Molard Noir**.

Below, the sturdy **Château de Bourdeau** (*private*), occupying a great location above a sweet little port, has survived since the medieval period rather better than the centre of **Le Bourget-du-Lac**, but this town's privileged medieval priory still stands, its muddy-green molasse-stone **church** built on the remains of a Roman temple. It contains a colourful 13th-century carved frieze, Christ riding into Jerusalem on a donkey resembling a rabbit. The **priory buildings** (*t 04 79 25 01 99; open July–Aug for guided tours via tourist office; adm*) were converted into a home for an American woman early in the 20th century. The grounds with their irreligious statues of naked ladies are now a public garden. Count Thomas II of Savoie had an important **castle** (*t 04 79 25 01 99, guided tours sometimes possible; adm*) closer to the lake, its ruins being restored to create a cultural centre focusing on Savoie's old forts. Le Bourget's **port** and **lakeside beaches** prove full of life, if somewhat suburban.

A tight road hugs the **east side of Lac du Bourget**, under wooded heights. The lake's main settlement, **Aix-les-Bains**, slopes up from the southeast corner. Beside the waters, you'll find a long **beach**, all manner of boats for cruises, restaurants and rampant urban development. This **port area** is in full expansion, the harbour offering an impressive 1,500 berths. In fact, the town has been awarded the coveted label of *Station Nautique* because of its exceptional facilities for sailing and watersports, the only French harbour not beside the sea to have received the distinction.

The new lakeside developments lies some distance below the old **thermal spa resort**. The hot sulphurous waters here were celebrated by the Celtic Allobroges, then the Romans built splendid baths. Forgotten for a vast period, in the early 1600s Henri IV brought a spark back to the place, while in the 18th century, grand new spa buildings went up. Napoleon's family enjoyed taking the waters, but the best-remembered French visitor was the sickly young Romantic poet Lamartine, who came in October 1816 and met Julie Charles, a young married woman suffering from tuberculosis. They fell madly in love and promised to meet again the following season. But Julie was too ill to make it back, dying before the end of 1817; the forlorn Lamartine immortalized her in his poetry, notably '*Le Lac*', under the name of Elvire.

Another famous visitor to Aix-les-Bains went by the subtle pseudonym of Countess of Balmoral. She was none other than Queen Victoria, and a whole British colony followed in her wake. The Anglo-Saxons didn't mix with the locals, but marked the place with their eccentricities. One story says Victoria was so appalled to see a donkey mistreated, she rescued it, packing it off to Buckingham Palace. Lavish villas and hotels were built for mega-wealthy visitors. The First World War killed the trend for fashionable spa resorts. The generous French health service has kept the place going, but it is now working hard to promote more tempting relaxation treatments.

Central Aix-les-Bains is something of an architectural jumble, but the town retains quite some style, and that curious spa mixture of sickness and celebration. Opposite the mistreated Art Deco facade of the **Thermes Nationaux** stand the remnants of two major Roman monuments, the **Arch of Campanus** and the **Temple of Diana**, with a **Musée Archéologique** (*tours via tourist office; adm*). On the guided tour of the town you're taken inside the rather grim if engrossing **Thermes Nationaux** (specializing in treatments for rheumatism) to peer at the dark remnants of the Roman baths beneath. Peek inside the outrageous **Grand Casino** nearby, opened by King Victor Emmanuel II in 1850. Some of the original mosaics by Salviati and the stained glass are still in place above the fruit machines and their addicts in this outrageous extravaganza, its theatre the first place in France to witness Wagner's *Tristan and Isolde*, in 1897, and still putting on events, not all as highbrow. Close by, the elegant **public gardens** exude a genteel air, Lamartine's statue recalling his tragic connection with the place. Followers of British royalty can pay homage to the severe statue of Victoria on a nearby square, and might seek out the modest English church beyond. Also discover **Place Carnot**, one of Aix-les-Bains' most enchanting squares.

Up the slope, truly palatial former hotels have been turned into apartments. The swanky contemporary **Thermes Chevalley** have also opened on high, catering in part for those in search of luxury treatments, with superb pools. The **Musée Faure** (*t 04 79 61 05 57; open 6 Jan–19 Dec daily 10–12 and 1.30–6; closed Tues and public hols; adm*), set in a grand hillside villa, contains an interesting and unusual selection of

Impressionist works, a bright room of contorted Rodin sculptures looking across to the vicious Mont du Chat, plus some rather miserable memorabilia of Lamartine.

At the southern end of the lake, industry has long triumphed on the flat plain leading to Chambéry, added to by business and research parks. But one corner of the lakeside has recently been spruced up with the landscaped **Site des Mottets** and its **Port des 4 Chemins**, little beaches and facilities for the sports-mad Savoyards on offer, but also explanations on Savoie's lake ecology and reed beds. However, Lac du Bourget having a muddy bottom in contrast to Annecy's sandy one, the waters remain murky.

Chambéry

Regional symbols of Savoie stand out prominently around Chambéry, notably the Savoyard flag, plus a bellicose heraldic black lion, another proud symbol of the house of Savoie. Melodramatic monuments also pay homage to local heroes. The place acquired political importance in the 13th century, suddenly elevated to regional capital. The line of Savoie lords saw to the considerable development of their head-quarters. In 1453 the duke came by a fabulous shroud said to have covered Christ's dead body. Displayed in Chambéry, it drew large numbers of pilgrims. But the expansionist French monarchy was pressing at the gates, briefly taking the place. The dukes moved to Turin for safety, taking their precious shroud with them. However, Chambéry remained an important Savoyard administrative centre, keeping senate and ducal treasury. French troops continued to harrass the place, though. Then, after the 1730s, in which Jean-Jacques Rousseau famously lived here, in the 1740s a Spanish army wrought devastation. Victor-Amédée III had much of the castle rebuilt in grand style. The French came back at the Revolution, making Chambéry capital of the large if shortlived *département du Mont-Blanc*. After Napoleon's defeat, the Savoyards regained control of their territories. Adventurer General Benoît de Boigne avoided the European upheaval altogether, fighting in India, making a considerable fortune there, ploughed back into civic provisions for Chambéry.

The pleasingly compact historic kernel is encased in broad, busy boulevards. If you land in town on the right day, start with a fascinating tour of the huge **castle** of the dukes of Savoie (**t** *04 79 33 42 47, tours organized via tourist office; open July and Aug Mon–Sat for tours at 10.30, 2.30, 3.30 and 4.30, Sept daily tour at 2.30 only, further tours during some hols; adm*), still an administrative city within the city, with a vast *Ancien Régime* front along with its imposing machicolated medieval towers, one with a chamber serving as a school room for the guides to give a Savoie history lesson. The aloof-looking **Sainte Chapelle** is where the 'Turin' shroud once lay. Despite a damaging fire, the chapel preserves fine 16th-century stained glass, even if Christ curiously changes face several times in his story. On certain Saturdays you're allowed up to the **bell-organ loft** perched way on high; and twice on most Saturdays (*at 10.30 and 5.30*), the extraordinary musician here presses the 70 bells into riotous tune.

Place du Château below is overseen by grand mansions and an arresting statue of the de Maistre brothers, passionate Savoyard writers. **Rue de Boigne**, a major arcaded shopping avenue of pink fronts, leads straight as an arrow to Chambéry's most famous monument, topped by Benoît de Boigne. More immediately, take picturesque, stocky **Rue Juiverie** or curving **Rue Basse du Château** to **Place St-Léger**, the most vibrant square in the centre, with its pinkish cobbles and fountains overseen by façades whose wooden shutters bring to mind Alpine chalets. Explore the maze of alleyways off the square, stumbling across *trompe l'œil* decoration, a Chambéry speciality. One end of **Place St-Léger**, **Rue Croix d'Or**, lined with major houses, has a fine selection of shops, continuing along **Rue d'Italie** beyond the fancy 19th-century **theatre**, lit up at night to flattering effect, like much of central Chambéry.

Tucked away in its own square between **Place St-Léger** and **Rue Croix d'Or**, the well-concealed **cathedral** originally formed part of a medieval Franciscan abbey, built in sober style, apart from the Flamboyant Gothic door. But brace yourselves for the dizzying *trompe-l'œil* tracery splashed all over the interior, like the wildest neo-Gothic wallpaper, the 19th-century work of Vicario. Fragments of older wall paintings survive, while the treasury displays beautiful items. The substantial regional museum, the **Musée Savoisien** (*t 04 79 33 44 48; open daily exc Tues and public hols 10–12 and 2–6; adm*), sprawls across the rest of the former monastery, containing displays going back to prehistoric communities settled along Lac du Bourget 3,000 years ago. The Gallo-Roman section includes lots of little finds. One level is devoted to paintings, many connected with the region, the explanations filling in pieces in the jigsaw of Savoyard history. One room displays 13th-century murals ripped from the Château de la Rive – its secular illustrations, including an attack on a castle, are rare in medieval art. Further sections focus on Savoie rural communities and the Second World War.

Wide **Boulevard du Théâtre** leads to the de Boigne column and **Fontaine des Eléphants**, with its serene pachyderms unaware that they've lost their posteriors. **Boulevard de la Colonne** leads to further grandiose buildings, including the **Musée des Beaux-Arts** (*t 04 79 33 75 03; open daily exc Tues and public hols 10–12 and 2–6; adm*). Its Italian collections are particularly rich, a strong reminder of Savoie's connections across the Alps. A few well-known Flemish and French artists also get a look in. In the opposite direction from the de Boigne column, the burly arcaded barracks of the **Carré Curial** have been given a modern makeover, while the striking, striped curves of the **contemporary theatre** next door were designed by architect Mario Botta.

A steep two-mile route leads you into almost unspoilt countryside and the **Maison des Charmettes** (*t 04 79 33 39 44; open daily exc Tues and public hols 10–12 and 2–6, Oct–Mar 10–12 and 2–4.30; adm*), briefly home to Chambéry's most famous 18th-century resident, Jean-Jacques Rousseau, and still surrounded by sloping orchards with mountain views. The deeply confused young Rousseau arrived in Chambéry from Annecy (*see above*) with Madame de Warens, his most important mentor. She found him a job in offices working on the duke's map to establish an equitable tax system, but he resigned to follow his passion for music, which he taught in town. He and Madame de Warens then spent some of their happiest times renting Les Charmettes. Although he suffered a terrible physical attack here, he loved the place and, most importantly, through his voracious studies developed his *'magasin d'idées'*, a store of ideas from which sprang his radical thinking on equality, education, nature, and society's general will, opposed to individual freedom. The simple, faded interiors have

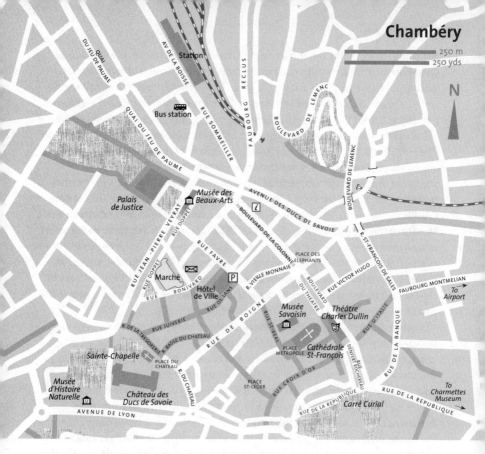

The map shows the following labels:

250 m
250 yds

N

Station
QUAI DU JEU DE PAUME
AV DE LA BOISSE
RUE SOMMEILLER
FAUBOURG RECLUS
BOULEVARD DE LEMENC
Bus station
QUAI DU JEU DE PAUME
RUE DOPPET
Musée des Beaux-Arts
AVENUE DES DUCS DE SAVOIE
BOULEVARD DE LEMENC
Palais de Justice
RUE JEAN-PIERRE VEYRAT
RUE DOPPET
RUE FAVRE
BOULEVARD DE LA COLONNE
PLACE DES ÉLÉPHANTS
R. ST-FRANÇOIS DE SALES
FAUBOURG MONTMELIAN
To Airport
Marché
RUE BONIVARD
Hôtel de Ville
RUE DE LANS
R. VIEILLE MONNAIE
BOULEVARD DU THÉÂTRE
RUE VICTOR HUGO
RUE
RUE DE BOIGNE
RUE ST-RÉAL
Musée Savoisin
Théâtre Charles Dullin
RUE D'ITALIE
RUE DE LA BANQUE
R. DE LA TRÉSORERIE
RUE JUIVERIE
R. BASSE DU CHÂTEAU
Sainte-Chapelle
PLACE DU CHÂTEAU
Cathédrale St-François
PLACE MÉTROPOLE
DENFERT ROCHEREAU
Musée d'Histoire Naturelle
Château des Ducs de Savoie
RUE DU CHÂTEAU
PLACE ST-LÉGER
RUE CROIX D'OR
Carré Curial
RUE DE LA RÉPUBLIQUE
RUE DE LA RÉPUBLIQUE
To Charmettes Museum
AVENUE DE LYON

retained a period charm. A few of his brilliant quotes are presented, but read world-changing works such as *La Nouvelle Héloïse*, *Emile* or *Du Contrat Social* to understand the man credited with bringing the world the rights of man, and damned for creating the creed of the vilest totalitarian regimes. Or try his autobiography, *Les Confessions*, a spanking good read. Rousseau has gone down as a champion of the Alps, seeing in them a reflection of awesome divine power, foreshadowing the Romantics.

Lac d'Aiguebelette and Avant-Pays Savoyard

Moving to more tranquil waters via the dramatic **Col de l'Epine** pass, charming **Lac d'Aiguebelette** lies discreetly west of Chambéry. Little boathouses line its reedy sides, and fishermen make the most of the exceptional catches. In summer, Aiguebelette has the warmest waters of the big lakes for bathing, although you have to pay for most of the **beaches**. Consider cycling the relatively unstrenuous 17km round the whole lake; for example, beside the Nances motorway exit, hire **bikes** at **Vertes Sensations** (*t 04 79 28 77 08 or 06 15 20 81 87, www.vertes-sensations.com*) – it also organizes canoeing, *via ferrata* and paragliding. The east bank road sticks to the lake, unlike the western one, but from there you look across to the spectacular **Montagne**

de l'Epine – walk to this summit along the GR9A trail. Down below the **Château de Chambost**, beautiful, restful restaurant terraces cluster on the southern waterside, looking out to the two lake islands. The mean local Christian legend has it that Jesus visited a town that once stood here, knocked at every door for charity, but was turned away by all except the poorest old woman. By way of punishment, he drowned the place, bar the hillocks on which the houses of the old woman and her daughter stood.

Beyond Lac d'Aiguebelette, the beautiful border land of the **Avant-Pays Savoyard**, once disputed territory, is now most calming, with far more cows than people, producing mountains of Emmenthal and Tomme de Savoie. North of Aiguebelette, **Novalaise** has one of the most significant cheese cooperatives. Stop at the **Col de la Crusille** for mesmerizing views down on the Dauphiné, the ruins of the **Château de Montbel** a tempting destination for walkers. The nearby ruined **Château de Rochefort** retains memories of one of the most notorious smugglers in this frontier zone, 18th-century Louis Mandrin. To confound the authorities, he supposedly even shoed his horses back-to-front! He was caught at this castle, and executed in Valence. Close to the **Col du Banchet**, the **Grottes de Dullin** were caves where Mandrin hid merchandise and arms. The listed church at **Dullin** hides enticing features.

Down on the flats, seek out the **Château de Montfleury** (*t 04 76 32 92 71, July–Aug daily 1–6, May–June and Sept weekends and public hols 2–6; adm*), somewhat neglected by time, its 13th-century tower and *Ancien Régime* wings having served 30 years as a holiday home. It was then taken over by a painter-cum-collector who has crammed it with his brash works and a massive display of objects, most impressive of which are the weapons and armour. To the north, the village of **St-Maurice-de-Rotherens** lies below **Mont Tournier**, highpoint of the frontier **Pays de Guiers**. Climb to the ruined medieval castle for majestic views. The cute little **Musée de la Radio Galletti** (*t 04 76 31 76 38; open July–Aug Mon, Thurs and weekends 3–6, May–June and Sept Sun 3–6; adm*) tells the story of a pioneering 20th-century engineer here.

The fish-rich frontier **Guiers river** joins the Rhône close to picturesque **St-Genix-sur-Guiers**, bits of its medieval ramparts still standing. The town's name is linked to a slightly sickly cake, *brioche de St-Genix*, deliberately breast-shaped, in honour of the 3rd-century Sicilian martyr Agatha, whose legend has it that she had her breasts cut off by cruel Romans for her faith – but they grew back. The figure was adopted in Savoie once the dukes had also become kings of Sardinia (*see p.14*). Watch out for the sweet, crunchy red lumps of praline in the brioche. South, **Le Pont-de-Beauvoisin** consists of two competitive, colourful towns mirroring each other either side of the Guiers, known for *chocolatiers* and furniture makers. The D921 via **Attignat-Oncin** with its rare traditional tanner (*t 04 79 36 00 26; open July–Aug tours Wed at 4, Sat at 3; adm*) leads south towards the stunning, daunting walls of the Chartreuse range.

Pre-Alpine Ranges

From Chartreuse to Vercors

The Isère Valley below the Western Belledonne 269
The Chartreuse Range 274
Grenoble 276
The Drac, Matheysine and Trièves 280
The Vercors Range 282

18

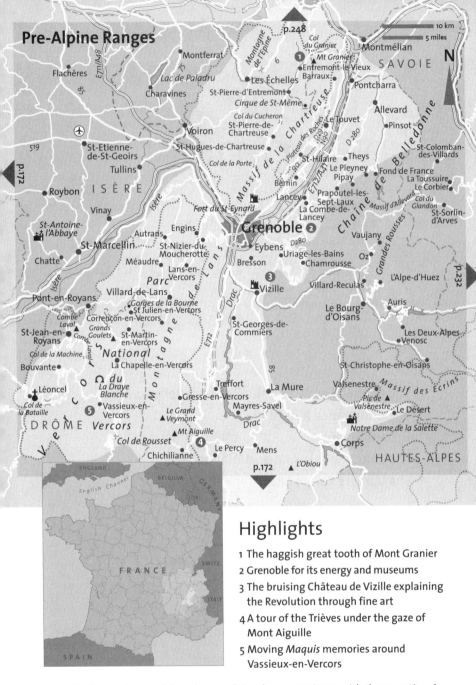

Pre-Alpine Ranges

Montferrat · Lac de Paladru · Charavines · Les Échelles · St-Pierre-d'Entremont · Cirque de St-Même · Col du Granier · Mt Granier · Entremont-le-Vieux · Barraux · Montmélian · SAVOIE · Pontcharra · Allevard · Pinsot · St-Colomban-des-Villards

Flachères · Voiron · St-Etienne-de-St-Geoirs · Tullins · Roybon · Vinay · St-Antoine-l'Abbaye · St-Marcellin · Chatte · Pont-en-Royans · Combe Laval · St-Jean-en-Royans · Bouvante · Léoncel · Col de la Bataille · DRÔME

Col du Cucheron · St-Pierre-de-Chartreuse · St-Hugues-de-Chartreuse · Col de la Porte · Le Touvet · St-Hilaire · Theys · Le Pleyney · Pipay · Fond de France · La Toussuire · Le Corbier · Col du Glandon · St-Sorlin-d'Arves

Fort du St-Eynard · Engins · Autrans · St-Nizier-du-Moucherotte · Méaudre · Lans-en-Vercors · Villard-de-Lans · Gorges de la Bourne · St-Julien-en-Vercors · Corrençon-en-Vercors · Grands Goulets · St-Martin-en-Vercors · La Chapelle-en-Vercors · La Draye Blanche · Vassieux-en-Vercors · Le Grand Veymont · Mt Aiguille · Col de Rousset · Chichilianne · Le Percy · Mens · L'Obiou

Grenoble · Bernin · Lancey · Prapoutel-les-Sept-Laux · La Combe-de-Lancey · Eybens · Bresson · Uriage-les-Bains · Chamrousse · Vizille · Villard-Reculas · Oz · Vaujany · L'Alpe-d'Huez · Auris · Le Bourg-d'Oisans · Les Deux-Alpes · Venosc · St-Christophe-en-Oisans · Valsenestre · Pic de Valsenestre · Le Désert · Notre Dame de la Salette · Corps · HAUTES-ALPES

St-Georges-de-Commiers · Treffort · Gresse-en-Vercors · Mayres-Savel · La Mure

Parc National du Vercors · Montagne de Lans · Isère · Drac

p.248 · p.172 · p.232 · p.172

10 km · 5 miles

Highlights

1 The haggish great tooth of Mont Granier
2 Grenoble for its energy and museums
3 The bruising Château de Vizille explaining the Revolution through fine art
4 A tour of the Trièves under the gaze of Mont Aiguille
5 Moving *Maquis* memories around Vassieux-en-Vercors

South of Savoie's great lakes, the pre-alpine drama continues with the sensational jagged ramparts of the Chartreuse and Vercors ranges, making up the mountainous, forested eastern half of the Dauphiné. Sandwiched between them, the historic capital of that former province, ever-expanding Grenoble, has squeezed out all over the big, flat crossroads of the Isère and Drac valleys. Not just Chartreuse and Vercors stand guard over the city – the Belledonne forms a massive snowy barrier to the east. The location is stunning, but then so is the whole of this area, even if its mountain roads count among the most daunting in France.

The Belledonne's western slopes (for the eastern side, *see* p.245) offer small ski domains in winter, and a narrow balcony of a tourist route in summer, with splendid walks to stunning high lakes. While this range is topped by traditional triangular Alpine peaks, amazing huge molar-shaped mountains mark the pre-alpine ones. Either end of the Chartreuse, the Mont Granier and Dent de Crolles match each other in haggish grandeur. The name Chartreuse may conjure up images of perilously potent monkish brews in poisonous green and yellow. But the most important historical fact is that the Chartreuse (or Carthusian) order of monks was created here in the 11th century by St Bruno, a medieval model for a tough life of work and prayer.

Grenoble, host of the Winter Olympics in 1968, may have the image of an ultra-modern city, but it also turns out to have a fantastic historic legacy. Drink in the past, and the studenty present, in the café- and restaurant-lined streets. The place is crammed with truly excellent museums. South, the Château de Vizille, built for the Dauphiné's great *Ancien Régime* Protestant leader, Lesdiguières, is now home to an engrossing museum tracing the French Revolution through art – there are claims that significant early revolutionary rumblings were heard in these parts. Vizille also lies along the Route Napoléon, recalling the *petit caporal*'s final desperate bid to reclaim power in Paris, coming over from his exile on Elba in 1815 on a last wave of popular support. This road cuts through the Matheysine, on the east bank of the Drac, a precipitous railway line above the river built expressly to carry coal from this beautiful former mining land. The other side of the Drac, the calmly gorgeous Trièves is overseen on one side by the dramatic Obiou, on the other by the Mont Aiguille, the latter perhaps the most photogenic of all France's pre-alpine molar-toothed tops, and linked to some of the earliest adventures in mountaineering.

Mont Aiguille is just one of the many extremely challenging peaks of the Vercors. From whichever side you approach this formidable natural fort, the roads to it are hair-raising. On high, you reach gentle plateaux dotted with small, open resorts, the pastures carpeted with the densest flora from late spring. But in these parts, many villages preserve terrible memories of the Second World War, when the Germans mounted a full-scale offensive to root out the Resistance fighters here. Some hid in the Vercors' huge caves, but not in the most spectacular, the Grottes de Choranche. The Vercors ends in the south with head-spinning drops into the Drôme valley.

The Isère Valley below the Western Belledonne

Overseen by the Chartreuse's massive teeth to the west and the Belledonne's almost eternally snow-tipped peaks to the east, this stretch of the Isère from Pontcharra to Grenoble offers a remarkably flat route in these tortured mountainous parts. It's known by the name of the **Grésivaudan**, the valley of Grenoble. In 1960, the

Getting Around

By air: Grenoble-St-Geoirs airport (t 04 76 65 48 48) lies *c.* 40km northwest of the city.

By train: Grenoble, hub of public transport for this chapter, is just under 3hrs from Paris-Gare de Lyon. Ordinary trains between Grenoble and Lyon take *c.* 2hrs.

By bus: From Grenoble, **Cars VFD** (t 08 20 83 38 33, *www.vfd.fr*) serve most directions with reasonable bus services.

Tourist Information

For general information on the Chartreuse range, try the **Association de Développement Touristique de Chartreuse**, t 04 76 88 64 00, *www.chartreuse-tourisme.com* or the **Maison du Parc**, 38380 St-Pierre-de-Chartreuse, t 04 76 88 75 20, *www.parc-chartreuse.net*.

For general information on the Vercors, contact the **Association pour le Développement Touristique du Vercors**, t 04 76 95 15 99, *www.adt-vercors.com*.

Pontcharra: 21 Rue Laurent Gayet, 38530 Pontcharra, t 04 76 97 68 08, e *ot.haut-gresivaudan@wanadoo.fr*.

Allevard: Place de la Résistance, 38580 Allevard, t 04 76 45 10 11, e *office@allevard-les-bains.com*.

Les Sept-Laux: Les Cortillets, 38190 Les Sept-Laux, t 04 76 08 17 86, e *station@les7laux.com*.

Uriage: 5 Ave des Thermes, 38410 Uriage, t 04 76 89 10 27, e *info@uriage-les-bains.fr*.

St-Hilaire-du-Touvet: 102 Route des 3 Villages, 38660 St-Hilaire-du-Touvet, t 04 76 08 33 99, e *o.t.st-hilaire-du-touvet@wanadoo.fr*.

St-Pierre-d'Entremont: 73670 St-Pierre-d'Entremont, t 04 79 65 81 90, e *ot.entremonts@wanadoo.fr*.

Les Echelles: Rue Stendhal, 73360 Les Echelles, t 04 79 36 56 24, *www.chartreuse-tourisme.com*.

St-Pierre-de-Chartreuse: 38380 St-Pierre-de-Chartreuse, t 04 76 88 62 08, *www.st-pierre-chartreuse.com*.

Grenoble: 14 Rue de la République, 38019 Grenoble, t 04 76 42 41 41, *www.grenoble-isere-tourisme.com*.

Vizille: Place du Château, 38220 Vizille, t 04 76 68 15 16, e *info@ot-vizille.com*.

La Mure: 43 Rue de Breuil, 38350 La Mure, t 04 76 81 05 71, e *tourisme.lamure@wanadoo.fr*.

Mens: Rue du Breuil, 38710 Mens, t 04 76 34 84 25, e *ot.mens@wanadoo.fr*.

Lans-en-Vercors: Place de la Mairie, 38250 Lans-en-Vercors, t 04 76 95 42 62, *www.ot-lans-en-vercors.fr*.

Autrans: Route de Méaudre, 38880 Autrans, t 04 76 95 30 70, *www.ot-autrans.fr*.

Méaudre: Le Village, 38112 Méaudre, t 04 76 95 20 68, *www.meaudre.com*.

Villard-de-Lans: 105 Chemin de la Patinoire, 38250 Villard-de-Lans, t 04 76 95 10 38, *www.ot-villard-de-lans.fr*.

Corrençon-en-Vercors: Place du Village, 38250 Corrençon-en-Vercors, t 04 76 95 81 75, *www.ot-correncon.fr*.

La Chapelle-en-Vercors: Place Piétri, 26420 La Chapelle-en-Vercors, t 04 75 48 22 54, e *ot.vercors@wanadoo.fr*.

river was canalized to put a stop to its impetuous mood swings, also letting cereals grow on the flats. On the safer slopes, walnuts, fruit trees, vines and cattle have traditionally shared the meagre space. But industry early took firm root too.

Pontcharra, in the border territory with Savoie, was the birthplace of Pierre Terrail, lord of Bayard, portrayed in the heroic version of French history as the ideal chevalier, *sans peur et sans reproche* (beyond fear or reproach), who valiantly served megalomaniac François I, even knighting the royal after his triumph at Marignano in Italy in 1516. The **Musée Bayard** in the **Château Bayard** (*t 04 76 97 68 08; open May–Sept daily exc Tues 2–6; adm*) above town relates his story. As to the landmark **Tour d'Avalon**, it recalls the 12th-century Carthusian Hugues d'Avalon, who went off to become Bishop of Lincoln and serve King Henry II of England. Up the Bens river, on the border between Dauphiné and Savoie, lay an outpost of the Grande Chartreuse, the **Chartreuse de St-Hugon**.

Vassieux-en-Vercors: Av du Mémorial,26420
Vassieux-en-Vercors, t 04 75 48 27 40.

Market Days

Grenoble: Daily exc Mon.
Allevard: Thurs morning.
Mens: Sat morning, plus Wed morning in
summer
Autrans: Wed morning.
Méaudre: Tues morning.
La Mure: Mon morning.
La Chapelle-en-Vercors: Thurs morning, plus
Sat morning in summer.

Where to Stay and Eat

Le Touvet ✉ 38660

Fontrier B&B, 81 Rue de la Charrière, Le Pré
Carré, t 04 76 08 42 30, f 04 76 08 56 43
(*inexpensive*). Pretty old-stone 18th-century
farm with charming rooms.

St-Pierre-d'Entremont ✉ 73670

**Hostellerie du Château de Montbel, t 04 79
65 81 65, f 04 79 65 89 49 (*inexpensive*).
Pleasant traditional village inn serving excellent food (*moderate*). *Closed Nov–mid-Dec;
restaurant closed Sun eve and Mon in low
season.*
**Chalet du Cirque de St-Même, t/f 04 79 65
89 28, *www.chalet-hotel.com* (*inexpensive*).
Modern, but in the local style, close to
superb natural sight, plus decent regional
cuisine (*cheap*).

St-Pierre-de-Chartreuse ✉ 38380

***Beau Site, t 04 76 88 61 34, **e** *hotel.beausite
@libertysurf.fr* (*moderate*). Good option in a
village with a number of pretty hotels.
Restaurant (*moderate*). Pool. *Closed
April–early May and mid-Oct– mid-Dec;
restaurant closed Sun pm, Mon and Tues.*
Pirraud B&B Pré Montagnat, t 04 76 88 65 44
(*inexpensive*). Stylish new chalet, traditional
style. *Table d'hôte* (*cheap*).

Grenoble ✉ 38000

****Park Hôtel, 10 Place Paul Mistral, t 04 76
85 81 23, *www.park-hotel-grenoble.fr* (*luxury–
very expensive*). Looking on to a picturesque
park, the luxury, quite central option. Refined
restaurant (*expensive–moderate*). *Closed
most Aug; restaurant closed weekend lunch.*
***Hôtel d'Angleterre, 5 Place Victor Hugo,
t 04 76 87 37 21, *www.hotel-angleterre.fr*
(*expensive*). Businesslike, opposite a busy
garden square . Some rooms with spa baths.
**L'Europe, 22 Place Grenette, t/f 04 76 46
16 94, **e** *hotel.europe.gre@wanadoo.fr*
(*inexpensive*). Good central location, in a
Haussmann-style block with wrought-iron
decoration but modern rooms.
L'Escalier, 6 Place Lavalette, t 04 76 54 66 16
(*expensive*). Excellent restaurant in characterful house close to the art museum,
serving classic French cuisine. *Closed Sat
lunch, Sun, and Mon lunch.*
Auberge Napoléon, 7 Rue Montorge, t 04 76 87
53 64 (*expensive*). Stylish little restaurant
where the Emperor once ate, by the central
garden. *Closed Sun and all lunchtimes exc*

Little remains of the 12th-century establishment, but the setting is awesome. The
Buddhist retreat now established here received the Dalai Lama in 1997.

Pressing into the Belledonne range, **Allevard** grew into a curious mix of steel town
and spa town, the mining past recalled at the **Musée Jadis Allevard** (*t 04 76 45 16 40;
open April–Oct daily exc Tues 10–12 and 3–6; adm*), and in a marked trail leading out of
town, the spa life and casino just about hanging on – in its heyday the place received
many celebrities. Gateway to the **Bréda valley**, the countryside around Allevard teems
with wild orchids. The villages up the valley have preserved their old character, **Pinsot**
holding on to its metal and milling traditions with the **Musée des Forges et Moulins**
(*t 04 76 13 53 59, www.membres.lycos.fr/forgesmoulins; open April–Sept Wed–Sun
10–12.30 and 2–5; adm*). The name of **Fond-de-France** acts as a reminder that this was
frontier territory with Savoie up to the mid-19th century. It's now a good point of

Sat, plus early Jan, early May and late Aug–early Sept.

La Voile Blanche, 4 Rue Pierre Duclot, t 04 76 44 22 62 (moderate). Fine regional cuisine at a reasonable price, plus a terrace. Closed Sun.

Le 5, Place Lavalette, t 04 76 63 22 12 (moderate). Trendy spot for light but lively lunch in the museum. Closed Tues.

Eybens ✉ 38320

★★★Château de la Commanderie, 17 Av d'Echirolles, t 04 76 25 34 58, e resa@ commanderie.fr (expensive–moderate). Little castle in lovely grounds just south of Grenoble. Terrace for summer dining (expensive). Pool. Closed late Dec–early Jan; restaurant closed Sat lunch, Sun pm and Mon.

Bresson ✉ 38320

★★★★Chavant, t 04 76 25 25 38, e chavant@ chateauxhotels.com (expensive). Reputable family hotel in sweet village south of town. Great restaurant (expensive), garden, pool. Restaurant closed Sat lunch, Sun pm and Mon.

Uriage ✉ 38410

★★★★Grand Hôtel, Place D.S. Hygie, t 04 76 89 10 80, e grandhotel.fr@wanadoo.fr (very expensive–expensive). A very grand Second Empire establishment with modern hydrotherapy centre and fabulous restaurant, Les Terrasses (very expensive). Closed Jan; restaurant closed July–Aug Wed, and Thurs lunch, rest of year Sun, Mon, and all lunchtimes exc Fri and Sat, plus late Aug.

Vizille ✉ 38220

★★★Château de Cornage, Chemin des Peupliers, t 04 76 68 28 00 (moderate). Bourgeois house in the Cornage hillside area north of the centre, plus fine cuisine (expensive–moderate). Restaurant closed Sun eve.

Le Percy ✉ 38930

Les Volets Bleus B&B, Hameau des Blancs, t 04 76 34 43 07 (inexpensive). Intense Trièves pleasures at this picturesque former farming property. Vaulted room for table d'hôte (cheap). Closed Nov–Easter.

Mens ✉ 38710

L'Engrangeou B&B, Place de la Halle, t 04 76 34 85 63 (inexpensive). Tasteful rooms above art gallery by the market. Table d'hôte (cheap).

Chichilianne ✉ 38930

★★Château de Passières, t 04 76 34 45 48, f 04 76 34 46 25 (inexpensive). Enchanting medieval castle with relaxed style and interesting art. A real find. Restaurant (moderate). Pool. Closed Oct; restaurant closed Sun eve and Mon out of season.

Sauze B&B, Ruthières, t/f 04 76 34 45 98 (inexpensive). Spacious rooms in a traditional farm in a hamlet 3km from main village. Table d'hôte in old barn (cheap).

Villard-de-Lans ✉ 38250

★★★Le Christiania, Av Prof Nobecourt, t 04 76 95 12 51, e hotel-le-christiania (expensive–moderate). Big modern family-run chalet with well-furnished rooms, many with private balconies. Gastronomic cuisine

departure for summer walks through the Massif d'Allevard to many spectacular high lakes (hence the additional name for the area of Les Sept Laux) and high passes . Geologists say the Belledonne peaks count among the oldest rocks in France, perhaps dating back 700 million years. Thousands of sheep congregate at the **Combe Madame** for summer grazing. The valley road turns up to the little ski station of **Le Pleyney**, one of the three making up the Belledonne ski terrain of **Les Sept-Laux** (see p.331).

Snaking along the mid slopes above the Isère between Allevard and Uriage, the D280 road is known as the Belledonne's **Route des Balcons**, twisting and turning through steep orchards, the odd vineyard below, sharp snowy peaks above. The village of **Theys** has preserved traditional architecture. Branch off for **Prapoutel** and **Pipay**, the two other resorts of Les Sept-Laux. Beyond these, the most uplifting way to appreciate the western Belledonne is to walk the GR549, passing by magical high lakes, and

(moderate). Covered pool. *Closed mid-April–mid-May and late Sept–mid-Dec; restaurant closed weekday lunchtimes outside holidays.*
Villa Primerose, 147 Av des Bains, **t 04 76 95 13 17, *www.hotel-villa-primerose.com* *(inexpensive)*. Charming bargain hotel. *Closed late April and Oct–mid-Dec.*

Corrençon-en-Vercors ✉ 38250
***Hôtel du Golf, **t** 04 76 95 84 84, *www.planete-vercors.com/hotel-du-golf* *(expensive)*. Smart. Restaurant *(moderate)*. Pool. *Closed April–early May and mid-Oct–mid-Dec; restaurant closed Sun eve and Mon outside main hols, plus lunchtimes Mon–Thurs in low season.*

St-Julien-en-Vercors ✉ 26420
***Domaine de Piache, Hameau de Piache, **t** 04 75 45 51 83, *www.traditional-legend.com/piache.htm* *(inexpensive)*. Calm beautiful retreat in traditional farm 1km from the village. Restaurant serving organic produce *(moderate)*. Archery available.

La Chapelle-en-Vercors ✉ 26420
Bellier, Av de Provence, **t 04 75 48 20 03, **f** 04 75 48 25 31 *(cheap)*. Chalet with spacious rooms with balconies. Alpine-style restaurant *(moderate)*. *Closed Nov–April; restaurant closed Tues eve and Wed out of season.*
Hôtel des Sports, Av des Grands Goulets, **t 04 75 48 20 39, *www.hotel-des-sports.com* *(cheap)*. Nice and simple. Restaurant *(moderate–cheap)*. *Closed late-Nov–Jan; restaurant closed Sun eve and Mon.*

St-Agnan-en-Vercors ✉ 26420
Auberge Le Veymont, Place du Village, **t** 04 75 48 20 19, **e** *leveymont@wanadoo.fr* *(inexpensive)*. Nice mountain feel to the simple rooms and restaurant *(moderate)*. *Closed mid-Mar–late April and late-Sept–Christmas.*

Vassieux-en-Vercors ✉ 26420
Auberge du Tetras Lyre, Rue Abbé Gagnol, **t 04 75 48 28 04, **e** *j.davion1@libertysurf.fr* *(inexpensive)*. Welcoming simple village chalet, rooms with balconies. Restaurant *(moderate–cheap)* putting the accent on local cuisine. *Closed mid-Nov–mid-Dec.*

Lente ✉ 26190
Hôtel de la Forêt, **t 04 75 48 26 32, *www.hotel-de-la-foret.com* *(inexpensive)*. Lost in the countryside. Very simple rooms, warm welcome and themed weekends, Good dishes *(moderate)* *Closed most Jan and Dec; restaurant closed Mon eve and Tues out of season.*

Col de la Machine ✉ 26190
Hôtel du Col de la Machine, at the pass, **t 04 75 48 26 36, *www.vercors.com/hotel-col-de-la-machine* *(inexpensive)*. Appealing family hotel. Excellent regional cooking *(moderate)*. Pool. *Closed mid-Nov–mid-Dec; restaurant closed Sun eve and Mon in low season.*

Bouvante ✉ 26190
*Auberge du Pionnier, Col du Pionnier, **t** 04 75 48 57 12, **f** 04 75 48 58 26 *(inexpensive)*. Simple rustic retreat beside a forest. Tasty country cooking *(moderate)*. *Closed Tues.*

peaks almost reaching 3,000m. A daring engineer, Aristide Bergès, found a way of raising **Lac du Crozet** higher in the 19th century, all the better to exploit it for *houille blanche*, white coal, or hydroelectric power. This was a major advance in turning the water power of the Alps into electricity. Bergès is honoured at the **Musée de la Houille Blanche** (being renovated) at **Lancey** back down beside the Isère. Above, once again on the Route des Balcons, the diminutive **Musée Rural d'Arts et Traditions Populaires** (**t** *04 76 71 48 09; open all year, by appointment only; adm*) at **La Combe-de-Lancey** offers an insight into peasant life in the Belledonne range alongside the village castle, its gardens accessible via the museum, offering particularly fine views across the valley. The D280 draws squiggles around the slopes east of Grenoble to land up at the still elegant old valley spa resort of **Uriage**. Between the two wars, it attracted glamorous literati, such as Gide and Colette, the latter one of several authors to feature the town under a thin literary disguise. **Chamrousse** far above counts among the very earliest ski resorts in France (*see p.330*).

Following the west bank of the Isère through the Grésivaudan, the N90 paralleling the motorway is rather industrial and commercial. Find the smaller roads above the hubbub to appreciate splendid vistas onto the Belledonne. By **Barraux**, a **fort** (*t 04 76 85 16 15 for details on tours*) was ordered by Duke Charles-Emmanuel I of Savoie at the close of the 16th century, but Protestant Lesdiguières secured it for the Dauphiné in 1598. It conserves terrible more recent memories as an internment camp during the world wars. **Ste-Marie-d'Alloix** is dedicated to the happier production of decent white wine, **La Flachère** to pottery. The **Château du Touvet** (*t 04 76 08 42 27, www.touvet. com; open mid-April–Oct daily exc Sat 2–6; adm*), a proudly family-owned manor in the Dauphiné style, boasts most elegant formal French gardens in a sensational setting. Take the D29, or a **cable car** from **Montfort** (*t 04 76 08 00 02; runs April–mid-Dec; adm*) that will whisk you up from the noisy valley to the otherworldly mid-slope **Plateau des Petites Roches**, beloved of hang-gliders, but also an uplifting spot for walkers, under the dramatic southern Chartreuse's Dent de Crolles. The views are stunning, reaching as far as Mont Blanc. **Bernin** below has held on to its vineyards. The comically named **Cascade de la Pissarole** along with the highly picturesque towers of the equally silly sounding **Manor of Craponoz** (*not open*) are tucked away in an enchanting spot.

The Chartreuse Range

The previous section skirted round the eastern side of the Chartreuse mountains. To the west, you can also avoid taking on this vicious range by following the main road from Chambéry to Voiron. While you can cower below the terrifying grandeur of the Chartreuse's limestone teeth along these routes, you can't get close to the hushed culture at the heart of the range. Here we accept the challenge of the central route through the Chartreuse. As its name indicates, the **Entremont** (Between the Mountains) **valley** cuts quite neatly through the middle, but to reach it from Chambéry you have to climb a formidable mountain road to the **Col du Granier**, wonderful glimpses on offer back down onto the Lac du Bourget. The awesome molar of **Mont Granier** towers over the north end of the range. In a cave below the summit, a huge cache of bears' bones was recently discovered. The reasons for this high spot of hibernation over many millennia are nicely explained at the new **Musée de l'Ours** (*t 04 79 26 29 87; open July–Aug daily exc Tues 10–12.30 and 3–7; May–June and Sept open pm only; rest of year open weekday pm, but closed weekends; adm*) in **Entremont-le-Vieux**, a cheese cooperative close by.

St-Pierre-d'Entremont, overseen by the ruins of the medieval **Château de Montbel** with their beautiful views along the Entremont valley, is the tourist nub of the Chartreuse, which was declared a regional nature park in 1995. The tourist office doubles as a **Relais du Parc**, presenting a brief overview of the range and its sights, and has a good craft shop, local herbs also on sale. To the east, the **Cirque de St-Même** (*May–1st week Sept parking charge and restricted numbers*) ends in a theatrical dead end of mountains named after a hermit who hid out here. Count an hour and a half for the walk round to the spectacular waterfalls, sources of the Guiers-Vif river.

You can reach the **Grottes des Echelles** (*t 04 79 36 65 95, www.animgrotte.fr; open mid-June–mid-Sept daily 10–5.30; Easter–mid-June and mid-Sept–Oct weekends and public hols 10–4.30; adm*) on the Chartreuse's western edge either by a very tortuous mountain road from Entremont-le-Vieux, or via the **Gorges du Guiers Vif** from St-Pierre-d'Entremont. To discover the two long narrow caves, you need to walk down a small canyon of a stone path, this *Voie Sarde* leading out of the Chartreuse dating back to Roman times. The folk hero of these parts, the smuggler Mandrin, has gone down in legend as a kind of *Ancien Régime* Robin Hood. The concretions in the second cave include some surprising natural phallic forms! At the end of the trail you emerge in the midst of a cliff with painterly views of the Avant-Pays Savoyard (*see* p.266).

Head for the southern half of the Chartreuse range via the **Col du Cucheron**. **St-Pierre-de-Chartreuse** consists of a scattering of countless charming hamlets on steep slopes, including a little ski resort. The village of **St-Hugues-de-Chartreuse** lies contentedly in a more open valley. The church, converted into a **Musée Départemental d'Art Sacré Contemporain** (*t 04 76 88 65 01, www.arcabas.com; open daily exc Tues 9–6; adm*), contains an intriguing cycle of paintings and decorations, the work of the artist Arcabas, who came here to work on three separate occasions, in 1952, 1973 and 1985. The display ends with the superb drama of the Last Supper.

You can't visit the **Couvent de la Grande Chartreuse**, headquarters of the Carthusian order of monks, and hidden away in its own circle of mountains, by foot. It's only visible from afar, but you can get an excellent picture of the order's history and punishing monastic life at the **Musée de la Grande Chartreuse** at **La Correrie** (*t 04 76 88 60 45, www.chartreux.org; open July–Aug daily 9.30–6.30, May–June and Sept daily 9.30–12 and 12–6.30; April and Oct daily 10–12 and 2–6; adm*) west of St-Pierre-de-Chartreuse, in a beautiful set of buildings constructed for the lay brothers. The story began when saint Bruno founded his strict order in 1084, along with six companions. Prior Guigues wrote down the statues in 1127. While the monks were devoted to a strict life of study and meditation, the lay brothers busied themselves with hard labour and mastered many crafts, including iron-working. The monks didn't live in abject conditions; you can visit their typical double-levelled cells at La Correrie. The Grande Chartreuse itself, to be admired in photos here, took on its magnificent forms, with its fine array of roofs and towers, when it was rebuilt after a fire in 1676. Banished at the Revolution, the Carthusians only returned to France and the Chartreuse range in 1940. Visitors are now encouraged to follow the example of the monks' search for peace and go on a walk in a valley beyond La Correrie designated a *zone de silence*.

For a very challenging walk reflecting the high drama of the Chartreuse , try the exhilarating way to the **Belvédère des Sangles**. South via the **Col de la Porte**, it's not such a difficult path up through meadows to **Charmant Som**, one of the best viewing platforms in the whole range. The **Fort du St-Eynard**, one of a rash of dramatic forts built by the French military after the disastrous rout by the Germans in the Franco-

Prussian war of 1870, stands in near-suicidal position at the southern tip of the Chartreuse. The precipitous view down on to Grenoble induces vertigo.

Grenoble

Encircled by such sensationally jagged mountain ranges, set at its flat junction of valleys leading off towards Savoie and Switzerland to the north, Provence and Italy to the south, and the Rhône Valley to the west, Grenoble was an obvious location for the commercial, cultural and intellectual capital of the Dauphiné region to grow. Unfairly burdened with a reputation for being uncompromisingly modern and industrial, it turns out to be a cosmopolitan place, with wonderful squares, and as many museums as there are months of the year, recalling its fascinating history.

Grenoble's Gallo-Roman predecessor was insignificant compared to magnificent Vienne on the Rhône (*see* p.155), under whose authority it lay, but by the 3rd century it was surrounded by substantial oval walls. Christianity got an early footing, as you can still see at the church of St-Laurent. In the medieval period, the bishops battled with local lords to oversee the city. The mighty counts of Albon took control. It was one of their number, Guigues IV, who was given the name of Dauphin (Dolphin), adopted by his descendants, the region they ruled becoming known as the Dauphiné. Dauphin

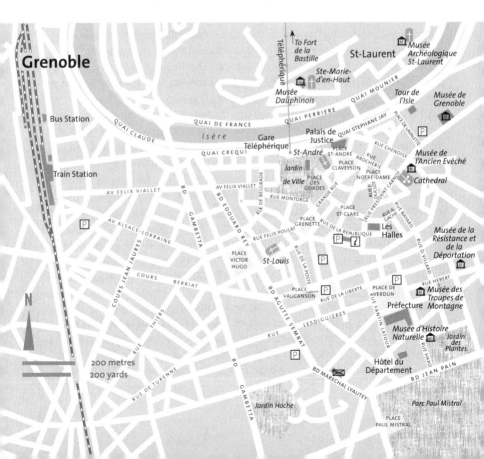

Humbert II established his council and treasury at Grenoble. Humbert created a university, but tragically overstretched himself, and was forced to sell the region – so French king Philippe V bought the Dauphiné in 1349, giving it to his eldest son. From that time on, the heir to the French throne would be known as the Dauphin. Only one, the future Louis XI, truly ruled the region before becoming monarch; it was he who created the Dauphiné *Parlement* or law courts in 1453.

The 16th-century Wars of Religion caused bitter fighting in the region, the fanatical Catholic Baron des Adrets wreaking devastation. But the leading Protestant Lesdiguières put his stamp firmly on Grenoble, securing it in 1590 on behalf of King Henri IV, extending the ramparts, ruling the place with firmness and defending the Dauphiné against Savoie. The Catholic Church hit back in the 17th century by building religious communities around town. However, in this period the city's merchants, and its libertines, also prospered. Despite its image of aristocratic elegance, as the *Ancien Régime* cracked up, Grenoble flared up. The celebrated *Journée des Tuiles* of 7 June 1788 was named after a riot in town brought about by the monarchy's attempt to close France's regional *Parlements*; protesters threw tiles from the rooftops at royal troops. The event has been interpreted by some historians as an important warning rumble before the Revolution. The three Estates of the Dauphiné gathered to call for a national meeting of the French Estates. Local boy Henri Beyle, better known by his pseudonym Stendhal, recorded his impressions of the Revolution in Grenoble before he went on to become one of France's greatest 19th-century novelists.

In fact, the Revolutionary period passed off relatively peacefully in town, just two people guillotined compared with a couple of thousand executed in Lyon. Napoleon caused a stir with his unexpected arrival via the Drac valley in 1815 on his brief last attempt to regain power. Through the 19th century, the city was massively fortified, notably with the building of the Fort de la Bastille high above the Isère.

Industrialization and working-class struggles came early. The rich adopted the Vinay company's ground-breaking moulded cement for extravagantly decorated apartment blocks. And skiing took off in the mountains around town; the first attempts to intro-duce the sport into France took place at Chamrousse east of the city. A major centre for the production of arms in the First World War, Grenoble's chemical industries developed enormously through the 20th century. During the Second World War, the city, as with much of the French Alps, was occupied by Italians. Although Pétain and other Vichy notables were warmly greeted when they visited, the town became the main centre of Resistance in the Alps, to be awarded the *Croix de la Libération* at the end of the conflict. With three universities now, Grenoble is most renowned for its scientific research facilities, while industry has expanded still further along its valleys. But pleasure is never far away: the city hosted the Winter Olympics in 1968 and it is the major gateway to the Alpine resorts in the Ecrins range.

On a tour of Grenoble, head first for the grand **Place Notre-Dame**, in the quarter where the bishops of Grenoble held sway in medieval times. The **cathedral** looks as if it's had to fight to stay on the square, with town houses shouldering in beside it. The stocky front is topped by a mighty, square brick 13th-century bell tower. The interior proves very plain apart from the showy tall ciborium (to store the eucharistic bread and wine) in the choir. From inside the edifice you can visit the adjoining **church of St-Hugues**, another grim early-Gothic building. While a new tramway was being prepared around here in the 1980s, vestiges were unearthed of earlier episcopal buildings, including a rare 5th-century baptistery, plus Gallo-Roman walls, all now well housed in the splendidly presented **Musée de l'Ancien Evêché** (*t 04 76 03 15 25, www.ancien-eveche-isere.com; open daily exc Tues 9–6 (Sun 10–7); adm*). The section on the Dark Ages boasts the magificent rare Vézeronce helmet. You can then follow the history of the medieval lords of the Dauphiné, and the foundation of three religious orders in early medieval times – not just the Chartreuse or Carthusian, but also the Antonine (*see* p.179)and the Chalais (absorbed by the Cistercian). The story then moves on to and beyond the glamorous *Ancien Régime* city aristocrats.

The even swisher modern **Musée de Grenoble** (*t 04 76 63 44 44, www.museede grenoble.fr; open daily exc Tues 10–6; adm*), the fine arts museum, stands on the eastern edge of the historic centre, near the river. Among the highlights are Perugino's *St Sebastian*, Giuseppe Cesari's *Portrait of an Architect*, Rubens' *Pope Gregory Surrounded by Saints*, and French works by Philippe de Champaigne, Vouet and Claude Lorrain, plus an extraordinary series of New Testament scenes by Zurbarán. David's 1780 *Tête de femme* looks like a precursor of Lucien Freud. Henri Fantin-Latour, an accomplished 19th-century artist from Grenoble, is reserved his own space. The museum also boasts one of the finest modern art collections in France outside Paris: there are good Fauvist and Cubist pieces, a few Matisses, and canvases by the likes of Léger and Modigliani. Major sculptures stand scattered in the garden.

West of the Musée de Grenoble lie the liveliest, most atmospheric **historic streets** of the city. Sumptuous residences built for members of the *Parlement* stand along **Rue Chenoise** and **Rue Brocherie**, which lead to the town's pretty **Place St-André**, overseen by the former **Parlement** building, beside the **church of St-André**. You might pause to watch the world go by from the terrace of the **Café de la Table Ronde**, which claims to be the second-oldest café in France. Adjoining **Place des Gordes** leads to the **Jardin de Ville**, a leafy garden created for Lesdiguières. His former house contains the weary little **Musée Stendhal** (*t 04 76 54 44 14; open summer Tues–Sun 9–12 and 2–6, rest of year Tues–Sun 2–6*), scarcely reflecting the passionate prose of the city's greatest literary son, although the ungrateful boy wasn't entirely complimentary about the place.

South of the historic core, a whole grand city went up from the mid-19th century, mimicking Parisian Haussmann style, but with many of the façades built in groundbreaking moulded cement. The most impressive set piece in the grid is the immense **Place de Verdun**, overseen by imposing civic and army buildings in a variety of pastiche styles, although the departure of Napoleon's statue, which once stood in the middle, left an empty feeling. One edifice contains the **Musée des Troupes de Montagne** (*reopening after renovation; t 04 38 37 44 04 for times*), dedicated to the heroics of the French elite mountain regiment, the *Chasseurs Alpins*. Not far off, the **Musée de la Résistance** (*t 04 76 42 38 53, www.resistance-en-isere.com; open daily exc Tues 10–6; adm*) is a very sobering, serious Second World War museum, with modern presentations. South beyond the ambitious **Muséum d'Histoire Naturelle** (*t 04 76 44 05 35, www.museum-grenoble.fr; open Mon–Fri 9.30–12 and 1.30–5.30, weekends 2–6;*

adm) covering the natural history of the Alps, you come to spacious, elegant gardens, the **Jardin des Plantes** with splendid greenhouses. The **Tour Perret**, a cement skyscraper by one of the pioneers in the genre, went up for a 1925 international exhibition on *houille blanche* ('white coal' as the French call hydroelectric power), such an important source of energy for the region's industrial development. Memories of the Winter Olympics also stand out around here, including the **Olympic bowl**.

North **across the Isère**'s steely grey waters, Grenoble's oldest church has been converted into the maze of the **Musée Archéologique St-Laurent** (*t 04 76 44 78 68, www.musee-archeologique-grenoble.com; closed for renovation–check times; adm*). So many layers of Christian buildings have been discovered one on top of another here that the architecture looks deeply confusing. In the 4th century, a Christian necropolis was established on the spot, just outside the city, protected from the floods of the Isère. At the end of the 5th century, a rectangular chapel went up. A rare little funerary church in the shape of a cross, with trefoil ends to each arm, was then built on the site in the 6th century. This was transformed in the 8th and 9th centuries, with a whole new church built on top. Following all this, in the 11th and 12th centuries the church was transformed as part of a Benedictine priory. Confused? Through the church's now floorless nave, amid a jumble of gaping tombs, set about identifying the different periods. Above, alarming swastikas feature among the early-20th century decorations on the ceiling; when they were painted in 1910 they were merely regarded as ancient solar symbols. Venturing into the labyrinth below, don't miss the crypt of St-Oyand, wolfish monsters and birds featuring among the foliage of its beautiful Carolingian carved capitals. Outside, the narrow **St-Laurent quarter**, with its massive 14th-century gateway, its 19th-century fortified terraces and its ethnic restaurants, has a more laid-back, alternative feel than central Grenoble. As to the quayside, it's lined with an absurd number of pizzerias, a reminder of the strong Italian links with the city.

A steep track up the hill takes you to the **Musée Dauphinois** (*t 04 76 85 19 01, www.musee-dauphinois.fr; open June–Sept daily exc Tues 10–7; rest of year daily exc Tues 10–6; adm*), set in a huge former convent, Ste-Marie-d'en-Haut, built in its prominent site during the Counter-Reformation by François de Sales' and Jeanne de Chantal's Order of the Visitation. Its nuns came from wealthy families, and the architecture has a spacious air, although the interiors have been much transformed, having served since the Revolution as prison, school, barracks and housing centre before being turned into a museum. However, the Baroque chapel has survived intact, covered head to toe with paintings depicting François de Sales' life (*see* p.250). The outrageous gilded retable with twisted columns is topped by a figure of God looking like a wild-eyed preacher. The museum has two interesting permanent collections, one on Alpine village life, the other devoted to the history of skiing, while temporary exhibitions on aspects of the Dauphiné are mounted in the other spaces.

The **bubble cars** taking you over the metallic grey-green waters of the Isère are the best way to reach **Fort de la Bastille**, which guards the city to the north. From the somewhat neglected fortified terraces way up on high, you'll see how far Grenoble has sprawled along the valleys around, and just how dramatically it's surrounded by high peaks. Down on the flat towards the railway station, **Le Musée des Automates** (*t 04 76 43 33 33, www.automatesanciens.com; open Jan–Dec daily 2–6.30; adm*) pays homage to one of the major French makers of automated puppets, Vaucanson of Grenoble, this place run by a man passionate about his craft. Further out along the Drac, **Le Magasin, Centre National d'Art Contemporain** (*t 04 76 21 95 84, www.magasin-cnac.org; take tramway towards Fontaine*) puts on major contemporary art exhibitions.

A couple of very smart addresses are worth seeking out in Grenoble's rampant suburbs. The **Musée Hébert** (*t 04 76 42 97 35, www.patrimoine-en-isere.com; open Jan–Dec daily exc Tues 10–6; adm*) occupies an *Ancien Régime* villa with views of the Belledonne peaks in the wealthy neighbourhood of La Tronche. As it was being restored recently, bold, rough *trompe-l'oeil* scenes were discovered in its rooms. But the place is dedicated to a 19th-century artist, son of a wealthy Grenoble lawyer. Although Hébert spent much of his life in Paris and Italy, his family left many of his works to the city. They include gorgeous male and female figures, somewhat in pre-Raphaelite style, including the most sensual of Joan of Arcs. While none of Hébert's major works depicted his native land, his watercolours did, a selection on show.

The **Château de Sassenage** (*t 04 76 27 54 44, www.domaine-de-sassenage.com, garden open July–Aug daily exc Mon 2–6; château open for many cultural events*) has kept its aristocratic head above the engulfing suburbs west of town. It sits below the soaring Vercors heights, looking across to the big-veined Chartreuse mountains. This spot was the seat, for almost 1000 years, of one of the mightiest families in Dauphiné history, lords of the Vercors and surrounding territories. The medieval castle was abandoned for a grand *Ancien Régime* edifice reminiscent of a Loire château. Beyond the wonky carved lions and the unfortunate-looking mermaid in a tub by the entrance, the interiors reflect 17th-century good living in the Dauphiné, with interesting regional furniture and paintings, well explained on an intelligent tour. The nearby **Cuves de Sassenage** (*t 04 76 27 55 37, www.sassenage.fr; open July–Aug daily 10–6; June and Sept Tues–Sun 1.30–6; April–May and Oct weekends 1.30–6; adm*), colourful caves you can visit to the sound of underground streams, became the focus of national fears in May 2002 when a group of schoolchildren was trapped inside by the sudden rise of the waters. New security measures are now in place along the narrow galleries carved into curious shapes by water erosion.

The Drac, Matheysine and Trièves

East below the formidable Vercors lies the quietly dramatic Drac valley. We take our section of the **Route Napoléon** (now the N85) the opposite way to *le petit caporal*, from Grenoble into the Matheysine, above the Drac's east bank. Head for the brutally massive **Château de Vizille**. Set in splendid **grounds** (*t 04 76 68 07 35, open June–Aug daily exc Tues 9am–10pm; April–May and Sept–Oct daily exc Tues 9–7; rest of year daily exc Tues 10–5; free*), this intimidating castle was built from 1600 to 1619 for Lesdiguières (*see p.277*), but now houses an engrossing **Museum of the French**

Revolution (*open April–Oct daily exc Tues 10–6; rest of year exc public hols and Tues 10–5; adm*). On 21 July 1788 it hosted the celebrated meeting of the representatives of the Dauphiné's three Estates in a ground-breaking act of independent cooperation between nobles, Church and bourgeoisie. The entrance hall contains a useful time chart, while throughout, paintings and models are fused with text to illustrate the complex different stages of the Revolution.

Heading straight south for La Mure, the upheaval of Napoleonic times is recalled at **La Prairie de la Rencontre** close to the **Lac de Laffrey**. The equestrian statue of the power-crazed Corsican stood for a while in the centre of Grenoble, then was consigned to this backwater, but one of significance – Napoleon's battalion from Elba encountered a royalist one supposedly loyal to King Louis XVIII. It's said the *petit caporal* flashed open his coat like a military Jesus, and the cry went up of '*Vive l'Empereur*', the monarchist troops changing sides on witnessing this apparition.

As an alternative to the N85, you can try hugging the **east bank of the Drac**. The once formidable river, compared in legend to a *drac*, or dragon, has in parts been exploited by industry and tamed by dams, the latter allowing people to practise water sports in its violently bright waters. One of the earliest electrified rail lines in France winds along a dramatic route like a mule track far above the river. Now serving simply as a tourist train linking St-Georges-de-Commiers and La Mure, the main function of the **Chemin de Fer de La Mure** (*t 08 92 39 14 26, www.trainlamure.com; runs April–Oct; adm*) when it was built was to transport coal from the Matheysine. This somewhat surprising mining history is recalled in the local museums, the under-ground **Mine Image** (*t 04 76 30 68 74, www.mine-image.com; open June–mid-Sept daily tours 10–5.30, May and late-Sept daily 2.30–4.30; April and Oct Wed and weekends 2.30–4.30; other months weekends 2.30–4.30; adm*) and the **Musée Matheysin** (*t 04 76 30 98 15; open May–Oct daily exc Tues 1–6.30; adm*), the latter at the busy sloping town of **La Mure** and covering other local craft traditions with style.

Further south down the Drac at **Mayres-Savel**, board **La Mira** (*t 04 76 34 14 56, e bateau.lamira@wanadoo.fr; operates mid-May–Oct; adm*) to appreciate the valley's drama by boat (with meal possible). Or for more elation, bungee jumpers experience a heady 100m drop from the dramatic **Pont de Ponsonnas** (*t 04 76 47 42 80 for reservations; open July–Aug daily, May–June and Sept–Nov weekends; adm*) a bit south of La Mure, billing itself as the number one site in Europe for the crazy sport.

Continuing down the Drac, **Corps** makes a pleasant last stop on the border with Provence, set beside the **Lac du Sautet**, created by another dam on the river, and offering another major expanse for water sports. A quite hairy mountain road leads up from Corps to **Notre-Dame-de-la-Salette**. The reason why this pilgrimage spot is perched at 1,800m is that two shepherds claimed to have witnessed a vision of the Virgin Mary up here in 1846. The 19th-century Church seizing on such opportunities, a whole new religious centre arose in the dramatic location. Today this remains one of the most important Catholic pilgrimage destinations in France. To enjoy unspoilt reflection on the majesty of nature, head east from La Mure via **Valbonnais**, allowing you to enter the **Ecrins National Park** via relatively quiet routes, hiking trails leading into the splendid mountains from the dead-end villages of **Valsenestre** and **Le Désert**.

Following the **west bank of the Drac** from Grenoble, you pass under the gaze of the Vercors' highest heights. The N75 route is stunning, but little roads west take you up onto the gorgeous slopes around the Gresse valley. **Treffort** down by the Drac has another landing stage for cruising on La Mira (*see* above). Head up to **Gresse-en-Vercors** for the walking trail to the top of that range's highest peak, **Le Grand Veymont** (2,342m). From this exceptional viewing point, you can see as far as Mont Blanc, while close up, you can spot perhaps the most isolated pasture in France, on top of the bald **Mont Aiguille** (2,086m), totemic symbol of the **Trièves**, the beautiful rumpled cereal lands between Vercors and Drac. Although called the Needle in French, this unmissable mountain sticks out much more like a vast exposed, isolated tooth. At the close of the 15th century, King Charles VIII passed this way on his Italian campaigning. On a whim, seemingly in a mood to conquer all he saw, he ordered Antoine de Ville, one of his lords, to organize the ascent of the totally inaccessible-seeming summit. But the exploit was achieved with the elaborate use of ladders. This event is often claimed in France to be the first example of French mountaineering. The village of **Chichilianne** sits in an exceptionally beautiful location below Mont Aiguille. The writer Jean Giono, well-known in France for his evocative novels on traditional rural life, set several of his books in the Trièves, hence the **Espace Jean Giono** (*t 04 76 34 78 23; open summer Tues, Thurs and weekends 4–7, rest of year Fri and Sat; adm*) at **Lalley**. The passes to the west lead across to the Drôme valley (*see* p.188).

Pleasantly laid-back **Mens** a bit to the east has an understated charm, an old, long-Protestant market town that hasn't spruced itself up yet. Stroll around to take in its little fountains, its covered market, its churches, and the delightful Belle Epoque **Café des Arts**, whose walls are covered with local landscapes. Local history and traditions are covered at the **Musée du Trièves** (*t 04 76 34 88 28, www.musee-trieves.com; open Jan–Dec daily exc Mon 3–7; adm*). **Terre Vivante** (*t 04 76 34 80 80, www.terrevivante. org; open May–Oct; adm*), well-hidden in the countryside out of town, proves an amazingly well-run ecological park encouraging environmentally friendly practices with exceptional good sense. East of the N75, lose yourselves in beautiful mountainous dead ends on the frontier with the Hautes-Alpes of northern Provence, marked by the majestic peak of the **Obiou** (2,790m).

The Vercors Range

Menacing peaks rising on all sides, the natural fort of the Vercors range that stretches southwest from Grenoble is only reachable by very disturbing roads from whichever way you approach. But once you've scaled the near-sheer walls, the high plateaux prove easier to travel round. The villages up top long remained cut off from the outside world. This hidden territory, offering caves for further protection, became a hide-out for Resistance fighters in the Second World War, leading to terrible Nazi attacks and extremely bitter memories. Gently developing its tourism, helped by a role in the 1968 Winter Olympics, in 1970 the Vercors became one of the earliest regional nature parks created in France.

Typically alarmingly steep roads lead up from the suburbs of Grenoble to the Vercors. Heading past the **Tour sans Venin**, a meagre remnant of medieval defence, make for **St-Nizier-du-Moucherotte,** a balcony of a village on the northern end of the range, with staggering views down on the city, up the Isère valley and as far as Mont Blanc. Overseen by three peaks known as the **Trois Pucelles** (Three Virgins), much of the village was destroyed in Nazi attacks, the **Nécropole** in its beautiful location well below the houses dedicated to the memory of those killed by Germans. The highest, eastern line of Vercors mountains reach over 2,000m. The only way to get close to them is via the GR91 hiking trail, part of the **Grande Traversée du Vercors** network (*www.traversee-vercors.com*) which you can join by St-Nizier. The route is accessible for mountain bikes and donkeys as well!

An alternative route up from Grenoble into the Vercors takes you along the **Furan valley**, past **Engins**, a village with an 11th-century church. The Vercors draws potholers with challenges such as the Gouffre Berger, its underground drop of more than 1,000m hidden to the west. Walkers are guided more easily by instructive signs to the fresh **Gorges du Bruyant**. Heading for Lans, you enter the gentle, quiet pasturelands of the northern Vercors, the scattered villages settled peacefully below long wooded spines to east and west still proudly recalling the parts they played in the 1968 Winter Olympics. In summer, the pure air and flower-filled meadows make this a good place to breathe easy. However, regardless of when you visit the **La Magie des Automates** (*t 04 76 95 40 14, www. magiedesautomates.com; open Jan–Sept and Nov–Dec daily 10–6; adm*) on the edge of **Lans-en-Vercors**, you are not allowed to forget the snowy season and Christmas. A mad collector of automata has created a plethora of scenes, not exclusively devoted to Father Christmas, cuddly bears and wolves featuring large.

A loop to the west takes you to typical open villages, **Autrans** keeping its lovely old-style feel, especially around the central square, despite having become a major centre of cross-country skiing. A *fromagerie* keeps Vercors cow cheese traditions going. See if you can visit the **Musée La Ferme de Martine et François** (*t 04 76 95 73 63; open by rendez-vous only; adm*), a traditional farm on the outskirts where you can discover much about Vercors farming ways and animals on the guided tour. **Méaudre** has a nice feel with its scattered hamlets, although modern constructions are spreading. Lively **Villard-de-Lans**, amid meadows, is a sporty resort all year round, signalled by its central ice-rink and outdoor wave pool. **Ludi Parc** (*t 04 76 95 06 95; open in summer*) offers the further attractions of a tree-top assault course, archery and summer bobsleighing on a section of the 1968 Winter Olympics track. **Corrençon-en-Vercors** at the end of the road is known for its beautiful golf couse.

In stark, chilling contrast, just a bit west, the hamlet of **Valchevrière** was wiped out by the Nazis, only ghostly ruins recalling this important, devastated Resistance hideout. The main D531 road west from Villard plunges through the **Gorges de la Bourne**. The sensational entrance to the **Grottes de Choranche** (*t 04 76 36 09 88, www.choranche.com; open Jan–Dec; adm*) hangs on a lip of rock sticking out from a massive, sheer face of forested mountainside. Two streams converge inside the caves, the main wonders of which are the delicate stalactites, *fistuleuses*, like spaghetti glued to the ceiling. Truly terrifying roads lead into the southern half of the Vercors from the Bourne valley, as frightening as any roller-coaster ride. The most notorious takes you along the side of the Vernaison gulley via the **Petits** and **Grands Goulets**, head-spinning distances above and below. The rival route forces you to cling to the side of the **Combe Laval**, with even more terrifying canyon views. Tucked away in a sensational location, members of the small Russian Orthodox community at the **Monastère St-Antoine** (*t 04 75 47 72 02; open daily 11.30–12.30 and 2–5; adm*) explain to visitors the rich iconography of the masterful recent murals decorating their church.

Up on the main plateau of the southern Vercors, a moving memorial and plaques at **La Chapelle-en-Vercors** reveal how this was one of the range's main villages martyred by the Nazis in 1944 as they tried to wipe out the Resistance groups on the high plateaux. **Vassieux-en-Vercors** was another. Some 600 Resistance fighters, along with around 200 villagers, were assassinated by SS soldiers who flew in silently in gliders. The horror is retold both at the passionately run, old-fashioned **Musée de la Résistance** (*t 04 75 48 28 46; open April–Oct daily 10–12 and 2–6; free*) in the reconstructed village, at the **Nécropole** (*open May–mid-Sept 10–12.30 and 1.30–6; free*), a cemetery with a memorial room showing a video on the war campaign, and up at the new-fangled **Mémorial de la Résistance** (*t 04 75 48 26 00, www.memorial-vercors.fr; open April–Sept daily 10–6; Jan–March Wed–Sun 10–5; Oct 10–5; winter school hols 10–12.30 and 2–5; adm*), snaking down the ridge from the Col de Lachau. All these make for deeply harrowing visits. Seeking refuge in the dark **Forêt de Lente** spreading west beyond the *Mémorial* are deer, chamois and mouflons.

You'll hear further horrific war tales on a visit into the bowels of the Vercors range at the **Grotte de la Luire** (*t 04 75 48 25 83; open July–Aug daily 9.30–6; April–June and Sept– Oct daily 9.30–12 and 1.30–6; adm*) east of Vassieux. North of the village, the massive **Grotte de la Draye Blanche** (*t 04 75 48 24 96; open high season daily 9–7, low season 9.30–12 and 2–5, closed All Saints'–Christmas; adm*) has revealed a lot about animal prehistory with all the remains unearthed here. But the most immediate excitement comes from the colour of the natural concretions and what's aptly nick-named a cascade in stone. For another long view of civilization in the Vercors, seek out the **Musée de la Préhistoire** (*t 04 75 48 27 81, www.prehistoire-vercors.fr; open July–Aug daily 10–6, April– June and Sept daily 10–12.30 and 2–6; Oct–Mar weekends 10–12.30 and 2–5; adm*) going back a quarter of a million years, but concentrating on Neolithic finds on the spot. The Vercors being a major area for *spéléologie*, potholing, contact the **Maison de l'Aventure** (*t 04 75 48 22 38, www.maison-aventure.com*) about possibilities.

The southeast heights of the Vercors are protected by their status as the **Réserve Naturelle des Hauts Plateaux du Vercors**, the largest nature reserve in France, jam-packed with Alpine flora. The huge fanning dorsal mountain of the Grand Veymont, the highest peak in the Vercors at 2,341m, oversees this secretive land. You can't reach this area by car, but even on the lower Vercors plateaus, from late spring you can enjoy the exceptionally dense carpets of mountain flowers.

Out west, the strong, stoical church of the **abbey of Léoncel** offers a calm halt before sensational twisting roads down from the range's heights. Whichever staggeringly dramatic road you take to leave the Vercors' southern heights, it comes as a shock going from the chilly, chilling cliff tops to the warm, dry territory of lavender and vine-yards of the southern *département de la Drôme* (*see* p.182).

Winter Sports

Dave Watts

Haute Savoie 287
Savoie: The Tarentaise Valley 302
Savoie: The Maurienne Valley 319
Isère 325
Ain 333

19

The Rhône-Alpes region includes the biggest ski areas and some of the best-known ski resorts in the world. It stretches from Châtel, Morzine and Avoriaz in the north to Alpe-d'Huez and Les Deux-Alpes in the south – with Val d'Isère, Courchevel and over 170 other resorts in between. No fewer than three Winter Olympics have been held in the Rhône-Alpes – in Chamonix in 1924, Grenoble in 1968 and Albertville in 1992. And no ski areas in the world come anywhere near to offering the extent and variety of, for example, the 200 lifts and 600km of pistes of the Trois Vallées or the 650km of the Portes du Soleil.

Whatever type of resort you want, you'll find it here, from those based on traditional mountain villages such as La Clusaz, Les Contamines and Valloire, to resorts which were purpose-built in high, snowy wildernesses in the 1960s and 1970s to allow you to ski straight from and right back to your accommodation. Prime examples of the latter include Flaine, La Plagne, Les Arcs and Le Corbier. You'll find chic expensive resorts with designer shops and fur coats, such as Megève and Courchevel 1850, those aimed at the budget traveller such as Les Menuires and Brides-les-Bains, and resorts that firmly target the family market like traffic-free Valmorel. You can even carry on skiing in summer on glaciers high above resorts such as Tignes and Les Deux-Alpes.

Constant improvement and innovation mean that the ski areas of the Rhône-Alpes always have something new to offer. For the 2004 season, for example, the world's biggest double-decker cable car holding 200 people and covering 2km in less than four minutes, opened to link the ski areas of Les Arcs and La Plagne to form a new joint area known as Paradiski with over 400km of pistes. At the same time, nine new lifts and five new pistes were built to link six existing resorts in the Maurienne valley with over 300km of pistes making up another new area known as Les Sybelles.

The lift systems in the region include some of the most modern in the world, with state-of-the-art high-speed gondolas holding over 30 people in each cabin, 8-seater chair-lifts and fast underground funiculars as well as the cable car referred to above, so queueing has largely become a thing of the past.

This section of the book looks at the main ski areas in the Rhône-Alpes, how their slopes suit expert, intermediate and beginner downhill skiers and boarders and at how the resorts that make them up differ in ambience and architecture.

As well as downhill skiing terrain, most resorts also feature cross-country skiing, which remarkably few British or North American guests try. They are missing out on a very different experience – cross-country skiing through winter-wonderland forests, around frozen lakes or on high plateaux makes a beautiful and peaceful change from the hurly-burly of crowded downhill pistes. But cross-country can also be a major aerobic work out – as you'll see from the lycra-clad athletes you'll sometimes find hurtling past you. And some areas of the Rhône-Alpes, such as the Vercors and the Monts-Jura mountain ranges, have become more renowned for their extensive and compelling cross-country terrain than for their downhill slopes.

Winter walking on cleared mountain paths and walking on snowshoes makes the mountains accessible for those who don't want to ski, as well as being popular with skiers too. Ice skating, especially on an outdoor rink in the midst of a village, makes a jolly après-ski activity, as does tobogganing down dedicated runs that may be floodlit after dark. More sedately, you may be able to take a horse-drawn sleigh ride.

Parapenting and hang-gliding have become hugely popular in many resorts and you can join a qualified instructor on a tandem flight from top to bottom of a mountain, soaring around on some thermals. For those of more nervous dispositions, sight-seeing flights around the mountains are available in some resorts by either helicopter or small aeroplane. Snowmobiling tours, ice driving courses, go-karting on snow, ice-climbing on frozen waterfalls or man-made pinnacles of ice may also be on offer. More specialized activities available include ice diving beneath a frozen lake (with a guide!) in Tignes and trying out the Olympic bobsleigh run in La Plagne. So quite apart from the eating, drinking and nightlife there's plenty to do than just ski.

For maps covering the main winter sports regions, see pp.214, 232, 248 and 268.

Haute Savoie

Portes du Soleil: Avoriaz, Châtel, Les Gets, Morzine, La Chapelle d'Abondance, Montriond, St-Jean d'Aulps – plus some Swiss resorts

Local hero Jean Vuarnet, now of sunglasses fame, won the gold medal in the Men's Downhill at the Walt Disney-orchestrated 1960 Winter Olympics in Lake Tahoe, California. Shortly afterwards he was entrusted with the development of Avoriaz, one of the first French purpose-built ski resorts, which opened in 1966 high above the traditional mountain town of Morzine. It was Vuarnet's dream to build a cross-border ski area, linking the pistes of Avoriaz to those of Les Crosets and Champéry, over the border in Switzerland – a dream that became a reality in 1968, when the *Portes du Soleil* (Gateways to the Sun) ski area was born.

Since then, development has been continuous and the **Portes du Soleil** now covers 14 resorts and claims 650km of pistes, over 200 lifts, 500 snow guns, more than 1,000 ski instructors and 100,000 beds. But each resort remains modest in size and has a local ski area with distinct character that is not lost in a homogeneous whole.

The Portes du Soleil vies with the Trois Vallées(see p.304) for the crown of being the world's largest ski area. While the Trois Vallées has 50km fewer pistes, they are truly linked by lift and pistes, whereas in the Portes du Soleil you have to catch a bus or walk quite a distance in a few places – so a fair verdict might be a tie!

The area as a whole can be classed as an intermediate's paradise, with mile after mile of easy-cruising blue and red runs and an interesting mixture of snow-sure runs above the tree line and pretty runs through the woods below. The main Portes du Soleil circuit can be skied in either clockwise or anti-clockwise direction and takes in Avoriaz 1800 and Châtel in France and Morgins, Champoussin and Les Crosets in Switzerland (in that order if you go clockwise). It makes a wonderful day's skiing if the snow is good – and a full day's worth too if you are tempted to linger over a long lunch at one of the many rustic mountain restaurants around. The circuit breaks down only at Châtel where, whichever direction you are travelling in, you need to take a short bus ride – the buses are frequent and free.

Portes du Soleil

Ski Area
Height of slopes 975m–2,275m
Number of lifts 206

Pistes 650km
green 13%
blue 38%
red 39%
black 10%

Tourist Information

Avoriaz 1800: t 04 50 74 02 11,
www.avoriaz.com.
Châtel: t 04 50 73 22 44, www.chatel.com.
Les Gets: t 04 50 75 80 80, www.lesgets.com.
Morzine: t 04 50 74 72 72, www.morzine.com.

Ski Schools

Avoriaz 1800: The British Alpine Ski School,
t 04 50 74 12 64, www.britishskischool.co.uk,
is very highly rated. Emery, t 04 50 74 12 64,
www.emeryproshop.com, is a specialist
snowboard school.
Châtel: the International School, t 04 50 73
31 92, www.essi-chatel.com, caters well for
English-speaking guests.

Les Gets: The original branch of the British
Alpine Ski School, t 04 50 79 85 42,
www.britishskischool.co.uk, is still run by
Scottish ski guru Hugh Monney.
Morzine: Former British snowboard champion
Becci Malthouse is a partner here in the
British Alpine Ski School, t 04 50 74 78 59,
www.britishskischool.co.uk – she is a top ski
instructor too.

Where to Stay

Avoriaz 1800
★★★Dromonts, t 04 94 97 91 91, www.
christophe-leroy.com (luxury–expensive).
Central and smartly renovated after a
takeover by celebrity chef Christophe Leroy,
whose summer base is St-Tropez. Excellent
food, two restaurants, cookery courses.

La Chapelle d'Abondance
★★Cornettes, t 04 50 73 50 24,
www.lescornettes.com (moderate). 2-star
rooms with 4-star facilities (pool, sauna,
stean, Jacuzzi), excellent great-value
restaurant, atmospheric bar popular with
locals. Family-run in idiosyncratic way
(showcases with puppets and dolls, doors
that unexpectedly open automatically).

The main disadvantage of the area is that it is relatively low for a big French ski area – with the slopes ranging from 975m to 2,275m (compared with 1,550m to 3,455m for L'Espace Killy, for example). So the snow quality can suffer in warm or dry weather. But when snow conditions are good, the area is a delight.

The main French resorts all have good beginner slopes and easy green runs to progress to. But experts will find steep slopes in relatively short supply. Most are in the Avoriaz 1800 area and include four 'snowcross' runs – an excellent concept, where effectively off-piste runs are left ungroomed but are controlled for avalanches (and closed if dangerous) and patrolled. This is normal in North America but in Europe most off-piste is entirely uncontrolled and you risk being killed by an avalanche whenever you slide off the marked trails. Nicknamed the 'Swiss Wall' because of its steepness and huge moguls, one (but not the only!) piste down into Switzerland from above Avoriaz 1800 will challenge even the most expert – but the more timid can ride a chairlift down and chuckle at the carnage below on the way.

Morzine is just off the main Portes du Soleil circuit but has a gondola up into it (which you have to ride down as well). Its main local slopes are on the opposite side of the valley on gentle, wooded slopes that link up with those of Les Gets.

Apartments

Many in **Avoriaz 1800** are showing their age and in need of renovation. **Falaise**, near the top of the village, has some of the smartest.

Catered Chalets

Ski Total, t (0870) 1 63 36 33, and **Ski Activity, t** (01738) 840888. Comfortable chalets in both Morzine and Les Gets.

Snowline, t (020) 88 70 48 07. Some very smart central chalets in Morzine.

Chalet Gueret, t (01884) 256542. Extremely luxurious, peacefully set out of town (with a minibus to transport you around).

La Ferme de Montagne, Les Gets, **t** 0800 072 3069. Gourmet cuisine, big rooms (most with sitting areas) and an outdoor Jacuzzi.

Eating Out

In the Resorts

Avoriaz 1800: Hotel Dromonts (*see* 'Where to Stay') has an inventive gastronomic restaurant and a cheaper bistro.

Châtel: Vieux Four does wonderful steaks and Savoyard specialities in a lovely rustic building right in the centre.

La Chapelle d'Abondance: Hotel Cornettes (*see* 'Where to Stay') has excellent-value set menus.

Morzine: La Taverne in Hotel Samoyede is highly regarded for the likes of lobster ravioli, truffle risotto and scallops.

On the Mountain

Avoriaz 1800: Of the clutch of rustic chalets in the hamlet of Les Lindarets, **La Crémaillière** offers excellent steaks with chanterelle mushrooms and a reliable *plat du jour*.

La Grenouille du Marais, near the top of the gondola up from Morzine, has tasty food, lovely views and atmosphere.

Morzine: Don't miss **Chez Nannon**, near the top of the Troncs chair between Nyon and Chamossière – good Savoyard food, a fine terrace for sunny days and a rustic interior for snowy ones.

Bars and Clubs

Avoriaz 1800: Yeti is popular as the lifts close. **Tavaillon** has Sky TV showing live sports. **Choucas** and **The Place** both have live bands.

Châtel: Tunnel, with a DJ or live music every night, is very popular with British guests. For an English-style pub, head for **Avalanche**. For a more French feel, try **Godille**.

Morzine: If dancing on tables in ski boots is your scene, head for **Crépuscule** when the lifts shut. For a quieter drink, try the **Boudha Café** with its Asian décor.

Perched above a dramatic, sheer rock face, **Avoriaz 1800** (the 1800 was added to the name in 2003 to emphasize its relatively high altitude) insists on cars being parked well outside the resort. From there, horse-drawn sleighs or snow-cats transport you and your luggage to your accommodation. Thankfully, the problem of horse mess has been cut since they now wear 'nappies' and staff on snowmobiles scoop up what escapes! A main snow-covered 'street', free of skiers and boarders as well as traffic, runs the length of the resort and the cliff face behind, prettily-lit at night, adds to the alpine ambience. The angular, high-rise buildings, distinctly 60s in style, fit in remarkably well with their mountain environment and their faded wood cladding adds a sense of age and style.

Eight hundred vertical metres below Avoriaz 1800, the traditional mountain town of **Morzine** is not unattractive, with nearly all buildings built in chalet-style. But it sprawls amorphously on both sides of a river gorge and if you are staying out of the centre, buses will be needed to reach both town and the lifts. Many UK chalet operators offer their own free mini-bus service to the lifts – worth looking for.

Just off the main road to Morzine and 6km away, the smaller old village of **Les Gets** makes a very atmospheric place to stay. The partly car-free centre, right by the slopes, has mainly traditional chalet buildings and plenty of tempting shops and restaurants. An outdoor ice rink adds to the 'winter wonderland' charm and there's a mountain music museum with barrel organs, music boxes and guided tours in English. But it takes a long time to reach the main Portes du Soleil circuit on skis – you have to get to Morzine, cross the town and take the gondola up towards Avoriaz 1800.

In the old village of **Châtel**, new unpretentious chalet-style hotels and apartments rub shoulders with old farmhouses where cattle still live in winter. Like Morzine, it has expanded over the years and now sprawls along the road in from Lake Geneva and the diverging roads out – up the hillside towards Morgins in Switzerland and along the valley towards the lifts up to the link with Avoriaz 1800. The gondola up to Super-Châtel and the pistes to Switzerland starts right in the village centre.

Unspoiled **La Chapelle d'Abondance**, 5km from Châtel, has its own small ski area and a gondola that links with Torgon in Switzerland (excellent views of Lake Geneva from there) and the slopes above Châtel. It is rather isolated so best for those with cars.

Grand Massif: Les Carroz, Flaine, Morillon, Samoëns, Sixt

Few ski areas contain such contrasting resorts as austere, concrete-block, purpose-built **Flaine** (the first resort in the area to become popular on the UK market) and the ancient mountain village of **Samoëns**, the only winter sports resort in France to be classified a *'Monument Historique'* – complete with its pretty central square, medieval fountain and ancient church.

They are among the easiest resorts in France to get to, being an hour or less by car from Geneva airport, and share one of the most under-rated ski areas in the Rhône-Alpes: 265km of varied pistes plus some excellent off-piste. And while the snow down towards the lower resorts can suffer if the weather is warm, the **high bowl** above Flaine often offers a paradise of fresh powder.

With almost 80 per cent of the area's pistes being classified blue or red, intermediates of all levels are guaranteed a great time. And if the snow is good throughout the area, cruising down to the valley villages can be a delight. One of the longest pistes in the Alps runs from above Flaine down to Sixt – the 14km easy, picturesque **Cascades blue** takes you right away from the lift system and all signs of civilization, dropping over 1700 vertical metres on the way. If you'd like to discover more about the local wildlife, don't miss the long **green Marvel run** to **Morillon 1100**, which has excellent signs along the way (in English as well as French) explaining all about the birds and animals you are likely to spot.

All the resorts have good nursery slopes (a lift ride above the villages in the cases of Samoëns and **Morillon**) for beginners, though Flaine's easy slopes do tend to have experienced skiers whizzing through them, which can be unnerving. Only Morillon has a good long, easy green to progress to (the Marvel run mentioned above). But there are plenty of easy blues.

Experts will love the area's off-piste. But beware: although much of it looks like it can safely be explored without a local guide, this impression is mistaken. Ravines and potholes abound in the bowl above Flaine but are often covered with a layer of snow and the terrain should be treated with the same caution that you would use on a

Grand Massif

Ski Area
Height of slopes 700m–2,480m
Number of lifts 75

Pistes 265km
green 12%
blue 41%
red 38%
black 9%

Tourist Information

Les Carroz: t 04 50 90 00 04, *www.lescarroz.com.*
Flaine: t 04 50 90 80 01, *www.flaine.com.*
Morillon: t 04 50 90 15 76, *www.ot-morillon.fr.*
Samoëns: t 04 50 34 40 28, *www.samoens.com.*

Ski Schools

Flaine: the **International School** (t 04 50 90
8441, *www.flaine-internationalskischool. com*)
has a good reputation for both group and
private lessons; and the small **Super Ski school**
(t 04 50 90 82 88, *www.flainesuperski.com*) is
run by two former French ski team coaches
and specializes in sessions for advanced and
expert skiers, offering race training as well
as ski improvement courses.

Where to Stay

Flaine
There are no real hotels, just a **Club Med** and
some **club-hotels** run by tour operators,
including **Crystal**, t 0870 160 6040, which
operates **Hotel Totem**.

Les Carroz
★★Bois de la Char, t 04 90 06 18, *www.hotel-
boisdelachar.com* (*moderate–inexpensive*). At
the top of the resort right on the slopes with
easy access to the gondola. Good food,
friendly staff.

Samoëns
★★★Neige et Roc, t 04 50 34 40 72, *www.
neigeetroc.com* (*moderate*). A short walk

from the centre and the gondola.
Welcoming, with tasty food, a sauna, steam
room, Jacuzzi and new indoor pool.

Apartments
Flaine: The **Forêt** and **Grand Massif** buildings
are attractively woody inside and have hotel
facilities such as a restaurant and bar.
Les Carroz: The newish **MGM apartments** are
smart, with indoor pool and sauna.

Eating Out

In the Resorts
Flaine: The welcoming **Michet Chalet** at the
foot of the pistes specializes in Savoyard
food, and the smart **Perdrix Noire** in **Forêt**
gets packed out.
Samoëns: **Pizzeria Louisiane** offers decent
pizzas and some highly alcoholic ice creams,
while **Chalet Fleurie** and **Chardon Bleu**, both
a car ride away in Verchaix, are worth the
journey.

On the Mountain
Chalet du Lac de Gers has a wonderfully
isolated position overlooking the frozen lake,
does simple inexpensive food and is a real
adventure in that you use their phone part-
way down the **Cascades piste** (next to a piste
map sign) and they come down with a
snowcat to tow you up while you hang on to a
rope. Above Morillon the rustic **Igloo** offers a
reliable *plat du jour*. And the 200-year-old
Chalet les Molliets near the bottom of the
Molliets chair is charmingly rustic with leather
boots and old ski sticks decorating the walls
and features Savoyard food as well as steaks
and other options.

Bars and Clubs

Flaine: The **White Grouse pub** has a big screen
TV, rock music and punters throwing drinks
back in happy hour. Later on, the more
French **Cimes Rock** is the liveliest place, with
live bands or karaoke.
Other Resorts: quieter more typically French
bars are the main option.

glacier. Touring is a possibility behind the Grandes Platières, and there are some scenic off-piste routes from which you can be retrieved by helicopter. All the black pistes on the map deserve their grading. The Gers drag lift serves great expert-only terrain, usually very quiet because of its position rather off the beaten track, outside the main Flaine bowl beyond Tête Pelouse. Two more serious black pistes run from Tête des Saix down towards Samoëns 1600 – most intermediates sensibly avoid these by taking the blue alternative.

When **Flaine** opened in 1968, its Bauhaus buildings designed by American architect Marcel Breuer and intended to blend in with the rocks that surround it, met with great acclaim. But to many eyes they don't blend in at all – in winter at least. Unusually for a ski resort, it is approached over a high pass, and Flaine suddenly springs into view below – a mass of grey concrete blocks at the bottom of an impressively snowy bowl. You'll love it or hate it but whatever your view on the architecture, it is compact and convenient. The main central square of **Flaine Forum**, the focal point of the resort, opens on one side to the slopes. Above it, connected by a lift that works day and night, **Flaine Forêt** has more apartments, shops and restaurants. The main gondola to the top of the Flaine bowl goes from Forum and the eight-seater chair, which links to pistes leading to the other villages of the Grand Massif, goes from Forêt. A shuttle-bus ride away and with no direct access to lifts or pistes, the newer development of **Hameau-de-Flaine** has been built in a much more conventional chalet style.

If you prefer a more traditional village setting, try **Les Carroz**, on the road up from the valley to Flaine before you get to the pass. Set on a wide sunny slope, this chalet-style resort has the lived-in feel of a real French village and life revolves around the village square with its pavement cafés, restaurants and interesting little shops. A choice of gondola or slow chairlift takes you up to the heart of the Grand Massif slopes – but they are a steep walk or shuttle-bus ride from some of the village centre.

The attraction of staying in the characterful old village of **Samoëns** increased dramatically from the 2003/4 season when a new eight-seater gondola, the Grand Massif Express, opened to whisk you from the edge of the village to the heart of the slopes at **Samoëns 1600** in just eight minutes. Before that you had to drive or catch a bus to and from **Vercland** above Samoëns to catch a gondola from there. You ride the new gondola down as well as there is no piste back to the village. It makes a pleasant change to stay in a real village with a life of its own outside skiing – with local bars, shops and restaurants. Samoëns was once a thriving centre for stonemasons and their work is evident in ornate carvings around the village centre. Samoëns 1600 has excellent nursery slopes and some accommodation too.

Morillon is a small, pretty, rustic village with a gondola up to the mid-mountain, modern mini-resort of Morillon 1100 which has been built in a quite attractive, low-rise style with slopes on your doorstep.

Chamonix Valley: Chamonix, Argentière, Les Houches (ski areas not linked), Vallée Blanche

Chamonix could not be more different from the archetypal high-altitude, purpose-built French resort, either in resort ambience or in the type of skiing on offer. The

The Vallée Blanche

No competent intermediate or expert skier should go to Chamonix without tackling one of the world's epic runs. When there's enough snow on the lower slopes, the Vallée Blanche is 24km long and descends 2800m vertically; often you have to stop 875m higher and catch the train down from Montenvers but even that curtailed version will be a day out to remember and brag about for the rest of your life. The standard gentle and easy route – so flat in places that boarders will find it too tedious to enjoy – resembles a green run for much of its length; you do this run for the spectacular scenery rather than the challenge of the slope. The views of the crevasses and *séracs* (huge pillars of ice) – and the rugged rock spires beyond – are simply mind-blowing. The trickiest part is right at the top; after you emerge from the Aiguille du Midi cable car, a tunnel takes you to a narrow ridge with sheer drops on both sides which you have to walk down while carrying your skis, not something for those who suffer from vertigo to attempt. There is (usually) a fixed guide rope for you to hang on to, and many parties rope up to their mountain guides (the walk can be avoided completely by taking the lifts up from the Italian side of Mont Blanc instead). After that, the run seems very easy and you can concentrate on admiring the spectacular glacial surroundings. If you want more challenging slopes there are plenty of alternatives to the classic route, of varying difficulty and danger.

The classic route can get very busy at times with up to 2,500 people a day doing it; but do not attempt it without a qualified mountain guide – dangerous crevasses lurk to swallow those not in the know and some of the snow bridges between them can be very narrow. Go early to avoid the crowds.

ancient town centre, steeped in the history of being a leading mountaineering centre for over 200 years (*see* p.23), oozes charm in a rugged way, with spectacular views from its pavement cafés of tumbling glaciers and Europe's highest peaks which seem to rise perpendicularly from the valley. As a first-time visitor you could be forgiven for wondering where on earth you could ski around here. The answer is much higher up and much further along the valley in both directions. The only run back to town (other than a nursery slope area at the bottom) is fearsomely steep and often closed and, although you can access ski slopes from near the town centre, a lot of the slopes are a bus or car ride away.

A gondola from near the centre heads up **Le Brévent** and links with **La Flégère**'s slopes, which can also be accessed by cable car from further up the valley. The sunny, largely south-facing pistes here have truly spectacular views over the valley to **Mont Blanc**, the **Aiguille du Midi** and numerous other memorable peaks. The spiky Aiguille du Midi itself is reached by a two-stage cable car which is a real feat of engineering and deposits you at a bone-chilling-cold altitude of 3840m; wrap up well before you make the ascent and think hard before removing a glove to take a photo at the top. Lots of pedestrians make the trip just for the experience and the views and those who intend to ski should not even dream of attempting to do so without a mountain guide – there is only off-piste here and the terrain is riddled with crevasses (known as '*slots*' by the local *braves*).

Chamonix

Ski Area
Height of slopes 1,035m–3,840m
Number of lifts 49

Pistes 152km
green 21%
blue 31%
red 35%
black 13%

Tourist Information

Chamonix: **t** 04 50 53 00 24,
www.chamonix.com.
Argentière: **t** 04 50 54 02 14,
www.chamonix.com.
Les Houches: **t** 04 50 55 50 62,
www.leshouches.com.

Ski Schools

ESF, **t** 04 50 53 22 57, *www.esf-chamonix.
com*, runs a great programme of all-day
Ski Fun Tours, featuring a different area
every day.
Compagnie des Guides, **t** 04 50 53 00 88,
www.cieguides-chamonix.com. Don't miss
a day out on the Vallée Blanche or other
glacier runs.

Where to Stay

There is a huge choice of hotels for a ski
resort, especially of good-value two-stars.

Chamonix
****Hameau Albert 1er, t 04 50 53 05 09,
www.hameaualbert.fr (*luxury–expensive–*).
The smartest place in town, a beautiful
centrally situated 100-year-old chalet with
some rooms in separate farmhouse and
chalet buildings in the grounds, indoor-
outdoor pool, sauna, Jacuzzi, excellent
restaurant with two Michelin stars.
**Arve, t 04 50 53 02 31, *www.hotelarve-
chamonix.com* (*moderate–inexpensive*).
Central, by the river, small newly decorated
rooms, fitness facility, sauna, climbing wall.

Argentière
***Grands Montets, t 04 50 54 06 66,
www.hotel-grands-montets.com (*moderate–
inexpensive B&B*). At the foot of the slopes by
the lifts, with great views from some of the
rooms, recently renovated, with lovely pool,
sauna, steam and gym. Has been B&B only
but was experimenting with outside
caterers serving dinner in summer 2004.

Les Houches
***Hôtel du Bois, t 04 50 54 50 35, *www.hotel-
du-bois.com* (*moderate*). Popular chalet-style
hotel, with good views of Mont Blanc massif
from half the rooms, pool and sauna.

Back in the valley, head up it towards the Swiss border and you reach **Argentière**, whose local mountain, the **Grands Montets**, accesses some phenomenal off-piste for experts. Even further up the road towards Switzerland you come to **Le Tour** and a gondola into the largely intermediate slopes of **Col de Balme**. Down the valley, in the opposite direction from Chamonix, **Les Houches** offers yet another skiing option (because of a local dispute, sadly not covered at the time of writing by the Chamonix Valley or Mont Blanc area lift passes). With all these options, many of them involving fairly lengthy journeys, having a car rather than relying on local buses gives you a lot more flexibility. It also allows you to try out other resorts covered by the Mont Blanc area lift pass, which include Megève, Les Contamines and even **Courmayeur** in Italy, easily reached through the Mont Blanc tunnel, although the toll isn't cheap.

Intermediates who like ski-in, ski-out convenience and mile after mile of perfectly groomed easy cruising runs would be happier in many other resorts. But intermediates looking for something out-of-the-ordinary, who relish the prospect of trying some steeper slopes or some off-piste and who fancy the prospect of exploring the

Minibus to take you to and from the slopes (and do airport transfers).

Apartments

There are plenty of the uninspiring cramped apartments typical of French ski resorts, but unusually also some very smart places. **Balcons du Savoy** on the slopes but close to the centre of Chamonix, **Ginabelle** near the train station, **Cristal d'Argentière** in the centre of Argentière and **Hauts de Chavants** near the slopes at Les Houches are all a cut above the norm, with relatively spacious well-furnished rooms and a swimming pool (some have saunas and steam as well).

Catered Chalets

A lot of small specialist Chamonix tour operators offer very high-quality personal service on top of comfortable accommodation, such as ferrying you around in minibuses and booking up mountain guides for you in advance. These include **Collineige**, **t** (01276) 24 262; **Bigfoot**, **t** 0870 300 5874, and **Huski**, **t** (020) 7938 48 44.

Eating Out

In the Resorts

Chamonix: For the best food in town head for the **Hameau Albert 1er** (*see* 'Where to Stay') which offers a *Maison de Savoie* fixed price menu as well as delicious *à la carte*.

L'Atmosphère lives up to its name, a rustically furnished *auberge* by the river which serves traditional as well as local speciality dishes. The **Cabane** serves good value classic dishes and there is a wide choice of ethnic restaurants serving food from Japan, China, India, Mexico, Spain and elsewhere.

On the Mountain

The beautiful old **Bergerie** at **Planpraz** on **Le Brevent** is by far the most attractive option in the area – with both self- and table-service sections, but it does get packed. The dull **Panoramic** at the top serves unremarkable food but has stunning views of Mont Blanc over the valley.

At the **Grands Montets**, the attractive modern **Plan Joran** has decent food and table- and self-service options, and the rustic **Chalet-Refuge du Lognan** offers spectacular views of the Argentière glacier.

Bars and Clubs

Chamonix: This is the place for the liveliest nightlife. Several bars in the centre get packed when the lifts close, including the **Choucas video bar**. Later on the partying crowd head for **The Pub, Wild Wallaby's**, **Mill Street Bar** and **Bar du Moulin** and then on to night clubs and discos such as **Dick's T-Bar**. For a quieter drink try **Dérapage**. **Argentière**: The **Office** bar is the focal point.

whole Chamonix valley, can have a wonderful time here. Col de Balme at one end of the valley and Les Houches at the other both offer excellent blue and red intermediate pistes, the former above the tree line and ideal for sunny days and the latter largely below the tree line and ideal for snowy ones. Le Brévent and La Flégère also have good cruising runs – but don't dream of trying the black runs down to the valley unless you are both competent and brave.

Beginners are catered for by various nursery slopes scattered along the valley floor. But they'd be better off learning elsewhere and saving Chamonix until they are experienced mountain people when they can truly appreciate the splendours of the terrain here. Experts will love the place. Indeed many fall so head-over-heels in love that they never return home – or only for the time it takes to quit the job, sell up and move out here. It's the off-piste that attracts them; plus the powder, the scenic grandeur, the nightlife and the food, of course. But the off-piste mainly. There's so much of it that no single run is worth describing here; suffice to say that you should hire a guide and explore, but do not explore without a guide – the terrain is riddled with dangers for the unwary. And options are plentiful; many top British mountain guides base themselves here and the local *Compagnie des Guides*, established over 150 years ago, is world renowned.

Chamonix has expanded into quite a sizable town and, though the centre remains charming with its cobbled streets and squares, lovely old buildings, grand hotels, fast-flowing river and pedestrianized areas, the periphery has more than its fair share of tacky 1960s and '70s architecture and traffic-choked streets. The choice of bars, restaurants and shops is large and varies from long-standing local enterprises to big-name international chains.

Staying centrally or way outside are the two best options and both Argentière and Les Houches make smaller-scale alternatives : pleasant villages with enough bars and restaurants to create a friendly local atmosphere. But neither is as centrally placed for exploring the whole valley.

Evasion Mont-Blanc: Megève, St-Gervais, le Combloux, St-Nicolas-de-Véroce

In 1916 **Megève** was singled out by Baroness Rothschild as the resort to develop into the French equivalent of chic St-Moritz in Switzerland and, after her Mont d'Arbois Palace hotel opened in 1921, the resort boomed and attracted more European royalty than anywhere else in high season. For a time in the 1960s and '70s its reputation faded as newer, more snowsure resorts were built. But now the beautiful people have returned, attracted by the charm of the exquisitely restored, traffic-free medieval centre with its cobbled streets, splendid church and designer shops. Together with St-Gervais it shares an extensive ski area, known as *Evasion Mont Blanc*, of gentle, prettily wooded slopes with stunning views all round, including wonderful close-up vistas of Mont Blanc. If only the town and slopes were 500m higher, Megève would fulfil many people's vision of the perfect ski resort. As it is, the price you pay for choosing such an idyllic setting is the chance of poor snow; but when there's snow in the village and fresh powder on the slopes you could be forgiven for thinking you had died and gone to Heaven.

Megève's pistes are perfect for its pampered clientele: mile after mile of well-groomed easy blue and red runs. Two of its three main mountains, Mont d'Arbois (which links with St-Gervais) and Rochebrune, can be reached from the centre of town and are linked by a cross-valley cable car but the third, La Jaillet, is a bus ride away. This third area, which links with runs above **Combloux**, should have seen the fruition by the time this book is published of a plan to build new lifts and pistes to link it with La Giettaz in the next valley on the road to La Clusaz. Timid intermediates will find easy cruising in all the sectors and there are gentle runs right from the top down to valley level. Those looking for more of a challenge can try the famous *Olympique* downhill run at Rochebrune – a wonderful undulating red run with snowmaking from top to bottom. And at Cote 2000 the black *Stade Descente* piste is often groomed to race-track perfection and open to all. Near the top of the Mont d'Arbois sector the Epaule chair accesses a fabulous red run along the ridge of the mountain, above the old village of **St-Nicolas-de-Véroce**, with jaw-dropping views of Mont Blanc in front of

Evasion Mont-Blanc

Ski Area
Height of slopes 850m–2,355m
Number of lifts 120

Pistes 450km
green 16%
blue 27%
red 40%
black 17%

Tourist Information

Megève: t 04 50 21 27 28, *www.megeve.com*.
St-Gervais: t 04 50 47 76 08,
www.st-gervais.net.
Combloux: t 04 50 58 60 49,
www.combloux.com.

Ski Schools

Megève: The long-established **International School, t** 04 50 58 78 88, *www.esimegeve. com*, is more popular with British guests that the main **ESF. White Sensations, t** 04 50 91 14 25, *www.white-sensations.com*, started by young highly-qualified British instructors a couple of seasons ago, is highly regarded and has grown rapidly.

Where to Stay

Megève
★★★★**Fermes de Marie, t** 04 50 93 03 10, *www. fermesdemarie.com* (*luxury–very expensive*). Ten minutes' walk from the centre, beautifully converted former farm buildings based round a 16th-century vaulted cowshed. Spa with sauna, Jacuzzi, pool and fitness room.
★★★**Ferme Hôtel Duvillard, t** 04 50 21 14 62, *www.ferme-hotel.com* (*very expensive– expensive*). Smartly restored farmhouse at the foot of the slopes right by the Mont d'Arbois gondola.
★★**Gai Soleil, t** 04 50 21 00 70, *www.le-gai- soleil.fr* (*moderate–inexpensive*). Comfortable, family-run, five minutes from the centre and Rochebrune gondola. Savoyard cooking and a 'giant *tartiflette*' evening once a week.

Catered Chalets
Stanford Skiing, t (01223) 477 644, specializes in Megève, and its creaky old Sylvana chalet hotel makes a cheap and cheerful base near the cable car up to Rochebrune.
Simon Butler Skiing, t 0870 8730 001, another Megève chalet specialist, offers tuition-based holidays (Simon is a ski instructor).

Eating Out

Megève

La Ferme de Mon Père, with three Michellin stars and 20 out of 20 from the Gault-Millau guide, is one of the very best restaurants in France, run by the famous chef Marc Veyrat who also has a wonderful restaurant in Annecy; it gets booked up weeks in advance. Exceptional food and wine but budget for a bill of a few hundred pounds a head.

For less astronomic prices and simpler food try **Mama Mia** (which has a wider-ranging menu than its Italian name suggests) and **Brasserie Centrale**. The **Phnom-Penh** makes a change from French and Savoyard food.

On the Mountain
Auberge du Côte 2000, at the foot of the slopes so easily accessible to pedestrian trade, serves some of the finest (and priciest) lunchtime food in a former farmhouse owned by the Rothschild family. **Alpette**, on top of the Rochebrune ridge, runs a snowcat service from the top of the gondola for pedestrians to sample its refined fair. **La Ravière**, a tiny hut in the woods near the La Croix drag in the Mont d'Arbois area, does an excellent set menu daily. Above St-Nicolas, several charming chalets offer simpler food at much more modest prices.

Bars and Clubs

The **Club de Jazz Les Cinq Rues** in Megève opens from teatime till late, attracts some big-name musicians and serves excellent (if expensive) cocktails. The **Palo Alto** nightclub in the casino can get busy. The **Cocoon**, **Apéritif** and **Roses** are popular with British guests. The **Pallas Café** attracts a younger crowd and **Megève Caves** a more mature age group.

you, the whole of Megève's ski area to the left and off-piste slopes leading down towards neighbouring Les Contamines to the right. The ski schools organize trips to ski the Vallée Blanche in Chamonix – competent intermediates who enjoy spectacular scenery should not miss this opportunity (*see* 'Chamonix' for more details).

If the snow is good, beginners will find Megève perfect: nursery slopes both at valley level and at altitude on all three mountains, lots of very easy green and blue runs to progress to and patient instructors who are used to dealing with neophytes. Not renowned as an area for expert skiers, Megève has few steep pistes worthy of their black status, the toughest being those from Mont-Joly and Epaule on Mont d'Arbois and the black mentioned above at Cote 2000. But if snow is good, there is worthwhile off-piste which remains untracked much longer than in many other resorts, as most Megève visitors have no desire to leave the perfectly manicured pistes. The steep wooded area under the second stage of the Princesse gondola on Mont d'Arbois and the more open bowls at Cote 2000 are especially worthy of exploration. If you hire a guide you can hike up from the top of the Mont-Joly chair and ski all the way down to the adjacent (but unlinked) resort Les Contamines. And the Mont Blanc area lift pass which covers Megève also allows you to explore the steep runs and off-piste of Chamonix (an easy car journey and excursions are often laid on).

Megève's beautiful and tranquil centre, based around the big church and open-air ice rink, contrasts sharply with its sprawling and traffic-choked outskirts. So it is best to stay in or close to the centre, where you can join the fur-coated and non-skiing crowd sipping coffee, window-shopping, taking rides in horse-drawn sleighs or just strolling around enjoying the ambience. Lunching is another major activity here and many of the 37 mountain restaurants scattered around the ski areas can easily be accessed by non-skiers – some will even send snowcats to pick customers up from the top of the nearest gondola. The resort rivals Courchevel for its choice of swish four-star hotels and Michelin-starred restaurants and you can spend a fortune living the high life here but there are plenty of more affordable options too.

For a much more down-to-earth holiday base, consider the handsome 19th century spa town of **St-Gervais**, set in a narrow river gorge, halfway between Megève and Chamonix, at the entrance to the side-valley leading up to St-Nicolas-de-Véroce and Les Contamines. Interesting food shops, cosy bars, thermal baths and an Olympic skating rink make St-Gervais a pleasant place to explore. If you have a car and want to make full use of all the resorts covered by the Mont Blanc lift pass it makes a much more central base. It also has direct access to the Mont d'Arbois ski area via a 20-person gondola from just outside the town and at the gondola mid-station, a small collection of hotels, private chalets and new apartments at **Le Bettex** are conveniently situated for the runs but have little evening animation. At the other side of St-Gervais from the gondola, a rack-and-pinion railway takes you to the slopes of Les Houches (*see* 'Chamonix') – you catch the railway back or, given enough snow, can ski back to St-Gervais off-piste. When the railway was built in 1904 the original idea was for it to go all the way to the top of Mont Blanc but, not surprisingly, it didn't quite make it.

Val d'Arly

Ski Area
Height of slopes 1,000m–2,070m
Number of lifts 42

Pistes 150km
green 29%
blue 33%
red 31%
black 7%

Tourist Information

Val d'Arly: **t** 04 79 31 06 82, *www.valdarly-montblanc.com.*

Espace Cristal

Ski Area
Height of slopes 1,230m–1,950m
Number of lifts 40

Pistes 90km
green 34%
blue 36%
red 25%
black 5%

Tourist Information

Les Saisies: **t** 04 79 38 90 30,
www.lessaisies.com.

Val d'Arly: Praz sur Arly, Flumet, Notre-Dame de Bellecombe; and Espace Cristal (in Savoie): Crest-Voland Cohennoz, Les Saisies

Val d'Arly's small, traditional villages, very close to Megève, on the road towards Albertville, have ambitious plans to link their two main ski areas to those of L'Espace Cristal from Christmas 2005 to form L'Espace Diamant. At the time of writing, however, these were still split into two.

Le Domaine Val d'Arly links the resorts of Praz sur Arly, Flumet and Notre-Dame de Bellecombe, while the ski areas of Crest-Voland Cohennoz and Les Saisies are marketed as **L'Espace Cristal**. The pistes of both suit intermediates and beginners best with lots of green and gentle blue and red pistes and very few challenging runs. The area sprang to fame for the 1992 Albertville Winter Olympics when cross-country events were held at the Mont Lachat area, shared by Les Saisies and Crest-Voland-Cohennoz. The 80km of trails here form one of the premier cross-country areas in the French Alps and other smaller loops dotted around the valley add variety.

The downhill slopes of **La Giettaz**, up the road towards La Clusaz, should be linked by the time this book is published to the Jaillet slopes of Megève, by new lifts and pistes due to open for Christmas 2004. La Giettaz's own slopes include some more challenging runs than is the norm in either Megève or Val d'Arly.

Les Contamines-Hauteluce

The charming unspoiled old village of Les Contamines, just a few kilometres from the macho slopes of Chamonix in one direction and the poodles and beautiful people of Megève in the other, makes a fine contrast to both. The compact centre with pretty wooden chalets, ancient church and weekly market in the square retains rural appeal, despite the resort as a whole having grown to spread thinly quite a distance over the valley. You can stay in the centre or near the lifts at Le Lay, a 1km bus ride away.

The resort's enviable snow record, said to be due to its proximity to Mont Blanc, together with a high proportion of shady northeast-facing slopes, means way above

Les Contamines

Ski Area
Height of slopes 1,160m–2,485m
Number of lifts 26

Pistes 120km
green 16%
blue 23%
red 40%
black 21%

Tourist Information

Les Contamines: t 04 50 47 01 58,
www.lescontamines.com.

Where to Stay

Les Contamines
★★★**Chemenaz**, t 04 50 47 02 44, *www.
chemenaz.com* (*moderate–inexpensive*) by the
gondola in Les Contamines, modern chalet,
only 3-star in town, with sauna and Jacuzzi.

average snow reliability until late on in the season. Although the majority of the
slopes (limited in extent compared with bigger-name resorts but still reasonably
substantial) suit intermediate cruising best, experts can enjoy some decent off-piste
and the Mont Blanc lift pass covers other resorts in the area, so you should not get
bored if you are prepared to travel. For beginners, the nursery slopes at both the
village and mid-mountain are fine but there are few easy green runs to progress to.
Several rustic mountain restaurants add to the area's appeal for a relaxing time.

Les Aravis: La Clusaz, Le Grand-Bornand, St-Jean-de-Sixt (skiing not linked)

Few other major French ski resorts can claim to be based around what are still,
essentially, genuine, unpretentious mountain villages that exude rustic charm and
Gallic atmosphere. And few others can be reached in an hour or so from Geneva
airport via the beautiful lakeside town of Annecy or in a leisurely day's drive from the
Channel ports. Combine these attractions with over 200km of largely intermediate
slopes, above and below the tree line, spread over five linked sectors in La Clusaz and
the separate Le Grand-Bornand area, and you can see why so many British families
have decided to buy homes around here. If it weren't for the altitude, or rather the
lack of it and therefore unreliable snow conditions, Les Aravis could attract many
more winter visitors. Snowmaking has been installed in recent years and is continu-
ally increased, but of course it makes no difference in mild weather.

Most intermediates will love **La Clusaz** if the snow conditions are good. Early intermediates will delight in the gentle slopes at the top of Beauregard and over on
La Croix-Fry at Manigod, with its network of tree-lined runs, and you can travel all over
the area on gentle, green pistes. L'Etale and L'Aiguille have more challenging but wide
blue runs while more adventurous intermediates will prefer the steeper red pistes
and good snow of the north-west facing slopes of La Balme and the long red down
Combe du Fernuy from L'Aiguille. Le Grand-Bornand is full of easy cruising blue and
red intermediate runs stretching in both directions above Le Chinaillon.

For beginners, the nursery slope at village level in La Clusaz could not be more
convenient and the other, more snowsure ones up the mountain at the top of the
Beauregard cable car and at Crêt du Merle are even better. The Beauregard area has

Les Aravis

La Clusaz: Ski Area
Height of slopes 1,100m–2,500m
Number of lifts 55

La Clusaz: Pistes 132km
green 29%
blue 32%
red 29%
black 10%

Le Grand-Bornand: Ski Area
Height of slopes 1,000m–2,100m
Number of lifts 39

Le Grand-Bornand: Pistes 82km
green 33%
blue 30%
red 30%
black 7%

Tourist Information

La Clusaz: t 04 50 32 65 00, www.laclusaz.com.
Le Grand-Bornand: t 04 50 02 78 00,
    www.legrandbornand.com.
St-Jean-de-Sixt: t 04 50 02 70 14,
    www.saintjeandesixt.com.

Ski Schools

La Clusaz: Two smaller schools provide good
    personal service: **Sno-Academie**, t 04 50 32
    66 05, www.snow-board.com, and **Aravis
    Challenge**, t 04 50 02 81 29, www.aravis-
    challenge.com (which includes off-piste and
    freestyle courses in its programme).
Le Grand-Bornand: **Starski**, t 04 50 27 04 69,
    www.esi-starski.com, is a small international
    school based in Chinaillon.

Where to Stay

La Clusaz
***Beauregard**, t 04 50 32 68 00, www.
    hotel-beauregard.fr (expensive–moderate),
    chalet-style buildings, with big pool, sauna,
    steam room, Jacuzzi and gym, on the fringe
    of the village. Good for families.

***Chalets de la Serraz**, t 04 50 02 48 29,
    www.laserraz.com (expensive–moderate)
    wonderful old chalet beautifully converted
    to a small hotel, set in a peaceful position
    4km from town, with a restaurant renowned
    for its excellent local cuisine.

Le Grand-Bornand
Croix Saint-Maurice, t 04 50 02 20 05,
    www.hotel-lacroixstmaurice.com
    (inexpensive–moderate), good value chalet
    in the heart of the old town right by the
    church and ski bus stop for La Clusaz.

Catered Chalets
None of the big tour operators feature
Les Aravis, but plenty of private chalets are
available, such as the old farmhouse out of
town now run by **Aravis Alpine Retreat**,
t (020) 8878 8760.

Eating Out

In the Resorts
La Clusaz: **Les Chalets de la Serraz** (see 'Where
    to Stay') has some of the best food in the
    region. In La Clusaz itself, the **Ecuelle** stands
    out for its Savoyard specialities.
Le Grand-Bornand: **La Ferme du Lormay** in the
    Vallée du Bouchet, 5km from Le Grand-
    Bornand, serves good-value local food with a
    heavy emphasis on cheese and polenta in an
    ancient Savoyard farmhouse.

On the Mountain
The aptly named creaky old **Vieux Chalet**
just above La Clusaz near the top of the
gondola is wonderfully peaceful for a leisurely
lunch, inside or out, and easily accessible for
pedestrians too. The **Vieille Ferme** at
Merdassier makes another splendid place for a
serious lunch away from hustle and bustle.

Bars and Clubs

La Clusaz: It doesn't really get lively except at
    weekends and peak season weeks. The
    Caves du Paccaly has live music, the **Pressoir**
    sports videos and **Pub Le Salto** Sky TV and
    draught Guinness. The **Ecluse** disco and **Club
    18**, which often has live bands, liven up later.

lovely gentle blue runs to progress to, including one long run around the mountain right back to the village. Le Grand-Bornand and St-Jean-de-Sixt also feature good beginner slopes. The La Clusaz piste map doesn't seem to have much to offer experts, but most of the sectors offer decent off-piste, all the more attractive for being ignored by most visitors – don't miss the excellent run down Combe de Borderan from L'Aiguille and the Combe de la Bellachat reached from the top of La Balme. La Balme also has several fairly challenging pistes above mid-mountain, including the seriously steep black Vraille run, which leads to the speed skiing slope. The Tetras on L'Etale and the Mur Edgar (named after Olympic hero and local boy Edgar Grospiron) run below Crêt du Loup on L'Aiguille have been reclassified as blacks, and rightly so. In Le Grand-Bornand the steepest runs, including the black Noire du Lachat, go from the top of Le Lachat.

Cross-country enthusiasts will love Les Aravis, with around 70km of prepared trails to choose between, including a lovely sunny area at the top of the Beauregard cable car in La Clusaz and in the Vallée du Bouchet at Le Grand Bornand.

Built beside a fast-flowing stream at the junction of several wooded valleys, La Clusaz's charming centre features old stone and wood buildings and a large church. Roads run from here in several directions, which is difficult to get to grips with initially and the new buildings blend in well with the old. It has grown into quite a large sprawling place now, offering facilities such as a huge open-air swimming pool with fabulous views of the mountains. Every Monday evening a jolly welcome meeting in the main square allows you to mingle with locals and fellow guests and sample local cheeses and *vin chaud*. **Le Grand-Bornand**, a ten-minute free bus ride away, exudes the feel of remaining a quiet, unspoiled mountain village based around its baroque church, despite having two gondolas up to the slopes. Much of the new development has taken place up the road at the chalet-style development of **Le Chinaillon**, served by chairlifts up into the skiing. Every week, local farmers open their doors to visitors and Wednesday is market day, with a special wholesale market of local Reblochon cheese as well. The small hamlet of **St-Jean-de-Sixt**, midway between La Clusaz and Le Grand Bornand, has a small slope for beginners and tobogganing.

Savoie: The Tarentaise Valley

Le Grand Domaine: Valmorel, St-François-Longchamp, Doucy-Combelouvière

If you have ever been to any of the Tarentaise resorts you will have driven past the turn-off to **Valmorel**, the major resort in the Grand Domaine ski area. That's what most people do, ignoring what is arguably the most sympathetically designed French purpose-built ski resort. It shares its slopes with two less popular and less attractive modern ski stations – St-François and Longchamp.

The ski area, though not as huge as its near neighbours, links the Tarentaise with the Maurienne valley and contains several distinct sectors divided by ridges and valleys either side of the Col de la Madeleine, which makes it interestingly varied and

Le Grand Domaine

Ski Area
Height of slopes 1,250m–2,550m
Number of lifts 56

Pistes 153km
green 33%
blue 39%
red 19%
black 9%

Tourist Information

Valmorel: t 04 79 09 85 55, *www.valmorel.com*.
Doucy-Combelouvière: t 04 79 22 94 17,
www.doucy-combelouvière.com.
St-François-Longchamp: t 04 79 59 10 56,
www.saintfrancoislongchamp.com.

Ski Schools

Valmorel: ESF, t 04 79 09 81 86, *www.esf-valmorel.com*, has an especially high
reputation for teaching children and
beginners.

Where to Stay

Valmorel
★★★Auberge Planchamp, t 04 79 09 97 00,
www. hotelplanchamp.com (*very expensive
–moderate*), on the slopes, just above the chair
lift out of Valmorel, smartest in town with
liberal use of pine, cosy bar area and open fire.

Catered Chalets
Valmorel: Crystal, t 0870 1606 040, and
Neilson, t 0870 333 3347, each have a couple
of chalets in Valmorel, targeted at families.

Eating Out

Valmorel:The Grange is the place for Savoyard
specialities, **Pizzeria du Bourg** for pizzas
cooked in a wood-fired oven and **Jimbo Lolo**
for steaks and Tex-Mex.

Bars and Clubs

Don't come here for lively *après-ski*. Bar and
restaurant terraces at the bottom of the main
slope back to Valmorel are good for a beer.
Later on, the **Clover** disco and karaoke bar and
Café de la Gare can get lively.

attractive to intermediates of all standards. The main Planchamp red run back to the
village, lined with snow-guns, can be quite challenging towards the end of the day if
the bumps have built up; for an easier option, take the alternative blue. Good intermediates should not miss the red and black in the Gollet sector and a day out to the
far end of St-François-Longchamp and back. The area also provides lots of scope for
trying a bit of off-piste beside and between the main pistes.

Experts won't find many pistes to challenge them: those from the top of the Mottet
chair and the nearby Riondet drag are some of the steepest and most interesting. But
you'll find plenty of little-skied off-piste. To make the most of it, hire a guide and explore
runs such as those along the fabulous north-facing valley from near the top of the
Lozière chair, where the snow stays good for long after a fresh snowfall. You can also
traverse from the top of the Gollet sector and ski down to the old village of **Les
Avanchers**, way below Valmorel, passing through forests and over streams on the way.

Few resorts can boast anything as good for beginners as the excellent nursery
slopes, isolated from better skiers racing through and yet right in the centre of the
village. Speedy progress can be made here and on very easy green runs higher up.

Valmorel's low-rise buildings, with liberal use of wood and coloured walls, and short
traffic-free main street lined with shops and restaurants, give the resort a cheerful,

family-friendly atmosphere, with almost a Disneyesque feel to it. The main high-speed chairlift out and piste back are at one end of the main street and at the other a step-on lift for pedestrians and skiers alike works until late to serve a number of higher accommodation 'hamlets' and the Pierrafort gondola. Below Valmorel, reached by a gentle blue and then even gentler green run and set prettily in the trees, **Doucy-Combelouvière** appeals to those looking for a quiet time. **St-François-Longchamp**, more starkly set just above the tree line, has more of a conventional purpose-built resort feel, with some chalet-style but mainly bigger, more block-like buildings.

Les Trois Vallées: Courchevel, La Tania, Méribel, Brides-les-Bains, St-Martin-de-Belleville, Les Menuires, Val-Thorens

Even the keenest skier or snowboarder will find the 600km of linked pistes and 1,400 sq km of skiable terrain that **Les Trois Vallées** boasts will keep them busy for a week. Indeed it would keep most people happy for a season. Nowhere else approaches this scale of ski domain, where you have to take your skis or board off only to have lunch or ride the gondolas or cable cars among the 200 lifts that can carry 260,000 people an hour. While Les Portes du Soleil claims 650km of pistes and over 200 lifts, there are gaps between its pistes where you have to walk or take a bus.

The dream of linking the Saint-Bon, Allues and Belleville valleys from Courchevel at one end to Val-Thorens at the other began in 1925 but was not fully realized until 1975. Since then the ski area has expanded yet again into the Maurienne valley beyond Val-Thorens and should really be renamed *Les Quatre Vallées*, but that would be a waste of the millions francs and euros that have been ploughed into the marketing of this vast commercial enterprise.

From early December until late April, you can usually explore the whole area. But the 3000m peaks and glaciers towering above Val-Thorens mean that this resort has one of the longest winter seasons in Europe, stretching from early November until May.

Intermediates of every standard will find the Trois Vallées a paradise, with over two-thirds of the pistes graded blue or red and most of them immaculately groomed every night. If you want to step out on to perfect corduroy-style pistes every morning without travelling 5000 miles to the USA, this is the place to head for. The area seems to be on a mission to match the high standards of service in US ski areas in general, and Courchevel has copied the useful US practice of having free maps available every morning showing which pistes have been groomed overnight. There is no point in picking out particular intermediate runs – suffice to say that wherever you go, you won't be disappointed. Beginners are well-catered for too, at all the major resorts, with good nursery slopes and easy green runs to progress to.

Many experts deride the Trois Vallées as being simply for intermediates. It is true that only 12% of the pistes are graded black. But among them are some real challenges. Courchevel offers the most steep black runs including the awesome *Grand Couloir*, near the top of the Saulire cable car, where the north-facing slope generally has excellent powder and is reached via a vertigo-inducing precipitous path. *Suisse* and *Chanrossa*, also near Saulire, are two of the longest, steepest mogul runs around. Lower down, leading to the lowest of Courchevel's villages, Le Praz, both *Jockeys* and

Les Trois Vallées

Ski Area
Height of slopes 1,260m–3,230m
Number of lifts 200

Pistes 600km
green 17%
blue 34%
red 37%
black 12%

Tourist Information

Brides-les-Bains: t 04 79 55 20 64, *www.brides-les-bains.com*.
Courchevel: t 04 79 08 00 29, *www.courchevel.com*.
Les Menuires: t 04 79 00 73 00, *www.lesmenuires.com*.
Méribel: t 04 79 08 60 01, *www.meribel.net*.
St-Martin-de-Belleville: t 04 79 00 20 00, *www.st-martin-belleville.com*.
La Tania: t 04 79 08 40 40, *www.latania.com*.
Val-Thorens: t 04 79 00 08 08, *www.valthorens.com*.

Ski Schools

Courchevel and Méribel: Highly rated British-run **New Generation**, t 04 79 01 03 18, *www.skinewgen.com*, staffed largely by go-ahead young, highly qualified British instructors, started in Courchevel in the 1990s and opened in Méribel a few years later and generates rave reviews from most customers. **Magic in Motion**, t 04 79 01 01 81 (Courchevel), t 04 79 08 53 36 (Méribel), *www.magicinmotion.co.uk*, started in Méribel and expanded to Courchevel and other Trois Vallées resorts and also has a good reputation.

Les Menuires and St-Martin-de-Belleville: There is little choice here except the **ESF**, t 04 79 00 61 43, *www.esf-lesmenuires.com* and, t 04 79 00 24 78, *www.esf-st-martin-belleville.com*.
La Tania: The **Magic in Motion** branch here is specially highly thought of for its teaching of children. t 04 79 01 07 85, *www.magicinmotion.co.uk*.
Val-Thorens: The **ESF**, t 04 79 00 02 86, *www.esf-valthorens.com*, has a special group to explore the pistes and off-piste of the whole Trois Vallées – you can join just for a day or for the whole week. **Prosneige**, t 04 79 01 07 00, *www.prosneige.fr*, runs everything from beginner and children's classes to heli-skiing and a 5-day off-piste course.

Where to Stay

Courchevel

You can spend a fortune staying in one of 14 plush 4-star hotels, but there are cheaper options too.

★★★★**Mélézin**, t 04 79 08 01 33, *www.amanresorts.com* (*luxury–room only*). On the piste just above the centre of 1850, extremely stylish and luxurious, with bathrooms overlooking superb views of the mountains. Pool, steam room, Jacuzzi, gym

★★★**Peupliers**, t 04 79 08 41 47, *www.lespeupliers.com* (*expensive*). Near the piste and lifts at 1300, beautifully renovated and much expanded old chalet with a good value restaurant serving a varied menu.

Méribel

★★★★**Grand Cœur**, t 04 79 08 60 03, *www.legrandcoeur.com* (*very expensive–luxury*). Wonderful old chalet just above village centre near piste, splendidly comfortable lounge with grand piano, sauna, steam room, Jacuzzi, gym.

Jean Blanc are entertaining blacks so long as the snow is good. In Méribel, head for the *Face* which was created as the ladies downhill run for the 1992 Olympics, or for the *Combe de Vallon*, which is a real test of stamina despite being graded as a mere red. In Les Menuires, head for the *La Masse* area where the steep blacks and reds usually have some of the best snow around because of their north-facing orientation. In Val-Thorens, for warp-speed cruising you can't beat the *Combe de Caron* run after it

★★Adray Télébar, t 04 79 08 60 26, *www. telebar-hotel.com* (*expensive*). Lovely ancient chalet, peacefully positioned in the woods by the piste above the village, with a popular restaurant (lunchtime as well as evenings).

Val-Thorens

★★★★Fitz Roy, t 04 79 00 04 78, *www.fitzroy hotel.com* (*luxury–very expensive*). Sumptuous modern *Relais et Châteaux* chalet on slopes in centre of resort with superb piste-side terrace, pool, sauna, steam room, salon.

★★★Sherpa, t 04 79 00 00 70, *www.lesherpa. com* (*expensive–moderate*). Smart, friendly new chalet near top of resort, with special offers for children sharing parents' room. Sauna, steam room, Jacuzzi.

Apartments

Courchevel: High-quality apartments include the **Forum** in the centre of 1850 and the **Montagnettes** in 1650.

Les Menuires: **Montagnettes** and **Alpages**, both in Reberty and the latter with a pool, are smart newish developments, far superior to the dire apartments in the central La Croisette area.

Méribel: **Fermes de Méribel Village** at the bottom of a chairlift in a new development 2km from Méribel centre are well-furnished with lots of beams and wood, good views, pool, sauna, steam room and gym.

Val-Thorens: A huge choice of smart new, well-furnished apartments – some of the best include **Oxalys** (with pool, sauna, steam room, Jacuzzi and excellent restaurant), **Montagnettes**, **Balcons de Val-Thorens** and **Village Montana**.

Catered Chalets

The Trois Vallées is the catered chalet capital of the world. Huge numbers of UK tour operators have chalets in all the main resorts (over 50 feature Méribel, for example).

Courchevel: 1850 is full of luxury chalets, and tour operators which specialize in them include **Flexiski, t** 0870 9090 754, **Lotus Supertravel, t** (020) 7962 9933, **Scott Dunn**, **t** (020) 8682 5050, and **Simply Ski, t** (020) 8541 2209. Down in 1650, **Le Ski, t** 0870 7544 444, has a varied selection of conveniently located, mid-market options.

Méribel: Check the position of chalets carefully – some are a long way from lifts and pistes (though many tour operators have mini-buses to shuttle guests to and fro). **Meriski, t** (01285) 648 515, has specialized in up-market Méribel chalets for over 20 years. Other deluxe options include **Descente International, t** (020) 738 438 54, **Lotus Supertravel, t** (020) 7962 9933, **Scott Dunn, t** (020) 86 82 50 50, **Snowline, t** (020) 88 70 48 07, and VIP **t** (020) 8875 1957. **Bonne Neige, t** (01270) 256 966, **Ski Activity, t** (01738) 840 888, **Ski Blanc, t** (020) 8502 9082 and **Ski Total, t** 0871 633 633, all have good chalets. **Mark Warner, t** 0870 7704 226, has a big chalet-hotel right on the piste at Méribel-Mottaret.

St-Martin-de-Belleville: **Chalets de St-Martin**, **t** (01202) 473 255, features self-catered as well as catered chalets.

Eating Out

In the Resorts

Courchevel: The **Bateau Ivre** and **Chabichou** in 1850 both have two Michelin rosettes and prices to match. The cosy **La Saulire** (also known as **Chez Jacques**) is more affordable and does Savoy specialities, while **La Locomotive** with railway-themed décor has an extensive and varied menu and the **Potinière** is a budget option for pizza, steak or pasta. In 1550, the **Petit Savoyard**, **Montagne** and **Eterlou** are close together and do good steaks as well as Savoyard

has been groomed – it will be well worth the wait for the cable car up, which is the only serious queue left in the Trois Vallées.

There is excellent off-piste to be explored with a guide – and most of it deserted compared with ski areas with a more macho image such as L'Espace Killy and Chamonix.

specialities. Down in 1300 the **Peupliers** (*see* 'Where to Stay') is building a good reputation since its refurbishment.

Méribel: Croix Jean-Claude down in Les Allues, a taxi-ride from the centre, serves good honest local food such as rabbit and lake fish in a pleasant rustic dining room, away from the bustle of the main resort. In Méribel itself the **Grand Cœur** (*see* 'Where to Stay') has the highest reputation for haute cuisine, **Chez Kiki** is famous for its charcoal-grilled meats, **Cro-Magnon** specializes in fondue, raclette and pizza.

St-Martin-de-Belleville: People come from miles around to the excellent cuisine of the prettily presented, traditonal *auberge* of **La Bouitte** in nearby St-Marcel which is famous for its *foie gras*, veal, cheeses and dessert trolley.

Val-Thorens: L'Oxalys opened for the 2002/3 season and has quickly built a reputation for having the best classic French cuisine in town and a superb views from its piste-side terrace. **Galoubet** is excellent for Savoyard specialities such as *pierrade* and *tartiflette*. For Tex-Mex try **El Gringo's**.

On the Mountain

Courchevel: Beware of the Chalet de Pierres and Cap Horn, two of the most expensive mountain restaurants in the Alps. Much better value are the friendly **Panoramic** (table- and self-service) at the top of the cable car to La Saulire, and the simpler menu (including excellent *omelette savoyarde*) and sunny three-tier terrace of **Bel Air** at the top of the gondola from 1650.

Méribel: The **Altibar** has a lovely peaceful sun terrace and a varied menu, the **Altiport** hotel terrace serves an excellent buffet and steak tartare, the **Chardonnet**, at the mid-station of the Mottaret-Saulire gondola, is a wonderful suntrap. For a cheaper, quicker option try **Rond Point**, just below the mid-

station of the Rhodos gondola, for the very tasty paninis.

Les Menuires: The old chalet of **L'Etoile**, on the piste just above the resort, with a rustic interior and sunny terrace, features waiters in traditional costume.

Val-Thorens: Bar de la Marine, on the Dalles piste, does good grills and *plat du jour*, has a decent wine list and a nautical theme.

Bars and Clubs

Courchevel: If you want lots of nightlife, head for 1850. **Jump**, at the bottom of the main pistes, is popular when the lifts close. Later on the exclusive **Caves** nightclub, with top Paris cabaret acts and sky-high prices and **Kalico**, with DJs and cocktails, get busy. The **Bergerie** does themed evenings of food, music and entertainment. Down in 1650 the **Bubble** and **Rocky's** bars are the focal points, with largely British clientele.

Méribel: Rond Point by the piste gets packed as the lifts close and often has live music; the **Taverne and Pub** in the main square and **Rastro** and **Downtown** at Mottaret attract the crowds too. Later on **Scott's**, in the main square, and **Dick's Tea Bar**, on the road below the centre, have dancing till late.

St-Martin-de-Belleville: Pourquoi Pas? piano bar with roaring log fire and comfy sofas is a great contrast with **Brewski's**, the other main bar with its wooden chairs and tables, photos of 1960s and '70s rock groups and occasional live bands – both are British-run.

Val-Thorens: The **Frog and Roastbeef** attracts a lot of British customers with its cut-price beer and often a live band at tea-time and claims to be the highest pub in Europe. The **Red Fox** has tea-time karaoke and also attracts the crowds. Later on, the **Underground** nightclub and **Malaysia** cellar bar are the places to head for.

Nearly all the major resorts in the area, which between them have 140,000 beds, have been purpose-built – some with more panache and style than others. At the northern end, in the Saint-Bon valley, the highest of Courchevel's four main villages, **Courchevel 1850** is one of the chicest and most expensive ski resorts in Europe, with more four-star hotels than any city in France outside Paris. When you consider they all have to make their money in a four-month season, it comes as no surprise that they charge sky-high prices. But the Paris jet set and, increasingly, nouveau-riche Russians, happily pay them. British guests tend to stay in more affordable catered chalets or self-catering apartments. Most buildings here are no more than three or four storeys and had wood cladding and pitched roofs added to improve their appearance for the 1992 Olympics.

Courchevel 1650, with its old village square and friendly, less up-market feel, has grown in a higgledy-piggledy fashion with different architectural styles either side of the road up the 1850. The food shops here are much better than in its up-market neighbour, with excellent butcher, baker and delicatessen. **Courchevel 1550** is set off the main road in a quiet position but its square block-like buildings and lack of animation means it lacks character and focus. The same cannot be said of the lowest village, **Courchevel 1300** (more commonly called **Le Praz**), which still retains an old village with narrow cobbled paths at its heart – though it was expanded hugely for the 1992 Olympics, which also resulted in a huge ski-jump hill being built at the foot of the slopes.

Gondolas are the main way out of each of the villages, though the rickety old pair from Le Praz badly need replacing (and hopefully will have been by the time you go).

Between Le Praz and Méribel, **La Tania** was built to house the press for the 1992 Olympics and its apartments and chalets, prettily set in the woods, now make a small, family-friendly resort with a traffic-free centre and an efficient gondola to the slopes.

There are few other resorts in the Alps that are as British as **Méribel** in the central Allues valley. Conceived and kick-started by Colonel Peter Lindsay in the 1930s and '40s, either side of the Second World War, many of its chalets are British-owned and the British population in winter appears to exceed the French. From the start, strict architectural guidelines were laid down limiting development to traditional wooden chalet-style – so the resort escaped the architectural excesses that so many other French resorts suffered from. But the place has been allowed to expand hugely across the mountainside, with much of the newer development a bus-ride from the slopes. **Méribel-Mottaret** is a rather soulless satellite a few kilometres up the valley with a traffic-free centre and convenient ski-in, ski-out accommodation.

Way below Méribel at an altitude of only 600m, the old spa town of **Brides-les-Bains** was very quiet in winter before a gondola was built linking it in 25 minutes to Méribel. It now makes a budget base from which to explore the slopes – but the last gondola back down leaves at around 5pm.

The old village of **St-Martin-de-Belleville**, the administrative capital of the third (Belleville) valley, has a lovely 16th-century church, prettily floodlit at night. In 1950 it didn't even have running water or electricity and while resorts around it developed in the 1960s and 70s, it wasn't until the 1980s that it was linked by a chairlift into the slopes – now replaced by a smart new gondola. The resort has expanded slowly with all new buildings in the original stone and wood style and still remains small, exuding the feel of a traditional village.

The next resort up the valley could not be in more stark contrast. There may be someone other than the tourist office director who has a good word to say about **Les Menuires**' original architectural style, but I have yet to meet them. The resort centre of La Croisette and its immediate neighbouring buildings are monstrous concrete blocks

– some of them huge – with cheaply-built apartments and a dire, dark and tatty indoor shopping and restaurant complex. Yes, they are trying to make the best of what they built by smartening it up and the newest developments of Reberty and Hameau des Marmottes have been built in smart traditional chalet style. But the central core is depressingly awful.

Further on up the road at the head of the valley **Val-Thorens** (at 2,300m Europe's highest resort) forms the most snowsure part of the Trois Vallées. Despite its bleak setting, high above the tree line beneath towering peaks, this purpose-built resort has a much more welcoming feel than Les Menuires, with smaller, mainly medium-rise and wood-clad buildings with car-free streets and squares and ski-in, ski-out convenience for most accommodation. When it's sunny here it makes an excellent base. When it's snowing hard, whiteout conditions can make it feel very inhospitable.

Paradiski: Les Arcs, La Grande Plagne, Peisey Vallandry

The world's largest cable car – a double-decker called the Vanoise Express which holds 200 people – opened in December 2003 to link two already famous ski areas. Spanning the 2km between Montchavin on the La Plagne slopes and Plan Peisey on the Les Arcs side in less than four minutes, it whisks you smoothly along, with stunning views towards the Plan Peisey side – be sure to face that way. The resulting joint ski *domaine*, christened **Paradiski**, leaps into the record books as one of the biggest in the world. Only the Trois Vallées and the Portes du Soleil can legitimately claim significantly more than Paradiski's 450km of pistes and 164 lifts. Arguably, in terms of total skiing terrain including off-piste potential, Paradiski beats them both.

Both **La Plagne** and **Les Arcs** are classic examples of 1960s purpose-built ski resort development on previously deserted, high snowfields. Over the last 40 years, they have both developed big networks of ideal intermediate cruising runs, perfectly suited to the mass-market clientele they have aimed to attract. Plenty of beginners learn their skiing and snowboarding skills happily here, though once you progress from the nursery slopes there are no really easy long green runs to move on to, which is less than ideal. For experts, black runs near the top of both La Plagne and Les Arcs present worthwhile challenges; and don't miss one of the longest pistes in the Alps

High-speed Thrills

In 1992, Olympic athletes hurtled down the bobsleigh run in La Plagne. Now you can experience the thrills of reaching over 100kph and negotiating the 19 banked bends of the 1.5km track, which is opened and floodlit several times a week. You have the choice of a solo mono-bob, an Olympic 4-man bob with you sandwiched between the fully-trained driver and brakeman or a slightly slower padded bob-raft where four tourists go it alone. In Les Arcs, the 1992 Olympians hit speeds of well over 200kph in the speed skiing event. Now anyone with the nerve can try the famous 'flying kilometre' here – an immaculately groomed steep slope above Arc 2000 reserved specially for the event. You'll be supplied with special long, straight skis, a helmet and goggles and win a bronze medal for hitting 110kph (nearly everyone does), silver for 130kph and gold for 150kph.

Paradiski

Ski Area
Height of slopes 1,200m–3,255m
Number of lifts 164

Pistes 420km
green 5%
blue 54%
red 28%
black 13%

Tourist Information

Les Arcs: t 04 79 07 12 57, *www.lesarcs.com.*
Peisey-Vallandry: t 04 79 07 94 28,
www.peisey-vallandry.com.
La Plagne: t 04 79 09 79 79,
www.la-plagne.com.
Montchavin-les-Coches: t 04 79 07 82 82,
www.montchavin-lescoches.com.
Champagny-en-Vanoise: t 04 79 55 06 55,
www.champagny.com.

Ski Schools

Les Arcs: Highly rated British-run **New
Generation,** t 04 79 01 03 18, *www.
skinewgen.com,* started a Les Arcs school in
2003/4 after establishing itself first in
Courchevel and Méribel – staffed largely by
go-ahead young, highly qualified British
instructors. **Spirit 1950,** t 04 79 04 25 72,
www.spirit1950.com, with bilingual instructors, opened in the new Arc 1950

development and has rapidly built a good
reputation. These now provide competition
for the previous main international school
Arc Aventures, t 04 79 07 41 28, *www.arc-
aventures.com.*
La Plagne: Evolution 2 in Montchavin, t 04 79
07 81 85, *www.evolution2.com,* **Oxygène** in
Plagne-Centre, t 04 79 09 03 99, *www.
oxygene-ski.com,* and **El Pro** in Belle-Plagne,
t 04 79 09 11 62, *www.elpro.fr,* all provide a
good personal service.

Where to Stay

There are very few hotels; most accommodation is apartments and chalets.

Les Arcs
★★★**Grand Hotel Mercure** (Arc 1800), t 04 79
07 65 00, *www.mercure.com (expensive).*
New and modern, locally judged to be worth
four stars.
★★**Vanoise** (Plan-Peisey), t 04 79 07 92 19, *www.
hotel-la-vanoise.com (moderate).* Modern
rooms, friendly staff, great views from
restaurant, close to cable-car to La Plagne.

La Plagne
★★**Glières** (Champagny-en-Vanoise), t 04 79 55
05 52, *www.hotel-glieres.com (moderate).*
Rustic, varied rooms, friendly welcome, 100m
from the gondola.

Apartments
There are thousands to choose from in each
resort. **Erna Low,** t 0870 7506 820, is the

from the top of Les Arcs' Aiguille Rouge cable car down to Villaroger – a total descent
of over 2000m vertical. Because most visitors to these resorts are intermediates, off-
piste in both areas tends to be deserted and becomes tracked out much less quickly
that in more macho resorts such as Val d'Isère. Good skiers willing to hire a guide will
love epic off-piste runs such as the north face of Bellecôte and the run over the Col du
Nant glacier to Champagny-le-Haut through the Vanoise National Park (both starting
from the La Plagne area) and the Combe de l'Anchette from the Grand Col above Les
Arcs to Villaroger.

None of Les Arcs' three main purpose-built traffic-free villages, named unimagina-
tively after their heights, can be described as attractive. Many of the big wood-clad
apartment blocks do however offer the convenience of allowing you to ski to and
from their doors. **Arc 1600,** the original Arc which opened in 1968, has the friendliest

official UK representative for both Les Arcs and La Plagne and can book apartments for you.

Les Arcs: Arc 1950's smart new development and **MGM's Alpages de Chantel** above Arc 1800 both have access to pools, saunas and gyms.

La Plagne: Montagnettes in Belle-Plagne and **MGM** in Aime-La-Plagne are spacious and well-furnished with good views.

Catered Chalets

Les Arcs: Ski Olympic, t (01302) 328 820 has a big chalet-hotel, **Ski Beat, t** (01243) 780 405 some attractive new chalets, and family-specialist **Esprit Ski, t** (01252) 618 300 some similar chalets and a nursery – all in the Peisey-Vallandry area.

La Plagne: Ski Beat, t (01243) 780 405 has a wide selection throughout the resort, **Finlays, t** (01573) 226 611 two smart chalets near Montchavin.

Eating Out

In the Resorts

Les Arcs: L'Ancolie, a delightful traditional *auberge* a five-minute taxi-ride below Peisey-Vallandry, serves generous portions of the best local produce, such as duck breast and rabbit, and offers excellent value menus. Don't miss the wild boar terrine if it's available. **Bois de Lune** in the woods at Montvenix, a taxi-ride below the Arc 1600, makes a lovely secluded location for an evening out.

La Plagne: The **Refuge** in Plagne-Centre, decorated with bobsleigh memorabilia, claims to be the oldest restaurant in La Plagne (dating from 1961) and serves a wide-ranging menu.

On the Mountain

Les Arcs: The charmingly rustic 500-year-old **Belliou la Fumée** at Pre-St-Esprit below Arc 2000 boasts a lovely log fire in the centre of the main dining room and a varied menu. **Chalets de l'Arc**, above Arc 2000, though quite large and only a few years old, has been built in traditional style and features interesting *plats du jour*, such as chicken in vinegar.

La Plagne: Chez Pat du Sauget, above Montchavin, and **Au Bon Vieux Temps**, just below Aime la Plagne, are both small, rustic huts – very cosy and jolly on a snowy day. **Roc des Blanchets** at the top of the Champagny gondola has beautiful views over to Courchevel and often offers free *Viperine* (a local liquor with a dead viper in the bottle) at the end of your meal.

Bars and Clubs

Les Arcs: In 1800 the **Red Hot Saloon** and **Jungle Café** both sometimes have live music and the **Fairway** disco rocks till 4am.

La Plagne: Mat's in Belle-Plagne resembles an English pub, **King Café** in Plagne-Centre gets packed and has a huge TV and occasional live music, **Mine** in Plagne-1800 attracts lots of Brits and boasts an old train and mining artefacts.

feel because of its setting in the trees and its fine views along the valley and towards Mont Blanc; it is also where the funicular up from Bourg-St-Maurice in the valley below arrives. By far the largest, with the widest variety of shops and restaurants, **Arc 1800** is the liveliest place to stay. **Arc 2000** sits bleakly on a shelf, way above the tree-line and consists of little more than a few giant blocks, including a Club Med. A much-hyped new village, **Arc 1950**, opened its first phase for winter 2003/4 and will continue to grow for the next ten years. Set just below Arc 2000 and linked by gondola lift till late at night, 1950 is the first European village to be created by Canadian resort developer Intrawest who specialize in building attractive resort villages. True to form Arc 1950's low-rise, chalet-style curved buildings made from local wood and stone, set around a cobbled pedestrian street, offer a much more pleasant environment than the other Arc villages. But the apartments themselves are disappointingly small and cramped – following the French norm rather the extra space you would get from similar developments in North America.

The new cable-car link to **La Plagne**, at the western end of the ski area, prompted rapid development over the last few years of low-rise chalet-style buildings. **Plan Peisey** and **Vallandry** are side by side, with the latter having more of a focal point, with a pedestrian ized square of shops and restaurants – a friendly, quiet place to stay and ideal for exploring the whole Paradiski area. For a more rustic base, the old village of **Peisey**, below here, is linked by lift but not piste and is still a largely unspoiled mountain village with few tourist trappings except a couple of restaurants.

At the La Plagne end of the cable-car link, the genuine old farming village of **Montchavin** has expanded in sympathetic style and makes a peaceful place to stay with a fair choice of shops and restaurants around its car-free centre. Just above it the new development of **Les Coches** has been built in similarly attractive chalet style. The contrast between these and the hideous, cheap, purpose-built original high-altitude La Plagne accommodation centre of **Plagne-Centre**, with its claustrophobic underground shopping malls and restaurants could not be starker. Two of the other high-altitude 'villages', **Plagne-Bellecote** and **Aime La Plagne**, give a similar impression of being slung up to provide budget accommodation with little regard for the environment – huge apartment blocks are what you see and what you get. Belle-Plagne is the most attractive of the purpose-built villages with low-rise buildings built toresemble typical Savoyard architecture.

At the southern end of the La Plagne ski area, furthest from the link to Les Arcs and way down in the valley at 1250m (compared with the 2000m or so of the purpose-built villages), **Champagny-en-Vanoise** makes another attractive place to stay. Like Montchavin it is based around an old mountain village but it doesn't have quite the same rural feel to it, perhaps because it has developed along a winding approach road. A powerful gondola whisks you up to snowsure slopes but you may have to ride it down as well because the runs home are often closed, as the snow suffers from their south-facing aspect and they have no snowmaking.

Espace San Bernardo/Sud Mont-Blanc: La Rosière and La Thuile (Italy)

Perched far above the most dramatic bend in the Isère valley, **La Rosière** occupies a sensational location with stunning views over to the slopes of the Les Arcs ski area on the other side of the gorge. Its attractive, purpose-built, chalet-style buildings, set among trees on sunny slopes, give it a very friendly feel and make the least well-known and smallest of the major Tarentaise resorts particularly appealing to families. Kids also love the friendly St Bernard dogs kept at the far end of the resort – a dead end in winter but open in summer when it forms the start of the Petit-St-Bernard pass over to Italy. Cross-border skiing to La Thuile in Italy forms another of the winter attractions and the joint area has recently been christened Espace San Bernardo.

La Rosière's own slopes are south-facing, which is unusual for a major French resort. But they can cope with the battering they get from the sun because of the unusually large amounts of snow they receive from storms funnelled up the Isère valley from the south-west. **La Thuile** in Italy, just over the Col de la Traversette frequently gets

Espace San Bernardo

Ski Area
Height of slopes 1,175m–2,610m
Number of lifts 36

Pistes 140km
green 12%
blue 36%
red 35%
black 17%

Tourist Information

La Rosière: t 04 79 06 80 51, www.larosiere.net.

Ski Schools

La Rosière: Evolution 2, t 04 79 40 19 80, www. evolution2.com, receives high praise and also organizes heli-ski groups

Where to Stay

La Rosière
**Plein Soleil, t 04 79 06 80 43 (moderate–inexpensive). A cheerful little hotel in the centre with small, cosy rooms and restaurant and great views.

Apartments
La Rosière: The relatively new Les Balcons, away from the centre at Les Eucherts, offer smart accommodation for larger groups in spacious apartments, some with wood-burning stoves and all with Jacuzzis.

Catered Chalets
La Rosière: For years Ski Olympic, t (01302) 328 820, was the only British chalet operator in La Rosière and it still has two rustic places set in the woods below the centre. It has also taken over a 2-star hotel in the centre and a newly built chalet on the edge. Family specialist Esprit Ski, t (01252) 618 300, has over ten chalets, all fairly central and all with access to reliable and comprehensive child-care facilities. Thomson, t 0870 606 1470, has two central nearly new chalet-apartments with sauna and crèche run by British nannies. Crystal, t 0870 160 6040, has three chalet-apartments in the same building.

Eating Out/Bars

Many people come down the mountain for lunch, where Relais du Petit St-Bernard and P'tit Relais are popular (evenings as well as lunchtime).

Of the handful of bars, Arpins has karaoke, but après-ski is generally quiet.

much less snow – though what it does get keeps in good condition because of the slopes being predominantly north-facing. But it is not unusual in cold weather to find hard icy slopes in Italy and deep soft snow in La Rosière. In warm weather, heading for Italy may be the best bet to avoid slush.

These cross-border options make La Rosière a good resort for intermediates. The top half of La Rosière's own slopes boast some fairly steep and challenging red runs while the lower half are mainly gentle blues and greens. Over in Italy, you'll be struck by how crazy it is not to have a standardized piste-grading system between countries (in fact, there isn't even one between resorts in the same country, but that's a different story). Most of La Thuile's red runs would be blue elsewhere and most of its blues would be green. Virtually the whole of the top half of the mountain on the Italian side is very easy cruising. Only the pistes down from mid-mountain to La Thuile village offer a significant challenge – a lovely red through the woods and a couple of genuinely steep blacks.

Nursery slopes both in the village centre and at Les Eucherts (which also has some accommodation), with a green run near the village and some gentle blues on the lower half of the mountain to progress to, make La Rosière a convenient resort for beginners. They'll enjoy the sunny setting and wonderful views over the valley too.

Experts will find little excitement in La Rosière. The steepest pistes are on the lowest slopes where the snow quality can suffer badly from the sun, down the *Marcassin* run to Le Vaz and down the *Ecudets* and *Eterlou* runs to Les Ecudets. The black runs down to La Thuile usually have decent snow and certainly offer a challenge. But all this doesn't add up to much. The real attraction for experts is the heli-skiing on offer from Italy (heli-skiing is not allowed from the French side). You can be dropped (with a guide, of course) on the Ruitor glacier for a splendid 20km off-piste run that ends up near Ste-Foy, a short taxi-ride from La Rosière. The upper part of this takes you through open powder fields with stunning views of crags and glaciers and the lower part meanders delightfully through the woods by a gurgling stream with summer dwellings dotted around.

La Rosière's buildings start along the winding road up from the valley town of Séez and culminate in the tiny resort 'centre' – which is actually the top of the approach road and foot of the main slopes. There isn't more to it than a few shops, bars, restaurants and hotels. The small scale of the resort and the pleasant, low-rise architecture contrast hugely with the hustle and bustle and big block-like buildings of nearby Tignes and La Plagne, for example.

Ste-Foy-Tarentaise

One of the great undiscovered gems of the Rhône-Alpes, tucked away just a short drive from big name resorts such as Val d'Isère, Tignes, Les Arcs and La Plagne, **Ste-Foy-Tarentaise** offers some of the most deserted off-piste terrain in the region. Ski instructors and mountain guides from the bigger resorts come here on their days off and bring their favourite clients to find untracked powder, days after the last snowfall. If you want to see it in its pristine form, go now. The company that runs the lifts in Val d'Isère is rumoured to be interested in buying up Ste-Foy's lifts (owned by the local commune) and if it does, the result is sure to be more people on the slopes.

You'll see the valley village of Ste-Foy-Tarentaise on the approach to Tignes and Val d'Isère, where a tiny road branches off for Villaroger and a chair-lift link-up towards Les Arcs. Carry on a short distance and you'll come across La Thuile; turn left here and you are on the approach road up to the Ste-Foy lift base (also known as Bonconseil) and a fledgling resort village.

Three successive quad chairlifts take you up to Col de l'Aiguille over the handful of deserted pistes on offer. It counts as a busy day in Ste-Foy if you see someone else on a chairlift in front of you and the few people who do come here don't normally do so for the pistes. If you want to stick to the marked trails, you'll end up skiing the same delightfully uncrowded slopes. The 1000m vertical of empty red runs are ideal for confidence-building and high-speed carving, while a couple of black runs and one blue add a bit of variety.

While not a great place for beginners, Ste-Foy has a small drag lift on the nursery slopes at the base, a green run to progress to from the top of the first chairlift and a gentle blue from the top of the second.

Ste-Foy-Tarentaise

Ski Area
Height of slopes 1,550m–2,620m
Number of lifts 5

Pistes 25km
green 8%
blue 15%
red 54%
black 23%

Tourist Information

Ste-Foy-Tarentaise: t 04 79 06 95 19,
www.saintefoy.net.

Ski Schools

Ste-Foy-Tarentaise: The ESF, t 04 79 06 96 76,
www.saintefoy.net/esf-a.htm, is the only
school and organises off-piste groups.

Where to Stay

Ste-Foy-Tarentaise
**Auberge sur la Montagne, t 04 79 06 95 83,
www.auberge-montagne.co.uk (moderate).
Just above the turn off at La Thuile, run by
British owners Sue and Andy Mac, lots of old
wooden beams, wholesome French food,
recently refurbished bedrooms. Sauna and
outdoor Jacuzzi.
**Le Monal, t 04 79 06 90 07, www.le-monal.
com (inexpensive). In the valley hamlet of
Ste-Foy-Tarentaise, basic rooms, bar popular
with locals, two restaurants.

Apartments
A few are available at the slopes, bookable
through the tourist office – see its web site.

Catered Chalets
Ste-Foy-Tarentaise: Premiere Neige, t 0709
200 0 300, has several good new chalets and
will transport you around to different ski
areas. Luxurious Yellow-Stone Chalet, t 04
79 06 96 06, has a huge living room with a
big stone fireplace, six double bedrooms,
sauna and a Jacuzzi with panoramic views
down the valley.

Eating Out

In the Resort
As yet there's nothing special at the resort of
Ste-Foy. Chez Mérie in the hamlet of Le Miroir
is delightfully rustic with a varied menu from
steaks to local specialities. The Grange in
Hotel Le Monal (see 'Where to Stay') has built
a fine reputation.

On the Mountain
Chez Léon at Plan Bois at the top of the first
chairlift, with good Savoyard specialities, a
charcoal grill and a terrace, is regarded as best.

Bars and Clubs

Don't come here for lively après-ski. The
Pitchouli at the ski station has table football
and sometimes live music of questionable
quality. The Hotel Le Monal bar is popular with
locals and typically French – a refreshing
change from many of the bars packed with
Brits and Scandinavians in nearby Val d'Isère.

Expert skiers and boarders will love the off-piste. You can see endless possibilities on
the front face from the chairlifts as you ride up and much of this is good for trying off-
piste terrain for the first time. But local guides will show you wonderful, long runs
from the top which take you away from all signs of civilization. One classic run takes
you down through the ruined old village of Le Monal and ends up on the road
between Ste-Foy and Val d'Isère. Another starts with a hike up to Pointe de la
Foglietta, and descends through trees and over a stream to the tiny village of Le Crot.
The possibilities are enormous – but you will need a guide.

Most visitors to Ste-Foy come just for the day and until the property developer
MGM started building a few chalets and apartments at the base of the lifts a couple

of years ago there were few other options. At the time of writing, it is still something of a building site with little more there than exceptionally smart, new, chalet-style buildings constructed of local wood and stone, the tourist and lift ticket offices, a cafe/bar, a small supermarket and a couple of ski shops (including the longest-established Zigzags, of which we've had wildly differing reports, from 'horrible staff' and 'rudest ski shop in the world' to 'very helpful and well-equipped with everything for off-piste'). To make the most of the scattered restaurant scene and nearby resorts, it's a good idea to have a car or to stay at one of the chalets which have minibuses to shuttle you around.

Espace Killy: Val d'Isère and Tignes

Local hero Jean-Claude Killy gained demigod status by winning three gold medals at the 1968 Grenoble Winter Olympics, went on to spearhead the organization of the 1992 Albertville Winter Olympics and was appointed President of the Coordination Commission for the 2006 Turin Winter Olympics. Between times he received the ultimate accolade of having one of Europe's best and most snowsure ski areas named after him. With **Val d'Isère** at 1850m, **Tignes** at 2100m and slopes (including two glaciers) going up to 3455m, L'Espace Killy boasts a longer season than virtually any other ski area in France, lasting from November till May. The Grande Motte glacier in Tignes also opens for summer skiing and boarding, though it can no longer boast of 365-day-a-year opening because of a late spring/early summer closure period; in winter the snow normally remains delightfully light and powdery here.

Constant improvement of the lift system has generally made lift queues a thing of the past. Powerful gondolas whisk you out of both Val d'Isère and Tignes-le-Lac and high-speed underground funiculars run from Val d'Isère to the top of Bellevarde and from Tignes-Val-Claret to the Grande Motte. High-speed chairlifts abound and one of the world's first eight-seater chairs serves the Tovière link from Val d'Isère to Tignes.

The 300km of pistes suit intermediates best. But beware: grading is inconsistent and you'll come across blues that would be reds elsewhere and reds that would be black. The runs at the top of all the sectors, but especially the Le Fornet and Solaise areas of Val d'Isère, offer the easiest cruising, whereas the runs back down to the valley tend to be the steepest of all. The long reds and blues from the Grande Motte to Tignes-Val-Claret and L'Aiguille Percée to Tignes-Les-Brévières are delightful for good intermediates and the run from Solaise to Le Laisinant in Val d'Isère can be wonderfully quiet, even on a busy day. Intermediates should also consider exploring some of the easy off-piste throughout the area with the help of a guide.

Only the brave should tackle the serious black runs, especially the *Face* run from the top of Bellevarde to Val d'Isère, which is often covered in huge moguls for much of its length. The *Face* was the venue for the 1992 Olympic downhill and judged by the racers to be too steep and dangerous (so the World Cup *Première Neige* downhill held in Val d'Isère every December reverted to the old *OK* piste from Bellevarde to La Daille).

Experts will love the steep on-piste challenges but, even more so, some of the best and most extensive lift-served off-piste terrain in the world. This extends right from one end of the ski area to the other with, at the Val d'Isère end, the fabulous *Col Pers* run from near the top of the Pissaillas glacier above Le Fornet which, if the snow is good, ends in the Gorges de Malpasset, where you ski over the frozen Isère river back to the Le Fornet cable car. At the Tignes end, as well as lots of routes off the Grande Motte glacier you can ski from Col du Palet all the way over the back and through the Vanoise National Park to Champagny, which is part of the La Plagne ski area.

For beginners neither resort is ideal. Both may have good nursery slopes, largely free of through-traffic of accomplished skiers and boarders, but Tignes offers no easy green runs to progress to and Val d'Isère no easy runs back down to the village – you'll have to catch the lifts back.

Espace Killy

Ski Area
Height of slopes 1,550m–3,455m
Number of lifts 97

Pistes 300km
green 15%
blue 46%
red 28%
black 11%

Tourist Information

Tignes: t 04 79 40 04 40, *www.tignes.net*.
Val d'Isère: t 04 79 06 06 60,
www.valdisere.com.

Ski Schools

Val d'Isère: Snow Fun, t 04 79 06 19 79,
www.valfun.com, was one of the first ski
schools here to cater specifically for English-
speakers and now has over 70 instructors.
Mountain Masters, t 04 79 06 05 14,
www.mountain-masters.com, has a mixture
of highly qualified British and French
instructors. The **Development Centre, t** 06 15
55 31 56, *www.tdcski.com*, was started for the
2002/3 season by four top young British
instructors and has quickly built a good
reputation. **Alpine Experience, t** 04 79 06 28
81, *www.alpineexperience.com*, and **Top Ski**,
t 04 79 06 14 80, *www.topskival.com*, both
specialize in off-piste guiding, organize
groups each morning and offer lessons in
the afternoons. **Misty Fly, t** 04 79 40 08 74,

www.mistyflyvaldisere.com, is a specialist
snowboard school (and shop).
Tignes: Evolution 2, t 04 79 06 86 94, *www.
evolution2.com*, has a good reputation.

Where to Stay

Val d'Isère
★★★★Blizzard, t 04 79 06 02 07, *www.
hotelblizzard.com* (*luxury–expensive*) right in
centre with indoor-outdoor pool and good
food.
★★★Samovar, t 04 79 06 13 51, *www.
lesamovar.com* (*inexpensive–expensive B&B*)
By gondola and funicular at La Daille, traditional and family-run with good food.

Tignes
★★★Village Montana, t 04 79 40 01 44, *www.
vmontana.com* (*expensive–moderate*). Stylish
new complex with outdoor pool above Le-Lac.
★★Arbina, t 04 79 06 34 78, *www.arbina.net*
(*moderate–inexpensive*) Right by the lifts in
Le Lac, with busy lunchtime terrace and
après-ski bar and good restaurant.

Apartments
Val d'Isère: Pierre&Vacances' rustic style, well
furnished Chalets du Laisinant are peacefully set at the bottom of a piste from
Solaise, near a bus stop 1km from the village
centre; its Val d'Isère Centre apartments,
near the shops and nightlife, have a sauna,
fitness room and outdoor pool. Local agency
Val d'Isère Agence, t 04 79 06 73 50,
www.valdisere-agence.com, has a large selection of places.

The two resorts contrast sharply in character. Set in a deep valley, way below the source of the Isère river and the Col de l'Iseran, one of highest passes in the Alps (shut in winter of course), **Val d'Isère** first developed as a ski resort in the early 1930s. Although the old village and an 11th-century church still form its heart, a huge amount of more modern construction has gone on, with largely ribbon development along the access road and by the '*front de neige*' (edge of the slopes). At the entrance to the village stands La Daille, an uncompromising area of high-rise blocks built of grey concrete and stone 'to blend in with the mountains in summer' but to many a horrendous eyesore. After that the buildings become largely low-rise, wood-clad and much easier on the eye. The tasteful, central, pedestrian-only Val Village area, built of

Tignes: **MGM's Ecrin des Neiges** in Tignes-Val-Claret has a welcoming reception with open fire, comfortable apartments and an indoor 'aquatonic' centre with spectacular views, sauna and steam room (separate fee). **Village Montana** (*see* 'Where to Stay') features apartments as well as hotel rooms.

Catered Chalets

Val d'Isère: There's a huge variety. Operators specializing in luxury chalets include **Lotus Supertravel**, **t** (020) 7962 99 33, **Scott Dunn Ski**, **t** (020) 8682 5050, and **VIP**, **t** (020) 8875 1957. **Finlays**, **t** (01573) 226 611, has a varied selection across the price range, as does Val d'Isère specialist **YSE**, **t** (020) 8871 5117. **Le Ski's**, **t** 0870 754 4444, great value group of chalets are just off the main street and **Ski Beat's**, **t** (01243) 780 405 smart five-unit chalet at La Daille. **Mark Warner**, **t** 0870 7704 226, offers four chalet-hotels, including one with a rooftop outdoor pool.

Tignes: More are coming on the market each year. **Total Ski**, **t** (08701) 633 633, **Ski Olympic**, **t** (01302) 328 820, and **Neilson**, **t** 9870 9099 099, each have several; and **Esprit Ski**, **t** (01252) 618 300 runs a chalet-hotel with childcare facilities.

Eating Out

In the Resorts

Val d'Isère: **Chalet du Crêt**, widely regarded as the best in town, in an old farmhouse near La Daille has a fixed-price menu starting with enormous *hors d'œuvres* spread, followed by a choice of main courses, cheeses and desserts. **Perdrix Blanche** in the centre of town is a busy brasserie with a wide-ranging menu.

Tignes: **Campanules** in Le-Lac has a smart restaurant with good service. **Pizza 2000** has reasonable prices and caters well for large parties (e.g. chalet staff's night off).

On the Mountain

Surprisingly for such a well-known area, good, atmospheric mountain restaurants are sparse.

Val d'Isère: **La Fruitière** at the top of the gondola from La Daille is the best up the mountain, with table-service and decorated with artefacts from a dairy in the valley. Down at the bottom of the gondola the cheaper **Les Tufs** does good pizza and, on the first floor, an excellent buffet.

Tignes: The recently built **Alpages** (self-service) and **Lo Soleil** (table-service) at the top of the Chaudannes chair on the eastern slopes both have excellent views over to the Grande Motte. On the western side, try the **Chalet de Bollin**, just above Val Claret.

Bars and Clubs

Val d'Isère: **Bananas** at the bottom of Bellevarde, with a sunny terrace and cosy wooden interior, beckons at the end of the day for a (relatively) quiet drink, with the basement bar of **Taverne d'Alsace** an attractive alternative. Later on, **Dick's T-Bar** springs into life as the main disco, with **Petit Danois** somewhat less frenetic.

Tignes: The **Crowded House** and **Fish Tank** in Val Claret, the **Arbina** in Le-Lac and **Harri's Bar** in Le Lavachet (near Le-Lac) are popular.

local wood and stone before the 1992 Olympics, features some smart shops and hotels and restaurants competing for attention by the nursery slopes. The resort has one of the most efficient free bus systems in the ski world (called the *Train Rouge*) which shuttles continuously along the main road and between all the major lift stations; it is also becoming more pedestrian-friendly year-by-year as more and more traffic restrictions are introduced.

But don't expect to practise your French much in Val d'Isère. In winter the place often seems to be dominated by British guests and workers. Over 60 UK tour opera-tors feature Val d'Isère in their programmes and between them run hundreds of catered chalets here – staffed largely by young British people wanting to spend the winter in the Alps. Many of the ski schools, shops, restaurants and bars are owned or staffed by Britons too.

Tignes has a much more French feel to it. The main parts – **Tignes-le-Lac** and **Tignes-Val-Claret**, a few hundred metres apart and separated by a lake (frozen in winter and used for cross-country, ice diving and even kite skiing) – were built largely in the 1960s and 1970s, high above the tree line in a spacious open bowl surrounded by spectacular peaks and glaciers. There have recently been attempts to smarten up the original stark, block-like buildings which were thrown up to allow functional, afford-able, ski-in, ski-out vacations rather than aesthetic pleasure and many now have wood cladding. Traffic has been rerouted or sent underground to make it less intru-sive and newer developments – such as in the Les Almes area of Le Lac – are being built in a more attractive traditional wooden chalet style. The old village of **Tignes-les-Brévières** (at 1550m, the lowest point in the Espace Killy) has been renovated to provide a much more atmospheric place to stay.

Savoie: The Maurienne Valley

Les Sybelles: Le Corbier, La Toussuire, Les Bottières, St-Jean-d'Arves, St-Sorlin-d'Arves, St-Colomban-des-Villards

For the 2003/4 season a major new ski area was formed by the building of nine new lifts and five new pistes linking the modern, purpose-built resorts of Le Corbier and La Toussuire via the L'Ouillon summit with the traditional old villages of St-Sorlin-d'Arves on one side of it and St-Colomban-des-Villards on the other. In terms of piste mileage, Les Sybelles, with 310km, rivals L'Espace Killy with a mere 300km. But the similarity ends there. Les Sybelles has pistes that are almost entirely suited to beginners and early intermediates. Unusually for such an extensive ski area, there is hardly a seri-ously challenging slope in sight.

Early and unadventurous intermediates can cruise the whole area on gentle blue pistes and almost as gentle reds, most of which are immaculately groomed each night. More adventurous types will soon tire of the lack of steeper slopes, so don't come here expecting another Les Arcs, Trois Vallées or L'Alpe-d'Huez and the variety they offer. About the steepest long run, *Vallée Perdue*, down the valley between La Toussuire and Le Corbier and graded black, justifies no more than a red grading for

Les Sybelles

Ski Area
Height of slopes 1,300m–2,620m
Number of lifts 73

Pistes 310km
green 18%
blue 40%
red 36%
black 6%

Tourist Information

Le Corbier: t 04 79 83 04 04,
www.le-corbier.com.
St-Colomban-des-Villards: t 04 79 56 24 53,
www.saint-colomban.com.
St-Jean-d'Arves: t 04 79 59 72 97,
www.saintjeandarves.com.
St-Sorlin-d'Arves: t 04 79 59 71 77,
www.saintsorlindarves.com.
La Toussuire: t 04 79 83 06 06,
www.la-toussuire.com.

Ski Schools

The local **ESF** is the only option in all the
resorts except La Toussuire, where the
International School, t 04 79 56 77 74,
www.esi-toussuire.com, offers an alternative.

Where to Stay

La Toussuire
***Soldanelles, t** 04 79 56 75 29, *www.
hotelsoldanelles.com* (*moderate–inexpensive*)
two minutes from main street, simple
rooms, pool, Jacuzzi and sauna.

St-Sorlin-d'Arves
****La Balme, t** 04 79 59 70 21, *www.hotel-
balme.com* (*moderate*) at the top of the
resort near the piste, basically furnished
rooms, lovely views.

Apartments
The main option in all these resorts.

St-Jean and St-Sorlin-d'Arves: **Crystal, t** 0870
1606 040, and **Thomson, t** 0870 606 1470,
both feature new apartments, including
some with pool and sauna.

Catered Chalets
Le Corbier: Equity, t (01273) 298 298, runs a
chalet-hotel near the centre with a popular
bar and prices which include lift pass, equipment hire and insurance.

Eating Out

In the Resorts
Le Corbier: Le Grillon, 3km away in the
Villarembert, makes a pleasant rustic
change from Le Corbier's tower blocks, with
traditional French food such as *magret de
canard* and *gratin dauphinois*.
St-Sorlin-d'Arves: Table de Marie features local
specialities.
La Toussuire: Envol, in a rustic hut near the
entrance to town, specializes in Savoyard
cuisine.

On the Mountain
St-Sorlin-d'Arves: The **Bergerie** at the top of
the main chair out of town has a big sunny
terrace with wonderful views, a rustic interior, reasonable prices.

Bars and Clubs

This is not the area to come to for lively
nightlife.
Le Corbier: Roches Blanches restaurant in the
centre includes a cosy bar area with
comfortable seating and an open fire. For
dancing, the **Président** gets busy only on
peak holiday periods.
St-Jean and St-Sorlin-d'Arves: The **Irish Pub** in
St-Jean lives up to its name and for a more
traditional French atmosphere head for the
Godille in St-Sorlin.
La Toussuire: The **Alpen Rock** nightclub, next to
the Envol restaurant can get lively in peak
periods. The **Tonneau** is one of several bars
that also sell food.

steepness. The highest point in the area, Les Perrons above St-Sorlin-d'Arves has some excellent long reds on both sides of the summit.

It is difficult to think of any ski area whose slopes are as well-suited to beginners as Les Sybelles. All the main resorts have good nursery slopes and long, easy greens and blues to progress to.

Experts should cross Les Sybelles off their shortlist, unless they want to rely on fresh snow making the easy off-piste near the pistes a powder playground. It simply lacks any on-piste challenge.

Le Corbier's eight tower blocks, typical of 1960s design, dominate the resort and reach as high as 19 storeys above underground walkways and shopping malls. But the traffic-free nature of the core of the resort at the foot of the slopes makes it very family-friendly – indeed it runs a French Family Championship each year with teams made up of mother, father and one child. Neighbouring **La Toussuire** just up the road grew up over a somewhat longer period, with many more low-rise buildings built in a hotch-potch of styles. The pedestrian-only main street, lined with shops, bars, restaurants and apartments, has the slopes behind one side, traffic behind the other and music and announcements from the radio station in the tourist office building piped out constantly through loudspeakers on the lampposts.

Slopes from above Le Corbier lead down towards **St-Jean-d'Arves** and a tasteful development of new chalet-style buildings near the lift base at La Chal. The original old village lies over the valley and has bus links to both here and the more substantial old village of **St-Sorlin-d'Arves** at the head of the valley. St-Sorlin has grown in ribbon-development fashion in the confined valley floor near the piste which runs along most of its length and has interesting local shops, a Baroque church and a year-round life outside the ski industry. At the opposite end of the ski area, a series of slow chairs and drags now connect the tiny old village of **St-Colomban-des-Villards** to L'Ouillon and the rest of the ski area. The roadside hamlet of **Les Bottières** below La Toussuire is even smaller.

Les Karellis

Set at a lofty 1600m, the modern, purpose-built resort of Les Karellis consists of little more that a clutch of block-like, flat-roofed apartment buildings with little in the way of charm. But what it lacks in that department is to some extent made up for by its interestingly varied, snowsure slopes with fine views of the Maurienne range.

Les Karellis

Ski Area
Height of slopes 1,600m–2,520m
Number of lifts 17

Pistes 60km
green 14%
blue 40%
red 32%
black 14%

Tourist Information

Les Karellis: t 04 79 59 50 36,
www.les-karellis.fr.

These offer more challenging intermediate runs than nearby Valloire and Valmeinier and a day trip to here, if you are staying at those resorts and have a car, is worth considering.

Valloire-Valmeinier

The old mountain villages of Valloire and Valmeinier 1500 and the tastefully-designed, modern purpose-built resort of Valmeinier 1800 share the most extensive slopes in the Maurienne valley and their contrasting characters adds considerable interest to the ski area. All are reached by a long winding road which eventually splits into two, high above the austere valley town of St-Michel-de-Maurienne.

Two gondolas from different parts of town access Valloire's two linked mountains. The Setaz sector's shady slopes, the lower part treelined and the upper section open, generally have the best snow and the toughest slopes. The broad, open, west-facing slopes of Crey du Quart offer a choice of routes to link to the Valmeinier valley. A gentle blue heads down from Grand Plateau to Valmeinier 1800, while an even

Valloire-Valmeinier

Ski Area
Height of slopes 1,430m–2,595m
Number of lifts 33

Pistes 150km
green 25%
blue 27%
red 37%
black 11%

Tourist Information

Valloire: t 04 79 59 03 96, *www.valloire.net*.
Valmeinier: t 04 79 59 53 69,
  www.valmeinier.com.

Ski Schools

Valloire: the **International School**, t 04 79 59 05 18, *www.esivalloire.free.fr*, has now been going over 20 years and provides an alternative to the ESF.
Valmeinier: the ESF, t 04 79 59 20 10, *www.esf-valmeinier.com*, is the only option.

Where to Stay

Valloire
★★★Aux Oursons, t 04 79 59 01 37, *www.hotel-les-oursons.com* (*expensive–moderate*) near the centre, comfortable, friendly, pretty dining room, teddy bears (*Ourson* means teddy bear), small pool, Jacuzzi and sauna.

Apartments
Valloire: The **Galibier** (1km from the centre but close to the piste and a chairlift) and central **Valmonts** apartments are both relatively new, with pool, sauna, steam room.
Valmeinier 1800: The **Pierre&Vacances** apartments are above average for the chain, right on the piste, with an outdoor pool and sauna.

Eating Out

Valloire: The **Gastilleur** restaurant in the Setaz hotel on the main street is the gourmet choice, while **Bistrot Chez Fred** serves reasonably priced brasserie food and gets so packed that they erect a canvas awning on the balcony to fit more people in. The **Grange** crêperie resembles a barn and the **Asile des Fondues** serves what you'd expect from the name in a beautiful old building with stone walls.

Bars and Clubs

Valloire: Few of the mountain restaurants are memorable and neither resort is the place to go for lively nightlife, though the **Touring Bar** attracts the teens and 20s with table football, a pool table and loud music.

gentler blue or green leads to the Armera chairlift which goes down and then up to Valmeinier 1500. The open, west-facing slopes above and between the two Valmeiniers, like the Crey du Quart slopes, get the full afternoon sun, so snow quality can suffer. Watch out for some tricky drag-lifts in the Valloire sectors, which can lift you in the air at the start.

The vast majority of the slopes are ideal for intermediates of all standards. For easy cruising, head for the Crey du Quart and Valmeinier sectors which have gentle blues and almost-as-gentle reds everywhere. The often deserted long, gentle *Armera* blue winds its way delightfully through the trees down from Crey du Quart towards Valmeinier 1500 and the Neuvache blue along the valley from Valmeinier 1800 is flat enough to be a green. The rather out-of-the way red Praz Violette piste from the top of the Combe drag-lift (which, be warned, has some very steep pitches and a huge bend of over 90° in it) can be a wonderful cruise away from the crowds. For more of a challenge, head over to Cretaz and try the highest runs, including the *Cascade* black which often has excellent snow.

All the resorts suit beginners well, with nursery slopes both at village level and up the mountain at the top of both Valloire's gondolas, followed by very easy green runs to progress to.

Experts will find the area limited. The long *Grandes Droze* black run can present a challenge when the bumps build up and the area beyond Valmeinier 1800 served by the Inversins chairlift and from Crey du Quart down into the Valmeinier valley have some decent off-piste if the snow is good.

The six day lift pass allows a cut-price day in the Trois Vallées (the Val-Thorens sector can be accessed easily by gondola from Orelle in the Maurienne valley, around 30 minutes away by bus).

Valloire still feels like a real mountain village with a year-round population of 1,000, an old church and square in the centre, *crêperies*, *fromageries* and reasonably-priced restaurants. Various events such as street markets and ice-carving competitions add to its lively ambience and because the Col du Galibier pass beyond it closes in winter the place is mercifully free of through traffic and its one-way system is there only because of its narrow streets. The much smaller old village of **Valmeinier 1500** has less life while its purpose-built satellite of **Valmeinier 1800** attracts most of the tourists. Started in 1986, its low-rise chalet-style buildings line the bottom and side of the main slope and fit in well with their surroundings.

Valfréjus

Tucked away in the woods above the valley town of Modane on the site of the old hamlet of Charmaix, the purpose-built resort of **Valfréjus** and its small ski area offer a peaceful alternative to more frenetic bigger places. The compact resort includes a couple of hotels, several apartment blocks, a handful of bars, restaurants and shops, all pleasantly built in local wood and stone in chalet style and centred around the foot of the gondola and chairlifts which take you up to the main focus of the ski area at Plateau d'Arrondaz, 2200m, 650m higher than the village.

Valfréjus

Ski Area
Height of slopes 1,550m–2,735m
Number of lifts 12

Pistes 52km
green 20%
blue 50%
red 10%
black 20%

Tourist Information

Valfréjus: **t** 04 79 05 33 83, *www.valfrejus.com*.

La Norma

Ski Area
Height of slopes 1,350m–2,750m
Number of lifts 118

Pistes 65km
green 30%
blue 22%
red 41%
black 7%

Tourist Information

La Norma: **t** 04 79 20 31 46, *www.lanorma.com*.

The mainly open bowls above Plateau d'Arrondaz and the tree-lined runs back down to the village offer lots of different blue run options, ideal for intermediate cruising. You can ski off both the front and the back of the top ridge and a wonderful long blue from the top at Punta Bagna, served by the second stage of the gondola, takes you right away from all the lifts amid scenic splendour and all the way down to the village, a descent of almost 1200m vertical. The main drawback for keen piste bashers is the limited extent of the area – but the lift pass covers La Norma too and buses run between the two resorts Monday to Friday. Experts will find the area of limited interest, apart from two steep, bumpy blacks down the front from Punta Bagna and some off-piste potential. Beginners are catered for by nursery slopes at both village and mid-mountain level, with a few green runs to move on to.

La Norma

La Norma, with its wood-clad low-rise buildings offering traffic-free ski-in, ski-out convenience, makes a quiet, family-friendly destination for those not looking for much of a challenge on the slopes. If you get bored with the local mainly easy intermediate pistes, the 6-day lift pass covers a day at nearby Valfréjus and a cut-price day pass for the Trois Vallées (accessed by gondola from Orelle in the Maurienne valley). There are bus links to each of these once a week, on different days. When you book an apartment you can do a half-board deal which supplies you with coupons to use at restaurants in the resort.

Val Cenis

The two traditional, unspoilt old villages of Lanslebourg and Lanslevillard have joined together for marketing purposes as Val Cenis, set by a road that in summer links over the Col de l'Iseran pass to mighty Val d'Isère. The contrast between sleepy little Val Cenis and brash and bustling Val d'Isère is sharp.

While **Lanslebourg** spreads along Route Nationale 6 (a dead end in winter, when the road over the Col du Mont Cenis becomes a piste), **Lanslevillard**, 100m higher and set

Val Cenis

Ski Area
Height of slopes 1,400m–2,800m
Number of lifts 22

Pistes 80km
green 21%
blue 23%
red 42%
black 14%

Tourist Information

Val-Cenis: **t** 04 79 05 23 66 (Lanslebourg),
t 04 79 05 99 10 (Lanslevillard),
www.valcenis.com.

Where to Stay

Val Cenis: specialist tour operator MGS,
t (01799) 525984, has a selection of apartments to rent.

off the road further up the valley, with an ice rink and swimming pool, exudes more
charm and convenience for the slopes. Thanks to strict controls in both villages, no
buildings of over three storeys exist and all exhibit a traditional style in stone or
wood. Between them they have 11 mainly 2-star hotels and 24 restaurants.

One lift from Lanslebourg and three from Lanslevillard take you into the shared
slopes, which are reasonably snowsure due to their north-facing aspect, snowmaking
on the lower runs and top height of 2800m. Above mid-mountain a good variety of
blue and red runs suit intermediates best and a top-to-bottom descent of 1400m
covers an impressive amount of vertical for a relatively small ski area. Although the
wooded lower half of the mountain includes a few red runs, most are easy blues and
greens, including Europe's longest green run, the 10km *L'Escargot*, ideal for beginners
to try out once they are off the village nursery slopes. The **Termignon ski area**, 10
minutes away by bus and covered by the 6-day lift pass (as is a day out in another
resort in the Maurienne valley), provides another 35km of mainly gentle intermediate
and beginner terrain.

Isère

Les Grandes Rousses: L'Alpe-d'Huez, Auris-en-Oisans, Oz-en-Oisans, Vaujany, Villard-Reculas

L'Alpe-d'Huez sprang to fame as one of the venues used for the 1968 Grenoble
Winter Olympics, the Games when French hero Jean-Claude Killy won all three Alpine
skiing event gold medals. After that it grew quickly in a seemingly unplanned way
and its buildings come in all designs. Four other main villages at lower altitudes and
with very different characters offer other bases to explore the large ski area (known
as the Grandes Rousses, though this name is not well-known in the UK), one of the
few in the Alps that is equally good for beginners, intermediates and expert skiers.

It advertises itself as the 'Island in the Sun' because so many of its slopes face south
or south-west. In cold wintry conditions this makes for great skiing and a wonderful
suntan but when the weather is warmer, the direct sun can turn the slopes slushy
later in the day and icy first thing. Extensive snowmaking covers around a quarter of
the slopes and helps keep these in good condition as long as it is cold enough at night

to use it. And the high Sarenne glacier and shady slopes above Vaujany and at Signal de l'Homme almost always offer good snow (the glacier offers summer skiing too).

With just over half the 230km of pistes classified blue or red, intermediates can cruise around the whole area easily. The main *Couloir* blue run from the top of the DMC gondola out of L'Alpe-d'Huez will please early intermediates so long as it isn't too crowded, as will the gentle blues from Signal and above Vaujany; all offer delightfully easy cruising. Many of the red runs in the area, such as those accessed from the Lièvre Blanc chair and the runs down to Oz and Vaujany, present serious challenges that suit more ambitious or confident intermediates best. They will also enjoy the 16km-long *Sarenne* run (*see* box, below) and being able to brag about it in the pub back home.

A large area of very gentle green slopes immediately above L'Alpe-d'Huez, served by 11 lifts covered by a special beginners' lift pass, makes the resort almost ideal for beginners. Sadly, despite this whole area being declared a slow skiing zone, many better skiers and boarders still flash through it too quickly. Above Vaujany a much smaller but good beginner area serves people staying locally.

Although L'Alpe-d'Huez lacks a macho image, experts will find plenty to keep them entertained – long and challenging black runs, some reds that ought to be black and serious off-piste options. A 300m tunnel below the top of the Pic Blanc cable car leads to three long blacks on the front side of the mountain, usually impressively mogulled, sometimes made even more tricky by the effects of the sun and with a start that requires nerve. The *Fare* run down to below Vaujany now has snowmaking and its north-facing aspect means the snow can be good despite its lack of altitude. If you hire a guide, excellent off-piste can be found all over the area, including descents starting over glaciers and ending around 2000 vertical metres lower.

Alpe-d'Huez spreads across an open mountainside, its hotchpotch of buildings including a futuristic church dating from the 1960s. If you had to pick a focal point, it would be the *Avenue des Jeux* near the centre, where you'll find the big outdoor swimming pool, ice-skating rink and some of the shops, bars and restaurants. A bus service (free with a lift pass) runs through the resort and a slow bucket lift is handy for getting you from much of the accommodation to the big DMC gondola at the top.

Pleasantly situated close to the most forested part of the area, a series of the wood-clad, chalet-style apartment blocks and a few shops, bars and restaurants make up **Auris-en-Oisans**. Its peaceful setting makes it a good family resort and easy access by

The World's Longest Black Run

Starting at 3330m from the top of the Pic Blanc cable car, the black *Sarenne* piste descends 2000m vertical over its 16km length making it one of the Alps' classic runs and the longest black run in the world. It gains its black grading because of its steep upper section, with stunning views and a section of seriously huge moguls that can be avoided by taking a recently-created easier option. The bottom half flattens out into what could be classed as an easy green with the spectacular rock faces of the Sarenne gorge rising up above you. Competent and adventurous intermediates will find the whole run well within their capabilities but boarders beware: you are likely to face a tiring scoot or walk out along the flat final section.

Les Grandes Rousses

Ski Area
Height of slopes 1,220m–3,320m
Number of lifts 87

Pistes 230km
green 35%
blue 27%
red 25%
black 13%

Tourist Information

L'Alpe-d'Huez: t 04 76 11 44 44, *www.alped-huez.com*.
Auris-en-Oisans: t 04 76 80 13 52, *www.auris-en-oisans.com*.
Oz-en-Oisans: t 04 76 80 78 01, *www.oz-en-oisans.com*.
Vaujany: t 04 76 80 72 37, *www.vaujany.com*.
Villard-Reculas: t 04 76 80 45 69, *www.villard-reculas.com*.

Ski Schools

L'Alpe-d'Huez: British instructor Stuart Adamson runs the highly acclaimed **Masterclass**, t 04 76 80 93 83.
Vaujany: We have had excellent reports of the ESF, t 04 76 80 71 80, *www.esf-vaujany.com*.

Where to Stay

L'Alpe-d'Huez
★★★★**Royal Ours Blanc**, t 04 76 80 35 50, *www.eurogroup-vacances.com* (*luxury–expensive*) central, luxurious, excellent fitness centre with Jacuzzi, pool and sauna.

Vaujany
★★**Rissiou**, t 04 76 80 71 00 (*moderate–inexpensive*) run by British tour operator Ski

Peak (*see* 'Catered Chalets'). Simple rooms, good food, nice bar popular with locals.

Apartments
L'Alpe-d'Huez: **Pierre&Vacances'** attractive and relatively new **Quartier des Bergers** apartments with pool and sauna are set near the Marmottes gondola.

Catered Chalets
Vaujany: **Ski Peak**, **t** (01428) 608 070, pioneered Vaujany on the UK market and now has several chalets, some quite luxurious, in both Vaujany and the hamlet of La Villette up the valley at the mid-station of the gondola. They have minibuses to shuttle you around.

Eating Out

In the Resorts
Crémaillère, **Au P'tit Creux** and **Génépi** in L'Alpe-d'Huez are all worth a look.

On the Mountain
The cosy **Chalet du Lac Besson**, peacefully set by a cross-country trail north of the DMC gondola mid-station and reached by the blue Boulevard des Lacs piste, has a sunny terrace and some of the best food on the mountain. **La Bergerie**, on the red run down to Villard-Reculas, with a log fire and ancient artefacts, offers good food and friendly service.

Bars and Clubs

L'Alpe-d'Huez is the place to stay if you want a lively time. British tour operators run bars such as the **Roundhouse** in Crystal's Hôtel Vallée Blanche and the **Underground** in Neilson's Hôtel Chamois – both get packed. The **Stage One** and **Igloo** discos liven up later on in the evenings. For a quieter time, head for a 4-star hotel bar or choose one of the lower villages.

car makes it good for drivers who want to try out other resorts such as Les Deux-Alpes and Serre Chevalier which are included on a 6-day lift pass.

Purpose-built Oz-en-Oisans station, above the attractive old village of **Oz-en-Oisans**, has two powerful gondolas into the slopes – one arrives above L'Alpe-d'Huez, the other above Vaujany, making it a very convenient place to stay. While still quiet, Oz has developed into a fair-sized place with attractive chalet-style buildings of wood and stone and a skating rink as well as a choice of restaurants, bars and sports shops.

The old mountain hamlet of **Vaujany** suddenly found itself rich beyond its wildest dreams when a hydroelectric power operation was built on its land in the 1980s. It spent some of this new-found wealth on a huge cable car (at the time the world's biggest) towards L'Alpe-d'Huez and a two-stage gondola to its local slopes - and the local bed base is small enough to mean you'll never find a queue. While the hamlet has grown into a village and tasteful modern buildings rub shoulders with the old stone houses, it retains much of its old-world charm and you may still find chickens in the street. It also boasts a new sports centre including a big swimming pool, a new village centre by the lifts (with smart ski shop, café, deli and underground car park) and excellent childcare facilities.

A high-speed chairlift built a few years ago to Signal, above L'Alpe-d'Huez, resulted in the rustic old village of **Villard-Reculas** gradually being renovated and developed into a resort. A few new apartment blocks have been built and cow sheds and barns converted to join a couple of bars and restaurants and a small hotel. But it remains essentially a quiet and peaceful backwater.

Les Deux-Alpes (linked to La Grave)

As far as the skiing is concerned **Les Deux-Alpes** would be more appropriately named *'Une Alpe et Un Peu'*. The main slopes rise up steeply along the eastern edge of the long, sprawling, narrow resort village and culminate in the Glacier du Mont de Lans, which reaches 3570m. Now that's a real *Alpe*. The other side of the main road the second ski area of Pied Moutet reaches a mere 2100m, less than 500m above the resort itself. Most people stick to the eastern side, itself linked at the top by snowcat to the cult resort of **La Grave**, where virtually all the slopes are off-piste. Les Deux-Alpes welcomes large numbers of British guests and its glacier opens for business in summer as well as winter, attracting lots of snowboarders who love its terrain-park and half-pipe. Many come on special 'camps' where tuition is included in the package.

The main ski area resembles the village in that its shape is long (high) and narrow. The main Jandri Express gondola isfollowed by the Dôme Express underground funicular to take you almost 1800m vertical above the village. But this is no Trois Vallées, Espace Killy or even L'Alpe-d'Huez: instead of opening up a huge playground of lifts and pistes as in these bigger resorts, your choices are restricted to heading down again or playing on a handful of 'spur' lifts that take you to one side or the other of the main route. At one point the mountain narrows down to form essentially just a single run, which can become extremely crowded.

Intermediates who don't mind skiing the same runs repeatedly can have a good time here. The higher runs generally have good snow and some great fast cruising, especially on the mainly north-facing pistes served by the chairlifts off to the sides, where you can often pick gentle or steeper terrain as you wish. But avid piste-bashers will explore all there is to offer in a couple of days and many visitors take the opportunity of excursions to other resorts covered for a day on the six-day lift pass, such as L'Alpe-d'Huez (to which there's a helicopter as well as a bus link) and Serre-Chevalier.

Les Deux-Alpes

Ski Area
Height of slopes 1,300m–3,570m
Number of lifts 58

Pistes 200km
green 24%
blue 39%
red 24%
black 13%

Tourist Information

Les Deux-Alpes: **t** 04 76 79 22 00,
www.les2alpes.com.

Ski Schools

Les Deux-Alpes: This branch of the **ESF, t** 04 76
79 21 21, *www.les2alpes-esf.com*, has a better
reputation than most, and the **Primitive**
snowboard school, **t** 06 07 90 71 35, teaches
advanced riders half-pipe and off-piste skills
as well as beginner/intermediate classes.

Where to Stay

Les Deux-Alpes
★★★★**Bérangère, t** 04 76 79 24 11 (*expensive–
moderate*). Despite a rather dreary exterior,
inside it is the smartest in town, with pool,
sauna, steam room, Jacuzzi and gym; on-
piste at less convenient north end of town.
Restaurant serves delicious lamb and lobster.
★★★**Chalet Mounier, t** 04 76 80 56 90, *www.
chalet-mounier.com* (*expensive–moderate*).
Smartly modernized old farm building at
southern end of town near the Diable
gondola. Extras include pool, sauna, steam

room, Jacuzzi, gym and a splendid Michelin-
rosetted restaurant.

Apartments
The **Alpina Lodge**, right by the slopes near
the ski school meeting place, is the smartest
in town.

Catered Chalets
Mark Warner, t 0870 770 4226, has taken
over the smart Marmottes hotel at the foot of
the quiet Pied Moutet slopes, which it runs as
a chalet-hotel with facilities including pool,
sauna, steam room, Jacuzzi, bowling alley,
table tennis and pool table. It suits families
well and has its own childcare facility.

Eating Out

In the Resort
The **Chalet Mounier** and **Bérangère** are two
of the best places (*see* 'Where to Stay'). At the
other end of the price scale try the **Vetrata**,
Spaghetteria or **Smokey Joe's** (which also does
a good English breakfast).

On the Mountain
The **Pastorale** at the top of the Diable gondola
and the newer **Chalet de la Toura** with its big
terrace and efficient table-service near the
Toura chair are the pick of a poor bunch.

Bars and Clubs

Les Deux-Alpes: There's no shortage of lively
places. The **Rodéo Saloon** attracts crowds of
rowdy *après-skiers* who like watching people
being flung off the mechanical bucking
bronco. The **Windsor Pub** sells a wide selection
of beers and whiskies, **Smithy's** features live
bands and DJs, **Corrigans** Irish Pub is popular
and **L'Opera** nightclub livens up later on.

Less confident intermediates will love the quality of the snow and the gentleness of
most of the runs on the upper mountain. Their problem might lie in finding the pistes
too crowded, especially if poor snow in other resorts results in people being bussed
in. At the end of the day, you can ride the Jandri Express down or take the long
winding green back to town. Unless you are competent, confident and enjoy icy or
slushy moguls beware of the more direct short black runs back home, except on the
rare occasion when one has been groomed.

A string of drag lifts (some of them free to use even without a lift pass) and one chairlift line the bottom of the slope by the village and serve an excellent spacious and gentle area for beginners. After that beginners can head for the glacier and its fine array of very easy slopes – but bad weather can close these top lifts and novices might find the blue runs on mid-mountain intimidating because of better skiers and boarders flashing past them at speed.

The most challenging black pistes include the aptly named *Super Diable* and the *Grand Couloir* from Tête Moute and the runs down to town (where you can often see those not up to it tumbling long distances without their skis). But off-piste opportunities form the area's main attraction for experts. The Chalence itineraries from just below the top of the Jandri Express to the Fée chairlift can be great fun in good snow, as can the area between the Fée and Thuit chairs. More serious routes that end well outside the lift network, with verticals of over 2000m, can be tackled with a guide, including outings across the glacier to the awesome slopes of La Grave and down to the small valley village of St-Christophe.

Although no Alpine beauty, Les Deux-Alpes has avoided the worst excesses of many purpose-built resorts; rather than being planned, it gives the impression of having grown haphazardly over the years, with a wide range of building styles, from old chalets through 1960s blocks to more sympathetic recent developments. It looks better as you leave than as you arrive along the road from the north, because all the balconies face the southern end of town. Hotels, apartments, bars and shops line the busy main street and the parallel one that completes the one-way traffic system and although the village lacks a real centre, a couple of focal points are evident.

The area around the tourist office and the Jandri Express, near the middle of the resort, boasts an outdoor ice rink and some good restaurants and bars. The village straggles north from here, becoming less convenient the further you go, though a free shuttle-bus saves some very long walks from one end of town to the other. **Alpe de Venosc**, at the southern end, has many of the best bars and nightspots, the most character, the fewest cars, the best shops and the Diable gondola up to the tough terrain around Tête Moute. The resort is one of the liveliest in France for après-ski, which goes on until the early hours.

Another gondola from the Alpe de Venosc end of town descends steeply down the side of the Vénéon valley to the old village of **Venosc**, where craft shops and studios line the cobbled streets (*see* p.246).

Belledonne: Chamrousse and Les-Sept-Laux (skiing not linked)

Jean-Claude Killy hurtled to victory in the 1968 Olympic men's downhill in the resort of Chamrousse in the Belledonne massif, just to the south-east of Grenoble. This functional family resort, popular with day-trippers from Grenoble, boasts a wide variety of terrain within its limited area. The slopes above **Chamrousse 1750** (also known as **Roche Béranger**) suit early intermediates and beginners best, with easy blue cruising runs, a few green runs and an area of nursery slopes right by the village. From the upper part of the mountain more challenging red runs head down towards the other main village of **Chamrousse 1650** (also known as **Le Recoin**), some of which

Chamrousse

Ski Area
Height of slopes 1,400m–2,250m
Number of lifts 26

Pistes 77km
green 17%
blue 43%
red 20%
black 20%

Tourist Information

Chamrousse: t 04 76 89 92 65,
   www.chamrousse.com.

Les-Sept-Laux/Prapoutel

Ski Area
Height of slopes 1,350m–2,400m
Number of lifts 25

Pistes 100km
green 11%
blue 38%
red 43%
black 8%

Tourist Information

Les-Sept-Laux: t 04 76 08 17 86,
   www.les7laux.com.

are floodlit for night skiing. On the cable-car ride from Chamrousse 1650 to the summit of Croix de Chamrousse, you look down on the area's black runs, including the famous Olympic pistes, which offer interesting challenges for experts, among them fairly long runs of 850m vertical down to Casserousse at 1400m. Cross-country enthusiasts can try the 40km of attractive trails on the Plateau de l'Areselle at 1500m.

The other major downhill resort in the Belledonne, **Les-Sept-Laux**, with a slightly larger piste network, lacks the same extent of challenging black runs but is popular with intermediates and beginners. Most accommodation, shops, bars and restaurants have been purpose-built at **Prapoutel**, at the western end of the ski area where the slopes benefit from the afternoon and evening sun. From there slopes spread along the mountain eastwards to **Le Pleynet** where the slopes attract the morning sun, with **Pipay** in the centre being a popular base for day-trippers from Grenoble, with chairlift access to the heart of the pistes. Intermediates will find pistes to suit them throughout the area – the easy route marked on the piste map in yellow will help you explore from one end to the other. The main interest for experts lies in the off-piste.

Vercors: Villard-de-Lans/Corrençon-en-Vercors, Lans-en-Vercors, Méaudre and Autrans (skiing not linked)

Unspoilt villages in the beautiful Vercors Regional Natural Park, just to the south-west of Grenoble, turn into winter wonderlands from December to March and offer skiing holidays with a quieter pace and more genuinely French countryside feel to them than the big resorts of the Alps; prices here are much lower too. Cross-country is as important and more extensive than downhill skiing and, for downhillers, the area is best for those who are looking for a peaceful relaxing holiday rather than clocking up as much mileage on the snow as possible.

The biggest downhill resort, the charming old market town of **Villard-de-Lans** which, together with its smaller rustic neighbour Corrençon-en-Vercors, shares a very respectable 130km of pistes, took off as a tourism destination early last century with

Villard-de-Lans/Corrençon-en-Vercors

Ski Area
Height of slopes 1,160m–2,170m
Number of lifts 25

Pistes 130km
green 15%
blue 31%
red 23%
black 31%

Tourist Information

Villard-de-Lans: t 04 76 95 10 38,
  www.villarddelans.com.
Corrençon-en-Vercors: t 04 76 95 81 75,
  www.villarddelans.com.

Lans-en-Vercors

Ski Area
Height of slopes 1,020m–1,810m
Number of lifts 14

Pistes 40km
green 35%
blue 41%
red 24%

Tourist Information

Lans-en-Vercors: t 04 76 95 42 62,
  www.ot-lans-en-vercors.com.

Méaudre

Ski Area
Height of slopes 1,010m–1,600m
Number of lifts 10

Pistes 18km
green 38%
blue 31%
red 23%
black 8%

Tourist Information

Méaudre: t 04 76 95 20 68,
  www.meaudre.com.

Autrans

Ski Area
Height of slopes 1,050m–1,650m
Number of lifts 16

Pistes 18km
green 59%
blue 12%
red 23%
black 6%

Tourist Information

Autrans: t 04 76 95 30 70,
  www.ot-autrans.fr.

the popularity of its 'clean air and milk' health cures; the milk came from the local Villarde breed of cows. Skiing started here in 1925 and it hosted the World Skiing Championships in 1931 and part of the Winter Olympics in 1968. The area's latest hero, local girl Carole Montillet, became the first Frenchwoman to win an Olympic gold medal in the prestigious downhill event when she triumphed in Salt Lake City in 2002.

Intermediates will find plenty of blues and greens to keep them interested and wonderful views, especially over the Lac du Pré above Villard-de-Lans and of the Alps and Mont Blanc from the top of the highest lifts. Beginners have ideal nursery slopes right by **Corrençon-en-Vercors** and at Les Glovettes above Villard-de-Lans. Experts can enjoy no fewer than eight black runs, mainly on the higher slopes above Corrençon-en-Vercors, and some off-piste.

The 160km of tracks on the High Vercors Nordic site, which includes what in summer is an 18-hole golf course, has become one of the leading cross-country areas in France. There's even a Nordic ski adventure park, with bumps, ridges, jumps and bends, popular with experienced and beginner Nordic skiers, and a 30km Royal Chrono circuit where you can compare your time with, say, Olympic champion Raphaël Poirée.

A huge amount of money has been invested in recent years in snowmaking machinery to ensure good snow (so long as it's cold enough) in both the downhill and cross-country areas.

On the road from Grenoble to Villard-de-Lans, you pass through the village of **Lans-en-Vercors**, with the second largest downhill ski area in the Regional Park, though with only 40km of pistes it is hardly huge and it has no black runs. Its two cross-country areas offer 68km of trails. **Méaudre**, a tiny, charmingly unspoilt village just to the north of Villard-de-Lans, and **Autrans**, larger and a little further north again, both have even smaller areas of downhill slopes but their main claims to fame are their cross-country facilities. Méaudre's two areas, one right by the village and the other 300m higher at Les Narces, total 100km and Autrans' varied trails total 160km. Autrans is famous for cross-country skiing, especially thanks to the great race called the *Foulée Blanche*, taking place every year in January.

Ain

Monts-Jura: Mijoux/La Faucille, Lélex/Crozet (skiing not linked)

Just to the northwest of Geneva, the unspoilt Monts-Jura resorts offer a relaxingly low-key winter holiday with magnificent views over Lake Geneva and towards Mont Blanc. The two neighbouring resorts of **Mijoux** and **Lélex** sit at the foot of their small and separate downhill ski areas, Mijoux-La Faucille and Lélex-Crozet, with gentle slopes which suit beginners and intermediates best. Neither is high (with a maximum altitude of 1680m and the valley at 900m) which means that the snow can suffer in times of shortage and in warm weather, though snowmaking on Lélex-Crozet helps. The 120km of cross-country trails in both the Valserine valley and on the more snowsure La Vattay plateau are more than double the length of the downhill pistes and make the area a popular destination with cross-country enthusiasts. Other popular activities here include snowshoeing and dogsledding.

Monts-Jura

Ski Area
Height of slopes 900m–1,680m
Number of lifts 28

Pistes 50km
green 37%
blue 30%
red 22%
black 11%

Tourist Information

Monts-Jura: t 04 50 20 91 43, *www.monts-jura.com.*

Cross-country Skiing

Because most British and non-European skiers usually learn downhill skiing when they first visit the Alps and then visit the mountains for only one or two weeks a year, very few try cross-country skiing. Those who do frequently become hooked by the peace and tranquillity of it compared with downhill, as it allows you to get away from the crowds and the lift systems and into the forests, on and around frozen lakes and onto high plateaus. Compared with downhill, cross-country skiing also appeals to those in search of an aerobic work-out; while the ski lifts take a lot of the effort out of downhill skiing, it's your own energy that gets you up the hills of a cross-country trail. The lightness of the skis and the comfortable shoes you wear compared with the heavy skis and bindings and stiff plastic boots of downhill equipment form another attraction for many people.

There are two main types of cross-country skiing (which is increasingly becoming known as '*ski nordique*' rather than '*ski de fond*' in France). The most common one involves gliding along in grooves in the snow, one for each ski, that have been prepared by special machines – it looks at first sight rather like walking on skis but in practice there's much more to it than that, and lessons to teach you the basics are a must if you are to get the most out of the sport. The other main style is more like skating on skis on tracks that have been prepared specially for that purpose – that's the type you see on TV for most of the main Nordic competitive races and biathlons.

With over 200 special Nordic skiing areas and 11,000km of prepared and secured pistes, cross-country is booming in France. While most ski resorts have some cross-country facilities, a few specialize in this activity. In the Rhône-Alpes, these include: Vercors, Monts-Jura, Le Grand Bornand with Les Confins in Les Aravis, Plateau des Glières and Praz de Lys in Haute Savoie, Domaine d'Agy (Morillon and Les Carroz) and Les Saisies. As well as skiing, most *Espace Nordique* areas also offer other activities such as walking paths, dogsledding and snowshoeing, have detailed maps showing all the trails and their own ski pass. In the Rhône-Alpes, area passes are available allowing you to try cross-country throughout the region – for example, throughout Savoie or Haute Savoie. The *Espace Nordique* areas also offer original tours and courses with the local ESF.

For more information about Nordic skiing visit *www.ski-nordic-france.com*, where you'll find details of Nordic areas including piste maps, costs and links to the relevant resort websites. For contact details on Vercors, Monts-Jura, the biggest Nordic areas in Rhône-Alpes, and Les Saisies (Val d'Arly/Espace Cristal) *see* the relevant chapters.

Other Nordic Skiing Areas

Les Glières Plateau: Cross-country skiing centre at Thorens-Glières **t** 04 50 22 45 63
La Clusaz Les Confins Plateau: Nordic area centre at La Clusaz, **t** 04 50 02 47 43
Agy/Les Carroz: Agy Nordic Centre at St-Sigismond, **t** 04 50 34 27 53
Praz de Lys: Nordic Centre at Taninges, **t** 04 50 34 25 05
Le Semnoz: Nordic Ski Centre at Leschaux, **t** 04 50 01 16 48
Savoie: Grand Revard **t** 04 79 25 80 49

Language

Everywhere in France the same level of politeness is expected: use *monsieur, madame* or *mademoiselle* when speaking to everyone (and never *garçon* in restaurants!), from your first *bonjour* to your last *au revoir*.
For food vocabulary, *see* pp.31–34.

Pronunciation

Vowels
a/à/â between *a* in 'bat' and 'part'
é/er/ez at end of word as *a* in 'plate' but a bit shorter
e/è/ê as *e* in 'bet'
e at end of word not pronounced
e at end of syllable or in one-syllable word pronounced weakly, like *er* in 'mother'
i as *ee* in 'bee'
o as *o* in 'pot'
ô as *o* in 'go'
u/û between *oo* in 'boot' and *ee* in 'bee'

Vowel Combinations
ai as *a* in 'plate'
aî as *e* in 'bet'
ail as *i* in 'kite'
au/eau as *o* in 'go'
ei as *e* in 'bet'
eu/œu as *er* in 'mother'
oi between *wa* in 'swam' and *wu* in 'swum'
oy as 'why'
ui as *wee* in 'twee'

Nasal Vowels
Vowels followed by an **n** or **m** sound nasal.
an/en as *o* in 'pot' + nasal sound
ain/ein/in as *a* in 'bat' + nasal sound
on as *aw* in 'paw' + nasal sound
un as *u* in 'nut' + nasal sound

Consonants
Many French consonants are pronounced as in English, but there are some exceptions:

c followed by *e, i* or *y*, and *ç* as *s* in 'sit'
c followed by *a, o, u* as *c* in 'cat'
g followed by *e, i* or *y* as *s* in 'pleasure'
g followed by *a, o, u* as *g* in 'good'
gn as *ni* in 'opinion'
j as *s* in 'pleasure'
ll as *y* in 'yes'
qu as *k* in 'kite'
s between vowels as *z* in 'zebra'
s otherwise as *s* in 'sit'
w except in English words as *v* in 'vest'
x at end of word as *s* in 'sit'
x otherwise as *x* in 'six'

Stress
The stress usually falls on the last syllable except when the word ends with an unaccented **e**.

Useful Phrases

hello *bonjour*
good evening *bonsoir*
good night *bonne nuit*
goodbye *au revoir*
please *s'il vous plaît*
thank you (very much) *merci (beaucoup)*
yes *oui*
no *non*
good *bon (bonne)*
bad *mauvais (e)*
excuse me *pardon, excusez-moi*
Can you help me? *Pourriez-vous m'aider?*
My name is... *Je m'appelle...*
What is your name? *Comment vous appelez-vous?* (formal)
How are you? *Comment allez-vous?*
Fine *Ça va bien*
I don't understand *Je ne comprends pas*
I don't know *Je ne sais pas*
Speak more slowly *Pourriez-vous parler plus lentement?*
How do you say ... in French? *Comment dit-on ... en français?*

Help! *Au secours!*
doctor *le médecin*
hospital *un hôpital*
emergency room *la salle des urgences*
police station *le commissariat de police*
No smoking *Défense de fumer*

Shopping and Accommodation

Do you have...? *Est-ce que vous avez...?*
I would like... *J'aimerais...*
Where is/are...? *Où est/sont...*
How much is it? *C'est combien?*
entrance *l'entrée*
exit *la sortie*
open *ouvert*
closed *fermé*
push *poussez*
pull *tirez*
money *l'argent*
traveller's cheque *un chèque de voyage*
post office *la poste*
stamp *un timbre*
phonecard *une télécarte*
postcard *une carte postale*
Do you have any change? *Avez-vous de la monnaie?*
shop *un magasin*
central food market *les halles (f)*
pharmacy *la pharmacie*
aspirin *l'aspirine (f)*
condoms *les préservatifs (m)*
insect repellent *un produit insectifuge*
sun cream *la crème solaire*
tampons *les tampons hygiéniques (m)*
Do you have a room? *Avez-vous une chambre?*
Can I look at the room? *Puis-je voir la chambre?*
How much is the room per day/week? *C'est combien la chambre par jour/semaine?*
single room *une chambre pour une personne*
twin room *une chambre à deux lits*
double room *une chambre pour deux personnes*
... with shower/bath *... avec douche/salle de bains*
... for one night/one week *... pour une nuit/une semaine*
bed *un lit*
blanket *une couverture*
cot (child's bed) *un lit d'enfant*
pillow *un oreiller*
soap *du savon*
towel *une serviette*

Transport, Driving and Directions

How can I get to...? *Comment puis-je aller à..?*
When is the next...? *A quelle heure est le prochain...?*
What time does it leave (arrive)? *A quelle heure est-ce qu'il part (arrive)?*
From where does it leave? *D'où est-ce qu'il-part?*
Do you stop at...? *Est-ce que vous passez par...?*
How long does the trip take? *Combien de temps dure le voyage?*
A single/return ticket (to...) *un aller* or *aller simple/aller et retour (pour...)*
aeroplane *l'avion*
berth *la couchette*
bus *l'autobus (m)*
bus stop *l'arrêt d'autobus (m)*
car *la voiture*
coach *l'autocar*
coach station *la gare routière*
flight *le vol*
on foot *à pied*
port *le port*
railway station *la gare*
ship *le bateau*
taxi *le taxi*
delayed/on time *en retard/à l'heure*
platform *le quai*
date-stamp machine *le composteur*
timetable *l'horaire (m)*
left-luggage locker *la consigne automatique*
ticket office *le guichet*
ticket *le billet*
customs *la douane*
seat *la place*
breakdown *la panne*
driver *le chauffeur*
entrance *l'entrée (f)*
give way/yield *céder le passage*
hire *louer*
driving licence *un permis de conduire*
motorbike/moped *la moto/le vélomoteur*
no parking *stationnement interdit*
petrol (unleaded) *l'essence (sans plomb) (f)*
road *la route*
roadworks *les travaux (m)*
This doesn't work *Ça ne marche pas*
Where is...? *Où se trouve...?*
left *à gauche*
right *à droite*

Glossary

abbaye abbey
abside apse
arc-boutant flying buttress
ardoise slate
arrondissement city district
auberge inn
autel altar
aven swallow hole (vertical hole in the rock)
bas-côté aisle (which can also be a *collatéral*)
basse-cour (for château) outer courtyard; (for farm) farmyard
bastide a new town founded in the Middle Ages; usually rectangular, with a grid of streets and an arcaded central square; sometimes circular in plan
beffroi tower with a town's bell
bergère wing chair (more frequently means shepherdess, though)
bien national property of the state
boiserie(s) (en plis de serviette) (linenfold) wood panelling
cachot prison cell; dungeon
canonnière loophole for gun
castrum a rectangular Roman army camp, which often grew into a permanent settlement
cave or *caveau* wine cellar
chaire pulpit
châtelain(e) lord of a château (lady of a château)
chemin path
chemin de ronde parapet walk, wall walk, rampart walk
chœur choir (in architecture as well as music)
cintre arch (also coat hanger)
clé (or clef) de voûte keystone or boss (architecturally speaking)
clocher-mur the west front of a church that rises high above the roofline for its entire width to make a bell tower
col pass
(escalier en) colimaçon spiral (staircase)
collégiale collegiate church
colombage half-timbering
colombier dovecot

(les) combles attic, loft, garret; roof timbers
commanderie local headquarters of a knightly order (like the Templars or Knights Hospitallers), usually to look after the order's lands and properties in an area
commune in the Middle Ages, the government of a free town or city; today, the smallest unit of local government, encompassing a town or village
(les) communs outbuildings
corps de logis main building
côte coast; on wine labels *côte, coteaux* and *costières* mean 'hills' or 'slopes'
cour court; courtyard (a *cour d'honneur* is the principal courtyard of a château)
cours wide main street, like an elongated main square
couvent convent or monastery
cul-de-lampe sculpted pendant at the bottom of a rib or vault
domestique as an adjective, domestic, but just as commonly used as a noun meaning servant
donjon castle keep
douves (sèches) (dry) moat
écluse canal lock
église church (see also *temple)*
enceinte defensive enclosure (also means pregnant)
enfeu niche in a church's exterior or interior wall for a tomb
enfilade series of linked rooms
estampe engraving (*sur bois* = woodcut)
fabrique folly (more commonly, manufacture or factory)
fenêtre à meneaux mullioned window
fossé ditch
fraise strawberry, but also ruff
fusain charcoal
géminé twin
gentilhommière manor
gisant sculpted prone effigy on a tomb
gîte self-catering accommodation
gîte d'étape basic shelter for walkers

Grande Randonnée (GR) long-distance hiking path

grange farm

grotte cave

(les) halles covered market

herse portcullis; (in agriculture) harrow

historié historiated (decorated with flowers or figures or animals, often telling a story in pictures)

hôtel originally the town residence of the nobility; by the 18th century became more generally used for any large, private residence; also a hotel

hôtel de ville town hall

investir to invest, but also to besiege

lavoir communal fountain, usually covered, for the washing of clothes

lucarne dormer, attic or gable window

magnanerie silk-producing farm

mairie town hall

la maison ordinary word for a house, but also a euphemism for a château, which it would be too vulgar to refer to directly

maquis Mediterranean scrub; also used as a term for the French Resistance in hiding during the Second World War

mascaron an ornamental mask, usually one carved on the keystone of an arch

mécène patron

modillon a stone projecting from the cornice of a church, carved with a face or animal figure

ogive diagonal rib (in architectural vaulting); an *arc en ogive* is a lancet arch

parlement a regional law court before the Revolution, with members appointed by the king; by the late *Ancien Régime, parlements* exercised a great deal of influence over political affairs

(nom à) particule name with a handle (i.e. nobleman's name indicated by a '*de*' or '*du*' in front of the surname)

pech hill

pignon gable (*avoir pignon sur rue* = to have a shop in a prime position or to be prosperous)

place square

pleurant weeper, mourner

poêt hill

pont-levis drawbridge

porte cochère carriage entrance

poudre de succession 'powder of inheritance' (euphemism for poison)

poutre beam

presqu'île peninsula

primitif early master (in painting)

puy high point (also *pujol*)

retable a carved or painted altarpiece, often consisting of a number of scenes or sculptural ensembles

rez-de-chaussée (rc) ground floor (US first floor)

rinceau(x) ornamental foliage, foliated scroll

romain Roman (note difference from *roman*)

roman Romanesque (10th-12th century architectural style characterized by rounded arches); as a noun, a novel

sablière beam, stringer

sens de la visite generally not sense of the visit, but direction to follow on the visit

sens interdit no entry

sens unique one way

temple Protestant church (more usually than a temple)

tomber en quenouille to pass into the female line or fall to the distaff

tourelle turret

transi in a tomb, a relief of the decomposing cadaver

travée bay (in church architecture); span (of bridge)

trumeau the column between twin doors of a church portal, often carved with reliefs

tympanum semicircular panel over a church door; often the occasion for the most ambitious ensembles of medieval sculpture

verdure tapestry representing trees or foliage as the main motif (more commonly means greenery or salad vegetables!)

vieille ville historic, old quarter of town

village perché hilltop or hillside village

visite libre unaccompanied visit, not free visit (which would be *visite gratuite*)

vitrail (plural: vitraux) stained glass window(s)

voûte vault or arch (*en anse de panier*: basket-handle arch; *d'arête*: groined vault; *en berceau*: barrel vault; *en éventail*: fan vault; *d'ogives*: ribbed vault; *en plein cintre*: semicircular arch)

Index

Main page references are in **bold**.
Page references to maps are in *italics*.

abbeys and monasteries 9–10
  Abondance 223
  Aulps 223
  Bodon 194
  Bourg-en-Bresse 86–7
  Hautecombe 9, **261**
  Léoncel 284
  Notre-Dame-des-Dombes 88
  Peillonnex 216–20
  St-Antoine 284
  St-Pierre 67–8
  Tamié 258–9
  Trappe d'Aiguebelle 189
  Valcroissant 188
Abondance 223
accommodation 50–1
  see also under individual places
Aignoz 206
Aiguebelette 253, **265**
Aiguèze 148
Aiguille du Midi 293
Aiguilles d'Arves 244
Ailhon 142
Aillon valley 260
Aillon-le-Jeune 253, **260**
Aime 240
Ain 208–10
  winter sports 333–4
airlines 36–7, 40
Aix-les-Bains 7, 17, 253, **261–2**
Alba-la-Romaine 144
Albertville 235, **237–8**, 258
Albon 153
Alex 256
Alix 98
Allan 169
Allement dam 209
Allevard 271
Allier 132
Allinges-le-Neuf 216
Allinges-le-Vieux 216
Allymes 204
Ambérieu-en-Bugey 204
Ambierle 111, **114**
Ambronay 208
Ampère, André-Marie 104
Ampuis 160
Ancien Régime 13–15, 23
Andance 161
Annecy 19, 25, **249–56**, *250*
Anneyron 161

Annoisin-Chatelans 202
Annonay 15, 24, **132**
Anse 102
Anthy-sur-Léman 218, **220**
Antraigues-sur-Volane 129, **135**
Aoûste 185
Apremont 259
Arâches 225
Aravis 225
Arbent 209
Arbin 259
Arc valley *see* Maurienne
architecture 8, 14
Arcoules 160
Ardèche *126*, **127–48**
  gorges 147–8
  north *130*, 131–6
  south 136–48, *137*
  sports and activities 128, 138
  wine 144
Ardent 223
Ardoisière des 7 Pieds 223
Arêches 234, **237**
Arenthon 256
Argentière 230, 294
Argentine 245
Arginy 100
Arlempdes 112, **124**
Ars-sur-Formans 89–90
Artemare 201, **205**
Astrée 23
Attignat-Oncin 266
Aubenas 136–9
Aubres 186
Aucelon 187
Aulan 196
Aulps 223
Auris-en-Oisans 325–8
Aussois 235, **243**
Autrans 283
  winter sports 331–3
Avant-Pays Savoyard 266
Avenas 97, **98**
avens
  de la Forestière 147
  de Marzal 147–8
  d'Orgnac 146–7
  see also caves
Avérole valley 242
Aviernoz 225, 252
Avoriaz 223
  winter sports 288, 289
Avrieux 243
Avrissieu 201
Avully 216

Bâgé-le-Châtel 84
Bagnols-en-Beaujolais 98, **102**
Balazuc 144–5
Banne 143
Barbie, Klaus 19–20, 78
Baronnies 193–6
Barrage de l'Esseillon 243
Barrage de Génissiat 210
Barrage de Grangent 118
Barrage de Villerest 113
Barraux 274
Barre, Raymond 62
Barret-de-Lioure 196
Bas-en-Basset 122
Bastie d'Urfé 12, **115**
Beauchastel 165
Beaufort 234
Beaufort-sur-Gervanne 187
Beaufortain 236–7
Beaujeu 97, **99**
Beaujolais 26, *92*, **93–106**
  festivals 98
  wine 94–5
Beaulieu 140
Belle Epoque 16–18
Bellecombe-en-Bauges 260
Belledonne 330–1
Bellegarde 210
Bellevaux 220
Belleville 100
Belley 201, 206
Bérard waterfall 230
Bergès, Aristide 17, 273
Berlioz, Hector 24–5, 174–5
Bernard of Clairvaux 9, 23
Bernard, Claude 101
Bernin 274
Bessans 235, **242**
Besse 246
Bézorgues valley 135
Bidon 148
Billebaudez en Beaujolais Vert 99
Billième 258
Bionnassay 228
birdlife 88, 194
Blay 238
Bodon 194
Boëge 216
Boën-sur-Lignon 115–16
Boffres 129
Bolozon 209
Bonne valley 246
Bonneval 238
Bonneval-sur-Arc 235, **242**
Bonneville 224

Borée 124
Bossan, Pierre 17
Bossieu 176
Boucieu-le-Roi 133
Boudin 237
Bouligneux 88
Boulogne 136
Bourbon dynasty 10
Bourdeaux 184, **187**
Bourg-Argental 132
Bourg-en-Bresse 85–7
Bourg-St-Andéol 154, **168–9**
Bourg-St-Maurice 237, **240**
Bourget, lake 205–6, 260–3
Bourgoin-Jallieu 174
Bourne gorge 283
Bouvante 273
Bouvesse-Quirieu 200
Bozel 239
Brandes-en-Oisans 246
Brangues 202
Brantes 195
Bréda valley 271
Brégnier-Cordon 203
Brénaz 205
Brénod 205
Bresse *80*, **81–7**
Bresson 272
Brides-les-Bains 304–9
Briennon 113
Briord 203
Bronze gorge 224
Brou 86
Brouilly 100
Bruyant gorge 283
Buellas 85
Bugey 199, **203–10**
Buis-les-Baronnies 186, **195**
Bully 103, **113**
Burdignin 216
Bussières 114
Cap Plein Air 185
Capetian dynasty 8, 10
capons 81
Capvignes 100
Carnot, Sadi 17
Carolingian dynasty 7
Carthaginians 7
Cascade de la Pissarole 274
Cascade du Ray-Pic 135
Catherine de' Medici 12
Catholic Church 7, 8, 12–13, 14
caves 48
 Balme 202
 Balmes 243
 Chauvet 6
 Choranche 283
 Draye Blanche 284
 Dullin 266
 Echelles 275
 Huguenots 147
 Labalme 209
 Luire 284
 Madeleine 147
 Pic 205
 St-Marcel 148

Thaïs 6, 179
Tunnels 147
 see also avens
Céladon 23
Celliers 238
Celts 6
Cerdon 208–9
CERN 211–12
Cervérieu 205
Cervières 120
Césarges 176
Ceyzériat 207
Ceyzérieux 201
Chabrillan 182
Chaize 100
Chalamont 87
Chalencon (Ardèche) 134
Chalencon (Drôme) 188
Chalencon (Loire) 122
Challes-les-Eaux 253, **259**
Chalmazel 111, **120**
Chambéry 253, **263–5**, *265*
Chambles 118
Chambonas 143
Chambost 266
Chamelet 102
Chamonix 20, 23, **230**, **296**
 winter sports 292–6
Champagne-en-Valromey 205
Champagny-le-Bas 239
Champagny-d'en-Haut 239
Champdieu 116
Champdor 205
Champoly 120
Chamrousse 274
 winter sports 330–1
Chanay 206
Chanaz 252, 258
Chandolas 145
Changy 114
Channel Tunnel 37, 39
Chanousia gardens 241
Chantemerle 238
Chapelle de l'Hermitage 162
Chaponost 105
Charavines 177
Charentay 100
Charix 210
Charlemagne, Emperor 7
Charles IX 13
Charles VIII 11
Charles X 16
Charlieu 109–13
Charmant Som 275
Charmes-sur-Rhône 154, **165**
Charnay 103
Chartreuse de Bonnefoy 124
Chartreuse liqueurs 30, 178
Chartreuse mountains 274–5
Chartreuse de St-Hugon 270–1
Chaspinhac 112
château
 Allinges 216
 Allymes 204
 Arenthon 256
 Arginy 100

Aulan 196
Avully 216
Boulogne 136
Chaize 100
Chambost 266
Chantemerle 238
Chaumont 257
Chèze 134
Clermont 257
Délphinal 202
Ferney 211
Fléchères 89
Gabelle 196
Grangent 118
Grignan 189–90
Jarnioux 101
Lachassagne 103
Lavoûte-Polignac 122
Longpra 178
Menthon 255–6
Miolans 259
Montbel 274
Montellier 88
Montfleury 266
Montmelas 101
Montrond-les-Bains 117
Montrottier 256–7
Pierreux 100
Polignac 122
Retourtour 133
Ripaille 221
Rive 259
Roche 113–14
Rochebaron 122
Rochebonne (Ardèche) 134
Rochebonne (Beaujolais) 102
Rochefort 266
Rochetaillée 104
Roure 146
Rubins 225
St-Marcel-de-Félines 114
St-Paul-en-Cornillon 118
St-Vidal 122
Sothonod 205
Suze-la-Rousse 191–2
Talaru 120
Thorens 225
Tours 102
Touvet 274
Vaugirard 116
Ventadour 140
Virieu 176
Vizille 280–1
Vogüé 144
Châteaubourg 163
Châteaufort 258
Châteauneuf-sur-Isère 162
Châteauneuf-sur-Rhône 169
Châtel 223
 winter sports 290
Châtillon (Beaujolais) 103
Châtillon (Savoie) 260
Châtillon-sur-Chalaronne 85, **88–9**
Châtillon-en-Diois 185, **188**
Châtillon-en-Michaille 201
Chatte 178

Chaudieu 260
Chaumont 257
Chautagne 258
Chavannes-sur-Suran 208
Chazay-d'Azergues 103
Chazelles-sur-Lyon 117
cheese 29, 120, 226, 236
Chénas 96
Chessy-les-Mines 103
chestnuts 29, 135
Chèze 134
Chézery-Forens 210
Chichilianne 272, **282**
Chignin 259
Chintreuil, Antoine 83
Chirols 140–1
Chiroubles 97–8
Chonas-l'Amballan 153
Christianity 7, 8, 12–13, 14
church opening hours 48
cinema 25, 76
Cirque de Fauconnière 210
Cirque du Fer à Cheval 224
Cirque de Gens 145
Cirque de St-Même 274–5
Cize 209
Clairette de Die 182
Clansayes 169
Claveisolles 99
Clement V, Pope 59
Clermont 257
Cléry 259
climate 44
climbing 48
Cliousclat 154, **165–6**
Clochemerle 26, 93
Cluny 8
Cluse des Hôpitaux 204
Cluses 224–5
Cogny 101
Cohennoz 299
Col des Aravis 226
Col d'Aussois 239, 244
Col de Balme 294
Col du Banchet 266
Col de Béal 120
Col de Berthiand 209
Col de la Colombière 226
Col de Crie 99
Col de la Croix de Bauzon 141
Col de la Croix de Fer 245
Col de la Croix-Fry 226
Col de la Crusille 266
Col du Cucheron 275
Col de l'Epine 265
Col de l'Escrinet 135
Col d'Ey 194
Col de la Faucille 201, 211
Col du Galiber 245
Col du Glandon 245
Col du Granier 274
Col de l'Iseran 241–2
Col de Joly 236
Col de Joux 224
Col du Lautaret 245
Col de Lèbe 204–5

Col de Leschaux 260
Col de la Loge 120
Col de la Machine 273
Col de la Madeleine 238
Col de Méraillet 237
Col du Mont-Cenis 242–3
Col des Montets 230
Col de Perty 195
Col du Petit St-Bernard 241
Col de la Porte 275
Col des Portes 203
Col de Rousset 188
Col des Saisies 236
Col de la Seigne 237
Col de Tamié 258
Coligny 207–8
Collonges-au-Mont-d'Or 98, **104**
Colombier-sous-Pilat 129
Combe de Malaval 246
Combe de Savoie 258–9
Combloux 219, **227**
winter sports 296–8
Commelle-Vernay 111
Condas 112
Condorcet 186
Condrieu 153, **160**
wine 158–9
Conflans 235, **238**
Confrançon 85
Conjux 260
consulates 45
Contrevoz 201
Conzieu 206–7
copper mining 106
Corbonod 206
Cordon 219, **227**
Cormet de Roseland 237
Cornas 159
Corps 281
Corrençon-en-Vercors 273, **283**
winter sports 331–3
Côte de Brouilly 100
Côte Roannais 114
Côte Rôtie 158, 160
Coteaux du Lyonnais 104
Coteaux du Tricastin 190
Côtes du Forez 115
Côtes du Rhône-Villages 191
Counter-Reformation 12
Courchevel 239
winter sports 304–9
Courmayeur 241, 294
Courtes 82
Couvent de la Tourette 105
Coux 135
Couzon-au-Mont-d'Or 104
Crémieu 199–202
Cressin-Rochefort 206
Crest 182–5
Crest-Voland 219, **227**
winter sports 299
Crêt de l'Œillon 131
Crêt de la Perdix 131
crime 44
crocodile farm 169
Croix Rampeau 104

cross-country skiing 334
Crozes-Hermitage 159
Crozet 273
winter sports 333
Cruas 165
Cruet 259
Crussol castle 163
Cuisiat 207
Culoz 206
cycling 42, 49
Dancé 113
Dardilly 104–5
Dark Ages 7
Davézieux 133
Défilé de Donzère 168
Défilé de l'Ecluse 212
Défilé de Pierre Châtel 258
Défilé de Ruoms 145
Défilé des Trente Pas 189
Delphinal 202
Dent du Chat 261
Désaignes 133
Désert de Platé 225
Die 182, 184, **187–8**
Dieulefit 185, **189**
Dini, Paul 101
disabled travellers 44–5
Divonne 19, 201, **211**
Dombes *80*, 81, 82, **87–90**
Dorne valley 135
Dortan 209
Douce-Plage 163
Doucy 239
Doucy-Combelouvière 302–4
Doussard 256
Drac 281
Dranse de Morzine 223
driving in France 40–1
driving licences 41
Drobie valley 141
Droisy 257
Drôme 172, 173
festivals 184
north 175, 180–1
south 182–96, *183*
Duingt 256
Dullin 266
E111 forms 45
Ecole 260
Ecrins National Park 245, 281
Edict of Nantes 13
electricity 45
embassies 45
Engins 283
Ennuye valley 194
Entremont 274
entry formalities 39
Epierre 245
Espace Cristal 299
Espace Killy 316–19
Espace San Bernardo 312–14
Espahy 124
Essalois 118
Esseillon 243
Estivareilles 120
Estrablin 152

Etables 153
Etoile-sur-Rhône 165
Eurostar 38–9
Evaison Mont-Blanc 296–9
Eveux 105
Evian-les-Bains 19, 20, 218, **221–2**
Evosges 204
Excenevex 220
Eybens 272
Eygalayes 186
Eyrieux river 134
Faugères 142
Faverges 258
Faverges-de-la-Tour 200
Feissons 238
Ferme da la Forêt 82
Ferney-Voltaire 201, **211**
Ferrassières 186, **196**
ferries 37–8
Fessy 216
festivals 46, 98, 152, 184
Feurs 117
Firminy 119
Flaine 225, 291
   winter sports 292
Flaxieu 206
Fléchères 89
Fleurie 97
Flumet 219, 227
   winter sports 299
Fond-de-France 271–2
Fontcouverte 245
food and drink **28–34**, 45, 81, 143
   see also under individual places,
   wine, cheese
Forêt de Lente 284
Forêt de Saou 187
Forez plain 115–19
Foron valley 216
Fort l'Ecluse 212
Fort de l'Esseillon 243
Fort Marie-Christine 243–4
Fort de Ronce 243
Fort du St-Eynard 275
Fort St-Gobain 243
Fort de Tamié 259
Forteresse de Couzan 120
François I 12
François de Tournon 12
Frangy 257
Franks 7
Fréjus tunnel 244
Frenay, Henri 77
Gabelle 196
Garnier, Tony 18, 76
Genestelle 136
Germagnat 208
Gesse-en-Vercors 281–2
Gex 201, **211**
Giffre 223–4
Gigors-et-Lozeron 187
Gimel peat bog 131
gîtes 51
Givors 151, 155
Glières 225–6
Glueyre valley 134

golf 49, 161, 167
gorges
   Ardèche 147–8
   Arly 227
   Bourne 283
   Bronze 224
   Bruyant 283
   Cluse des Hôpitaux 204
   Diosaz 230
   Dranse 223
   Eygues 194
   Fier 257
   Guiers Vif 275
   Pont du Diable 223
   Ste Baume 168
   Toulourenc 196
Graix 131
Gran Paradiso Park 241
Grand Colombier 258
Grand Massif 290–2
Grandes Rousses 245
   winter sports 328–8
Grands Montets 294
Grange-Chartron 99
Grangent 118
Granges-lès-Beaumont 177
Gras 144
Greeks 6
Grenoble 271–2, **276–80**, *276*
   history 7, 10, 15, 276–7
   Winter Olympics 19
Grésivaudan 269–70
Grésy-sur-Isère 252–3, **259**
Grignan 185, **189–90**
Grospierres 140
grotte see caves
Guignol puppets 16, **24**
Guigues dynasty 9
Gumières 120
Gutenberg Bible 69
Habères 216
Hameau-de-Flaine 292
Hannibal 7
Haut Chablais 223–4
Haute Savoie *214*, **215–30**
   winter sports 287–302
Hautecombe 9, **261**
Hauteluce 236
   winter sports 299–300
Hauterives 177, **180**
Hauts Plateaux du Vercors 284
Hautville-Lompnes 204
health 45, 47
Henri II 12
Henri III 13
Henri IV 13, 60
Hermitage 159
Herriot, Edouard 18
Héry 227
history **6–20**
   Ancien Régime 13–15, 23
   Belle Epoque 16–18
   Celts 6
   Christianity 7, 8, 12–13, 14
   Dark Ages 7
   Hannibal 7

Italian Wars 11–13
   Medieval Period 8–11
   Napoleon Bonaparte 15–16
   prehistory 6
   Revolution 15, 61
   Wars of Religion 11–13, 60
   World Wars 18, 77–8
horse-riding 49
Hospice du Petit St-Bernard 241
hotels 50–1
   see also under individual places
Huguenots 12
Huguenots caves 147
Hundred Years War 10
Innocent IV, Pope 59
insurance 45, 47
Internet access 48
Isère *172*, **173–81**, *175*, **269–74**
   Upper Isère 237–42
   winter sports 325–33
Isle d'Abeau 174
Isle Crémieu 199–203
Italian Wars 11–13
Izernore 209
Izieu 203–4
Jacobins 15
Jacquard, Joseph 16
Jaillance 182
Jarnioux 101
Jarrier 245
Jarsy 260
Jasseron 207
Jaujac 140
Jeansagnière 111
Jesuits 14
Jongieux 252, **258**
Jonzieux 132
Joseph 124
Journans 207
Joyeuse 142
Joyeux 88
Jujurieux 208
Juliénas **94–5**, 96
Jura 211, 333
Knights Templars 8
La Bastie d'Urfé 12, **115**
La Bâtie-Montgascon 203
La Bénisson Dieu 113
La Bérade 246
La Brégoule 164
La Chambotte 260
La Chapelle d'Abondance 288, **290**
La Chapelle St-Romain 258
La Chapelle-en-Vercors 284
La Chaudière 184
La Chavade 141
La Clusaz 226
   winter sports 300–2
La Combe-de-Lancey 273
La Compôte 260
La Correrie 260, 275
La Côte d'Aime 240
La Côte St-André **174–6**, 176–7
La Faucille 333
La Féclaz 260
La Flachère 274

La Flégère 293
La Garde-Adhémar 154, **169**
La Giettaz 227
La Grande Plagne 309–12
La Grave 246
La Gurraz 241
La Meije 246
La Mira 281
La Mulatière 84
La Mure 281
La Norma 324
La Pacaudière 114
La Plagne 240
La Prairie de la Rencontre 281
La Roche-sur-le-Buis 195
La Roche-sur-Foron 224
La Rosière 235, **241**
  winter sports 312–14
La Sône 179
La Tania 304–9
La Terrasse-sur-Dorlay 131
La Thuile 312–14
La Tour-du-Pin 174
La Toussuire 245
  winter sports 319–21
La Voulte-sur-Rhône 165
Labastide-de-Virac 140, **146**
Labeaume 145
Lacenas 101
Lachassagne 103
Lachau 196
Lacoux 204
Lafarge 14
Laffrey, lake 281
Lagnat 257
Lagorce 145
lakes
  Aiguebelette 265
  Annecy 251, **255–6**
  Barterand 206
  Bourget 205–6, 260–3
  Chambon 246
  Chevril 241
  Crozet 273
  Devesset 133
  Genin 210
  Grangent 118
  Issarlès 124
  Laffrey 281
  Léman (Geneva) 220–2
  Mont Cenis 243
  Montriond 223
  Paladru 177
  Point Vert 203
  Roseland 234, **237**
  St-Martial 124
  Sautet 281
  Vallon 220
  Vert 228
Lalley 282
Lalouvesc 133
L'Alpe d'Huez 246
  winter sports 325–8
Lamartine 16
Lamastre 129, **133**
Lanas 144

Lanches 240
Lancrans 210
Landry 240
language **335–6**
  menu reader 30–4
Lans-en-Vercors 283
  winter sports 331–3
Lanslebourg 235, **242**
Lanslevillard 235, **242**
L'Arbresle 105
Largentière 139, **142**
lavender fields 26, 186–7
Lavoûte-Polignac 122
Le Bessat 131
Le Bois d'Oingt 102
Le Bourg d'Oisans 246
Le Bourget-du-Lac 261
Le Bouschet 134
Le Brévent 293
Le Châtel 235, **244–5**
Le Châtelard 260
Le Cheylard 134
Le Chinaillon 226
Le Cohennoz 227
Le Corbier 319–21
Le Corbusier 19
Le Crozet 114
Le Désert 281
Le Fayet 293
Le Grand Abergement 205
Le Grand Colombier 205
Le Grand Domaine 302–4
Le Grand Veymont 282
Le Grand-Bornand 226
  winter sports 300–2
Le Mas 141
Le Miroir 241
Le Monal 241
Le Monastier-sur-Gazeille 124
Le Moulin 241
Le Pègue 192
Le Percy 272
Le Pêt d'Ane 113
Le Petit Abergement 205
Le Pleyney 272
Le Poët-Laval 185, **189**
Le Poët-Sigillat 194
Le Pont-de-Beauvoisin 266
Le Pouzin 154
Le Puy-en-Velay 112, **122–4**
Le Tour 294
Le Touvet 271
Le Villaron 242
L'Ecot 242
Lélex 210
  winter sports 333
Lente 273
Léoncel 284
Les Aravis 300–2
Les Arcs 240
  winter sports 309–12
Les Avenières 203
Les Bauges 258–60
Les Bottières 319–21
Les Carroz 291
  winter sports 292

Les Chapieux 237
Les Contamines-Montjoie 228
  winter sports 299–300
Les Crottes 146
Les Cuillères du Royans 179
Les Deux-Alpes 246, 328-30
Les Etages 246
Les Evettes 242
Les Gets 223
  winter sports 289–90
Les Glières 225–6
Les Grandes Rousses 245
  winter sports 325–8
Les Houches 230, 294
Les Ilettes 225
Les Karellis 321–2
Les Marches 259
Les Menuires 304–9
Les Pilles 186
Les Plans d'Hotonnes 205
Les Pontières 237
Les Saisies 234, **236**, 299
Les Sept-Laux 272
Les Sybelles 319–21
Les Trois Vallées 287–8, 304–9
Les Vans 139–40, **143**
Les-Sept-Laux 330–1
Lescheraines 260
liqueurs 30, 178
L'Isle d'Abeau 174
L'Isle Crémieu 199–203
Lochieu 205
Loire *108*, **109–24**
Longpra 178
Loubaresse 141
Loubet, Emile 18
Lozes 243
Luc-en-Diois 188
Lucey 258
Ludi Parc 283
Luire caves 284
Lumière brothers 17, **25**
Lupé 131
Lyon 25, *54*, **55–78**
  Abbaye St-Pierre 67–8
  Amphithéâtre des Trois Gaules
    73
  aquarium 74
  Atelier de la Soierie 72
  Auditorium 75
  botanical gardens 75
  Boulevard de la Croix Rousse 73
  Célestins theatre 70
  Centre Commercial 75
  Centre d'Histoire de la
    Résistance et de la
    Déportation 75
  churches
    Basilique St-Martin d'Ainay 74
    Cathedral (*Primatiale*) of St
      John 64
    Chapelle de la Trinité 70
    Notre-Dame de Fourvière 63
    St-Bonaventure 70
    St-Bruno 73
    St-Georges 66

St-Nizier 69
St-Paul 65
St-Polycarpe 73
St-Vincent 66
cinema 25, 76
Cité Internationale 74
Civilisation Gallo-Romaine 64
Cour des Voraces 73
Cours Roosevelt 75
Crédit Lyonnais skyscraper 75
Croix-Rousse 72–3
culture 58
eating out 57–8
Eue de la Charité 71
Fourvière Hillside 63–4
Gallo-Roman Lyon 63–4
Gerland Park 76
getting around 56
getting there 56
Halle Tony Garnier 75–6
Halles 75
history 8, 14, 15, **55–62**
Hôtel de la Couronne 69
Hôtel de Gadagne 65–6
Hôtel des Lions 65
Hôtel-Dieu 74
Interpol headquarters 74
Jardin des Chartreux 73
La Mouche quarter 75
Lyon-Perrache station 74
markets 56
Medieval city 64–6
Montée de la Grande-Côte 73
museums
    Art Contemporain 74
    Art Sacré 63
    Arts Décoratifs 71–2
    Beaux-Arts 67–8
    Civilisation Gallo-Romaine 69
    Confluences 74
    Historique de Lyon 66
    Hospices Civils de Lyon 74
    Imprimerie 69
    Lumière 76
    Marionnette 66
    Tissus 71
    Urbain Tony Garnier 76
nightlife 58
opera house 67
Palais de Bondy 66
Palais du Commerce 70
Palais de Justice 66, 75
Palais St-Jean 66
Parc des 4 Rives 75
Part-Dieu quarter 75
post office 74
Préfecture 75
Presqu'île de Lyon 67–72
Renaissance city 64–6
Resistance movement 77–8
Rhône banks 74–6
Roman theatres 63–4
St-Georges quarter 66
Saône banks 66–7
shopping 56
Sofitel hotel 74

swimming pool 75
Tête d'Or park 74–5
Théâtre des Ateliers 66
Tour Rose 65
tourism 20
tourist information 56
town hall 67
Villa Lumière 76
where to stay 56–7
zoo 75
Macheville 133
Magnieu 206
Maison du Patrimoine de Hières-
    sur-Amby 202
Malataverne 154
Malartre, Henri 104
Malleval 131, **160**
Mandy mill 134
Manigod 219, **226**
Mantenay-Montlin 82
Manthes 180
Marais de Lavours 206
Marcy 103
Marcy-l'Etoile 98, **105**
Marcy-sur-Anse 98
Marguerite of Austria 11
Marie de'Medici 13
Marie-Christine fort 243–4
markets 47
Marlhes 132
Marsanne 166
Mas de la Vignasse 145
Massif Central 6
Massif du Tanargue 141
Maurienne 242–5
    winter sports 319–25
Mauves 163
Mayres-Savel 281
Méaudre 283
    winter sports 331–3
Megève 227
    winter sports 296–8
Meillerie 222
Meillonnas 201, **207**
Menoge valley 216
Menon valley 195
Mens 272, **282**
Menthon-St-Bernard 255–6
menu reader 30–4
Méouges valley 196
Mercurol 162
Méribel 239
    winter sports 304–9
Merovingian Period 7
Merpuis 209
Mesozoic Era 6
Meyras 141
Mézilhac 141
Mieussy 224
Mijoux 201, **210–11**
    winter sports 333
Miolans 259
Mionnay 85
Mirabel 143
Mirabel-aux-Baronnies 186, **194**
Mirmande 154, **166**

Modane 244
Mollans-sur-Ouvèze 186, **194**
monasteries see abbeys and
    monasteries
money 47
Monsteroux 174
Mont Aiguille 282
Mont Blanc 15, **23**, 227–8, **229**, 293
Mont Buet 230
Mont Cenis 243
Mont de la Charvaz 258
Mont Charvin 227
Mont du Chat 258
Mont Chaussitre 131
Mont Chiniac 133
Mont-Denis 244
Mont Gerbier de Jonc 124
Mont Granier 259, 274
Mont Lozère 141
Mont Mézenc 124
Mont Myon 207
Mont Nivigne 207
Mont d'Or 103–4
Mont Pilat 130 131–2
Mont Pourri 240
Mont Revard 260
Mont St-Rigaud 99
Mont Salève 216
Mont-Saxonnex 224
Mont Thonier 266
Mont Tourvéon 99
Mont Ventoux 195
Mont-de-Lans 246
Montagne de l'Aup 188
Montagne du Gros Foug 258
Montagne du Matin 114
Montagne des Princes 257
Montagne du Semnoz 259
Montagne de Souhait 203
Montagne de Vuache 257
Montagny 105
Montalieu 202
Montarcher 120
Montbel 274
Montbrison 116
Montbrun-les-Bains 196
Montcet 85
Monte Bianco 241
Montélimar 154, **166–7**
Montellier 88
Montferrat 177
Montfleury 266
Montgolfier brothers 15, **24**, 132, 133
Montlambert 259
Montmelas 101
Montmélian 259
Montpezat-sous-Bauzon 141
Montréal 142
Montrevel 82, 84
Montriond 287
Montriond, lake 223
Montrond-les-Bains 111, **117**
Montrottier 98, **106**
Montrottier, château de 256–7
Monts du Forez 115, 120–1
Monts-Jura 211, 333

Monts du Lyonnais 105
Monts de la Madeleine 109, 114
Montségur-sur-Lauzon 185
Montseveroux 174
Montverdun 115
Morancé 98
Moras-en-Valloire 180
Morestel 200, **202–3**
Morgon 99
Morillon 290, 292
Mornant 105
Morzine 219, **223**
    winter sports 288, 289
Motz 252, 258
Moulin à Vent 96
Moulin, Jean 77–8
Mourguet, Laurent 16, **24**
Moûtiers 238
museum opening hours 47
Mussolini, Benito 18
Myans 259
Nantua 209–10
Napoleon Bonaparte 15–16
national holidays 48
Naves 143
Nâves-Parmelan 225
Nécropole 283
Nernier 220
Néronde 114
Neuville-sur-Ain 209
Neyrac-les-Bains 139, **141**
Nid d'Aigle 228
Noailly 111
Noirétable 120
Notre-Dame-d'Ay 133
Notre-Dame-de-Beaumont 88
Notre-Dame-de-Bellecombe 219, **227**
    winter sports 299
Notre-Dame-de-la-Délivrance 101
Notre-Dame-des-Dombes 88
Notre-Dame-de-l'Hermitage 120
Notre-Dame-des-Neiges 141
Notre-Dame-de-Parménie 178
Notre-Dame-de-la-Salette 281
Novalaise 266
Novalaise-Lac 253
Noyer 260
Nyons 185–6, **192–3**
Obiou 282
Odenas 100
Oignin valley 209
Oingt 98, **102**
Oisans 245–6
Oncieu 204
Ontex 261
opening hours 47–8
Ouvèze river source 195
Ouvèze valley 194–5
Oyonnax 209
Oz-en-Oisans 325–8
Païolive forest 143
Panissières 114
Paradiski 309–12
paragliding 49
Parc Animalier de Courzieu 106
Parc Animalier du Merlet 230

Parc de la Droséra 120
Parc Naturel du Chambaran 180
Parc des Oiseaux 88
Parc Walibi 203
passports 39
Passy 228
Pavia, battle of 12
Pavin brothers 14
Pays de Gex 210–12
Pays des Trois Vallées 176
Paysalp 220
Payzac 142
Peaugres safari park 133
Peillonnex 216–20
Peisey Vallandry 309–12
Peisey-Nancroix 240
Pélussin 131
Pennes-le-Sec 187
Pérouges 85, **87–8**
Philippe le Bel 10
Pic de Chenavari 165
Piéchut, Barthélemy 26
Piégon 194
Pierre Châtel 258
Pierre Menta 237, 240
Pierre-sur-Haute 120
Pierrelongue 194–5
Pierreux 100
pilgrimage sights 17
Pinsot 271
Pipay 272
Pius VI, Pope 16
Pizay 97
Plaine de la Bièvre 174
Plaisians 186
Planzolles 142
Plateau de Coiron 135, 144
Plateau des Glières 225–6
Plateau de Larina 202
Plateau des Petites Roches 274
Plateau de Retord 205
Pointe de la Grande Casse 239
Poleymieux 104
police 44
Polignac 122
Pollieu 206
Pommiers 102, **133**
Poncin 209
Pont-d'Ain 208
Pont d'Arc 147
Pont du Diable 223
Pont de l'Isère 153
Pont-des-Pierres 210
Pont-en-Royans 179
Pont-de-Vaux **83**, 84
Pontaix 187
Pontcharra 270
Portes du Soleil 287
Portout 260
post offices 48
Pouillat 208
Pouilly-sous-Charlieu 110–11
Pouilly-les-Feurs 114
Pourcharesse 142
practical A–Z **44–52**
Pralognan-la-Vanoise 235, 239

Pranles 134
Prapoutel 272
Praz sur Arly 299
Pre-Alpine Ranges 268, **269–84**
Pressiat 207
Privas 129, **134–5**
Protestantism 12–13, 134
public holidays 48
Pussy 238
Puygiron 189
Queige 237
Quintenas 133
Rabelais, François 12, 60
railways 38–9, 40
Recoubeau Jansac 185
Réginié-Durette 99
religion 7, 8, 12–13, 14
Rémuzat 194
Replonges 84
restaurants see food and drink
Retournac 122
Retourtour 133
Revermont 207–8
Revolution 15, 61
Rhône valley 22, 1, **151–70**
    festivals 152
    Lyon to Lac Léman 198, **199–212**
    wine 158–9, 191
Ribes 140, **141–2**
Richerenches 191
Rimon-et-Savel 187
Ripaille 221
Rive 259
Roannais 113–14
Roanne 111
Roche 113–14, **120**
Rochebaron 122
Rochebonne (Ardèche) 134
Rochebonne (Beaujolais) 102
Rochecolombe 144
Rochefort 266
Rochefort-en-Valdaine 189
Rochegude 185, **192**
Rochemaure 165
Rochessauve 129
Rochetaillée (Ardèche) 131
Rochetaillée (Beaujolais) 104
Romanche valley 246
Romanèche-Thorins 96–7
Romans 6–7, 55–7
Romans-sur-Isère 177, **181**
Ron des Fades 142
Ronzières 102
Roure 146
Roussas 169
Rousseau, Jean-Jacques 15
Rousset-les-Vignes 192
Route des Belvédères 161–2
Route de la Lavande 186
Route Napoléon 280
Route d'Olivier 194
Royans 179
Royans-Vercours 179
Roybon 180
Rubins 225
Ruffieu 201, **205**

Ruffieux 252, **258**
Rumilly 257
Ruoms 145
Sablières 141
Saillans 187
St-Agnan-en-Vercors 273
St-Agrève 129, **133**
St-Alban-Auriolles 140, **145**
St-Alban-de-Montbel 253
St-Amour 93-4
St-André-de-Bâgé 84
St-André-de-Chalencon 112, **122**
St-Antoine 284
St-Antoine-l'Abbaye 177, **179–80**
St-Auban-sur-l'Ouvèze 186, **195**
St-Barthélemy-de-Vals 161
St-Benoît-en-Diois 187
St-Bonnet-le-Château 112, **121**
St-Bonnet-le-Courreau 112, **120**
St-Bonnet-le-Froid 129
St-Chef 203
St-Christophe-en-Oisans 246
St-Colomban-des-Villards 319–21
Ste-Croix 187
Ste-Croix-en-Jarez 128–9, **131**
St-Cyr-sur-Menthon 84
St-Désirat 160–1
St-Didier-sur-Chalaronne 89
St-Donat-sur-l'Herbasse 181
St-Etienne 14, **118–19**, *119*
St-Etienne-du-Bois 87
St-Etienne-de-Lugdarès 141
Ste-Eulalie 112, 124
St-Eynard 275
St-Félicien 133
Ste-Foy-l'Argentière 105
Ste-Foy-Tarentaise 241
   winter sports 314-16
St-François-Longchamp 238
   winter sports 302–4
St-Galmier 111, 117
St-Geirges-des-Hurtières 245
St-Genest-Malifaux 129
St-Genix-sur-Guiers 266
St-Geoire-en-Valdaine 178
St-Georges-en-Couzan 111-12
St-Georges-d'Espéranche 176
St-Germain-sur-l'Arbresle 103
St-Gervais 219, **228**
   winter sports 296–8
St-Gingolph 222
St-Gobain 243
St-Haon-le-Châtel 111, **114**
St-Hugues-de-Chartreuse 275
Ste-Jalle 194
St-Jean-d'Ardières 97
St-Jean-d'Arves 319–21
St-Jean-d'Aulps 287
St-Jean-du-Chevelu 252
St-Jean-de-Belleville 239
St-Jean-de-Maurienne 235, **244**
St-Jean-de-Muzols 161
St-Jean-sur-Reyssouze 82
St-Jean-en-Royans 179
St-Jean-St-Maurice-sur-Loire 113
St-Jean-de-Sixt 300–2

St-Jean-des-Vignes 103
St-Jeoire 220
St-Jeoire-Prieuré 259
St-Jorioz 256
St-Joseph 159, 163
St-Julien-Molin-Molette 129, **132**
St-Julien-du-Serre 129
St-Julien-en-Vercors 273
St-Just 169
St-Just-St-Rambert 112, **117**
St-Lager 100
St-Laurent-les-Bains 141
St-Laurent-sous-Coiron 143
St-Laurent-d'Oingt 102
St-Laurent-sur-Saône 83–4
St-Marcel caves 148
St-Marcel-d'Ardèche 169
St-Marcel-de-Félines 114
St-Marcellin 178
Ste-Marie-d'Alloix 274
St-Martial 112
St-Martial, lake 124
St-Martin-d'Ardèche 148
St-Martin-de-Belleville 239
   winter sports 304-9
St-Martin-du-Mont 207
St-Maurice-d'Ardèche 140
St-Maurice-des-Chasaux 209
St-Maurice-sur-Loire 111
St-Maurice-de-Rotherens 266
St-May 194
St-Montan 168
St-Nazaire-en-Royans 179
St-Nicolas-la-Chapelle 219, **227**
St-Nicolas-de-Véroce 219, **228**
   winter sports 296–8
St-Nizier-du-Moucherotte 282–3
St-Ondras 177
St-Paul-en-Cornillon 118
St-Paul-Trois-Châteaux 154,
   169–70
St-Paul-de-Varax 88
Ste-Paule 102
St-Péray 159, 163
St-Pierre 67-8
St-Pierre d'Albigny 259
St-Pierre-de-Boeuf 160
St-Pierre-de-Chartreuse 271, **275**
St-Pierre-de-Curtille 261
St-Pierre-d'Entremont 271, **274**
St-Pierre-la-Palud 106
St-Pierreville 129, **134**
St-Pons 140
St-Rambert-d'Albon 161
St-Rambert-en-Bugey 204
St-Régis du Coin 132
St-Remèze 148
St-Romain-en-Gal 155
St-Romain-de-Lerps 163
St-Romain-le-Puy 116
St-Sorlin-sur-Arve 245
   winter sports 319–21
St-Sorlin-en-Bugey 204
St-Symphorien-sur-Coise 106
St-Thomé 144
St-Trivier-de-Courtes 82

St-Trivier-sur-Moignans 85
St-Uze 161
St-Victor-sur-Loire 118
St-Vidal 122
St-Vincent-de-Barrès 165
Salavre 207
Sallanches 225
Salles-Arbuissonas 101
Samoëns 219, **224**, 291
   winter sports 292
Sanilhac 139
Saou 184, **187**
Saut de la Drôme 188
Sauvain 120
Savoie
   Beaufortain 236–7
   counts of 9, 10–11, 12, 13–14
   Great Lakes *248*, **249–66**
   Haute Savoie *214*, 215–30,
      287–302
   Maurienne 242–5, 319–25
   Oisans 245–6
   sports and activities 218
      see also winter sports
   Tarentaise 237–42, 302–19
   Vanoise valleys *232*
   wine route 257–9
Sciez-sur-Léman 218, **220**
Scourtinerie 193
Second Empire 17
Séderon 196
Séez 241
Seguin, Marc 16, 132
Sermoyer **83**, 84
Serrières 153, **160**
Serrières-sur-Ain 209
Serrières-de-Briord 203
Servoz 230
Sevrier 256
Seyssel 206, 257
Seythenex 258
shopping
   Lyon 56
   opening hours 47
   useful phrases 336
Sièvres 143
silk industry 61
Sisteron 196
Site des Charmes 83
Site des Mottets 263
Sixt 290
Sixt-Fer-à-Cheval 224
skiing *see* winter sports
Sollières-Envers 243
Songieu 205
Sothonod 205
Soyans 187
Soyons 153, **164**
spa centres 49
specialist holidays 52
speed limits 41
sports and activities 48-9
   Ardèche 128, 138
   golf 49, 161, 167
   Savoie 218
      see also winter sports

Stendahl (Brillat-Savarin) 15
Suze-la-Rousse 185, **191–2**
Tain-l'Hermitage 153, **161**
Talaru 120
Talloires 252, **256**
Taluyers 105
Tamié 258–9
Taninges 224
Tarentaise 237–42
   winter sports 302–19
Taulignan 192
telephones 48
temperature chart 44
Termignon 243
Ternand 102
Terre Vivante 282
TGV 38–9
Theizé 98
Theys 272
Thines 143
Third Republic 17
Thollon-les-Mémises 218-19
Thônes 219, **226**
Thonon-les-Bains 218, 220, **221**
Thorens 225
Thorrenc 161
Thueyts 141
Tignes 241
   winter sports 316–19
Tossiat 207
Tour de Crest 182–5
tourism 19–20
tourist information 50
Tournon-sur-Rhône 153, **162**
Tours 102
Touvet 274
Trappe d'Aiguebelle 189
travel **36–42**
   disabled travellers 44–5
   entry formalities 39
   getting around 40–2
   getting there 36–9
   specialist holidays 52
   useful phrases 336
Treffort 207, 281
Trévoux 90
Trièves 282
Trois Becs 185–6
Trois Pucelles 283
Trois Vallées 287–8, 304–9
Troisgros 113
truffles 29, 170
Ugine 227
Urban II, Pope 8, 59
Urfé, Claude de 12
Uriage 272, **273–4**
Usclades-et-Rieutord 112
Usson-en-Forez 120-1
Uzer 139
Vacheresse 223
Vagnas 140
Vaison-la-Romaine 194
Val d'Arly 299
Val-Cenis 324-5
Val d'Isère 241
   winter sports 316–19

Val-Thorens 304–9
Valaurie 154, **169**
Valbonnais 281
Valchevrière 283
Valcroissant 188
Valdo, Pierre 9
Valdrôme 188
Valence 153, **163–4**
Valfréjus 323–4
Vallée d'Aulps 223
Vallée de Belleville 239
Vallée Blanche 293
Valloire 245
   winter sports 322–3
Vallon, lake 220
Vallon-Pont-d'Arc 140, **146**
Vallorcine 230
Valmeinier 322–3
Valmorel 239
   winter sports 302–4
Valois dynasty 10
Valouse 186
Valréas 191
Valromey 205
Vals-les-Bains 136, **138–9**
Valsenestre 246, 281
Valserine 210–12
Valvignières 144
Vandeins 85
Vanoise valleys **232**
Vassieux-en-Vercors 273, **284**
Vaugirard 116
Vaujany 325–8
Vaux-en-Beaujolais 97, **100–1**
Vauxrenard 98
vegetables 29
Vénéon valley 246
Venosc 235, **246**
Ventadour 140
Venterol 192
Vercheny 187
Vercland 292
Vercors 282–4
   winter sports 331–3
Vergongeat 207
Vernay, Georges 160
Vernoux 83–4
Vesancy 211
Veyrier-du-Lac 252, **255**
Veyrines 133
Vianney, Jean-Marie 16–17, 89–90,
   105
Victor-Emmanuel I 16
Victoria, Queen 17
Vienne 7, 152, **155–60**, *156*
Villard 216
Villard-sur-Doron 237
Villard-de-Lans 272–3, **283**
   winter sports 331–3
Villard-Reculas 325–8
Villars-les-Dombes 88
Ville-sur-Jarnioux 101–2
Villefranche-sur-Saône 98, **101**
Villeperdrix 194
Villié-Morgon 97, **99**
Vinay 178

Vinéum 162
Vinezac 139, 142
Vinsobres 191
Vions 258
Virieu 176
visas 39
Viuz-en-Sallaz 220
Viviers 167–8
Vizille 272, **280–1**
Vogüé 144
Voiron 178
Volane valley 135
Volerie du Forez 116
Voltaire 15
Vongnes 206
Vonnas 84–5
Vonsobres 185
Vulmix 240
vultures 194
walking 42, 49
walnuts 29
Wars of Religion 11–13, 60
water sports 49
when to go 44
where to stay 50–1
   useful phrases 336
   see also under individual places
wine 30
   Ardèche 144
   Beaujolais 94–5
   Bugey 206
   Clairette de Die 182
   Côte Roannais 114
   Coteaux du Tricastin 190
   Côtes du Forez 115
   Côtes du Rhône-Villages 191
   Pétillant de Gravelles 207
   Rhône valley 158–9, 191
   Savoie wine route 257–9
   Vinéum 162
Winter Olympics 19
winter sports 17, 19, 49, **286–34**
   Ain 333–4
   cross-country skiing 334
   Haute Savoie 287–302
   Isère 325–33
   Maurienne Valley 319–25
   Tarentaise valley 302–19
   see also sports and activities
World Wars 18, 77–8
Yenne 258
Yvoire 218, **220**
Yzeron 106

You handle the slopes, we'll handle the rest.

Basel | **Geneva** | **Grenoble** | **Lyon**
Servicing Rhône-Alpes

Visit our website to book your
in resort accommodation, ski hire, transfers,
sports insurance and more.

Many regional departures — check website for details.

easyJet.com
Come on, let's fly!

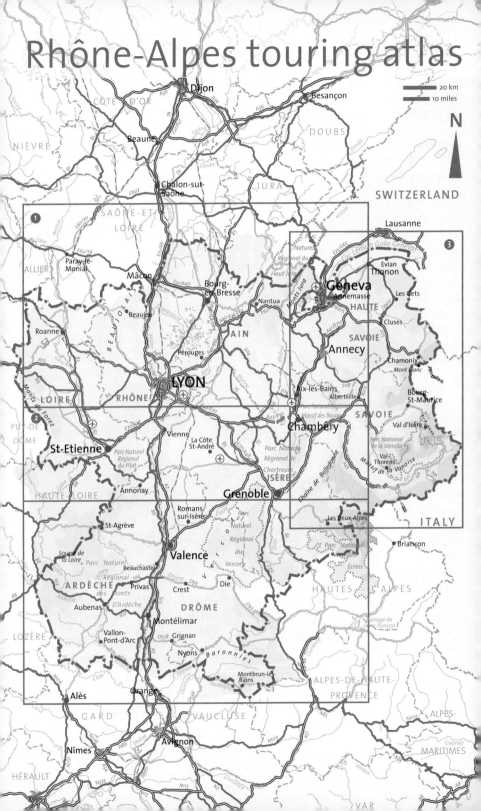

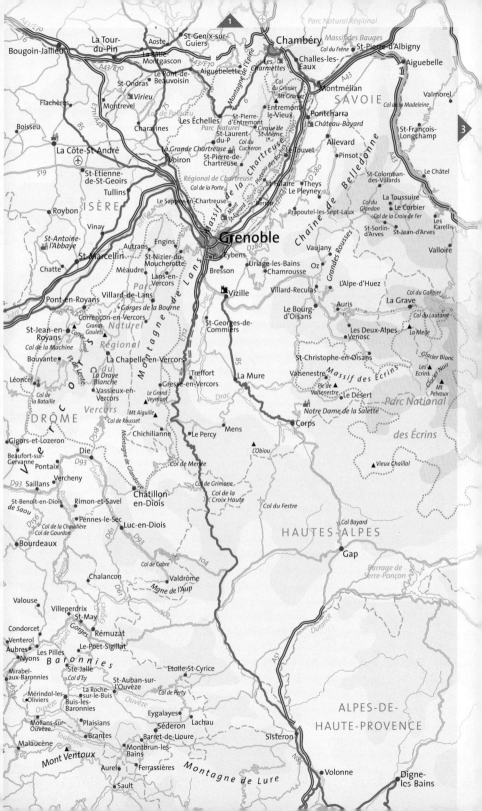

FRANCE

Philippe Barbour, Dana Facaros
& Michael Pauls

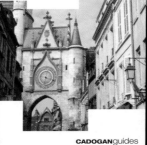

CADOGANguides

LOIRE

Philippe Barbour

BRITTANY

Philippe Barbour

flying visits
FRANCE

*great getaways by
budget airline, train & ferry*

CADOGANguides

CADOGANguides

Also available:
Buying a Property:
  France
Corsica
Côte D'Azur
Dordogne & the Lot
Gascony &
  the Pyrenees
Normandy

London–Paris
Paris
Provence
Short Breaks in
  Northern France
South of France
Working and Living:
  France

CADOGANguides

RHÔNE-ALPES
F R A N C E

Enjoy sun-filled holidays in beautiful surroundings

This delightful region of France with spectacular scenery offers you the opportunity to enjoy a wide variety of sports, including canoeing and other water sports, cycling & walking or simply exploring its picturesque towns and villages.

After a day in the invigorating fresh air and sunshine you can relax & watch the world go by at a pavement café or return to your campsite for a friendly Barbecue.

Easily reached by the main autoroutes and only about 8 hours from the Eurotunnel and main ferry ports.

With 940 campsites, long seasons, a wide variety of accommodation (including bungalows for the whole family) and a wide variety of activities to choose from there's sure to be somewhere in the Rhône-Alpes just for you.

We are here

Paris

St Etienne

Lyon

Geneva

Valence

Nîmes

Montpellier